AARON COPLAND AND HIS WORLD

AARON COPLAND
AND HIS WORLD

EDITED BY CAROL J. OJA AND JUDITH TICK

PRINCETON UNIVERSITY PRESS
PRINCETON AND OXFORD

Copyright © 2005 by Princeton University Press

Published by Princeton University Press, 41 William Street,
Princeton, New Jersey 08540
In the United Kingdom: Princeton University Press,
3 Market Place, Woodstock, Oxfordshire OX20 1SY

All Rights Reserved

For permissions information, see page xii.

Library of Congress Control Number 2005927155

ISBN-13: 978-0-691-12470-4 (paperback)
ISBN-10: 0-691-12470-1 (paperback)
ISBN-13: 978-0-691-12469-8 (cloth)
ISBN-10: 0-691-12469-8 (cloth)

British Library Cataloging-in-Publication Data is available

This publication has been produced by the Bard College Publications Office:

Ginger Shore, Director

Francie Soosman, Cover design

Natalie Kelly, Design

Text edited by Paul De Angelis and Erin Clermont

Music typeset by Don Giller

Printed on acid-free paper. ∞

pup.princeton.edu

Printed in the United States of America

1 3 5 7 9 10 8 6 4 2

To Vivian Fine, composer,

and Minna Lederman, editor, music
journalist, and cultural activist—

two women of modern music
who brought the editors close to
Copland's world

Contents

PART III
COPLAND'S INNER CIRCLE

PART IV
ANALYTIC PERSPECTIVES

PART V
POLITICAL EDGES

Contents

Acknowledgments

It is an honor to contribute to the series of books connected with the Bard Festival of Music, under the inspiring leadership of Leon Botstein. As with all the titles in this series, the production schedule has been unusually tight, and we are grateful for the high-level professionalism of everyone involved. Our authors were exemplary in their nimble responsiveness and unfailing good humor under very tight deadlines. And we were fortunate to work with an extraordinary editorial and production staff, especially the highly expert Paul De Angelis, Natalie Kelly, and Ginger Shore in the Bard Publications Office, as well as Erin Clermont, our first-rate copy editor. Irene Zedlacher was most helpful as well. Special thanks go to Emily Abrams, a graduate student in musicology at Harvard University, for exceptional editorial assistance.

We are also grateful to Gary Duehr, a professional photographer in the Boston area, for working to improve the quality of the photo of Aaron Copland and Arthur Berger that is published here and to Ellen Berger for providing the image. Also, we extend thanks to George Boziwick at the Library of the Performing Arts at Lincoln Center for assembling the complete correspondence of Copland and Berger.

Permissions

The following copyright holders have graciously given their permission to reprint musical excerpts from copyrighted works.

Works of Copland

Appalachian Spring © Copyright 1945 by The Aaron Copland Fund for Music, Inc. Copyright renewed. Boosey & Hawkes, Inc., Sole Publisher & Licensee.

"Ballade of Ozzie Powell," The Aaron Copland Fund for Music, Inc., © copyright owner.

Billy the Kid © Copyright 1941 by The Aaron Copland Fund for Music, Inc. Copyright renewed. Boosey & Hawkes, Inc., Sole Publisher & Licensee.

The Cummington Story. Reprinted by permission of The Aaron Copland Fund for Music, Inc., copyright owner.

A Lincoln Portrait © 1943 by The Aaron Copland Fund for Music, Inc. Copyright renewed. Boosey & Hawkes, Inc., Sole Publisher & Licensee.

Music for the Theatre © Copyright 1932 by The Aaron Copland Fund for Music, Inc. Copyright renewed. Boosey & Hawkes, Inc., Sole Publisher & Licensee.

Music for Radio (Prairie Journal) © Copyright 1940 by The Aaron Copland Fund for Music, Inc. Copyright renewed. Boosey & Hawkes, Inc., Sole Publisher & Licensee.

Piano Fantasy © Copyright 1957 by The Aaron Copland Fund for Music, Inc. Copyright renewed. Boosey & Hawkes, Inc., Sole Publisher & Licensee.

Piano Sonata © Copyright 1942 by The Aaron Copland Fund for Music, Inc. Copyright renewed. Boosey & Hawkes, Inc., Sole Publisher & Licensee.

Piano Variations © Copyright 1932 by The Aaron Copland Fund for Music, Inc. Copyright renewed. Boosey & Hawkes, Inc., Sole Publisher & Licensee.

First Symphony © 1928 by The Aaron Copland Fund for Music, Inc. Copyright renewed. Boosey & Hawkes, Inc., Sole Publisher & Licensee.

Three Moods © Copyright 1981 by The Aaron Copland Fund for Music, Inc. Copyright renewed. Boosey & Hawkes, Inc., Sole Publisher & Licensee.

Twelve Poems of Emily Dickinson © Copyright 1951 by The Aaron Copland Fund for Music, Inc. Copyright renewed. Boosey & Hawkes, Inc., Sole Publisher & Licensee.

Sonata for Violin and Piano © Copyright 1944 by The Aaron Copland Fund for Music, Inc. Copyright renewed. Boosey & Hawkes, Inc., Sole Publisher & Licensee.

Symphony for Organ and Orchestra (a.k.a. Symphony No. 1) © Copyright 1931, 1963 by The Aaron Copland Fund for Music, Inc. Copyright Renewed. Boosey & Hawkes, Inc., Sole Publisher & Licensee.

The Tender Land © Copyright 1954, 1956 by The Aaron Copland Fund for Music, Inc. Copyright Renewed. Boosey & Hawkes, Inc., Sole Publisher & Licensee.

Works of Stravinsky

Rite of Spring (Le Sacre du Printemps) © Copyright 1912, 1921 by Hawkes & Son (London) Ltd. Copyright Renewed. Reprinted by permission of Boosey & Hawkes, Inc.

Symphony of Psalms © Copyright 1931 by Hawkes & Son (London) Ltd. Copyright Renewed. Revised version © Copyright 1948 by Hawkes & Son (London) Ltd. Copyright Renewed. Reprinted by permission of Boosey & Hawkes, Inc.

· · ·

The following copyright holders have graciously granted permission to reprint or reproduce the following copyrighted material. Acknowledgments for some additional works also appear under some of the figures or in the notes.

Langston Hughes, "Weary Blues" and "Ballad of Ozie Powell," from *The Collected Poems of Langston Hughes* by Langston Hughes, © Copyright 1994 by The Estate of Langston Hughes. Used by permission of Alfred A. Knopf, a division of Random House, Inc.

Marsden Hartley, *Indian Compositon*, The Frances Lehman Loeb Art Center, Vassar College, Poughkeepsie. Gift of Edna Bryner.

Ruth Keahey, *El Saloon Mexico*, Copland Collection, Library of Congress. The Aaron Copland Fund for Music, Inc.

Quotations from previously unpublished letters by Lincoln Kirstein © Copyright 2005 by the New York Public Library (Astor, Lenox, and Tilden Foundations).

Quotations from *Rodeo* typescript and "American Ballet by Agnes de Mille," Agnes de Mille Collection, Jerome Robbins Dance Division, The New York Public Library for the Performing Arts. Reprinted by permission of the Agnes de Mille Foundation.

Quotations from Marilyn Hunt's interview with Eugene Loring, Oral History Archive, Jerome Robbins Dance Division, The New York Public Library for the Performing Arts. Reprinted by permission of the Eugene Loring Estate.

Quotations from letters by Aaron Copland, photographic reproductions of those and other letters, photographs of Aaron Copland and Leonard Bernstein in 1941, as well as other writings of Aaron Copland: The Aaron Copland Fund for Music, Inc., © copyright owner. Quotations from letters by Leonard Bernstein and photographic reproduction of those and other letters, © Copyright Amberson Holdings LLC. Used by permission of The Leonard Bernstein Office, Inc. Photograph of Aaron Copland and Leonard Bernstein in 1985 by Walter H. Scott.

Arthur Berger's letters to Aaron Copland: reprinted by permission of Ellen Berger. Photo of Copland and Berger together in 1954 courtesy Ellen Berger. Copland's letters to Berger, The Aaron Copland Fund for Music, Inc., © copyright owner.

Typescript with proposed titles for *Music for Radio* and Copland's telegram from Mexico, Copland Collection, Library of Congress, The Aaron Copland fund for Music, Inc., © copyright owner. Quotations from letters by Theodore Chanler reprinted by permission of the Theodore Chanler Estate. Quotations from letters by Roy Harris reprinted by permission of the Roy Harris Estate. Quotations from letters by Roger Sessions reprinted by permission of the Roger Sessions Estate. Quotations from letters by Davidson Taylor reprinted by permission of the Davidson Taylor Estate. Quotations from letters by Deems Taylor reprinted by permission of the Deems Taylor Estate.

Richard Wilbur, "A Wall in the Woods: Cummington," from *Mayflies: New Poems and Translations* (Harcourt, 2000).

Norman Rockwell, *Freedom of Speech* (*Saturday Evening Post* story illustration of February 20, 1943): Norman Rockwell Art Collection Trust, The Norman Rockwell Museum at Stockbridge, Massachusetts.

Three images from *Sunday Showcase: Can Culture Explode* (May, 1966 television program) and transcription of *Aaron Copland Meets the Soviet Composers*: Channel Thirteen/WNDT.

Between Memory and History:

An Introduction

CAROL J. OJA AND JUDITH TICK

It is quite true what Philosophy says: that Life must be understood backwards. But that makes one forget the other saying: that it must be lived forwards. The more one ponders this, the more it comes to mean that life in the temporal existence never becomes quite intelligible, precisely because at no moment can I find complete quiet to take the backward-looking position.

— Søren Kierkegaard

Aaron Copland's legacy stands between memory and history. An active presence on the musical scene for the bulk of the twentieth century, Copland interacted with most of the major figures in American composition, performance, publishing, and music journalism from 1924, when he returned to New York after studying in France, until the early- to mid-1980s, when he gradually retreated from public life because of deteriorating health. He died in 1990. No self-absorbed isolate, Copland was very much a public figure, a man "generous in his personal relations," as his close friend and colleague Arthur Berger recalled, who "also wanted to make this a better place for the American composer in general."[1] This value lives on after his death through the Aaron Copland Fund, established through a bequest by the composer for ongoing support of contemporary American classical music, and Copland House, which sponsors composer residencies and concerts. Copland's goal was to provide American composers with the creative and practical space for producing their art, to help them forge a sense of solidarity, and to make them competitive in an international new music arena. All this was grounded in an abiding sense of public spirit and an intense engagement with the contemporary world, traits that define Copland's cultural contribution as much as his compositions. *Aaron Copland and His World* appears at a turning point in reassessing that legacy.

As time passes, fewer and fewer authors are in a position to speak about Copland from personal experience. Among our contributors, Vivian Perlis stands out as the one who knew him best, especially through her work with Copland on a two-volume fusion of oral history and autobiography (published in 1984 and 1989). Others included here knew him briefly or casually. But for most, he represents the past. Thus a composer whose work was first interpreted by composer contemporaries, beginning with Virgil Thomson in his 1932 portrait in *Modern Music,* then by partisan followers, most notably Arthur Berger in his *Aaron Copland* of 1953 and Julia Smith in her biography of Copland from 1955, has now moved into an entirely new phase of historical inquiry.[2]

As of the early twenty-first century, enough time has gone by not only to witness but also to reflect on the stages of change that have characterized the reception of Copland and his music. Taste has shifted away from serialism toward a postmodern openness to breaking barriers between "popular" and "classical," "Western" and "non-Western," bringing with it multivoiced waves of tonal revisionism. Along the way, skeptical postwar modernists, who assessed Copland as "old-fashioned" or "conservative," have themselves been absorbed in the cycles of history. In the 1960s, recalls one composer of a generation then in its twenties, Copland was often dismissed as being "not serious" because "real music was an intellectual exercise, a kind of exclusive discipline shared by a few initiates, like nuclear physics."[3] In the ensuing decades, what once seemed absolute truth has come to be viewed as an attitude shaped by a particular intellectual environment—an attitude with the integrity of its own moment. At the same time, the roots of Copland's legacy reach ever more deeply into a vast country's vulnerable sense of its common national self. "Choose Copland," Julia Smith was told when searching for a dissertation subject. Her teacher Frederick Jacobi, a composer active in Copland's primary organization, the League of Composers, explained, "He has accomplished more than any of the rest of us. Not that we haven't all tried hard—very hard—but somehow or other Copland has struck the 'American' note."[4]

Today we live in an era when "diversity" has become a watchword. Yet through Copland's music, in ways still only partially understood, his vision of "America" has attained the status of artistic consensus that allows it to express and indeed shape representations of our national character, even at a time when cultural critics question whether such a concept has either validity or utility. Who would have predicted that almost fifty years after its composition a "Ballet for Martha" would comfort a nation in the aftermath of 9/11?

There are many reasons why scholars are engaging anew with Copland. Since his death, his substantial collection of personal papers and music manuscripts has been moved out of the basement of his home in Peekskill, New York, and become available at the Library of Congress; much of it is now easily accessible online through the American Memory Project. At the same time, Howard Pollack's magisterial *Aaron Copland: The Life and Work of an Uncommon Man* (1999) initiated a major reassessment of Copland's contribution within the shifting contexts of his times. The centennial year of Copland's birth in 2000 played yet another revisionist role, witnessing festivals devoted to his work, conferences, celebratory nationwide birthday events, and new recordings, which transported many hitherto unfamiliar works into the spotlight. The number of doctoral dissertations about Copland and his music continues to increase, many fueled by the recent rise of cultural studies, with its interdisciplinary attention to the setting of a life and its impact as much as to analysis of artistic output.

As a result, new angles of critical vision within humanistic disciplines have made it possible to explore with both sensitivity and objectivity aspects of Copland's life and work that hitherto remained speculative or obscured. These include such relatively uncharted topics as the sexuality of a man who wrapped himself in a cocoon of personal privacy. Both Paul Anderson's essay about the influence of André Gide on Copland and Vivian Perlis's account of the friendship between Copland and Bernstein speak in different ways to this issue. Other recent trends in scholarship— from the exploration of ethnic identity to that of politics, film, and the implication of geography on a creative life—illuminate hazy vistas. Howard Pollack ranges widely over Copland's life and work, reflecting on his identity as a Jew; in the process, he records a long period in which anti-Semitism and pride in ethnicity produced paradoxes of reception. Beth Levy focuses on what she describes as "an unprecedented upheaval in the understanding of race in general and Jewishness in particular," using *Music for Radio* to speculate how Copland's musical and cultural assimilation took place. Elizabeth Crist takes the position that progressive politics suffuse Copland's musical sensibility from the very beginning of his compositional career, rather than first rising up in the 1930s, as historians have recounted it. Neil Lerner explores affinities between Roosevelt's famous "Four Freedoms" speech and Copland's score for *The Cummington Story*, discovering in the process that a film made for propaganda purposes by the Office of War Information has become crucial to the people of Cummington, Massachusetts, and their sense of local history.

Throughout, implicit ironies abound in how the meaning of the term *American* has shifted. Many authors in this volume treat the term as political discourse, and the cumulative effect projects various character-izations of Copland—most notably, political subversive versus flag-waving patriot—as points of congruity between the reception of art and political change. For Copland, composition was in part an act of citizenship. Much of his music was conceived in an era when political engagement was paramount for American artists, yet a certain discreet veneer often kept the edges soft and the underlying story partially hidden. He negotiated a landmine of labels, where in one decade they were used to galvanize the masses and in another they could lead to ostracism. "By its very nature, political vocabulary is unusually ambiguous and flexible," writes the political historian David Green, adding that "whoever shapes public understanding of the labels thereby shapes the nature of political discourse."[5] Or to dart back to Kierkegaard, whose words open this introduction, "Once you label me you negate me."

In Copland's case, the labels have at times produced large frames for critical judgments about his music. There is the austere Copland and the accessible one, the composer of abstract compositions and the one who drew on folk tunes. In part, these classifications were put in place through the writings of Arthur Berger, but they were also promulgated by Copland himself, even as he expressed frustration about them. "It occurred to me," he reflected in a 1979 public interview with one of the editors, "that maybe [in the 1930s] we could write a music that would be true to ourselves and yet have a wider potential audience."[6] As the years passed, he was assessed as either graced or afflicted with this duality. Two close readings of Copland's compositional methods appear here to clarify the relationship of works that have been historically opposed rather than juxtaposed—to wit, *Appalachian Spring* and the Piano Sonata. Elliott Antokoletz discusses the former in an essay exploring Copland's manipulation of folk materials, particularly in comparison to the European composers Bartók and Stravinsky. Meanwhile, Larry Starr delves into the Piano Sonata, reflecting on Copland's tendency to produce "sui generis" compositions. While this distances the Piano Sonata from *Appalachian Spring*, Starr also sees a close relationship between them. "The Piano Sonata had its origins in the same kind of impulse to speak directly to, and of, his time that motivated Copland's 'Americana,'" declares Starr. Thus our book challenges assumptions about the relationship between modernism and tradition, treating "radical" and "conservative" as contingent categories of inquiry.

While many of our authors consider the meanings of "American" within politics and style, Martin Brody treats the term as a philosophical category, a focal point through which Copland engaged the great aesthetic questions of his time. By comparing Copland's thinking with that of Sessions and Berger, Brody illuminates stylistic decisions as well as posing a "radical question" indirectly articulated by Copland: "What were the prospects for a national musical culture in a nation of immigrants?" He further links Berger's descriptions of the "quality" of Copland's harmony within a sophisticated aesthetic position related to Berger's understanding of American "neoclassicism." At one of Berger's last public discussions about Copland, which occurred during a presentation for an undergraduate class taught by one of the book's editors in 2002, he noted the contradictions between his own aesthetic perspective and that of the composer he so admired. "Copland didn't care about such abstract things as professional philosophical aesthetics," Berger remarked. At the same time, Berger still displayed sustained interest in focusing on the concept of "qualities" as a way of discussing Copland's harmonies. He then played chords from one of the Emily Dickinson songs to illustrate the nature of Copland's transformative voicings.[7]

Thus *Aaron Copland and His World* also highlights the role of Arthur Berger in so many aspects of Copland's reception. Not only did Berger establish parameters for our understanding of Copland's music through his 1953 study, but he directly engaged Copland in a dialogue over his stylistic eclecticism. This issue is one of many recorded in correspondence between the two men, scrupulously edited by Wayne Shirley, which is published here in it is entirety for the first time. The letters extend from 1933 to 1982. Copland and Berger enjoyed a rich, multifaceted relationship, one of mentor and disciple, critic and subject, close friends. And their correspondence yields many of the jolting juxtapositions so frequent in America. "The other night, while walking down Hollywood Blvd.," wrote Copland to Berger in 1943, "I happened on a copy of the *Partisan Review*. Imagine my surprise when I came upon your piece on the Sonata."

This volume also adds to the primary sources about Copland through two sets of intriguing documents. Melissa de Graaf contributes a transcript of a post-concert discussion between Copland and the audience at a Composers' Forum concert in 1938. There Copland appeared entirely at home in a kind of classical-music town-meeting format. Meanwhile, Emily Abrams provides tools for a new kind of media research with an annotated catalogue of Copland's appearances on television beginning in 1958. Her work has implications beyond this volume, for only recently have scholars begun to explore the potential of media materials about modern classical music in any systematic way. In addition, she transcribes one show, *Aaron Copland Meets the Soviet Composers*, produced by WGBH in Boston in 1959, which was the result of a Cold War cultural exchange.

Three interdisciplinary essays by noted scholars outside of music focus on art, dance, and expressive culture in general. The art historian Gail Levin, whose own contribution to Copland scholarship was recently described as "arguably the first substantial interdisciplinary study of Copland by a scholar outside musicology," discusses affinities between Copland's music and Mexican modernism.[8] In a pioneering survey of Copland's vital relationship to modern dance, Lynn Garafola brings her deep understanding of dance history to Copland's three major ballets, explaining the shared modernist values of these art forms. And cultural historian Morris Dickstein illuminates Copland's world within the context of his intellectual and creative peers during the turbulent 1930s.

Finally, Leon Botstein offers an essay on Copland that is both conclusion and coda. Expanding upon ideas raised throughout the book, Botstein comments on some of the major themes of identity and politics already discussed. His candid portrait of Copland's personality as a musical leader is enhanced by a wider frame of reference against which various aspects of Copland's musical practices take on new meaning. We see Copland in the context of Mahler, Bartók, and a host of other European composers, as well as the more familiar Thomson and Ives.

As a whole, we hope our volume contains enough dissent and consent about Copland to parallel his own ability to welcome multiple interpretations of his music. This is crucial to sustaining the viability of his legacy. Not only does Copland's life and work stand at the crossroads of memory and history, but his "America" does as well. Does that America still exist? Who can identify—either now or in the future—with the leanness and loneliness of the Copland landscapes? Who will recognize the archetypal Anglo-American hymn skeletal structures of his melodic language? Statistics based on the 2000 United States Census highlight the sea changes the country is undergoing, from rural to urban, Euro-American to Latin American.

Thus by standing at a nexus of memory and history, this book also questions what the country was, is, and will be. Yet we believe Copland's legacy will endure because of the universality of human experience expressed through his music. For all the emphasis on the nuances embedded in the term "American," Copland's music reaches beyond national borders. Perhaps it is not too much of a reach, therefore, to claim that we and our authors share Copland's hopefulness about humanity in general and art in particular. No matter how dark the moment—and certainly the composer of *Connotations* was hammering out a warning—Copland remained a believer in the ideal that music could contribute to our understanding of democratic space. If our volume resonates with the tensions inherent between past and present, looking backwards and forwards at the same time, then we are responding to Copland's cultural mission, imbued with a kind of pragmatist optimism so beautifully expressed by his older contemporary, the philosopher John Dewey, who wrote this message in 1934:

To be fully alive the future is not ominous but a promise; it surrounds the present as a halo. . . . But all too often we exist in apprehensions of what the future may bring, and are divided within ourselves. . . . Art celebrates with peculiar intensity the moments in which the past reinforces the present and in which the future is a quickening of what is now.[9]

NOTES

1. Arthur Berger, "Aaron Copland 1900–1990," *Perspectives of New Music* 30, no. 1 (1992): 296–98.

2. Virgil Thomson, "Aaron Copland: American Composers, VII," *Modern Music* 9, no. 2 (January–February 1932): 67–73; Arthur Berger, *Aaron Copland* (New York: Oxford University Press, 1953); Julia Smith, *Aaron Copland: His Work and Contribution to American Music* (New York: Dutton, 1955). The passage of time has of course affected perspectives on the entire generation of American composers born around 1900, which with the death of Leo Ornstein in 2002 passed completely into history. Some crucial figures from the next generation are gone as well—notably Leonard Bernstein (d. 1990) and, most recently, Arthur Berger (d. 2003).

3. Jon Deak, interview with Meryl Secrest, n.d., as quoted in her *Leonard Bernstein: A Life* (New York: Knopf, 1994), p. 305. Here Deak is articulating an opinion about what he observed during the 1960s, and he includes Bernstein alongside Copland.

4. Smith, *Aaron Copland*, p. 3.

5. David Green, *Shaping Political Consciousness: The Language of Politics in America from McKinley to Reagan* (Ithaca, N.Y.: Cornell University Press, 1987), pp. 2, ix.

6. Aaron Copland, interview by Carol J. Oja, CUNY Graduate Center, New York, May 8, 1979. Excerpts published as "Aaron Copland and Minna Lederman: American Music in the Thirties," *Institute for Studies in American Music Newsletter* (November 1979): 6.

7. The statement about Copland and "abstract things" was made in conversation with Judith Tick, January 23, 2003. The piano demonstration of Copland's chords occurred during a guest appearance by Berger at a seminar taught by Tick at Harvard University in October 2002.

8. Jennifer DeLapp, review of *Aaron Copland's America: A Cultural Perspective*, ed. Gail Levin and Judith Tick, *Music Library Association Notes* 58, no. 2 (December 2001): 365.

9. John Dewey, *Art as Experience* (New York: Minton, Balch & Co., 1934), p. 18.

PART I

SCANNING A LIFE

Copland and the Prophetic Voice

HOWARD POLLACK

Although many observers long have been intrigued by the fact that Aaron Copland, one of our most distinctively American composers, was Jewish, this in and of itself has received little critical attention. The dearth of commentary regarding Copland's Jewish background seems especially surprising given the recent proliferation of Copland scholarship spurred by the composer's death in 1990, and the subsequent cataloguing of his voluminous papers at the Library of Congress, not to mention his centennial in 2000, which brought in its wake dozens of symposia, festivals, and other events.

Admittedly, the connections between Copland and his Jewish heritage, both in terms of his life and his work, are oblique. Copland's parents were both Jewish immigrants from Lithuanian Russia, but his mother, Sarah, emigrated to the States as a very young child in the 1860s and grew up largely in Dallas, Texas, and his father, Harris, arrived in New York in the 1870s, his surname changed from Kaplan to Copland as early as that; so the process of acculturation was well under way by the time Aaron, the youngest of five, was born in Brooklyn in 1900. Further, because his parents ran a small department store, they left him to the care of his older siblings, especially his sister Laurine, a lively girl on her way to becoming a car-driving, golf-playing Long Island suburbanite. And the Washington Avenue neighborhood in which the Coplands lived, at the time called southern Bedford though today considered part of Crown Heights, was, at least in the very early 1900s, not particularly Jewish.

The Coplands retained their Jewish identity, nonetheless. Sarah and Harris occasionally spoke Yiddish, and the family attended an Orthodox congregation, Congregation Baith Israel, in Brooklyn's Cobble Hill area. Harris even served for a period as the synagogue's president, while Aaron's oldest brother Ralph supervised its Sunday School. Aaron became

· 1 ·

a bar mitzvah there. The Coplands also celebrated various Jewish holidays, even keeping a separate set of Passover dishes. They were, explained Copland, "more traditional than religious, but observant."[1]

However, in adult life, although retaining strong memories of the music he heard in the synagogue and at Jewish weddings, Copland evidenced little direct connection with Judaism or Jewish culture. He was neither religious nor observant. He rarely attended a synagogue service. In fact, in a 1974 letter, he reminded a young friend that he had "resigned from the Jewish church."[2] His will specified that his funeral service, if any, be "non-religious." His friend and protégé, Leonard Bernstein, would tease him by saying that he was not a "real Jew."[3] To all appearances, and by all accounts, he was what many might call a secular humanist.

Moreover, Copland rarely explored Jewish subject matter in his work. The exceptions included a setting of the poem, "My Heart Is in the East," written by a friend of his youth, Aaron Schaffer (1918), and whose seemingly Zionist text must have resonated for Copland to some extent; a Lament for cello and piano (1919), after one of the traditional melodies for the Hebrew hymn, "Adon Olom"; *Four Motets* for chorus (1921), based on his own arrangement of biblical texts; the piano trio *Vitebsk* (1928), inspired by S. Ansky's play *The Dybbuk*; a setting of the Jewish-Palestinian folk song "We've Come" ("Banu") (1938); and an a cappella choral work based on the opening section of Genesis, *In the Beginning* (1947). One might add his incidental music to Irwin Shaw's *Quiet City* (1939), a play that addresses such issues as assimilation and anti-Semitism. In addition, at age sixteen, just at the beginnings of his compositional pursuits, Copland planned an "imaginary oratorio" with sections including "The Burial of Moses" and "Song of Miriam."[4] This side of his output clearly paled both in size and importance to his involvement with American themes and subjects, or at least those that were not specifically Jewish.

Furthermore, of those works with explicit ties to Judaism, only four date from his maturity, and three of these—"We've Come," the incidental music to *Quiet City*, and *In the Beginning*—were commissioned as such. Copland possibly even fashioned himself at the outset of his career as something of a Jewish composer before moving on in other directions. But in any case, as it turned out, *Vitebsk* proved his only mature work on a Jewish theme undertaken on his own initiative, and that piece reflected on the social conditions of East European ghetto life as opposed to the legacy of ancient Israel or the Jewish-American experience. "What preoccupied me was the fact that America had not found its voice as Germany and then France had in producing composers in the music world," he once stated. "The Jewish national aspect had never preoccupied me."[5]

Copland's slim catalogue of explicitly Jewish works is potentially misleading, however, since he mostly wrote instrumental music with abstract
or fairly neutral titles, so that their meanings are inherently elusive, certainly to the listener, and possibly to the composer himself. Over the
years, many sensitive and knowing listeners were struck by connections
between Copland's music and the Old Testament, in particular the biblical prophets, an association all the more surprising considering that
this same music was regarded as avant-garde and cosmopolitan; moreover, nothing in his music explicitly pointed to this connection aside
from the movement "Prophecy" that concluded a 1934 orchestral work,
Statements. "He is a prophet calling out her sins to Israel," wrote his friend,
colleague, and rival Virgil Thomson, for instance, in a seminal 1932 article on the composer. "He is filled with the fear of God. His music is an
evocation of the fury of God. His God is the god of battle, the Lord of
Hosts, the jealous, the angry, the avenging god, who rides upon the
storm."[6] Thomson, it must be said, was overplaying his hand in this
article, and duly tempered such remarks in later years; but he always
maintained the idea that Copland was essentially "the Jewish preacher telling
people right and wrong."[7]

Many other knowing listeners similarly identified Copland with the
Old Testament and biblical prophecy, especially in the years before such
works as *Rodeo* and *Appalachian Spring* dimmed such associations. Paul
Rosenfeld, like Thomson one of America's superior music critics of the early
twentieth century, wrote of Copland's music as "finely Hebraic, harsh and
solemn, like the sentences of brooding rabbis," while the brilliant pianist
John Kirkpatrick detected in Copland's 1941 Piano Sonata "a strong contact with the Old Testament, which evidently operates quite without the
composer's knowledge."[8] "That voice, the Mosaic voice," recalled Copland's
good friend Leo Smit, " . . . the first time I heard the opening of the Piano
Concerto, I thought of Moses blasting away on the mountaintop."[9] In his
landmark biography of Copland, Arthur Berger, discussing certain passages
of Copland, was reminded of "the psalmodic chants for the synagogue with
their biblical air of prophecy and gloom."[10] And yet another close friend,
Leonard Bernstein, spoke of "the prophetic statement" and "the reflective
mediation" found in all of Copland's music from the Piano Variations and
Billy the Kid to the Nonet and *Inscape*.[11]

Even without direct reference to anything biblical per se, Copland's
critics sometimes cast him in a quasi-prophetic light. After the premiere of
Connotations for orchestra, composed for the gala opening of New York's
Lincoln Center, one critic wryly observed, "For the majority of the audience, all over 35, if the ladies don't object to the sweep of the statement,

it was totally evident that Copland represented an assault on their nervous systems which they resented. . . . It is strictly accurate to declare that an audience paying $100 a seat and in a mood for self-congratulation and schmaltz hated Copland's reminder of the ugly realities of industrialization, inflation and cold war—which his music seemed to be talking about."[12]

Significantly, friends and journalists occasionally spoke of Copland as a "patriarch" or "prophet" or as a "musical Moses," although his smiling and sympathetic demeanor hardly fit one's expectations of an Old Testament prophet.[13] Leonard Bernstein, who first encountered Copland via the composer's Piano Variations (1930), gave the following account of meeting him at a concert in 1937:

> I could empty the room, guaranteed, in two minutes by playing this wonderful piece [the Variations] I had just learned by Aaron Copland, whom I pictured as a sort of patriarch, Moses or Walt Whitman–like figure, with a beard, because that's what the music says. It's hard as nails, as Moses was hard as nails, with his tablets and prophesying and shattering those two tablets of the Law, and then trying again. I had this kind of connection in my mind between Moses and Aaron. And so I was shocked to meet this young-looking, smiling, giggling fellow.[14]

On yet another occasion, Bernstein, comparing this "smiling, giggling" Aaron to his biblical namesake, spoke of "the mysterious anima of the brother Moses, the stern and stammering lawgiver" within: "It is as though the amiable, cultivated Aaron provided the public voice for the harsh and resolute prophet that rages within."[15] Robert Cornell, another friend, viewed the famous Copland affability at least in part as "a mode of self-protection."[16] According to a number of accounts, when displeased about something, Copland could glare in such a way as to make one stop dead in one's tracks. A few letters revealed this rather stern side. After a younger friend and colleague, David Diamond, made a scene one night after drinking too much, Copland wrote him a letter telling him that it was "imperative" that he seek medical treatment: "Everything else is unadulterated crap: the liquor that you 'like the taste of,' the arguments, the posturings, the abusiveness, the insults, the belligerencies, the later sophistries, self-justifications, and letters of explanations—all of it is just meaningless and senseless crap. The whole goddam thing spells one word: i-l-l. The remedy for illness is medical attention. Think it over and remember who it is that writes this to you."[17] In this letter—the best, David Diamond recalled, he ever received—one glimpses the same powerful moral presence often discerned in Copland's music, but rarely on display otherwise.

Other aspects of Copland suggested an affinity with the biblical prophets: his strong commitment to social justice and world peace; his interest in various nationalisms; his rejection of religious rites and orthodoxies; and his ascetisism (when the swami Nitya-Swarup Ananda visited him in his modestly furnished home in the hills of Cortlandt, New York, he remarked, "You are living here like a yogi").[18]

What, though, might be biblical or prophetic about Copland's music itself? Listeners who suggested such connections usually did so in the context of the music that seemed to express his inner self most directly—that for solo piano music. A speculative inquiry accordingly would explore possible ties between Copland and biblical prophecy by taking the solo piano music—in particular, the three major works in this area, namely, the Piano Variations (1930), the Piano Sonata (1941), and the Piano Fantasy (1957)—as fundamental reference points. As early, middle-period, and late works, respectively, these three pieces also conveniently span much of Copland's stylistic development: the Piano Sonata accommodates something of the folkloric interests that preoccupied him around 1940, while the Fantasy employs in its own way Arnold Schoenberg's twelve-tone method, which came into national vogue in the 1950s.

Whatever their differences, each of these piano works encompasses five distinct expressive modes that can be related to at least some aspects of biblical prophecy, represented here by the Book of Isaiah. These might be termed the declamatory, the idyllic, the agitated, the sardonic, and the visionary.

The Variations, the Sonata, and the Fantasy all open strikingly with powerful declamations marked by speechlike rhythms, brittle attacks, and leaping melodies, with only the sparest (if any) harmonies, as if to underscore the impression of a single spoken voice. No one ever had composed in a style quite like this before (Example 1). Such declamations can be found in a wide range of Copland works of various moods and functions, including one of his best-known pieces, the optimistic *Fanfare for the Common Man*, composed on commission during the Second World War as a patriotic morale booster.

Example 1. Copland, Piano Variations, p. 3.

Most of the commentators who spoke of the prophetic and biblical aspects of Copland's music probably had this unique declamatory style foremost in mind. The concision, the curtness, the severity, the fragmented phrases, the sheer force of the music: these traits seem closer to prophetic rhetoric, with its commands to hark and to wail, than to any concert music tradition. Compare the urgency, the insistence, and the stern and explosive severity of Copland's declamations with such a passage from Isaiah as, "Wash yourselves; make yourselves clean; remove the evil of your doings from before my eyes; cease to do evil, learn to do good; seek justice, rescue the oppressed, defend the orphan, plead for the widow" (I:16–17).[19]

Another highly personal but contrasting Copland trademark—his distinctively gentle pastoral mode—similarly echoes the prophetic tradition. His ballet score *Appalachian Spring*, to take only the most celebrated example, constitutes what might be the single most memorable musical idyll in the history of American music. Significantly, the work's choreographer, Martha Graham, suggested for the general mood of the opening of the ballet that the composer draw upon the opening of the Bible, that is, the creation story as found in Genesis (a text that Copland later used for his choral masterpiece, *In the Beginning*); she even planned, as Copland well knew, to intersperse spoken excerpts from the Book of Genesis in the course of the ballet's opening sections.[20] At the ballet's very start and elsewhere throughout his oeuvre, Copland evoked a deeply poignant and luminous purity by using the simplest materials in highly individual and novel but restrained ways; this includes a lovely set of variations on the Shaker hymn "Simple Gifts" for a depiction of a utopian community at work and at play, as found later in this same ballet. Something akin to this can be found in the piano music, especially in *Down a Country Lane*, but in the larger, more ambitious piano works as well, such as the second thematic area of the Piano Fantasy, a tender twelve-tone pastorale (Example 2).

Example 2. Copland, Piano Fantasy, p. 14.

The pastorale functions strongly in biblical prophecy as well. Isaiah dreams of "a return to simple, idyllic conditions," writes Robert Gordis, referring to Isaiah's famous lines: "They shall beat their swords into plowshares, and their spears into pruning hooks; nation shall not lift up sword against nation, neither shall they learn war any more" (II: 4).[21] Contrasting such idealism with Plato's vision of a utopia "safeguarded by a standing army," Gordis argues that such utopian pacifism represents a uniquely Jewish tradition, a tradition that Copland seems to have tapped in his own way.[22]

In yet another vein, Copland's music reveals a strongly agitated—or what one might also call a restless or nervous—quality. This trait can even be found in the complete ballet score to *Appalachian Spring*, for in preparing the popular ballet suite, Copland removed some of its more agitated sections, including the episode "Fear in the Night," choreographed by Martha Graham as a minister's hell-and-brimfire sermon. The Piano Fantasy also has a number of passages with directives like "restless, hesitant," "hurried and tense," "agitated," "uncertain," "violent," "furiously," and "insistent." Copland often communicates such ideas by impulsively and almost obsessively repeating short motives in halting and shifting metrical contexts against barely moving, often very dissonant harmonies (Example 3).

Example 3. Copland, Piano Fantasy, p. 6.

If not commonly associated with Copland, such restlessness is famously characteristic of the troubled, often anguished prophets, quick to remind people of God's wrath, as in this passage from Isaiah (XXI: 3–4): "Therefore my loins are filled with anguish; pangs have seized me, like the pangs of a woman in labor; I am bowed down so that I cannot hear, I am dismayed so that I cannot see. My mind reels, horror has appalled me; the twilight I longed for has been turned for me into trembling."[23] Some theologians have argued that such restlessness marks a principal distinction between Judaism, with its anticipations and hopes for the Kingdom of God, and Christianity, with its sense of salvation and fulfillment attending the arrival of Jesus. Significantly, in his depiction of the settling of the American frontier, *Billy the Kid*, Copland resorts to a high degree of tension, suggesting that the settlers have not so much found a promised land as they are still in the process of seeking one.

Copland also proved a great satirist and often a particularly sardonic one. *Billy the Kid*, for example, contains a grotesquely ironic depiction of the settlers after they gleefully capture Billy, who, in this mythic telling of the story, represents outcast and downtrodden members of society. The music's humor derives from the banality of the material set within a discordant, somewhat bitonal context. A similarly edgy, rather black humor characterized Copland's music from the beginning of his career—as in works like "Jazzy" from *Three Moods; The Cat and Mouse* for piano; and the ballet score *Grohg* (Example 4).

Example 4. Copland, "Jazzy," *Three Moods*, p. 7.

The prophets also employed sarcasm, especially, as often the case with Copland, to make a moral point. Isaiah writes: "The daughters of Zion are haughty, and walk with outstretched necks, glancing wantonly with their eyes, mincing along as they go, tinkling with their feet" (III:16), and taunts the King of Babylon by exclaiming: "How you are fallen from heaven, O Day Star, son of Dawn!" (XIV: 12).[24] The authors of Isaiah no doubt would have relished Copland's bleakly humorous distortion of "The Star-Spangled Banner" in his balletic parody of the American judicial system, *Hear Ye! Hear Ye!* (1934).

Finally, one encounters passages in Copland—often at the conclusion of his works—that seem nothing less than visionary. Robert Silverman admired Copland's ability, in the coda to the Piano Sonata, to depict "a serenity far beyond normal human experience," while Dika Newlin, in a reference to both the endings of the Sonata and Fantasy, spoke of "wide-flung sonorities gradually dissolving into nirvana" (Example 5).[25] One finds a similar visionary quality at the end of *Appalachian Spring*, as well as in the concluding movement of *Statements* for orchestra, a movement entitled, as mentioned, "Prophecy." In all these instances, the music suggests a state of transcendence, if not some sort of cosmic vision.

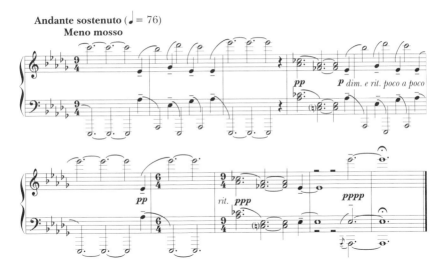

Example 5. Copland, Piano Sonata, third movement, p. 28.

The biblical prophets were of course themselves great visionaries. The Book of Isaiah, for example, comprises in large part a series of oracles and predictions, as in the passage: "Arise, shine; for your light has come, and the glory of the Lord has risen upon you. For behold, darkness shall cover the earth, and thick darkness the peoples; but the Lord will arise upon you, and his glory will appear over you. Nations shall come to your light, and kings to the brightness of your dawn" (LX: 1–3).[26] The convergence and conflation of past, present, and future, as found in biblical prophecy, can be seen perhaps as analogous to that sense of time-lessness found in the epilogues of Copland's great piano pieces.

Other works by Copland support and reinforce these suggested connections with biblical prophecy. In the popular *Lincoln Portrait* for speaker and orchestra (1942), Copland, who prepared the text himself, created a spoken narrative that intensifies the biblical overtones of Lincoln's words, with Copland standing in relation to Lincoln as the prophets do to the Lord: "Lincoln was a quiet man. Abe Lincoln was a quiet and a melancholy man. But when he spoke of democracy, this is what he said: He said: 'As I would not be a slave, so I would not be a master.'" The music, meanwhile, presents those five expressive modes outlined here, now cast in the context of Lincoln's life: the declamatory for Lincoln's moralistic pronouncements; the idyllic for his early youth in Kentucky and Indiana; the agitated for his wartime activities; the sardonic for his political career; and the visionary for his prophecy "that this nation, under God, shall have a new birth of freedom; and that government of the people, by the people, and for the people, shall not perish from the earth."

Another, even more evocative connection with biblical prophecy informs one of Copland's towering accomplishments, the *Twelve Poems of Emily Dickinson* (1949–50). Copland, who wrote relatively few songs, stumbled across the still relatively unknown Emily Dickinson in the late 1940s; drawn to her work and life, he set twelve of her poems for voice and piano, thereby creating a song cycle that represents not only his most imposing work in this area, but one of the masterpieces of the American vocal repertory.

Numerous commentators have reflected upon this fruitful albeit unexpected collaboration between Copland and Dickinson. No one yet has explicity suggested biblical prophecy as a possible bond, yet various Dickinson scholars have placed the poet's work in exactly that context, most notably Beth Maclay Doriani in her 1996 monograph, *Emily Dickinson: Daughter of Prophecy*. According to Doriani, the tradition of Judeo-Christian prophecy—here embracing a long line of Christian figures from Jesus to Emerson, but very much including the biblical prophets, above all Isaiah, who was one of Dickinson's favorite authors—profoundly shaped the content, form, and style of Dickinson's work in a number of ways: in its intensity, colloquialness, incisiveness, and vividness; in its exclamations and pauses; in its fondness for paradox and indirection; in its depth, passion, sobriety, and moral vision. "The Judeo-Christian prophetic tradition, broadly defined," writes Doriani, "provided Dickinson with a voice to speak about her own vision of spirituality and her experiences of human suffering."[27] This also included, says Doriani, setting herself apart from society in order to better communicate and enlighten her community through a circle of sympathetic initiates. After visiting Dickinson's home in Amherst, Copland noted with interest that she was able to view the "main crossroads of her town" from her bedroom window, which, he writes, "must have given her some idea of what was going on in the outside world."[28]

Significantly, the aforementioned Copland modes, said to have some prophetic resonance, are not only on ample display in the Dickinson songs, but trenchantly suit and illuminate the poetry: the declamatory in "Sleep is supposed to be"; the idyllic in "Nature, the gentlest mother" and "When they come back"; the agitated in "There came a wind like a bugle" and "I felt a funeral in my brain"; the sardonic in "Why do they shut me out of Heaven?" and "Going to Heaven!"; and the visionary in "The world feels dusty" and "The Chariot."

If Copland's music somehow mirrored or absorbed biblical prophecy, to what extent could this have been intentional? Discussing his *Symphonic Ode*, a major orchestral work completed in 1929, Copland stated that although he attempted to project an "American quality," he also had in mind "a—shall we say Hebraic—idea of the grandiose, of the dramatic and the tragic, which was expressed to a certain extent in the Organ Symphony."[29] Copland's use of the word *Hebraic* in conjunction with such adjectives as *grandiose, dramatic,* and *tragic* arguably points to the Old Testament and its prophets. That the early *Organ Symphony* (1924) was his first major work and the *Symphonic Ode*, the piece that initiated his association with prophecy (L. A. Sloper, reviewing the premiere in the *Christian Science Monitor*, supposed the work's opening section to represent "the majesty of the ancient Hebrews" and its climactic finale, "the August Prophets") further suggest that the absorption of Jewish traditions constituted a fundamental and intentional aspect of Copland's artistic makeup.[30]

In this attempt to find a place for the "Hebraic" amid the tradition of Western art music, Copland drew on the Jewish vernacular, including liturgical cantillation and davening, the dance music at weddings, and the shofar calls on the high holidays; but he also owed much to three admired composers who themselves appropriated biblical traditions: Ernest Bloch, Gustav Mahler, and Igor Stravinsky. In terms of his mature style, he plainly was particularly beholden to Mahler and Stravinsky; but something of his commanding moral presence and exhortatory passion may have been indebted as well to Bloch, a composer most associated in the public imagination with biblical prophecy, and one to whom Copland felt especially close before falling under the spell of Stravinsky and Mahler while a student in Paris.[31]

However, these connections also highlight differences. Mahler stood more clearly in the tradition of the isolated and suffering nineteenth-century poet-prophet; Stravinsky, in the more objectively modernist tradition, showed a marked interest in the revitalization of ritual; and Bloch came to represent the more nationalist aspects of the Jewish tradition. Copland warned the young Leonard Bernstein specifically against emulating these three composers as well as himself, but in a work like—tellingly enough—the *Jeremiah Symphony* (1940), Bernstein established himself as an eclectic inheritor of all four musical lines.[32]

In plain distinction to Mahler, Stravinsky, and Bloch, Copland subjected his "Hebraic" ideas to an overarching interest in developing a distinctly American music and in exploring specifically American themes and materials. Copland might have been speaking of himself when he wrote that his Jewish-French colleague Darius Milhaud proved that a composer could "remain profoundly national and at the same time profoundly Jewish."[33] As already suggested by consideration of the *Lincoln Portrait* and the *Dickinson Songs*, such confluence may have been particularly congenial in Copland's case because American culture and society had a deep-rooted orientation toward biblical prophecy, one that surfaced with particular intensity in the years just prior to the Civil War—the same period of American history that most attracted Copland. *Appalachian Spring*, for instance, takes place in an antebellum Shaker community and uses a hymn, "Simple Gifts," that dates from around 1848. Most of the American tunes that Copland selected for his two sets of Old American Songs (1950, 1952) similarly date from the years just prior to the Civil War.

Nor was Dickinson the only nineteenth-century American with ties to prophecy to engage Copland's attention. He frequently quoted Emerson and periodically thought about setting the poetry of Whitman to music. Harold Clurman, speaking of the strong left-wing sympathies that he, Copland, and other friends shared, placed such political leanings in the context of "the humanistic traditions of the Emerson, Thoreau, Walt Whitman epoch," referring to three figures with strong prophetic associations.[34]

Copland's prophetic inclinations, drawn presumably from his Jewish heritage but intersecting with national American preoccupations, arguably allowed the creation of a Jewish-American art that spoke to and for the country as a whole, with *Billy the Kid* a tragic account of the settling of a promised land; *Appalachian Spring* a tale of Eden and its fall; *Lincoln Portrait* a celebration of an American Moses; and the *Dickinson Songs* a profound dialogue with an American Miriam. In this sense, Copland wound up writing his "Burial of Moses" and "Song of Miriam" after all. The extent to which his Jewish-American music could impress listeners at home and abroad as quintessentially American no doubt underscores affinities between American and Jewish traditions, though it points, above all, to Copland's own remarkable achievement.

NOTES

1. Aaron Copland, interview by Martin Bookspan, April 29, 1980, transcript, Aaron Copland Collection, Music Division, Library of Congress.

2. Phillip Ramey to Aaron Copland, May 8, 1974, ibid.

3. Phillip Ramey, interview by author, May 9, 1994, cited in Howard Pollack, *Aaron Copland: The Life and Work of an Uncommon Man* (New York: Henry Holt, 1999), p. 28.

4. Ibid., p. 33.

5. Copland, interview by Martin Bookspan.

6. Virgil Thomson, "Aaron Copland," *Modern Music* 9, no. 2 (1932): 67.

7. Virgil Thomson, *Virgil Thomson* (New York: Da Capo, 1966), pp. 276–77; Aaron Copland and Vivian Perlis, *Copland: 1900 Through 1942* (New York: St. Martin's/Marek, 1984), p. 199.

8. Paul Rosenfeld, *Discoveries of a Music Critic* (New York: Harcourt, Brace, 1936), p. 334; John Kirkpatrick, "Aaron Copland's Piano Sonata," *Modern Music* 19.4 (1942): 246.

9. Aaron Copland and Vivian Perlis, *Copland Since 1943* (New York: St. Martin's Press, 1989), p. 251.

10. Arthur Berger, *Aaron Copland* (New York: Oxford University Press, 1953), p. 52.

11. Leonard Bernstein, "Aaron and Moses: Copland at 75," *Findings* (New York: Simon and Schuster, 1982), pp. 314–16.

12. Robert J. Landry, "Philharmonic Hall's Historic Preem: Glam, Traffic Jam and Copland Capers," *Variety*, September 26, 1962.

13. See Pollack, *Aaron Copland*, pp. 521, 657 n. 12.

14. Leonard Bernstein, quoted in Copland and Perlis, *Copland: 1900–1942*, p. 337.

15. Bernstein, "Aaron and Moses," p. 315.

16. Robert Cornell, interview by author, July 29, 1995.

17. Aaron Copland, letter to David Diamond, February 17, 1947, Copland Collection.

18. Nitya-Swarup Ananda, quoted in Pollack, *Aaron Copland*, p. 28.

19. "Isaiah," *The New Oxford Annotated Bible* (New York: Oxford University Press, 1991), p. 868.

20. Pollack, *Aaron Copland*, p. 395.

21. "Isaiah," p. 869.

22. Robert Gordis, *Poets, Prophets, and Sages: Essays in Biblical Interpretation* (Bloomington, Ind.: Indiana University Press, 1971), pp. 264–65.

23. "Isaiah," p. 892.

24. Ibid., pp. 871, 885.

25. Robert Silverman, liner notes, Copland, *Piano Sonata,* Orion ORS 7280; Dika Newlin, "The Piano Music of Aaron Copland," *Piano Quarterly* 111 (1980): 11.

26. "Isaiah," p. 949.

27. Beth Maclay Doriani, *Emily Dickinson: Daughter of Prophecy* (Amherst, Mass.: University of Massachusetts Press, 1996), p. 5.

28. Copland and Perlis, *Copland Since 1943*, p. 158.

29. Edward T. Cone, "Conversation with Aaron Copland," *Perspectives of New Music* 6.2 (1968): 64.

30. L. A. Sloper, review of Copland's *Symphonic Ode, Christian Science Monitor,* February 2, 1930, quoted in Julia Frances Smith, *Aaron Copland: His Work and Contribution to American Music* (New York: Dutton, 1955), pp. 138–39.

31. Pollack, *Aaron Copland*, p. 36.

32. Ibid., pp. 194, 522.

33. Copland, "What Is Jewish Music?" *New York Herald-Tribune,* October 2, 1949.

34. Harold Clurman, *The Fervent Years: The Group Theatre and the Thirties* (New York: Da Capo, 1941, 1975), pp. 290–92.

Founding Sons:

Copland, Sessions, and Berger on

Genealogy and Hybridity

MARTIN BRODY

> The idea was entirely original with me.
> —Aaron Copland

In his deceptively genial autobiographical "sketch," "Composer from Brooklyn" (1939), Aaron Copland elaborated an enigma, the riddle of his immaculate artistic conception. The story began in an unlikely setting:

> I was born on a street in Brooklyn that can only be described as drab. It had none of the garish color of the ghetto, none of the charm of an old New England thoroughfare, or even the rawness of a pioneer street. It was simply drab. . . . I am filled with mild wonder each time I realize that a musician was born on that street.[1]

A site of perennial, multinational, and multiethnic immigration ("peopled largely by Italians, Irish, and Negroes"), Copland's birthplace nonetheless reminded him only of a vaguely designated, decidedly un-American location, defined by class rather than ethnicity: "one of the outer districts of lower-middle-class London." The composer puzzled over the incongruous scene; he must have been aware, however, that it exemplified a distinctly American predicament and a new kind of cultural milieu, what the literary scholar Philip Fisher has called "American democratic social space":

Open to immigration and flooded by immigrants in the century between 1820 and 1920, America was a patchwork of peoples. . . . With no shared religion, no deep relation to a common language, no shared customary way of life with its ceremonies and manners, no single style of humor or common inherited maxims and unspoken rules, the continental nation lacked just those features that any Romantic theory of the nation-state required. The radical choice to people the continent rapidly through immigration so as to "hold the land" by force of numbers blocked the patient creation over time of a historically or racially unified people. If patience and selection were historically essential, Americans were not, and would never be a *Volk*.[2]

The "mild wonder" registered by Copland in the famous opening sentences of "Composer from Brooklyn" reflected a long-standing perplexity about the nature of cultural identity and hierarchy in the United States, a diverse, postcolonial society. In amiably introducing himself and his neighborhood, Copland insinuated a radical question: What were the prospects for a national musical culture in a nation of immigrants?

In "Composer from Brooklyn," Copland ever more insistently identified the answer to this question with his own personal development and artistic fate, eliding considerations of aesthetics, ideology, and musical technique in favor of a characteristically American fable of new beginnings, hard work, good luck, and common sense. Conflating his family origins with his inauspicious birthplace, he elaborated a trope of originality: "[N]o one had ever connected music with my family or with my street," he flatly stated. "The idea was entirely original with me."[3] A paragraph later, he persevered: "Music as an art was a discovery I made all by myself."[4] And again, a few sentences later: "I distinctly remember with what fear and trembling I knocked on the door of Mr. Leopold Wolfsohn's piano studio on Clinton Avenue in Brooklyn, and—once again all by myself—arranged for piano lessons."[5]

After staking his claim as a solitary American original, the narrator of "Composer from Brooklyn" presented himself as a trailblazer, pursuing a new kind of American Dream and mapping the "virgin soil" of American musical culture.[6] Events unfold almost magically, as the eager protagonist continued to be "filled with a mild sense of wonder," now evoked by an unbroken string of good fortune. To study harmony with Rubin Goldmark in 1917 was a "stroke of luck" (since he was "spared the flounderings that so many American musicians have suffered through incompetent teaching at the start of their theoretical training"). And then, just when he was compelled to face the prospect of traveling abroad to continue his studies, Copland stumbled across an announcement for a new music school at Fontainebleau. The first to apply, he was once again pressed into pioneering service: "No one to my knowledge had ever before thought to study composition with a woman. The idea was absurd on the face of it. . . . [H]ow would it sound to the folks back home?" Linking the questions of foreign and female influence, Copland could deflect the debate over nationalism and internationalism in favor of a more ecumenical cosmopolitanism. He reported that he received an impeccable education from Nadia Boulanger, while steeping in the culture of Paris, the epicenter of modern art and music—without subordinating himself to an overbearing male master or the ethos of a rigid patrilineal tradition.

As the composer from Brooklyn describes the years after his return home from France, the narrative compression of incidents into mythic events becomes dizzying. An unexpected and unexpectedly sympathetic phone call from the much-admired critic Paul Rosenfeld left an afterglow of nationalistic sentiment: "I couldn't have been more surprised if President Coolidge had telephoned me." His relationship with Serge Koussevitzky, which developed just when the Russian émigré became music director of the Boston Symphony, was "a stroke of extraordinary good fortune for me and for American music generally." And so it goes, again and again. At the end of the 1939 version of the "sketch," Copland emerged as the first American composer to be fully assimilated into an urban American concert culture still consecrated to the Old World. Even more, as he blossomed into artistic adulthood his musical maturation became ever more closely identified with that of American music. While ascending in the cultural hierarchy, he transformed it, reshaping the institutions of American music and representing more and more far-ranging aspects of American experience. The catalogue of recent works that closed the 1939 version of the essay revealed an impressive range of genres, media, audiences, and collaborations. It spoke to and for the American experience in the broadest and boldest of terms:

> *El Salón México* is an orchestral work based on Mexican tunes; *The Second Hurricane* is an opera for school children of high school age to perform; *Music for Radio* was written on a commission from the Columbia Broadcasting Company especially for performance on the air; *Billy the Kid,* a ballet written for the Ballet Caravan, utilizes

simple cowboy songs as melodic material; *The City, Of Mice and Men,* and *Our Town* are scores for the films.

In a final peroration, Copland could claim that the "reception accorded these works in the last two or three years encourages me to believe that the American composer is destined to play a more commanding role in the musical future of his own country."[7] A young man, pointedly from Brooklyn, had triumphantly become the composer of America.

Forty-five years after the publication of "Composer from Brooklyn," Copland and Vivian Perlis produced an autobiographical book, *Copland: 1900–1942*. Revisiting his drab Brooklyn street in the latter autobiography, he lays out an entire Bildungsroman of New York Jewish immigrant experience—one that qualifies the story of a culturally neutral place and a pristinely self-invented person told in "Composer from Brooklyn."[8] The picture that emerges, of a large, close-knit, industrious, and upwardly mobile immigrant family engaged in a prosperous business, is anything but drab.[9] In the busy environment of the Coplands' department store on the ground floor of their house, the gregarious Aaron finds both a strong "central core" of domestic life and also a theatrical arena (with a "wide audience"), a "larger world than would have been supplied by a mere 'home.'"[10] His father somehow manages to become an elder and eventually the president of one of the oldest synagogues in Brooklyn, even while working in the family store twelve hours a day, six and a half days a week, straight through the Jewish Sabbath. His mother is "everything a maternal parent should be," an even-tempered parent and zealous coworker in the family business.[11] And his "uncolorful" neighborhood was in fact a place with intricate cultural mores and clear ethnic fault lines. The walk to school at Public School 111 took him through an Irish neighborhood: "'dangerous territory.' A Jewish boy had to watch out for himself."[12]
Copland also warmly recalls the music making that occurred in his parents' home and the constancy of their support, however anxious he was that his father might disapprove of his artistic calling. "My parents always had a kind of basic confidence in me—'If he thinks he can do it, let him do it.'"[13] Perhaps most decisively, he reminisces profusely about a charismatic comrade-in-arms, a "kindred spirit with whom I could share my yearnings and aspirations." Copland met Aaron Schaffer during the summer of 1916 at the Fairmont Hotel, "a gathering place for well-known Jewish literary people," in Tannersville, New York.[14] A "young intellectual" with an impressive pedigree (the "son of a respected rabbi in Baltimore, and himself a student at Johns Hopkins University concen-

trating on French and French literature"), Schaffer became a fast friend who corresponded with Copland for several years.[15] "Big Aaron" not only urged Copland to stay true to his burgeoning artistic ideals, but he inspired a powerful lust to travel to France. "If only you could come to Paris with me," Schaffer gushed, in a letter to Copland, written in 1919 (two years before Copland learned of the new music school at Fontainebleau), "wouldn't we be two happy Bohemians!"[16]

In the following, I want to consider the conceptual space between the self-representations of "Composer from Brooklyn" and Copland's later, more expansive autobiography—and to suggest that the narrator of "Composer from Brooklyn," far from denying the story of his ancestry, chose to mark it enigmatically in representing himself as a new kind of cosmopolitan immigrant American artist: the delegate of immigrant experience *in toto* rather than a particular group, and thus, the composer who could speak to and transform America's democratic social spaces.[17] Copland explicitly developed the conceptual underpinnings of this project in his 1952 Norton Lectures, *Music and Imagination* (which I want to read as a third kind of autobiography, one that interweaves personal anecdotes and reflections with a far-ranging critical and historical narrative). In the penultimate lecture, "The Musical Imagination of the Americas," he attempted to trace a map of America's complex, postcolonial, immigrant musical geography and to chart its hybrid genealogy—thus recasting himself as the artistic son of an African as well as a European diaspora.

In imagining an American concert music born out of diverse cultural sources, Copland identified himself with a crowd of New York bohemian artists and intellectuals self-consciously striving to redefine and domesticate the idea of culture during the 1920s and '30s. "[Alfred Stieglitz's] gallery was the hang-out for younger artists such as photographer Paul Strand, painters John Marin and Georgia O'Keeffe (later Stieglitz's wife), Waldo Frank and other writers I met at Paul Rosenfeld's apartment," he later recalled. Copland saw a special role for himself in this illustrious group. "They were all aware that music lagged behind the other arts, and they took it for granted that I, as the contemporary composer among them, would do something about the situation."[18] As the cultural historian Susan Hegeman has proposed, the writers and artists in and around the Stieglitz milieu created a new rhetoric of culture to address "a particular descriptive need in the modernist movement [that spoke to] problems [such] as immigration and assimilation; the personal experiences of group belonging and alienation; and questions of what constituted the best, or purest, expressions of a group of people, be they the 'folk,' the nation, or a region in the nation."[19] This new model of culture offered a modus operandi to map American social space in light of the diversity and fluidity of its groups and regions (in contrast to an ideology on the German model: one of genealogical purity and an evolutionary model of cultural development and personal *Bildung*). In his highly influential book, *Our America* (1919), Waldo Frank imagined a postcolonial, pan-American geography of different ethnic groups, regions, and classes, each engaged in a momentous struggle to fulfill its destiny. Invoking the panoptical figure of Whitman, the paradigmatic genius of America's democratic vistas, he conferred a preeminent role on the American artist, who might empathically channel the diversity of American experience and imaginatively grasp the whole. The magisterial Whitman adumbrated Frank's transcultural humanism. But the promise embodied in the poet from Brooklyn would not be realized until all Americans completed an arduous spiritual journey, which Frank described in fervid language that surely must have stirred the young Copland: "When all our people have at last come through suffering to longing, and then to the release in life, they will find in them music. And it will be American."[20]

Seeking this American music in himself (always, it seems with the imposing model of Whitman in mind), Copland confronted fundamental questions: Could the multiregionalism of American society be marked in a musical semiotic—and to what audience would this sign system speak? How might American music incorporate its non-European sources, not as subordinate if salutary "Others," but as coequal aspects of a postcolonial idiom? How would a historically conservative and Eurocentric concert culture adapt in an American musical culture that embraced its diverse immigrant origins? The urgency of such questions was intensified by a pressing, transnational crisis in modern music, preeminently figured in the premise of emancipated dissonance (which challenged the idea of a universal source of musical coherence in the elaboration of a "chord of nature"). Under the pressure of a pervasive modernist challenge to the ontology of music, as well as the demands of an inspiring if complicated new model of American culture, a young American composer might well feel like both a pioneer and an orphan. "The gods of the fathers were ridiculous or dead," Waldo Frank fervidly declared in *Our America*.[21] Copland echoed the sentiment near the close of *Music and Imagination*: "Gradually, by the late twenties, our search for musical ancestors had been abandoned or forgotten, partly, I suppose, because we became convinced that there were none—that we had none. We were on our own, and something of the exhilaration that goes with being on one's own accompanied our every action."[22] However, if the paternal deities had disappeared, the search (and nostalgic hope) for a usable past remained vital. Even as he recalled the youthful exhilaration of being liberated from one set of musical parents, Copland attempted to show how a perennially immigrant American composer might *choose* his ancestors: mining a variety of artistic traditions and repeatedly reinventing his musical lineage as he asserted a new course for his nation's musical culture—in effect, recasting himself as both a founder and a son.[23]

However, the tension between genealogical trees and multicultural maps (or, alternatively, between ideologies of purity and hybridity or models of cultural evolution and cultural diversity) would prove difficult to resolve. Copland reached a point of blockage at the close of "Musical Imagination of the Americas" as he approached a deep conceptual fault line within modernism, one that played out dramatically in a long-festering dispute between him and his erstwhile collaborator Roger Sessions. I will discuss the argument between Copland and Sessions below; then, I will juxtapose both Copland's and Sessions's positions on the ancestry of American composition with a reading of a few excerpts from a groundbreaking work of the second generation of Copland reception, Arthur Berger's monograph, *Aaron Copland*. Invoking pragmatism, Berger sought a musical idiom that might be both hybrid and "pure," while distancing himself from grand historical narratives or cultural theories.[24] However, the younger composer-critic was not thereby able to bring peace to the fractious community of American composers. Nor could he evoke Copland's Whitmanian largesse or Sessions's patrician hauteur as he contemplated Our Musical America.

I. "Our America"

The European cultures, swept to America and there buried, were half-killed by the mere uprooting. They were never American; they could never live *in* America.

—Waldo Frank, *Our America*

The title of Copland's penultimate Norton lecture, "The Musical Imagination of the Americas" in itself affirmed the composer's staunch, cosmopolitan Pan-Americanism and challenged the prevailing Euro-ethnic genealogy of American concert culture (as well as counterbalancing the East-West trajectory of his own family's story).[25] The lecture that followed was entirely ecumenical in its attitude toward North and South American relations. The two continents, Copland argued, are united by a shared experience of colonization: "In both North and South America it was only natural that from the beginning the musical pattern followed lines which are normal for lands that are colonized by Europeans."[26] Although the Latin American composers, Chavez and Revueltas, successfully channeled the spirit of the Americas' precolonial music, the search for indigenous American origins was almost entirely futile. Nonetheless, Copland concurred with Waldo Frank in proposing that the American musical imagination should not be focused on the colonizer's culture (even though Copland and presumably much of his audience at Harvard were themselves the product of a European diaspora). Rather, the imagination of the Pan-American composer, northern or southern, was *colonial*, nurtured by a cross-fertilization of diverse immigrant legacies with no fixed hierarchy.

The hallmark of this convergence was a new kind of musical rhythm, in which the European contribution was modest. "There seems to me no doubt that if we are to lay claim to thinking inventively in the music of the Americas our principal stake must be a rhythmic one," Copland asserted in an extended consideration of the mixed sources of Pan-American rhythm. Moreover, he concluded, "we owe the vitality and interest of our rhythms in large measure to the Negro in his new environment."[27] In elaborating, he carefully distinguished between the polyrhythmic structures in American music and a variety of European examples of polymetric complexity, which he located primarily in late-fourteenth-century polyphonic music and the Elizabethan madrigal.[28]

The question of how contemporary composers had assimilated their African patrimony, however, proved complicated. In addressing it, Copland repeatedly hedged, struggling toward a conclusion that was literally difficult for him to conceive. "We of the Americas learned our rhythmic lessons largely from the Negro. Put thus baldly it may be said, with some justice perhaps, that I am oversimplifying. But even if I overstate the case the fact remains that the rhythmic life in the scores of Roy Harris, William Schuman, Marc Blitzstein, and a host of other representative American composers is indubitably linked to Negroid sources of rhythm."[29] In elaborating this hesitant claim, Copland provided little clarification of his anxious imagery of teachers and students, Europe and Africa, and cultural miscegenation. Rather, he rehearsed an incongruous trope of nature versus culture: while African rhythm comes directly from the human body, European rhythm has been entirely sublimated into the body of mature musical forms. Transported by a mythic vision of the African rhythmic "gift," he described "a conception of rhythm not as mental exercise but as something basic to the body's rhythmic impulse . . . an insistence that knows no measure, ranging from a self-hypnotic monotony to a riotous frenzy of subconsciously controlled poundings."[30] He contrasted this attribute of lower consciousness to an entirely genteel European counterpart, "applying always to a phrase of music—as the articulation of that phrase."[31] The racialism of this scenario is tempered at least by a pervasive insistence that the contemporary Euro-ethnic composer is eager to learn from his Afro-ethnic predecessor. However, even as he suggested that the imagination of the American composer, inspired by African-American rhythm, has been freed to think of rhythm autonomously from the structural pitch hierarchies of European music, he immediately prevaricated: "This, of course is not meant to be taken as literally true, but merely indicates a tendency on our part," he cautioned, as if to reassure himself, and perhaps his upper-crust audience at Harvard, that the American composer is not immune to the refined harmonic treasures of the European heritage.[32]

Copland's inchoate effort in "The Musical Imagination of the Americas" to account for the African sources of the rhythmic inspiration of contemporary American concert music demonstrated the stubborn problems of cultural origins, identity, and value facing a composer-theorist of postcolonial American music at midcentury. The musical diversity of the Americas might be an inexhaustible resource, but it also threatened to produce an irreconcilable jumble of clashing elements. The potential to produce hybrid musical idioms—to draw on a rich variety of parent cultures—might be the distinguishing feature of American music, but this capacity would not easily yield a refined mode of expression or even a clear technical foundation to rival the great traditions of Europe. In "The Musical Imagination of the Americas," Copland found no triumphant resolution of the problem. At the close of the lecture, the unresolved questions of American ethnic particularism and cultural synthesis come back to haunt him when, in a characteristic gesture of inclusiveness, he acknowledged an alternative perspective: the "universalist ideal" represented by Sessions, Piston, and Barber—one that "belittles the nationalistic note and stresses 'predominantly musical values.'"[33] As he magnanimously acknowledged this competitive vision, Copland arrested the development of his own argument. Neither overtly challenging nor endorsing the opposition of "universal" and "national," he made no effort (other than by punctuation) to question the phrase "predominantly musical values." He even worried out loud that his search for a colonial history and a postcolonial model of American music might merely be a neurotic fantasy, the product of "a deep psychological need to look for present signs [of] the unadulterated American creation." The lecture then quickly closed with an unsettling caveat—that American optimism, "[if] it is not to be mere boyish exuberance . . . must be tempered . . . by a reflection of the American man . . . as he appears to us with all his complex world about him."[34] Copland, who had confidently called for "an indigenous music of universal significance" near the beginning of his talk, suggested at its end that the hope for a characteristically American music might be "mere boyish exuberance"; the nationalist impulse might be too "narrow"; the nationalistic note too shrill.[35] Without a clear program for integrating the various musical impulses of the Americas into a stable, refined, and generally intelligible form of expression, Copland seemed unable to resolve the dialectal opposition of "indigenous" and "universal" in his conception of American music.

Thus, he seemed, at least momentarily, to internalize the position of Roger Sessions, an old friend who had become an ideological nemesis. For Sessions, the remedy of America's deficiencies was unambiguous: an *exile* rather than an *immigrant* cosmopolitanism, the paradigm of which was not an assimilated immigrant, self-consciously creating a hybrid, postcolonial dialect, but an émigré exile, who—having come to the United States during a period of upheaval and crisis in Europe—had resolutely held on to his native culture and spoke the most refined dialect of his native musical "language." By the mid-1940s, Sessions's representative exile was Arnold Schoenberg, whom he cast not only as a paternal figure for young American composers and a model artistic citizen (a composer of "uncompromising integrity and independence . . . still the most dangerous enemy of the musical status quo"), but also an agent of the sublime, who had internalized a great tradition and led music through a great crisis (and to the advent of the twelve-tone method):

> The truly immense achievement of Schoenberg lies in the fact that his artistic career embodies and summarizes a fundamental musical crisis. More than any other composer he led the crisis to its culmination. He accomplished this by living it through to its furthest implications. But he also found technical means which could enable composers of his own and later generations to seek and find solutions.[36]

Ironically, Sessions's internationalism (often seen as a "sophisticated" alternative to the naïveté of "Americanism") had come to evoke a kind of nostalgic, crypto-nationalist ethos of unbroken genealogical lines and pure cultural tradition on the German model. In Schoenberg, however, Sessions had found a heroic individual who could stand, simultaneously, for Old World *Kultur* and American patriotism—a conscientious objector to "mass" subjectivity and culture who would allow Sessions to rehabilitate a neo-Romantic Weltanschauung while muting its neo-nationalistic undertones.

In "The Musical Imagination of the Americas," Copland provided no fully developed alternative to Sessions's model of exile cosmopolitanism (with its rationalization of the twelve-tone method and its genealogical link, via Schoenberg, to the Viennese tradition). However, Copland returned to the nagging question of musical sources in the final Norton lecture of *Music and Imagination*, "The Composer in Industrial America," where he adumbrated a resolution of his previous ambivalence. His model was the incorporation of folk melody or hymn tunes, a less charged prototype of cultural hybridization than the synthesis of African rhythm and European pitch structure that he had previously considered. However, rather than invoking a reassuring example (e.g., Bach's harmonization of chorale tunes) or evoking the trope of genealogy in any other way, Copland shifted conceptual models, reaching for something more ambitious:

> What, after all, does it mean to make use of a hymn tune or a cowboy tune in a serious musical composition? There is nothing inherently pure in a melody of folk source that cannot be effectively spoiled by a poor setting. The use of such materials ought never be a mechanical process. They can be successfully handled only by a composer who is able to identify himself with, and reëxamine in his own terms, the underlying emotional connotation of the material. A hymn tune represents a certain order of feeling: simplicity, plainness, sincerity, directness. It is the reflection of those qualities in a stylistically appropriate setting, imaginative and unconventional and not mere quotation, that gives the use of folk tunes reality and importance. [37]

Hymn tunes might appear to offer a simple genealogical link to Europe, but the American cosmopolitan, immigrant composer could claim no "pure" relationship to them, because he or she was in no simple sense a child of Europe. The imaginative work of the immigrant composer (and listener) *always* involved an unconventional distillation and recontextualization of expressive qualities from an intuitively grasped "order of feeling," because *all* musical material could be thought of as indigenous, all new musical creation an experiment in recontextualization. To grasp the order of feeling, then, was necessary but not sufficient; the *compositional* imagination also required self-awareness and abstraction. Moreover, the process of sparking the postcolonial musical imagination (identification with the appropriated material, abstraction and an awareness of difference, and then recontextualization) would not yield either a reified compositional technique, a fixed cultural map, or a stable relationship to artistic forebears, but rather a heightened self-awareness, comparable to what the artist and philosopher Adrian Piper has called "self-confounding":

> The aim of appropriat[ing Afro-ethnic sources] would be not to exploit deliberately the Other's aesthetic language but to confound oneself by incorporating into works of art an aesthetic language one recognizes as largely opaque to one; as having a significance one recognizes as beyond one's ability to grasp. . . . The cross-cultural appropriation of alien formal devices reminds one of one's subjectivity. Self-consciousness of this kind is a necessary condition of innovation.[38]

Copland might not have grasped all of the terms of Piper's analysis, any more than Piper would endorse his essentialist description of African-American rhythm. However, for Copland (who would be called before the House Un-American Activities Committee only a year after completing his stint as Norton lecturer), the effort to channel the order of feeling in a wide variety of musical sources would not dispel the historical and ideological facts of cultural and political difference. And the composer who wrote so much eloquent and warm regionalist music had also equated modernism with "a new spirit of objectivity."[39] (In incorporating "indigenous" sources to produce works such as *Rodeo* or *El Salón México*, the Composer from Brooklyn might also be acutely aware that he was transforming the sonority of the "European" orchestra even as he sublimated American folk materials into concert music.) What is refined, then, in the American composer's struggle to develop techniques of musical hybridization is the composer's moral sense, the capacity for empathic connection, as much as the composer's "craft," per se.[40] The musical imagination of the Americas is inseparably linked to the ethical imagination of the Americas.

II. "The Field of the Aesthetic"

The whole panorama presented to us through our senses, the surface of our experienced world, is the field of the aesthetic.
—D. W. Prall, *Aesthetic Analysis*, 1936

Taking Copland's music as his subject, Arthur Berger also pondered the diversity of America's musical sources and, like Copland, delineated a process of analysis, abstraction, and hybridity as a *modus operandi* for the creation of music that would be both modern and American.[41] For Berger, however, the endpoint of this exercise was not an enlargement of the moral imagination or a search for artistic parents in America's diverse regional and ethnic sources, but rather an ever-finer attunement to the pristine moment of aesthetic experience, unfettered by either cultural theory or the semiotics of national, regional, or ethnic identity. For Copland's history and topography of cultural differences (encoded in diverse artifacts and organized into orders of feeling) Berger substituted an open field of changing structural distinctions projected by physically and emotionally resonant tones.

The hallmark of Berger's aesthetic was the moment of pure artistic epiphany. Thus, midway through his monograph on Aaron Copland, he made a curious suggestion. Considering musical developments between 1920 and 1950 (the period in which the entire corpus of Second Viennese School twelve-tone music had appeared), Berger pondered a microstructural detail of compositional technique and wondered whether it might come to be seen as a touchstone of artistic value. "The matter of chord spacing may possibly turn out to be one of the great musical contributions of the last few decades," he proposed, "and Copland stands close to Stravinsky among those who are most responsible for it."[42] In an era of emancipated dissonance, Copland had mastered the art of "sparing tones," effectively emancipating the consonance, so that "spaces in the pitch continuum may be presented for their own wonderful luminousness." To demonstrate this principle, Berger offered five examples, all but one a single, striking chord, and all but one taken from Copland. The sequence of chords progresses incrementally, marking a time-lapse picture of vanishing chromaticism and dissonance: first a trichord of no inherent tonal provenance, then partially and fully diatonic collections, and finally a pristine G-major triad. This demure triad (placed next to a talismanic sonority in Berger's musical universe, the "revelational" opening E-minor triad of *Symphony of Psalms*) exemplifies Berger's critical claim that "new ways of presenting old triads lead to unanticipated qualities" (Example 1).[43]

For Berger, the production of new "qualities" was a crucial project of modern music, and Copland's luminous chords were paradigmatic. This involved a process of abstraction and recombination—a dismantling of conventionalized structures and then an act of reconstruction using their component parts: "new ways of presenting old triads." Liberated from the norms of tonality, Copland had produced chords with new spatial dispositions and pitch doublings, yielding evanescent new sonorities. As he contemplated the "subtle gradations of beauty" revealed when the composer's imagination lights on the ephemeral aspects of sound, Berger

Example 1. Berger's Example 25A–E, from *Aaron Copland* (Oxford University Press, 1953).

was momentarily carried away by the prospects for a new narrative of musical modernism.

> The extraordinary progress in chord-formation from Chopin and Schumann to Strauss and Debussy fastened itself upon a progress in the direction of ever more chromatic harmonies. But what if these advances in chord-formation were to be applied to diatonic harmonies as well? Imagine the vast new areas that would be opened by this means![44]

Intentionally or not, Berger recalls the story of modern music told by Schoenberg in the essay "Composition with Twelve-Tones (I)," in which he invokes another pantheon of musical geniuses (Wagner, Strauss, Mussorgsky, Debussy, Mahler, Puccini) to rationalize a gradual "emancipation" of dissonance.[45] But for Berger, this and other such teleological models, whether producing a mandate for dissonance or an art of noise, are the work of extremists. "Radical musical theorists insist that the only new direction for music is atonality or the replacement of tones by percussion. How wrong they are."[46] By contrast, Berger imagines an unbounded range of new possibilities, revealed when a composer dared to decouple the "extraordinary progress in chord-formation" made by nineteenth- and early-twentieth-century European masters from their concurrent "progress in the direction of ever more chromatic harmonies."

In fulfilling this anti-teleological project, Berger imagined himself to be working shoulder to shoulder with Copland. Writing to the elder composer in 1943, almost a decade before he published *Aaron Copland*, Berger described an example of how he had attempted to produce "new qualities" in his own music—by disentangling previously fused elements of European music through his own art of "sparing tones":

> I do not have any regret, however, about the pure white-note phase
> I went through. I felt that from Wagner thru Webern, the skips and
> rhythmic asymmetry remained inseparable from chromaticism and
> that new qualities were available by using some of these devices dia-
> tonically and within a regular meter.[47]

Although Berger never laid out a complete theory of musical qualities, he invoked the concept repeatedly throughout *Aaron Copland*. He praised Copland's Piano Variations as a rare case of sustained compositional invention, in which the unfolding of an entire composition could evoke the epiphanic experience of an unanticipated quality: "This was one of those instances when what Jacques Maritain calls a 'new type-analogy of the beautiful' seemed to have been revealed to us—namely, a new way of re-arranging existing musical materials to make 'the brilliance of form . . . shine upon matter.'"[48]

However, Berger was most explicit about the sources and effects of new qualities when he concentrated on local events, surface sonorities so fresh and riveting that they inspired ever more concentrated auditory attention (Example 2).

In describing the "Theme" of the Copland Piano Variations, Berger even conflated performance and composition as creative activities, insisting that the sound surface is a primary source of aesthetic value. Although he did not explicitly mention the resonance effect indicated in the score (the silently held C♯, another kind of doubling that produces a bracing surface quality), his description of the music, as performed by Copland himself, focused on the primacy of the individual, resonating sound: "He dwelt on

Example 2. Berger's Example 3, from *Aaron Copland* (Oxford University Press, 1953).

every tone, as if to distil the last ounce of sonority out of it—which was as it should be, since there were so few tones. (This style sets the pattern for the performance of all his piano works, which seem to depend somehow on the resonance lingering between one key and the next.)"[49]

In a recollection published in 2002, a half-century after his Copland book, Berger again recalled the "lingering resonance" of this performance and the significance that the opening notes of Copland's *Variations* had held both for him and Roy Harris. "We [Berger and Harris] decided together that it was not only the smallest rhythmic unit that occupied the American composer but indeed the *single note*, as if we were forging a tradition from the very source, starting at the beginning of time."[50] The creation of a new quality in a single pitch or chord, and the revelation it intimated, might thus outweigh the creation of an entirely new musical syntax—even the twelve-tone method itself.

Berger's American Dream of a primal, prehistorical sonority may seem hard to square with his effort to situate Copland (and his chords) next to Stravinsky. The opening sound of the *Symphony of Psalms* seems an incongruous emblem of the American composer, yearning to be released from the burdens of history.[51] Berger never fully resolved this incongruity, but he found the basis for a rapprochement in the idea of "aesthetic quality" as developed by the pragmatist philosophers John Dewey and David Prall. During the early 1930s, Berger had zealously participated in an extraordinary mini-academy that had formed around Prall at

Harvard—a prodigious group that included Leonard Bernstein, the painter Robert Motherwell, the poet Delmore Schwartz, and the critic Harry Levin.[52] Three decades later, Berger remained sufficiently identified with and immersed in Prall's work to write the introduction to the second edition of the philosopher's magnum opus, *Aesthetic Analysis*. In his introduction, he recalled the stunning impact the philosopher had on his group and lamented that Prall had not had more influence on the American scene as a whole. "For those of us striving for a better understanding of art [the publication of *Aesthetic Analysis* in 1936] was an immensely sobering experience. It seems remarkable that after all these years Prall's example should have so little effect."[53]

For Prall (as for Dewey) qualities were produced through the cognitive faculty of "consummation," which he described as the condensation of "the intricate and infinite matrix of natural flux" into evanescent but discrete experiences: "Only as we can sum infinite minute perceptions into large clear ones; or, to speak more literally and in more modern terms, only as we become aware of felt qualitative content, are we even conscious."[54] Dewey had described this process as a "rhythm of struggle and consummation," an open-ended dialectic that was modeled in the work of art: "The real work of art is the building up of an integral experience out of the interaction of organic and environmental conditions and energies."[55] The goal of this ongoing work was an enrichment of human experience, not by internalizing a fixed set of idealized cultural values, but by engaging in the enterprise of perception itself, concentrating on the qualities imminent in fluid transactions between perceiver and perceived.[56] For Dewey and Prall, as well as Berger, aesthetic experience was active, occurring on the fine line between concept and percept; and it was panoramic, engaging the entire domain of experience. However, it was also ephemeral: aesthetic knowledge was distinct from "anaesthetic" knowledge precisely to the degree that it was constituted without recourse to instrumental reasoning, ideological overlays, high theory, or reified histories. In *Aesthetic Analysis*, Prall worried repeatedly about the nature and scope of the conceptual baggage required to focus the experience of a quality without hypostatizing it. "The difference between perceiving clearly and understanding distinctly is not the great difference that we are sometimes led to think it," he acknowledged, but immediately added: "The most obvious fact about knowing works of art is that direct apprehension is the final adequate knowledge that we want."[57] Whatever concepts are brought to bear on aesthetic experience, they must not violate the intuition of perceptual immediacy.

In his introduction to *Aesthetic Analysis*, Berger echoed his mentor, insisting on the primacy of "directly felt appearance" and the capacity to stay on the surface: "As reasonable human beings we are capable, when we analyze our experience, of distinguishing between the direct and immediate apprehension of qualitative relations and our other preoccupations."[58] However, his taxonomy of chords in Example 25 of *Aaron Copland* (see Example 1, page 28) adumbrates a far more original contribution to a pragmatist theory of modern music.[59] Berger implied that an individual chord, such as the opening sonority in *Symphony of Psalms*, could produce the epiphany of a new quality, even before it had a context in a piece of music, not simply because of some prehistorical, primal, or otherwise essential quality, but because the chord evoked a diverse and consummately usable past: its freshness was set in relief against an unbounded history of prior triadic sonorities. The *Psalms* chord is stunning because it is not like any triad that has been heard before, and yet it is still experienced as a triad.

The recipe for a hybrid musical genealogy that Berger mentioned in his letter to Copland ("Webern" contours and rhythm combined with "American" diatonicism) suggests a general principle: the cross-fertilization of musical structures—a recombination of elements that challenges reified musical conventions—as a means of producing new sonorities and triggering experiences of new qualities. Copland's pretty G-major triad, in Berger's Example 25E, was emblematic, a genomic prototype for producing new qualities by recombining disparate structural particles. If neoclassicism was inherently hybrid in nature, it might also be American, at once returning to the primal source of musical resonance and evoking the whole panorama of the musical past in an ongoing process of recombination and self-reinvention.

Berger never said all of this in one place, nor did he describe qualities so metaphorically. However, he invoked Prall often in his essays; the concept of aesthetic qualities is at the heart of his analysis of Copland's achievement. At various points in *Aaron Copland* he explicitly linked the "qualities" of Copland's music with the synthesis of hybrid sources. He approvingly cited Paul Rosenfeld's "keen" insight, in 1929, that Copland's music blended (in Rosenfeld's words) "leanness, slenderness of sound with a strain of grandiosity," evoking "Wagnerian fatness, thickness, and heaviness." For Berger, this synthesis of elements was "still one of the things that invests [Copland's] music with a quite special and intriguing quality."[60] Elsewhere, speaking on his own authority, Berger grandly summarized Copland's capacity to incorporate a hybrid mix of preexisting elements to produce a personal quality and an American idiom:

By the mid-forties, Copland had not only absorbed elements of the American West into his musical language, but also New England hymnody and Shaker music among other sources. All of these, along with jazz, his first love, yielded an amalgam that for quite a number of years we recognized on the one hand as Copland and on the other as American music.[61]

At various points along the way in *Aaron Copland,* Berger carefully emphasized that the consummately American composer was not merely a "skilled folklorist." He praised Copland's "exceptional degree of selectivity, transformation, and abstraction through which the essence of the material as well as a specific attitude, heightened emotion, ingenuity, and personality are conveyed."[62] However, Berger (unlike Copland in *Music and Imagination*) focused his discussion on the wide range of Copland's techniques of compositional abstraction. Copland's folk sources, no more or less than the works of the European canon, were made up of molecular structures—in Berger's discussion they were, more often than not, triads or otherwise stacked thirds—that can be broken down and recombined to produce new qualities of resonance while evoking a memory of their origins. Thus Copland produced an "indigenous substratum" in his music, a modern American idiom made up of synthetic, hybrid qualities that could frame a variety of regional found objects: folk songs or hymns, cowboy tunes, or Latin American dances. Berger could hardly fault this achievement, and he concludes his Copland book with a caveat to both expert and untutored listeners:

> It is natural for the average listener to delight in music based on folk songs, and to credit the composer for the appeal that these by themselves possess. It is just as natural for the experienced listener—who is justified in a way—to regard one folk adaptation as very much like any other. Copland's case requires a further perception on the part of both.[63]

For Berger, however, this "further perception" always moves away from the world as given toward a world reconstructed—toward recombination and abstraction at the micro-level. His appraisal of the success of Copland's experiments in musical hybridity was correlated with the degree of their "consummation"—that is, with the extent to which indigenous sources were sublimated into culturally neutralized, "autonomous" aesthetic events, capable (he often seems to suggest) of producing a surprising quality of resonance or articulation. The trace elements of indigenous sources in Copland's music were eloquent not because of their interest as cultural signifiers per se, but because they marked the path of an ingenious process of abstraction. Conversely, remnants of "indigenous" culture that were not adequately subjected to compositional abstraction would smudge the aesthetic surface and distort the experience of aesthetic quality.

In *Aaron Copland*, Berger turned skeptical most often when he was confronted with an unadulterated musical quotation or an otherwise inadequately sublimated indigenous thing-in-itself, whether its source is Cuba, Appalachia, or the Wild West. For Berger, such ethnic or regional signifiers did not indicate an enlarged empathic capacity but rather a passive relation to the past—or even worse, artistically dubious motives: "[Copland] was very much concerned over the foreign market, South America in particular, and he spoke of the need for some local stamp so that our music would be recognizable there," he proposed in discussing Latin American musical materials. Elsewhere he described Copland's incorporation of folk music, whatever its beneficial artistic effects, as "an aspect of his campaign to achieve a simple style and a content that would engage the interest of a wider audience."[64] About this campaign itself, Berger was unambiguous. At the culmination of a passage on Copland's populism, he uniquely loses his composure:

> The vein of optimism and patriotic sentiment, formerly confined to Rotarians and conservative artists, became *the thing* in the ranks of the *avant-garde,* and even composers who were unaware of the sociological origins fell in line, responding to what they thought was a purely creative trend. In their cries of "America I love you," beating their breasts, they sometimes outdid the Rotarians. Copland has never gone to this extreme, but came precariously close to it in *Lincoln Portrait.*[65]

The sources of Berger's evident ire in this passage are complicated; his crowd of Rotarians might easily have included more than a few Stalinist fellow travelers.[66] My point here is that Berger's theory of qualities rendered an ethos of musical hybridity far different from that of Copland's, with its correlative principle of empathic connection to the "order of feeling" of a cultural other. As Berger makes clear elsewhere, in a discussion that doesn't involve Copland, the expression of musical qualities and emotion requires an erasure of the "outside world":

Tones themselves are, to start with, emotionally toned. A high, loud sound has its aura of excitement, however limited or diluted that may be under certain conditions. . . . A composer's choice of a high sound to complete a formal pattern involves an accompanying, probably unconscious, approval of the feeling that comes in its wake. It is a feeling, moreover, that is not a mere matter of association like the relation of most words to their object. If the listener can resist assimilating the sound to anything obvious in the outside world, its function and meaning will be precisely what they are by virtue of its place within the music's structure.[67]

The "universality" of this model is panoramic, unimpeded by any fixed genealogy or cultural boundary. However, it reverses the implicit logic of Copland's *Music and Imagination*. For Copland, there is a rhythm of conceptual struggle leading to *empathic* consummation—the latter resulting when the effort to integrate cultural differences yields a heightened sensitivity to others. For Berger, there is a rhythm of struggle leading to a consummation *via abstraction*: the evaporation of identifying cultural markers that might inhibit the autonomous aesthetic experience.

Coda: "I, of course, love both."

In the opening of *Aaron Copland*, Arthur Berger offered a bit of wry, homespun historiography, a dutiful condensation of the elder composer's self-representation in "Composer from Brooklyn." "It has long ceased to be a norm for composers to appear on the scene as 'descendants' . . . of a long line of illustrious musicians," Berger suggested. In place of this outdated genealogical trope, he conjured up the image of a dispossessed but undaunted waif: "the portrait of a young man clamoring for musical education, passionately seeking contact with serious musicians, struggling for sheer existence in a milieu consecrated to quite other things." Such a person is "not uncommon nowadays," Berger continued, adding a dry peroration: "to this class of individuals Aaron Copland belongs."[68] Unlike the Composer from Brooklyn, Berger's Copland was not a solitary, triumphant pioneer but rather a member of an embattled class of individuals—artistically orphaned sons and daughters, aspiring to secure the foundations of their art but stuck, it seemed, in a purgatory of "clamoring," "seeking," and "struggling." At midcentury, Berger already seemed aware that he could produce no model of structure or culture that would contain the diversity of America's music.

Indeed, his aestheticism, grounded in Prall's idea of qualities and inflected by his skeptical populism, would often mark a barrier between him and Copland. Despite their differences, however, and the increasingly fragmented subcultures of American music that they inhabited, they sustained a deep and consistently sympathetic bond—one that is movingly manifested in five decades of correspondence.[69] However, at one point in this long and warm dialogue, the underlying conflict surfaced, and the generally serene Copland turned feisty. "The other night, while walking down Hollywood Blvd., I happened on a copy of the *Partisan Review*," he wrote to Berger in the spring of 1943. "Imagine my surprise when I came upon your piece on [my] Piano Sonata. I wonder what made you not tell me about it—just neglect? Or was it 'fright' at my reaction?" He proceeded to chide Berger for "rather overdo[ing] the dichotomy between my 'severe' and 'simple' styles. The inference is that only the severe style is really serious. I don't believe that." The letter closes with a uniquely unvarnished judgment and a twist of the knife:

> (After reading [Alfred] Kazin's book [*On Native Grounds*] I've come to the conclusion that Stravinsky is the Henry James of composers. Same "exile" psychology, same exquisite perfection, same hold on certain temperaments, same lack of immediacy of contact with the world around him). . . . I don't think he's in a very good period. He copies himself unashamedly, and therefore one rarely comes upon a really fresh page—for him, I mean. I know this is blasphemy in the Berger household, but there it is—so make the most of it.[70]

Copland was probably aware of Henry James's hold on Berger's temperament, but his cool remarks on Stravinsky were surely meant to chill his younger friend, who responded with a torrent of qualifications:

> I am somewhat perturbed by the fact that neither P[artisan] R[eview] nor M[odern] M[usic] discussions of your Sonata bring out the tremendous warmth that I have toward it. It has become a really deep part of my experience—you know, the kind of thing that runs through your head and elicits a certain emotion. It may be that shortcomings are more tangible. By the fact that they do not become part of the unity, they glare out. And so one tends to dwell on them. Moreover, I sort of assume that everyone else thinks you're as good as I think you are. Also, people know I think you're good, and they know how much I like you aside from your musical achievements. . . . And mainly, words of praise are so cheap now.

Suggesting that things would be set straight by the mentor's return to his East Coast milieu, Berger momentarily became maudlin: "The sun kind of sets for many of us when you're away and we all get rather disparate."[71]

Copland did not go back east immediately, but his correspondence with Berger quickly turned genial again, as the younger man continued to generate the material that would culminate in his *Aaron Copland*. The wound, however, did not entirely heal. Copland recalled Berger's critique at the end of *Music and Imagination*, in a closing rebuke to his critics and an encomium to the diversity of American music.[72] Berger, for his part, revisited the incident in the opening essay of *Reflections of an American Composer*, quoting his *Partisan Review* essay and Copland's response at length, insisting again that there was a "sharp dichotomy between [Copland's] two approaches," and even invoking the salutary figure of Henry James.[73] As in his many previous writings on Copland, Berger continued to question the use of indigenous materials: "Works that lean heavily, for example, on compiled folk music—even those of Stravinsky and Bartók—are liable to give up their secret too easily."[74] But his longtime friend and correspondent the Composer from Brooklyn preferred to put his secrets out in the open. Writing to Berger in 1958, he gratefully acknowledged the publication of yet another essay about his music by offering a droll, conspiratorial comment on the polarization of the American musical scene: "You probably will please neither school: those who want a subjective, impressionist, historical appraisal; or those interested only in a thorough series breakdown from start to finish." His characteristic conclusion: "I, of course, love both."[75]

NOTES

Special thanks to Carol Oja and Judith Tick for their many insights and great patience in editing this essay; to Wayne Shirley for generously providing a pre-publication draft of his edition of the Copland-Berger correspondence; to Katharine Park and Alice Friedman for many discussions of the material presented here.

1. Aaron Copland, "Composer from Brooklyn: An Autobiographical Sketch," in *Aaron Copland: Selected Writings 1923–1972*, ed. Richard Kostelanetz (New York and London: Routledge, 2004), p. xix. "Composer from Brooklyn" originally appeared in *The*

Magazine of Art (1939) and was reprinted in *The New Music: 1900–1960* (New York: W. W. Norton, 1968).

2. Philip Fisher, *Still the New World: American Literature in a Culture of Creative Destruction* (Cambridge, Mass.: Harvard University Press, 2000), pp. 33–4.

3. Copland, "Composer from Brooklyn," p. xix.

4. Ibid., p. xx.

5. Ibid.

6. The pertinent passage: "I had left my drab Brooklyn street as a mere student with practically no musical connections. I was returning there [from France in 1924] in much the same state. As far as I was concerned, America was virgin soil." Ibid., p. xxiii. Although Copland refers to his own naïveté, the image burnishes his self-representation as an American original.

7. Ibid., p. xx, xxii, xxiv, xxvi.

8. Aaron Copland and Vivian Perlis, *Copland: 1900 Through 1942* (New York: St. Martin's/Marek, 1984).

9. In *Copland: 1900 Through 1942*, Copland felt compelled to defend his previous description: "To my surprise, the idea of a composer of so-called serious music being born on a drab street seems to have caught the fancy of many a commentator." However, in recalling his boyhood in the latter autobiography, he tones down his rhetoric: "To any boy living there it would have seemed like an ordinary Brooklyn street." Ibid., p. 16.

10. Ibid., p. 15.

11. Ibid., p. 18.

12. Ibid., p. 19.

13. Ibid., pp. 22–23. The anxiety that the young Copland felt about his wish to pursue a musical career are unsurprising, given the family's overwhelming work ethic and its aspiration for upward class mobility.

14. Ibid., pp. 24–25. The cultural geography of Catskills resorts in the early decades of the century warrants further consideration. The area around Tannersville, located in the northern Catskills, was a gathering spot especially for patrician, cosmopolitan Jews, many of German extraction: an upscale milieu for Copland, the offspring of a Russian-Lithuanian family of merchants.

15. Ibid., p. 24.

16. Ibid., p. 35.

17. In retelling and interpreting the stories of Copland's autobiographies, I'm mindful of my own complicity in eliding issues of sexuality from the narrative. I don't mean to minimize the personal or broader analytic importance of sexual difference in attempting to understand either Copland or music, but rather to focus on a different aspect of identity: how Copland and his cohort grappled with the relationship between America's postcolonial past and its culturally diverse present—and thus the genealogy of American music (in terms of race, ethnicity, and region) and its constellation of questions.

18. Copland and Perlis, *Copland: 1900–1942*, p. 125.

19. Hegeman brilliantly analyzes the process of domesticating the idea of culture in the United States during the first half of the twentieth century. The vision of culture she describes developed from the interlocking perspectives of scholars in the emerging field of cultural anthropology, culture criticism, and literature. See Susan Hegeman, *Patterns for America* (Princeton, N.J.: Princeton University Press, 1999). Carol Oja discusses the importance of Frank's historiography, specifically his vision of America as a latent culture only fully emerging in the twentieth century, as a strong influence on Paul Rosenfeld, among others. See Carol J. Oja, *Making Music Modern: New York in the 1920s* (Oxford, Eng.: Oxford University Press, 2000), p. 306. In *Aaron Copland's America* by Gail Levin and Judith Tick (New York: Watson-Guptill, 2000), pp. 13–14, Levin also calls attention to the impor-

tance of Frank as a model for artists and critics including Copland and Rosenfeld. (She notes also that Copland had been an avid reader of *The Dial* and an advocate of ideas presented there long before he personally met a number of its authors in Stieglitz's gallery.) Levin discusses the significance for Frank, Rosenfeld, and others of incorporating Native American or African art as an exercise in self-estrangement, a precondition for cultural renewal. I will consider Copland's thoughts on the matter in the following text and notes.

20. Waldo Frank, *Our America* (New York: Boni and Liveright, 1919), p. 188. In the passage in question, Frank elaborates an image of Leo Ornstein as a kind of musical American Moses, traveling on the path revealed by the godly Whitman, but not yet having arrived in sight of the Promised Land. The young Copland might well have read his own future in this fervid rhetoric. (See the discussion of the Copland-Frank connection in Pollack, *Aaron Copland*, p. 104, ff.)

21. Ibid., p. 223. Apropos of the death of the fathers: Hegeman suggests that Frank's *Our America* "reworked [Van Wyck] Brooks's schemas in such a way as to transfer American identity from the historical to the spatial axis, and it offered up a schema of spatial sites, both real and hypothetical, for imagining the transformation of American culture." (Susan Hegeman, *Patterns for America*, p. 104.) I will argue that Copland (at least the Copland of the Norton Lectures) is stuck conceptually somewhere between Brooks's temporal and Frank's spatial models: that is, searching the postcolonial cultural geography of the Americas for an adequately coherent "usable past" that is continuous and integrated with a modern, cosmopolitan present—rather than "opting out of the very sites associated with troubled modernity" as Hegeman describes Frank's polemic, p. 94.

22. Aaron Copland, *Music and Imagination* (Cambridge, Mass./London: Harvard University Press, 1980), p. 106.

23. One of the subtexts of this discussion is that Copland's invocation of imagery of genealogy distinguishes the rhetoric of the "cosmopolitan, immigrant American" composer from tropes of "exoticism." Copland also seems to be striving to work up a measured alternative to a prevalent rhetoric of cultural diversity as warfare and triumph (e.g., George Antheil's proclamation of "the victory of the Slav over the German, and the Negro over the Slav" announced in "The Negro on the Spiral, or a Method of Negro Music" [1934], reprinted in *Modernism and Music*, ed. Daniel Albright [Chicago/London: University of Chicago Press, 2004], pp. 389–90).

24. Berger was, of course, a proud member of Copland's self-described circle of younger composers; however, the relationship between the two was complicated. If Waldo Frank (with Whitman) seems especially apposite to Copland's intellectual formation as an "ethnographer" of the Americas, Berger is an unapologetically highbrow, analytically inclined thinker, on the model of the Trotskyite, often Jewish, New York critics who founded and sustained the *Partisan Review*. Obsessed with questions of the aesthetic surface, Berger was far more concerned with sequestering elite modernism from the encroachments of mass culture than with embracing the cultural diversity of the Americas.

25. The Waldo Frank quote used above can be found on p. 223 of *Our America*.

26. Copland, *Music and Imagination*, p. 79.

27. Ibid., p. 83.

28. Ibid., pp. 83–84.

29. Ibid., pp. 84–85. Among the various issues that Copland doesn't pursue here is the diversity of compositional thought among the composers in his "representative" group. As Arthur Berger noted, recalling Roy Harris's ideas about American rhythm (which Copland has in mind in the passage under consideration), the concept of a distinctly American rhythm did not always translate into practice in clear-cut ways: "It is odd that Harris's hypothesis in regard to what defines the American sense of rhythm did not seem

to have much of an effect on his own music, to the extent at least that I could judge."
Arthur Berger, *Reflections of an American Composer* (Berkeley: University of California
Press, 2002), p. 24.

30. Copland, *Music and Imagination*, p. 84.

31. Ibid., p. 85.

32. Ibid., p. 87. Copland's discussion of African-American rhythm warrants comparison with the commonplace tropes of cultural hybridity associated with Tin Pan Alley
and the musical theater in the 1920s and '30s. For example, consider this cheerful pronouncement, from the renowned Broadway lyricist, Yip Harburg: "[Harold] Arlen's
hallmark is his synthesis of Negro rhythms and Hebraic melodies. They make a terrific
combination, a fresh chemical reaction. George Gershwin did this too, in his own brilliant
way. Gershwin and Arlen created a new sound in American theater music by combining
black and Jewish elements." "Yip" Harburg, "From the Lower East Side to 'Over the
Rainbow,'" in *Creators and Disturbers: Reminiscences by Jewish Intellectuals of New York*, drawn
from conversations with Bernard Rosenberg and Ernest Goldstein (New York: Columbia
University Press, 1982), p. 146. As I am arguing, Copland reaches for a more magisterial
and generalized (but also anxious) vision of postcolonial, cultural hybridity. The unsolved
question of hybridity, refinement, and cultural evolution resurfaces often, especially
strikingly in Leonard Bernstein's "What About That Great American Symphony?"—a
playful imaginary dialogue between himself and an unidentified Broadway producer
that appeared in *The Joy of Music* (New York: Simon and Schuster, 1959), pp. 40–51.
Bernstein compares the German *Singspiel* and the ensuing rise of symphonic music in the
eighteenth century to the mid-twentieth-century American musical theater and the
emerging concert music of the United States—suggesting that the musical theater might
be a perennial breeding ground for elite concert music. By extension, he implied that
the hybrid musical idioms bred in the musical theater might eventually infuse American
symphonic music. Of course, the traffic between musical theater and concert music
flowed in both directions. Bernstein's *West Side Story*, a masterpiece of the cosmopolitan
immigrant imagination, is an object lesson in hybridity and the evocation of diverse
sources—preeminent among them Stravinsky and Copland. For example, the entrance
of the Jets in the Prologue of *West Side Story*: the octatonic harmony there and the
contour of its famous opening vibraphone/alto sax melody, tersely and ironically echo
Petrushka's *furioso* "curses" near the beginning of the second tableau of Stravinsky's modernist masterpiece, while also evoking cool jazz (particularly the Modern Jazz Quartet)
and, in the finger snaps produced by the Jets themselves, the embodied sound of the
urban outsider in the form of "beat" as well as gang culture. Indeed, the Bernstein of
West Side Story can be seen as yet another kind of founding son, integrating Copland's
Whitmanesque, self-aware inclusiveness and Berger's concept of hybrid qualities.

33. Copland, *Music and Imagination*, pp. 94–95. In the progression of cultural models proposed in "The Musical Imagination of the Americas," there is an intervening term
between Copland's postcolonial model and his discussion of "universalism"—a shift to
imagery of geography, which follows Copland's exploration of the colonial history of the
Americas. Invoking the vastness of the American continents and nations and their intra-
national, regional idioms, Copland discusses Villa-Lobos and Ives, Douglas Moore and
Virgil Thomson (pp. 92–94). Copland tacks away from postcolonial history in order to
provide a comprehensive review of the competing tendencies in American musical life;
however, he also implicitly registers a tension between the geographical and historical aspects
of a postcolonial model of culture.

34. Ibid., p. 95.

35. Ibid., p. 79.

36. Roger Sessions, "Schoenberg in the United States," p. 369, and "Some Notes on Schoenberg and 'The Method of Composition with Twelve Tones,'" pp. 372–73, in *Roger Sessions on Music, Collected Essays*, ed. Edward T. Cone (Princeton, N.J.: Princeton University Press, 1979). It should be noted that Sessions had already worked up some of the rhetoric he invoked to describe Schoenberg in writing about a previous European émigré father figure, Ernst Bloch. (See "Ernst Bloch" in *Roger Sessions on Music*.) In turn, as Paul Anderson has suggested, the novel *Jean-Christophe* (written by Bloch's friend Romain Rolland), which had also made a big, but perhaps not as significant impression on Copland, was a primary source for Sessions's vocabulary of resolute artistic individualism. (See Paul Anderson, *An Analysis of the Aesthetic Writings of Aaron Copland and Roger Sessions*, Ph.D. diss., Brandeis University, 2004, p. 18ff.) In shifting to the paternal figure of Schoenberg, however, Sessions could also adapt the Viennese master's historical rationalization for the development of the twelve-tone method and the strong model of genealogical continuity that it carried.

37. Copland, *Music and Imagination*, p. 104.

38. Adrian Piper, "The Logic of Modernism," *Out of Order/Out of Sight*, vol. 2 (Cambridge, Mass./London: MIT Press, 1996).

39. Aaron Copland, *Our New Music* (New York: McGraw Hill, 1941), p. 5. The pertinence of Copland's ideas about "objectivity" was suggested to me by the discussion of Copland's intellectual formation in Paul Anderson, *An Analysis of the Aesthetic Writings of Aaron Copland and Roger Sessions*.

40. Howard Pollack in *Aaron Copland* notes that the reception of *Billy the Kid* focused on the question of a Jewish New Yorker's uncanny ability to depict the American West. Pollack cites Copland's affable response, late in life: "'Every American has a feeling of what the West is like—you absorb it,' he explained to *Newsweek* in 1976. . . . He also related this achievement to 'Jewish adaptability' and 'the melting pot aspect of American life'" (p. 325). As I am arguing here, Copland developed his extraordinary capacity for musical depiction in relation to the work of a number of other "adaptable," often Jewish, artists and culture theorists. The complex rapprochement of modernist ideas and cultural hermeneutics that they developed deepened the meaning of terms such as "the melting pot aspect of American life," and demonstrated how questions of assimilation and difference could lead to new aesthetic models.

41. Epigraph: D. W. Prall, *Aesthetic Analysis*, 1st ed. (New York: Thomas Y. Crowell, 1936), p. 6. Further references to *Aesthetic Analysis* will refer to the second edition, 1964, for which Arthur Berger wrote the introduction.

42. Arthur Berger, *Aaron Copland* (New York: Oxford University Press, 1953), pp. 70–71.

43. Ibid., p. 71.

44. Ibid., p. 70.

45. "Composition with Twelve-Tones (I)," *Style and Idea: Selected Writing of Arnold Schoenberg*, ed. Leonard Stein (New York: St. Martin's Press, 1975), pp. 216–17.

46. Berger, *Aaron Copland*, p. 70.

47. Arthur Berger, letter to Aaron Copland, August 5, 1952, in this volume, p. 209.

48. Berger, *Aaron Copland*, p. 43.

49. Ibid., p. 45. As Judith Tick has suggested to me, the fixation on the individual tone that Berger describes here seems to echo Dane Rudhyar's metaphysical proclamations on the "gospel of tone." See Oja, *Making Music Modern*, 103ff. and Judith Tick, *Ruth Crawford Seeger: A Composer's Search for American Music* (New York: Oxford University Press, 1997), p. 48ff. In adapting Prall's theory of aesthetics to modern music, Berger found a conceptual framework that allowed him to jettison metaphysics while still contemplating the potent effects of individual sonorities.

50. Berger, *Reflections of an American Composer,* p. 23.

51. Stravinsky was, of course, a very different kind of cosmopolitan exile than Schoenberg. The Russian master's "lifelong anti-humanism—his rejection of all 'psychology,'" to borrow Richard Taruskin's apt formulation, made him an unlikely father figure, however strong his influence on more than a few American composers may have been. See Richard Taruskin, *Defining Russia Musically: Historical and Hermeneutical Essays* (Princeton, N.J.: Princeton University Press, 1997), p. 391. In discussing Stravinsky, Berger generally shied away from questions of subjectivity, focusing rather on the relationship between Stravinsky's "formalism" and criteria of musical expressivity.

52. Berger often discussed the importance of his studies with Prall and the group of students in his circle (see, for example Berger's introduction to the second edition of *Aesthetic Analysis,* p. x).

53. Prall, *Aesthetic Analysis,* pp. ix–x.

54. Ibid., p. 8.

55. John Dewey, *Art as Experience, The Later Works, 1925–53,* ed., Jo Ann Boydston (Carbondale, Ill.: Southern Illinois University Press, 1969–91), vol. 10, p. 29, p. 70.

56. Robert Westbrook paraphrases Dewey's position on the relationship of art and daily life in *Art and Experience*: "Industrial capitalism fostered an even greater 'chasm between ordinary and esthetic experience' by draining everyday social life of aesthetic quality. In modern society 'the hostility to association of fine art with normal processes of living is a pathetic, even a tragic, commentary on life as it is ordinarily lived. Only because that life is usually so stunted, aborted, slack or heavy laden, is the idea entertained that there is some inherent antagonism between the process of normal living and creation and enjoyment of works of esthetic art" (p. 34). Robert B. Westbrook, *John Dewey and American Democracy* (Ithaca, N.Y./London: Cornell University Press, 1991), p. 400.

57. Prall, *Aesthetic Analysis,* p. 39.

58. Ibid., p. xix.

59. Berger hints at the difference between his conception of "aesthetic quality" and Prall's in his introduction to *Aesthetic Analysis.* Speaking of the philosopher's conception of the overtone series as a "natural intrinsic order," Berger writes: "Prall, who is, I fear, carried away by the neatness of this natural source and veers to the traditional line of music theory a bit too closely for comfort, is bound to be construed by musical readers as having committed what is known as the 'naturalistic fallacy'" (pp. xxiv–xxv). Among the suspicious "musical readers" of Prall that Berger probably had in mind was Milton Babbitt, a music thinker who repeatedly criticized the naturalization of music theory via the overtone series. Berger never posited his own antiessentialist ontology of qualities, preferring, rather, a loose, intuitive, heuristic approach to the question. Nonetheless, Berger's project of conceptual reconstruction—like Babbitt's (modeled on the *Aufbau* of the logical positivists)—could be described in Lucian Krukowski's terms as an "effort" at divestiture of the ideological strictures of the past [which] became tantamount to a reinvention of the enterprise." (Lucian Krukowski, "Aufbau and Bauhaus: A Cross-Realm Comparison," *Journal of Aesthetics and Art Criticism* 50/3 (Summer 1992): 197. It might be argued that Berger's reconstruction of Copland's hybridity, using the technology of Prall's pragmatism, is analogous to Babbitt's reconstruction of Sessions's embrace of Schoenberg, using the technology of logical positivism—but that is an idea for another occasion.

60. Berger, *Aaron Copland,* p. 40.

61. Berger, "Nationalism," in *Reflections of an American Composer,* p. 57.

62. Berger, *Aaron Copland,* pp. 57–58.

63. Ibid., p. 96.

64. Ibid., p. 57.

65. Ibid., p. 29.

66. See Martin Brody, "Music for the Masses: Milton Babbitt's Cold War Music Theory," *Musical Quarterly* 77, no. 2 (Summer 1993): 161–92. See also note 28.

67. Arthur Berger, "Rendezvous with Apollo," in *Reflections of an American Composer,* p. 55.

68. Berger, *Aaron Copland*, p. 3.

69. See Wayne Shirley's edition of the correspondence in this volume.

70. Copland to Berger, April 10, 1943. Thanks to Wayne Shirley for identifying the reference to Kazin's *On Native Grounds*.

71. Berger to Copland, April 12, 1943.

72. See Copland, *Music and Imagination,* pp. 108–9.

73. Although Berger does not quote Copland's previous disparaging reference to Henry James in his review of the incident, he cites James as the authority who had best captured the pleasure of art that is "tougher and more challenging." Berger quotes a favorite parenthetical passage from *The Wings of the Dove*: "(The enjoyment of a work of art . . . is greatest, it is delightfully, divinely great, when we feel the surface, like the thick ice of the skater's pond, bear without cracking the strongest pressure we throw on it.)" See Berger, "Composers and Their Audience in the Thirties," *Reflections of an American Composer,* p. 15. James's image of the felt surface would evoke Prall's "aesthetic surface" for Berger.

74. Berger, *Reflections of an American Composer,* p. 15.

75. Copland to Berger, April 9, 1958, in this volume, p. 215.

PART II

COPLAND'S GREATER CULTURAL WORLD

"To Become as Human as Possible"

The Influence of André Gide on Aaron Copland

PAUL ANDERSON

> I do not claim, of course, that neutrality (I was about to say: indecision) is a sure sign of a great mind; but I do believe that many great minds have been greatly disinclined to . . . conclude—and that to state a problem properly is not to suppose it solved in advance.
>
> —André Gide, *The Immoralist,* Preface

As he traveled to Paris in June of 1921, Copland felt an extraordinary sense of anticipation. Born into a family of Jewish Russian immigrants who operated a department store on a "simply drab" street in Brooklyn, Copland had resolved by the age of fifteen to rise above the tedium of his inherited existence.[1] He therefore embraced every cultural experience he could procure within his limited sphere of opportunity. He sought out unusual music in libraries, engaged a composition instructor, and attended whatever "meager contemporary musical events" he could find in New York, all the while longing for the experiences that only France could provide.[2] When the Palace at Fontainebleau announced openings for a small number of American music students, Copland was the first to apply and the first to be accepted. His enthusiasm is palpable in his autobiography, written more than sixty years later:

> Arriving at twenty on French soil, my expectations were dangerously high, but I was not to be disappointed. . . . It was the time of Tristan Tzara and Dada; the time of André Breton and surrealism; it was when we first heard the names of James Joyce and Gertrude Stein, T. S. Eliot and Ezra Pound, and also of the French writers Marcel Proust and André Gide. . . . All kinds of artistic activities were bursting about me, and I was determined to take it all in as fast as possible.[3]

During his studies at Fontainebleau, Copland became acquainted with Nadia Boulanger, who was serving on the faculty. After some initial skepticism, arising partly from her gender, Copland became a devoted advocate of her ideas and pedagogical skill.[4] At the end of the summer term at Fontainebleau, he relocated to Paris to study with Boulanger for the next three years.[5]

Boulanger participated in the tradition, popular in France at the time, of gathering her students one evening each week to discuss art and culture in an informal setting. The topics of her Wednesday soirées were by no means limited to music, as Copland later noted: "She was the friend of Paul Valéry and Paul Claudel, and liked to discuss the latest works of Thomas Mann, of Proust, and André Gide."[6] Copland subscribed to the *Nouvelle Revue Française*, and enrolled in literature classes at the Sorbonne. He and his roommate, Harold Clurman, frequented bookshops in the hopes of seeing one of the great authors of the day.[7] By the summer of 1923, Copland had chosen a favorite among those authors: in a letter to Boulanger from Germany, he wrote, "I must explain to you that my friend Clurman and myself are ardent 'disciples' of Gide."[8]

This admiration endured throughout Copland's life. Quotations from Gide appear throughout his prose. His understanding of homosexuality and his sense of sexual identity were profoundly shaped by his exposure to Gide's writings. His personal library at the end of his life, which now resides in the Library of Congress, contains thirty books by Gide, far more than by any other author.[9] Gide's writings clearly had a profound influence on Copland.

But this influence is all the more striking because Gide's ideas and rhetorical methods served different purposes in his own life than they did in Copland's. While both men sought to embrace contradictory beliefs, Gide framed this activity in terms of conflict, while Copland spoke in terms of reconciliation. Gide's works portray a wrenching internal struggle fought openly on the stage of his literature, and which took its toll on his social standing and on some of his most cherished relationships. Copland, on the other hand, gave no indication that he endured such a conflict—his adoption of Gide's ideas served rather to enlarge his social circle and to increase his professional opportunities. The fact that Copland found Gide's ideas to be useful under circumstances so different from his own is a testament to the broad applicability of those ideas.

"The rules of morality and the rules of sincerity"

One of the earliest indications of a specific Gide influence on Copland's thought appears in a 1927 journal entry. In order to appreciate the significance of this entry, we must first consider the nature of Gide's moral dilemma.

Throughout his childhood, Gide had struggled with the rigidity of his parents' religious practice. His father, a professor of law at the Sorbonne, had been nicknamed "Vir Probus" or "Morally Upright Man" by colleagues at the university, and his mother, who raised him after his father's death in 1880, subscribed to an extreme form of Protestantism, which Gide considered to be harsh and unhealthy.[10] His first major work, *The Notebooks of André Walter*, which he wrote at the age of twenty-one, was intended as a proposal of marriage to his cousin Madeleine, who was devoutly religious. She rejected the proposal, mortified that he would publicize personal details of their close friendship.[11]

In the same year, he met a man who would exert a significant counterbalance to his mother's strict morals: British playwright Oscar Wilde. Wilde encouraged Gide to embrace the pleasures of life, including giving full expression to his homosexual desires. In 1895, while on vacation in Algiers, Gide immersed himself in Wilde's philosophy, taking a newfound delight in simple pleasures and engaging in sexual relations with an Arab boy.[12] But Gide's giddy fascination with his new way of life was traumatically interrupted by the news that his mother was dying in France.

He returned to Paris in time to be with his mother before her death. Soon after her funeral, he married Madeleine and sought to adopt a lifestyle that would conform to his mother's expectations.[13] But the marriage, which he and Madeleine agreed never to consummate, did not eradicate Gide's homosexual yearnings as he had hoped. He soon found himself in a confusing situation—married to a woman with whom he was emotionally in love, while indulging his sexual desires with men to whom he felt no such commitment.[14]

His writings convey a profound struggle with these irreconcilable convictions: a sincere belief in the goodness of earthy pleasure and a longing for moral purity through self-denial. Pairs of books, some of which he wrote concurrently, argue opposite sides of the question. In an early journal entry, written just weeks after he met Wilde for the first time, he wrote, "Like an invalid turning over in his bed in search of sleep, I am restless from morning till night, and at night my anxiety awakens me. . . . I am aware of a thousand possibilities in me, but I cannot resign myself to want to be only one of them."[15] Eight days later, he clarified the nature of his anxiety: "I am torn by a conflict between the rules of morality and the rules of sincerity."[16]

"My normal self"

In a 1927 journal entry, Copland outlined a similar struggle:

> I have two principles of living which seem apparently, and possibly are actually, contradictory. First: everything is good which makes me act otherwise from my normal self. Second: Never do anything which betrays my true nature.
>
> The first tells me to get drunk, the second tells me that if I get drunk, I betray my true nature.
>
> The ideal would be for my true nature to tell me to leave my normal self. But if it doesn't, should I force it? There's the problem.
>
> (Make list of examples of the first rule and of the second, thus: the first says to live adventurously, the second to live carefully. The first says experience everything since all experience is good; the second says experience only that which is admirable and good.)
>
> To-night it seems to me that I should force myself a little, like one forces a child to take music lessons for the sake of finding any possible latent talent; that is, get drunk twice anyhow if only to prove to myself conclusively that it is not in my true nature to get drunk. (This has other applications!)
>
> My ever present fear is that by thinking that I know myself, i.e., my <u>normal</u> self completely, I may circumscribe whatever latent possibilities I may have.[17]

The passage conveys a kind of naive apprehension, as contrasted with the profound agitation of Gide, but its content is remarkably parallel: a recognition that contradictory tendencies coinhabit the author, necessitating unwelcome judgments. Copland makes an important distinction between his "normal self" (representing his habitual patterns) and his "true nature" (representing his potential). In the final sentence, he acknowledges a fear that becomes a central theme—perhaps *the* central theme—in his aesthetic thought: complacency breeds stultification. The only way to ensure against a pattern of lost opportunities is to seek out and embrace experiences that run counter to your instinctive tendencies (your "normal self").

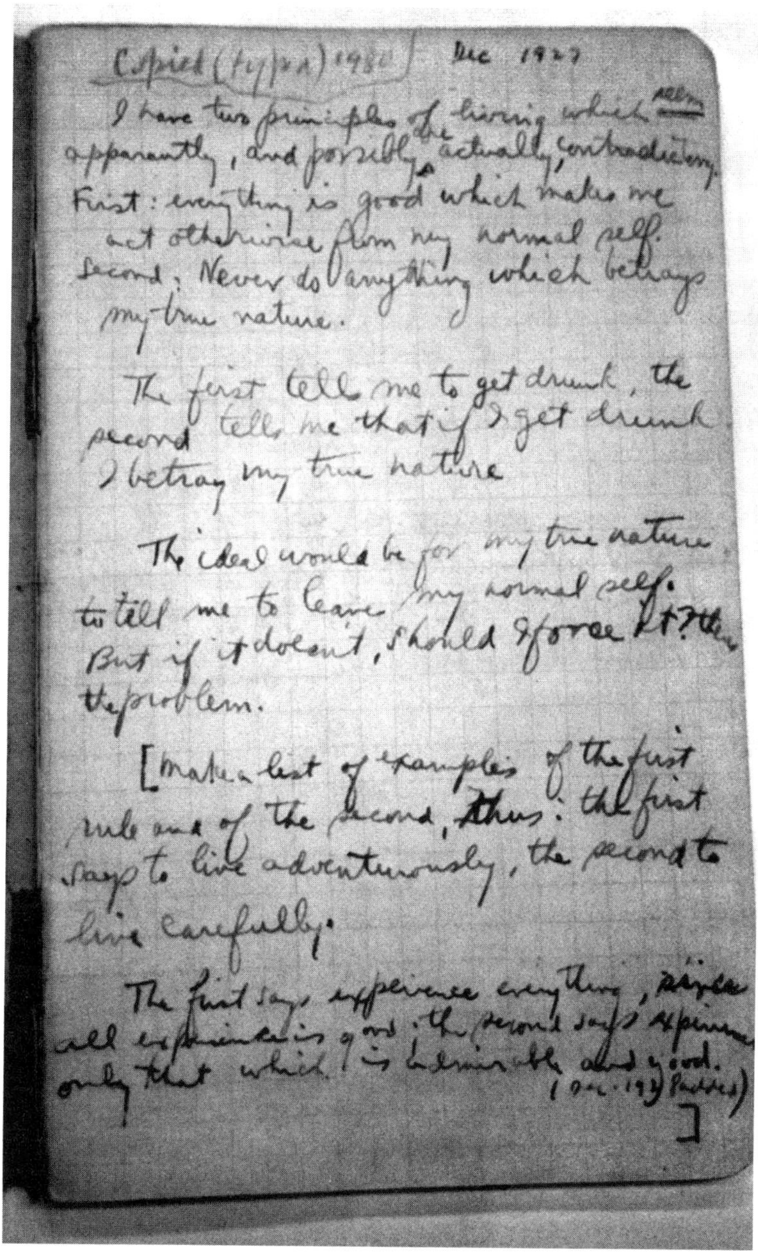

Copied (typed) 1980   Dec 1927

I have two principles of living which apparently, and possibly actually, contradictory. First: everything is good which makes me act otherwise from my normal self. Second: Never do anything which betrays my true nature.

The first tells me to get drunk, the second tells me that if I get drunk I betray my true nature

The ideal would be for my true nature to tell me to leave my normal self. But if it doesn't, should I force it? There's the problem.

[make a list of examples of the first rule and of the second, thus: the first says to live adventurously, the second to live carefully.

The first says experience everything, since all experience is good; the second says experience only that which is admirable and good.
(Dec. 1927 Paris)]

Figure 1. Copland's December 1927 journal entry. A part of this page is quoted in Aaron Copland and Vivian Perlis, *Copland: 1900 Through 1942*, which explains the annotation on the top left of the manuscript: "Copied (typed) 1980."

The following passage in the same journal, dated March 1928, further develops this theme and identifies the source of Copland's ponderings: "Gide says, 'Those who differ from me most, attract me most.' I might have written that. . . . My imagination takes fire when I am given a glimpse of the workings of a being different from myself. Our differences throw into a stronger light my true self."[18] As an extension of the previous entry, Copland makes clear that his goal of increased self-awareness is achievable only through exposure to the unfamiliar.

Corydon: "The pledge of a deliverance"

Gide's writings were meaningful to Copland because they exposed him to unfamiliar ideas. Copland carefully studied Gide's apology for homosexuality, entitled *Corydon*, because it provided him with new strategies of thinking about his sexual identity.[19] Unlike the other Gide volumes in his library in which he made few markings, Copland's copy of *Corydon* is filled with underlined passages and margin notes, made in pencil. Additional notes appear on a sheet of paper inserted in the book.[20]

The precise date of these notes is not clear. However, it is likely that Copland made them in 1924, his last year as a student in Paris. The book was first released to the public in that year, causing no small stir among literary circles.[21] As an admirer of Gide, Copland would certainly have been aware of the controversy and interested in its source. Copland's copy of the book is in fact a 1924 edition. Furthermore, his margin notes indicate a young man, anxiously exploring questions of sexuality and personal identity.

The marginalia reveal Copland's deep interest in Gide's ideas, an interest so personal that it engenders careful consideration and questioning. Some of Gide's arguments meet with Copland's immediate approval, others with skeptical curiosity, and still others with emphatic rejection (evidenced by such exclamations as "Rot!" and "Bunk!").[22]

The book consists of four imaginary dialogues between the first-person narrator and his friend Corydon, who is himself writing a defense of homosexuality. Consistent with his rhetorical style, Gide's narrator plays the role of a skeptic, to whom Corydon argues his case, appealing first to biological phenomena, then to cultural precedents (almost entirely from ancient Greece), to provide evidence for the thesis that homosexual activity is contrary neither to nature nor to the interests of society.

Corydon makes his case by extremes, arguing in one section, for example, that men are intrinsically more attractive than women and, in another section, that men should be encouraged to engage in homo-

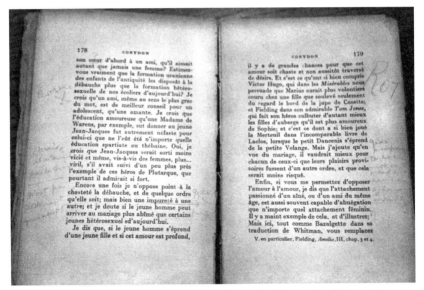

Figure 2. Two pages from Copland's copy of *Corydon*, illustrating his margin notes. See Table 3 for a transcription of these marginalia.

sexual relations in order to shield women from undesired quantities of sexual activity.[23] Copland contemplates both assertions with some skepticism. On page 125, when Gide asserts that women dress beautifully to compensate for their own deficiencies, Copland muses, "In ancient times, did not men dress beautifully too?" And on page 173, when Gide makes an implicit distinction between homosexuals and heterosexuals, Copland is quick to note the contradiction with an earlier passage: "Yes, but Gide suggests that everybody might be, should be homosexual for the sake of the woman!"[24]

Another controversial topic that attracted Copland's attention was Gide's model of the relationship between sexual desire and art. Gide claims that artistic expression arises from surplus male sexual energies.[25] Copland considers the implications of Gide's theory on an inserted sheet of paper:

Anagenetic—simply means the formation of tissue (fat) etc. The female uses her surplus "sexuality" for the physical profit of the race (to feed her child etc.) The female is anagenetic.

The male is catagenetic. He uses his surplus (useless physically) sexual powers in artistic endeavor etc. . . .

Afterthought—when woman uses her sexuality for her pleasure and not for her progeny she too may become catagenetic ("artistic"). Perhaps that is why in these days of much birth control in educated circles there are coming to be so many woman-artists.

Although he does not explicitly propound this view in his published writings, Copland indirectly refers to this theory on more than one occasion. In an essay on his former teacher, Nadia Boulanger, he notes the lack of any women among the great composers of history.[26] And in a 1952 lecture at Harvard University, he addresses the topic briefly during a discussion on the nature of the creative mind:

> I have sometimes wondered whether this problem of the successful shaping of musical form was not connected in some way with the strange fact that musical history names no women in its roster of great composers. There have been great women musical interpreters, but thus far—I emphasize, *thus far*—no examples of women composers of the first rank. This is a touchy subject, no doubt, but leaving aside the obscure and various reasons for the historical fact, it appears to indicate that the conception and shaping of abstract ideas in extended forms marks a clear boundary between the creative mind and the interpretive mind.[27]

Copland discreetly leaves the "obscure and various" reasons for this phenomenon unspoken. He may or may not have continued to give credence to the theory suggested to him by *Corydon*. But he is clearly fascinated by the lack of "great" women composers, and he conspicuously ignores the obvious explanation that social structures had precluded the recognition of a female "great composer" prior to that time. Instead, he seems to be convinced that the reason arises out of fundamental differences between men and women.

But while these theories stimulated Copland's thought, his primary concern in reading *Corydon* was with the book's central thesis: that modern society ought to abandon its condemnation of homosexual conduct. His most favorable comments appear on pages 175 through 178, near the end of the fourth dialogue, in which Gide argues that the prohibition of homosexuality engenders immoral conduct, whereas social acceptance would promote integrity.

Gide begins by asserting that "lust" is neither specifically heterosexual nor homosexual in nature, and that "virtue," in either case, "consists in mastering it." But in a culture that labels all homosexual activity as immoral, those with a "homosexual inclination" are reduced to "an academy of hypocrisy, cunning, and disrespect for law."[28] ("Bravo!" writes Copland on that page.) When Gide argues that "Greek morality" is more conducive to chastity and virtue than existing societal norms, Copland writes jubilantly, "Gide le puritain!"[29] He clearly concurs with Gide's argument but also seems to find it ironic that a defender of homosexuality could be simultaneously a defender of chastity.

By far the most important effect of *Corydon* in Copland's life was that it provided a logical framework within which homosexuality could be acceptable and even desirable. Gide concludes the book with a defense of the classic Greek relationship in which an older man serves as both mentor and lover to a younger man. Copland clearly adopted this model in his own romantic relationships, as documented by Howard Pollack in his biography of the composer.[30]

Gide hoped that his book would help young readers to find peace with themselves, and it appears to have accomplished just that for Copland.[31] Gide also contended that the book was liberating for him personally:

> It's precisely when one refuses to grant any importance to the sexual question that it threatens to take on too much. [This question] ceased to bother me from the day I decided to consider it up front, to truly deal with it. *Corydon*, far from attesting to an obsession . . . is the pledge of a deliverance. And who can say how many, with one stroke, this little book also delivered?[32]

However, the publication of the book did not by any means mark the ending of Gide's strivings with "the sexual question." Madeleine, who had previously discovered his infidelities, accepted neither his logic nor his avowal of unchanged affection toward her. After her death, Gide wrote a book in her memory, reaffirming his abiding love for her and mourning her inability to understand or accept that love.[33] Thus, although Gide's rational discussion of homosexuality may have provided Copland with a framework for contentment in his intimate life, such contentment proved to be unattainable for Gide himself.

"The varieties of human experience"

Whether or not Gide took seriously his hypothesis that art is a by-product of the sexual impulse, he clearly saw art as an extension of life, an extension that ought to reflect the most extreme possibilities in living. In an early collection of essays, he asserted that art arises out of "the pressure of overabundance, it begins where living is no longer a sufficient expression of life."[34] He sought in several books, most notably *Lafcadio's Adventures*, to craft a truly gratuitous crime, committed with no motive by a character who obtained no advantage from it. His intention in these endeavors was to experience as much of life as possible, if only vicariously, in order "to become as human as possible."[35]

Of course, by publishing his work, Gide knew that he was subjecting his readers to the same extreme experiences. This he did intentionally, with the same goal: "It is not in offering a solution of certain problems that I can render a real service to my reader, but in forcing him to meditate himself on these problems, of which I do not admit the possibility of any solution that is not individual and personal."[36] He wrote the book *Corydon*, "not to solicit pity [but] to DISTURB."[37] The artist's raison d'être is to "oppose," and thus to "initiate."[38] Gide believed that exposure to diverse and even unpleasant stimuli was a necessary step to self-understanding and personal fulfillment.

Copland described art in similar terms, as illustrated by this passage from the conclusion of his autobiography, published in 1989: "Composers don't write music to console their audiences as though they were composing lullabies. They write music to stir people up, to make them think about the varieties of human experience depicted in their work."[39] The wise listener will seek out and embrace unusual and even disturbing aesthetic experience: "Those who really love music have a consuming passion to become familiar with its every manifestation," he wrote in a 1941 essay.[40] And in 1954, he asserted that "we needlessly impoverish ourselves" when we restrict our listening to the familiar and conventional, precisely mirroring an aphorism of Gide: "I always feel I am impoverishing myself when I limit myself."[41]

Like Gide, Copland believed that exposure to a diversity of experience results in increased self-awareness. In the third of his Norton lectures, for example, he proffers an answer to the question, "Why is it so important . . . that I compose music?"

> The reason for the compulsion to renewed creativity, it seems to me, is that each added work brings with it an element of self-discovery.

I must create in order to know myself, and since self-knowledge is a never-ending search, each new work is only a part-answer to the question "Who am I?" and brings with it the need to go on to other and different part-answers. Because of this, each artist's work is supremely important—at least to himself.[42]

And Copland does not settle for an art that benefits only its creator. On the same page, he provides the obvious corollary: "And just as the individual creator discovers himself through his creation, so the world at large knows itself through its artists, discovers the very nature of its Being through the creations of its artists."[43] Experience, then, opens the door to self-discovery, and it is the mandate of art to facilitate this process.

Copland's advocacy for new music rests upon this model of creativity. A dynamic aesthetic experience will, by definition, challenge and stretch its audience, and performers ought to plan their concerts with that fact clearly in mind. "A narrow and limited repertoire in the concert hall results in a narrow and limited musical experience," he writes in a Norton lecture.[44] And in the London *Sunday Times* on October 12, 1958, he argues that performers need to program more contemporary music "to relieve the stylistic monotony of their programs. I have never known a public concert of variegated make-up that wasn't enlivened by ten minutes of controversial music. Even those who are sure to hate it are given something to talk about."[45] In the same article he appends a warning: the existing "apathy" in programming concerts, if it were to continue, would eventually lead to "the complete stagnation of music as an art."[46] Performers bear a heavy responsibility, inasmuch as they, through their timidity, not only deny the public access to vital experiences but also condition that public not to expect those experiences. Audiences require a "balanced diet," and performers are obligated to ensure the provision of adequate aesthetic nutrition.[47]

For the same reason, composers should strive for breadth of content. Just as Gide prided himself on creating many characters who differed significantly from one another, Copland judged the music of other composers based in part on the number of distinct "moods" they were able to evoke.[48] The music of Ives, for example, earns Copland's praise for its "richness and depth of emotional content."[49] Franz Liszt, on the other hand, incurs Copland's censure for repeatedly evoking only five "moods," and always separately, never commingled.[50] Likewise, after some early experimentation with jazz, Copland concluded that it was fundamentally inferior to serious music because it was essentially limited to two "moods": the blues and a frenzied hysteria.[51]

A related indicator of emotional richness lies in the music's susceptibility to multiple interpretations. When asked to interpret his *Symphonic Ode* in 1931, for example, Copland responded with the following quotation from Gide:

> Before explaining my book to others, I wait for them to explain it to me. To wish to explain it first would be to restrain its meaning prematurely, because even if we know what we wish to say we cannot know if we have said *only* that. And what interests me especially is what I have put into my book without my own knowledge.[52]

And in a Norton lecture, he expresses the same thought in his own words:

> An English critic, Wilfred Mellers, has found in the final movement of my Piano Sonata "a quintessential musical expression of the idea of immobility." "The music runs down like a clock," Mellers writes, "and dissolves away into eternity." That is probably a very apt description . . . , although I would hardly have thought of it myself. . . . I admit to a curiosity about the slightest cue as to the meaning of a piece of mine—a meaning, that is, other than the one I know I have put there.[53]

Copland goes on to assert that the existence of divergent viable interpretations is a mark of greatness—a piece that cannot be understood in multiple ways lacks "richness of meaning."[54]

Copland wholeheartedly concurred with Gide's thesis that self-awareness was a product of extreme experience and that it was the role of art to provide such experience. Throughout his writings, whether addressing the listener, the performer, or the composer, Copland consistently urged experimentation and broad-mindedness in the service of this principle.

"Inside and outside . . . at the same time"

In spite of his emphasis on extreme experience, Copland also encouraged a certain detachment on the part of the composer. In the book *Our New Music*, for example, he defines modern music as "the expression in terms of an enriched musical language of a new spirit of *objectivity*, attuned to our own times."[55] Various composers, including Stravinsky and Chávez, earn Copland's praise for their "impersonal approach" and "objectification of sentiment."[56] He even argues, on one occasion, that Berlioz is relevant for our day specifically because of his "subtle calculation."[57] This emphasis on objectivity as a criterion for the valuation of modern music is a manifestation of a French Symbolist influence on his aesthetic thought.

Symbolism was one of the most significant literary movements in Paris during the years Copland lived there. Under the tutelage of Stéphane Mallarmé, many of the most prominent authors of the day, including Paul Valéry, Paul Claudel, and Marcel Proust, sought carefully calculated effects as a reaction against the Romanticism of the previous generation. To the Symbolists, the goal of the artist was not simply to portray exceptional experience, but to portray it in an exceptional way. Unskilled authors, wrote Mallarmé,

> take the thing just as it is and put it before us—and consequently they are deficient in mystery: they deprive the mind of the delicious joy of believing that it is creating. To name an object is to do away with the three-quarters of the enjoyment of the poem which is derived from the satisfaction of guessing little by little: to suggest it, to evoke it— that is what charms the imagination.[58]

And so the Symbolists elevated "charm" or "beauty" above content as the supreme criterion of artistic stature, and they consequently cultivated a clinical precision in their creative process.

Early in his career, Gide was closely connected with the Symbolists, regularly attending Mallarmé's Tuesday soirées. But following his 1895 trip to North Africa, he forcefully renounced the movement, citing its detachment from life. By focusing on deliberate effects, the Symbolists deprived themselves of the rich experiences that might result from unbridled interaction with the world around them. "My great grievance against [the movement]," he wrote in 1926, "is the little curiosity it showed in the face of life. . . . Poetry became for them a refuge; the only means of escape from hideous realities."[59]

Although Copland wholeheartedly endorsed Gide's imperative of direct involvement in experience, he also considered Symbolist detachment to be an important element of creative endeavor. In his third Norton lecture, he explains how these two characteristics coexist in his theory of creativity. A composer engaged in creative endeavor places himself in a paradoxical state: "One half of the personality emotes and dictates while the other half listens and notates. The half that listens had better look the other way, had better simulate a half attention only, for the half that dictates is easily disgruntled and avenges itself for too close inspection by fading entirely away."[60] Copland's composer, then, maintains a degree of self-awareness while at the same time yielding to his own subconscious impulses. He must be "inside and outside the work at the same time."[61] He must cultivate the quality Schubert attributed to Beethoven: a "superb coolness under the fire of creative fantasy."[62]

Copland employs similar terms in his description of the listening process:

> There is something about music that keeps its distance even at the moment that it engulfs us. It is at the same time outside and away from us and inside and part of us. In one sense it dwarfs us, and in another we master it. We are led on and on, and yet in some strange way we never lose control. It is the very nature of music to give us the distillation of sentiments, the essence of experience transfused and heightened and expressed in such fashion that we may contemplate it at the same instant that we are swayed by it. When the gifted listener lends himself to the power of music, he gets both the "event" and the idealization of the "event"; he is inside the "event," so to speak, even though the music keeps what Edward Bullough rightly terms its "psychical distance."[63]

Like the composer, Copland's ideal listener fuses the contrasting attributes of objective contemplation and active participation.

Gide's commitment to direct experience impelled him to reject Symbolist objectivity. Copland, on the other hand, maintained a deep respect for the Symbolist aesthetic and developed a model of the creative process as a paradoxical synthesis of Gidean immersion and Symbolist detachment. He insisted on their perpetual coexistence in both composing and listening. While no musician may fully comprehend the process by which he or she achieves this marriage of objectivity and involvement, it is, for Copland, the essence of the creative experience.

"Two opposing theories have been advanced . . ."

But while Copland's attitude toward Symbolism differed from Gide's, his description of the creative process actually illustrates another aspect of Gide's influence. For in this description, Copland reveals his adoption of one of Gide's defining characteristics: the ability to simultaneously embrace contradictory ideas. Gide advocated the exploration of opposing points of view in order to acknowledge the complexities of the underlying questions. Copland adopted this approach as well, employing sometimes counterintuitive language as he attempted to validate opposing ideas.

For example, in his first Norton lecture he makes an argument with such a curious logic that the reader wonders what he might have hoped to accomplish by it:

> Two opposing theories have been advanced by the aestheticians as to music's significance. One is that the meaning of music, if there is any meaning, must be sought in the music itself, for music has no extra-musical connotation; and the other is that music is a language without a dictionary whose symbols are interpreted by the listener according to some unwritten Esperanto of the emotions. The more I consider these two theories the more it seems to me that they are bound together more closely than is generally supposed, and for this reason: music as a symbolic language of psychological and expressive value can only be made evident through "music itself," while music which is said to mean only itself sets up patterns of sound which inevitably suggest some kind of connotation in the mind of the listener, even if only to connote the joy of music making for its own sake.[64]

As a formal argument, the passage fails miserably. The two theories as he defines them are patently irreconcilable—music either makes explicit reference to nonmusical entities or it does not. "Music itself" is not really "music itself" if imbued with explicit symbolism, and "the joy of music making for its own sake" hardly qualifies as an "extramusical connotation."

What, then, was the objective of these rhetorical gymnastics? On a superficial level, the passage could be interpreted as a product of his accommodative personality: he had friends in both camps and didn't want to alienate any of them. But a significant assertion, which immediately precedes the passage quoted above, suggests a deeper motivation for the exercise: "I have seldom read a statement about the meaning of music . . . that did not seem to me to have some basis in truth."[65] Thus, his attempt to reconcile the irreconcilable emanated not only from an *interpersonal* accommodation but from a deep-rooted *philosophical* accommodation which deplored a rejection of any principle that might have some validity.

Copland's desire to endorse opposing ideas led him in some cases to advocate a balance between extreme positions. For example, near the end of the fourth Norton lecture, in addressing the role of the audience in the artist's work, he quotes British musicologist Edward Dent:

> Is [the composer] to write for himself only, to express his own indi-viduality and then throw it in the face of the world with a "take it or leave it," or is he to regard his genius as something he holds in trust

for the betterment of his fellow-creatures? That of course has always been the fundamental problem of all composers since Beethoven—the relation of the artist to the outside world.[66]

Professor Dent's description makes evident his own bias in favor of the latter approach, but Copland adopts a more measured view in his commentary on the passage: "As I see it, there are really two questions involved here: first, that of the artist and his conscience—out of what inner conviction is he composing; and second, the artist and his communication—what musical language must he use in order to reach whatever audience he thinks may potentially be his?" Copland allows that composers may vary in their emphasis on each of these questions, but he insists that there is a danger in the appeasement of one to the exclusion of the other; thus, "the twelve-toners have a program, but little hope of reaching a popular audience; and the *progressivistes* have a potential audience, but no guarantee that they can invent a fresh musical manner appropriate to its needs."[67]

Copland's treatment of this topic echoes Gide's argument in a collection of essays entitled *Nouveaux Prétextes*, which Copland owned. In the book, Gide insists that "the artist cannot do without a public," and decries the tactic of the typical modern artist: "Turning his back on his time, [he] expects from the future what the present denies him." But lest his position be misunderstood, Gide goes on to criticize popular artists who, "wanting a public at any price, buy a cut-price one from the mob."[68]

This insistence on accommodating both sides of a difficult question resulted in a nuanced assessment of the Soviet Union on the part of both Gide and Copland. Gide, who was a lifelong advocate of communism, was horrified at the oppression he observed on a 1935 visit to the country. He wrote two harsh criticisms of the Soviet government following that journey. But he continued to believe in the ideals of communism although he disapproved of its specific implementation in the Soviet Union.[69] Copland likewise sympathized with the communist movement during the 1930s and wrote admiringly of the work of Soviet composers in his 1941 book *Our New Music*.[70] But in his 1968 revision of the book, he reversed his earlier position, declaring that "musical creativity in the USSR has been stultified" because its composers failed "to face up to the musical realities of our day."[71] Still, in a Norton lecture, Copland acknowledges the complexities facing both the composers and the governments of communist nations:

I must reluctantly admit that there are many disturbing factors in a situation that is anything but clarified. But how could it be otherwise? The only possible alternative would be for the composer to remove himself from all contact with the life about him, and that would be worse. No, we must expect Europe's music to reflect the many different tensions that characterize its political and spiritual life, for that is the only healthy way for it to exist.[72]

And so Copland, like Gide, made every effort to embrace contrasting ideas about complex issues. Like Gide, he refused to adopt a simplistic approach to the relationship between the artist and the public, arguing that integrity and accessibility were both important values. Likewise, while he criticized Soviet composers for their own lack of adventurousness, he also acknowledged the importance of their participation within their own social structure. In acknowledging and accepting divergent points of view, Copland evidences his internalization of Gide's tolerance for contradiction. As Gide wrote in a 1922 journal entry: "Hardly a day goes by that I don't throw everything back into question."[73]

"I could enjoy going back and forth . . . "

Copland's adoption of this ideological accommodation, together with the imperative of diversity of experience, served as the basis for significant career decisions that distinguished him significantly from his peers. Because these decisions also mirrored Gide's approach to his own craft, we will first consider the practical implications of these principles in Gide's literary career.

Gide used his writings to explore extreme versions of his own contradictory convictions. For example, in *The Fruits of the Earth* (1897) he endorsed a hedonistic lifestyle to a fictional young follower, but immediately after completing it, began to write *Saul* (1903), in which he illustrated how such indulgence resulted in the downfall of a great king. In the novel *The Immoralist* (1901) the main character destroys his marriage through his licentiousness, but in the companion volume *Strait Is the Gate* (1909) the protagonist carries her religious fervor to masochistic extremes.

Gide resisted attempts to pigeonhole his views based upon individual works. As he asserted in 1909, "If anyone thinks that in my latest work he has finally grasped what I am like, let him think again: it's always from my last-born that I am the most different."[74] And in 1926, he explains that even in a deliberately one-sided book such as *Strait Is the Gate*, "there is, for whoever consents to read well and without prejudice, the critique of the book within the book itself, as it should be."[75] He harbored no illusions about the consequences of such an approach and even declared on one occasion his ambition to "win for each work a new public."[76] Thus, while his literary diversity grew out of a desire to explore the extremities of experience, it also enabled him to evade simplistic classification.

Copland likewise took pains to avoid being easily categorized. After establishing himself as a serious composer in the 1920s, he deliberately sought to appeal to a broader audience. By 1937 he had begun to market himself as a film composer, and by 1939 he had secured a contract to score the film *Of Mice and Men*.[77] Although many of his colleagues would have considered such an assignment to be beneath their dignity, Copland approached the task with humility: "I was an outsider to Hollywood, but I did not condescend to compose film music; I worked hard at it. Perhaps this is why I was accepted."[78] After completing the score, he surprised both his Hollywood acquaintances and his "serious" colleagues by returning to New York. "There seemed to be an idea that once one went to Hollywood, he was lost forever to the rest of the music world! But I could enjoy going back and forth to California occasionally without moving there. It was such a nice change from New York—the weather was beautiful, and the pay was good."[79]

His catalogue is remarkably diverse; it includes ballets, an opera for high school students, a serial piano quartet, and several film scores. Contrary to the best efforts of musicologists, his works defy division into chronological periods.[80] From the 1930s through the 1970s, he composed pieces with varying degrees of sophistication. He expressed bewilderment at efforts to partition his work into categories:

> In my own mind there was never so sharp a dichotomy between the various works I have written. Different purposes produce different kinds of work, that is all. The new mechanization of music's media has emphasized functional requirements, very often in terms of a large audience. That need would naturally induce works in a simpler, more direct style than was customary for concert works of absolute music. But it did not by any means lessen my interest in composing works in an idiom that might be accessible only to cultivated listeners.[81]

Like Gide, Copland deliberately sought diversity in his artistic output and disapproved of simplistic descriptions of his work. Perhaps his reason for pursuing so many varied composing opportunities is best expressed in a letter he wrote to William Schuman, declining an opportunity to join the faculty of the Juilliard School in 1945: "My deepest inner concern," he writes, "seems to be a need to think of myself as free to move about when and where I please and to let my mind dwell solely on my own music if I happen to feel that way."[82] Consistent with the fear he expressed in his 1927 journal entry, he continued to worry about undermining his development by limiting his options.

The net effect of these career decisions was to dramatically increase Copland's prominence and influence. Despite a brief period of professional difficulty associated with his appearance before the McCarthy subcommittee in 1953, Copland enjoyed steadily increasing celebrity during the 1950s and 1960s with its attendant privileges, including visits to the White House, numerous performances of his music both in the United States and internationally, and the receipt of the Presidential Medal of Freedom in 1964.[83] In the last decades of his life, he increasingly pursued conducting opportunities, spoke frequently in public, appeared on television and radio, and received numerous awards and honorary degrees.[84] Although these activities displaced composing almost entirely after 1970, he justified these pursuits by citing Gide's admonition "that each person should follow his own natural instincts."[85]

And so Copland's willingness to accept divergent views manifested itself in wide-ranging professional pursuits that enabled him to achieve a level of prominence far surpassing that of his peers.

In conclusion, what Copland ultimately inherited from Gide was a kind of ideological modesty, a tentativeness born of a recognition of his own limitations and of the complexities of life. Gide's stated objective "to become as human as possible" thus denotes not only the pursuit of personal growth through exposure to diverse stimuli, but more important, an awareness and acknowledgment of one's own imperfections. We have observed varied manifestations of that principle: in Copland's early fears of unrealized potential, in his exploration of sexuality, and finally in his conception of the nature of art and his consequent professional decisions.

Other authors clearly made their mark on Copland's aesthetic thought, including the Symbolist poets. But the significance of this Gidean tentativeness for Copland was that it provided a basis for amalgamating these disparate philosophies into an ideological framework within which he could make constructive professional decisions. In Gide's world, this tentativeness may have arisen out of a struggle between painfully irreconcilable convictions, but for Copland, the principle provided a serviceable foundation for a successful career as perhaps the most prominent American composer of the twentieth century.

Table 1. Direct References to Gide in Copland's Writings

Letter to Nadia Boulanger, 1923

During my stay in Salzburg, I read André Gide's new book on Dostoievsky. (I must explain to you that my friend Clurman and myself are ardent "disciples" of Gide.) He says many interesting things concerning the Frenchman's need of logic and its relation to "la grande ligne." I must tell you one quotation he makes from the German, Rathenau, which I think eminently true. Rathenau says that it is because she has never consented either to sin or to suffering that America has no soul.

Letter to Nadia Boulanger, 1924

Forgive me for making this a "business letter." I should have preferred telling you about other things—our jazz-bands, for instance, or Gide's "Corydon," but I'll leave it for another letter.

Journal, 1928

Gide says, "Those who differ from me most attract me most." I might have written that. . . . My imagination takes flight when I am given a glimpse of the workings of a being different from myself. Our differences throw into a stronger light my true self.

Our New Music, **1941, p. 114**
(Also appears in the 1968 revision of the book, *The New Music,* p. 79.)

[Speaking of Hindemith's dual role as composer and theorist:] The danger is obvious—given the formula, the creator is likely to underestimate the unconscious part of creation—what André Gide calls "la part de Dieu."

Music and Imagination, **1952, p. 46**

There is an unconscious part in each work—an element that André Gide called *la part de Dieu.*

Copland on Music, **1960, p. 86**

[From an essay on Nadia Boulanger:] She was the friend of Paul Valéry and Paul Claudel, and liked to discuss the latest works of Thomas Mann, of Proust, and André Gide.

Copland 1900–1942, **1984, p. 56**

It was the time of Tristan Tzara and Dada; the time of André Breton and surrealism; it was when we first heard the names of James Joyce and Gertrude Stein, T. S. Eliot and Ezra Pound, and also of the French writers Marcel Proust and André Gide. . . . All kinds of artistic activities were bursting about me, and I was determined to take it all in as fast as possible.

Table 1 continued

Copland 1900–1942, **1984, p. 65–66**

On Wednesday afternoons she [Nadia Boulanger] held class meetings for her students, *déchiffrage* classes, where new works were read at the piano by some bright student. They would be discussed and enthused about, or dismissed. At other times we sang Monteverdi and Gesualdo madrigals, which were virtually unperformed at that time. Also, the latest literary and artistic works were examined: Kafka, Mann, Gide, Pound. Those Wednesday afternoons became an institution.

Copland 1900–1942, **1984, pp. 75–76**

I familiarized myself with the monthly *La Nouvelle Revue Française*, which featured French writers such as Gide and Proust, and I occasionally saw these figures at the bookshops. Harold and I felt that we were living in a very civilized atmosphere. There was much more than music going on, and we were well aware of it.

Copland 1900–1942, **1984, p. 166**

In another connection, André Gide has well expressed my meaning: "Before explaining my book to others, I wait for them to explain it to me. To wish to explain it first would be to restrain its meaning prematurely, because even if we know what we wish to say we cannot know if we have said *only* that. And what interests me especially is what I have put into my book without my own knowledge." The exploration of the subconscious in Gide's writings was one of the influences moving me toward a style in which my music was to stand as pure and absolute, limited in no way by programmatic or extramusical connotation.

Copland Since 1943, **1989, p. 267**

As a young man, one of the writers who had impressed me was Gide. I remember him writing that each person should follow his own natural instincts. For me, it seemed natural and comfortable to do several different things.

Table 2. Books by Gide in the Copland Library

1. *André Gide*. Éditions du Capitole (numbered #897).
2. *Ainsi soit-il ou les jeux sont faits*. Gallimard, 1952.
3. *Amyntas*. Gallimard, 1925.
4. *Attendu que . . .* Charlot, 1943.
5. *Les Caves du Vatican*. Nouvelle Revue Française, 1922.
6. *Les Contemporains*. Capitole, 1928 (numbered edition).
7. *Corydon*. Nouvelle Revue Française, 1924.
8. *Un Esprit non prévenu*. Éditions Kra, 1929.
9. *Et nunc Manet in te*. Ides et Calendes, 1947.
10. *Les Faux-monnayeurs*. Gallimard, 1925.
11. *Feuillets d'automne*. Mercure de France, 1949.
12. *L'Immoraliste*. Mercure, 1923.
13. *Incidences*. Nouvelle Revue Française, 1924.
14. *Journal, 1939–1942*. Gallimard, 1946.
15. *Journal, 1942–1949*. Gallimard, 1950.
16. *Journal des faux–monnayeurs*. Gallimard, 1927.
17. *Les Nourritures terrestres*. Gallimard, 1921.
18. *Nouveaux Prétextes*. Mercure, 1921.
19. *Les Nouvelles Nourritures*. Gallimard, 1935.
20. *Paludes*. Gallimard, 1926.
21. *Prétextes*. Mercure, 1923.
22. *Retouches à mon retour de l'U.R.S.S.* Gallimard, 1937.
23. *Le Retour de l'enfant prodigue*. Gallimard, 1932.
24. *Retour de l'U.R.S.S.* Gallimard, 1936.
25. *Robert*. Gallimard, 1930.
26. *Saül*. Gallimard, 1922.
27. *Si le grain ne meurt, II*. Nouvelle Revue Française, 1924 (3 vols.).
28. *La Symphonie pastorale*. Gallimard, 1925.
29. *Voyage au Congo: Carnets de route*. Gallimard, 1927.
30. *Le Voyage d'Urien*. Gallimard, 1929.

Also, the following book by André Gide and J. L. Barrault:
31. *Le Procès: Pièce tirée du roman de Kafka*. Gallimard, 1947.

NOTE: A list of all books in the Copland library is available on the Library of Congress website, http://lcweb2.loc.gov/service/music/eadxmlmusic/eadpdfmusic/mu002006_x.pdf.

Table 3. Selected Margin Notes in Copland's Copy of *Corydon*

Copland's copy was the edition published by Éditions de la Nouvelle Revue Française, 1924. The English edition is the translation by Richard Howard published by University of Illinois Press, 2001.

Page in Copland's Copy	Page in English Edition	Reference Text (Gide)	Copland's Markings
Front cover			Inscription on top right-hand corner in ink (all other markings are pencil). Corner of cover is ripped, so the inscription is illegible.
49	29	I refuse to admit that he might have invented [a homosexual tendency] if he's healthy, precisely because I do not acknowledge this taste as a spontaneous one except among those who are inverted, degenerate, or sick.	Copland circles the word <u>invertis</u>, and draws an arrow to his comment at the top of the page: "'invertis' here seems to mean, people who have <u>inverted</u> (or perverted) themselves."
49	30	And you will permit me to remark that this taste, moreover, can scarcely be inherited, for the plausible reason that the very act which would transmit it is necessarily a heterosexual act.	Question mark beside this paragraph.
70–71	44	Yet whereas in the female this extra substance is immediately utilized for the race, what happens to it in the uncastrated male? It becomes material for variation. Here, I believe, is the key to what is called "sexual dimorphism," which in almost all the so-called superior species makes the male into a creature of show, or song, or art, of sport, or of intelligence—a creature of play.	Writes, "dimorphe . . . two forms = purely physical and 'spiritual' = art etc. etc." Also writes: "mâle entier = uncastrated male"
72	45	The most one can say is that these dimorphic characteristics attain their finest development in the so-called higher species only when seminal expenditure is reduced to its minimum. Chastity, on the other hand, is not of great advantage to the female.	Writes, "Does this mean that the 'artist' must reduce his seminal expenditure to the minimum?"

Table 3 continued

Page in Copland's Copy	Page in English Edition	Reference Text (Gide)	Copland's Markings
92	59	[Corydon asserts that traditional theories of the mating instinct are inaccurate, inasmuch as homosexual behavior is observed in numerous species of animals.] Each of these modest "observers," confining his attention to the species he is studying, discovers such behavior and believes he must regard it as a monstrous exception.	Writes, "'instinct sexuel' does not exist? What is meant is that in so far as 'instinct sexuel' signifies the force that impels animals to fecundate."
96	62	It is very difficult to suppose that an *observation* can be the result of chance, and that it occurs to the mind as the fortuitous answer to a question the brain has not asked.	Underlined, with two vertical lines beside the passage.
102	66	The sexual instinct is as undetermined in the female as in the male. . . . The male, for his part, does not desire precisely the female, and still less "procreation," but simply pleasure. Both of them quite plainly seek sexual pleasure.	Writes, "Scandale! (Is this supposed to be NEW? It was my opinion long ago!)"
103	67	Waste, from the point of view of utilitarian finality. But it is upon this waste that art, thought, and play will be able to grow and to flourish.	Underlines, "*déchet.*" Writes, "waste."
106–7	69–70		Page is inserted, with the following text: Pages 70, 71 Very difficult! Anagenetic—simply means the formation of tissue—(fat) etc. The female uses her surplus "sexuality" for the physical profit of the race (to feed her child etc.) The female is anagenetic.

Table 3 continued

Page in Copland's Copy	Page in English Edition	Reference Text (Gide)	Copland's Markings
			The male is catagenetic. He uses his surplus (useless physically) sexual powers in artistic endeavor etc. Man to be an "artist," according to this theory must not use up his surplus sexuality—he must "réduire la dispense séminale a son minimum." Chastity has its uses for the male. Not for the female. (Page 72) Afterthought—When woman uses her sexuality for her pleasure and not for her progeny she too may become catagenetic ("artistic"). Perhaps that is why in these days of much birth control in educated circles there are coming to be so many woman artists. (See footnote, p. 107.)
110	71	But, in return, will you for your part acknowledge that homosexual tastes no longer seem to you so contrary to nature as you claimed this morning?	Writes, "chez les animaux."
125	84	[Quoting Darwin:] *I was much disappointed in the personal appearance of the women; they are far inferior in every respect to the men. . . . The women appear to be in greater want of some becoming costume even than the men.*	Writes, "Women dress beautifully because they are themselves less beautiful! (But in ancient times did not men dress beautifully too? There is an economic cause for the plainness of men's dress.)"
126	85	Stevenson, for instance, . . . in speaking of the Polynesians acknowledges that the beauty of the young men greatly exceeds that of the women.	Writes, "assassin!!"

Table 3 continued

Page in Copland's Copy	Page in English Edition	Reference Text (Gide)	Copland's Markings
127	86	Whereas among animals the male's efflorescence can be transmitted only to the male, *women certainly transmit most of their characters, including beauty, to their offspring of both sexes.* [Again quoting Darwin]	Writes, "We do not love Beauty. The most beautiful boy (the boy I recognize as most beautiful is no more desirable than any girl). Sexual attraction a matter of desire not of beauty. Desire cannot be explained by beauty. Rats!"
127–28	86	[The narrator speaking to Corydon:] If you are not susceptible to feminine beauty, so much the worse for you, and you have my sympathy—but don't go trying to convince me of general aesthetic laws based on a sentiment which, despite all you can say, will remain an individual one.	Writes, "This argument is interesting; it is not pertinent."
135	91	[Quotes Goethe:] *Pederasty is as old as humanity itself, and one can therefore say that it is natural, that it resides in nature, even if it proceeds against nature. What culture has won from nature will not be surrendered or given up at any price.*	Writes, "Pederasty = Boylove (simply). Sodomy = (Boylove with intercourse) — I think Gide weakens his case for the homosexual by talking about the simple pederast alone. (See footnote page 11.) Is a defense of Boylove necessary? No, since it is only exalted friendship."
139	94	(You see that I am dropping the argument of a lesser beauty, because I do not think that sexual attraction is necessarily dependent upon it.)	Writes, "ah Ha! some sense."
146	99	I do maintain that, in most cases, the appetite which awakens in the youth is not of any very specific urgency; that he experiences pleasure in whatever form it is offered, no matter by which sex, and that he	Writes, "C'est la question. Gide's <u>pleasure</u> theory of sex is not so new as his use of it."

Table 3 continued

Page in Copland's Copy	Page in English Edition	Reference Text (Gide)	Copland's Markings
		owes his habits more to outside influences than to the promptings of desire.	
147	99	[The narrator to Corydon:] If each boy were left to himself and if outside reprimands did not interfere—in other words, if civilization were to slacken—homosexuals would be even more numerous than they are.	Writes, "Yes, why not experiment?"
147	99	[The narrator to Corydon:] Now it is my turn to serve up Goethe's words: *What culture has won from nature will not be surrendered or given up at any price.*	Writes, "Weak, very weak."
172	118	I tell you, the shameless stimulation of our popular imagery, theaters, music halls, and a host of publications serves only to lure woman away from her duties; to make her into a perpetual mistress, who no longer consents to maternity.	Writes, "Bunk! Pourquoi?"
173	119	If you please, we'll leave aside the inverts for now. The trouble is that ill-informed people confuse them with normal homosexuals.	Writes, "Yes, but Gide suggests that everybody might be, should be homosexual for the sake of the woman!"
175	120	Obviously, if you make the thing itself a crime. But that is just what I hold against our morality; as I hold public censure of unmarried mothers responsible for three-quarters of all abortions.	Writes, "Bon!"
175	121	It is really staggering to see to what degree, in matters so serious, so urgent, so vital to the country, people prefer the word	Writes, "Trés bien! Bravo!"

Table 3 continued

Page in Copland's Copy	Page in English Edition	Reference Text (Gide)	Copland's Markings
		to the thing, appearance to reality, and readily sacrifice the supply of goods to the window dressing.	
178	123	Again, I'm not comparing chastity with debauchery of any kind, but one kind of impurity with another.	Writes, "Gide le puritain!"
179	123	I'm saying that if the young man falls in love with a young woman and if this love is authentic, then there is every chance that this love is a chaste one, not immediately crossed by desires.	Writes, "ROT"
179	123	But I add that, with regard to marriage, it would have been better, and less dangerous, for each of these young men if their temporary pleasures had been of another kind.	Writes, "Gide proposes to do away with even real diseased men by homosexuality!"
180	124	I am saying that this love, if it is authentic, tends toward chastity.	Writes, "???"
181	125	I believe that nothing can be better for him than a lover of his own sex. I believe that such a lover will jealously watch over him, protect him, and himself exalted, purified by this love, will guide him toward those radiant heights which are not to be reached without love.	Writes, "<u>Interesting</u>"
182	125–26	From thirteen to twenty-two . . . is for the Greeks the age of loving friendship. . . . Only after that does the boy . . . turn his thoughts to women.	Writes, "But this is what often actually happens, isn't it?" Lower on the page, writes, "Here things take on a different aspect. A new aspect. Worth thinking about anyway."

NOTES

1. Aaron Copland, *Our New Music: Leading Composers in Europe and America* (New York: McGraw-Hill Book Company, 1941), p. 212. From a 1939 essay entitled "Composer from Brooklyn: An Autobiographical Sketch." This essay is also included in Gilbert Chase, *The American Composer Speaks* (Baton Rouge: Louisiana State University Press, 1966). Note that Copland later published a revised version of the book as *The New Music: 1900–1960* (New York: W. W. Norton, 1968). The revisions were significant—whole chapters were replaced and numerous editorial passages were added. Hereafter, I will refer to the earlier version of the book wherever possible. I will reference the later version only when the text in question does not exist in the earlier version.

2. Aaron Copland and Vivian Perlis, *Copland: 1900 Through 1942* (New York: St. Martin's/Marek, 1984), pp. 25–35. See also *Our New Music*, pp. 213–17.

3. Copland and Perlis, *Copland: 1900–1942*, p. 56.

4. "No one to my knowledge had ever before thought of studying composition with a woman. This idea was absurd on the face of it. Everyone knows that the world has never produced a first-rate woman composer, so it follows that no woman could possibly hope to teach composition." Copland, *Our New Music*, p. 218.

5. Copland and Perlis, *Copland: 1900–1942*, pp. 48–50, pp. 61–70.

6. Aaron Copland, *Copland on Music* (New York: Doubleday & Company, 1960), p. 86.

7. Copland and Perlis, *Copland: 1900–1942*, pp. 75–76.

8. Aaron Copland, letter to Nadia Boulanger, August 12, 1923, Aaron Copland Collection, Music Division, Library of Congress, Box 248, Folder 8 ("Boulanger 1920–1924"), available online at http://memory.loc.gov/music/copland/corr/corr0059/0003v.jpg.

9. See Table 2 for a list of Gide's books in the Copland Library.

10. André Gide, *If It Die . . . : An Autobiography*, trans. Dorothy Bussy (New York: Vintage International, 2001), pp. 8–9. George D. Painter, *André Gide: A Critical Biography* (New York: Atheneum, 1968), pp. 2, 28–29.

11. Painter, *André Gide*, pp. 9–13.

12. Ibid., pp. 17, 25–26, 29.

13. Ibid., pp. 26–29.

14. Gide did have serious extramarital relationships (ibid., p. 119). However, as noted later in the essay, he reaffirmed after Madeleine's death that he believed he felt a love for her that transcended all other relationships, a love so pure that physical intimacy would have degraded it. See Gide, *Et Nunc Manet in Te*, trans. Justin O'Brien (New York: Alfred A. Knopf, 1952), pp. 48–49.

15. André Gide, *The Journals of André Gide*, trans. Justin O'Brien (New York: Alfred A. Knopf, 1955) I:18.

16. Ibid., I:19.

17. Aaron Copland, Diary, Copland Collection, Box 243, Folder 11, pp. 1–2. Part of this passage is quoted in Copland and Perlis, *Copland: 1900–1942*, pp. 140–41.

18. Copland, Diary, p. 3. Also appears in Copland and Perlis, *Copland: 1900–1942*, p. 141. Perlis reports that when Copland reviewed these journal entries "some fifty-four years later," he "hooted with laughter at their naiveté, but remarked that they still make sense" (p. 140).

19. Sexual issues are an important part of Gide's influence on Aaron Copland, although Copland was attracted to Gide's writings before becoming aware of Gide's views on sexuality. Obviously, merely touching on the topic raises numerous questions, many of which I do not address in this essay. I have deliberately chosen not to emphasize such issues as Gide's contribution to the gay rights movement, the treatment of *Corydon* within gender studies literature, and Copland's lifelong concealment of his own sexual orientation.

My primary purpose in this essay is to highlight the ideological axioms that Copland inherited from Gide, and to illustrate how those axioms became the bedrock of Copland's worldview. In my estimation, a more extensive treatment of any one of those other topics would have required a prolonged detour that would detract from my central thesis. Readers who would like more information about *Corydon* might begin with Alan Sheridan's discussion in the book *André Gide: A Life in the Present* (Cambridge, Mass.: Harvard University Press, 1999), pp. 371–80. For more information about Copland and sexuality, see the chapter entitled "Personal Affairs" in Howard Pollack's *Aaron Copland* (New York: Oxford University Press, 1953), pp. 234–56.

20. The other books in which markings appear are *Incidences* and *Robert*. However, in both of these cases, the markings are limited to lines beside paragraphs. *Corydon* is the only book in the collection with actual text written in the margins. In Copland's copy of *Corydon*, about one-quarter of the pages have notes in the margins (42 out of 182.) See Table 3 for a partial inventory of Copland's markings in the book.

21. Painter, *André Gide*, pp. 85–86. An incomplete first edition (only the first two dialogues) was published privately in 1910. It consisted of only twelve copies. A complete second edition was printed privately in 1920 (only twenty-one copies). That edition was finally released to the public in 1924. The initial print run of 5,500 copies sold quickly, and was followed immediately by a second run of 8,000 copies. See George William Ireland, *André Gide: A Study of His Creative Writings* (Oxford, Eng.: Clarendon Press, 1970), p. 310.

22. Marginalia, pp. 171, 172, and 179 of Copland's copy of *Corydon*. See Table 3.

23. André Gide, *Corydon*, trans. Richard Howard (Urbana: University of Illinois Press, 2001), pp. 80–86, 91, 103–6, 116–19.

24. In reference to the paragraph beginning "If you please, we'll leave the inverts aside for now . . . " Gide, *Corydon*, pp. 119–20.

25. Gide, *Corydon*, pp. 44–45.

26. Copland, *Copland on Music*, pp. 84–85. The distinction that he draws between music and the other arts in this passage is noteworthy:

> Actually Nadia Boulanger was quite aware that as a composition teacher she labored under two further disadvantages: she was not herself a regularly practicing composer and in so far as she composed at all she must of necessity be listed in that unenviable category of the woman composer. Everyone knows that the high achievement of women musicians as vocalists and instrumentalists has no counterpart in the field of musical composition. This historically poor showing has puzzled more than one observer. It is even more inexplicable when one considers the reputation of women novelists and poets, of painters and designers. Is it possible that there is a mysterious element in the nature of musical creativity that runs counter to the nature of the feminine mind? And yet there are more women composers than ever writing today, writing, moreover, music worth playing. The future may very well have a different tale to tell; for the present, however, no woman's name will be found on the list of world-famous composers.

27. Aaron Copland, *Music and Imagination* (Cambridge, Mass.: Harvard University Press, 1952), pp. 43–44.

28. Gide, *Corydon*, p. 120 (p. 175 in Copland's copy).

29. Ibid., p. 122 (p. 178 in Copland's copy).

30. Pollack, *Aaron Copland*, pp. 234–36.

31. Ibid., p. 234.

32. As quoted in Hal May and Susan M. Trotsky, eds., *Contemporary Authors* (Detroit, Mich.: Gale Research Inc., 1988), vol. 124, p. 178 (originally from Gide, *Journals*, III:252).

33. Gide, *Et Nunc Manet in Te*. Consider also the following passage from his *Journals*, dated January 6, 1933 (before Madeleine's death, but after the publication of *Corydon*):

"Every time I see her again I recognize anew that I have never really loved anyone but her; and even, at times, it seems to me that I love her more than ever."

34. As quoted in Frederick John Harris, *André Gide and Romain Rolland: Two Men Divided* (New Brunswick, N.J.: Rutgers University Press, 1973), p. 60.

35. André Gide, *Pretexts*, ed. Justin O'Brien (New York: Meridian Books, 1959), p. 31.

36. As quoted in Painter, *André Gide*, p. 96 (originally from the *Journal of the Counterfeiters*).

37. As quoted in May and Trotsky, *Contemporary Authors*, p. 177, from an undated journal entry.

38. As quoted in Martin Seymour-Smith and Andrew C. Kimmens, eds., *World Authors* (New York: H. W. Wilson Company, 1996), II:974 (originally from Gide's *Journals*, 1937.)

39. Aaron Copland and Vivian Perlis, *Copland Since 1943* (New York: St. Martin's Press, 1989), p. 424. A similar passage (with a slightly harsher tone) appears in the 1959 essay, "The Pleasures of Music": "The use of music as a kind of ambrosia to titillate the aural senses while one's conscious mind is otherwise occupied is the abomination of every composer who takes his work seriously." Copland, *Copland on Music*, p. 26.

40. Copland, *Copland on Music*, p. 204. Consider also this similar passage from a 1959 essay: "The same people who find it quite natural that modern books, plays, or paintings are likely to be controversial seem to want to escape being challenged and troubled when they turn to music. In our field there appears to be a never-ending thirst for the familiar, and very little curiosity as to what the newer composers are up to. Such music-lovers, as I see it, simply don't love music enough, for if they did their minds would not be closed to an area that holds the promise of fresh and unusual musical experience." Ibid., p. 44.

41. Ibid., pp. 67–68. Gide, *Pretexts*, p. 322.

42. Copland, *Music and Imagination*, p. 41.

43. Ibid.

44. Ibid., p. 19.

45. Copland, *Copland on Music*, p. 264.

46. Ibid., pp. 264–65.

47. Copland, *Music and Imagination*, pp. 19–20. Consider also the following passage from *Copland on Music*, pp. 268–69, which addresses the same topic with exactly the same metaphor: "Present programming tends to stultify and mummify our musical public. Under such conditions we composers are strongly tempted to ask: What are you doing to our audiences? Frankly, we have very little confidence when we bring our pieces before such audiences. Often we sense that the audience that listens to us is not the right audience for our music. Why? Because they have not been musically nurtured and fed properly, with a resultant vitamin lack of musical understanding." He encourages experimental programming in other passages as well, including the third Norton lecture (*Music and Imagination*, p. 57).

48. Gide, *Pretexts*, p. 323.

49. Copland, *Our New Music*, p. 159.

50. Copland, *Copland on Music*, p. 124. See also his description of the three moods in Milhaud, p. 83 of *Our New Music*.

51. Copland, *Our New Music*, p. 88. See also his discussion of the topic in *Copland on Music*, 49. And on p. 26, in a separate essay, he posits that serious music is "serious" or significant specifically because of its broad "emotional range."

52. Copland and Perlis, *Copland: 1900–1942*, p. 166. The original source of the quotation is André Gide's preface to one of his novels, *Paludes* (Paris: Gallimard, 1920). The translation is by Copland.

53. Copland, *Music and Imagination*, p. 46. Consider also the following journal entry, which appears in *Copland on Music*, p. 131: "Nothing pleases the composer so much as to have people disagree as to the movements of his piece that they liked best. If there is enough disagreement, it means that everyone liked something best—which is just what the composer wants to hear. The fact that this might include other parts that no one liked never seems to matter."

54. Copland, *Music and Imagination*, p. 49.

55. Copland, *Our New Music*, p. 5 (italics added). References to "objectivity" as a defining characteristic of modern music abound in Copland's writings. See also the passage on p. 116 of the same book: "It was firmly established that new music, in whatever style, was to be objective in attitude, clearly conceived, and contained in emotional expression."

56. Copland, *Copland on Music*, p. 193 (Stravinsky). Copland, *Our New Music*, p. 203 (Chávez). See also *Copland on Music*, pp. 93–94, in which he cites Marcel Proust as he describes his fascination with Stravinsky's "wrong" notes that sound so right.

57. Copland, *Copland on Music*, pp. 114–16. See also the passage on Berlioz in the Norton Lectures (Copland, *Music and Imagination*, p. 35). Note also that, in the passage on Chávez cited above, Copland identifies "the rejection of Germanic ideals" as one of the "major traits of modern music."

58. As quoted in the Preface to Mallarmé's *Collected Poems*. Consider also the following similar passage, quoted on p. 257 of the same volume: "Paint not the thing itself but the effect it produces. I say: a flower! and outside the oblivion to which my voice relegates any shape insofar as it is something other than the calyx, there arises musically, as the very idea and delicate, the awe absent from any bouquet."

59. Edmund Wilson quotes this passage in *Axel's Castle: A Study in the Imaginative Literature of 1870–1930* (New York: Charles Scribner's Sons, 1940), p. 257. The quotation comes originally from André Gide, *Journal des Faux-Monnayeurs*, p. 53. Alan Sheridan points out that in spite of Gide's explicit condemnation of Symbolism, the influence continued to play a role in his writings, most notably in his use of *mise en abîme* (a story within a story). However, in spite of the persistence of certain elements of Symbolism in his rhetorical methods, he consistently affirmed his rejection of the movement. Sheridan, *André Gide*, pp. 110–11.

60. Copland, *Music and Imagination*, p. 43.

61. Ibid., p. 46.

62. Ibid. Consider also Copland's description of the music of Mozart: "Mozart in his music was probably the most reasonable of the world's composers. It is the happy balance between flight and control, between sensibility and self-discipline, simplicity and sophistication of style that is his particular province." *Copland on Music*, pp. 107–8.

63. Ibid., p. 10. Immediately following this passage, Copland quotes one of the Symbolists, Paul Claudel, using the words "expectation and attention" to refer to a concert listener. Copland sees this choice of words as validating his conception, inasmuch as the term "expectation" implies openness while "attention" suggests a critical awareness.

64. Ibid., pp. 11–12.

65. Ibid., p. 11.

66. Ibid., p. 74.

67. Ibid., p. 75. See also Copland's discussion of total serialism in *Music and Imagination*, pp. 69–70.

68. As quoted in Sheridan, *André Gide*, p. 202. Originally from the 1903 lecture "The Importance of the Public," which was included in André Gide, *Nouveaux Prétextes: Réflexions sur quelques points de littérature et de morale* (Paris: Mercure, 1911), pp. 28–44.

69. Sheridan, *André Gide*, pp. 624–25. Painter, *André Gide*, pp. 114–16.

70. Copland, *Our New Music*, pp. 120–23.

71. Copland, *The New Music*, pp. 84–85.
72. Copland, *Music and Imagination*, pp. 76–77.
73. As quoted in May and Trotsky, *Contemporary Authors*, p. 173 (from a 1922 journal entry).
74. Ibid., p. 177 (from a 1909 journal entry).
75. Ibid., p. 176 (from a 1926 journal entry).
76. Ibid., p. 179 (from a 1922 journal entry).
77. Copland and Perlis, *Copland: 1900–1942*, pp. 270–71, 297.
78. Ibid., p. 300.
79. Ibid. Copland unabashedly admitted, on multiple occasions, the role of monetary considerations in his relationship with Hollywood. In his autobiography, he introduces his discussion of film music in the following way: "All things considered, especially financial, June 1937 seemed like a good time to accept Clurman's invitation to visit Hollywood to try for a film contract. I had followed George Antheil's column in *Modern Music*, 'On the Hollywood Front,' with great interest. 'Something is going on in Hollywood,' Antheil wrote. 'Composers may remain aloof to it, but only at the peril of being left behind, esthetically perhaps as well as financially'" (Copland and Perlis, *Copland: 1900–1942*, p. 270). And in response to questions about his 1966 "signature" music for a CBS television series, he wrote, "I was puzzled when people asked why I bothered composing for television. Although I never accepted assignments that did not interest me, there was another factor to consider: Somebody had to pay the rent!" (Copland and Perlis, *Copland Since 1943*, p. 347).
80. Julia Smith identified three periods: French-Jazz (1924–29), Abstract (1929–35), and American Folksong (1935–44). See Julia Smith, *Aaron Copland: His Work and Contribution to American Music* (New York: E. P. Dutton, 1955). But note that he composed *Statements* and *El Salón México* simultaneously, that his Piano Sonata is sandwiched between the score to the movie *Our Town* and the ballet *Rodeo,* and that he wrote his Piano Quartet, his *Twelve Poems of Emily Dickinson,* and the first set of *Old American Songs* all in the year 1950.
81. Copland, *Music and Imagination*, pp. 108–9.
82. Copland and Perlis, *Copland Since 1943*, p. 316.
83. Ibid., pp. 304–6, 315, 344–46.
84. Ibid., pp. 388–98, 402–4.
85. Ibid., p. 267.

Copland and American Populism in the 1930s

MORRIS DICKSTEIN

When I was growing up in New York in the 1940s and early '50s, the remnants of Popular Front politics and culture were still around us, so much a part of the landscape that I scarcely noticed them. For our parents, who had come to the United States as immigrants when they were young, the Depression and the New Deal remained daily facts of life, influencing their anxieties as well as their life choices. New Deal legislation dealing with housing, Social Security, and the rights of labor created a safety net that was quickly taken for granted, as were "progressive" ideas in general, but without allaying basic fears about the next paycheck, the next rental payment. But caution was mingled with pride, for ordinary people felt that the New Deal had offered not only aid and hope but a new level of self-respect. The common man had come into his own. On the cultural side, radio programs like *The Goldbergs*, *I Remember Mama*, and even *Amos 'n' Andy* affirmed ethnic pride while creating cross-cultural bonds that helped bring immigrant groups into mainstream, though some of the actors would soon fall victim to the blacklist.

New York City politics still has a Popular Front tinge. Fiorello La Guardia, a liberal Republican of mixed Italian and Jewish background, served as mayor on a Fusion ticket until 1945. I remember the commotion when he came to dedicate a playground near my school, a tiny piece of the vast array of public works created under the New Deal. In East Harlem, the American Labor Party, which supported Henry Wallace for president in 1948, continued to reelect a maverick congressman, Vito Marcantonio, through 1950. In every election season, banners across the *Jewish Daily Forward* building, which towered over the Lower East Side, promoted the candidates of the social-democratic Liberal Party, which had recently split off from the ALP. At the Waldorf-Astoria Hotel in March 1949, some eight hundred cultural figures, including Arthur Miller, Lillian Hellman, Aaron Copland, the young Norman Mailer, and, from the Soviet Union, Dimitri Shostakovich, met to discuss war and peace in what proved to be the swan song of Soviet-American wartime amity. A small group of intellectuals, led by Sidney Hook, Dwight Macdonald, Mary McCarthy, and the young Irving Howe, confronted the participants over the state of freedom in the Soviet Union. It was a signal moment in an atmosphere that was already tense with the Cold War. A few months later, riots greeted those who attended a concert by one of the best-known icons of the Popular Front, the black singer and actor Paul Robeson, in Peekskill, New York.

My father, though not especially political, was a loyal member of a CIO union that co-sponsored the concert. An uncle of mine, a Communist who belonged to Sidney Hillman's Amalgamated Clothing Workers, drove up to hear Robeson, whom he idolized, and to show solidarity with his old comrades. His wife, my mother's younger sister, was so terrified at the violence they encountered, which the local police did nothing to prevent, that she pressured him to withdraw from any political activity. And if the old Left were not already on the defensive, a few months later the Rosenberg spy case broke upon the world. For the next three years, until the couple was executed, their fate captured the fearful attention of immigrant Jews like no other story. Except for blacklists, spy cases, and congressional hearings, which searched out the remnants of the 1930s Left, the culture and politics of the Popular Front effectively disappeared, except in the nostalgic recollections of those involved, for whom it remained the great adventure of their lives.

For Aaron Copland, 1949 represented the culmination of his time in Hollywood, with his score for *The Heiress* winning an academy award. By 1950 his work turned quietly—but dramatically—back to the concert hall, with the first set of *Old American Songs* and the Piano Quartet. But soon he too was hauled before a congressional committee to account for his political leanings in the 1930s and early '40s, when he wrote the music for *The North Star*, a pro-Soviet wartime film written by Lillian Hellman and produced by Samuel Goldwyn. Unlike some other witnesses, he gave answers that were as direct and plain-spoken as his music. But as a composer for the concert hall he was much less vulnerable to being blacklisted than a Hollywood actor or director

A few years later I became a student at Columbia University, home to many anti-Communist New York intellectuals who had been critical of the rhetoric and politics of the Popular Front, including Lionel Trilling, F. W. Dupee, Richard Hofstadter, and Robert Gorham Davis. Once sympathetic to Marxism themselves, they, like other writers appalled by the conditions of the Depression, attacked the Popular Front first from the Left as a middlebrow culture that had lost its radical edge, then from the

Right as an obedient front for Soviet interests in a patriotic American guise. In the gray mood of the late 1950s, when these issues had grown too remote to understand, my friends and I were irresistibly drawn to everything that the Cold War and McCarthyism had plowed under—indeed, to whatever would annoy our teachers most. We searched for old discs by Robeson and more recent ones by the Red Army Chorus, which had visited America during the Cold War thaw of the post-Stalin years. By then the Robeson albums were almost impossible to find. When I inquired around 1960 at Columbia Records, once Robeson's label, a vice president wrote to me that they had *never* put out any recordings by him, though I later found one, which I still have, while rifling through a secondhand bin in the British crown colony of Gibraltar. But I also came to share my instructors' view that most Popular Front literature was flat-footed and propagandistic in its social realism, many cuts below the intransigent modernist writing that now enthralled me.

By the 1980s, when I began studying the cultural history of the Depression years, the ambivalence I felt as an undergraduate still seemed writ large in the scholarship.[1] In the wake of the hopes and failures of the New Left, many of us were once again attracted to the 1930s as a period of political engagement, social consciousness, and radical struggle. As the gap between the rich and poor began to widen and selfish greed came back in fashion, the social policies initiated during the Depression shimmered like a beacon of sympathy for the underdog. But the arts of the Depression years all too often seemed dated by stale agit-prop techniques, and crippled by an aesthetic conventionality designed to appeal to the least demanding audience. Teaching this material in the 1980s and 1990s required special pleading, and our students, for whom even the 1960s had faded into myth, were easily bored. At the same time, some works produced in the 1930s seemed so unforced, so natural, that even young readers with little sense of history could connect with them immediately.

The songs of Woody Guthrie sounded musically primitive to a generation schooled on rock, but they were bracingly direct and spontaneously appealing. The words were always fresh, and the musical idiom had survived in western ballads and talking blues, but also in the work of later troubadours like Bob Dylan, as Dylan himself so often acknowledged. Dylan had arrived on the Greenwich Village scene in the early 1960s, when the folk culture, populated by aging radicals and young wanabees, was almost a lifeline back to the thirties. This was the moment (1962) when John Steinbeck, another enduring icon of the thirties, belatedly received the Nobel Prize for Literature. Though scorned by highbrow critics, his novels retained their universal appeal, though the social situations they dramatized so effectively had long since changed. In the wake of the vigorous new civil rights movement, Richard Wright's portrayal of racial oppression and hatred in *Native Son* and *Black Boy* had lost none of its power, nor had Henry Roth's story of a boy growing up on the Lower East Side in the first decade of the twentieth century—the inimitable *Call It Sleep*. The left-wing convictions of these writers did not make their work formulaic or destroy its power to communicate across the decades. Their social commitment, so typical of Depression writing, in no way conflicted with their artistic integrity; instead it gave their work fire and energy. By the early sixties, the revival of radicalism and the new interest in ethnicity, especially among blacks and Jews, rekindled interest in their work.

Call It Sleep, one of the great novels of the century, was in many ways a special case, for it was controversial among leftist critics, then forgotten until it was rediscovered in the sixties.[2] Roth's conversion to Communism came only as he was finishing the book in 1933, and the political discipline that came with his new worldview had a stultifying effect on his efforts as a writer. (His next novel did not appear until sixty years later.) With its tightly woven texture, recurring symbols, and interior monologues, *Call It Sleep* shows the influence of Joyce, Eliot, and the modernism of the 1920s. As a psychological narrative, amazing in its sensitivity to a child's view of the world, it seemed self-indulgent to some Marxist critics. Yet the story, besides being deeply personal, was also a document of the recent American past: immigration, the hardscrabble life of the ghetto, with its babble—or Babel—of cultures and languages. Roth had responded not only to Joyce's experiments with language and point of view but to his keen re-creation of everyday life in a modern city.

This was a time of transition for Aaron Copland as well. In 1934, the year that *Call It Sleep* was published, he too struck a curious balance between modernism and populism. That year he wrote *Statements*, in many ways a culmination of his modernist language of the 1920s, and *Hear Ye! Hear Ye!*, the first and least known of a series of ballets, the genre that eventually made him a household name. Along with *Call It Sleep* and other enduring works of the thirties, Copland's music fractures our conventional narrative of the period, the one first laid out by F. Scott Fitzgerald in 1931 in "Echoes of the Jazz Age" and Malcolm Cowley three years later in *Exile's Return*. In this canonical view, the twenties were the age of high spirits and expatriate adventures, reflected in wild artistic experiments, "the religion of art," as Cowley described it scornfully. In the thirties, however, the money ran out: the prodigals were forced to return home and buckle down, and most of them did. Moreover, says Cowley, "Paris was no longer the center of everything 'modern' and aesthetically ambitious in American literature."[3] The social misery of the Depression made them face up to the moral exigencies of American life; it pressed them to pay serious attention to an everyday world they once dismissed with irony or contempt. Larky irresponsibility gave way to a quickened social conscience, experimentation to documentation, surrealism to a new realism. The party was supplanted by the Party.

While some careers in the arts conformed to this conversion pattern, many did not, Fitzgerald's among them; he came home, but not to become a proletarian writer. The culture of the Popular Front was long seen as a (lamentable) result of this shift, but even the turn toward populism, especially after 1935, was part of a much wider development that went far beyond the new cultural policy of the Communist Party. It extended to Hollywood, which in a sense had always been populist, reaching out to the largest number of ordinary Americans, but also to a wide array of government-sponsored cultural programs, including the Treasury Department's Section of Fine Arts, which commissioned murals and sculpture for federal buildings and for 1,100 post offices across the country; Roy Stryker's Photography Unit of the Resettlement Administration, which movingly documented the effects of the Depression in the American heartland; and, most extensively, the art, music, theater, and writers' projects of the Works Progress Administration (WPA), a relief agency. The Federal Writers' Project alone put out more than 800 volumes, the best known of which were guides to all 48 states as well as many localities. Never had so much information been amassed by so many writers about the most mundane features of American life, a literary parallel to the vast array of public works that were constructed by the WPA across the nation.[4] FDR himself embarked on a more personal form of populism, using an intimate conversational tone in his fireside chats to make the chief executive a less remote figure, better able to reach ordinary Americans.

Stylistically, the new populist arts picked up important strands of modernism as well as social realism, as in such committed theater productions as Marc Blitzstein's Brechtian musical *The Cradle Will Rock* and other experimental work by the boy wonder Orson Welles and his producer, John Houseman.[5] Like others in his generation, Copland fused modernism with populism, seeking a fresh, clean, spare, yet colorful sound as he turned more directly to American subjects. The focus on American life, creative use of native traditions, went back several decades. In the 1930s it included a more varied body of fiction, journalism, poetry, painting, illustration, popular music, concert music, dance, theater, film, and photography than most critics acknowledged. As early as 1942, in an eloquent tribute, Alfred Kazin devoted the concluding chapter of *On Native Grounds* to the "enormous body of writing about the American scene that is one of the most remarkable phenomena of the era of crisis." He wrote that "it testified to an extraordinary national self-scrutiny."[6] His own book, beginning with its title, belonged with this literature and arose from the same impulse. Writers like Lewis Mumford in *The Brown Decades* (1931), Van Wyck Brooks in *The Flowering of New England* (1936) and *New England: Indian Summer* (1940), and Carl Sandburg in *The People, Yes* (1936) and his multivolume biography of Lincoln (1926–39) were taking stock of vigorous American traditions at a time when morale was low and faith in the system, as well as faith in the future, had taken a terrible beating.

Aaron Copland's career needs to be seen in this political and literary framework. On the surface it appears to be a prime example of the Exile's Return, the transformation of the experimental '20s modernist into a socially conscious, far more accessible '30s artist. Copland was never an expatriate, but he spent three formative years in Paris between 1921 and 1924, absorbing European culture, studying composition, and relishing the spunky novelties of the modernist scene dominated by Stravinsky, Joyce, Schoenberg, Picasso, Cocteau, Diaghilev, and younger composers like Milhaud, Satie, and George Antheil, Copland's brash American contemporary. "The sheer glamour of the period exerts a magic spell," Copland later wrote. "The very word 'modern' was exciting. The air was charged with talk of new tendencies, and the password was originality—anything was possible."[7] Yet Copland, like Malcolm Cowley, maintained that living in Paris made him more American, stimulating him to create music that would spring from his own roots, as Europeans so clearly were nourished by theirs. Even Stravinsky, the most influential modernist, had turned toward folk material, as Joyce relished popular songs. At the same time the French avant-garde was transfixed by all things American, which seemed to them quintessentially modern: the urban crowds, the skyscrapers, the clean, functional lines of the machine, the informal, egalitarian manners, the lack of tradition (or low respect for it), even the hostility to art and culture. The fetishization of art could thwart the innovative spirit of the living. Americans were seen as instinctively pragmatic. Irreverence was their birthright, classlessness their privilege: they were happily uncultured, even downright primitive.

As Picasso had been taken with African sculpture and masks, Copland's Paris of the 1920s was enamored of blacks and especially jazz. Soon after he and his friend Harold Clurman returned to the States, the city made a cult of the black American dancer and singer Josephine Baker and *La Revue Nègre*, as can be seen in Paul Colin's strikingly stylized modernist posters. In the same year, 1925, Copland used jazz rhythms and snatches of familiar tunes (like "The Sidewalks of New York") in the "Dance" section of his *Music for the Theatre*. The equally lively "Burlesque" section reminded Roy Harris of "whorehouse music." Copland was partly inspired by the vulgar but irresistible singing and mugging of Fanny Brice, whose Jewish vamps were as deliciously exaggerated as Baker's half naked, chocolate-colored primitives.[8] By reaching out to the spirit of the theater, jazz, popular music, and burlesque, Copland composed a kind of "Broadway Boogie-Woogie," with those two animated sections joined by a bluesy interlude. As Copland's biographer Howard Pollack remarks, this middle section introduces that "lonely, night-in-the-city ambience so characteristic of the mature composer."[9] By developing brief but easily recognizable melodic motifs with sparkling orchestral color, he anticipated the ballet works of the late '30s and early '40s that would establish his American sound and make him a permanent classic. Like Gershwin and Cole Porter, Copland captured the propulsive energy and high spirits of the twenties and then gave it a deeper meaning in the pinched conditions of the Depression, when a choreographer like Balanchine could go back and forth between ballet and Broadway, and choreography itself became an expressive way to overcome inertia and get people moving.

The new interest of American artists in the neglected wealth of the American scene developed all through the 1920s. On his return from Paris, Copland developed close links to the circle around Alfred Stieglitz, the great photographer and impresario of modern art, as well as to Paul Rosenfeld, Stieglitz's loyal spokesman and eloquent house critic. Before the war, Stieglitz had promoted both European and American modernists at his celebrated gallery at 291 Fifth Avenue, which closed in 1917. But the galleries he opened from 1921 onward, including An American Place, featured only American artists, perhaps because the Europeans Stieglitz had first exhibited, included Cezanne, Brancusi, and Picasso, had not only dominated the Armory Show of 1913 but now enjoyed worldwide renown. Moreover, influential cultural critics like the younger Van Wyck Brooks had argued that American life was either too genteel or too crassly materialistic to nurture great achievements in the arts, a sentiment many expatriate writers shared. Stieglitz and Rosenfeld, on the other hand, looked back to Whitman for an authentic American art that rejected European models and were influenced by D. H. Lawrence's conviction that American writers had already broken new imaginative ground in their explorations of both the continent and their own psyches.

This Lawrentian argument was pursued by Rosenfeld in his most important book, *Port of New York: Essays on Fourteen American Moderns* (1924); by the poet William Carlos Williams in his ambitious prose work, *In the American*

Grain (1925); and by Hart Crane in his uneven Whitmanesque epic, *The Bridge* (1930). Copland was attracted to the work of Crane and Williams and grew especially close to Rosenfeld, who was primarily a music critic, though *Port of New York* focused on painters and a few writers, among them Williams, Sandburg, and Sherwood Anderson. Rosenfeld in turn became a great admirer of Copland's music. This was hardly to be expected since Rosenfeld was unsympathetic to jazz and especially to the crowd-pleasing concert pieces of George Gershwin, to which Copland's jazz-inflected scores were sometimes compared. His 1929 essay on Copland, though written long before Copland's popular works were composed, helped set the terms by which his music would be appreciated. Rosenfeld stressed its "leanness, slenderness of sound," combined with "a strain of grandiosity." He described the liveliness, "the decided motoriness," of Copland's rhythm, even in its slow moods, and emphasized the kinetic vitality that would later become a hallmark of Copland's ballet scores. "What one means by this motoriness of Copland's, is its strong kinesis, its taut, instinctive 'go.' Wistful or burlesque, slow or fast, his pieces have enormous 'snap.'" It is revealing that Rosenfeld, a mandarin stylist, reaches for colloquial terms (set off by single quotation marks) to evoke this strikingly American yet also modern quality in Copland's work. He connects it to the machine ("the hiccoughing beat" of the jazzy Scherzo of Copland's first symphony, he finds, "iterated with a mad mechanic joy"), to the new archi-tecture, with its wiry steel skeleton, and to American energy in general, "all that's swift and daring, aggressive and unconstrained in our life."[10]

While this describes what Copland had already done, it could be read as a program for work he had yet to do, from the austere virtuosity of the Piano Variations (1930), which thrilled young composers and performers like Leonard Bernstein, becoming a benchmark for the new music, to the folk-inspired *El Salón México* (1932–36), *Billy the Kid* (1938), *Rodeo* (1942), and *Appalachian Spring* (1944). Students of thirties culture commonly contrast this kind of audience-friendly populism—melodic, familiar, accessible—with the insouciant modernism of the 1920s or the aggressive experimentalism of the early 1930s, which produced not only the Piano Variations, which ordinary listeners often found forbidding, but also severe proletarian fiction and poetry, which attracted few readers. There was also a mammoth novel like Dos Passos's *U.S.A.* trilogy (1930–36), a collage of history, biography, jour-nalism, and fiction without genuinely individualized characters.

The aesthetic radicalism of Copland or Dos Passos paralleled the politi-cal radicalism of the Left during the early thirties, the peak years of the Depression, before the official turn toward the Popular Front in 1935. Yet Dos Passos's sweepingly ambitious novel follows directly from the concern with the American scene promoted by the Stieglitz circle and exemplified by writers like Williams and Crane, and even F. Scott Fitzgerald in the twenties. For them, America became a challenge, an enigma—something to be unraveled and explained by exploring its founding myths and popular traditions. They looked for the themes and folkways that might make sense of American culture. For Copland, as for many writers and visual artists, the burgeoning populism of the post-1935 period, far from representing a sharp reversal of direction, had deep roots in the modernism of the 1920s and the radicalism of the early 1930s.

Part of the turn toward populism was anthropological. Along with an interest in jazz and the blues came a recovery—or was it partly an invention?—of folk culture. Stemming from the nineteenth-century search for national roots, this fascination with folklore, which came late to the United States, took shape in the twenties but grew in the thirties. Ethnomusicologists like Charles Seeger, John Lomax, and his son Alan Lomax traveled through the rural South to record and transcribe music that belonged to oral traditions that could soon be lost. As early as 1927, Carl Sandburg retrieved and published a huge collection of folk songs, *The American Songbag*. Pioneering folklorists such as Constance Rourke, B. A. Botkin, and Zora Neale Hurston collected humor, tall tales, legends, and folk wisdom, including the stories Hurston brought together in *Mules and Men* (1934) under the tutelage of her mentor, Franz Boas. Later, after fieldwork in Haiti, she began gathering material in her native Florida for the Federal Writers' Project.

A key feature of the twenties avant-garde was a rebellion against middle-class gentility in the name of earthiness, authenticity, and frank sexual expression. These projects reflected the critical spirit of D. H. Lawrence, whose influence, along with Freud's, was pervasive. Sherwood Anderson's *Winesburg, Ohio* (1919) was a deeply personal ethnography of an American town, with an accent on the unfulfilled lives of its inhabitants and the longings of its clumsy but sensitive young protagonist, who records their stories but escapes at the end. Jean Toomer's *Cane* (1923), an idiosyncratic mixture of poetry and prose, sank deep into the loam of the author's native Georgia in a way that fascinated both the young modernists, who published his work in *The Liberator*, and the future writers of the Harlem Renaissance. *Cane* found an unlikely echo in the work of an aristocratic white southerner, DuBose Heyward, whose immersion in Gullah culture would lead to his evocative portrayal of Charleston's Catfish Row. He would see the story of *Porgy and Bess* through its transformations from novel to Broadway play to Gershwin's 1935 folk opera.

Of all the Harlem Renaissance writers, none better achieved a folk-like simplicity than Langston Hughes in his first two books of poems, *The Weary Blues* (1926) and *Fine Clothes to the Jew* (1927). Well before the "forgotten man"—the neglected veteran who had served his country—and the "common man" were elevated into myth by the onset of the Depression, Hughes used colloquial American speech to direct his poems and prose to ordinary readers. His language and rhythm were deceptively simple, intentionally evading the literary. Moreover, Hughes tried to bring the very cadence of jazz and the blues into his jingly rhythm, as in the title poem of the first volume:

> *Droning a drowsy syncopated tune,*
> *Rocking back and forth to a mellow croon,*
> *I heard a Negro play.*
> *Down on Lenox Avenue the other night*
> *By the pale dull pallor of an old gas light*
> *He did a lazy sway . . .*
> *He did a lazy sway . . .*
> *To the tune o' those Weary Blues.* [11]

Another strain of Hughes's "Americanness" turned up in a poem that appeared in Alain Locke's 1925 anthology *The New Negro*. "I, too" echoed Whitman, beginning, "I, too, sing America." Written in the voice of the "darker brother" who is sent to eat in the kitchen, it predicts that one day he would find his place at the table. [12] A much longer poem from 1925, "America," focuses on the "little dark baby" and the "little Jew baby" as they both struggle for acceptance. Hughes writes in lines so short, almost hypnotically repetitive, that they create a drumlike cadence: "We come / You and I, / Seeking the stars. / You and I, / You of the blue eyes / And the blond hair, / I of the dark eyes / And of the crinkly hair. / You and I / Offering hands / Being brothers, / Being one, / Being America." [13]

The motif of the brotherly handshake, the mutual recognition across barriers of race and class, became one of the central images of the Popular Front and part of the insignia of the industrial labor unions. Even in his best-known poem on this theme, "Let America Be America Again" (1936), whose dark refrain is that "America never was America to me," Hughes concludes with the shaky confidence that the dream is not quite dead, that "America will be!" [14] This faith culminated in Earl Robinson's 1939 cantata *Ballad for Americans*, made famous by Paul Robeson, and in his 1943 anthem "The House I Live In," with lyrics by Abel Meeropol, which was sung by Robeson but also most effectively by Frank Sinatra in a short film of 1945 by that name. The introductory verse of "The House I Live In" begins, in classic Popular Front fashion, "What is America to me?" It goes on to describe the little ordinary things enjoyed by "all races and religions," all sharing the same house, the same nation. Under the banner of democracy, where each individual has "the right to speak my mind out," inequalities of wealth, distinctions of class, race, or religion are subdued, to be replaced by that warmhearted abstraction, the people: "But especially the people / That's America to me." In the movie—written by a future member of the Hollywood Ten, Albert Maltz, and directed by an old Hollywood pro, Mervyn LeRoy—Sinatra sings this with such force and lyrical conviction as to make its sugary sentiments unexpectedly concrete, teaching a lesson in tolerance to a rowdy group of young boys.

As his congressional inquisitors would later remind him, Copland was a longtime fellow traveler who remained deeply involved with left-wing causes between 1932 and 1949. He even won a prize for setting a May Day song in 1934. But the motivation for his turn toward populism and Americana was not strictly political. Copland had always wanted to create an intrinsically American music, but he also came to feel that there was a limited audience for avant-garde writing, which itself had lost its buoyant experimental edge, in part because the Depression had altered the national mood. His response to a shifting cultural climate was typically pragmatic, as was his turn away from left-wing politics after 1949. Like a painter disenchanted with the museum as a mausoleum for the elite, he felt confined by the concert hall, looking instead to theater, films, and dance to get in touch with a wider public. To reach this audience, he accepted the artistic challenge of "an imposed simplicity" and the personal challenge of collaboration, even when he knew that his work would have to play a subsidiary role.[15] Writing his first Hollywood film score for Lewis Milestone's adaptation of Steinbeck's *Of Mice and Men* (1939), he mused that "it seemed a strange assignment to write music that is actually meant to be uninteresting."[16] To make sure his music was heard, he rarely failed to adapt it—especially the ballet music—into orchestral suites that proved to be enduringly successful in the concert hall.

When intellectuals of the 1940s and 1950s assailed Popular Front culture, they often linked it with technology, new media, and mass audiences. They saw it as hopelessly middlebrow, a dumbing down of art into toothless entertainment. To them it represented a deluge of mechanical and commercial art swamping the real thing. Some modernist critics of the 1920s like Edmund Wilson and Gilbert Seldes had welcomed the new popular arts. But now, as the thirties ended, *Partisan Review* writers like Clement Greenberg and Dwight Macdonald launched attacks on kitsch and mass culture that were rooted in their anti-Stalinist politics. These became the first volleys in a culture war that would rage throughout the early postwar decades.

The new avant-garde of the 1940s would define itself against post office murals, movie culture, tonality, program music, representational realism or regionalism, and progressive messages of any kind. This assault reopened and widened the modernist break between high art and popular taste. It would be pointless to describe it as a gross injustice to thirties art or a blind resistance to new forms of mass communication. Every modern generation defines itself against its predecessors; postwar artists, some of whom began as WPA artists and social realists, were no exception. But Copland embraced the opportunity to seek out native resources to paint a picture of American life, and he set about trying to do this in fresh ways, giving full play to his own distinctive musical voice. *Billy the Kid*, choreographed by Eugene Loring, was one of a series of American-themed ballets commissioned by Lincoln Kirstein's Ballet Caravan, including Virgil Thomson's *Filling Station*. Here was a Jewish New Yorker, working on rue de Rennes in Paris with two collections of western tunes that Kirstein had pressed on him—achieving what the Left called a "united front" in his own artistic identity. Copland later recalled his initial qualms: "I have never been particularly impressed with the musical beauties of the cowboy song as such." He noted that "it is a delicate operation to put fresh and unconventional harmonies to well-known melodies without spoiling their naturalness." He kept in mind "my resolve to write plainly—not only because I had become convinced that simplicity was the way out of isolation for the contemporary composer, but because I have never liked music to get in the way of the thing it is supposedly aiding."[17]

It was typical of the populist artist of the late 1930s to try to communicate more directly and to undertake cooperative projects, making use of familiar or accessible materials. Popular artists rarely saw themselves in Romantic terms as lone creators striving for utter originality. If they were lucky and gifted, they struck a new note by combining, synthesizing, and collaborating. Virgil Thomson undoubtedly paved the way for Copland's use of folk material with his *Symphony on a Hymn Tune* and especially with his wonderful scores for Pare Lorentz's government-sponsored documentaries, *The Plow That Broke the Plains* (1936) and *The River* (1937). Or so he often claimed. In an ambivalent but incisive essay on Copland in *Modern Music* in 1932, Thomson, reflecting on the melancholy fate of the modern composer, concluded prophetically, "Simple clarity is what we need, and we will get it only by a radical simplification of our methods of composition."[18]

Clarifying and simplifying, reaching out to a wider audience, promoting some form of communal bonding, finding a distinctive native style, and doing this with freshness and vitality—these were some hallmarks of the

Group Theatre, created by Copland's lifelong friend Harold Clurman, which sought to combine honest emotion with radical protest. But the populist turn can best be seen in the New Deal Arts Projects, including the Treasury Department mural commissions starting in 1934 and the WPA Federal Arts Project starting in 1935, which decorated so many official buildings across America with scenes from American history and contemporary life. Some of these scenes offended local mores. Others were mocked by critics for their impersonality or figurative conservatism. In her challenging book on post office murals, *Wall-to-Wall America* (1982), Karal Ann Marling argues that high-art standards of aesthetic autonomy and originality are irrelevant to these works. For the painters, as for the government that commissioned them, the murals were less a work of art than a compact with the community and with popular feeling. The emphasis was on the story they told, not the form. "The mural remained a painting, but it was a painting last; first, it was a depiction of objects and scenes, a picture, a symbol, an event."[19] The artist turning from the easel to the mural was like the composer moving from the concert hall into the theater or the movie palace. This was an experiment in the democratization of art for a mass audience. Marling suggests that the murals should be compared to movies, not to paintings in museums. The murals, like Hollywood movies, relied on the "collective archetype, which aligned their aesthetic with mass culture." She argues that "movies were successful—and profitable—in direct proportion to their ability to arouse and stimulate the latent content of the popular imagination. Movies spoke to everybody, at 25¢ a head, in a familiar tongue, the imagistic argot of the people. The cowboy, the hood, the common man, and the Midwestern farmer were instantly recognizable amalgams of operative myth, fiction, legend, and half-remembered dreams of childhood."[20]

Before the government programs, the best-known examples of such mythmaking artists were the Mexican muralists, especially Diego Rivera, whose Rockefeller Center murals were destroyed in 1933 because he had included the head of Lenin, and the titanic Midwestern populist Thomas Hart Benton, whose highly stylized scenes of ordinary Americans had a huge impact on New Deal artists. Here too we can see parallels to Copland. Benton had begun as a modernist but later turned sharply against modernism, especially abstract art, while adapting some of its techniques to the portrayal of realistic scenes. Like other regionalist painters, Marling claims, Benton worked less from life than from the stereotypes of the popular media. His figures were so recognizable in part because they were generalized rather than individualized; to achieve the typical, the sense of the collective, they relied on a stock of images familiar from films, cartoons, and photographs. In *America Today* (1930), Benton's great set of murals for the New School in New York, "the figures, drawn like animated cartoon characters, defy orthodox anatomy," says Marling. "Benton's farmers and floozies diagram kinetic energy poised for release."[21]

Copland's use of Mexican tunes in *El Salón México* and cowboy songs in *Billy the Kid* and *Rodeo* can be usefully compared to Benton's reliance on archetypal, easily recognizable images borrowed from popular culture, though Copland, with unfailing musical taste, invariably gave them an unspoiled feeling that transcended stereotype. Both artists were reaching for the elusive figure of the common man, to whom Copland paid such dignified tribute in his famous *Fanfare* of 1942. And both evoked tremendous energy from their use of popular material. "*America Today* is essentially plotless but achieves a comparable unity through Benton's forceful contention that energy is the hallmark of American life," according to Marling. "As the Depression deepened, the dynamism of the New School murals promised that this powerful race of doers could find a way out."[22]

Like so much populist art of the late 1930s, Copland's ballets are based on the same optimistic principle. In a period of continuing stagnation, they aim to get people moving again, to stimulate their high spirits. Copland did not set out deliberately to cheer people up, only to reach them more directly, but his buoyant music, such as the "Hoe-Down" in *Rodeo*, invariably makes listeners want to kick up their heels. Copland instinctively understood why dance—from Busby Berkeley and Fred Astaire to Balanchine and Martha Graham—grew into such a prime passion of the Depression years, when ballet was democratized and Americanized. The figure of Billy the Kid also fits in easily with the outlaw stereotypes so popular during the Depression, such as the Bonnie-and-Clyde characters in Edward Anderson's novel *Thieves Like Us* (1937) and Fritz Lang's *You Only Live Once* (1937), or the charismatic criminals played by Jimmy Cagney, with the same "snap," the electric sense of vitality, that Rosenfeld praised in Copland's music.

Copland's populist works, like Benton's murals, form chapters of an ongoing saga of the common man that produced not only literary creations like Steinbeck's characters but screen personalities that would endure for half a century. For Frank Capra in his celebrated populist movies made between 1936 and 1946 the common man was personified by actors like Gary Cooper and Jimmy Stewart, playing the naive but determined everyman, as well as a brilliant galaxy of character actors like Walter Brennan, while his female counterpart was the spunky working girl played by Barbara Stanwyck or Jean Arthur. In Fritz Lang's first two American movies, *Fury* (1936), an anti-lynching film, and *You Only Live Once*, the common man was impersonated by Spencer Tracy and Henry Fonda, both of whom would become bywords for rock-ribbed integrity.

John Ford would cement Fonda's image by casting him as Tom Joad and then as Abe Lincoln, the ultimate historical forerunner of the common man, as Whitman was the literary forerunner. More class-conscious directors turned to John Garfield and Sylvia Sidney as ethnic working-class figures, beloved by Popular Front audiences. These actors had already developed their personalities on the New York stage. The Group Theatre aesthetic associated with Clurman, Lee Strasberg, and Clifford Odets was making inroads into Hollywood. It infiltrated war movies, which focused on the ordinary dogface rather than the combat hero. It would triumph after the war in the hands of Elia Kazan, Arthur Miller, Marlon Brando, and the Actors Studio. In different ways, Stanley Kowalski and Willy Loman brought the common man into the postwar era, while Blanche DuBois conveyed the forlorn romanticism of an earlier time.

Copland's initial film projects, his scores for *Of Mice and Men* (1939) and *Our Town* (1940), involved literary projects that were part of the same populist bent toward Americana and the common man. Yet his music always had a singular authenticity that is missing from the work of composers like Earl Robinson or Elie Siegmeister, who exploited American material because they had a message to deliver or because the Party steered them in that direction. Much of Popular Front art was not only message-ridden but smacked of condescension and insincerity, an ersatz simplicity that patronized its subjects and came off as anything but natural. This was what makes the work of Copland, Benton, Steinbeck, Capra, John Ford, Walker Evans, James Agee, Marc Blitzstein, Woody Guthrie, and even Virgil Thomson so refreshing.[23] They made genuine art with what, for others, was little more than a political program, even a form of middle-class slumming.

Because Depression conditions were so extreme, social tourism became endemic to the decade. Writers and journalists of every kind were intrigued by how ordinary Americans were getting by. Long before the official populism of the second half of the decade, writers like Edmund Wilson, who had just published a book on international modernism, took to the road to report on how people were doing; he filed his stories for *The New Republic*, where he had served in the 1920s as literary editor. As published in book form, *The American Jitters* (1932) was the best of Wilson's travel books, and along with *To the Finland Station*, his 1940 history of revolutionary ideas, was the closest he came to writing truly effective narrative, a good deal closer than his own fiction. In one sketch, for example, "A Bad Day in Brooklyn," he explores the stories of three separate people who, at their wits' end, try to kill themselves on the same day, showing how even their suicide attempts prove haplessly ineffectual. In "Two Protests," he makes a pointed juxtaposition between a protest meeting of activists and intellectuals, which he describes at considerable length, and a spontaneous act of desperation by a Sicilian immigrant, a man with a wife, infant child, and no job, who kills his landlord when he hounds him for the rent, a story Wilson recounts in a few stark, uninflected paragraphs almost as an afterthought. Avoiding emotion or explicit commentary, Wilson takes on the inflections of a hard-boiled writer to convey some harsh ironies that beset the lives of ordinary Americans during the lowest days of the Depression.

This kind of committed journalism continued in different forms all through the 1930s: in oral histories collected by members of the Federal Writers' Project, which led to such acclaimed volumes as *These Are Our Lives* (1939), thirty-five stories of southern tenant farmers; in text-and-photo books covering some of the same ground by Agee and Evans, Margaret Bourke-White and Erskine Caldwell, Dorothea Lange and Paul Taylor, Edwin Rosskam and Richard Wright; or in what Marshall Berman, in an essay on Studs Turkel, called the "We-the-People-Talk book," composed of interviews and conversations in which ordinary men and women, customarily silenced by history, find their voice, as they rarely did in the journalism that preceded, where their stories were filtered through the interpretive prose of the writer.[24] An important example of committed journalism was *The People Talk* (1940) by Benjamin Appel, a genuine hard-boiled writer, who took to the road by car and put together a collage of people and viewpoints so spare, so free of comment or interpretation, that it makes Wilson look garrulous. Here the writer himself completely disappears.

Appel's book in some ways is the purest example of 1930s populism. Its dedication page reads: "By the People / and / For the People," at once a political echo and an assertion of democracy, as if the People themselves could assume collective responsibility, without literary intervention.[25] James Agee took this documentary impulse even further when he recorded his resistance to using words at all in *Let Us Now Praise Famous Men*: "If I could do it, I'd do no writing at all here. It would be photographs; the rest would be fragments of cloth, bits of cotton, lumps of earth, records of speech, pieces of wood and iron, phials of odors, plates of food and of excrement. Booksellers would consider it quite a novelty; critics would murmur, yes, but is it art; and I could trust a majority of you to use it as a parlor game."[26]

Copland's populism and his treatment of the American scene are at the furthest remove from the impersonal realism sought by Wilson, Appel, and Agee, and achieved most powerfully by great 1930s photographers like Walker Evans. When Copland worked on *El Sálon México* or *Danzón Cubano*, he understood that he was working from the outside, not strictly as a tourist, but with popular materials, which he did not hesitate to transpose into his own voice. Like Virgil Thomson, he felt that music cannot simply transcribe or invent but must also seduce. His western ballets were frankly grounded in mythology, not actuality; working with Martha Graham on *Appalachian Spring* (1944), he knew he was helping her shape a myth by way of rhythm, expressive passion, and physical movement. His use of the Shaker hymn "Simple Gifts" ("'Tis the gift to be simple, 'tis the gift to be free"), which points to what was most admired about the Shaker way of life, was almost a credo for the simplifying approach he had taken since the mid-1930s and, as Howard Pollack remarks, "had connotations relevant to the work's larger themes of peace, war, remembrance, and national identity."[27]

No concert audience has ever needed to know the program of this ballet to appreciate its music, which sums up all Copland had been trying to achieve for almost a decade, and perhaps as far back as his integration of jazz and pop materials in the 1920s. "The entire score," notes Pollack, "represents an absorption of the vernacular—suitable to a script so steeped in a wide range of American myth and folklore. It often gives the impression of folk music, so much so that listeners are often surprised to discover that it uses only one folk tune."[28] Where *Billy the Kid* evoked a life of risk and violent adventure and *Rodeo* had the dizzying energy of a country square dance, the music for *Appalachian Spring*, especially the variations on the Shaker melody, is stately, vibrant, often slow and tense, but always immensely dignified, with the same grandeur and solidity as *Fanfare for the Common Man*. If *Rodeo* anticipates *Oklahoma!*, also choreographed by Agnes de Mille, *Appalachian Spring* reminds me of Walker Evans's eloquent, deeply humane photographs; they make other treatments of rural folk look corny or condescending. This quiet dignity is especially impressive in Copland's original chamber score, without the color and brilliance of the orchestral suite of 1945. In either version, *Appalachian Spring* marks the culmination of Copland's populism and his exploration of American themes.

In its heyday in the 1890s, American populism was an agrarian rebellion against eastern bankers, plutocrats, and industrialists. In the Europe of the 1920s and 1930s, populism took a fascist turn and became a frightening mass ideology of blood and soil. When Kenneth Burke, at the first American Writers' Congress of 1935, suggested substituting "the people" for "the workers" or "the masses" in the propaganda of the Left, he was reminded by one critic that it was "historically associated with demagoguery of the most vicious sort." But Burke insisted that "the symbol of 'the people'" was both "closer to our folkways" and contained "connotations both of oppression and of unity."[29] In the cultural wing of the Popular Front, a battery of socially concerned writers, artists, composers, choreographers, and photographers, abetted by the cultural programs of the New Deal, created a left-wing populism that could be urban as well as rural, that lent dignity to common people, recaptured lost elements of our history and folk heritage, instilled energy and hope into people who were suffering from fear and privation, and tried to bridge gaps of sympathy and understanding between different races, classes, and regions. For some "the people" was an empty symbol, a tactical appeal to an undifferentiated mass that did not truly exist and to traditions that were largely imaginary or simply recast in a "progressive" image. But at its best, until postwar anticommunism set out to destroy its influence, the new populism brought important chapters of the American past alive; it made many Americans far more aware of how others lived and suffered during the Depression; it gave political energy to a more inclusive liberal tradition, and cemented communal bonds that carried over into the national war effort. Aaron Copland was shaped by this movement as much as he helped bring it into being. He had anticipated it in the 1920s and continued to pursue it through the 1940s and even beyond. Despite the aesthetic and political backlash against populist art, his key works, like Gershwin's and Ellington's, helped create the American sound. Beloved by audiences, echoed by the younger composers he helped nurture, his music became an enduring part of the nation's cultural life.

NOTES

1. For an overview of this ongoing research, see my essay "Depression Culture: The Dream of Mobility," in *Radical Revisions: Rereading 1930s Culture*, ed. Bill Mullen and Sherry Linkon (Urbana, Ill.: University of Illinois Press, 1996), pp. 225–41.

2. First published in 1934 by a publisher that soon went bankrupt, *Call It Sleep* was reprinted in hardcover by a small publisher in 1960s but did not gain wide attention until a paperback edition was issued by Avon Books in 1964. Reviewed on the front page of *The New York Times Book Review*, a first for a paperback, it went on to sell a million copies.

3. See F. Scott Fitzgerald, "Echoes of the Jazz Age," *The Fitzgerald Reader*, ed. Arthur Mizener (New York: Scribner's, 1963), pp. 323–31, and Malcolm Cowley, *Exile's Return: A Literary Odyssey of the 1920s* (1934; New York: Viking, 1956), p. 284.

4. For a detailed history of the Federal Writers' Project, see Jerre Mangione, *The Dream and the Deal: The Federal Writers' Project, 1935–1943* (Boston: Little, Brown, 1972).

A general introduction to the New Deal arts projects can be found in Milton Meltzer, *Violins & Shovels: The WPA Arts Projects* (New York: Delacorte, 1976). See also William E. Leuchtenburg, *Franklin D. Roosevelt and the New Deal, 1932–1940* (New York: Harper & Row, 1963), pp. 124–28. Among public works Leuchtenburg records that the WPA built 2,500 hospitals, 5,900 school buildings, 1,000 airport landing fields, and nearly 13,000 playgrounds—in short, the precious public infrastructure for the next half century and beyond.

5. On the variety of creative work associated with the Popular Front, see especially Michael Denning, *The Cultural Front* (London: Verso, 1997), though Denning, to counteract old stereotypes about realism and documentary, casts his net perhaps *too* widely, turning even *Citizen Kane* into a Popular Front movie. The emphasis on documentary is best formulated in William Stott, *Documentary Expression and Thirties America* (New York: Oxford, 1973). A much more jaundiced view of the Popular Front, reflecting both the early critiques of intellectuals and a later New Left radicalism, is developed by Richard H. Pells, *Radical Visions and American Dreams* (New York: Harper & Row, 1973), pp. 292–329.

6. Alfred Kazin, *On Native Grounds: An Interpretation of Modern American Prose Literature* (1942; Garden City, N.Y.: Anchor, 1956), p. 378.

7. Aaron Copland and Vivian Perlis, *Copland: 1900 Through 1942* (New York: St. Martin's/Marek, 1984), p. 55.

8. Ibid., p. 120.

9. Howard Pollack, *Aaron Copland: The Life and Work of an Uncommon Man* (New York: Henry Holt, 1999), p. 129.

10. Paul Rosenfeld, "Aaron Copland," in *Musical Impressions: Selections from Paul Rosenfeld's Criticism*, ed. Herbert A. Leibowitz (New York: Hill and Wang, 1969), pp. 249, 250, 252.

11. Arnold Rampersad, ed., *The Collected Poems of Langston Hughes* (New York: Vintage, 1994), p. 50.

12. Ibid., p. 46.

13. Ibid., p. 52.

14. Ibid., pp. 189–91.

15. Copland and Perlis, *Copland 1900–1942*, p. 316.

16. Ibid., p. 299.

17. Ibid., p. 279.

18. Virgil Thomson, "Aaron Copland," in *A Virgil Thomson Reader* (1981; New York: E. P. Dutton, 1984), p. 22. Thomson's piece is at once shrewd, competitive, and marginally anti-Semitic, with its undue emphasis on Copland's Jewish origins. "His melodic material is of a markedly Hebrew cast," says Thomson, strangely. "Its tendency to return upon itself is penitential" (p. 20). But the unflappable Copland hardly ever took offense. Moreover, Thomson's essay includes incisive comments such as these: "By coloristic I mean it is made out of harmonic and instrumental rather than melodic devices. This compilation is picturesque and cumulative. It tends to augment its excitement, to add to weight and tension. His dominant idea of form is crescendo" (p. 20). Some of this could be usefully applied to music Copland had not yet written.

19. Karal Ann Marling, *Wall-to-Wall America: A Cultural History of the Post-Office Murals in the Great Depression* (Minnneapolis: University of Minnesota Press, 1982), p. 14.

20. Ibid., p. 90.

21. Ibid., p. 40.

22. Ibid., p. 41.

23. Though Thomson was a Paris-trained cosmopolitan who based his first two opera on witty librettos by Gertrude Stein, his music took strength from his deep Midwestern roots.

24. See Marshall Berman, "Studs Terkel: Living in the Mural," *Adventures in Marxism* (London/New York: Verso, 1999), pp. 65–68.

25. See Benjamin Appel, *The People Talk: American Voices from the Great Depression* (1940; New York: Touchstone, 1982).

26. James Agee and Walker Evans, *Let Us Now Praise Famous Men* (1940; New York: Ballantine Books, 1966), p. 12.

27. Pollack, *Aaron Copland*, p. 398.

28. Ibid., p. 399.

29. Quoted in Daniel Aaron, *Writers on the Left: Episodes in American Literary Communism* (1961; New York: Columbia University Press, 1992), pp. 290–91.

From the New York Avant-Garde to

Mexican Modernists:

Aaron Copland and the Visual Arts

GAIL LEVIN

Less than two years before the centennial of his birth, an art museum invited me to commemorate Aaron Copland with an exhibition of my choice.[1] That proposal led me to consider which visual artists, if any, had intersected with the composer. Turning to the two-volume autobiography that Copland wrote with Vivian Perlis, I read in a letter to his parents written aboard ship en route to France in 1921, that he considered himself "very lucky in being seated next to three French people, who always converse in French. One is an old priest, another a painter, and a young woman who has attended college in America. They are very nice to me and always encourage me when I try to splash some French."[2] Copland went on to comment that he had spent "a great deal of time with one of them, the painter, who is a man of about 30 and has been giving me the most valuable information about Paris."[3]

Commenting decades later on this letter, Copland recalled that the painter was Marcel Duchamp, "who meant nothing to me, despite the fact that in 1913, at the New York Armory Show, he had sent the art world into a tizzy with his *Nude Descending a Staircase*."[4] Copland went on to report (both in his letters home and in later commentary) how Duchamp had impressed him, tried to discourage him from study at Fontainebleau, and taken him out several times in Paris. The French artist—Copland described him as "exactly the sort of person I wanted to meet"—merited only one sentence in Howard Pollack's masterful biography.[5] Thus I wondered if there might be something to learn by looking for other connections between Copland and visual artists. In ensuing research, I discovered a number of interlocking relationships with significance for the composer's creativity and career. This essay draws upon my previous study as well as unpublished documentation that has come to my attention since.[6]

Although Copland made many friends within circles of visual artists and their patrons, he was extremely modest about his own knowledge of the visual. Of his time in Paris, he told Perlis: "I knew the painters were very active, but I have never been as close to painting as to literature."[7] But he did learn about the painters through his then roommate and lifelong friend, Harold Clurman, who recalled of himself and Copland: "We were very serious about the arts," and asserted, "I learned a great deal about painting because we also knew painters."[8] Still, Copland insisted, "If I had been more visual-minded I would have gone to many more exhibitions than I did."[9] Clurman, who was already writing reviews by 1922, felt confident enough to comment upon visual artists' work for the Ballets Suédois—from Gerald Murphy's sets, scenario, and costumes for *Within the Quota*, with jazz-inflected music by Cole Porter, to Fernand Léger's African-inspired sets for *Création du Monde*, a collaboration which also included the writer Blaise Cendrars and the composer Darius Milhaud.[10] Since Copland also attended these performances by the Swedish Ballets, we can assume that the two roommates discussed the company's programs.

Back in New York in 1924, after three years in Paris, Copland got to meet the critic Paul Rosenfeld, whose essays on music and art in *The Dial* he particularly enjoyed. After hearing Copland play at the League of Composers, Rosenfeld called him to say that he liked his music and began inviting the young composer to dinners at his Irving Place apartment. There Copland met others in the avant-garde, many closely engaged with visual art, including the critics Lewis Mumford, Waldo Frank, and Edmund Wilson, as well as the painter and poet e.e. cummings and other notable visual modernists, including Alfred Stieglitz, Georgia O'Keeffe, Paul Strand, Rebecca Salsbury Strand, and Florine Stettheimer (whose dinners Copland also attended).[11] Years later Copland recalled: "Waldo Frank's book of 1919, *Our America,* challenged writers to bring America into the modern art movement. Alfred Stieglitz was the unofficial leader of this group. His gallery was the hang-out for younger artists such as photographer Paul Strand, painters John Marin and Georgia O'Keeffe (later Stieglitz's wife), Waldo Frank and other writers I met at Paul Rosenfeld's apartment."[12]

Although Rosenfeld is known to have come to modernism through music, he supported avant-garde artists such as Marsden Hartley, a painter, poet, and essayist of the Stieglitz circle, whose abstract painting *Indian Composition* (1914), with its self-consciously Native American theme (painted in Berlin), hung in his collection. Rosenfeld also purchased one

Figure 1. Marsden Hartley, *Indian Composition*, 1914.

of Hartley's calla lily paintings in 1921.[13] The artist Richard Hennessy recalls that Copland owned a photograph of Hartley.[14] Poets such as Hart Crane, Marianne Moore, and Alfred Kreymborg often read at Rosenfeld's dinners, at which Copland played his compositions.[15]

Copland, who wrote supportively of Rosenfeld's critical brilliance, insisted, "I owe him a special debt." He noted that "the American scene in particular was a consuming interest of Rosenfeld's. He believed passionately in the emergence of an important school of contemporary American composers."[16] Here Copland recalls statements Rosenfeld made in *The Dial*, calling for works that "speak to the American of what lies between him and his native soil."[17] This emphasis on building an American culture is what Copland may well have absorbed from the artists at Rosenfeld's dinners, even if rivalries for their host's attentions were occasionally an undercurrent on these evenings.

Mainly members of the Stieglitz coterie, these vanguard visual artists were calling for an art that would be American. According to Edmund Wilson, Rosenfeld respected Stieglitz to the extent that "it was difficult, if not impossible, to persuade him to pay attention to any contemporary American painter who was not a protégé of Stieglitz,' and if Stieglitz had excommunicated a refractory or competitive disciple, Paul, following the official directive, would condemn him."[18]

While Stieglitz had formerly included African tribal and avant-garde European art (by such artists as Matisse, Picasso, and Picabia) along with American art at his first gallery, known as 291 and closed in 1917, he showed only Americans at the Intimate Gallery, opened in 1925.[19] The very name of Stieglitz's last gallery, An American Place, which he opened in December 1929, emphatically attests to this continuing commitment. In recalling those who frequented An American Place, Stieglitz's last companion, Dorothy Norman, listed "the composers Edgar [sic] Varèse, Ernest Bloch or Aaron Copland" as well as Harold Clurman, who was by then published as both a music and a theater critic.[20]

In fact, Clurman remained close to Stieglitz until the latter's death in 1946. Copland's connection to Stieglitz was more complicated. Although Norman, who was both a writer and photographer, reportedly complained to Paul Bowles in 1934 about what she perceived as Copland's "complete lack of sympathy for Stieglitz," she must have gotten over her pique.[21] Ultimately, she became a patron of Copland's, helping to underwrite the production of his opera *The Second Hurricane* in 1937. As late as 1954, Copland wrote to friends that Norman would be hosting a post-production party for his opera *The Tender Land* (with libretto by his young lover Erik Johns).[22] Norman shared leftist sympathies with Copland and served with him, Stieglitz, and others on the board of Clurman's Group Theatre, which was founded to present contemporary plays of social significance and to develop the art of the theater and acting. Meanwhile, since 1933, Clurman had been publishing theater reviews in the Communist newspaper *The Daily Worker*, under the pseudonym Harold Edgar. Norman worked with Clurman, Waldo Frank, and other supporters of Stieglitz, all of whom were active in leftist politics, to revitalize and reposition Stieglitz during the politically charged 1930s, when Stieglitz, born in 1864, was already in his late sixties. They attempted to link Stieglitz's antimaterialism to Marx, despite the fact that the photographer, who had developed his ideas during the 1890s, had been a philosophical anarchist.[23] They sought to replace his isolated focus on "Americanism" with active opposition to Fascism, which was then gaining strength in Germany and Spain. In a volume of essays published in tribute to Stieglitz in 1934, Clurman described Stieglitz's gallery as a "collective" and asserted, "We must create collectives which will include artists of our own kind, and be associated with groups of related workers."[24]

Stieglitz defended his own view of his political identity when, in 1935, Waldo Frank expressed disappointment that he refused to join the Communists: "I have always been a *revolutionist* if I have ever been anything at all," he explained, noting, "In reality, I am much more *active* in a revolutionary sense than most of the so-called Communists I have met."[25] Frank, who had attempted a collaboration with Copland, whom he invited to compose the music for his unrealized play *Malva*, himself became disillusioned with Communism by 1937.[26]

Although Stieglitz rarely spoke out directly about politics during this period, he joined John Dewey, Lewis Mumford, and Lincoln Steffens in lending his name to the Advisory Committee of the Artists' Committee of Action, a leftist group that emerged when members of the John Reed Clubs and others united to protest the destruction of Diego Rivera's mural at Rockefeller Center.[27] On May 1, 1934, Stieglitz not only demonstrated with this group, lobbying Mayor La Guardia for a municipal art gallery, but he also addressed a mass meeting of a thousand people at the New School for Social Research. He must have been pleased, for he later referred to this as one of the "Red Letter Days" of his life.[28] At the same time, Stieglitz remained the anarchist committed to the individual worker rather than unions and organized collective action. In 1934, he suggested as much when he withdrew from the new Artists' Union.[29]

Stieglitz and Copland's mutual friend Rosenfeld was, however, more than aloof from leftist politics. In an article in *Scribner's*, Rosenfeld attacked a writers' manifesto (drawn up by Edmund Wilson, Waldo Frank, and Lewis Mumford in 1932) stating that America had come to a dead end and calling for "a new human order."[30] Among the signers was his friend the novelist Sherwood Anderson, who wrote to him in 1933: "Perhaps you are disgusted with me that I seem to have gone over to the Communists. I haven't really. . . . I began going around to the factories. That I presume led my going toward Communism. I got so ashamed sometimes, doing nothing, always standing aside."[31] Half a year later, Anderson, who had attended a large Communist Party conference in Europe in 1932 and published a pro-labor novel, *Beyond Desire*, wrote Rosenfeld and asked, "How can I help feeling, Paul, that it is you fellows in your isolation who are failing in the real Communist spirit."[32]

Thus, no matter how aloof from politics Stieglitz and Rosenfeld might have chosen to be, their friends on the political Left challenged them to join the struggle that so many faced during the Depression. Copland's intellectual milieu, like that of many composers in New York, moved toward leftist activism during the 1930s. Perlis wrote: "Copland was not by nature a political person; he joined neither the Socialist nor Communist Party, but for a time in the early 1930s he was what might be called a fellow traveler. When questioned about his leftist activities, his answer is simply, 'It seemed the thing to do at the time.'"[33]

One might expect evidence of Copland's involvement in important leftist cultural activities to be well documented among his extensive papers at the Library of Congress. Yet the relative paucity of documents for this kind of association probably represents the composer's defensive response to red-baiting by the House Un-American Activities Committee and Senator Joseph McCarthy. Copland, who was called to testify before the Senate Permanent Subcommittee on Investigations of the Committee on Government Operations on May 26, 1953, did not leave much documentation linking him to leftist politics and activist friends. One can only speculate whether such evidence ever existed or whether Copland destroyed documentation as "incriminating" during a time of right-wing persecution of prominent left-wing Americans.

What remains today to link Copland most conspicuously to the cultural Left are two published pieces in the communist journal *New Masses*. As is well-known, in May 1934, *New Masses* published Copland's winning entry in a contest to set music to the poem "Into the Streets May First," by Alfred Hayes. Music by the contest winner was intended for use at the Second Annual American Workers Music Olympiad, scheduled to take place the following April. In the November 1934 *New Masses*, Copland reviewed *The Workers Song Book No. 1* published by the Workers Music League, an organization founded in 1931 and affiliated with the American Communist Party. He pronounced it "the first adequate collection of revolutionary songs for American workers."[34] Still another document of Copland's sympathies with the Left survives in a letter to his friend Carlos Chávez in Mexico. Copland wrote about a year after winning the contest, observing, "I noticed that you are beginning to play music from Soviet Russia. I should very much like to make a trip there. (Have you seen my Communist song 'Into the Streets May First'? It has been republished in Russia.)"[35]

The absence among Copland's papers of documents referring to his friendship with Diego Rivera, a politically active artist if ever there was one, probably results from the political repression of the McCarthy era. In fact, most of Copland's close connections with visual artists appear to have drawn sustenance from their shared enthusiasm for leftist politics.

Rivera had already figured in discussions among the first American avant-garde by 1915, when Marius de Zayas opened his Modern Gallery at 500 Fifth Avenue and soon showed paintings by Rivera paired with examples of Pre-Conquest Mexican Art. Rivera, like Copland, developed an interest in folk culture. He claimed his real "master" was the popular Mexican engraver of illustrations for broadsheet ballads, José Guadalupe Posada, whose shop was near the art school he attended as a teenager.[36] Rivera developed a friendship with Posada, whom he admired as a great artist of the people.

Copland likely met Rivera through their mutual friend Chávez. The two composers had first became acquainted in the autumn of 1926, during Chávez's second stay in New York, when he was rooming with the painter and printmaker Rufino Tamayo in a tenement on Fourteenth Street.[37] By then, both Copland and Chávez had spent time in Paris. And both were committed to create a new American art that could stand on its own, apart from European traditions.

Copland and Chávez each composed music with qualities that appealed to Rosenfeld, whose artistic philosophy reflected that of the Stieglitz coterie. In his book *By Way of Art* (1928), Rosenfeld praised Chávez for the "original aspects of his work," which "makes us feel America," and commends "his passion for the relics of Aztec culture as well as the forms of existing life."[38] In an adjacent essay on Copland, Rosenfeld, while not yet wholly convinced, nonetheless noted: "Copland stands to-day as one of the most independent, able and promissory of the new American composers."[39] Rosenfeld followed up the next year in his book *An Hour with American Music*, which included two more juxtaposed essays on Chávez and Copland, about whom he wrote: "For while Copland's work is plainly that of a young man, wanting mellowness, wide inclusivity, and the warmest intensity, it is indubitably autonomous; and symbolic of the new world on every hard green page of it."[40] The music of Chávez, Rosenfeld proclaimed, was "manifestly un-European." Perhaps he was thinking of the painting he owned by Hartley (Hartley had also written about preserving Native American culture), with its Native American theme when he emphasized Chávez's connection "with the American soil and the savage chants of the Indians. Himself part Amerindian, the atonal sing-song of his lyrical themes strongly recalls the crowing and cackling of the red-man in his dusty pueblos."[41]

Even in New York, Chávez and Tamayo kept up their interest in Native American culture and shared a mutual sympathy for the Mexican revolution and the resulting new government's art initiatives. Tamayo, too, had an interest in music; he played the guitar and sang Mexican folk songs about the aims and ideals of the new government's reforms.[42] The two Mexicans held musical recitals in New York that featured songs by Chávez performed by Lupe Medina, with Tamayo on guitar. One of Tamayo's closest friends was another Mexican expatriate, Miguel Covarrubias, the artist and illustrator, who performed his *corridos*, emotional songs similar to American country and western ballads.[43]

Covarrubias met various avant-garde composers in New York, including Copland's friend George Antheil, whom he caricatured in 1927; that same year, Copland was one of the pianists who performed an Antheil composition for ten pianos at Carnegie Hall.[44] We can confirm that Copland knew Covarrubias by 1929, since he wrote to Chávez, noting, "I met [ran into] Covarrubias who told me that the rumors that you were no longer with the Conservatory were false."[45] Another link was their mutual friend Colin McPhee.

Chávez's "use of folk material in its relation to nationalism" seemed to Copland in 1928 to be a defining trait of modern music.[46] The folk music that Copland had heard in the company of his Mexican friends in New York seemed even more available and appealing when he first visited Mexico in 1932. By then, Copland was attracted to the model of popular accessibility, which became an important ideal of the political Left. He began composing *El Salón México*, which he said was inspired in part by *Cancionero Mexicano*, a collection of Mexican folk songs illustrated by Tamayo and published as a book in 1931 by Frances Toor, an American anthropologist living in Mexico City. Toor, then the leading source on Mexican folk culture, published *Mexican Folkways,* a bilingual magazine about the value of Mexico's folk art and traditional culture. Copland's friends Rivera and Tamayo were among her contributors. She presented a copy of this book to Copland in 1932, which, acknowledging its significance, he donated to the Library of Congress in 1957, together with his manuscript for *El Salón México.*

So vivid was the experience of composing *El Salón México* that Copland wrote an article about it, illustrated with photographs of Mexican musicians taken by Victor Kraft, his young companion at the time.[47] He said that he had first heard about the club El Salón México in art historian Anita Brenner's guidebook to Mexico, in which she described a "Harlem type night-club for the peepul [*sic*], grand Cuban orchestra, Salón México."[48] But years later, Copland would credit his composer friend with the memorable encounter: "When Chávez took me to an unusual night spot called El Salón México, the atmosphere of this dance hall impressed me, and I came away with the germ of a musical idea."[49] Perhaps Copland first read about El Salón México and then asked Chávez to take him there.

Years later the composition inspired by the visit to the Mexican night-club caught the imagination of the young singer Jimmy Turpin, who sent

Copland a watercolor caricature by Ruth Keahey entitled *El Saloon Mexico* (1944). She depicted the American composer playing a piano in a Mexican saloon. Copland's distinctive profile ("his impressive beaked head") and characteristic grin are easily identifiable.[50] As he plays, a cat chases a mouse across the top of the piano, making a playful reference to *The Cat and the Mouse,* an early Copland piano piece composed in 1920. The audience depicted in this caricature—a man seated at the bar wearing a red serape and wide sombrero, the gun-toting cowboy standing at the bar beside a spittoon, and the bartender with his handlebar mustache—symbolize the attainment of popular accessibility that preoccupied Copland during the 1930s.[51]

To Copland at the time, Mexico seemed to offer "something fresh and pure and wholesome—a quality which is deeply unconventionalized," as he wrote to a friend, adding, "Mexico was a rich time. Outwardly nothing happened and inwardly all was calm, yet I'm left with the impression of having

Figure 2. *El Saloon Mexico* by Ruth Keahey.

had an enriching experience. It comes, no doubt, from the nature of the country and the people. Europe now seems conventional to me by comparison."[52] Copland further reflected about what made Mexico so special: "The source of it I believe is the Indian blood which is so prevalent. I sensed the influence of the Indian background everywhere—even in the landscape. And I must be something of an Indian myself or how else explain the sympathetic chord it awakens in me. Of course I'm going back some day."[53]

But he was most grateful to Chávez for coaxing him to visit Mexico, and wrote to him: "As soon as we crossed the border I regretted leaving Mexico with a sharp pang. It took me three years in France to get as close a feeling to the country as I was able to get in three months in Mexico. I can thank you for this, for without your many kindnesses, the opportunity for knowing it and loving it so well would never have come. I think always of my returning soon."[54]

It was through Chávez that Copland had met many of the country's leading modernists—not only Tamayo, Covarrubias, and Rivera, but also the Mexican composer's protégé, Silvestre Revueltas. Chávez in 1928 became the government-appointed director of the country's leading orchestra (until 1949) and the National Conservatory of Music (until 1934); he told Rivera's biographer Bertram Wolfe in 1937, "Diego has only two friends in artistic circles here [in Mexico, after Rivera returned], Miguel Covarrubias and me. We are his friends because we have no reason to be jealous of him."[55] Chávez was less militantly communist than muralists such as Rivera or David Alfaro Siqueiros or Revueltas, who joined the Communist-dominated League of Revolutionary Writers and Artists.[56]

Still another link between Rivera, Copland, and other contemporary composers was Ernest Bloch, whose daughters Lucienne, an artist, and Suzanne, a composer, met Diego and his wife, the painter Frida Kahlo, soon after the couple's arrival in New York in late 1931. The couple came for Diego's solo show at the newly founded Museum of Modern Art and stayed for the commission he received from the Rockefellers to paint a mural at Radio City (Rockefeller Center). Lucienne was so taken with Rivera that she became one of his assistants. Rivera's mural project (1932–34) coincided with Bloch's commission by Gerald Warburg to compose a musical setting for a reformed synagogue in New York. Bloch titled the piece *Avodath Hakodesh* (Sacred Service).

Copland and Bloch appeared together in a program entitled "An Evening of Hebrew Sacred and Folk Music" at the Euclid Avenue Temple in Brooklyn on April 3, 1934.[57] Rosenfeld had written about Bloch as a Jewish composer who "opened himself up to the genius of his race."[58] This consideration finds an echo in Copland's own comments about

Bloch, whom he once discussed in contrast to the "charmed atmosphere" of Milhaud: "When darkly colored, it takes on a deeply nostalgic connotation. Since this nostalgia is shared by none of his French confrères, I take it to be a sign of Milhaud's Jewish inheritance. That he is not so racial a composer as Bloch or Mahler seems natural if we remember that his ancestors settled in Provence in the 15th century, so that his Jewishness has long been tempered by the French point of view."[59]

If Copland and Bloch received backing in New York from a devoted network of Jewish supporters and patrons, Rivera had to deal with a much more controlling, white Anglo-Saxon Protestant at the top echelon of New York's high society.[60] The mural project's facilitator was Nelson Rockefeller, whose family was one of the richest in the world. The Rockefellers, through Nelson, commissioned and convinced a reluctant Rivera to produce a mural for the RCA Building in Radio City on the theme of *Man at the Crossroads Looking with Hope and High Vision to the Choosing of a New and Better Future*. Because he accepted this 1933 commission, the Communist Party attacked Rivera as a painter for millionaires, motivating him to prove what a Communist he was.[61] Rivera submitted to the Rockefellers an elaborate verbal description as well as a sketch of the planned mural. In the passage about the center section, he wrote: "The Worker gives his right hand to the Peasant who questions him, and with his left hand takes the hand of the sick and wounded Soldier, the victim of War, leading him to the New Road." He omitted to note that the Worker would be Lenin himself, and in the accompanying preliminary sketch his face was not recognizable.[62]

After the Rockefellers ordered the destruction of the mural because Rivera refused to remove the clearly identifiable image of Lenin, the artist ran out of money and luck. "His assistants and other friends such as Aaron Copland and Walter Pach threw a party, had a whip-round and paid for tickets for Rivera and Frida to sail on the SS *Oriente* for Veracruz, via Havana," wrote Rivera's most recent biographer, Patrick Marnham, though he does not document his precise source.[63] Hayden Herrera, in her biography of Kahlo, also refers to "Rivera's friend the U.S. composer Aaron Copland," likewise citing no source.[64]

Among the others who pitched in to give Rivera his going-away party was the artist Ben Shahn, who had served as one of Rivera's assistants at Rockefeller Center. A Jewish immigrant from Lithuania just two years younger than Copland, Shahn had much in common with Copland, including a significant stay in Paris during the 1920s and leftist political sympathies. Shahn depicted musical themes with allegorical intentions. Erik Johns recalled that Copland especially liked Shahn's work.[65]

More documentation of the mutual friendship of Copland, Rivera, and Chávez comes from previously unpublished material. The art critic Rosamond Bernier has given me her own account of their relationship. Then a college student, she was to meet all three men in Mexico City in 1936: "I met Aaron Copland the summer of 1936 when I went to Mexico for the first time on vacation from Sarah Lawrence. My father was head of the Board of the Philadelphia Orchestra and in that capacity invited the various guest conductors and soloists to our house. We had entertained Carlos Chávez when he conducted in Philadelphia, so when I was to go off to Mexico, my father wrote to Chávez that I was arriving."[66]

Chávez had been in Philadelphia for the March 31, 1932, premiere of his ballet *Horsepower* with sets and costumes designed by Rivera. Known as *H.P.*, this ballet, according to Chávez, contrasted the machine age of the industrial North with the traditional agrarian life it affected in "a symphony of sounds around us, a revue of our times."[67] Copland found "many of the usual modern trends" in "the symbolic machine-age music at the end of the ballet."[68] Rosenfeld saw that the two Mexicans had produced something significant: "Indeed, Chávez's music like Rivera's painting thrills us with the prospect of the great role Mexico may play in the development of an American culture."[69] On the occasion of this visit to the United States, his third, Chávez convinced Copland to journey to Mexico City for an all-Copland concert, the first ever given anywhere, on September 2, 1932. He not only conducted Copland's music, but he spoke to the audience about Copland as a significant composer who had absorbed his distinctive American culture.[70]

The friendship between Chávez and Copland enabled Bernier to meet Copland for the first time, an occasion she vividly recounts: "At my hotel in Mexico City I found a note from Chávez inviting me to come to a rehearsal of his orchestra, the Sinfonica de Mexico. Of course I went, to find the rehearsal already in progress, with a tall, rangy figure sitting at the piano, bouncing up and down, beaming with pleasure as he played Copland's jazzy Piano Concerto. It was the composer himself. Frida Kahlo and Diego Rivera were also sitting in on the rehearsal. Afterwards, Carlos introduced me to everyone."

Bernier's recollections confirm that Copland was friendly with both Rivera and Kahlo: "I was thrilled to meet Copland and he seemed pleased by my enthusiasm. We all chatted, and it ended by Frida and Diego inviting me to come to the concert with them and sit in their box. After the concert we all went out for supper." Further testimony about Copland's friendship with Kahlo is suggested by the fact that, during 1938, he displayed a Covarrubias caricature of her in his spartan loft at 113 West

Sixty-third Street in Manhattan. This drawing of Kahlo hung in a place of honor, along with a Mexican rug pinned to the wall and photographs of his Mexican composer friends Chávez and Revueltas.[71]

Their Mexican encounter inaugurated the friendship of Copland and Bernier, which lasted until his death. She remembers fondly Copland's delight when she responded to a longing he had expressed, while in Mexico, for one of his favorite things:

> I was completely enchanted by Aaron and remained enchanted for the next fifty years. He told me he was living in a small town about four hours drive from the city, Tlaxcala. It was cheap, a good place to work. The old upright piano he rented was adequate, he was used to the electricity cuts, and working by candlelight when that happened. But the one thing he missed, he said, was marmalade. He did like marmalade with his breakfast and there was none to be had in Tlaxcala. I acted immediately, and had soon rounded up an obliging boy friend to drive me to Tlaxcala, along with a large carton of marmalade jars. Aaron was astonished at my arrival and gave that wonderful toothy grin of his. He was working on his opera for high school kids, "The Second Hurricane." He sat down at the piano and played me the whole score, singing all the parts. . . . I loved it. I particularly loved "Gip's Song," and sometimes I would sing snatches of it to Aaron.

Copland subsequently scored "Gip's Song" for Bernier, who played the harp, and her first husband, Lew Riley, who played the guitar, and gave it to them as a wedding gift in 1937.[72] Copland's generosity and gift for nurturing friendships is apparent both in this instance and in his willingness to help Rivera in his moment of need.

Copland's support of Rivera was strengthened by their shared political ideals during the 1930s, but it also suggests that Copland did not follow any specific Communist Party line, for in 1929, the Mexican Communist Party expelled Rivera and the Conference of Revolutionary and Proletarian Writers at Kharkov in Ukraine subsequently condemned him for "advocating a right-wing program."[73] Rivera also criticized contemporary Soviet art, which he saw as dominated by academic painters he called "intellectual lackeys of Sir Joseph Stalin."[74]

Despite criticism of Rivera's position by the Party, he benefited from support by many sympathetic artists, composers, and writers in New York. Among the many who sent Rivera messages of solidarity and support over the mural episode was Stieglitz.[75] Close to Stieglitz, and much more active on the Left, was the photographer Paul Strand, one of the modernists that Copland first met through Rosenfeld and Frank. Strand was friendly with both Copland and Chávez, whom he photographed in 1931.

Writing about this time, Copland recalled: "Clurman was deeply involved with the Group Theatre, which he had started in 1930, and the Stieglitz crowd was still going strong. Several of them lived in the neighborhood, so I saw them often, and by now, Paul Strand, Orson Welles, Mary and Ralph Steiner [photographer], William Lescaze [architect], and Carl Van Vechten [photographer, novelist, and critic] were also my friends."[76] In New York in 1932, Van Vechten not only photographed Copland but also Diego Rivera and Frida Kahlo, and Rosa Covarrubias, the wife of Miguel, whom he first met in 1923. Copland and Strand saw each other during the summer of 1931, when both were guests at the Group Theatre's summer location in Brookfield Center, Connecticut.[77]

Strand first met Chávez in Taos during the summer of 1932. Since the composer served as chief of the Mexican government's Department of Fine Arts in the Secretariat of Education, he helped Strand become an official photographer and filmmaker for the government. Thus empowered, Strand could use his art to serve the most oppressed classes, his longtime goal. Soon after he arrived in Mexico City in late 1932, Chávez arranged for his recent photographs of New Mexico to be shown at the Sala de Arte of the Secretariat of Education. Marsden Hartley was then living in Mexico on a Guggenheim fellowship and helped hang Strand's show, which opened on February 3, 1933. Although Copland was in Mexico for four months, from September 2, 1932, he just missed seeing the exhibit.

With changes in the government in Mexico (the election of a new president, Lazaro Cardenas) Chávez suddenly found himself out of favor after many years. Copland wrote to Chávez on August 28, 1935, commiserating with him about the difficult period he was enduring: "Paul Strand came back last June with news of your struggles and since then I have often wondered [how] the new political situation in Mexico has been affecting you and your plans. I have always remembered our conversation on top of the pyramids of Tlotihuacan when you told me that the future—whatever it was to be—did not frighten you. I believed you then—and it has given me confidence that you will know how to manage even in these difficult times."[78]

Copland, too, was able to manage well during the Depression. By the mid-1930s, he had found yet another vanguard salon, where he connected with a different circle of visual artists, art critics, art dealers, and, most important, patrons of the arts. This was at the New York brownstone of

Kirk and Constance Askew on East Sixty-seventh Street. He directed the Durlacher Brothers art gallery on Fifty-seventh Street and she was a beautiful and wealthy New Englander. Regulars at the Askews' included Van Vechten; e.e. cummings; the art critic Henry McBride; the art dealers Marie Harriman, Pierre Matisse, and Valentine Dudensing; Chick Austin, a Harvard-educated painter and director of the Wadsworth Atheneum in Hartford; the composer Virgil Thomson; the choreographer Agnes de Mille; and the art collector and ballet impresario Lincoln Kirstein.[79]

It was at one of the Askews' evenings that Kirstein commissioned Copland to compose a cowboy ballet (with choreography by Eugene Loring) based on the popular book, *The Saga of Billy the Kid* by Walter Noble Burns (1938). Copland, who did not journey west for his research, would later boast how he composed *Billy the Kid* in an apartment on rue de Rennes in Paris.[80] To another of the Askews' evenings, Copland took Rosamund Bernier, who recalls meeting the Surrealist painters Salvador Dali and Pavel Tchelitchew, who were regulars there.[81] Copland became so interested in Surrealism that he kept a book by its leading writer, André Breton, all his life.[82]

Thus, during the 1920s and 1930s, Copland shared aesthetic and political ideas with many visual artists as well as with their most supportive critics and patrons. Several of those in his milieu recognized this communality, which became the basis for their friendship. Copland's concerns with popular accessibility and American identity encouraged his repeated explorations of folk music which would, in turn, parallel quests by visual artists to examine folk art. Experiments with folk culture proved a fertile source not only for Copland but also for some of the visual artists he met and admired, from Hartley to Tamayo and Rivera.

NOTES

1. The exhibition, "Aaron Copland's America," took place at the Heckscher Museum of Art, Huntington, N.Y., November 4, 2000 – January 21, 2001. See the exhibition catalogue: Gail Levin and Judith Tick, *Aaron Copland's America: A Cultural Perspective* (New York: Watson-Guptill Publishers, 2000).

2. Aaron Copland and Vivian Perlis, *Copland: 1900 Through 1942* (New York: St. Martin's/Marek, 1984), p. 42.

3. Copland to his parents, letter of June 10, 1921, Aaron Copland Collection, Music Division, Library of Congress.

4. Copland and Perlis, *Copland: 1900–1942*, p. 43.

5. Howard Pollack, *Aaron Copland: The Life and Work of an Uncommon Man* (New York: Henry Holt, 1999), p. 45.

6. The reference is to Levin and Tick, *Aaron Copland's America.*

7. Copland to Perlis, interview transcript (taped 1975–76). Copland Collection, Box 226, Folder 5, p. 73.

8. Copland and Perlis, *Copland: 1900–1942*, p. 57; Harold Clurman to Louis Schaeffer, "Reminiscences: An Oral History," in Marjorie Loggia and Glenn Young, eds., *The Collected Works of Harold Clurman* (New York: Applause Theatre Publications, 1994), p. 958.

9. Copland to Perlis, interview transcript, p. 106.

10. Clurman, *Collected Works*, "American Night at the Swedish Ballet," p. 1005.

11. See Levin and Tick, *Aaron Copland's America*, pp. 29–30 and 35, for a discussion of these dinners and who attended.

12. Copland and Perlis, *Copland: 1900–1942*, p. 125.

13. See Paul Rosenfeld to Alfred Stieglitz, letter of September 19, 1921, Alfred Stieglitz Papers, Yale Collection of American Literature, Beinecke Rare Book and Manuscript Library, Yale University. For Hartley's *Amerika* series, see Gail Levin, "Marsden Hartley's 'Amerika' Between Native American and German Folk Art," in *American Art Review* 5 no. 2 (Winter 1993): 120–25, 170–72.

14. Author's interview with Richard Hennessy, May 2000. His art remains in Copland's collection at Copland House, in Cortland Manor, N.Y.

15. Hart Crane to Grace Hart Crane, letter of November 30, 1924, in Thomas S. W. Lewis, *Letters of Hart Crane and His Family* (New York: Columbia University Press, 1974), p. 378. Crane recorded one of the dinners at which Copland performed on November 29, 1924.

16. Aaron Copland in *Paul Rosenfeld: Voyager in the Arts*, ed. Jerome Mellquist and Lucie Wiese (New York: Creative Age Press, 1948), p. 168.

17. Paul Rosenfeld, "American Painting," *The Dial* 71 (December 1921): 649–70.

18. Edmund Wilson, "Paul Rosenfeld: Three Phases," in Mellquist and Wiese, *Paul Rosenfeld*, p. 9.

19. Contrary to Howard Pollack's claim that Clurman "visited 291 once a week after his return from Paris," Clurman was only sixteen when Stieglitz closed 291. In addition, Clurman returned from study in Paris in 1924, so the Intimate Gallery, which opened the following year, must have been the first of Stieglitz's galleries that Clurman visited. See Pollack, *Aaron Copland*, p. 100.

20. Dorothy Norman, *Alfred Stieglitz: An American Seer* (New York: Random House, 1973), p. 196. For a discussion of Bloch and Stieglitz, see Levin in Levin and Tick, *Aaron Copland's America*, p. 53.

21. Copland and Perlis, *Copland: 1900–1942*, p. 258. Paul Bowles to Copland, 1934, Copland Collection; Pollack, *Aaron Copland*, p. 90.

22. Aaron Copland to Irving and Verna Fine, letter of March 19, 1954, Copland Collection. This and several other letters are available online as part of the Library of Congress's American Memory project. The digital identification number is copland corr0646.

23. See Susan Noyes Platt, *Art and Politics in the 1930s: Modernism—Marxism— Americanism, A History of Cultural Activism During the Depression Years* (New York: Midmarch Arts Press, 1999), pp. 4–5; and Gail Levin, "Kandinsky's Debut in America," in *Theme & Improvisation: Kandinsky & the American Avant-Garde*, ed. G. Levin and M. Lorenz (Boston: Bulfinch Press, 1992), p. 10.

24. See Harold Clurman in Waldo Frank et al., *America and Alfred Stieglitz: A Collective Portrait* (New York: Doubleday, 1934), p. 135.

25. Alfred Stieglitz to Waldo Frank, letter of July 6, 1935, Waldo Frank Papers, Van Pelt Library, University of Pennsylvania, Philadelphia, as quoted in Edward Abrahams,

The Lyrical Left and the Origins of Cultural Radicalism in America (Charlottesville, Va.: University Press of Virginia, 1986), p. 97.

26. See Alan Trachtenberg, ed., *Memoirs of Waldo Frank* (Amherst, Mass.: University of Massachusetts Press, 1973), pp. 185–87.

27. Andrew Hemingway, *Artists on the Left: American Artists and the Communist Movement 1926–1956* (New Haven: Yale University Press, 2002), pp. 86–87.

28. Alfred Stieglitz to Lionel Reiss, May 24, 1934, Stieglitz Collection. For a discussion of Stieglitz's politics and a photo (originally published in *Art Front*) by Lucienne Bloch of Stieglitz at this demonstration, see Platt, *Art and Politics in the 1930s*, pp. 3–9.

29. See Alfred Stieglitz to Hugo Gellert, October 28, 1934, and Alfred Stieglitz to Waldo Frank, July 6, 1935, Stieglitz Collection, as cited by Dickran Tashjian, *William Carlos Williams and the American Scene 1920–1940* (Berkeley: University of California Press, 1978), p. 151.

30. For the manifesto, see Edmund Wilson to Theodore Dreiser, letter of May 2, 1932, in Edmund Wilson, *Letters on Literature and Politics 1912–1972*, ed. Elena Wilson (New York: Farrar, Straus and Giroux, 1977), p. 222.

31. James Schevill, "The Glitter of Communism," in *The Achievement of Sherwood Anderson,* ed. Ray Lewis White (Chapel Hill, N.C.: University of North Carolina Press, 1966), pp. 147–48; and Sherwood Anderson to Paul Rosenfeld, letter of January 20, 1933, in Mellquist and Wiese, *Paul Rosenfeld*, pp. 227–28.

32. Mellquist and Wiese, *Paul Rosenfeld*, p. 232. See also White, *Achievement of Sherwood Anderson*, p. 258.

33. Copland and Perlis, *Copland: 1900–1942*, p. 218.

34. Aaron Copland, *"Workers Sing!" New Masses*, November 9, 1934, 28–29.

35. Aaron Copland to Carlos Chávez, letter of September 30, 1935. Chávez Papers, New York Public Library; photocopy is in the Copland Collection, Digital ID copland corr0199. No such Russian publication is mentioned in Copland bibliographies.

36. Bertram Wolfe, *The Fabulous Life of Diego Rivera* (New York: Stein and Day, 1963), p. 33.

37. Copland to Perlis, interview transcript, Copland Collection, Box 226, Folder 6, p. 209.

38. Paul Rosenfeld, "The Americanism of Carlos Chávez," in *By Way of Art* (New York: Coward-McCann, 1928), pp. 279–80.

39. Rosenfeld, "Copland Without the Jazz," in *By Way of Art*, p. 269.

40. Paul Rosenfeld, *An Hour with American Music* (Philadelphia: J. B. Lippincott Company), p. 127.

41. Rosenfeld, "Carlos Chávez," in *An Hour with American Music*, pp. 144–45. For Marsden Hartley on Native American culture, see his "The Red Man," in Hartley, *Adventures in the Arts* (New York: Boni and Liveright, 1921), pp. 13–29.

42. Robert Goldwater, *Rufino Tamayo* (New York: Quadrangle Press, 1957), pp. 18–19.

43. Adriana Williams, *Covarrubias* (Austin: University of Texas Press, 1994), p. 21.

44. Copland and Perlis, *Copland: 1900–1942*, p. 127; Aaron Copland, "George Antheil," *League of Composers Review* 2, no. 1 (January 1925): 26. Covarrubias's caricature of Antheil appeared in the *New York Sun* on April 9, 1927.

45. Aaron Copland to Carlos Chávez, letter of November 21, 1929, Copland Collection.

46. Aaron Copland, "Composer from Mexico: Carlos Chávez," in 1900–1960 (New York: W. W. Norton, 1968), *The New Music*: pp. 145–46. This is a revised version of Copland's article on Chávez that appeared in *The New Republic*, May 2, 1928.

47. Aaron Copland's "The Story Behind *El Salón México*" is in the Copland Collection, although not listed in Joann Skowronski, *Aaron Copland: A Bio-Bibliography* (Westport, Conn.: Greenwood Press, 1985). Pollack, *Aaron Copland*, p. 625, n. 22, dates the article ca. 1939 and identifies it as having been "written on the occasion of the 1939 Victor release of the work."

48. Anita Brenner, *Your Mexican Holiday: A Modern Guide* (New York: G. P. Putnam's Sons, 1932), p. 59.

49. Copland and Perlis, *Copland: 1900–1942*, p. 216.

50. Minna Lederman Daniel described Copland's appearance to Vivian Perlis in ibid., p. 112.

51. See Aaron Copland, "Composer from Brooklyn: An Autobiographical Sketch," in *An Aaron Copland Reader: Selected Writings 1923–1972*, ed. Richard Kostelanetz (New York: Routledge, 2004), pp. xxvi–xxvii.

52. Copland to Mary Lescaze, letter of January 13, 1933, Copland Collection. Digital ID copland corr0707.

53. Ibid.

54. Copland to Carlos Chávez, letter of January 2, 1933, Copland Collection.

55. Wolfe, *Diego Rivera*, p. 352.

56. Pollack, *Aaron Copland*, p. 220.

57. Copland and Perlis, *Copland: 1900–1942*, pp. 376–77, n. 23. Copland, identified as a "brilliant young Jewish composer," played *Prayer (Motet)*.

58. Paul Rosenfeld, "The Music of Ernest Bloch," *The Seven Arts* 1 (1917): 416.

59. Aaron Copland, in "Music Between the Wars (1918–1939) (1941, 1968), reprinted in Kostelanetz, *Aaron Copland: A Reader*, p. 43.

60. Copland's network of Jewish patrons and supporters included, besides Rosenfeld and Norman, such luminaries as Alma Morgenthau Wertheim, founder of the Cos Cob Press and Copland's first music publisher; Minna Lederman, editor of *Modern Music*, the journal of the League of Composers; Claire Reis, executive director of the League of Composers; and Clifford Odets, playwright.

61. Wolfe, *Diego Rivera*, p. 322.

62. Ibid., p. 321.

63. Patrick Marnham, *Dreaming with His Eyes Open: A Life of Diego Rivera* (New York: Alfred A. Knopf, 1998), p. 259. Marnham, whose book does not have source notes, states in an e-mail (2000) to the author that he found this information in the papers of Rivera's first biographer, Bertram Wolfe, in the Hoover Institution Archives, Stanford University, Box BW113-8.

64. Hayden Herrera, *Frida: A Biography of Frida Kahlo* (New York: Harper & Row, 1983), p. 83. Hayden Herrera, in a telephone conversation with the author, September 23, 2004, recalls that her source for this statement may have been Lucienne Bloch, whom she interviewed in the 1970s.

65. Author's interview with Erik Johns, January 30, 2000, New York.

66. Rosamond Bernier, e-mail to Gail Levin, August 18, 2000. All quotations from Bernier that follow are from this source.

67. Carlos Chávez, quoted in Robert L. Parker, *Carlos Chávez: Mexico's Modern-Day Orpheus* (Boston: Twayne Publishers, 1983), p. 6.

68. Aaron Copland, "Composer from Mexico: Carlos Chávez," in *The New Music*, p. 148.

69. Paul Rosenfeld, "The Americanism of Carlos Chávez," p. 282.

70. Pollack, *Aaron Copland*, p. 221.

71. Ibid., p. 94, based on his interview with David Diamond, February 10, 1996.

72. Copland and Perlis, *Copland 1900–1942*, p. 268.

73. For Rivera's history with the Communist Party, see Hemingway, *Artists on the Left*, p. 27.

74. Diego Rivera, "The Position of the Artist in Russia Today," *Arts Weekly* 1, no. 1 (March 11, 1932): 6–7.

75. Wolfe, *Diego Rivera*, p. 329.

76. Copland and Perlis, *Copland: 1900–1942*, p. 192.

77. Ibid., p. 219.

78. Copland to Carlos Chávez, letter of August 28, 1935, Copland Collection. Digital ID copland writ0018, Box 200, Folder 19.

79. Nicholas Fox Weber, *Patron Saints: Five Rebels Who Opened America to a New Art 1928–1943* (New York: Alfred A. Knopf, 1992), p. 181.

80. Aaron Copland, "Notes on a Cowboy Ballet," Copland Collection.

81. Copland and Perlis, *Copland: 1900–1942*, p. 267.

82. André Breton, *Situation du surréalisme entre les deux guerres* (Paris: Éditions de la Revue Fontaine, 1945), now in the Copland Collection.

Making an American Dance:

Billy the Kid, Rodeo, and *Appalachian Spring*

LYNN GARAFOLA

Few American composers had a longer or more intimate association with dance than Aaron Copland. He discovered it as an exciting form of theater art in Paris during his student years, which coincided with the heyday of Serge Diaghilev's Ballets Russes and Rolf de Maré's Ballets Suédois. In the Paris of the early 1920s new music and ballet were synonymous. Stravinsky, Prokofiev, and Falla were stars of the "Russian" troupe; Satie, Milhaud, and Honegger of the "Swedish" one. In 1923, like so many other young composers, Copland attended the revival of Stravinsky's *Rite of Spring* and the first performance of his *Les Noces*, as well as the premiere of Milhaud's *La Création du Monde*. Copland's first orchestral score, which he began in Paris, was a ballet. Although it was never produced, he recycled parts of it in his 1929 *Dance Symphony*, an independent orchestral work, and his 1934 ballet for Ruth Page, *Hear Ye! Hear Ye!*. "Ballet was *the* big thing in Paris during the 1920s," he told Phillip Ramey in 1980. "One of the first things I did upon arriving in Paris in 1921 was to go to the Ballets Suédois, where I saw Milhaud's *L'Homme et son Désir*."[1]

Copland discovered ballet in the aftermath of Diaghilev's modernist revolution. Through his successive choreographers—Michel Fokine and Vaslav Nijinsky before World War I, Léonide Massine, Bronislava Nijinska, and George Balanchine during and after the war—Diaghilev transformed not only what ballet looked like but also how it sounded. With his impetus the one-act ballet became the modernist standard. He jettisoned the choreographic formulas identified with Marius Petipa and late-nineteenth-century Russian tradition—the pas de deux and variation, the divertissement, the *grand pas* that presented the dancers by rank climaxing in the appearance of the ballerina and her partner, the division of dances into "numbers," and the mime scenes that "explained" the dramatic action. These conventions shaped ballet music as well as choreography; they determined the structure of the score, the sequence of the dances, the duration of individual numbers, the time signature, and the expressive quality. Even in *The Sleeping Beauty* (1890), a turning point in the development of music for the ballet, Tchaikovsky only partly transcended the conventions that tied his work to Petipa's.

As Diaghilev and his choreographers abandoned the old formulas, they looked for new music. Fokine, following the lead of Isadora Duncan, pieced together *Chopiniana* (1908) (renamed *Les Sylphides* by Diaghilev in 1909) from the waltzes and mazurkas of Chopin: music with a dance rhythm even if it was composed for the concert hall. Diaghilev himself adopted this strategy, as Balanchine did later, assembling scores from preexisting music, with varying degrees of editorial intervention. At the same time, Diaghilev began to commission new works, creating a body of twentieth-century music for the ballet stage that has yet to be surpassed. His great discovery was Stravinsky, his "first son," as he called him, but he also commissioned scores from Debussy, Ravel, Prokofiev, Falla, Satie, Poulenc, and many others.[2] Although these scores had a libretto, they were independent of the dance structure and step text. Music had become the "floor" of a ballet, the base on which to build the dance. In divorcing the ballet score from the choreographic text, Diaghilev made ballet music something "real" composers wrote, with a life beyond the stage. Numerous works of the twentieth-century concert hall began life as ballets.

Although this new music flourished above all in Europe, echoes could be heard in the United States. John Alden Carpenter teamed up with Diaghilev alumnus Adolph Bolm for several productions, beginning with *The Birthday of the Infanta*, a "ballet-pantomime" produced in 1919 by the Chicago Grand Opera Company. This was followed in 1922 at New York's Town Hall by *Krazy Kat*, a "jazz pantomime" inspired by George Herriman's popular comic strip.[3] Carpenter's *Skyscrapers*, choreographed by Sammy Lee (following the action laid out by the composer and scene designer, Robert Edmond Jones) and produced in 1926 by the Metropolitan Opera, was actually commissioned three years earlier by Diaghilev.[4] Interesting as these ballets may have been, none survived as stage works, although *Skyscrapers* remains alive as a concert work.[5]

Although dance flourished on the American commercial stage, it had yet to gain recognition as a concert form. Many "art" dancers went to Paris; those who stayed home pursued concert work between jobs in vaudeville. Moreover, prior to the mid-1920s, concert dance adhered to the prewar "Greek" and "exotic" styles popularized by Duncan, Denishawn, and their imitators. American concert dance was thus far from "modern," as this term was understood in the postwar years.

The appearance of a new generation of concert dancers in the late 1920s transformed the American dance world. Breaking with their predecessors, dancer-choreographers such as Martha Graham and Doris Humphrey began to create works that acknowledged the modernist revolution in music, the visual arts, and choreography. The first of these emerging modern dancers to use Copland's music was Helen Tamiris in *Lull* (1929), *Sentimental Dance* (1930), and *Olympus Americanus* (1931). Martha Graham followed with *Dithyrambic* (1931), a solo choreographed to Copland's Piano Variations, which premiered during a season that also included pieces by Schoenberg and Villa-Lobos.[6] "Surely only an artist with an understanding of my work," Copland later wrote, "could have visualized dance material in so rhythmically and complex and thematically abstruse a composition."[7] The "modern dance," as people were beginning to call the new form, was linked from the start to modern music.

Another early dancer to use Copland's music was Ruth Page. Ballet-trained and Chicago-based, a veteran of the Anna Pavlova company, and a protégée of Adolph Bolm, Page was remarkably open to modern work. As ballet director of the Chicago Grand Opera Company, she often commissioned music by contemporary composers, and she worked closely with Nicolas Remisoff, the Russian modern designer who had collaborated with Bolm throughout the 1920s. Her technical approach was similarly broad-minded. Sometimes she donned the tutu and pointe shoes of a ballerina. Just as often she took them off and danced like a modern.[8] She couldn't have done this in New York, where ballet and modern dance belonged to warring camps. Perhaps it was because the stakes were higher in Gotham, the epicenter of the new modern dance but also the country's ballet capital, with a strong—and growing—Russian presence. And she had few scruples about borrowing from the popular stage.

By 1934, when Page commissioned *Hear Ye! Hear Ye!* from Copland, national identity had become a pressing issue for citizens throughout American society. Dancers were also part of this conversation, and in their case the issue took the form of a question: What was American dance? For the moderns, the answer was self-evident. It was what they did (and what they sometimes called "the American dance"). It was definitely not ballet, born in Renaissance courts and financed by absolute monarchs and czars, a form scripted in hierarchy and disciplined through technique—an inheritance alien to the free, American, democratic body. "All the dogma of the ballet was either rejected out of hand or transformed or adjusted to new urgencies and concepts," recalled José Limón, a dancer-choreographer who began to study at the Humphrey-Weidman studio in 1929:

The all-important barre was done away with, much as Protestant reformers did away with altars, statues, and crucifixes. The basic barre exercises were performed in the middle of the studio. Stretches were done standing or sitting on the floor. Nobody pointed his toes. The movements of the torso took on a new and crucial importance. . . . Movement was no longer decorative but functional. . . . It had to dig beneath the surface to find beauty, even if this meant it had to be "ugly." The elegant contours of ballet were twisted and distorted. . . . Away with the debris of a decadent past: an austere, even stark, simplicity was in order.[9]

Hear Ye! Hear Ye! (1934) was set in a courtroom, with three different witnesses giving strikingly different accounts of the murder of a cabaret dancer. There was a big cast, including a "suggestively attired and writhing bevy of chorus girls" (in the words of one New York critic), lawyers, jurymen, a Mae West–type nightclub hostess, a maniac, and Page as the murder victim. Jazz permeated the score. Distorted segments of "The Star Spangled Banner" highlighted the theme of legal corruption and a parody of Mendelssohn's "Wedding March" the cynicism of the newlyweds.[10] Lurid headlines—"MURDER!" "GUILTY!" "RED-HOT JAZZ!"—flashed on an overhead screen.[11] Like many left-wing dances of the early 1930s, *Hear Ye! Hear Ye!* had a contemporary urban setting and a critical edge. To be sure, Page's cabaret dancer had little to do with the homeless shop girls and striking miners of Workers' Dance League concerts.[12] But the ballet took place in a city; it was filled with the characters and sounds of urban life, as well as its violence.

Not everyone equated modern dance with American dance. Among the dissenters was Lincoln Kirstein, the patron extraordinaire who invited Balanchine, a Russian émigré choreographer, to the United States in 1933 and stood by him until his death fifty years later. Along the way they founded the School of American Ballet (1934) and the New York City Ballet (1948). Like so many artists and intellectuals, Kirstein fell in love with ballet because of the Ballets Russes. Kirstein was rich and immensely cultured, a writer and collector of contemporary art, a Harvard man, a man who today would be called queer, a member of the junior committee of the Museum of Modern Art, and a leftist. He went everywhere, saw everything, heard everything. Strongly opinionated, he treated modern dance like a bête noire; he hated its cult of personality, rejection of tradition, and individualized "systems" of movement.[13] At the same time, he was dismayed by the resurgence of the so-called international or post-Diaghilev Ballet Russe companies whose wildly successful whistle-stop tours of the

United States in the 1930s under Sol Hurok's management trumpeted the idea that ballet was "Russian."

It was in this climate that Kirstein made his debut as an impresario. In 1935 the American Ballet, his first company with Balanchine, opened in New York. The reviews were tepid. John Martin, the powerful dance critic of the *New York Times* who supported the idea of an indigenous ballet troupe, threw down the gauntlet. Why import Balanchine, a Russian who had spent most of the previous decade in France, to develop an American company? "The problem resolves itself into one fundamental decision," Martin wrote. "Is the organization to attempt the fulfilment of its original policy of developing an American ballet, or is it to follow the direction of its present season and go on being merely 'Les Ballets Americains'?"[14]

Kirstein raged, but the following year he launched a small touring ensemble called Ballet Caravan. Everything about the Caravan was American: the personnel—meaning the dancers, designers, composers, *and* choreographers—and the subject matter, conveyed in titles like *Pocahontas*, *Yankee Clipper*, and *Tom*, a ballet based on *Uncle Tom's Cabin* that Kirstein tried for years to produce. Just as Diaghilev had yoked the idea of Russianness to modernism—a strategy adapted by the movement known as British ballet, as well as by companies such as Rolf de Maré's Ballets Suédois and Antonia Mercé's Les Ballets Espagnols—so Kirstein sought to do this with American material. In his case the subject matter drew on a national folklore redefined by the Left during the era of the Popular Front; in 1936 "Communism Is Americanism of the 20th Century" became the party's election slogan.[15] Although his later autobiographical writings ignore politics, Kirstein was a committed leftist in the 1930s. He wrote for publications such as *The Nation*, *New Theatre*, and *TAC Magazine*, with close ties to the Communist-oriented Left.[16] He joined the League of American Writers, was active in the John Reed Club, organizations later identified as Communist fronts, and was later "named" by friendly witnesses testifying in hearings before the Dies and other committees investigating "un-American" activities.[17] The protagonists of his ballets— cowboys, sailors, a gas pump attendant—belonged to the new breed of American working-class heroes popularized in proletarian dramas like *Stevedore*.

"When Lincoln Kirstein, director of the Ballet Caravan, asks you to write a ballet for him it is a foregone conclusion that you are going to tackle an American subject," Copland wrote in an essay about the genesis of *Billy the Kid*, which seems to have been used for publicity purposes.[18] For years Kirstein had been dreaming up ideas for ballets, including a "mass of suggestions" from popular and literary sources, few of which were stage-worthy.[19] Once the Caravan was launched, he was fired with energy, signing up collaborators, tutoring the untried choreographers, and managing the company of fifteen dancers, which—in a burst of leftist fervor—he tried to run as a collective. (It didn't work. The dancers wanted more structure.)[20] After two seasons, the summer touring company became a year-round ensemble, with Kirstein even making plans to present chamber operas. Among the titles bandied about were Henry Brant's and Cecil Helmy's *Miss O'Grady* and Copland's *The Second Hurricane.*[21]

It is unclear when Kirstein became interested in William Bonney, the desperado known as Billy the Kid, "who went west with his mother, killed twenty-one men . . . before he had lived twenty-one years, and was shot by his best friend, turned sheriff."[22] He later told dance historian Nancy Reynolds that Martha Graham's *American Document,* which premiered in 1938, a little more than two months before *Billy,* had influenced the creation of the ballet.[23] Certainly, *Document* was a work he admired. In a review published in *The Nation* he called it the "most important extended dance creation by a living American," no small praise, given his general disdain for modern dance.[24] It is mentioned in Graham's letters to him, sometimes in conjunction with Kirstein's *Memorial Day,* another project from 1937–38 that failed to materialize.[25] Subtitled "Dances for Democracy in Crisis," *Memorial Day* was a drama for dancers, epic in scale, about the conflict that had torn apart an earlier America, the Civil War. Like *Document,* the detailed scenario for *Memorial Day* incorporated a number of historical texts—speeches by Abraham Lincoln (Second Inaugural Address) and Henry David Thoreau ("Plea for Capt. John Brown"); a letter by Walt Whitman to a bereaved mother; prayers, poems, testaments, and reports about slavery and the Civil War—the "crisis" referred to in the subtitle. The costume sketches, included with the scenario, were by Jared French, who designed *Billy the Kid.* According to the title page, Copland was to write the music, and Lew Christensen, Erick Hawkins, and Eugene Loring—all Ballet Caravan members at the time—were to share the choreography. *Memorial Day* thus anticipated the team responsible for *Billy*—Loring, French, and Copland. At the same time, *Memorial Day* reveals to what extent Kirstein's vision of American history was politically engaged, emphasizing collective action rather than the heroics of individuality.

By 1937, Kirstein announced in *Blast at Ballet,* his impassioned defense of American ballet, Copland was on board for *Billy.* "Now we are working on Aaron Copland's *Billy the Kid,* Elliot Carter Jr.'s *Pocahontas,* and a contemporary treatment of the Minotaur legend, more modern Nazi than ancient Greek, with music by Charles Naginski, who sometime after starting our ballet, won the Prix de Rome."[26] But it wasn't until the following year that Copland found time to write the music. By then he had seen French's costume designs and discussed the action with the choreographer.[27] Kirstein, ever one for sharing sources, "slipped" Copland books of cowboy tunes. While in London for the International Society for Contemporary Music festival, Copland received the scenario and "Notes on Billy the Kid's Character" that Loring, doubtless with assistance from Kirstein, had compiled. Then, in Paris, in a studio on rue de Rennes, he sat down to compose.[28] The ballet premiered the following October.

Billy opens and closes with a horizontal trek across the stage, a march in silhouette of pioneers, invoking the millions who went west in the aftermath of the Civil War. The idea for this processional, Kirstein told Vivian Perlis, came from Graham, and is almost certainly the link with *American Document*, which also began and ended with "a parade of participants, using gestures borrowed from minstrel strut and cake-walk."[29] "Loring starts his ballet," Kirstein wrote in an advance piece in *The Dance Observer*, "not with Billy, but rather with the empty prairie, set with the bare silhouette of cactus columns. To a swelling march, the people who came across our plains move across our stage."[30] The scenes that follow are terse, rapid, and cinematic. Billy appears, a child clinging to his mother's skirts as she moves among the pioneer women, dance hall girls, cowhands, and Mexicans of a frontier town. His mother is slain, the accidental victim of a brawl; he plunges a knife into her murderer, avenging her, and a killer is born. In the episodes that follow he kills again and again. His victim is always the same, a character called Alias, who is sometimes a cowhand, a land agent, a sheriff, or Indian guide. The program note describes him as "the symbol of those men whom Billy shot with never one second of guilt, remorse or fright," but Loring later said he was the "evil" in Billy's nature—"what he tries to annihilate [but] cannot."[31] The tale moves toward its inevitable climax. Billy is captured, goes to jail, escapes, makes love to a sweetheart on the edge of the desert, and is shot. The Mexican women grieve, but in a reprise of the opening, the pioneers trek on. Billy is no more than a minor episode in the march of history.

In the 1970s, in an oral history for the New York Public Library, Loring described his collaboration with Copland. First, he (Loring) did the research. Then he made a simple dramatic outline. Next he wrote out all the incidents with timings. This was then given to Copland, who used the material to draft what he called "musical ideas." When the two met again, they discussed "what music . . . should be used where." Occasionally they differed. "I was rather astounded when the march was in 3/4," Loring recalled, "and I questioned that because I had an idea that a march should be in 6/8 or 4/4. . . . He reminded me that 'My Country 'Tis of Thee' is in 3." Sometimes practical considerations dictated where an idea would be used. Loring would say, "I like this idea for this event." Copland would say, "'But you want . . . three minutes. . . . And this . . . idea will not develop for three minutes.'" Once the order was established, Copland began to compose. Later, as the ballet neared completion, Copland made short cuts and small additions to accommodate the choreography. "It was a marvelously compatible collaboration," Loring remembered with pleasure.[32]

Many of the cowboy tunes that Kirstein had given Copland ended up in the music. "Old Granddad," "Git Along Little Dogies," "The Old Chisholm Trail," "Old Paint," "Oh Bury Me Not on the Lone Prairie," and others gave a distinctly American texture to the ballet. They were in the "very fabric of the score," as Chicago dance critic Ann Barzel wrote after the premiere, affecting and easy to hear, a form of plain speech rendered magical by the artist.[33] Similar textures were also woven into the choreography. Like Copland, Loring did his homework. His Mexican girls dance a *jarabe*; the revelers after Billy's arrest a Texas two-step. Work gestures abound in the opening march, and when Billy plays cards with his pal Garrett, one can almost see the cards slapping a rude table. The cowboys ride their horses with the raised knee of a child's gallop—a gesture both familiar and emblematic. And there is a casualness and loose-jointed ease in the dancing that seems very American.

In later years, Loring claimed that *Billy* "owed as much to modern dance as to ballet."[34] Like modern work of the 1930s, much of the movement is weighted rather than light, angular as opposed to rounded, and full of percussive punch. Feet can be flexed or pointed, and the dancers often work in parallel rather than in turnout. Whole families of ballet steps have disappeared, as well as pointe shoes (with one exception) and ballet arms. And only in Billy's duet with his sweetheart, the sole lyrical interlude, do we encounter the expansiveness and flow of a classical adagio, with its idealizing lexicon of lifts and pointe work. Elsewhere, when formal ballet steps are used—as in the triple pirouette–double tour phrase performed by Billy before he kills—they serve a gestural function, revealing something about his character. For Loring, ballet movement can tell only the fragments of a story or a very traditional one.

Except for some silent footage shot in 1939 in Chicago, little survives of the original production of *Billy*.[35] The ballet that exists today in repertory and in recordings stems from the version revived—and revised—by Loring for Ballet Theatre in 1940.[36] The original Billy had sixteen dancers. When Kirstein sold the production and the performance rights to Ballet Theatre, Loring more than doubled the size of the cast to thirty-five. He

DANCE OBSERVER

Vol. V, No. 8   OCTOBER, 1938   Fifteen Cents per Copy

EUGENE LORING *as Billy the Kid.*   *(George Platt Lynes)*

Eugene Loring as Billy the Kid on the cover of the October 1938 issue of *Dance Observer.* Founded by Louis Horst, Martha Graham's music director and composer of several of her early works, *Dance Observer* covered—and championed—modern dance. Private collection.

beefed up the number of good guys. The bigger cast, he said, "made the marches at the beginning and at the end much more spectacular."[37] However, it also detracted from the exemplary character of the story, which the spareness had underlined. Now, instead of six Dance Hall Girls, Mexicans, and Ranchers' Wives, there were three dance hall girls alone, real people rather than a collection of frontier types.

The original choreography was highly stylized. As John Martin commented in his Sunday column after the New York premiere, Loring's "medium is essentially a heightening and an abstraction of acting, . . . a kind of pantomime that has been rhythmically abstracted from natural gesture with great beauty and ingenuity."[38] One sees this clearly in footage from the original production. When Loring as Billy performs the riding gesture, he repeats it and phrases it, as if to say, "So what? Take that! And that!" In the dance that follows the battle, the revelers stomp and turn mechanically; their bodies are rigid, their faces blank, and they hold their arms to the side like marionettes. The grace notes of conventional expressiveness—linking steps, *épaulement*, turnout, soft wrists and elbows—are absent. Here, and elsewhere, Loring transforms the characters into American primitives, the stylized figures of folk art. "My dance form," Loring once said, "the musical form used in dance, does not parallel the music. It parallels it in spirit and in counts and that kind of thing, but the form is not equal, not parallel."[39] Copland's thumping music, as mechanical and insistent as a merry-go-round, offers a parallel to Loring's modernist populism. Neither celebrates *Billy*'s unthinking folk or sentimentalizes the narrative; neither aims for local color or realism. The ballet is a radical retelling of the familiar story, within a framework of historical necessity. "Billy the Kid is not the hero of this ballet," Kirstein wrote before the premiere,

but rather . . . the times in which he lived. He was a heroic type, yet he was not unique. He was typical in so much as he reflected many others like him. He could not have existed except for his particular historical epoch. This was the peak of our expanding frontier, before the law came, and when your only security was in your trigger-finger. Billy represented the basic anarchy inherent in individualism in its most rampant form.[40]

The ballet ends, not with Billy's death but, to quote Kirstein again,

with a new start across the continent, . . . one more step achieved in the necessary orderings of the whole generation's procession. It's a flag-raising, more than a funeral. Billy's lonely wild-fire energy is replaced by the group force of the many marchers.[41]

Over the years this critical edge has been lost.

In later years Kirstein put the ballet out of his mind. "I don't recall much about *Billy*," he told Vivian Perlis, "because I don't want to. I didn't like what the ballet became after I agreed to let Ballet Theatre do it."[42] Kirstein apparently never forgave Loring for abandoning Ballet Caravan for Ballet Theatre and taking *Billy* away from him.[43] But Kirstein remained devoted to Copland. In 1941 he produced a second Caravan work to the composer's music—*Time Table*, set to *Music for the Theater*, with choreography by Antony Tudor.[44] In 1945, from Third Army Headquarters in Germany, he wrote Copland, asking for a ballet "that will be the first thing I will produce on kissing native shores."[45] Kirstein returned to the subject the following year, proposing a ballet, to be choreographed by Balanchine, that would be "nothing more (or less) than an absolute musical work."[46] In 1953, he proposed yet another project, this one for Jerome Robbins, who had choreographed *The Pied Piper*, to Copland's *Concerto for Clarinet and String Orchestra*, for the New York City Ballet in 1951.[47] Finally, in 1954, as managing director of City Center, Kirstein produced Copland's opera *The Tender Land*, which Robbins directed. Kirstein never lost his admiration for the composer of Ballet Caravan's finest work.[48]

When *Billy* came into the world, Americana was not synonymous with what Richard Taruskin has called "an ingratiating white-bread-of-the-prairie idiom that could be applied ad libitum to the higher forms of art."[49] For artists and intellectuals associated with the Left, an American subject, even a western subject, did not necessarily call for celebration. Doris Humphrey's *New Dance Trilogy* (1935–36) and Martha Graham's *Chronicle* (1936) and *American Document* (1938) were all deeply critical of American life, although they revealed a tendency toward abstraction and avoided the literal representation of American subject matter. Where the literal depiction of Americana did appear was in ballet, above all in works like *Union Pacific* (1934) and *Ghost Town* (1939), which had a score by Richard Rodgers, produced by the touring Ballet Russe companies, which were coming under fire for the absence of American works in their repertory.

Everything changed with the approach of World War II. Nostalgic visions of hearth and home emanated from the Office of War Information, to which leftists and New Deal liberals gravitated now that the United States and the Soviet Union were allies. In his 1941 State of the Union Address, President Roosevelt spoke of the "Four Freedoms," which Norman

Rockwell depicted in *The Saturday Evening Post* as rural America eating together, worshipping together, and comforting each other in the circumscribed space of the home. Audiences cheered performances of *American Legend* (1941), an Americana sampler that included a classic square dance choreographed by Agnes de Mille, who also danced a hoedown.[50] Modern dancers like Jane Dudley and Sophie Maslow, who had once choreographed odes to Lenin and championed the urban oppressed, now turned their eyes to Appalachia and choreographed dances with titles like *Harmonica Breakdown* (1941) and *Dust Bowl Ballads* (1941). Although visual artists were rapidly turning away from the figurative, choreographers—with the major exception of Balanchine—were embracing it, above all as a celebratory vision of America.

In 1942, four years to the day after the premiere of *Billy the Kid*, the Ballet Russe de Monte Carlo gave the first performance of *Rodeo*. Still in active repertory today, it was the quintessential Americana ballet; only *Fancy Free*, choreographed two years later by Jerome Robbins, surpassed it, although the America it depicted was urban—sailors on shore leave in wartime New York. Subtitled "The Courting at Burnt Ranch," *Rodeo* was set in Texas, around 1900, an idyllic land of open spaces, cowboys, and their sweethearts. The ballet was by Agnes de Mille (niece of the Hollywood mogul), the music by Copland, the sets by Oliver Smith (who later designed *The Tender Land*), and the costumes by Kermit Love (of later Muppets fame). The program note described the ballet as follows:

> Throughout the American Southwest, the Saturday afternoon rodeo is a tradition. On the remote ranches, as well as in the trading centres and the towns, the "hands" get together to show off their skill in roping, riding, branding, and throwing. . . .
>
> The afternoon's exhibition is usually followed by a Saturday night dance at the Ranch House. The theme of the ballet is basic. It deals with the problem that has confronted all American women, from earliest pioneer times, and which has never ceased to occupy them throughout the history of the building of our country: how to get a suitable man.
>
> The material of the ballet is redolent of our American soil.[51]

De Mille's protagonist is the Cowgirl, plucky, spunky, in love with the Head Wrangler; a tomboy in jeans who hangs around the corral and gets under foot, a misfit in dungarees who finally puts on a dress. "Everyone is stunned," de Mille wrote in the libretto:

The Wrangler steps forward to invite her to dance, but the [Champion] Roper pushes him aside and paces the girl into frenzies of brilliant footwork. She flushes and shines, giving as good as she takes, the star of the party. The Wrangler is . . . on the point of kissing her when he is intercepted by the Roper who decides to kiss her himself. . . . She falls into his arms with the happy recognition that it was he all along she has been wooing, if without knowing it.[52]

It was an upbeat ballet, with a happy ending, "the Taming of the Shrew—cowboy style," de Mille said, and audiences loved it.[53] When the ballet opened in New York, the house exploded in laughter and applause, and de Mille, who had insisted upon dancing the Cowgirl herself (to the dismay of the Ballet Russe management) took curtain call after curtain call. (She says twenty-two, her biographer seventeen.)[54]

Outside the theater the war dragged on. In her memoir *Dance to the Piper*, de Mille recalled the atmosphere on the road with the Ballet Russe during the months leading up to the premiere:

July moved into August, August into September. The United States lost the Aleutians. Rommel had all but reached the Nile, the Japanese were hard upon New Zealand. We knitted and rehearsed and gossiped back across the continent in cars that were shunted aside to let trainloads of tanks take the right of way, and trainloads of men, some in uniform, but all with intent lost faces. . . . All of America was quickening, was affirming itself, was searching its heart.[55]

De Mille's own fiancé, Walter Prude, was shipped out. And as the curtain rose at the Met, the Battle of Guadalcanal was raging.[56] *Rodeo* expressed nostalgia for a settled, safe America; it celebrated the myth of a world that never was, a rural community untouched by the social and economic disruptions of the twentieth century.

Far more than *Billy the Kid*, *Rodeo* is a folk ballet. Copland used folk tunes throughout, and as Howard Pollack points out, they typically appear in their entirety and in relatively traditional settings. The score also features original music in folk style, "to the point that one cannot be sure, without consulting the original sources, where a folk tune leaves off or resumes."[57] De Mille worked much the same way, with certain dances coming directly from vernacular sources, with very little change. Among these was a "running set," a classic square dance performed to the sound of clapping hands, running feet, and the cries of a caller. There was a tap cadenza, a hoedown, waltzes, the one-step, and a Texas minuet—the fixings of a real Saturday-night shindig. Theater, not authenticity, was her goal. She was a born storyteller, a master of the quick character sketch. Abstraction was alien to her temperament; she wanted flesh-and-blood people, even if the picture of them was only skin deep. She used gesture brilliantly, the telling piece of stage business (like a squint or a slap) or gait (de Mille wanted her cowboys bowlegged) that conveyed what someone was all about. She could be very funny. However much she identified with the Cowgirl, she also poked fun at her—at the adoring way she gazed at the Chief Wrangler, at her awkwardness and lack of social graces, her stubbornness and bravado. The fun was gentle, because the Cowgirl dances her heart out and always tries again. De Mille's characters were American because they moved with an American inflection and accent, even if the dancers themselves were from all over Europe.[58]

Riding movements added to the choreographer's American lexicon. De Mille had been working at them for years, long before she saw *Billy the Kid*. She described them as "neither realistic nor imitative."

When performed correctly they suggested the high vigorous emotions of riding. But they were very difficult because the dancer had always to look as though he were propelled by an unseen animal. . . . The very essence of the movement was shock, spasm and effort.[59]

"Move from the solar plexus and back," she shouted at her would-be cowboys. "Think of athletes . . . of throwing a ball, from your feet, from your back, from your guts." De Mille rolled on the floor, "lurched, contorted, jackknifed, hung suspended and ground [her] teeth," until she "broke them technically."[60] There was much that recalled modern dance—the use of parallel, the freedom of movement in the back and the spasmodic movements of the torso, the relaxed foot (because cowboys in boots don't point). The stylized roping gestures added to the American "feel" of the choreography.

Far more than *Billy*, *Rodeo* has the spectacular excitement of ballet. The cowboys fly across the stage in leaps; they jump, jog, and spin. De Mille packs the choreography with ballet steps—*chassés, fouettés, sissonnes*, and all kinds of multiple pirouettes. For all the cowboy overlay, the exuberance of the opening scene lies in her delivery of old-fashioned bravura, coupled with her sense of space. In an early version of the scenario she speaks of the characters being "dwarfed by space and height and isolation," adding, "One must be always conscious of the enormous land on which these people live and of their proud loneliness."[61] Oliver Smith's backdrop for the opening scene, fences receding into the distance under a glowing red-orange sky, captured this vastness. But it comes across best in the dancing—in the groups that sweep across the stage, one after another, jumping with exhilaration, circling, rushing down the diagonal, or moving in unison, in a thrilling demonstration of male power.[62] Critics praised de Mille's craft. "In nothing she has previously done," wrote John Martin, "has Miss de Mille exhibited so much pure choreographic skill and resourcefulness."[63] Edwin Denby, writing in *Modern Music*, found the dances "full of quick invention . . . the best we've had on the prairie subject and the best Miss de Mille has done." He also commented on the ballet's sense of place, and how "the flavor of American domestic manners" was "especially clear in [its] . . . desert landscape." . . . "The dance, the music, the décor. . . . each are drawn to that same local fact with affection; and so they have a mysterious unity."[64]

Rodeo, to the extent that it was about the curbing of female independence, anticipated the postwar ideology that sent Rosie the Riveter back home. De Mille herself was divided. On the one hand, she really did believe that the Cowgirl—and ordinary women like her—could only find happiness as a wife and mother, whatever the pull of the open range. De Mille herself opted for something different. The granddaughter of social reformer Henry George, who advocated a single tax on land to eliminate poverty, she wanted it all—and pretty much got it. She married, had a son, and pursued a successful career as a ballet and Broadway choreographer. (Her first show, *Oklahoma!*, choreographed in 1943, grew out of *Rodeo* and, with its "dream ballet," was a turning point in Broadway history.) Nevertheless, *Rodeo* isn't about life on the ranch, it's about a girl trying to keep up with the guys, then outdancing them.

Nothing could be further from the heroine of Martha Graham's *Appalachian Spring*. Graham calls her the Bride, although no marriage ceremony takes place. She stands with her Husbandman, a farmer, in the clearing of a half-built house, surrounded by kin, a pioneer woman on the brink of happiness but not entirely at peace with herself or her world. The work premiered in 1944 at the Library of Congress. It was Copland's third ballet on an American subject in a half-dozen years, and his best known, a prestigious commission from Elizabeth Sprague Coolidge. The following year it opened in New York. Only days before, Copland had received the Pulitzer Prize, and the war in Europe had ended. Stories about "GI Joes" coming home began to replace the war news.[65] A paean to hearth, home, and the American heartland, to enduring American values and rural community, *Appalachian Spring* was an idyll of domesticity, and it caught the mood of the country brilliantly.

It didn't start out that way. In early drafts of the scenario (or "script," as Graham called it), it was closer to *American Document* and to Kirstein's unproduced *Memorial Day*. Like *Memorial Day*, Graham's new work was about the Civil War; it had a fugitive slave character, references to Harper's Ferry, and a section, "Moment of Crisis," that echoed Kirstein's subtitle, "Dances for Democracy in Crisis." As in *American Document*, there was an Indian Girl/Pocahontas figure, the theme of religious fanaticism, and spoken texts (in this case, from the Book of Genesis), eliminated at Copland's suggestion.[66] The Civil War theme had contemporary as well as historical resonances. The Office of War Information, for instance, published posters linking the words of Abraham Lincoln about a world half-slave and half-free to the struggle against Nazi tyranny.[67] As Marta Robertson has pointed out, World War II "was central to Graham's initial concept of *Appalachian Spring*," and at one point she even called the

A "family" group from *Appalachian Spring*, 1944: (from left) Martha Graham (Bride), May O'Donnell (Pioneer Woman), Merce Cunningham (Revivalist), and Erick Hawkins (Husbandman). Photo by Chris Alexander. Jerome Robbins Dance Division, The New York Public Library for the Performing Arts, Astor, Lenox, and Tilden Foundations.

work "House of Victory."[68] In letters to Mrs. Coolidge, Graham spoke of her new work as part of the war effort, as meeting a civic responsibility. For example, on September 15, 1943 she wrote:

> I also feel that I have an obligation at this time. I must do something for the world that is constructive in so far as it is within my small power to make it so. Either that or I should be doing some actual work to help the war. While my performances cannot be called entertainment as a more popular medium is, nevertheless there may be something in them that will permit people to use certain parts of themselves that are immortal to man. If I can make them feel alive and conscious of themselves for one instant, even though it has been through the means of what might be called tragedy in theatre then I have fulfilled my duty in part to the world at this time.[69]

Despite the emphasis on domesticity and celebration, *Appalachian Spring* was a work of serious art. Unlike *Rodeo*, it had a dark undertow, anxieties tucked away and bursts of fanaticism that rippled the surface. To be sure, both were choreographed by women, who viewed their protagonists from a distinctly female perspective (and also identified with them). However, in both atmosphere and aspiration, *Appalachian Spring* is closer to *Billy the Kid* than *Rodeo*. All three celebrate the American experience, but where *Rodeo* is uniformly upbeat, "a lyric joke," as de Mille put it, *Appalachian Spring*, like *Billy the Kid*, discloses a netherworld of evil that threatens the American Eden.[70] The "House of Victory" scenario made this tension clear, juxtaposing sections of communal celebration—"Eden Valley," "Wedding Day," "The Lord's Day"—with those of loneliness and apocalypse—"Fear in the Night," "Day of Wrath," "Moment of Crisis."[71] Graham's casting underscored this moral dimension. Yuriko, one of the original Followers, had been in a Japanese-American internment camp, and her presence in the cast represented a quiet challenge to racism here and abroad.[72] As in *Billy*, space was a source of ambivalence. Bound up in the myth of the West and the epic of American expansion, the open space promised freedom, as Graham herself had suggested in a 1935 solo, *Frontier*. But it was also fraught with danger. In *Billy*, the range was a killing ground, where sheriffs served the cause of American expansion, clearing the land of its native peoples and desperados living outside a newly imposed law. In *Appalachian Spring*, the home—like the Bride's impending marriage—delimits the space of imaginative possibility. "This has to do with living in a new town," Graham wrote in an early script, "some place where the first fence has just gone up. . . . It should all by theatrical clarity add up to a sense of place."[73] For much of the action, the Bride gazes outward, scanning the world beyond that first fence, registering the separation between safety and freedom. Whatever the pull of the unknown, she never once steps outside the domestic space.

In creating the work's sense of place, Graham was indebted to her collaborators. Both Copland and Noguchi shared her modernist vision, and the spare beauty of their contributions gave *Appalachian Spring* a distinction that set it apart from its predecessors—both Graham's as well as Kirstein's. Indeed, Kirstein's dream of creating an American *Gesamtkunstwerk*, a total art work that would rival Diaghilev's all-Russian productions of *Petrouchka* and *Les Noces*, was more fully realized in *Appalachian Spring* than in any Ballet Caravan work, including *Billy the Kid*. In part, this reflected the quality of Graham's imagination, her ability to see the "inner frame" or "bone structure" of her subject, to move from the historical particular to the "happenings [that] flow from generation to generation," to create legends that seemed truer to life than any document.[74] Graham also had a refined sense of design. Although she eschewed sets until the mid-1930s, she reconceived the dancing body as a stylized, modernist object. Critics joked about her long tube-like costumes, which clung to the body and dramatized the expressive torso—a badge of identity for modern dance, as the tutu was for ballet.

Unlike Kirstein, Graham had little interest in painted decor, and when she began to use sets, they were functional and uncluttered, more concerned with space than with illustration and color. Now, thanks to Noguchi, her stage acquired a visual identity and became an artwork in its own right—analogous to the best of Diaghilev's productions. Certain ideas for *Appalachian Spring* emanated from Graham herself. Among these was the Shaker connection; an early version of the scenario refers to the Mother's "Shaker rocking chair"; another speaks of the climactic hymn as representing a "Shaker meeting," while also referring to "the spare beauty of fine Shaker furniture" that "Grant Wood has caught . . . in some of his things"—a rare allusion by Graham to a painter.[75] Noguchi made the rocking chair referred to by Graham part of the set and used a minimal frame to suggest both a home in the making and the simplicity of Shaker objects to evoke the plainspoken men and women of Graham's imagined America. "I attempted through the elimination of all non-essentials to arrive at an essence of the stark pioneer spirit," Noguchi wrote.[76] Copland, for his part, incorporated one of the most famous Shaker hymns, "Simple Gifts," into the music; in keeping with the more sober tone of the work (especially when compared to *Rodeo*), it was the only folk tune he used. In *Blast at Ballet*, Kirstein had likened Graham to "Shaker architecture and woodcarving"; elsewhere, he compared her "individual expression at once beautiful and useful" to a "piece of exquisitely realized Shaker furniture or homespun clothing."[77] Graham was certainly aware of what Kirstein was writing about her in the late 1930s. They had met a few years earlier, and according to her biographer, Agnes de Mille, "he became addicted." He took to "hanging around," wrote about her in a way that made no secret of his admiration, and as her few surviving letters to him make clear, she regarded him as a friend.[78] Kirstein missed the Washington and New York premieres of her new work. "Everyone says *Appalachian Spring* is glorious," he wrote to Copland from Germany shortly after the first New York performance. "How I long to hear it."[79] In 1947 and 1948 he commissioned Noguchi to design two works for Ballet Society. And in 1952, Edwin Denby wrote to Kirstein urging him "to go hard after *Appalachian Spring*" for the New York City Ballet.[80] For reasons that remain unclear, the revival never materialized.

Appalachian Spring was one of several Graham scores underwritten by the Elizabeth Sprague Coolidge Foundation in the early 1940s. Like Copland, the other recipients of Mrs. Coolidge's largesse—Darius Milhaud (*Imagined Wing*), Paul Hindemith (*Herodiade*), Carlos Chávez (*Dark Meadow*), and Samuel Barber (*Cave of the Heart*)—were serious composers with varying inclinations toward modernism and identified with ballet.[81] Their presence on Graham's roster of composers signaled a major shift in her work since the late 1930s away from modern dance as a recital form toward a type of dance theater that had more in common with ballet of the period. In making that transition, Graham abandoned key tenets about the relationship of music and dance, as this was understood by modern dancers of the 1930s. Among these notions was the primacy of dance. As Graham wrote in 1937, describing the revolt of the moderns against the "ornamented forms of impressionistic dancing": "Dance accompaniment and costume were stripped to essentials. Music came to be written on the dance structure. It ceased to be the source of the emotional stimulus and was used as background."[82] Graham's influential music director, Louis Horst, who composed many of her early scores, elaborated: "We are now at a period where the dancer dominates—as she should—and has grown to be absolutely independent. She does the dance and creates the rhythm for it. She then gets a composer to write the music upon the form she has created. Naturally, this will make the music secondary."[83] One can only speculate about the reasons for the shift in Graham's musical taste in the late 1930s, and Kirstein's part in it. Not only was he close to her in this period, but he had been urging her since 1935 to get rid of her "unmelodic and trivial" music.[84] In 1941, she commissioned *Punch and the*

Judy from Robert McBride, who had written the music for *Showpiece*, produced in 1937 by Ballet Caravan and choreographed by Erick Hawkins, a former Kirstein protégé who was now Graham's partner. Finally, in 1942, Hawkins approached Mrs. Coolidge, setting in motion the process that ultimately transformed Graham's repertory, aligning it musically with post-Diaghilev modernist ballet.

Although Graham had been stridently anti-ballet in the 1930s, her choreography for *Appalachian Spring* represented a melding of ballet, folk, and modern idioms analogous to *Billy the Kid* but rooted in modern dance. The Followers skip, circle, and jump with the lightness of ballet dancers and even wear soft ballet slippers. The Husbandman does pirouettes, sissonnes, attitude turns, and even barrel turns (a classical virtuoso jump for men), although they are frequently performed in parallel and the feet are sometimes flexed. The Bride's duets with the Husbandman feature lifts, and like a traditional pas de deux incorporate solos for the partners. Loring's riding step appears (Hawkins, who must have incorporated them into the Husbandman's role, was a Cowboy in the original *Billy*), and Graham seems to have lifted the Followers' cupped hand flutter from the dream scene in *Oklahoma!*, which de Mille had choreographed the previous year. Modified turnout is used throughout, and everyone joins hands in the culminating figure of a joyous square dance. Only Graham's solos are built on the signature movements of her technique, the falls and contractions that hint at the Bride's private anguish. As in virtually all of her works, Graham here is both the protagonist and hero of the drama; the narrative is her quest for knowledge. Indeed, even in *Appalachian Spring*, the most transparent of her mature works, the action may be taking place wholly in her mind. The title came from a phrase in "Powhatan's Daughter," the same section of Hart Crane's poem *The Bridge* that inspired the 1936 Ballet Caravan production *Pocahontas*, with a score by Elliott Carter.

"Ballet for Martha" was how Copland referred to *Appalachian Spring* before Graham decided upon a title, and he kept the phrase as a subtitle when the score was published. In his mind it belonged with *Billy* and *Rodeo*, despite the somewhat different technical emphasis. It had acquired both the character and the stature of an American *ballet*, a work that seemed to narrow—if not repair—the breach between ballet and modern dance. By 1944 such a rapprochement seemed to lie within the range of possibility. As early as the mid-1930s, much to Kirstein's annoyance, some modern-dance choreographers were referring to their longer group compositions as "modern ballets."[85] In 1941, critic George Beiswanger called for Ballet Theatre to absorb the Humphrey-Weidman dances into its proposed "modern repertory" of American works.[86] In 1947 Lucia Chase wrote to Humphrey about acquiring *With My Red Fires* for the company or even choreographing a new work for Nora Kaye.[87] Ballet Society, which Kirstein founded with Balanchine in 1946 to further the development of "lyric theater" (Ballet Caravan and the American Ballet had collapsed in 1941) commissioned a work by Merce Cunningham, sets from Noguchi, and scores from Elliott Carter (*The Minotaur*, 1947), John Cage (*The Seasons*, 1947), Stravinsky (*Orpheus*, 1948), and others, in addition to presenting Gian Carlo Menotti's operas *The Medium* and *The Telephone* (the latter a world premiere) in 1947.

In this melding, Copland's Americana works played a key role. In different ways, *Billy the Kid*, *Rodeo*, and *Appalachian Spring* each created a dance for Americans, a language and an idiom that summed up a liberal-left idea about nationality, provided a way of incorporating vernacular material into an "art" idiom (be it ballet or modern dance), and situating such work within the European modernist succession. By the late 1940s American subject matter would disappear, and many choreographers would abandon narrative altogether and, like Copland, embrace more opaque forms of expression. By then, they had no need to prove themselves. The Ballet Russe companies had lost their edge; the Diaghilev inheritance had run dry or been absorbed into national traditions. During his years in Paris, Copland "wouldn't have dreamed of missing a new ballet by Stravinsky. His works were the most interesting and sensational in the Diaghilev repertory. . . . The essential Russianness of those scores suggested to me that it might be possible to create an American atmosphere in music."[88] With Copland as their partner, Loring, de Mille, and Graham created a repertory that drew on Diaghilev's powerful legacy—transforming rather than imitating it, bending it to American needs and giving it an American inflection. In this undertaking Copland's work served as a model, the exemplar of an art that was both serious and accessible, that acknowledged vernacular traditions but treated them as elements of a fine art. If Jerome Robbins could write in 1945 that the ballet had put on "dungarees" and left the "hothouse [to] become in America a people's entertainment," it was in part because Copland had showed the way.[89] His music had helped American dance become a serious American art.

NOTES

1. Phillip Ramey, "Copland and the Dance," *Ballet News* 2, no. 5 (November 1980): 8. Text copyright *Ballet News* 1980; reprinted courtesy of *Ballet News*, with permission.

2. Richard Buckle, *Diaghilev* (London: Weidenfeld and Nicolson, 1979), p. 450.

3. For Bolm's collaborations with Carpenter, see Suzanne Carbonneau, "Adolph Bolm in America," in *The Ballets Russes and Its World*, ed. Lynn Garafola and Nancy Van Norman Baer (New Haven: Yale University Press, 1999), pp. 227–32. See also the chapters on *The Birthday of the Infanta* and *Krazy Kat* in Howard Pollack, *Skyscraper Lullaby: The Life and Music of John Alden Carpenter* (Washington/London: Smithsonian Institution Press, 1995).

4. For the genesis and reception of the ballet as well as a discussion of its evolution and later fate, see Pollack, *Skyscraper Lullaby*, chaps. 13 and 14.

5. During the 2002–2003 season, *Skyscrapers* was programmed by the American Symphony Orchestra, Leon Botstein, music director. The work is included on *Skyscrapers and Other Music of the American East Coast School*, London Symphony Orchestra, Kenneth Klein, Angel CDC-7 49263 2. However, as Pollack points out, the recording is not complete and lacks an "authentic, idiomatic ease in the jazzy passages." Ibid., p. 247.

6. For a list of Graham's works, see Alice Helpern, "The Technique of Martha Graham," *Studies in Dance History* 2, no. 2 (Spring–Summer 1991): 36–49; for Tamiris, see Christena L. Schlundt, "Tamiris: A Chronicle of Her Dance Career 1927–1955," *Studies in Dance History* 1, no. 1 (Fall–Winter 1989–1990): 70–154. For *Lull*, which Schlundt does not mention, see the program for her "Dance Recital" at the Martin Beck Theatre, New York, April 7, 1929, Programs (Tamiris, Helen), Jerome Robbins Dance Division, New York Public Library for the Performing Arts (hereafter DD-NYPL). Although the music that Tamiris used is not identified in the programs, Pollack, in his biography of Copland, suggests that *Sentimental Dance* was done to the piano piece *Sentimental Melody; Slow Dance* and *Olympus Americanus* to another piano work, *Passacaglia* (Howard Pollack, *Aaron Copland: The Life and Work of an Uncommon Man* [New York: Henry Holt, 1999], p. 154). Another early Tamiris work to Copland music, which neither Schlundt nor Pollack mentions, is *Dance on an Ancient Theme*, presented at Washington Irving High School, New York, February 20, 1932, in the Students Dance Recitals series.

7. Aaron Copland and Vivian Perlis, *Copland Since 1943* (New York: St. Martin's Press, 1989), p. 30.

8. For Page's career, see John Martin, *Ruth Page: An Intimate Biography* (New York: Dekker, 1977); Ruth Page, *Page by Page*, ed. Andrew Mark Wentink (Brooklyn: Dance Horizons, 1978).

9. José Limón, *An Unfinished Memoir*, ed. Lynn Garafola, introduction by Deborah Jowitt (Hanover/London: Wesleyan University Press, 1999), pp. 21–22.

10. Jerome D. Bohm, "Ballet Series Is Opened Here by Ruth Page," *New York Herald Tribune*, March 2, 1936.

11. For Copland's description of the ballet and response to it, see Aaron Copland and Vivian Perlis, *Copland: 1900 Through 1942* (New York: St. Martin's/Marek, 1984), pp. 233–35.

12. For the radical dance movement in the 1930s, see Ellen Graff, *Stepping Left: Dance and Politics in New York City, 1928–1942* (Durham, N.C.: Duke University Press, 1997), and Lynn Garafola, ed., "Of, By, and For the People: Dancing on the Left in the 1930s," *Studies in Dance History* 5, no. 1 (Spring 1994), which also includes a selection of reviews by Edna Ocko, the preeminent left-wing dance critic of the 1930s. Founded in 1932, the Workers Dance League was an umbrella organization to further the development of workers' dance groups. The League sponsored concerts and contests (called Spartakiades) and included groups from Boston, Chicago, Newark, and Philadelphia, although New York was the

movement's center. In 1935 the Workers Dance League changed its name to the New Dance League, in an attempt to "dissociate itself from the amateurism that the term 'worker' was beginning to denote" (Graff, *Stepping Left*, p. 112). Two years later the New Dance League, the Dancers Association, and the Dance Guild amalgamated to form the American Dance Association, a political organization devoted to securing dancers' rights, promoting world peace, and fighting fascism. The New Dance Group, one of the original constituents of the Workers' Dance League, continues to offer classes in New York City. Throughout the 1940s and 1950s The New Dance Group remained faithful to the League's progressive agenda.

13. See, for example, his review of Martha Graham, "Prejudice Purely," *New Republic*, April 11, 1934, 243–44, and his essay "Crisis in the Dance," *North American Review* (Spring 1937): 80–103. For an overview of Kirstein's career, see Nancy Reynolds, "In His Image: Diaghilev and Lincoln Kirstein," in Garafola and Baer, *The Ballets Russes and Its World*, pp. 291–311; for his connection with the Left, see Lynn Garafola, "Lincoln Kirstein, Ballet Caravan, and the 1930s," *Dance Research* (in press).

14. John Martin, "The Dance: The Ballet," *New York Times*, March 10, 1935. The season repertory included revivals of *Errante*, *Dreams*, and *Mozartiana*, all staged by Balanchine for his Paris-based company, Les Ballets 1933. *Errante* had music by Schubert ("Wanderer" Fantasy) and designs by Pavel Tchelitchew; *Dreams* (or *Les Songes*, its original French title), music by Antheil (replacing the original Milhaud score), and designs by Derain; *Mozartiana*, music by Tchaikovsky (Suite No. 4, "Mozartiana") and designs by Christian Bérard. The new works were the now classic *Serenade*, to Tchaikovsky's Serenade in C for String Orchestra (sets by Gaston Longchamp, costumes by Jean Lurçat); *Alma Mater*, to music by Kay Swift (sets by Eugene Dunkel, costumes by John Held, Jr.); *Reminiscence*, to music by Godard (designs by Sergei Soudeikine); and *Transcendence*, to Liszt's *Mephisto Waltz*, Ballade, and various Hungarian rhapsodies (sets by Longchamp, costumes by Franklin Watkins). For Martin's other reviews of the season, see "American Ballet Makes Its Debut," *New York Times*, March 2, 1935; "American Ballet Opens Second Bill," *New York Times*, March 6, 1935. For a sampling of criticism of the individual ballets, see Nancy Reynolds, *Repertory in Review: Forty Years of the New York City Ballet*, introduction by Lincoln Kirstein (New York: Dial, 1977), pp. 36–44.

15. For the American Ballet and Ballet Caravan, see Anatole Chujoy, *The New York City Ballet* (New York: Knopf, 1953), chaps. 5–8; *Thirty Years: Lincoln Kirstein's The New York City Ballet* (New York: Knopf, 1978), pp. 40–80; Reynolds, *Repertory in Review*, pp. 36–62. See also Kirstein's two-part "Transcontinental Caravan," *Dance*, February 1939, 14–15; March 1939, 8, 38. The "Communism Is Americanism" slogan appeared on a card issued by the Communist Party during the 1936 campaign; it is reproduced in Eric Foner, *Give Me Liberty! An American History* (New York: W. W. Norton, 2004), p. 840.

16. For a list of Kirstein's published writings, see Harvey Simmonds, Louis H. Silverstein, and Nancy Lassalle, *Lincoln Kirstein: The Published Writings 1922–1977: A First Bibliography* (New Haven: Yale University Library, 1978).

17. This information is culled from Kirstein's FBI file, released under the Freedom of Information Act, as well as a response dated March 23, 1953, to a Rockefeller Foundation request for name checks on several individuals, including Kirstein, associated with City Center (RF12, 200R, City Center, Box 392, Folder 3391). These and other connections are discussed in my *Dance Research* article, "Lincoln Kirstein, Ballet Caravan, and the 1930s," forthcoming.

18. The essay, "Notes on a Cowboy Ballet," is reproduced in *Aaron Copland: Selected Writings 1923–1972*, ed. Richard Kostelanetz (New York: Routledge, 2004), pp. 239–41. A typescript of the same essay with the notation "EXCLUSIVE FEATURE" is in DD-NYPL, Clippings (*Billy the Kid*). Another typescript, in the Copland Collection (Box 200, Folder 19), has the following notation: "Ed. note: Mr. Copland's ballet 'Billy the Kid' will

have its first performance this Wednesday evening, May 24th, as one of the American Lyric Theatre Ballet presentations by the Ballet Caravan." Although Kostelanetz gives a 1938 date for this essay, it was probably written for the New York premiere of the ballet on May 24, 1939, at the Martin Beck Theatre. Copland reused some of this material in Copland and Perlis, *Copland: 1900–1942*, pp. 278–80.

19. Kirstein, *Thirty Years*, p. 71.

20. Ibid., pp. 70–71; Debra Hickenlooper Sowell, *The Christensen Brothers: An American Dance Epic* (Harwood Academic Publishers, 1998), pp. 123–24. Both Lew and Harold Christensen were members of Ballet Caravan.

21. Chujoy, *New York City Ballet*, p. 92. Neither of these works was produced by Ballet Caravan, although Loring's *City Portrait* (1939) had a score commissioned from Brant, and the composer had orchestrated the Godard music for the American Ballet's *Reminiscence* (1935). Brant also wrote the music for *The Great American Goof*, which Loring choreographed for Ballet Theatre in 1940.

22. Lincoln Kirstein, "About 'Billy the Kid,'" *The Dance Observer*, October 1938, 116.

23. Nancy Reynolds, ed., *Ballet: Bias and Belief—Three Pamphlets Collected and Other Dance Writings of Lincoln Kirstein* (New York: Dance Horizons, 1983), pp. 59–67.

24. Lincoln Kirstein, "Martha Graham at Bennington," *The Nation*, September 3, 1938, 230.

25. Graham's letters from this period, all undated, are in the Lincoln Kirstein Papers, DD-NYPL, Box 6, Folder 101. Kirstein's detailed scenario for *Memorial Day*, with Jared French's designs, are in the Copland Collection at the Library of Congress. According to Vicki Goldberg, in a short article about the "sheaf of watercolor sketches" discovered by archivists sifting through the collection, the project dates from 1937 or 1938 ("A Dance in Aquarelle," *Civilization*, February–March 1998, 34). However, since the material is undated, it is impossible to establish its exact relationship to *Billy the Kid* and *American Document*. Why the project was dropped is a mystery. One possible reason is that Copland did not want to write the music; another, that Kirstein was unable to raise the funds to produce it; a third, that the conception was so grandiose as to be unworkable. My feeling is that Kirstein lost interest in the project early on, since he never bothered to recover French's sketches and include them in his donation of American Ballet and Ballet Caravan set and costume designs to the Museum of Modern Art (where French's *Billy the Kid* designs are still housed). I am grateful to Vicky Risner, who first brought the *Memorial Day* material to my attention and made it possible for me to borrow several images for the 1999 exhibition *Dance for a City: Fifty Years of the New York City Ballet* at the New-York Historical Society.

26. Kirstein, "Blast at Ballet" in Reynolds, *Bias and Belief*, p. 202. *The Minotaur*, with music by Naginski, was another project that failed to materialize, although Kirstein produced a ballet with the same title but music by Elliott Carter in 1947 for Ballet Society. A "dramatic ballet in two parts," the 1947 *Minotaur* had choreography by John Taras and designs by the Spanish artist Joan Junyer. Although "Blast at Ballet" was published in 1937, Kirstein clearly wrote much of it in 1936, the year that *Pocahontas* premiered.

27. Three of French's designs—"Alias as Guide," "Alias as Mexican," and "Alias as Sheriff"—are reproduced in Gail Levin, "Aaron Copland's America," in Gail Levin and Judith Tick, *Aaron Copland's America: A Cultural Perspective* (New York: Watson-Guptill, 2000), pp. 82–83.

28. Copland and Perlis, *Copland: 1900–1942*, pp. 278–80. The scenario and "Notes on Billy the Kid's Character" are in the Eugene Loring Papers, DD-NYPL, Box 5 (Choreographic Notes: *Billy the Kid*). Also included among these materials are cast lists, floor plans, movement notes, a detailed synopsis, breakdown of scenes and time plot, and excerpts from books such as Theodore Roosevelt's *Ranch Life and the Hunting Trail* (1896) and Agnes C. Laut's *Pilgrims of the Santa Fe* (1931). The abundance of materials would seem

to support Loring's contention that "Lincoln did not do the book. What he did was . . . [hand] me the book by Walter Noble Burns, *The Life and Times of Billy the Kid* . . . and in his gruff manner . . . said, 'See if you can make a ballet out of it.'. . . [T]he rest of the work is totally mine. . . . [T]here was no kind of real close connection between Kirstein and myself on it." Marilyn Hunt, interview with Eugene Loring, 1975, DD-NYPL, Oral History Archive, pp. 35–36 (hereafter Hunt-Loring). However, it is clear from various accounts that Kirstein conceived not only the idea for the ballet but also what might be termed its larger ideology. Although many standard reference works, including Gerald Goode's *The Book of Ballets: Classic and Modern* (New York: Crown Publishers, 1939), Cyril W. Beaumont's *Supplement to Complete Book of Ballets* (London: Putnam, 1942), and Nancy Reynolds's *Repertory in Review*, list Kirstein as author of the ballet's book, no librettist is credited on the Caravan souvenir program or playbills. Chujoy, in the chronological checklist at the end of *The New York City Ballet*, credits Kirstein with authorship of all the Caravan libretti.

29. Copland and Perlis, *Copland: 1900–1942*, p. 284; Kirstein, "Martha Graham at Bennington," p. 230.

30. Kirstein, "About 'Billy the Kid,'" p. 116.

31. The playbill for the premiere at the Civic Theatre, Chicago, on October 16, 1938, is in the *Billy the Kid* clippings file, DD-NYPL. Playbills for other performances are in the American Ballet Caravan program file, DD-NYPL. For Loring's view of Alias, see Hunt-Loring, pp. 40–41.

32. Hunt-Loring, pp. 43–45. Howard Pollack's account of the collaboration (*Aaron Copland*, p. 321) draws on Richard Schottland's taped interview with Loring, also in the DD-NYPL, rather than Hunt's oral history; hence, the different wording.

33. Ann Barzel, "Ballet Caravan," *Dance*, December 1938, 36.

34. Richard Philp, "Billy the Kid Turns Fifty: An American Dance Document," *Dance Magazine*, November 1988, 42.

35. The New York Public Library for the Performing Arts' Dance Division has a number of recordings of the ballet. The oldest footage was filmed by Ann Barzel in Chicago in 1938, although it was spliced together with footage of the 1940 Ballet Theatre production. Still, it is possible to tell the two productions apart because the 1938 one was shot from the house and the 1940 version from the wings. The ballet was produced by the "TV-Radio Workshop of the Ford Foundation" in 1953 and televised on *Omnibus*; this version had an introduction and voiceover by the choreographer. In 1976 the PBS series *Dance in America* telecast the ballet as performed by American Ballet Theatre.

36. The name of the company was later changed to American Ballet Theatre.

37. Hunt-Loring, p. 61.

38. John Martin, "The Dance: 'Billy the Kid,'" *New York Times*, May 28, 1939.

39. Hunt-Loring, p. 46.

40. Kirstein, "About 'Billy the Kid,'" p. 116.

41. Ibid.

42. Copland and Perlis, *Copland: 1900–1942*, p. 284.

43. In a letter to Copland written in November 1940, Kirstein explains that he is willing to sell the sets and costumes to Ballet Theatre, but not give them to the company as an outright gift; he also says that there is a good possibility that he will revive the ballet sometime soon. Kirstein makes some very disparaging remarks about Loring, who had left Ballet Caravan to join Ballet Theatre the previous year and presumably wanted to restage his most famous ballet (Kirstein to Copland, November 11,1940, Copland Collection, Box 257, Folder 21). It should be noted that companies, not choreographers, owned the performance rights to ballets at this time.

44. *Time Table* premiered at the Teatro Municipal, Rio de Janeiro, on June 27, 1941, although an open dress rehearsal was held on May 29, 1941, at Hunter College before the

company's departure for South America. The ballet, according to Nancy Reynolds, "concerned wartime partings and reunions at a railroad station." Tudor told her: "I prefer to find music first and then look for an idea, since the other way around is terribly difficult. . . . This ballet was considered to be so 'American,' but you know we have armies in England, and it could just as well have happened there. I saw such things in World War I. And my costumes were roughly that period. The three girls were sort of flappers. It wasn't sad, because at the end a husband comes home just as the boyfriend leaves, on the same train" (quoted in Reynolds, *Repertory in Review*, 63). See pp. 63–64 for reactions to the revival by the New York City Ballet in 1949.

45. Kirstein to Copland, June 16, 1945, Copland Collection, Box 257, Folder 21.

46. Kirstein to Copland, December 1, 1946, ibid.

47. Kirstein to Copland, June 25, 1953, ibid.

48. For Kirstein's heartfelt expression of thanks to Copland shortly before the premiere of *Billy*, which he praised as the finest score the company had ever had, see Kirstein to Copland, September 19, 1938, ibid.

49. Quoted in Pollack, *Aaron Copland*, p. 531.

50. Carol Easton, *No Intermissions: The Life of Agnes de Mille* (Boston: Little, Brown, 1996), pp. 172–73.

51. Program, Ballet Russe de Monte Carlo, Metropolitan Opera House, New York, October 16, 1942, DD-NYPL, Programs (Ballet Russe de Monte Carlo).

52. Agnes de Mille, "Rodeo," typescript, Agnes de Mille Collection, DD-NYPL, Box 36.

53. Agnes de Mille, "American Ballet by Agnes de Mille," typescript, ibid.

54. Agnes de Mille, *Dance to the Piper* (Boston: Little, Brown, 1951), p. 233; Easton, *No Intermissions*, p. 194.

55. De Mille, *Dance to the Piper*, p. 226.

56. "Heavy Jap Forces Shell Guadalcanal" and "Guadalcanal Battle Rages; Major Sea Fight in Making" were the front-page headlines of the *New York Sun* on October 16 and 17, 1942, respectively.

57. Pollack, *Aaron Copland*, p. 367.

58. Casimir Kokich, the Head Wrangler, was Yugoslavian; Frederick Franklin, the Champion Roper, English; and Lubov Roudenko, who replaced de Mille, Bulgarian.

59. De Mille, *Dance to the Piper*, p. 218.

60. Ibid.

61. De Mille, "American Ballet."

62. The ballet returns periodically to the repertory of American Ballet Theatre, which acquired the performance rights in 1950. *American Ballet Theatre: A Close-Up in Time*, produced by WNET/13 in 1973, has a good production of Scene 1. Two photographs by Roger Wood, taken in England in 1950 (when American Ballet Theatre was on tour) are reproduced in Levin, "Aaron Copland's America," pp. 96–97.

63. John Martin, "'Rodeo' Presented by Ballet Russe," *New York Times*, October 17, 1942, p. 10.

64. Edwin Denby, "With the Dancers," *Modern Music* 20, no. 1 (November–December 1942): 53. Denby, who wrote the libretto for Copland's *The Second Hurricane* in 1936, began writing dance criticism for *Modern Music* the same year. During World War II, he replaced Walter Terry as the dance critic of the *New York Herald-Tribune*. Regarded as the finest dance critic of the period, Denby was an eloquent champion of Balanchine's early work.

65. In the *New York Times* the "Pulitzer Awards" were announced on the same front page with the triumphant headline, "The War in Europe Is Ended! Surrender Is Unconditional; V-E Will Be Proclaimed Today," May 8, 1945. For typical GI stories, see "From Khaki to Civvies: The Transition of GI Joe," *New York World-Telegram*, May 15, 1945.

66. Copland and Perlis, *Copland Since 1943*, p. 32; Pollack, *Aaron Copland*, pp. 394–95.

67. Foner, *Give Me Liberty!*, p. 867.

68. Marta Elaine Robertson, "'A Gift to be Simple': The Collaboration of Aaron Copland and Martha Graham in the Genesis of *Appalachian Spring*,'" Ph.D. diss., University of Michigan, 1992, p. 132. For an analysis of Graham's scenarios and the evolution of the characters and action, see chapter 3, "*Appalachian Spring*: The Biography of a Ballet."

69. Graham to Coolidge, September 15, 1943, uncatalogued box, joint materials related to *Appalachian Spring* from both the Elizabeth Sprague Coolidge Collection and the Music Division's Copland Collection, Library of Congress. For Graham's correspondence with Coolidge (although not this letter), see Wayne D. Shirley, "For Martha," *Ballet Review* 27, no. 4 (Winter 1999): 64–95.

70. De Mille, "American Ballet."

71. For a list of the sections, see Robertson, "'A Gift to be Simple,'" Table 4, p. 209.

72. For Yuriko, see the interview in Robert Tracy's *Goddess: Martha Graham's Dancers Remember* (New York: Limelight, 1997), pp. 100–11.

73. Martha Graham, "Name? Version 1," script sent by Graham to Copland in summer 1943. Copland Collection, Box 255, Folder 22.

74. Ibid.

75. Martha Graham, "House of Victory," script sent to Copland, May 16, 1943; and "Name? Version 1." Copland Collection, Box 255, Folder 22. For the connection with Grant Wood, see Levin, "Aaron Copland's America," pp. 99–100.

76. Quoted in Robert Tracy, *Spaces of the Mind: Isamu Noguchi's Dance Designs* (New York: Limelight, 2000), p. 44. *Appalachian Spring* was filmed in 1959 with Graham as the Bride, Stuart Hodes as the Husbandman, Bertram Ross as the Revivalist, and Matt Turney as the Pioneer Woman. A video of the recording is available on *Martha Graham—An American Original in Performance*, distributed by Kultur.

77. *Blast at Ballet*, in Reynolds, *Bias and Belief*, p. 249; *Martha Graham: The Early Years*, ed. Merle Armitage (Los Angeles, 1937; rpt. New York: Da Capo, 1978), p. 32.

78. Agnes de Mille, *Martha: The Life and Work of Martha Graham* (New York: Random House, 1991), pp. 229, 239. For Graham's letters to Kirstein, see note 26 above.

79. Kirstein to Copland, June 16, 1945. Copland Collection, Box 257, Folder 21.

80. Denby to Kirstein (1952). Kirstein Papers, DD-NYPL, Box 4, Folder 69.

81. Milhaud composed numerous ballets in the 1920s and 1930s, including *L'Homme et son Désir* (1921) and *La Création du Monde* (1923) for the Ballets Suédois, *Le Train Bleu* (1924) for Diaghilev's Ballets Russes, *Salade* (1924) for the Soirées de Paris, and *La Sagesse* (unproduced) for Ida Rubinstein. Hindemith's best-known ballets were *Nobilissima Visione* (or *St. Francis*) (1938) for the Ballet Russe de Monte Carlo and *The Four Temperaments*, commissioned by Balanchine in 1938 for the American Ballet, although not produced until 1946. Chávez's *H. P.* (*Horse Power*) was produced by (although not written for) Catherine Littlefield's Philadelphia-based civic ballet company in 1932.

82. "Graham 1937," in Armitage, *Martha Graham*, p. 86.

83. Quoted in "Lloyd 1935," Armitage, *Martha Graham*, pp. 89–90.

84. Lincoln Kirstein, "The Dance: Some American Dancers," *The Nation*, February 27, 1935, 258.

85. Lincoln Kirstein, "Crisis in the Dance," *North American Review*, Spring 1937, 99.

86. Marcia B. Siegel, *Days on Earth: The Dance of Doris Humphrey* (Durham, N.C.: Duke University Press, 1993), p. 228.

87. Ibid., pp. 228–30.

88. Ramey, "Copland and the Dance," p. 10.

89. Jerome Robbins, "The Ballet Puts on Dungarees," *New York Times*, October 14, 1945.

PART III

COPLAND'S INNER CIRCLE

Dear Aaron, Dear Lenny:

A Friendship in Letters

VIVIAN PERLIS

Aaron Copland and Leonard Bernstein met on Copland's thirty-seventh birthday, November 14, 1937. A few months later, a letter arrived from the nineteen-year-old Harvard student to "Dear Aaron," signed "Leonard Bernstein." So began a correspondence that chronicles the lives and careers of two of the most influential musical figures of the twentieth century. The exchange between Copland and Bernstein continued through fifty years and ended with a letter from Bernstein in 1988 to "My Dearest Aaron," signed "All My Love, Lenny." Within those years, salutations included: Dear Lensk, Old Charmer, Young Charmer, Aaron best of all, Hello Pal, Aronchen Liebchen, Aaron Foremost of Men, Dear Philharmoniker, Dear Judge-nose, Most August Diabolus, Dearest M.D., Dear Sorely-missed A. These personal letters provide an inside view of an extraordinary relationship that affected both composers deeply, and in turn, influenced American music over a long period of time.

At the start, the tone is of student and mentor; the correspondence then traces the friendship as it evolved—and deepened. The letters on both sides are spontaneous, articulate, informative, and affectionate. Bernstein is—as Bernstein was—effusive and confessional, playful and brash. By comparison, Copland appears restrained, but his pleasure in life, music, and people is apparent. A vivid picture emerges of two exceptional musicians, as well as of their relationship with each other and of their colleagues during the late Depression, through World War II, and beyond.

Copland at thirty-seven was the recognized leader of American contemporary music. He had experienced a full creative life before meeting Bernstein, including a few notable jazz-inspired works (what his colleague Virgil Thomson called "Copland's one wild oat"), followed by abstract pieces such as the Piano Variations, *Statements for Orchestra*, and the *Short Symphony*.[1] Like many artists in the 1930s, Copland experienced a politically active period, participating in the Communist-controlled Composers Collective and nearly joining the Socialist Party. Always influenced by the world around him, Copland was affected by the heated political scene at the New School for Social Research where he taught music appreciation courses.[2] He had fallen in love with a handsome young man named Victor Kraft, who became his long-term partner, and through composer Carlos Chávez, he and Kraft experienced Mexico together in 1932. When Copland met Bernstein in 1937, he already had his inner circle of friends—Harold Clurman, Carlos Chávez, and a group of admiring younger composers.[3] He had an advocate conductor, Serge Koussevitzky, and a mentor since the Paris years, Nadia Boulanger. As a leading figure in the League of Composers, Copland advised its director, Claire Reis, and Minna Lederman, editor of the League's magazine, *Modern Music*. Copland even had a "girlfriend" in Rosamond ("Peggy") Bernier—"the only woman I might have married."[4] Why at this time of his life did Copland welcome a new relationship with a young Harvard student named Leonard Bernstein?

The answers are not simple, either on a personal or professional level. There were many differences, not least in age and personality. Bernstein was mercurial, flamboyant, handsome, and bisexual. Copland was steady, dignified, modest, and homosexual. The differences stimulated rather than discouraged their friendship. From several explicit passages in their letters, it is clear that Copland and Bernstein shared an intimate relationship. While lasting for only a brief time in the early forties, it had an enduring impact on the quality of their affection and the depth of their loyalty. Musically, they had much in common and trusted each other completely. The discovery of exceptional creative talent is rare—each recognized it in the other and valued what they had found.

When Copland and Bernstein first met, America was well into the Great Depression and the uneasy years preceding World War II. The change from the twenties to the thirties precipitated by the Wall Street crash of 1929 had been abrupt and substantial. As George Orwell wrote, "Suddenly we got out of the twilight of the gods into a sort of Boy Scout atmosphere of bare knees and community singing."[5] When compared to the glamour and excitement of the Roaring Twenties, the poverty-stricken thirties were grim, but as Copland later explained, the Great Depression did not directly affect him. He had had no permanent home since boyhood, nor did he have a taste for luxuries or material belongings. Copland's room at the Empire Hotel cost $3.25 a week and was sufficient for his needs; his nearby loft, where he could use a piano without disturbing the residents, was described by Harold Clurman as "that dismal sanctuary on Sixty-third Street."[6] The loft was in a shabby building where Lincoln Center now stands. On the floor below was a chocolate factory. The space was sparsely furnished and there was never much to eat, but it was a loft before such places became stylish—talk was lively and young composers enjoyed being part of the artistic scene and hearing the latest gossip, musical, political, and personal. Victor Kraft stayed there when in New York City, as did Bernstein and others on occasion.

Copland was fond of saying, "It was great to be twenties in the twenties," but in style and bearing, he resembled the thirties—"plain," as Bernstein often described him, with one suit, one coat, a beret, and modest surroundings. Bernstein, on the other hand, although poor as students tend to be, seemed a holdover from the Jazz Age—a handsome party boy, reminiscent of Gershwin, who enjoyed being center stage at the piano, living high with an "anything goes" attitude, romantic and more often than not in love, a melodramatic figure, a refreshing splash of brilliant color in the pale gray of the Depression.

The First Meeting

The afternoon of November 14, 1937, found Bernstein on a train from Boston to New York City with his Harvard friend I. B. Cohen. He had borrowed the money for this rare trip in order to attend the New York debut of Anna Sokolow, a dancer he had seen and admired in Boston. How Bernstein came to be seated next to Copland that evening is not known. Was it really as coincidental as Bernstein described? The young Bernstein knew about Copland and even played his Piano Variations, which Arthur Berger had introduced him to, and he was ready to surprise the older composer by playing this daunting piece that very evening. Whether partially planned or serendipitous, the first meeting of the two musicians makes a very good story as told by Bernstein:

> On my right sat this unknown person, with buck teeth and a giggle and a big nose, of a charm not to be described, and when I was introduced to him, and found that it was Aaron Copland next to whom I was sitting, I could have been blown away—I was blown away! Because I had become a fanatic lover of the Piano Variations, and in fact I had learned them and spoiled many a party by playing them. I could empty the room, guaranteed, in two minutes by playing this wonderful piece by Aaron Copland, whom I pictured as a sort of

patriarch, Moses or Walt Whitman–like figure, with a beard, because that's what the music says. . . . And so I was shocked to meet this young-looking, smiling, giggling fellow, whose birthday it happened to be. Aaron was giving a party for himself at his loft. He invited everyone in that row, which were all sorts of people like Virgil Thomson, Paul Bowles, and Edwin Denby, poets and literary people, musicians, the photographer Rudy Burckhardt, and of course Victor Kraft. It was my real introduction to New York and to the elite artistic community. It was there Aaron discovered I was his great fan and that I knew the Piano Variations. He said, "You do? A junior at Harvard knows . . . I dare you to play it." And I said, "Well, it'll ruin your party, but . . . " So I played it, and they were all—he particularly—drop-jawed. And it did not empty the room.[7]

That is the how their friendship started, and from then on, Bernstein never forgot a Copland birthday. He came to think of "14" as a meaningful number and "November 14" as a magical date. It was an extraordinary coincidence when on that very day in 1943 a young aide was called upon to conduct the New York Philharmonic in place of an ailing Bruno Walter. His name was Leonard Bernstein, and suddenly, on Aaron Copland's forty-third birthday, he was a star.

(Facing page and below) Leonard Bernstein and Aaron Copland, 1941.

The Correspondence

The Aaron Copland and Leonard Bernstein Collections are housed in the Music Division of the Library of Congress. They include music manuscripts, papers, photographs, and correspondence. The letters of Copland to Bernstein total 111 and can be found on the Internet; Bernstein's to Copland number 114 and are not publicly available.[8] Most are ink autographs; a few are typewritten. Copland's letters were dated; most of Bernstein's were not. At an unknown time before Copland's papers were transferred from his home to the Library of Congress, he reviewed his letters from Bernstein and supplied approximate dates. Brief segments are blackened out, most probably by Copland, for personal reasons.

Both correspondents wrote fluently, not for posterity, but directly to each other. In keeping with Bernstein's excessive nature, his letters tend to be longer than Copland's. One is six pages, for example, with thirteen numbered points of information and requests. As their careers escalated, both men traveled widely and often did not see each other for long periods of time. Writing was their prime method of communication. For Copland especially, correspondence was his principal connection to the outside world, as telephoning may have been for others. Copland's writing style varies considerably depending on the recipient and date. He had an innate talent for what was appropriate, both in musical and literary pursuits. Always aware of his audience, he could adapt to a wide range of circumstances.

Copland's confident and easygoing manner was often misleading. He was a careful person with a reticence about overt displays of emotion or speaking about himself. In conversations and interviews, he would substitute the third-person "we" or "one" for "I." Those who knew Copland well invariably described him as "a very private person." Letters, being a step away from the actual presence, provided the extra measure of privacy for Copland to write about himself and to share experiences and explore ideas. Here is an excerpt from a letter to Leonard Bernstein from Havana, Cuba. (NOTE: In the excerpts from their letters that follow, Bernstein is identified as LB, Copland as AC. Approximate dates are in brackets. Ellipses indicate cuts made by the author.)

AC: [April–May 1941]
I wish you were here to share the music with me. I have a slightly frustrated feeling in not being able to discuss it with anyone; and a sinking feeling that no one but you and I would think it so much fun. . . . I've sat for hours on end in 5¢ a dance joints, listening. Finally

the band in one place got the idea, and invited me up to the band platform. "Usted musico?" Yes, says I. What a music factory it is! Thirteen black men and me—quite a piquant scene. The thing I liked most is the quality of voice when the Negroes sing down here. It does things to me—it's so sweet and moving. And just think, no serious Cuban composer is using any of this.

clean copy. _Please_ be archi-particular about dots, dashes, dynamics, etc. — as it saves endless time later when you reach the proof-correcting stage. The sooner the better on this.

3. I have a lecture to do in Boston on the 12th (Thursday) and will probably stay over for Kouss' concert on Fri (the 13th) Where will you be then? I promised to spend Sat. (the 14th) up at Larchmont with the Bill Schumans. But if you are coming thru town then I don't want to miss seeing you. So write your plans so soon like you know them.

What did you do all week without your shaving and tooth brush?

The second movement is done. Yippee!

Work hard — but not too hard — and think of me often as do I of you

love

A.

295 Huntington Av
Boston 1941?

Faron, Liebchen, won't you come to Boston
for Quiet City, which sends it quiet
message to all loving Boston hearts
this Fri & Sat. ? Oh I know you've
heard it before; but what a good excuse
it provides! Are you too busy? No.

I never thought it possible to
miss one person so thoroughly as I have you.
And if you come — please come — won't
you bring a copy of the Buenos Aires Sonata?
My studio hungers for your blessing —
    love
    Lenny

The Early Letters

Bernstein's letters from 1938 until Harvard graduation in the spring of 1939 were sent from Cambridge; Copland's mostly from New York City on Hotel Empire stationery. The earliest letters are signed with full names and are addressed to "Dear Leonard" or "Dear Aaron."

The first from Bernstein was typical—a dense and passionate four-page diatribe against almost everything, including Hitler, "a mad man strutting across borders, " and Harvard, "with these horrible musical dolls who infest the place."

LB: [March 22, 1938]
Goddammit, Aaron, why practice Chopin Mazurkas? Why practice even the Copland Variations? The week has made me so sick, Aaron, that I can't breathe anymore. The whole superfluousness of art shows up at a time like this, and the whole futility of spending your life in it. I take it seriously—seriously enough to want to be with it constantly till the day I die. But why? . . . Excuse this outburst, Aaron, but the whole concatenation of rotten, destructive things has made me very angry and disappointed. . . . Thank God for you. Our last hope is in the work you are doing.

Leonard Bernstein

AC: March 23, 1938
Dear Leonard, What a letter! What an 'outburst'! Hwat a boy! It completely spoiled my breakfast. . . . As for your general 'disappointment' in Art, Man and Life I can only advise perspective, perspective and yet more perspective. This is only 1938. Man has a long time to go. Art is quite young. Life has its own dialectic. Aren't you always curious to see what tomorrow will bring?

Of course, I understand exactly how you feel. At 21, in Paris, with Dada thumbing its nose at art, I had a spell of extreme disgust with all things human. What's the use—it can't last, and it didn't last. The next day comes, there are jobs to do, problems to solve, and one gets gradually inured to things. At my advanced age (37) I can't even take a letter like yours completely seriously. But I'm glad you wrote it, if only to let off steam. Write some more!

After hearing Copland's *El Salón México* performed by Koussevitzky and the Boston Symphony Orchestra (October 14, 1938), Bernstein wrote a letter showing remarkable insight into the range of Copland's work.[9]

LB: [October 20, 1938]

It's going to be hard to keep this from being a fan letter. The concert was gorgeous—even the Dvorak. I still don't sleep much from the pounding of [notation of phrase from El Salón México] in my head. In any event, it's a secure feeling to know we have a master in America. . . . [Clifford] Odets, true to form, thinks the Salon Mexico "light," also Mozart except the G minor Symphony. This angers me terrifically. I wish these people could see that a composer is just as <u>serious</u> when he writes a work, even if the piece is not defeatist (that Worker word again) and Weltschmerzy and misanthropic and long. "Light piece," indeed. I tremble when I think of producing something like the Salon.[10]

Bernstein's trenchant understanding of Copland's music was an important factor in Copland's acceptance of the young musician's friendship. Copland did not like being perceived as a split musical personality. "I'm only *one* me," he would say with a laugh in casual conversation. He found himself in the position of promoting the "neglected children" in his catalogue, while also protecting the popular pieces from being considered "lightweight." His colleagues preferred the Piano Variations and the *Short Symphony*. The popular pieces were almost an embarrassment to those who considered Copland the leader and the hope for American concert music. Composer and early Copland biographer Arthur Berger said, "Aaron took exception . . . to the sharp distinction I made between his music for an elite audience and his music for a larger public. He thought I was perhaps responsible for starting the whole idea of a bifurcation in his output."[11] Only the Mexican composer Carlos Chávez recognized that the composer was not divided into Copland the Serious and Copland the Popular. Chávez saw no inconsistency in conducting the premieres of such diverse pieces as the *Short Symphony* and *El Salón México*. Others, such as Elliott Carter and David Diamond, dismissed the popular side of Copland's *oeuvre*—they worried that, once in Hollywood, he would be lost to their musical world forever. Bernstein, however, argued fiercely with mutual friends that Aaron would never completely go "Hollywood."[12]

In preparation for his senior thesis before graduation in April 1939, Bernstein wrote to Copland at length with numerous questions and theories about nationalism, jazz, and American composers.

LB: [November 19, 1938]

In the midst of ten million other things I'm writing a thesis for honors . . . the subject is Nationalism in American music—presumably a nonentity but on the whole a vital problem.[13] We've talked about it once or twice. You said, "Don't worry—just write it—it will come out American—

The thesis tries to show how the stuff that the old boys turned out (Chadwick, Converse, Shepherd-Gilbert-MacD.—Cadman(!), etc.) failed utterly to develop an American style or school or music at all, because their material (Negro, American Indian, etc.) was not common—the old problem of America the melting pot. . . . I will try to show that there is something American in the newer music, which relies not on folk material, but on a native spirit (like your music, and maybe Harris + Session's [sic]—I don't know), or which relies on a new American form, like Blitzstein's. Whether this is tenable or not, it is my thesis, and I'm sticking to it.

Now how to go about it? It means going through recent American things, finding those that sound for some reason, American and translate that American sound into musical terms. I feel convinced that there is such a thing or else why is it that the Variations sound fresh and vital and not stale and European and dry?

This is where you can help, if you would. What music of what other composers in America would support my point, and where can I get hold of it? Would the music of Harris? Or Ives? Or Schuman? Or Piston? Or Berezowsky? . . .

AC: Dec 9, 1938
I know I'm late in answering but I've been swamped with things to do and your letter asked so many questions! . . . It would be so much better to do this *viva voce* than by letter, could it wait till then for my grandfatherly advice? You sound as if you were very much on the right track anyhow both as to ideas and composers' names. Don't make the mistake of thinking that just because a Gilbert used Negro material, there was therefore nothing American about it. There's always the chance it might have an 'American' quality despite its material. Also, don't try to prove too much. Composing in this country is still pretty young no matter how you look at it.

As early as his letter of 1938 about *El Salón México*, Bernstein expressed the wish to study with Copland:

I want seriously to have the chance to study with you soon. My heart's in it. Never have I come across anyone capable of such immediate absorption of musical material, possessing at the same time a fine critical sense with the ability to put that criticism into words—successfully. This is not rot. The little demonstration you gave with those early things of mine proved it to me conclusively.

Bernstein became Copland's only private student over a long period, and Copland was Bernstein's only real composition teacher. Their exchanges were often by mail, but also when Bernstein came to New York City they played piano four-hands, including Copland pieces from score before publication, among them *Billy the Kid*, *Rodeo*, and the Clarinet Concerto. Copland said, "It's funny; in the beginning I didn't take him very seriously as a composer, because he could do everything, and that was just one more thing that Lenny could do."

Bernstein showed Copland all of his early works, but "now, he'd think it would be more natural for me to bring what I was writing to him!"[14] It is surprising to consider a time when Leonard Bernstein needed help to find employment. Copland contacted several associates in the music world, but success came only from his publisher, Boosey & Hawkes, who agreed to pay Bernstein twenty-five dollars for a piano reduction of *El Salón México*.[15]

Copland offered to split the royalties.

LB: [August 29, 1939]
No jobs No future
Two momentous things
I've just finished the Salón México reduction—it's fine.
I've just finished my Hebrew song for mezz sop. and ork. I think it's my best score so far (not much choice). It was tremendous fun.
Under separate cover, as they say, I'm sending the Lamentation for yr. dictum. Please look at it sort of carefully—it actually means much to me. Of course, no one will ever sing it—it's too hard, and who wants to learn all those funny words? . . .
I'm not sending the <u>Saloon</u>, as you couldn't read my hasty script, anyway."[16]

Copland was frequently asked about the lack of Jewish materials in his music. This critique of Bernstein's "Lamentation" reveals some of Copland's thinking on the subject:

AC: [n.d.] Thursday

Dear Lenny—Of course it's the best thing of yours I've seen so far. . . . . I like best the beginning and end (from the Andante). The middle part seems less spontaneous and somewhat stiff in the joints. You seem too busy with your motif—too intent on doing the utmost with it—and consequently a little academic about it. The beginning and end, on the other hand, are warm and obviously 'felt.' (The final twelve measures are swell.)

There are certain drawbacks, of course, to adopting a Jewish melos. People are certain to say—'Bloch'. But more serious, the general 'ambiance' is bound to sound familiar to most ears. As far as I can judge by your music thus far, you are hopelessly romantic as a composer. It was clever to have adopted the 'Jewish' manner in this piece and thereby justify the romanticism of the piece . . . But somehow, someday, that richness of feeling that I call romantic will have to be metamorphosed so that it comes out more new-sounding, more fresh.

One last criticism. Your orchestration, which is excellent in spots, nevertheless remains spotty. It doesn't seem particularly as if you had conceived it as a whole. That is, it doesn't flow smoothly— . . . And I don't like your use of the piano (don't murder me!). . . . Of course, I'll change my mind about the whole piece as soon as you play it for me. When will that be?

P.S. Write more music!

Spring and summer of 1939 found Bernstein "all wrapped up in the Cradle," Marc Blitzstein's agit-prop theatre piece, *Cradle Will Rock* [LB: Spring 1939]. Copland and Kraft took a summer place in Woodstock and became friendly with Benjamin Britten and Peter Pears who lived close by. In his letters, Bernstein agonized over his future, his education, work, living arrangements, and a wide range of personal problems. Copland responded calmly, "Don't worry . . . Something is bound to turn up." "You arouse a long dead messianic complex in me. Do you mind being saved?"

LB: [July 30, 1939]

Last night I almost wrote you a very desperate letter. I was desperate. Having to do with those in the songwriting industry is no fun. And no success. . . . The crowning disappointment was when I went up to the Juilliard School to see about a conducting fellowship and found I was a month too late for application. Can something be done? Or do I turn in desperation to the possibility of Curtis. . . . Don't worry about Messiahing me.

The Forties

The largest number of letters and the most open and intimate were written in the 1940s. Bernstein closed his writings with "I miss you terribly," or even "I miss you more than I can say" or "I miss you like my right arm." Letters came from "Philly" where he did indeed attend the Curtis Institute until graduation, when he moved to New York City and worked at Harms, Inc., music publishers. Bernstein sincerely believed that Copland was our greatest American composer. He played all the piano music and piano parts, from the Piano Variations on, and was critical of other musicians' performances; he was particularly known for the Piano Sonata, which he claimed was his favorite Copland piece.[17] Admiring as he was, Bernstein did not hesitate to criticize his mentor. Compliments, often excessive, carried a sharp edge. For example, he played the Variations for Isabelle Vengerova at Curtis and reported to Copland that she didn't like them; *El Salón México* "has a turgid and theatrical ossia at the end of the slow middle section that I tried to fix . . . which is, I'm afraid, a bit dull even in the orch. Don't take it too hard." As for Copland's Third Symphony, the final movement was full of "*plauderei*" (German for "chatter") and must thereafter be performed with the cut Bernstein had made without permission.[18] Copland patiently listened to suggestions but acted on very few of them. As much as he admired Bernstein's musical abilities and convictions, he was protective when it came to his music. He agreed to the cut in the Third Symphony on musical grounds. However, without being confrontational, Copland would quietly turn away from recommendations. About *El Salón México*, he wrote simply (May 6, 1943), "The 2-piano Salon is out . . . It looks very pretty . . . But V[Victor] is upset because you (we) forgot to add the dedication!" And when Copland did not respond to the following, Bernstein wrote again. Still no answer.

LB [1941?]
Aaron—I never thought it possible! I have just conceived an idea for a piano version of Billy. It would be a kind of paraphrase in the style of the Liszt ones (formally only, I mean), probably a messy juxtaposition of tunes; but I think I can make it work by fooling around with it a little. You likee? You thinkee Boosee likee?

Performances were also targeted for criticism.

LB [1942?]

Just a few words apropos of the Lincoln Portrait performance. . . . Koussevitzky didn't do as well by it as I had expected. The opening was too agitated because he divided his beats—there was no feeling of tranquility and space. He missed a few cues (or passed them up) like "disenthrall" ourselves; and usually simply waited for the end of a speech and then played music. But the sum total was good—the impression was very exciting, and the audience was charmed. Why must you be in Hollywood? Although, after the parade of bowing composers (Billy + Barber) [William Schuman and Samuel Barber] it was very distinguished of you not to be present—a sort of special-ness, you know. It's a fine piece, my love, despite all the repetition.

Bernstein attended performances while Copland was on his first long tour of South American countries in 1941 for the State Department, fol-lowed by extended periods in Hollywood to compose music for the films *Of Mice and Men* and *The North Star*. Bernstein reported to Copland about performances, among them his own of the Piano Sonata. John Kirkpatrick played the premiere, but when Bernstein performed it for the Town Hall Music Forum in February 1943, he played the Sonata twice on the same program and later recorded it. Bernstein was searching for opportuni-ties to conduct and wrote to Copland, "God, I want much." Six months before Bernstein's famous conducting debut, Copland wrote, "Don't for-get our party line—you're heading for conductoring in a big way—and everybody and everything that doesn't lead there is an excrescence on the body politic" [May 6, 1943]. Copland was so sure of Bernstein's tal-ent that he showed little surprise at Bernstein's dramatic success with the New York Philharmonic in 1943. Bernstein was disappointed; he had always looked to Copland for approval, as he wrote ca. 1942: "I'll prove myself to you yet!" For once, Copland's equanimity irritated him.

In 1944, Copland returned to Mexico and wrote eloquent descrip-tions of the small town he and Victor inhabited.

AC: August 11, 1944

Peggy's sister Heather brought us to Tepoztlan, and we fell for it. I was saying to Victor the other day what an amazing experience it would be for you to take a plane and come directly here with no stopover in Mexico City. It would be like stepping off into the middle ages. . . . All this settling in has taken endless time and energy. It makes no sense unless I settle here for life. I would at that, except that it's impossible to get a New York Times ever. And what about you? Have you written me all? You'd better.

Copland had introduced Bernstein to his friends and colleagues. Many became his young friend's supporters. Bernstein had a driving need to be the center of attention for everyone. First and foremost was Koussevitzky; eventually he and "Lenushka" became as close as father and surrogate son. Similarly, after Copland put him in touch with Nadia Boulanger, from not knowing her at all, Bernstein was the one at her bedside when she died.[19] Copland's friends became Bernstein's—David Diamond, Claire Reis, Frankie and Bill Schuman, Verna and Irving Fine, and Peggy Bernier. Bernstein soon made himself known to Copland's friend "Benjie" Britten. When Copland was in Hollywood, Bernstein even tried to be part of Victor Kraft's life. They played squash and Bernstein convinced Kraft to go to California to be with Copland, writing to say that it would be good for both of them and "I wish it could be me." Copland did not seem disturbed or displaced by Lenny's takeovers. In fact, he enjoyed sharing anecdotes and experiences about Koussevitzsky ("Kouss," "Koussie," or "the Boss") and their many summers at Tanglewood.

The only hint of annoyance was in connection with Peggy Bernier. Copland had mentioned her in a letter to Bernstein, and was later surprised to receive a note from the south of France, the top half signed "Peggy," the lower half "Lenny":

Peggy Bernier: [n.d., end forties]
Well what do you know . . . that Lenny Bernstein bought himself a grey silk dressing gown in Barcelona, and off to Marjorca he went with his sister and Peggy Riley . . . he sings Copland . . . and I listen and remember . . . Actually I came on this trip on condition that he sound like Aaron at least once a day. Which he does. In fact we are all being Aaron so much of the time that we thought you should know about it . . . sent with just as much love as ever from Peggy

LB:
Dearest Judge-Nose of them all,
Well what do you know . . . Armed with that Peggy Riley Rosamond Margaret Rosenbaum Bernier and that intrepid Shirley Bern[stein] and a brand new dachshund named Henry and filled with corridas and flamencos and Spanish fly we have betaken our weary selves to a cove, very <u>intime</u>, no competition as Peggy puts it, and spend all

our time reenacting Aaronisms and giving out with Aaroniana and swimming and . . . curing our sundry neurotic diseases . . . and we suddenly decided that very little in life moves us as much as Aaron Copland. . . . Lensk

AC: October 2, 1950
So you're in Eze, eh? . . . Is Peggy still on the Riviera? If so, give her my love. I hope to see her in Paris in May—or maybe in Rome before that?

LB: [1951]
Seen Peggy? No letter from her rather perplexes me. My love to her if you see or write her.

Letters from the Fifties

From the time of Bernstein's debut with the New York Philharmonic, he was never again out of work—invitations came from all over the globe. Copland also traveled for long periods of time—another South American tour, lecture and teaching engagements. Letters took a long time to reach their destination and sometimes were forwarded or lost in transit. Bernstein wrote from Israel:

LB: May 21, 1950
So much time goes by: I don't know you any more—not even through your music, which is not exactly forthcoming. I played your violin sonata with a fine fiddler here the other day, and had a real old-fashioned nostalgic kick. Those faraway days when the C♯ was holy and the form so surprisingly right. Where's your music? God knows we need it. There hasn't been a real exciting American premiere in years. . . . What's up? Movies? Dickinson? A piano concerto? Eric + Victor: You?[20]

Israel is lovely, weather delightful, concerts fine, Heifetz in top form, Roy Harris 3rd successful, the people gay & forward-looking. I miss you.

AC:
Why is it that when I am in Hollywood you're in N.Y. and when you're in Hollywood I'm in Mexico and—no doubt when you're in Mexico I'll be in Russia. It doesn't seem right. It's amazing how often

I think of you in this Aztec No Man's Land. Just think, not a single soul in all this town has ever heard of you or me. And I moan when I think how good it would be for you to spend a month in this utter tranquility.

As Americans moved past World War II and into the different but dangerous Cold War, many artists and intellectuals felt uneasy and anxious, reaching for security in their personal lives. Bernstein, determined to make a change in his frantic conducting life, wrote on March 15, 1951, "I'm quitting conducting next month, for at least two years. . . . I've never felt so happy and strong about a decision: it will be so good to get in contact with myself again, live a little more innerly. . . . Do I have your Papal blessing?" Copland and Bernstein became even more aware of the changing times with the death of Serge Koussevitzky in 1951. The Berkshire Music Center at Tanglewood had been their base for many years, but now the directorship of the Music Center and Tanglewood's future were uncertain.[21] There is no letter in the Bernstein or Copland Collections about the death of the man who meant so much to them.

There were other substantial changes; Copland wrote Bernstein with the news that Victor Kraft had decided to marry and live in Mexico. Victor had suffered from a lack of confidence in his work as a photographer and uncertainty about his identity. In one of the few letters from Copland to Kraft that survives, Copland expressed himself more emotionally: "I am pretty much convinced that I'm not good for you. (I get a lump in my throat as I write it)" [n.d.].[22]

Bernstein himself, who agonized about his sexual orientation, also chose marriage and family. He became engaged to Felicia Montealeagre Cohn. They married in September 1951 and for the first few years, lived in Cuernavaca, Mexico:

LB: October 18, 1951
The piano has arrived. I have written an extra aria for Captain Hook (what shit!) to grace the new road production of Peter Pants, and am now starting on the long hard road of writing some real things. . . . The main stem is still that old devil theatre, and I have to see just what my connection with it is. I still haven't seen the score of the piano quartet, and long to. Isn't there something you can do?

What word from Victor? Does he find marriage as fascinating as I do (what a word for marriage)? Actually it is the most interesting thing I have ever done, though there are times when one's interest must be that of a person in an audience, or one would go mad. It is full of compensations and rewards, and reveals more to me about myself than anything else ever has, including a spotty array of analysis. . . . Dear old Judge-nose, I miss you.

In 1951, Copland stayed in Cambridge to work on the Charles Eliot Norton Lectures he was to deliver during the 1951–52 academic year at Harvard. Stravinsky and Hindemith had delivered Norton Lectures, but this was the first time a native-born composer had been chosen for the Poetry Chair. Copland's Norton Lectures were published as the book *Music and Imagination*.[23]

AC: November 5, 1951
These old Norton Lectures are paralyzing all my other activities—including letter writing. It was wonderful to hear from you. Wouldn't want you to be completely swallowed up by marriage! . . . Every stone in Cambridge reminds me of you. Also I.B. Cohen at the Faculty Club. . . . Did you hear the recording of the Piano Quartet on the back side of the Clar. Concerto? . . . I'm jealous of you in Cuernavaca. (Have you seen my house in Tepotzlan yet?)

The November 14, 1952, birthday letter was a reminder that the two composers had met fifteen years earlier and that Bruno Walter had celebrated Copland's birthday "most spectacularly eight years ago by getting sick." When the Bernsteins went to purchase a phonograph in Mexico they found the recording mentioned by Copland of the Clarinet Concerto and Piano Quartet.[24]

LB: [1952]
I am disappointed in the Concerto, and I think it may be a little on account of the performance. I remember it as being so much fun when you struggled with it on the piano (of course everything is more fun when YOU do it on the piano with your apologetic grin), and Benny's performance is ghastly and student-like, I think. But there is also something that does quite satisfy about the score, despite its evident beauties. The opening is still ravishing, and I find to my dismay that it is in places less like Satie than like the Rosenkavalier trio. *Tant mieux,* say I, though surprised not a little. Strange, in fact, how many touches of Strauss there are: there is even a slight Don Quixote feeling here and there. I still disapprove of the cadenza, finding it cute but arbitrary, but it is the last part that disappoints me because the last part was so much fun. Of all things, the form doesn't seem to work.

But the quartet, ah there is another matter. I rejoice particularly in the scherzo, because I think it is the longest sustained piece
of continuity you have written in a long time, and it is really continuous, yes really, and it goes and goes in a remarkably convincing
way. I feel rather close to the tonal way in which you are handling
tone-rows (I've done it too, here and there), and I find that this
movement is a real triumph. The last movement is beautiful too in
a way which has already become awfully familiar to Coplandites, so
that it is not such a thrill as the second. And the first is lovely but I
never did go for you and fugues, especially here where the opening is so reminiscent of the third Hindemith Quartet. Imagine,
Hindemith: Who'da thunk it? but it makes a fine piece, especially
for records, because you want to hear it again and again (of course
with two or three mambos in between). And I still think you are a
marvelous composer.

Dear Aa, it was a real joy to have your letter and I miss you and
hope you will continue to write and have a long happy life and write
zillions more like the Piano Quartet.

Bernstein's letter contradicts the usual impression that he was totally
against serialism and particularly Copland's use of the twelve-tone method.
Bernstein's Norton Lectures in 1973 affirmed his belief that tonality is a
basic premise of all music.

Copland continued as director of the Music Center at Tanglewood.
Bernstein spent most summers at the family home in Martha's Vineyard.

LB: July 19, 1954
I miss you. That's the long + the short of it. I don't miss Berlioz or
the crowds or the pewpils or the scenery or the meetings on the
green, green furniture of Seranak, or even the hot crowded Monday
Forums. I miss you, ecco. And Lukas. I want to hear about things
like how the Piano Concerto (yours) went . . . and dirty gossip, and
what of next year, and how is Tender Land going. Me, I stay on this
heavenly island, intending never to leave except to Venice for a week
in Sept to conduct my new piece with Isaac. It's finished, imagine,
and all orchestrated except for the finale. Man, I need you around
for some solid criticism. . . . Candide crawls along: it's the hardest
thing I ever tried, and—you won't believe this—it's very hard trying
to be eclectic.

Following Koussevitzky's death, Copland began to conduct more—the maestro never wanted his protégé to take time away from composition. When asked how he learned to conduct, Copland said that "Lenny" gave him some tips and told him to study. By the end of the decade, Copland was conducting his first pair of concerts with the Boston Symphony Orchestra while Charles Munch was on vacation. "What would dear old Kouss have said?" In about 1959 Bernstein saw Copland conduct on television:

LB: [n.d.]
Man, you've improved incredibly! Clarity, meaningfulness of beat, ass not extruding. Only problem: die head too much in die score. You must to know die musik better (or at least trust yourself more). But the big thrill was hearing the Symphony #1 again—what a scherzo! Want to succeed me at the Philh?

Letters: The Sixties

Letters were sent from various destinations during the sixties. From London, Copland wrote, commenting on the lack of American music on Bernstein's programs. "Maybe you could squeeze in ten minutes worth in front of the Mahler—what do you think?" Several exchanges were made between them as Copland's sixtieth birthday neared. Copland wrote, "Listen—just in case you're still mulling over birthday shindigs— Bill Schuman has 'reserved' Nov 14."

LB: [1959/60?]
I have a better idea, which is something nobody else can do for your 60th, and that is to make a whole TV show for the kids [the Young Peoples' Concerts with the New York Philharmonic] on the subject of the Venerable Giggling Dean. Imagine, Judge-Nose for one hour, coast-to-coast. This will happen on the 12th of November at noon in Carnegie Hall, and probably be telecast the following day. I want you to participate, do you hear?! Either to conduct a piece, or play the piano, or maybe narrate the Lincoln piece, or maybe conduct same with me sixty other conflicting homages on the same day.

I sorely miss T'wood also. My love to it, and its inmates. No, I haven't written a note.

Copland appeared on Bernstein's television program as planned, November 12, 1960. When Lenny told the young people that he felt he could have written Copland's music himself, his elder friend's quick retort was "Yes, but he didn't—I did!"

Bernstein had a history with Copland's opera for young people, *The Second Hurricane*. He had produced it many years earlier when still at Harvard. In 1960 it was revised by Bernstein as a television production, and a recording was about to be released.

LB: [1960]

Today I must write, because last night I heard the test-pressing of the 2nd Hurricane recording which will be out in time for your birthday. It's badly engineered in places, especially when there is choral complexity . . . —but in general I think you'll be delighted. Of course it's similar to the TV version, with me narrating, reserving a line or two of dialogue here and there, and cutting "Fat's Song" plus 2 other small cuts. But mainly I'm writing because I'm so impressed all over again with the music. It is lovely and endlessly fresh. Neither the simplicity nor the grandeur stales. Felicia loves it; Jamie and Alexander sing it marvelously by the yard. I hope you like it; it will be our November release on Columbia, along with Billy and Rodeo, making a delightful, gay, (though costly) birthday package!

When the New York Philharmonic commissioned Aaron Copland to compose a piece for the inauguration of the orchestra's new hall at Lincoln Center, Copland knew he was Leonard Bernstein's choice. The score of *Connotations* is dedicated to him. Copland was determined to compose an important work for the gala premiere [September 23, 1963]. He thought back to Koussevitzky asking for a "big piece" when the *Symphonic Ode* and Third Symphony were commissioned, and he aimed for a brassy extroverted sound that would reflect the contemporary architecture of the new building and the future of the performing arts center in New York City. *Connotations* was Copland's first twelve-tone work for orchestra. Whatever Copland expected, it was not the almost dead silence of the first-night audience and the negativity of the critics, who were almost unanimous in rejection of the work. A recording of the world premiere was not the best quality, but it was the only recording of this important Copland work for thirty years. Copland responded to a question of why he composed severe and unfriendly pieces: "You have to be pretty convinced about what you are doing; otherwise, there are many reasons for not doing it! No financial gain, no good criticism in the papers the next morning. You really have to be brave in that sense, and the bravery comes from the conviction."[25]

Copland was confident in his use of the twelve-tone method and used it again a few years later for another commission from Bernstein and the Philharmonic, this time the 125th anniversary of the orchestra.

AC: [August 2, 1967]:
Dear Lensk, Just finished the new piece for the 125th. Thought you'd like to know! I'm calling it <u>Inscape</u>. Of course I don't have to explain to you "vhat dot means"—but everybody else wants to know. Lasts about 12 min., and ends, (Oy)—quietly. I plan to be at the rehearsals. . . . Will we have a chance to giggle over the pages together? Or do you step right off the plane to the hall?? I can't wait to hear <u>you</u> do it.

The reviews following the premiere (September 13, 1967) were mixed. Bernstein, never convinced Copland should be using the twelve-tone method, nevertheless played and recorded *Inscape* and wrote his November 14 birthday letter.

AC: [November 17, 1967]
What a beautiful letter you wrote me for my birthday! I shall treasure it always. And what a deep satisfaction it is for me to know that we've sustained our feeling for each other all these many years. It's a joy—that's what it is. And just imagine what it means to me to see you prepare and conduct my music with such devotion and love and musical sensitivity.

When Bernstein turned fifty, Copland wrote from Tanglewood:

AC: August 26, 1968
Tanglewood, where your spirit hovers. But it always hovers, wherever I go. American music would have a different 'face' without you. Have a good tour—and always and always I love you dearly!

Aaron

Late Letters

A break between Copland and Bernstein came when Bernstein wrote a tribute in *Hi-Fidelity* magazine in honor of his friend's seventieth birthday. Bernstein's familiar pattern of praising with more than faint criticism is repeated here—but to publish it as a birthday commemoration (of all things) was to hurt Copland and cause a rift between them. In the article, Bernstein traces the "Schoenberg syndrome, embraced by the young, who gradually stopped flocking to Aaron. . . . The effect on him—and therefore on American music—was heartbreaking. He is, after all, one of the most important composers of our century. . . . The truth is that when the musical winds blew past him, he tried to catch up—with 12-tone music—just as it was becoming old-fashioned to the young. . . . Happy Birthday, Aaron. We miss your music."[26]

No apology followed. Nor was there a confrontation. In five years, Bernstein wrote an article in honor of Copland's seventy-fifth. This time, he lavished unreserved praise on all of Copland's output, making special mention of the Piano Variations: "From *Billy the Kid* to *Inscape*, from *El Salón México* to the *Nonet*, those *Variations* are the key. . . . I love all this music, in all its degrees of severity and charm."[27]

AC: July 1, 1975
Dear Lensk! I've just read your piece for the fourth time! I'm delighted—moved—touched—overwhelmed—It's so brilliantly conceived and executed that I can only hope it is all true. But true or not it's a prose poem that only you could write—and I bless you for it.

A few letters followed. Copland apologized for not coming to Bernstein's "Songfest" due to a snowstorm—"After all, I am 77!" Another, from September 5, 1978, expressed deep regret that he could not attend the "Remembrance" for Felicia, Bernstein's wife, who had died after a long and difficult illness.

As Copland's Alzheimer's disease accelerated in the 1980s, his activities became increasingly limited and his letters to Bernstein ended. Bernstein's last letter to Copland was written fifty years since they first met.

LB: November 14, 1988
My Dearest Aaron:
May God, wherever he is, bless you today and every day forever—
All my Love, Lenny

Both composers died in 1990 within a few months: Bernstein October 14, Copland December 5. "A Concert Remembering Lenny" was held at Carnegie Hall. Fittingly the date was November 14, Aaron Copland's birthday and the anniversary of their first meeting—history had come full circle. The event was an extraordinary musical and personal outpouring to the "superstar" of American music—as in life, Bernstein took center stage, while Copland's presence was felt from behind the scenes, as he marked the occasion of his ninetieth birthday at home.

This remarkable correspondence immediately conjures images of Aaron and Lenny, in their lives apart, and as they were together—icons of American music. They are tangible reminders that it is the details of life that make history—Copland's beret, Bernstein's cuff links. The letters are filled with information and rich with commentary. But their most distinctive feature is the expression of loyalty and affection that places this correspondence among the most notable and touching of our times.

Copland and Bernstein at Tanglewood, 1985. Photo by Walter H. Scott.

NOTES

Oral History, American Music (hereafter OHAM) at Yale University contains an extensive archive of recorded materials on Aaron Copland. These include the following: 15 hours of recorded oral history interviews with the composer (342 pages of transcript), Peekskill, N.Y., 1975, 1976; 1978, 1979, 1982; 24 hours of acquired interviews (some transcribed); 67 interviews with those who knew Copland, 1984 to l987; 4 hours of video interviews, 1976, 1982, 1984; master tapes for 1985 television documentary *Copland: A Self-Portrait* (outtakes donated to Library of Congress); photographs; and miscellaneous research materials.

    1. Virgil Thomson, "Aaron Copland (American Composers VII)," *Modern Music* 9, no. 2 (January–February 1932): 67–73.

    2. For Copland and politics, see Aaron Copland and Vivian Perlis, *Copland: 1900 Through 1942* (New York: St. Martin's/Marek, 1984), Interlude III, pp. 217–30.

    3. Among his many younger composer colleagues, Copland was close to Arthur Berger, Irving Fine, Lukas Foss, and William Schuman.

    4. Rosamond Bernier was Peggy Rosenbaum when she met Copland in Mexico while on college vacation in 1936. See Rosamond Bernier interview by Vivian Perlis, New York City, February 3, 1983, OHAM, edited for Copland and Perlis, *Copland: 1900–1942*, pp. 266–69.

    5. Quoted in Copland and Perlis, *Copland: 1900–1942*, p. 217; originally in George Orwell, "Inside the Whale," in *The Collected Essays, Journalism, and Letters of George Orwell, I: An Age Like This, 1920–1940* (London: Secker & Warburg, 1968), p. 510.

    6. Harold Clurman interview by Perlis, New York, May 20, 1979, OHAM.

    7. Leonard Bernstein interview by Perlis, Fairfield, Conn., September 22, 1983, OHAM, edited for Copland and Perlis, *Copland: 1900–1942*, pp. 334–41. Also Copland and Bernstein video interview by Perlis, Washington, D.C., 1979, excerpted in the television documentary *Copland: A Self-Portrait*, coproduced by Ruth Leon and Vivian Perlis, directed by Allan Miller, PBS, 1985. Bernstein also tells the story in *Findings* (New York: Simon & Schuster, 1982), pp. 284–91.

    8. Segments of the Copland and Bernstein letters were published in Humphrey Burton, *Leonard Bernstein* (New York: Doubleday, 1994) and Howard Pollack, *Aaron Copland: The Life and Work of an Uncommon Man* (New York: Henry Holt, 1999). The author is grateful to the Leonard Bernstein Estate for permission to read the correspondence in its entirety and to publish segments of the letters in this article.

    9. See Lawrence Starr, "Copland's Style," *Perspectives of New Music* 19 (1980–1982): 68–89; and Aaron Copland, "The Story Behind 'El Salón México,'" *Victor Record Review* 1, no. 22 (1939): 4–5. Conductor Michael Tilson Thomas has addressed the issue of stylistic similarities in various Copland pieces; for example, Copland Workshop, Zankel Hall, New York City, November 19, 2003.

    10. See facsimile of Bernstein's letter to Copland about the 1938 performance of El Salón México in Copland and Perlis, *Copland: 1900–1942*, p. 249.

    11. Arthur Berger interview by Perlis, Cambridge, Mass., November 13, 1981, OHAM, quoted in Aaron Copland and Vivian Perlis, *Copland Since 1943* (New York: St. Martin's Press, 1989), 209.

    12. In more recent times, the pendulum has swung in the opposite direction, with scholars and critics viewing the more accessible ballet and film music scores as essential Copland.

13. Titled "The Absorption of Race Elements into American Music," the thesis appears in full in Bernstein, *Findings*, pp. 36–99.

14. Aaron Copland interview by Perlis, Peekskill, N.Y., November 19, 1979, OHAM.

15. Bernstein also made a two-piano arrangement for Boosey & Hawkes. In 1935 pianist John Kirkpatrick, who arranged several Copland works, made a two-piano version of *El Salón México* before Bernstein's commission from Boosey & Hawkes. See John Kirkpatrick Papers, Yale Music Library, New Haven.

16. Copland and Bernstein referred to *El Salón México* as "The Saloon" or "The Old Saloon." Boosey & Hawkes did not receive the Bernstein reduction until many months after this letter was written.

17. Bernstein interview by Perlis, September 22, 1983.

18. See facsimile of letter, Bernstein to Copland, May 27, 1947, about conducting the Third Symphony in Prague, Aaron Copland and Vivian Perlis, *Copland Since 1943*, p. 70.

19. For a description see Bruno Monsaingeon, *Mademoiselle, Conversations with Nadia Boulanger* (Paris: Carcanet Press Limited, 1985), pp. 117–19.

20. "Eric" was Erik Johns, Copland's partner for several years during the 1950s. Johns was a dancer and painter, and worked with Copland as librettist for *The Tender Land* under the pseudonym Horace Everett.

21. For the Tanglewood years see Copland and Perlis, *Copland: 1900–1942*, Interlude IV, pp. 305–20.

22. Facsimile of segment from Copland to Victor Kraft to be published in Vivian Perlis and Libby Van Cleve, *Voices of America's Musical Century*, vol. 1 (New Haven: Yale University Press, Fall 2005).

23. Aaron Copland, *Music and Imagination* (Cambridge, Mass.: Harvard University Press, 1952).

24. The recording was released by Columbia Masterworks (ML 4421) in 1951 and contains the Clarinet Concerto performed by Benny Goodman with the Columbia Orchestra conducted by Copland, and the Piano Quartet performed by the New York Quartet.

25. Aaron Copland interview by Perlis, Peekskill, N.Y., March 9, 1976, OHAM.

26. Leonard Bernstein, "Aaron Copland at 70: An Intimate Sketch," *Hi-Fidelity*, November 1970: reprinted in Bernstein, *Findings*, pp. 284–91.

27. "Aaron and Moses: Copland at 75," *Schwann Catalog* June 25, 1975: reprinted in Bernstein, *Findings*, pp. 314–16.

Aaron Copland and Arthur Berger

in Correspondence

EDITED AND INTRODUCED BY WAYNE D. SHIRLEY

"Write a guy—no?" Copland asks Arthur Berger in a letter sent from Cannes in July 1955. The correspondence between the two composers is consistently interesting and often revelatory. Seeing Berger as an astute and articulate critic of his music, Copland comments on his works more freely to Berger than he does to other correspondents. And Berger's opinion—valuing the thornier scores over the more accessible—is important to Copland: Copland's joke in a letter to Leonard Bernstein that his *Letter from Home* will be "too distingué for P[aul] W[hiteman, who commissioned the piece] and not distingué enough for the Arthur Bergers of this world" is a compliment in disguise.[1] It is not an accident that when Copland dedicated his *Twelve Poems of Emily Dickinson* to "twelve composer friends" he chose to honor Arthur Berger with the final song, "The Chariot," in which the creator ascends to heaven.

What follows is the entire extant correspondence between Aaron Copland and Arthur Berger.[2] Copland's side of the correspondence is preserved in the Arthur Berger Collection at the New York Public Library for the Performing Arts; Berger's side in the Aaron Copland Collection in the Music Division of the Library of Congress.[3]

Some letters from this correspondence clearly did not survive. Copland tended to shed letters he received while traveling, thus that of Esther Berger of January 1951 with the "B.B. vituperations," received while Copland was at the American Academy in Rome and referred to in his letter of March 2, 1951, is no longer extant. We do not know whether "B.B." was Benjamin Britten, what the vituperations were, or whether it was one of the Bergers or B.B. who did the vituperating. But while they were not traveling both Copland and Berger had the instinct to preserve letters (and file them rationally, which is so useful to the student of correspondence.)

The back-and-forth between two composers of similar but not identical musical points of view gives a flavor of musical life that the "Selected Letters" of a single figure cannot provide.

As the years go on the correspondence becomes less frequent. This is partly the result of technological progress: long-distance telephoning became less of an extravagance and more of a regular way of communication. It also reflects the fact that both Copland's and Berger's lives increasingly involved much more routine correspondence—Berger as a member of a university faculty, Copland as a board member of several institutions. The opening of Copland's letter to Berger of November 20, 1964—"I haven't received a letter like yours from anyone in years!"—reflects Copland's nostalgia for the old days of long, interesting letters. His apology later in the same letter—"I should love to reply in kind, but the naked truth is that I am swamped with things to do in the next few weeks"—attests to the fact that for Copland such replies were things of the past.

Aaron Copland and Arthur Berger, August 1954. Photo courtesy Ellen Berger.

All letters here are presented complete, save for secretarial notations of address of recipient ("Mr. Aaron Copland // R.F.D. 1 // Peekskill // New York // AB/ds."). Thus a series of dots in the text is always the writer's punctuation, never an indication of omissions to the text. Series of dots in the footnotes, on the other hand, are editorial. Typos have been silently corrected: otherwise spelling is as it appears in the letters ("inclosure," "memoires"). We have also respected Copland's habitual omission of apostrophes when he wants to sound informal—("And of course theres always Modern Music"). No attempt has been made to impose on the correspondence the Princeton University Press's style manual concerning titles of pieces, books, and periodicals. ("Billy and Our Town, and somewhat in Lincoln.") Postscripts have been placed at the end of the letter, wherever they may appear in the original. Editorial additions appear in brackets.

Annotations assume that the reader knows the basic facts of Copland's life and works but cannot always remember what happened when. They assume less knowledge of Berger's career, but do not attempt a detailed biography. At the time of Copland's first letters Berger was a student of Walter Piston; during 1941 he was teaching at Mills College; from the later 1940s to 1953 he was earning a living as music critic for the New York *Sun* (to 1946) and *Herald Tribune* (1946–53). In 1953 Berger, the self-proclaimed "pathological New Yorker" (letter of March 10, 1941) moved to Cambridge, Massachusetts, where he lived for the remainder of his life. He taught at Brandeis University in Waltham until his retirement in 1980; he died in 2003.

1. Copland to Bernstein, August 25, 1944, Leonard Bernstein Collection, Music Division, Library of Congress.

2. Three items that might be considered part of the correspondence have been omitted for considerations of space: two letters of Esther Berger to Copland (neither of them about the "B.B. vituperations" Copland mentions in his letter of March 2, 1951) and a letter of Berger's to the members of the advisory board of *Perspectives in New Music*. These three items are in Aaron Copland Collection, Music Division, Library of Congress.

3. The writer thanks the staff of both these institutions. He especially thanks George Boziwick of the New York Public Library and Kevin LaVine of the Library of Congress, both of whom went far beyond the usual standards of librarianly helpfulness (which is high in both institutions) in assisting with this paper. He also wishes to thank the Aaron Copland Fund for Music and Ellen Berger for giving permission to publish this correspondence; to Carol Oja for encouragement and suggestions; to George Boziwick for photocopies; and the Princeton University Press for agreeing that, as a "document" rather than a paper, this correspondence could be printed *in extenso*.

Copland to Berger
Typed postcard, postmarked May 23, 1933, New York NY 12

Last get-together[1] of season—Saturday at 8:30—60 Washington Mews. . . .
No polemics if possible. . . . First public performance of Copland's "Short
Symphony."[2] Bring your own latest opuses if you like. No destructive
criticism invited, only the other kind

A.C.

1. That is, of the Young Composers Group, led by Copland, which included, besides Berger, Henry Brant, Israel Citkowitz, Lehman Engel, Vivian Fine, Irwin Heilner, Bernard Herrmann, Jerome Moross, Elie Siegmeister, and, "for a while at the beginning," Paul Bowles. Arthur Berger, *Reflections of an American Composer* (Berkeley: University of California Press, 2002), p. 29.

2. Perhaps in a version for piano: certainly not a full-scale performance complete with Heckelphon.

Copland to Berger
Handwritten letter

Lavinia, Minn.

Aug 6 1934

Dear Arthur:

Duly flattered at your starting your 'series' with the Variations.[1] What
else are you planning to take up—why cant we use one of the series in
'Modern Music'?

The Variations were written during 1930, though I had the initial
germ as early as 1928. In January of 1930 I took a house in Bedford, New
York and lived there until July. I remember working very concentratedly
on them during those six months. There was more work in Yaddo during Aug–Nov. 1. of that year. I played it for the first time in N.Y. at a League
Sunday afternoon concert in January 1931. (It has never been performed
in Berlin.) Martha Graham heard it at that concert. While its true that I
did not play from notes at that concert and even did not have it written
down in a <u>definitive</u> version (i.e., in ink), what I played was essentially
the present printed version with two exceptions [:] the dynamics were less
varied, and one of the variations near the end was recast in a somewhat
different form—also to vary the dynamic scheme. (Virgil Thomson still
thinks I play it too 'hard'!) That first version was written down—Martha
Graham uses it for her Dythrambic(?)[2]

The second American performance was at that Yaddo Festival. (There had been one in England in Dec. 1931.) At Yaddo, for the first time, I had the impression that the audience was 'getting it.'

I think it important in connection with the Variations that you point out that, as happens with so much American music, it has been heard only by the 'inner circle.' It has never been performed in N.Y. in the ordinary musical channels and has never been written about (or heard, to my knowledge) by any of those first-line music critics who never tire of generalizing about 'our American music.'

Glad to hear you were satisfied with Yaddo,—and that Yaddo (sic.)[3] was satisfied with you.

Always
Aaron

1. Berger's article "The Piano Variations of Aaron Copland," in *The Musical Mercury* 1, no. 3 (August–September 1934): 85–86. Berger was the editor of the magazine, and the article was meant to be the first of a series on American composers. The next issue (October–November 1934) contained an article by Berger on the songs of Charles Ives; the series ceased after this.

2. Copland is questioning the spelling of "Dithyrambic," not the accuracy of the statement.

3. Copland's "(sic.)," not an editorial one. "Yaddo was satisfied with you": Berger had reviewed an earlier Yaddo festival for the New York *Daily Mirror* (*Reflections of an American Composer*, p. 30): perhaps he had been thanked for his favorable review.

Copland to Berger
Handwritten letter on Hotel Empire stationery. From the context it is clear that the year is 1939, even though another hand has dated the letter, in pencil, "41."

March 26

Dear Arthur—

Your letter came at a very busy time for me—so busy in fact, that its taken me almost a month to get around to acknowledging it! Sorry—but I know you'll understand.

The book[1] is out—the opera[2] isn't. Since seeing you I've finished a ballet for Kirstein (which they are doing here with orchestra on May 20);[3]—an "Outdoor Overture" for high school orchestra;—stage music for Orson Welles 'Five Kings' Shakespeare;[4]—and now I'm busy completing a movie score for a Steiner film[5] and stage music for Irwin Shaw's "Quiet City." You can see its been a busy winter. . . .

By all means use my name in any applications you like. As far as knowing about jobs that are open—there is faint hope of that as most people connect me with composers only. However I'll keep my ears open.

If you are in N.Y. next winter I shall do my best to get you a column on the New Republic. They've had nothing about music since P. Rosenfeld left. (BH Haggin is ensconced in the Nation—so theres no hope there.) And of course theres always Modern Music.

Since you're coming home in another month or so I won't bother to write mere gossip and news. Look forward to seeing you both on your return.

Always

Aaron

1. *What to Listen for in Music* (New York and London: McGraw Hill, 1939).

2. *The Second Hurricane*; "out" in this context means "published," not "performed." C.C. Birchard was in the process of publishing the score.

3. *Billy the Kid*. The first performance with orchestra was actually May 24.

4. That is, Orson Welles's condensation of Shakespeare's history plays to a single evening.

5. Ralph Steiner's *The City*.

Berger to Copland
Typed letter, 1941

Mar. 10

Dear Aaron:

I have heard "The Second Hurricane" for the first time. I was in Boston when it was first given in N.Y. and I have hitherto relied on the piano score, of which I have been quite fond. But the orchestration in its simple and direct way has many delightful surprises and adds considerably to my fondness of this little work of yours. My wife heard the N.Y. performance, and found that this performance, as one might expect, fell considerably short of the New York one.[1] For a refugee, Goldschmitt caught on to the American spirit of the music to a considerable degree and conducted with much zeal. The word emphasis, however, was rather poor. The versification is so direct and so well underlined by the music, that there is little reason why every word should not be understood. Yet, even knowing the words, I often found them hard to distinguish. Some of the delightful syncopations, such as wonDERful did not come off, being sung rather as dotted quarter and eighth.

I have had occasion to lecture on and analyze (!) your little opera, and always found myself enjoying it, especially when I could illustrate—

singing in my New Yorkese, which I think is rather the quintessence of your musical prosody and emphasis. I neglected to tell my students, however, that the social content of your work (quote Siegmeister) is a plea for solidarity, nor do I think any of the S.F.[2] audience got this. Or maybe a few got the allusions to the organizer. (I hope you realize that I have a very broad grin on as I write these things.)

I had the curious experience of witnessing, in public performance the other day, a work I have written for woodwind quartet in three movements.[3] Members of the S.F. Symphony played it and did a fairly good job considering that they worked very little. I say I felt curious, first because I'm still not used to the idea of myself as a composer—altho I like what I'm doing now better than anything I've done before with music. I'm used to being on the sidelines while my friends compose. Also strange is the business of visualizing what something will sound like, and whether the instruments can play what you write. I was pleased to see that my visualization was not far off and that there were no notes the instruments could not play.

The quartet is to be played again at the Composers Forum along with three Yeats songs—the first of which I showed you last summer. You objected that the songs didn't show off the voice enough. The other two songs make up somewhat for this lack. And also, since they are now scored for flute, clarinet, bassoon and violin, the soloist is in a sense much less a soloist, but one chamber musician in a chamber ensemble. The Forum will make recordings of these works at the performance on long playing discs,[4] and I am going to try to get my works re-recorded on small discs.

A difficult situation has come up here. Esther and I have been very friendly with the Milhaud's, we like them very much and they have acted as if they like us. Milhaud's salary has been paid by Mrs. Coolidge, who will not however, continue to do so next year. Milhaud and I have been teaching much the same work, and since Mills can pay for only one of us, it is quite natural that Milhaud and not myself will be retained. I hope you understand that I do not bear any personal grudge against Milhaud. This is a social problem which far exceeds individuals. It is the duty of society to provide a more stable base for refugees than merely a year's salary following which they are left high and dry.

In the meantime, the prospect of returning east is at once attractive and, if I remain without a job, frightening. I do not feel altogether comfortable out here. I seem to have my roots cut off. On the other hand, the peace of mind, the free time my job gives me for composing, the magnificent country, and the proximity of the Milhauds are all extenuating circumstances. But when all is told, I'm a pathological New Yorker.

Do you think I'd have a chance to get a fellowship to study with you in composition at the Berkshires this summer. I'm going to fill out blanks and also see what I can do with the Harvard people.

I've used your name as a reference in applying for college and university positions. I hope you don't mind. I think you once gave me permission to use it in the past.

Yours,

[signed] Arthur

1. That is, the first production of *The Second Hurricane*, given at the Henry Street Settlement House in New York. Its first performance was on April 21, 1937.

2. San Francisco.

3. The Quartet in C Major, written that year.

4. That is, large 78 rpm discs of the kind used for radio transcriptions: not "long-playing" in its post-1948 meaning.

----·----

Copland to Berger
Handwritten letter

Larchmont, NY
March 19 '41

Dear Arthur:

Thanks for the long letter with all the news about the Hurricane. There's something about your report that makes me feel it's the real dope about the performance. Wish I could have seen it.

I was of course rather shocked to hear the denouement of the Milhaud 'visit.' Here again, your philosophical calm is somehow more effective than the usual 'ranting.' Nevertheless it seems a pity that it should have turned out that way. Naturally, if anyone writes me for reference, they'll get it.

I'm delighted you had the idea about the Berkshires. I don't know how free they are going to be with their scholarships this year, but you've certainly got a good start towards one. (Decisions are made rather late—hope you don't mind.)

Nice about the performances of your pieces. Good or bad one's got to hear them.

I'm living up here temporarily in order to finish a book for fall publication[1]—Modern Music is what it's all about.

My best to Esther.

Aaron

1. *Our New Music: Leading Composers in Europe and America* (New York/London: McGraw Hill, 1941).

Berger to Copland
Typed letter

April 25, 1941

Dear Aaron:

Thanks for a really sympathetic letter. Nothing has turned up for me yet, but I'm starting to get used to the idea of being one of the 10,000,000 unemployed. I'm rather resigned to some such prospect as Yaddo in the winter—if it's more possible for married folk to crash those hallowed gates in the winter.

I am trying to get one of my graduate students, who teaches at a high school in the suburbs here, to do the Outdoor Overture. He seems to be having difficulty in getting information as to the instrumentation, fees, etc. If you get a chance will you have your publisher send me the details at Mills.

My former student and very good friend, J.B. Middleton,[1] whose piano sonata I showed you last year, will apply for a fellowship at the Music Center.[2] I think you had some objections to the sonata I showed you, but you recognized his talent. That was a very early work which unfortunately, as a result of academic requirements of a thesis, had to be cast in a form larger than he could sustain at the time. His modernism has been considerably subdued this year since he's studying with Milhaud. He's a real person, very bright, and a good pianist, excellent musician, extremely direct, and my choice among young composers in the Bay region here. Incidentally, he's giving a concert at Mills at which he is to play Hindemith, Chavez, Bartok, Poulenc, Milhaud, the Stravinsky two-piano Concerto (with assistant) and he is also considering your Variations. This is a free concert. What is the present status of copyright on your Variations. He is also doing several concerts on his way east, some of which will be neither public nor educational but war-relief.

I hope you can take a few moments off the book to answer some of these queries. I am still thinking of Berkshire, myself. Davison[3] has given me his blessing in the matter and I have written to Judd. What about the orchestral requirement? I only have a short movement for strings and pianos, and the same goes for Middleton.

Regards,
[signed] Arthur

1. Jean B. Middleton studied under Copland at Tanglewood in 1941. His Symphony in C Major was published in 1962: he remains otherwise a shadowy figure.

2. The Berkshire Music Center.
3. Archibald T. Davison of the Harvard music department.

Copland to Berger
Typed letter on Hotel Empire stationery

May 8, 1941

Dear Arthur:

Your letter came while I was vacationing in Havana—and incidentally finishing a book.[1] Thats why I'm a little late with the reply.

I'm hoping to see you up at the Berkshires. I gave Mrs. Grant the O.K. as far as I was concerned. The rest is between the two of you. As far as I know, nothing has come in the way of an application from J.B. Middleton (I may be wrong about this). If he plans to do anything he had better do it fast as the class is almost full. In general we are aiming for a more experienced type of composer than I imagine Middleton to be, but I have an open mind.

I'll tell Boosey Hawkes to write you about the OUTDOOR OVERTURE. There is no fee for performances of the Variations except over the radio.

In haste,—but with all best wishes etc

[signed] Aaron

1. *Our New Music.*

—·—

Berger to Copland
Typed letter on Mills College stationery

May 9, 1941

Dear Aaron:

I seem to be bombarding you with letters. And each time I do[1] I feel the guilt of retarding progress on the forthcoming critique of contemporary music.

Dr. Edwin J. Stringham, Queens College, Flushing, N.Y., has asked me to have my references write to him immediately—which may or may not mean that something is brewing in that direction. I hope this will not be too much trouble for you.

Both my students and myself have derived great pleasure from analyzing your harmonic structure in the Variations and Second Hurricane. They are especially keen about those major triads ascending, blues fashion, and false-relation-wise, in minor thirds—viz. "It's wonderful,"[2] and the sequences in Salon Mexico.

I have had some duplicates of my Woodwind Quartet in case you would like me to submit something re the Berkshire fellowship. I also have a recording of it which was made at the Forum performance—altho not too badly played (accurately, but on the slow side), the recording is terrible. The reproduction does not warrant the terrific expense of making duplicates, but I have one copy which has been an aid in making revisions—adjusting the timing, repetitions, etc. Perhaps you will give me the chance to play the records for you when I am east—about the middle of June.

The prospects for next year are still pretty dismal.

I suppose you heard that Charles Jones is getting married—to one of my students in composition. Not a "composer"—the undergraduates have to take composition whether they want to or not. She is nevertheless a pretty good musician.

Yours,
[signed] Arthur

P.S. I hope you save copies of your letters of recommendation for me, so that you do not have to reconstruct them each time.

1. Berger writes "And each time I do see I feel. . . ."

2. Presumably the spot from cue 8 to cue 11 of the second number in *The Second Hurricane*, though this does not in fact match Berger's description.

—·—

Berger to Copland
Typed letter, 1941, probably July

3850 Amundsen Av.
New York City

Dear Aaron:

I should have written long ago to thank you for the fellowship and to beg forgiveness, etc., for turning it down after any trouble you might have gone to on my behalf. But I left Mills in haste & became involved in a rather busy summer session. The North Texas State Teachers College has the distinction—whatever it may be worth—of being the largest state teachers college in the world. They have a good choral tradition there, which comes near equalling the Westminster.[1] There are lots of high school teachers there, and I talked Copland. I came quite near getting you a Dallas performance of the Hurricane—I think Dallas could find the material, the interest and the backing. But the young man, who was to do it there, got an appointment in El Paso in a college. He's still anxious, and is playing with the idea of combining college and high school groups (i.e., the soloists and parents[2] from college) in El Paso. What do you think? Also, this is quite aside from the present case, but what attitude do you have towards performance with piano. It sounds rather well on the piano.

I hope to be up to the Berkshires for a short visit in Aug., but in the meantime I'd be grateful if you could help me on a matter that may ease my mind up for the fall. As a former Yaddo-ite do I address Mrs. Ames directly about being there in the winter. And do you think Esther and I have any chance for this? Or have you lost touch with this sort of thing.

You may be interested to know that the President of the Mills music club announced at the final dinner before a large assembled audience that "thanks to Mr. Berger they were now all for Copland." I lug my name in here because I do want you to know how I feel about you qua composer and how I have been bearing the torch.

Yours,

[signed] Arthur

I should have added above that the completion of my thesis (for Harvard PhD) and potential book on Stravinsky ought to be a concrete enough project for Yaddo.

Your Variations went over quite well, [in ink: "(see inclosure)"][3] except that there were the usual bewildered many. I thought he played it perhaps better than anything else on the program. He will repeat it at Illinois Wesleyan College, Bloomington Ill. the 22nd. The dissonance helped the outdoor carrying power in Texas.

---

1. Westminster Choir College in Princeton, N.J.

2. That is, the adult chorus.

3. The enclosure is no longer with the letter.

Copland to Berger
Handwritten postcard postmarked July 27, 1941, Stockbridge, Mass.

Dear Arthur:

Nice to know you're planning to visit us again. I no longer have any pull at Yaddo, but I know that Mrs. Ames is the person to address.

Thanks for all the good propaganda work.

Yours

Aaron

Copland to Berger
Typed letter

Hollywood, April 10, 1943

Dear Arthur:

The other night, while walking down Hollywood Blvd., I happened on a copy of the Partisan Review. Imagine my surprise when I came upon your piece on the Sonata.[1] I wonder what made you not tell me about it—just neglect? Or was it 'fright' at my reaction? Anyhow it was lots of fun to be surprised like that. Subsequently Victor[2] wrote me that you had mentioned it to him.

I don't know what others will think, but I liked it. My one objection is that it came to a rather sudden end, just as things were getting along. Were you cramped for space? It gives that impression.

There are a few things I'd like to comment upon. One is the meaning of my articles and "pronunciamentos." When I call for a "style that satisfies both us and them," I am mostly trying to goad composers on toward what I think is a healthy direction. I am emphatically <u>not</u> laying out an a priori plan for my own future compositions. I reserve the right always to practice not what I preach, but what the muse dictates.

I think also that for the sake of drawing sharp distinctions you rather overdo the dichotomy between my "severe" and "simple" styles. The inference is that only the severe style is really serious. I don't believe that. What I was trying for in the simpler works was only partly a larger audience; they also gave me a chance to try for a home-spun musical idiom, similar to what I was trying for in a more hectic fashion in the earlier jazz works. In other words, it was not only musical functionalism that was in question, but also musical language. I like to think that in Billy and Our Town, and somewhat in Lincoln, I have touched off for myself and others a kind of musical naturalness that we have badly needed—along with "great" works.

The reference to David's and Harold's[3] building up the "thinned out musical substance" needs to be expanded to be clear. I didn't understand it myself. But I'm sure they were pleased with the plug!

Did Victor tell you Stravinsky had me and Antheil to dinner? (After reading Kazin's book[4] I've come to the conclusion that Stravinsky is the Henry James of composers. Same "exile" psychology, same exquisite perfection, same hold on certain temperaments, same lack of immediacy of contact with the world around him.) He was extremely cordial with us. We played the Symphony[5] from off-the-air records, and S. complained bitterly about some of Stokowski's tempi. I don't think he's in a very good period. He copies himself unashamedly, and therefore one rarely comes upon a really fresh page—for him, I mean. I know this is blasphemy in the Berger household, but there it is—so make the most of it.

I hear glamorous reports of parties at the Berger household that make my mouth water. Apparently the Guggenheim fiasco didn't completely floor you. And everyone speaks of seeing you both at all the concerts there are, so you must have a lot to write me about. Please do, because I'm homesick like hell!

[in ink] Love to Esther,
Aaron

1. "Copland's Piano Sonata," *Partisan Review* 10, no. 2 (March–April, 1943): 187–90.
2. Viktor Kraft.

3. David Diamond and Harold Shapero.
4. Alfred Kazin, *On Native Grounds*.
5. Stravinsky's *Symphony in C* (1940).

Berger to Copland
Typed letter

Apr. 12, 1943

Dear Aaron:

Why I haven't written? I guess it is my normal inertia with respect to letter-writing, mixed in alloy of a certain fright as to your reaction and a certain insecurity as a result of my draft and job status. But I did mean to write and let you know about the article, and as a precaution I told Victor to write, just in case I procrastinated. Anyway, it's so much nicer that you saw it unmotivated. I get awfully tired of the feeling that one writes into a void, and that no one sees it unless told. Most of my literary friends have seen this without being told, and they seem to like it.

I want very soon to do a "definitive," that is, complete article on you (with your consent) and for that I should like to get together with you.[1] I want to plan the next few articles I do, for a book on contemp. music in general, so that while using them for magazines, I can also submit them to a publisher to get an advance. In the event of such an article, we can iron out your objections and exceptions to the present one—some of which are a matter of insufficient expansion on my part.

I put "severe" and "serious" in quotes with the intention of attributing them to others, more than to myself. In one case I used "allegedly" and elsewhere I thought I had used so-called, but it seems to have gotten lost somewhere. I guess the quotes aren't really enough. As to a strict dichotomy, I tried to avoid this at the beginning of the third paragraph. I do, however, tend to separate your two styles more than you do, I'm sure. And you yourself said to me, about seven years ago, that naturally one could not expect music done to order with a specific deadline to be like music composed over a long period—that is, over a period equivalent to the necessary time for its own fulfillment. But anyway, you and what you think, do not really count. You're only the composer, the traditional "medium thru which some higher power expresses itself," and that stuff, etc. etc.

As to the reference to your article, that was one of those shots in the dark which may or may not refer to yourself. But the fact that you should be thinking consciously about it, may indicate some unconscious concern in your own work. Moreover, you did say "we shall have to find a style, etc." And you actually have been doing that sort of thing in your own music. I don't see how this can be denied. Lincoln doesn't "write down" and appeals to some of us and them. What I expect next is to see you try some of the larger symphonic proportions, a la Shostakovich, without his exaggerated elephantine 19th century bulk and prolixity. In this case, the music would not simply appeal to us by virtue of its sensitivity and good taste, but would "satisfy us" in our desire for a certain complexity which makes it possible for us to live with music and find ever new and absorbing facets which we might not have noticed at first—little things hidden away in corners, concealed meanings, things in inner voices.

This brings me around to the last point about the "thinned-out" medium—and I do not expect you to agree with me on this score, since you would probably be acting differntly[2] if you did. David[3] was not pleased with this allusion to him, because he wants people to dwell on the "beauty" of his music, and he is obsessed with a normal musician's contempt for and fear of anything intellectual, as if it were a sin. Whereas to me, the intellectual element is only to be condemned when it excludes the emotional element. After all, the end in life is balance. For example, there is nothing bad about a love for the material and sensual in life, unless this love becomes so great a pre-occupation that it drags one down into the realm of materialism and sensuality to such an extent that the enjoyment of any other aspect of human behavior is excluded.

My failure to enlarge upon this was partly due to lack of space, and partly to the fact that specific musical reference was called for. And such reference would be out of place in a general publication, and moreover, should be illustrated with specific citations. Anyway, it's a thing which many people who know your music seem to understand and feel. I have expanded on it in Modern Music,[4] altho here, my piece was cut somewhat at the last minute. For example: "the lack of absorbing elements" "in certain slow sections"[5] the paucity of arpeggios and scales, the plea for a "wider dialectic play of contradictory elements."[6] What is so tantalizing is that this lack is one of the things that make your music so unique and desirable.

To make this more precise, I originally indicated, in P.R.,[7] a contrast between your Sonata and David's Two-piano Concerto, but I thought it was too much to assume an intimate acquaintance with the latter. I pointed to the abundance (in fact too much) of scales and arpeggio material in David, which made possible "the various levels of significance." Or for example, in the opening of the allegro of Mozart's Dissonance Quartet, K. 465 (after the slow intro.), we have what seems at first a common pom-pom-pom-pom-pom, repeated note accompaniment, which soon, however, branches off for itself in a beautiful curve which has an interest even aside from the melody. When we first hear the work, we enjoy the melody with the interest of the accompaniment as something which is certainly there, but which is somewhere in the back of consciousness. As we hear the work more, and we have "gotten" the melody, our attention focuses on this glorious accompaniment, and still later there is more enjoyment as we get the two as one thing. Don't take this metamorphosis of our listening as a literal process. But something like this may occur.

To me, the important thing is not the sum or extent of one's achievements, but the achievement. And I would like to see you now write the big work: a concerto, or cantata, or symphony. The encouraging thing in your case is the constant progression when so many others seem to be in retrograde. I must confess that I liked the Symphony (Igor's) but it - wasn't the big experience that I expected it would be. But then, I've heard it but once, and I detected a certain hectic rush for the notes on the part of the players, and I wondered just how much Stokie[8] was responsible for the starting and stopping. Or maybe, as I suspect, Igor has overdone the classical device of the capricious interruption as a means of ending one idea and going to the next.

Please don't quote me as saying Igor is in retrograde. It's just that I expected the Symphony to be the big thing. The Danses Concertantes, however, looks wonderfully clear in score, and I look forward to hearing it.

As to your attitude towards the Symphony—have you heard it much? May I remind you of your initially cool attitude towards the Psalms,[9] Persephone, and (I believe) Jeu de Cartes? I think we are governed a lot at first by what we think he ought to do next, and are somewhat blinded to what he does. But maybe I'm wrong. This is all pure conjecture.

I am somewhat perturbed by the fact that neither my P.R. nor M.M.[10] discussions of your Sonata bring out the tremendous warmth that I have towards it. It has become a really deep part of my experience—you know, the kind of thing that runs through your head and elicits a certain emotion. It may be that shortcomings are more tangible. By the very fact that they do not become part of the unity, they glare out. And so one tends to dwell on them. Moreover, I sort of assume that everyone else thinks you're as good as I think you are. Also, people know I think you're good, and they know how much I like you aside from your musical achievements. And I always fear they may attribute enthusiasm to personal feelings. And mainly, words of praise are so cheap now since they are dissipated so freely on so many unworthies. In any case, I hope I do not appear as bad as Virgil, dissecting a thing coldly and ruthlessly, and then saying he likes it.

Things musically here may appear more glamorous from afar than they really are. The sun kind of sets for many of us when you're away, and we all get rather disparate.[11] The main thing seems to be a small controversy over Israel's article.[12] I think Virgil misses the point. On the other hand, the implications of certain dangerous historical generalizations leave Israel open to such objections as Virgil's. It would be far better had Israel said this is true here and here and there. Moreover, "abstract" is such a debatable word now, that one ought to define precisely what one means by it before using it. For example, to me, the basic musical relationships as indicated by the overtone series are abstractions, and they do not become concrete (the opposite of abstract) just because they are "natural." Yet Israel touches here upon an excellent point in reference to Schoenberg. I would have made a distinction between a tendency towards speech and one towards song. Certainly modern music has become less abstract in its desire to mimic speech (Wagner, Moussorgsky, Debussy, Berg, and even the later Schoenberg). On the other hand, there has been a certain abstraction in Schoenberg, in respect to songfulness, which[13] can be defined in one sense as something concrete, since singing is something normal and natural to everyone, even if song itself is a certain abstraction or stylization with respect to speech. The most remarkable thing about Israel's article is the careful style—too careful for anything which we go through quickly for the meaning (as contrasted with something we dwell upon and re-read—a poem or novel—for the feeling as directly presented through the precise words and juxtapositions). [added in pen:] It seems rather wasted here.

Schuman has achieved a real low in his Free Song.[14] An indication of his musical taste is his choice of words. I don't think Whitman ever wrote anything worse than the words Schuman singled out from all the good stuff to choose from. "Pour down your unstinted nimbus, sacred moon."[15] I suppose a composer doesn't think verbally, so he is not to be blamed too much for his choice of words. But Schuman duplicates the feeling of the words he picks, instead of attempting to improve upon them. Also, it is significant that most of the great works of the past were remarkably successful in their texts: the Bach Passions, Gluck, Mozart's operas, the Ninth, even Persephone.[16]

You see what happens when I write a letter? I really must stop this now, and I haven't even had a chance to talk about "Lincoln" which I enjoyed in two concert hearings more than I expected I would. Some things disturb me about the text, which, I'm afraid, makes it rather occasional, unless it's possible later to drop it. I don't think it (the text) will sustain repeated hearings as poetry might have—even tho it's remarkably good stuff. Did you indicate a sort of iambic-anapest delivery simultaneously with the forte dotted eighths and 16ths around "The occasion is piled high with difficulty – – –" It's hard to hear the words when they are synchronized so closely with the loud chords of the orchestra here. I must look at the score. And I'd also like to study the Short Symphony; or better first, perhaps, (it might be easier) the Sextet.[17] Can I borrow this from Victor.

There's a possibility of a regular reviewing job (a pretty good one, not on the Trib. where I'd be about 4th or 5th string with the dregs). This is for next season if I'm not drafted. The problem is, how to get along till then. With free-lance work, I did not earn enough to get thru the summer and music work stops now. It's especially difficult to get a job with my present 3A status verging on 1A.

Finished my Serenade[18] about 8½ minutes, after all this time (too many other things unfortunately diverted me from it, so I really did not work on it for all of 9 months, as it seems). Benny[19] says he'll play it in June, but there now seems a possibility that he'll do "Jane Eyre" in Hollywood, at that time.

Your letter tells me very little about what you're doing, but Victor keeps me posted. I suppose you'll be gone a long time, since your picture seems to be assuming mammoth proportions. Bourke-White seems a nice touch.[20]

If you have had the patience to read this far, you will probably congratulate yourself on not receiving my verbose letters more often.

Yours,

[signed] Arthur

Regards and love from Esther.

1. Berger's "definitive" article appeared in *The Musical Quarterly* 31, no. 4 (October 1945): 420–47, as "The Music of Aaron Copland."

2. Probably a joke rather than a typo.

3. David Diamond.

4. "Once Again, the One-Man Show, 1943," a review article in *Modern Music* 20, no. 3 (March–April 1943): 175–82.

5. These last four words were added in pen.

6. Berger notes in pen in the margin "in Modern Music": meaning that the considerations mentioned in this sentence were cut from his article in *Modern Music*.

7. "Copland's Piano Sonata," *Partisan Review*.

8. Leopold Stokowski.

9. The *Symphony of Psalms*.

10. Modern Music.

11. Not a typo for "desperate"; rather, we all wander off in different directions.

12. Israel Citkowitz, "Abstract Method and the Voice," *Modern Music* 20, no. 3 (March–April 1943): 147–51.

13. Noted in pen, "song"; that is, "which" = song rather than songfulness.

14. William Schuman's *A Free Song* (Secular Cantata no. 2) for chorus, baritone, and orchestra, first performed on March 26, 1943, by the Boston Symphony Orchestra. (Berger would have heard it in the BSO's New York City concert of April 3, when it shared a program with the *Lincoln Portrait* and Samuel Barber's *Essay no. 1 for Orchestra*.) *A Free Song* went on to win the first Pulitzer Prize in music.

15. The final line of the first movement of *A Free Song*. To be just to Whitman (and to Schuman), the word *nimbus* has been set up earlier in the poem (and the piece).

16. Stravinsky's *Perséphone*, with a text by André Gide.

17. Copland's Sextet is an arrangement of his *Short Symphony*.

18. *Serenade Concertante* for violin, woodwind quartet, and small orchestra. It was first performed in 1945. Its 1951 revision was published in 1958 by C. F. Peters.

19. Bernard Herrmann.

20. Distinguished photographer Margaret Bourke-White had been doing some still photography for *The North Star*. (See Copland's letter to Berger of August 3, 1943.)

Berger to Copland
Typed letter

62 Barrow St. NYC
July 30, 1943

Dear Aaron:

I hope you didn't find my last letter to you too pedantic and dispassionately dissecting. I guess it's the academic in me that comes to the surface from time to time.

Since May I have been editing a monthly record magazine called LISTEN. It is syndicated through music dealers (who put their names on the cover) and reaches an incredibly large public of some 30,000 readers. I work on it about 1 1/2 weeks per month (write almost everything in it since there is no money for contributors) and it pays me in fair proportion to the length of time I work on it. So while it still doesn't solve the whole living problem, it is a reliable nucleus which I can supplement with free-lance work (if I were only a little more energetic I think I could get a good deal more in the way of odd assignments).

I started conservatively with feature articles on Grieg and Gilbert-Sullivan, boring within in the notes at the back of the book for the "cause."

For the August issue, I have been more daring: Stravinsky.[1] And the publisher was so pleased with this idea that, after my meek suggestion, I got him to believe that it was he who wanted American composers for the Sept. issue (Copland, Piston, Harris).[2] The magazine is gotten up fairly attractively (tho, through a switch of art man, it has suffered somewhat), and so I would welcome from you Victor's latest and best pictures, as soon as possible. (Has Boosey got these?) I prefer the action kind, and in this line, the best I've seen is the one with the negatives at the piano in Ewen's book.[3] But I'd rather use something new, and better, if possible. I would appreciate a selection of pictures, and I'll return those I do not use, if you're short. Also, bring me up to date on Coplandiana.

I was quite amused with the opportunity I had to plug new music in a trade paper, which is also edited by the same firm as LISTEN and which goes to all the dealers in the country (called Record Retailing). The editor disobeyed my instructions by putting my name to it, since I did it very much in the spirit of mimicking the type of thing that is expected in the way of trade style. In a subsequent issue I recommended your apprec. book[4] for window display.

The publisher's office is in Mt. Vernon, and I never get there, and they are lax in following out my orders, but I hope they do send you the Stravinsky issue when it's out. I picked up what Mellers had to say about the adaptability of your music to records in Kenyon[5] (in my so-called "Chatter" column).

Now the following is more urgent: The New Republic asked me to contribute the music article to their series Civilization in War-time.[6] I take it, this is a general survey of almost everything happening now, indicating incidentally how the evolution might be conditioned by the war. That is to say, there is not merely a one to one relationship—e.g., propaganda music and war. It seems to me you will have lots of suggestions, and while you must be very busy orchestrating and finishing up,[7] I wonder if you couldn't indicate some possible tracks, if only in a telegraphic form. I think the tendency of things like Lincoln Portrait can be related to this subject, and of course there was the meeting of ACA[8] at Miss Ziloti's. Anything new in this connection about yourself? Can you tell me more specifically what you did for the movie—what about the songs you wrote for it? I suppose David has news from Marc.[9]

In between these chores I'm trying to write a piano sonata.[10] I am also thinking of writing some articles towards a book on new music so I can have something definite to show publishers and foundations, while at the same time, perhaps, selling them to magazines. The [article on] American music is less practical, in a way, unless I can take a couple of years off, because there is so much data and so many concepts to wade through before the essential thread can be found. And I don't want to do another Tasker Howard.[11]

Don't stay away too long, and good luck with the Violin Sonata. Regards for Victor, and to both of you from Esther.

[signed] Arthur

1. "Igor Stravinsky," *Listen: The Guide to Good Music* (August 1943): 3–8.

2. "American Composers: Aaron Copland, Roy Harris, Walter Piston," *Listen* (September 1943): 3–8.

3. David Ewen, ed. *The Book of Modern Composers* (New York: Alfred A. Knopf, 1942), p. 461. Copland is at the piano correcting proofs (probably white-on-green proofs rather than "negatives") of the two-piano version of the *Danzón Cubano*. The photograph, by Victor Kraft, is the one which was finally used as an illustration for the article.

4. *What to Listen for in Music*.

5. "American Music (an English Perspective)," *The Kenyon Review* 5, no. 3 (Summer 1943): 357–75; or possibly "Music Letter from England," *The Kenyon Review* 5, no. 1 (Winter 1943): 118–22. In both of these articles Mellers speaks of Copland's music in terms of "the microphone"—primarily radio and film—rather than of "records."

6. This became "Music in Wartime," *The New Republic*, February 7, 1944, 175–78.

7. The music for the film *The North Star*.

8. American Composers Alliance.

9. David Diamond and Marc Blitzstein.

10. No piano sonata exists among Berger's acknowledged works; nor is there a piano piece from 1943.

11. Berger had complained about John Tasker Howard's *This Modern Music* in a review, "On Modern Music, But for Whom?" in *Modern Music* 20, no. 1 (November–December 1942): 64–65.

Copland to Berger
Typed letter on Samuel Goldwyn stationery

Aug 3, 1943

Dear Arthur:

I've been carrying your April letter around with me for months, and now your new one gives me incentive to answer promptly. There['s] nothing like being asked for one's picture for producing letters! There are a couple of photos at the ACA office. Thats your best bet as I have very few with me here, and Victor has taken no new ones in recent months. Mr. Goldwyn has a few prize ones made by Margaret Bourke-White but they are being saved for a glamorous occasion.

Nice to hear about your connection with the record world. God knows the record world is an important one, and they can stand a little boring from within.

I'm up to my neck in movie music at the moment so must reply briefly.

After waiting around for the film five months they have dropped it in my lap and want the score in a hurry. Since there is to be more than an hours worth of it I have a considerable job on my hands. Jerry Moross is organizing a small army of orchestrators and copyists to get ready for a September recording.

Thats the main news. I have also finished two movements of a Violin Sonata, and started a ballet for Martha Graham.

For your New Republic survey: the most impressive thing I've heard about in regard to producing music for the war is being engineered by Oscar Hammerstein in New York in connection with a Music War Council which is a branch organization of the Theatre Wing. (I'm not sure of all these titles.) No doubt you know of their work already. The Treasury Dep't. took on Roy Welch as a musical advisor—so perhaps he has news for you. Goossens series of Fanfares in Cincinnati[1] was an exception. In general, damn little has been done to make use of the talent of serious composers in the War effort—or that is my impression anyway.[2] Marc has what amounts to an Army Fellowship for the writing of a musical masterpiece celebrating the Air Force.[3] Anyway I have that on the "best authority." I suppose writing film music for pictures about the heroic Russian resist-ance[4] is a kind of related "fellowship."

I picked up the Mellers article at the same stand that I found your P.R. article.[5] It was very flattering, I must say. I think he hits certain things off marvellously well, particularly when he uncannily tells me just how I felt at the moment of composing. But I wish he were more readable, and less wordy. I'll really never be fully content until you do a full length piece. You know you can sell it anyday in advance to the Musical Quarterly—or so I think.

I'll be back when I finish the picture—if I don't go to Mexico for a few weeks vacation, first. Victor is there now.

Someday I'll write that <u>big</u> symphony you asked for in April.

Love to Esther.

[signed in red art-pencil] Aaron

1. Which included Copland's *Fanfare for the Common Man*.

2. Neither Berger nor Copland mentions the League of Composers' series of commissions of short orchestral works on aspects of the war, a project that produced Charles Ives's *They Are There!*, Bohuslav Martinů's *Memorial to Lidice*, William Grant Still's *In Memoriam: The Colored Soldiers Who Died for Democracy*, Bernard Herrmann's *For the Fallen*, and pieces by others including Carpenter, Cowell, Milhaud, and Piston. Copland, who had been approached for a composition for this series, declined, pleading the press of work for *The North Star* and his as yet unnamed ballet for Martha Graham.

3. This became *Symphony: The Airborne*.

4. Such as *The North Star*, the film Copland was working on.

5. Copland may have thought Berger was referring to Mellers's article "Language and Function in American Music," published in *Scrutiny* 10, no. 4 (April 1942): 346–57. The Copland Collection in the Library of Congress contains Copland's copy of *Scrutiny* (with only the pages of Mellers's article cut!), but neither issue of *The Kenyon Review*. P.R. refers to *Partisan Review*.

Berger to Copland
Typed letter on (New York) *Sun* stationery

May 1, 1944

Dear Aaron:

Your Violin Sonata has been singled out for re-hearing by the Critics Circle. The other works are quartets by Imbrie, Thompson[1] and Leroy Robertson. The NBC quartet may do these three at the end of May, possibly full or partial broadcast, possibly just private hearing for small invited group. Would you consider coming down to play your sonata with Ruth Posselt if date is convenient for you when it is arranged? Or do you have any other suggestion? I am asking you this as a member of the Awards Committee, and would appreciate answer as soon as possible. You can wire me collect at home (29 E. 28).

Lenny's Symphony,[2] Norman's[3] "Magnificat" & Schuman's String Symphony got the orchestral selection for performance May 11, 11:30 P.M. by NBC. How are you and how are your lectures[4] being received? And when will I see you for more than a fleeting moment?

Yours,
[signed] Arthur

1. Andrew Imbrie, Randall Thompson.
2. Bernstein's *Jeremiah* Symphony.
3. Norman Dello Joio.
4. Copland was lecturing at Harvard.

Copland to Berger
Handwritten letter

Tepoztlan,
Morelos,
Mexico
Sept. 8, 1944

Dear Arthur,

Theres no particular point to this letter—only a sort of blind instinct that if I can elicit a letter from you I can thereby keep in touch with the musical center of the world. Tepoztlan is definitely off the main road. In fact its about 400 years behind the procession. I doubt whether they even ever heard of Schostie,[1] as Harold[2] would say. And even if they heard of him, I doubt whether they'd care.

I found out most about the place by reading a book about it, written by an American, of course.[3] He spent 8 months here 15 years ago, before the road was opened. You can't find out much from the Indians themselves, they're so tight-lipped. The Mexico City Mexicans say they are unfriendly, but I suspect they are just shy. In any case my presence here is remarkable only because no American has lived here since Redfield wrote his book.

I imagine life here is closest to Italian hill town life, or what I suppose Italian hill towns are like. No newspapers and no radios, no telephones and no telegrams. That simplifies life considerably. Theres no traffic because the streets are unpaved. A kind of pitter-patter of bare feet on rock can be heard all day through. It's the women on their daily round. The men wear guaraches, but then they only work in the fields, and are mostly not to be seen until around 5 in the afternoon, when they emerge to make conversation with their friends on the corner of their street. Nights are dark—there's no electricity. In spite of that, twice weekly there is a kind of public dance that takes place in the open air market. It's the only modern touch in town—and I can't say it's very gay. Instead of doing jarabes and huapangos I was amazed to see them attempting a kind of Tepoztlan version of a fox trot. The nearest movie house is 15 miles away, but obviously its had its effect. The "jazz" is better than the dancing—perhaps because Redfield mentions phonographs with horns when he was here. But the whole thing is hardly conducive to inspiring a Salon Tepozteco.

I don't suppose you're interested in any of this, but at least it tells you where I am. Esther will be relieved to know that our house is quite perfect—complete with cook and gardener, <u>and</u> a bathroom. I have a separate studio with a baby grand. Unfortunately the old days are gone when one used to pay $8. a month for the whole thing—but then, you can't have everything.

We are only two hours from Mexico City so I have heard the Sinfonica[4] several times. Chavez played a piece of Revueltas' called Ventanas (Windows). Its very amusing to listen to—chuck full of orchestral color— but the form isn't very good, I'm afraid. He was like a modern painter who throws marvelous daubs of color on canvas that practically takes your eye out, but it doesn't add up. Too bad—because he was a gifted guy.[5] Also heard a Symphony No. 1 by young Pablo Moncayo.[6] He adds a gentle note to what is generally the grim or boisterous Mexican palette, but the whole thing is still rather unformed, despite charming moments. I am disturb[ed to][7] note that there doesn't seem to be any younger generation of [Mex-]ican[7] composers—fellows in their twenties, I mean. Galindo[8] and Moncayo are the thirty generation. I spoke to Chavez about it, but he doesn't seem to have any explanation. It may be lack of [an] outstanding composition teacher—nobody who teaches really seems to know his stuff. Chavez and Revueltas went abroad and the young men stay home. Something ought to be done about it.

What goes on where you are—thats really the point of this letter. I feel as if I had been gone for ages, and everything has changed. Of course it hasn't, but I need reassuring. Kolodin[9] isn't back from the wars, is he? Have you been composing anything? Has anybody been composing anything? I wrote a seven minute piece for Whiteman's[10] commission called "Letter from Home." Its very sentimental, with five saxophones that are sometimes five clarinets and sometimes four flutes—but it <u>modulates</u>!

Now all I have to do is to take care of the Koussie commission.[11]

Love to Esther from me and Victor.

Aaron

PS. Wild coincidence. Just came back from the P.O. and found a letter including the two I sent you in 1934 and 1943.[12] Very amused to reread them. <u>Now</u> I see why I wrote you—trying to get printed, thats all!

---

1. Dmitri Shostakovich, whose *Leningrad* Symphony had created a sensation in the United States. He had made the cover of *Time* in July 1942.

2. Probably Harold Clurman. (The expression sounds like a Shaperoism, but Harold Shapero was "Sonny" in most of Copland's correspondence.)

3. Robert Redfield, *Tepoztlán, a Mexican Village: A Study of Folk Life* (Chicago: Univer-

sity of Chicago Press, 1930). Copland may also have known a second book on the same village: Stuart Chase's *Mexico: A Study of Two Americas* (New York: Macmillan, 1931).

4. The Orquesta Sinfónica de México, conducted at that time by Carlos Chávez.

5. Silvestre Revueltas had died on October 5, 1940.

6. Pablo Moncayo (1912–1958) had studied with Copland at Tanglewood in 1942.

7. Page 2 of this letter torn in upper-right corner.

8. Blas Galindo (1910–1993) had studied at Tanglewood with Copland in 1941 and 1942.

9. Irving Kolodin.

10. Paul Whiteman.

11. Which became the Third Symphony.

12. *Letters of Composers: an Anthology,* *1603–1945,* ed. Gertrude Norman and Miriam Lubell Shrifte (New York: Alfred A. Knopf, 1946) included Copland's letters to Berger of August 6, 1934, and April 10, 1943. The letter that prompted this P.S. was doubtless from one of the editors of the anthology asking Copland's permission to publish the two letters and including transcripts.

Copland to Berger
Handwritten letter on Republic Productions stationery

April 6 1948

Dear Arthur:

Thought you'd be interested in the enclosed.[1] It happened last night. Your performance was only fair—I thought the tempi were all a shade too fast. The piece wears well—and seems that its being played everywhere. Thats nice!

Thought of sending you various addenda for your lists: but I imagine you've seen most of it: Kubly's piece in the April Esquire,[2] mine in the Times Mag.,[3] Donald's in Musical America (I'm writing him about it;)[4] and Finklestein's in last month's Mainstream.[5]

The job is done.[6] We preview tonight up in Santa Barbara. I'll be home next week. Best to Esther.

Aaron

1. No longer with the letter. Probably a program including the Berger Quartet in C Major for woodwinds.

2. Herbert Kubly, "America's No. 1 Composer," *Esquire,* April 1948, 57, 143–45.

3. "The New 'School' of American Composers," *The New York Times Magazine,* March 14, 1948, 18, 51–54.

4. Donald Fuller, "A Symphonist Goes to Folk Sources," *Musical America* 68, no. 3 (February 1948): 29, 256, 397.

5. Sidney Finkelstein, "Notes on Aaron Copland," *Masses & Mainstream* 1, no. 1 (March 1948): 89–91.

6. *The Red Pony.*

Berger to Copland
Typed letter on New York *Herald Tribune* stationery, 1949

Tuesday

Dear Aaron:

The Lange piece is up in type, and just happened to be the size of the hunk that had to be cut to make the Sun. piece fit space, and the Milhaud bit was stuck on to fill up the difference. Just one of those things, but it will certainly get in my next column. Thanks for the dope.

Would you prefer I not use the "rumor" about your choral piece for Kouss.; I've known of it for some time, and wonder if it can't be spilled now that the dinner announcement is out.[1] Or is it a secret? If not, what are the details—the text?

Your imminent departure for Europe is a challenge for me. You have every right not to believe it, but I have every intention of getting you the biog. half of the book next week. The silly thing is there are[2] only two spots to fix up, and you could just as well see it as it is. So you might as well start thinking now of a little spot to fit me in next week, say lunchtime, either mid-town or around my way. If we make the appt. now, I'll surely be ready. Would you give me a ring about this when and if you have a spare moment?

Yours,
[signed] Arthur

1. Copland was sketching a piece for chorus and orchestra, "Let Us Now Praise Famous Men," for the twenty-fifth anniversary of Serge Koussevitzky's assuming conductorship of the Boston Symphony Orchestra. The work remained unfinished: its opening choral idea became the opening of *Canticle of Freedom*.

2. Berger writes "there're are."

Berger to Copland
Typed letter. The year "1950" has been entered in pencil by another hand.

June 28

Dear Aaron:

I should have realized your lovely lawn party was a kind of good-bye for a while party, and that you would be off to some hills or other. Perhaps I should have sent this to N.H.[1] in the hope that you would be back before Tanglewood, but Es reminds me you were to sublet your house in Palisades. Broder & Bill S. have done a final check-up on the MS[2] and have made their final suggestions (very few) to me, and it looks as if it will go full speed ahead late this summer. They want all sorts of pictures—baby, adolescence, Paris (how about that group with Virgil & Nadia, et al?), and the more artistic photos you have had taken more recently (some of Victor's, and how about the Penn in Vogue; and Hollywood, and how did Naomi Siegler's come out). Even if you haven't access to your things now, start thinking seriously about this, and round them up the first chance you can after Tanglewood. I'm afraid you'll be off to Rome before I can get my hands on them. Incidentally, what of the Amer. Academy in Rome project? When will you know, or do you already?

I wonder how that item on the Canadian Hockey Assoc. fellowships got in the Trib. instead of the Times, or didn't you notice. You so and so, why don't you send me some spicy items for MY column, too. True I have less space, but I'm supposed to pep up the page. I'll be in Tanglewood for the opening weekend of the festival (last part of July) staying with the Fines,[2] & will see you then.

[signed] Arthur

1. The MacDowell Colony in Peterboro, New Hampshire.
2. Nathan Broder, at that time associate editor of the *Musical Quarterly*, was serving as editor for Berger's book on Copland. Bill S. is William Schuman; the manuscript is that of Arthur Berger, *Aaron Copland* (New York: Oxford University Press, 1953).
3. Both Copland and Berger occasionally stayed with Irving and Verna Fine when they were at Tanglewood.

Copland to Berger
Typed letter on Berkshire Music Center stationery

July 1, 1950

Dear Artur [*sic*]:

Nice to get your note. I had been thinking about you. The photos for the book I can supply after I get into my house again on September first. There's a good one by Ralph Steiner, circa '33, that has never been used. I have the Penn, and the Sieglers, and plenty of others. Do you think they will want shots of ballet scenes, or film excerpts?

I got a good laugh out of your 'Hockey' reproach. For some reason I didn't think of you—I guess it was because I didn't think it was serious enough for your column—you see how I've got you categorized. I was plenty mystified when I saw the item in the Trib. Well I'll have to make it up to you by supplying some choice tidbit sometime soon.

Yes, I expect to be off to Rome around Jan 1. I'll be at the Academy[1] as music consultant for the fellows.

Had a quiet time at the Colony[2] in June. At Harold Spivacke's[3] insistence I started a Piano Quartet for Mrs. Coolidge's 25th Anniversary Festival in late October in Wash. It'll be a miracle if I finish in time,[4] so keep this out of the public prints until I'm sure.

Look forward to seeing you both up here. Love to E.

> [signed] Aaron

1. The American Academy in Rome.
2. MacDowell Colony.
3. Harold Spivacke was chief of the Music Division of the Library of Congress and thus in charge of the Coolidge Festival.
4. It was in fact finished nine days before the premiere.

Copland to Arthur and Esther Berger
Handwritten letter on American Academy in Rome stationery

> March 2 '51

Dear Arthur & Es:

Hello—and how are you both? Here it is March already—and I never thanked Esther for her Jan. letter with the B.B. vituperations.[1] (Made good reading—tho at the time I was quite unaware of all the shenanigans going on.)

I'm starved for news from N.Y. Because of the Paris Herald[2] there are no N.Y. Herald's around anywhere so I haven't seen the music page since I left. It's a deprivation! Aside from that, it's a soft life. Beautiful apartment, marvellous view, swell cook, Bechstein, etc. etc. Almost too soft . . .

I'm lecturing on American music in various cities in Italy, and arranging several chamber music concerts. The Rome radio has invited me to conduct an all-C—— concert in May. Since the orchestra is very good, it should be fun. (Leo[3] to do the Piano Concerto with me.)

Maybe youve heard?—I'm the Charles Eliot Norton Poetry Professor for next year at Harvard.[4] I was more surprised than anyone else could be at the choice. (Erik[5] thinks this last sentence indicates a severe case of false modesty!) So its back to Cambridge—at least for 5 1/2 months starting in October.

How is everything by you-all? What kind of a winter is it turning out to be? What does Broder give now as a date for the book?

> Best to you
> Aaron

P.S. You ought to see Ashley Pettis[6] in a priest's garb. Complete transformation!

1. Benjamin Britten? We do not have Esther Berger's letter to which this letter is a response.
2. The Paris edition of the New York *Herald Tribune*.
3. Leo Smit.

4. Copland's series of lectures became his book *Music and Imagination* (Cambridge, MA: Harvard University Press, 1952).
5. Erik Johns.
6. Pettis had been the producer of the Composers' Forum-Laboratory concerts in New York.

Copland to Berger
Handwritten letter on American Academy in Rome stationery

Apr 30 '51

Dear Arthur:

Thought you might be amused by seeing your piece in the Jerusalem Post. I was not responsible—just as surprised as you may be to see it.

Had a most stimulating 2½ weeks in Israel. Conducted In the Beginning at a concert on the shores of the Sea of Galilee. Very appropriate setting, no? Trouble was that it happens to be 2 kilometers from the Syrian border—and at 2:30 A.M. I was awakened by sporadic firing in the night—generally referred to as border incidents! I also sat with 30 Israeli composers for 5 days and listened to their music. Turned out that I am the first composer to have visited from abroad. (Up to now, they've only had famous interpreters.) Reception was <u>warm</u>, as you can imagine. I lectured in Tel-Aviv and Jerusalem. Visited Jaffa, Haifa, Acre etc.

Do you ever write anybody? If so, I'm a candidate.

Best to Es.

Aaron

P.S. When's our book due to come out? Do you want to talk to Denis Dobson about an English edition? I'll be in London end of May to conduct the Clar Concerto.

Berger to Copland
Typed letter

222 Willow St.
Southport, Conn.
Aug. 5, 1952

Dear Aaron:

Would you please send post-haste to Nat Broder[1] the transformation of the first three-notes of the theme of your piano quartet, as they occur in the second movement. The place I mean goes something like this:

I do not trust my memory as to exact rhythm, meter, dynamics, and tempo mark. Please indicate these all to Broder, and quote only the 3 notes. Also, give him the tempo mark for the beginning of the first movement, which, tell him, goes on Ex. 3. He already has the theme of the quartet for this example (Ex. 3). The example from the second movement is to be marked Ex. 4. These are for a review of your record at this late date for MQ.[2]

We both enjoyed being with you. I sincerely got a good impression of the Center, and I hope I conveyed it Sun. in my article. I took a certain impish pleasure in placing you on the spot to match L.D. as commentator on your 3rd Symph.[3] I have complete confidence that your remarks, if they get you to talk about it, will be much more specific—tho you do tend to be secretive about your work.

As to Stuckenschmidt's aspersion on me, my contention is thoroughly borne out by the quotations of Henze's "rows."[4] They remind me of nothing so much as the sequential studies we used to have in solfeggio to cover all the tones in the scale with their chromatic neighbor notes. Fi-sol, Ra-do, Sai-la, etc. I had the feeling about Henze first, and then Milton[5] corroborated it, tho we both feel he is very gifted. It is time that the whole subject of the system of Schoenberg & Webern, as part of a style and specific technique, were aired out, and the distinction made clear that twelve-tones adapt themselves to altogether different uses only distantly related to that system. Perhaps I will one day get Milton to collaborate with me on such an article, to give the stamp of authority.

At last I can concentrate entirely on the orchestra piece.[6] The Maestro's secretary[7] called to find out how it was going, and whether I'd have it by Sept. 15. I confessed that if I have the music sans orchestration by that time, I shall consider myself fortunate. My problem is one you faced a long time ago. Some people tell me I have struck on something personal, but I know it is not practical for large orchestra and large audiences, especially since I do not have the prestige of Schoenberg, Webern, Sessions & Krenek to get the necessary extra rehearsal time. This, among other things, is what makes it necessary for me to take stock at this point, and try some new tactic, while salvaging the personal element.

I think the skips in the woodwind duo[8] will work, given expert players and the "interested audience." Sorry there was no chance to play it for you. You will notice a few more sharps & flats. I do not have any regret, however, about the pure white-note phase I went through. I felt that from Wagner thru Webern, the skips and rhythmic asymmetry remained inseparable from chromaticism, and that new qualities were available by using some of these devices diatonically and within a regular meter. This is the answer I would have given you that night after you heard my second violin duo, if it had not been so late. The slow tempo on the recording in the second movement meant that each tonal element lingered too long, and therefore gave a sense of greater tonal staticness than I had originally calculated (for I had originally intended the faster tempo). I think you'll like it better a tempo and when you're in a fresher listening mood. The problem (and this goes to a certain extent for the woodwind duo too) is to negotiate the skips with the same ease as conjunct notes, and this is merely a matter of practice. I have, unfortunately, not the aura around me that gets me the 100 or so rehearsals considered the normal minimum for Schoenberg and Webern works when they were new. I was encouraged last season by the almost Debussyesque sweetness of Schoenberg's piano music as played by Steuermann.[9] It usually sounds so clangorous. Perhaps there's some hope for my music getting the calmness or light capriciousness I visualize for it in performance. The allegro of the second duo is much lighter and less austere than it sounded when you heard it. Now that I know it better I can approximate its proper character more. But I still have the hope I may get someone else to make the recording.

This was to be a brief note. As Alexei[10] would say, "sorry."

Yours,

[signed] Arthur

1. Broder was at that time associate editor of the *Musical Quarterly.*

2. Berger's review appeared in the *Musical Quarterly* 38, no. 4 (October 1952): 655–59.

3. Berger's article described a talk given by Italian composer Luigi Dallapiccola before the Tanglewood performance of his *Canti di Prigionia* and ended by saying ". . . Mr. Copland . . . will be represented on next Saturday's festival program and by that time, no doubt, Tanglewood students will have a direct channel into the workings of yet another composer's mind in the creative process."

4. Hans Heinz Stuckenschmidt (1901–1988), German music critic with a particular interest in serial composition, including those of German composer Hans Werner Henze (b. 1926).

5. Milton Babbitt.
6. *Ideas of Order*.
7. "The Maestro" is Dimitri Mitropoulos, who had commissioned *Ideas of Order*.

8. Berger's Duo for Oboe and Clarinet, written this year.
9. Eduard Steuermann, pianist, composer, and member of Schoenberg's circle.
10. Alexei Haieff.

—·—

Copland to Berger
Handwritten letter on Berkshire Music Center stationery, August 1952

Dear Arthur

Flabbergasted by the unusual length of your letter!

This is our final week—all is hectic as you remember it—and since I could make neither head nor tail of your 'Broder' request, I am sending the score (just arrived) so you can indicate to Broder what you need, and incidentally be haunted by the 12 tones of my series.[1]

Love to Es
Aaron

P.S. No time now to comment on your own comments. You're obviously in a fighting mood—which is all to the good.

1. As Berger knew very well, Copland's series contained only 11 tones, and, with its emphasis on sequences of whole tones, was completely without the semitones Berger had suggested were overused by Henze in his rows (letter of August 5).

—·—

Berger to Copland
Typed letter

June 23, 1953

Dear Aaron:

We enjoyed seeing you and Victor. Hope we can do it again soon.

About the picture.[1] They'll use the candle-light one if they have to,[2] but if Victor gets a good new one in the next two weeks, there is still time. They feel that this square shape will mean reducing it quite a bit, and your head will be just a little detail in the composition.

Please get Victor to try some more, won't you? I am very anxious to have a brand new picture for the book. Will see you July first at the L of C,[3] and hope you have some encouraging news for me on this matter by then.

Yours,
[signed] Arthur

1. For Berger's book on Copland, which would finally appear this year.

2. They did, in fact, use "the candle-light one."

3. Library of Congress.

Copland to Esther Berger
Handwritten letter on Shady Lane Farm stationery

Dec 9 '53

Dear Esther:

I am always contactable chez Boosey-Hawkes—30 W. 57. The letter you forwarded[1] demonstrates the dangers of fulfilling the role of benevolent old man. I haven't the slightest idea what to do about it.

We have picked a name for the opera: <u>The Tender Land</u>. How you like? I've had good reactions to it—so I hope you both approve. (Its worse than naming a baby!) Production at the City Center is scheduled for the end of March.[2]

Think of me the next time you pass those Harvard Sq. bookshops.[3] Went into the 52nd St. Doubledays[4] to buy something and a stranger came up and asked me to autograph Arthur's book for an Xmas present. Good sign, no?

Love to you both,
Aaron

1. Not identifiable.
2. The premiere took place, in fact, on April 1, 1954.

3. Where Berger's book on Copland was now on sale.
4. A Fifth Avenue bookstore.

Berger to Copland
Typed letter on Brandeis University School of Creative Arts stationery, 1954

Mar. 15

Dear Aaron:

It seems I'm to do an article on "Tender Land" for Lincoln's magazine (Center)[1] after all, immediately following the opening so that it may be ready for the edition which goes to press Mon., April 5. I trust you will lend me a piano-vocal score for the occasion. Naturally, it would be very helpful if you'd send it to me here in Cambridge, but if for any reason this is too much trouble, or you prefer me not to see it before hearing it (since you seem so secretive about it all), I shall look forward to getting hold of one the night of the performance. You could give it to one of your scouts, or I could pick it up when I see you backstage, whichever is most convenient.

I have been asked to concentrate on the music, since there will have been a piece on the libretto in the previous issue. Have you finished yet?????

Best luck. Kupferberg,[2] incidentally, is going to Europe on a 6-week honeymoon, and will contact you another time about that Trib. article.

See you soon,
[signed] Arthur

1. This became "On First Hearing Copland's 'Tender Land,'" in *Center: A Magazine for the Performing Arts* 1, no. 3 (April–May 1954), pp. 6–8.

2. Herbert Kupferberg, writer on music at that time on the staff of the *Herarld Tribune*.

Copland to Arthur and Esther Berger
Handwritten Shady Lane Farm postcard, postmarked April 4, 1955, New York 17, NY

Dear Arthur & Es:

I'm having an 'off to Europe' party on Sat. (the 9th) at 4 30. Thought maybe you might be down for Easter. (Or maybe IF or HS)[1]

I have your copy of the Short Symph. and will hold onto it until I hear. Thought your piece read well in the Times.[2]

Best, Aaron

1. Irving Fine, Harold Shapero.

2. "Modern Symphonists," the *New York Times*, March 20, 1955.

Copland to Berger
Handwritten letter

Address until Aug 31: L'ORANGERIE
(Les Breguieres)
2e CANNES
Alpes-Mar[1]
July 17 '55

Dear Arthur:

I've been thinking of you a lot lately because I've been reading you in Hi-Fi[2] and in The Score.[3] (B & H had also sent me the Canticle mention).[4] Did I miss anything else?

I thought the Records resumé was good.[5] You seem to be developing a more 'intime' style in writing—a sort of fire-side-chat-manner which is all to the good, I think. Was especially noticeable in The Score piece, where some of it seemed directed just at the immediate 'family.' I expect you'll be getting repercussions therefrom—so steel yourself! (Only caught one error in the Hi-Fi piece—Webster Aitken plays a <u>D</u>♯ instead of a <u>D</u>♮—not vice versa.)

I hear you thought the Canticle poorly performed. I'm sure you were right. I heard a rehearsal and, as a result, feared the worst. K.L.[6] just ain't no conductor—between us. I'm anxious to hear it properly done some time.

I'm settled for the Summer in a villa overlooking Cannes and the sea. It's just idyllic. But I hope it produces some tough music!

Before that I was mostly in Paris, London and Baden-Baden.[7] I didn't manage to uncover any unsung heroes. I did finally hear a chamber work of Boulez—Le Marteau sans Maitre. (It had to have 50 rehearsals—on dit.) I thought it had some music in it—not just fascinating theories of organization. Wm. Glock[8] agreed; but we were definitely in the minority. On the other hand, Henze's Quartet was a mess.[9] New Music in Europe is beginning to take on a moyen âge life,—whatever vitality there is seems to be taking place underground, so to speak. No one at all is interested in 'just music.' First, it must have a sound,—interesting in and for itself; the over-all plan preferably based on some 12-tone-derived gimmick. (How clever of I.S. to combine 4 Trbni and 4 Str <u>with</u> diagrams, and yet write his own piece.[10]) Someday, I must try a special sound piece to see what it gives . . .

And what are you-all up to? How is the Louisville piece progressing?[11] How was the Brandeis Festspiel? Write a guy—no?

In the late fall I'm off to Scandinavia. Have concerts and lectures in all 4 countries. Also I'm conducting Short Symph for the 1st time in Europe in Baden-Baden, and the 3rd Symph. in Munich, both in Sept.

Love to Es

Aaron

1. Alpes-Maritimes.

2. "An Aaron Copland Discography," *High Fidelity* 5, no. 5 (July 1955): 64–69.

3. "Stravinsky and the Younger American Composers," *The Score*, no. 12 (June 1955): 38–46.

4. B&H, Boosey & Hawkes. *Canticle* mentioned in "The Pot of Fat: Chamber Opera Receives its Premiere—New Copland Work at M.I.T." *New York Times*, May 15, 1955. Copland's *Canticle of Freedom* had received its premiere on May 8. (*The Pot of Fat* is the title of Theodore Chanler's chamber opera.)

5. The *High Fidelity* discography.

6. Klaus Liepmann.

7. Copland had been a judge at the ISCM Festival at Baden-Baden, which ran from June 17 through 21. Established composers (not "unsung heroes") performed at the festival, including Chávez, Dallapiccola, Ibert, Schoenberg, and Carter (the last relatively new to European audiences but not to Copland).

8. William Glock, editor of *The Score*.

9. The String Quartet no. 2 (1952).

10. Igor Stravinsky's *In Memoriam Dylan Thomas*, for tenor, four trombones and string quartet. In the published edition the trombone parts in the Prelude are marked with brackets (the "diagrams" of Copland's letter) showing their use of the five-note row on which the work is based.

11. Berger's *Polyphony*, commissioned by the Louisville Orchestra, was finished in 1956.

———

Copland to Berger
Handwritten letter on Shady Lane Farm stationery

Apr 9 1958

Dear Arthur:

Sorry to have missed your Sunday night shindig, but I just couldn't make it, for reasons too complicated to go into here.

I've read your piece on the Fantasy[1] and was impressed by all the digging you must have done. I myself forget the various transformations of the series as soon as I've used them, so much of it was "news" to me,— tho not really. I was surprised at the discovery of the similarity of chords in Fantasy and Sonata. That was all unconscious. And a little surprised at your strong feeling in favor of the Piano Quartet. How nice.

As an article, you probably will please neither school: those who want a subjective, impressionist, historical appraisal; or those interested only in a thorough series breakdown from start to finish. I, of course, love both. — — —

I'm off to Chicago today to hear Reiner do an 18 min. suite for orch alone of The Tender Land. Then on to Wash. for a Boulanger Festival.

Best to Es

Aaron

1. "Aaron Copland's *Piano Fantasy*" in the *Juilliard Review* 5, no. 2 (Winter 1957–58): 13–27.

————

Berger to Copland
Typed letter on Brandeis University School of Creative Arts stationery

Oct. 15, 1959

Dear Aaron:

I have taken the liberty of giving you as reference for both Fulbright and Guggenheim. I have my sabbatical next year with half-pay, and will have to find some way of supplementing my income if I am to take the whole year off and do a substantial piece of work—the dreaded symphony,[1] which, as you once said (or were you quoting), is the "history of a man."

It seemed to me that writing you for permission to use your name would only make it necessary to write another [letter] later—and I could scarcely think of you refusing, in view of your constant willingness in this matter in the past.

Though I sent my Fulbright application in on time, I'm late, as you see, with the recommendations. I have been working very hard to finish the Fromm commission,[2] which I am now beginning to orchestrate for a group of 30 players (small orchestra). It is in two movements: Toccata & Variations, lasting some 25 minutes.

I trust you will attend to the inclosed at your earliest convenience. It is very important to me, and I would be most grateful to you if you kept this in mind. The ancillary research project is based on the assumption that European critics (a few) act as spokesmen for the composer more than our critics do.

We expect to be in NY the weekend of the 22d. Hope to see you and hear about your work.

Best regards,

[signed] Arthur

1. Berger adds in pen: "Note: the Symphony is for the Guggenheim project, not this one." The letter was sent with a form for the Fulbright application.

2. The *Chamber Concerto*.

Copland to Berger
Handwritten postcard of Leningrad

Leningrad, Apr 6 '60

Dear Es & Arthur:

Greetings from the nicest town so far. We've been in Tiflis, (Georgia) and Riga, (Latvia). Audiences are very cordial and no one turns a hair at our 'modernisms,' 'tho not a word said pro or con about the music itself. Lukas[1] doing his Symphony of Chorales here and me my Statements. First class orchestra. Best to you both. (Sorry to miss the May affair.)

Aaron

1. Lukas Foss.

Berger to Copland
Typed letter

19 Ash St.
Cambridge,
Nov. 2, 1964

Dear Aaron:

I'm in a highly retrospective mood these days—a kind of self-assessment that would have been more appropriate, I suppose, two years ago when I turned 50, except that at that time I was so deeply involved in getting Perspectives[1] on its feet (how deeply, no one, with the possible exception of Boretz,[2] will ever appreciate.) In any case, I thought of a day in the 1930s this afternoon while reading through, with great delight (and by no means for the first time), "Années de pélerinage." We were walking down Mass. Ave. towards Symphony Hall and you asked me how I liked Liszt. My reaction could scarcely have been more negative and your amazement scarcely more complete. I was perfectly sincere, except that my judgment was based on the most superficial acquaintance with the weakest examples of his work. Somewhere along the way I had been assured on "good authority" that Liszt was "out," and much as I admired you, your recommendation did nothing to shake my conviction. How exasperating I now, in turn, find this sort of thing: the young people who do not even, as I did, choose between Liszt and Mozart, Stravinsky, and Schoenberg (or, in current terms, Copland and Stockhausen), but rule it all out in favor of the "dernière cri." (Gosh, how old and solemn I sound.)

"If only Aaron could hear me now," I said to myself, because when no

· 217 ·

one's around and on my fine Steinway with its easy action I can play quite delicately. I suppose I flatter myself to think that you remember the incident or that my playing could atone for it. And yet I'm sure that it is among many little exchanges that contributed to the formation of the image you have of me, much as you'd be willing to grant that I now am far from the same, emaciated, insecure, inhibited, and in some ways frightened person that I was then. One thing that comes home to revisit me is my failure to give any attention to my image as a composer. Do you remember how hard my side-kicks in the "Young Composers Group" worked at this sort of thing? So much so that even you were taken in at times more than you should have been, while I was completely bamboozled into thinking I was no composer at all. The 2 piano pieces in the Lawson Gould album from 1933 are all that remain of that period,[3] since the other stuff was either lost or destroyed, tho there was not much of it. I'm not sure I ever showed you those pieces. I couldn't understand them, and when I showed it to my pals their reaction was such that I don't think I would have dared show them to you. Mainly, I couldn't play them. But as I think back, neither could they, for the most part, play their pieces (even Vivian[4] and her Inventions). They just had more talent in faking them.

I suppose I should be elated at having had so much success last summer, and tho I went reluctantly (the sacrifice of composing time, which you can well appreciate), I hope you are aware that I am very grateful to you for having invited me.[5] The recent performance of Polyphony at the BSO (which was brewing in Leinsdorf's mind last season) may very well have been clinched by Tanglewood. Did you catch the WQXR broadcast?[6] It went quite well, and I'm especially pleased that so much could be brought off after 2 1/2 hrs. rehearsal. The BSO strings drew attention to some lovely details that the Louisville LP,[7] excellent tho it is, was incapable of doing justice to.

But the odd thing about these successes (including two Sun. stories, the Globe as well as the one you saw in the Times) is that they do not seem to be much help in getting me either publication or a decent commission (I've been offered some thankless ones). As I look back at some pieces of the 40s I'm struck with how well they stand up. Since no one else says this, because hardly anyone listens (especially to that antediluvian stuff), I suppose it devolves upon me to say so myself, especially in the light of the fact that my music does not give up its secret easily: stylistically, it does not shock or knock one off his feet, but affords a certain complexity and detail if one is willing to live with it. (In that respect (i.e. detail and structure) I might say that I was interested in returning to your Piano Sonata recently, first movement especially, which we gave on our graduate exam for the Masters degree.) My first vn and piano duo which Leo[8] and Joe Fuchs used to play, still strikes me as a strong one both in detail and in large structure, and there are several piano pieces of which only a Rondo and the Bagatelles are published: 3 One-part Inventions, 4 two-part Inventions, 5 movements of a Partita; and others that I no longer stand behind. Except for the One-part inventions, this says nothing about the music written since Ideas of Order (1953)—all of that unpublished, too. Leonard Feist was talking of signing me up before the sale, but alas.

I suppose out of habit, in this retrospective mood, my reaction is to "go to Aaron" when problems like this come up. I have no reason to think you are in any position to help me in this situation. But if anything should come up or you have any ideas, keep this in mind. Aside from the fact that the stuff of the 40's seems pretty hopeless of getting to anyone's attention in not being in print now, I'm concerned about getting the new stuff into a form so that I do not have to handle the material and the reproductions myself. You probably have forgotten what a grind this is, if you ever knew what it was. I can't rely on Arnie[9] any more. He misplaces my masters—both Polyphony and the Chamber Music for 13 Players. The latter almost had to be cancelled. (It's a surprisingly good piece, a little gem, and I now have a tape from Tanglewood I'd like you to hear.)

The whole situation is such these days that you may think it downright silly of me to complain about being virtually a "neglected" composer,—and immodest and presumptuous as well. After all, as I am well aware, your position can scarcely be said to be properly and justly esteemed of late. But I suppose my feeling of dissatisfaction stems from a sense that despite sporadic successes I have never had more than a parochial following: a few friends and colleagues who find my mind interesting enough to take the trouble of listening to and investigating my music. I must say that I find a few members of the younger generation more willing to take me seriously, and while this is certainly the best kind of recognition (even if I do not interest the "far-out" crowd), it makes me think that part of the reason is that they can dissociate me from the figure of a journalist[,] which no one wanted to believe was consistent with being a good musician. Make what you will of these complaints and rest assured that I absolve you from any obligation to return with a consolatory compliment. My purpose in addressing them to you is simply to complete the picture: I share the general apprehensiveness that all of us feel with regard to what should be the shape and direction of our next work, but the results of my retrospection have been favorable with the regard to the quality of my music of the past, and I only regret that so few people really share the pleasure of this music with me. Sonny[10] may be right when he implies that this may be nothing more than a need to compensate for my personal loneliness.

You are no doubt wondering what is going on with Perspectives. Very complicated. But let me simply point out that in our earlier crisis a lack of any support from the board did not help my position any—and I was shocked and deeply hurt that this lack went so far as to culminate in a situation in which my resignation could be received without a vote of thanks for what I had done to get the magazine off to such an impressive start, even if it did not (how could it) please everyone. Now as a board member I feel it important to give Ben[11] the support I did not get, especially since my resignation was a blow to Ben that taught him a great deal. Tho I complained to you about the mathematical approach during the tensest days of the crisis, I now feel it must be met head on with attempts to understand it and make its practitioners make themselves clearer. If we have another viewpoint, let's be grownup about it, and defend it rather than strive to stifle theirs. In the next issue I discuss "technical" writing which you disapprove of.[12] Maybe this will give you occasion to state your reasons. My article also prompted the glossary that you have been urging—i.e., as you must know, it's in the works.[13] As a true liberal, either you must get into the controversy or, and I can sympathize [with] you, if it's not worth your time, let the adversary say his piece. (The Mellers book[14] had already been assigned to Cogan.)

Poverino, if you have gotten this far and read 50 percent, I congratulate you.

Love,
[signed] Arthur

1. The journal *Perspectives of New Music*, which first appeared in 1962.

2. Benjamin Boretz.

3. "Two Episodes: 1933," published in *New Music for the Piano*, ed. Joseph Prostakoff (New York: Lawson-Gould, 1963).

4. Vivian Fine.

5. Berger had taught at Tanglewood in the summer of 1964.

6. The Boston Symphony Orchestra's performance of Berger's *Polyphony* was broadcast on New York's radio station WQXR on October 10, 1964.

7. Louisville Records, LOU 58-4.

8. Leo Smit.

9. Probably master copyist Arnold Arnstein.

10. Harold Shapero.

11. Benjamin Boretz, who was now editor of *Perspectives of New Music*.

12. "New Linguistic Modes and the New Theory," *Perspectives of New Music* 3, no. 1 (Fall–Winter 1964): 1–9.

13. This became Edward T. Cone's somewhat mocking article, "A Budding Grove," *Perspectives of New Music* 3, no. 2 (Spring–Summer 1965): 38–46.

14. Wilfrid Mellers, *Music in a New Found Land: Themes and Developments in the History of American Music* (London: Barrie and Rockliff, 1964). The review, "Mr. Mellers' Trial, and Ours," written by Robert Cogan and Pozzi Escot, appeared in *Perspectives of New Music* 4, no. 1 (Fall–Winter 1965): 152–60.

Copland to Berger
Typed letter on Rock Hill stationery

November 20, 1964

Dear Arthur:

I haven't received a letter like yours from anyone in years!

But before I comment on it, let me begin by a piece of good news for you. In my capacity as Chairman of the Naumburg Recording Award Committee, I have been empowered to tell you that the Board of Directors have chosen two of your works for the Naumburg Recording Award in Chamber Music. They plan to record the Chamber Music for Thirteen Players and the Three Pieces for Two Pianos on one side of an LP. It is assumed that the two works together do not last more than the time allotted for one side.[1] As you can imagine, I am very pleased at the decision and want to be the first to congratulate you! I might add that the actual mechanics of who will perform the works and when they will be recorded is within the province of Columbia Records. Sooner or later you will probably have to have some correspondence with John McClure of Columbia Records or possibly Mr. Gerald G. Krimm who is Secretary to the Board of the Walter Naumburg Foundation, 157 East 74th St.

I am sorry I missed the broadcast of the Leinsdorf performance.[2] Unfortunately I don't get WQXR well in these parts and didn't want to hear a garbled version due to poor reception.

As for your letter, I should love to reply in kind, but the naked truth is that I am swamped with things to do in the next few weeks. Anyway, it was very pleasant and even flattering to think that you would write to me in the tone of the "olden" days. I'm sure you are quite justified in many of your complaints, and if I had any real solutions, I'd take time out to proffer them.

In any event, I'm going to be up in Boston for several weeks during late winter and spring, living in Cambridge while preparing a TV series for the National Educational Television Network.[3] This will give us time to chat, I hope, and I look forward to it.

All best,

[signed] Aaron

1. The recording, Columbia ML6359 (monaural)/MS6959(stereo), as it finally appeared in 1967, had one work of Arthur Berger and one of Richard Donovan on each side. It was Donovan's works, not Berger's, that went slightly over ideal timing for one side of an LP.

2. Of Berger's *Polyphony*, as mentioned in Berger's letter of Nov. 2.

3. This became the series "Music in the Twenties" for National Educational Television, with Copland as host and occasional conductor, broadcast in 1965. See Emily Abrams, "Copland on Television," in this book.

Berger to Copland
Typed letter

19 Ash St., Cambridge
Nov. 28, 1964

Dear Aaron:

Thanks for the wonderful news. In some intangible way it seems very curious indeed (psychic?) that you should have been in a position to offer this partial solution to one of my main gripes (relative inaccessibility of my music to students and interested parties owing to nonpublication). I have already heard from McClure. Incidentally, you were worried about the stops in the second movement of the 2-piano pieces which were selected. This was a conscious use of silence (a bit like my conscious interruption of cantabile lines which always used to disturb you—something like dismembering figures in abstract or semi-abstract painting, roughly). I think the second time around one has the proper [mind-]set to expect it and, I hope, accept it, too. Seeing the players in the hall helps, of course. But perhaps for the recording I can try to tighten up these pauses, or see that the performance makes them more convincing.

I should have assured you that I did not expect you to answer my outpouring, my thinking out loud. How would you go about it—it was so confused and touched on so many different things. I find myself from time to time writing such letters to let off steam, and then not sending—especially when they are to newspapers or magazines. I almost didn't send the one to you. Rather like Saul Bellow's Herzog.

Now that I have sent the letter to you, I realize that my dissatisfaction has a much deeper cause than simply a matter of acceptance. Since I wrote you I got up the courage to visit a publisher, instead of, as in the past, waiting for one to come to me. It seems news of the BSO performance had gotten to him, and Erich had himself mentioned the piece to this publisher.[1] So it looks promising, but I may want your advice before signing anything.

As far as listening to broadcasts, we're even, since I missed the Nonet.[2] I was en route to NY for a family affair. I do want very much to hear how it came out for large strings, and I hope I shall find someone with a good air-check. I'm delighted to hear you're coming here and that we'll have a chance to chat. Don't forget that my guest-room is at your disposal, tho I'll understand if you prefer to be off by yourself.

As ever,
[signed] Arthur

1. Erich: Erich Leinsdorf. *Polyphony* was later handled as a rental piece by Boelke-Bomart; it has never been published in the sense of being purchasable as notes on paper.

2. Copland's *Nonet* for strings was performed in its version for multiple strings by the New York Philharmonic under William Steinberg on November 19, 20, and 22, 1964. The performance of November 19 was broadcast.

—‧—

Berger to Copland
Typed letter on Brandeis University School of Creative Arts stationery

March 19, 1965

Dear Aaron:

A reminder to send me the score of that special recording of Connotations which I am very anxious to hear.

It was wonderful to see you the other night, and thanks again for the dinner.

Affectionately,
[signed] Arthur
Arthur Berger

—‧—

Copland to Berger
Typed letter

25th October, 1965

Dear Arthur:

Greetings from London, where I am in the midst of a conducting tour lasting in all six weeks. Will be back home in mid-November.

I am writing you about an event which is being planned for San Francisco in early March '66. I am going out there at the invitation of the Orchestra to put on three concerts of contemporary music, one chamber music, one chamber orchestra and one full orchestra. It is quite a project!

I remember the pieces for two pianos you played for me and would like to have them performed along with my NONET and the VARESE DESERTS. It turns out that there is an excellent two-piano team at the San Francisco State College in the persons of Bussotti and Nadas. They have agreed to do the pieces, and will probably be getting in touch with you directly in order to get hold of the music. Sometime after I am back, I should have a copy myself to examine, as I am supposed to say something about the pieces performed. I am pleased with this possibility of presenting the work in your old stamping-ground, and thought you would like to know about it, if you haven't already heard from San Francisco.

I hope you like your new living quarters and that all goes well.

All best,

[signed] Aaron

[in ink] P.S. As you can guess, this letter was dictated to a Boosey-Hawkes secretary!

———————

Berger to Copland
Typed letter on Brandeis University School of Creative Arts stationery
December 2, 1965

Dear Aaron:

I see from the society fashion columns in the <u>Times</u> that you are back.[1] Delighted that you are including my two-piano piece on the San Francisco program. I will get around to sending you a score before the month is over, but in the meantime I sent the material to California a good while ago.

Forgive the formality of this note.

In haste,

Arthur [secretarial signature]

1. "Fashions That Pass the Test of Time" (*New York Times,* November 19, 1965) by Bernadine Morris, reporting on a charity event at which Copland and Leonard Bernstein played two-piano music to raise funds for the MacDowell Colony. The article features a photograph of a (Stravinskyish-looking) Copland "with Mrs. Ernest Heller in a scoop-necked white brocade by Monte-Sano."

———————

Copland to Berger
Typed letter on Rock Hill stationery
February 9, 1966

Dear Arthur,

Damnation!! I recently heard from the managers of the San Francisco Symphony that the two pianists, Bussotti and Nadas, who had agreed to play your Three Pieces, have now reneged. Over the long-distance phone I had the impression that they were objecting to having the pianos "prepared."[1] Are they "prepared"?? And even if they are, what about it?

Well—whatever the reason, I'm damned disappointed, and obviously we owe you apologies.

Of course, we've all had this sort of thing happen, but it doesn't make it any better each time that it does. I'll be going out to the coast at the end of next week and will find out the gory details when I get there.

Damnation!!!

[signed] Aaron

1. Berger's *Three Pieces for Two Pianos* involve a moderate amount of Cagean "preparation."

Berger to Copland
Claire Reis asked a large number of composers to write letters for an album to be presented to Copland on his 70th birthday. This is Berger's typed letter, November 1970.

Cambridge, Mass

Dear Aaron:

It is good to have occasions like this for taking stock of all you mean to us, Aaron. Composers of my generation are much in your debt not only for the example your music has presented to us but also for what you have done to establish, through tireless efforts on the musical scene, an atmosphere in which we may pursue creative activities in this country with a sense that they finally command some respect. And yet, I should confess that trying to express myself on this matter is not easy, because I find myself reaching for words I have used in talking about you before—words that need no reiteration and that are out of place in a communication of this sort when they bear on your extraordinary responsibility to the precise curve of the heard musical line, since such words derive meaning from direct correlation with the music they refer to.

I am assuming that everyone knows how versatile you are and will not take me to imply any single-mindedness on your part. For I'm talking about words that endeavor to grasp at basic values, such as distinguish whatever you do regardless of the specific guise you may assume. If the same words still come to mind, moreover, it is not because you have not changed or because I have not come upon new ways of looking at your musical contribution. Indeed, I become more and more aware of the injustice that can be done to you by imposing too much insulation between "this kind of Copland music" and that, and I see you more and more as the unified, the whole musician, capable of expressing his devotion to the highest musical ideals in any number of ways—whether it be in music for the "interested" audience or for a wide, discriminating public, or in activities on behalf of the League of Composers or of young aspirants who need encouragement.

Let me use this occasion, therefore, to warmly congratulate you for your constant service in the cause of music—though I know only too well that there are many other ways in which you could be congratulated, and many other things you should be congratulated for. And the predicament I find myself in—wanting and yet not wanting to use the same words again to characterize this extraordinary trait in you—can thus be turned to advantage in the form of a moral. If outstanding achievement in the arts has always been remarkable, in our time it is still more remarkable for anyone, once having achieved, to continue to achieve. Your continued achievement adds a significant new dimension to the unbounded admiration we've always had for you.

Yours,

[signed] Arthur

Copland to Berger
Handwritten letter on 1538 L. Washington Street stationery

Jan 23 1971

Dear Arthur:

I've just re-read your birthday letter in the composer album I was given on Nov. 14. It's a beautiful statement, and I wanted to tell you how much I appreciated it. Reading it brings back the long years of our association, and how meaningful they were.

Also I wanted to thank you for your part in making my recent Brandeis visit so pleasant an occasion. Not forgetting the party at your house!

Best to Ellen.[1]—As ever, Aaron

1. Berger's second wife.

Copland to Berger
Typed letter on 1538 L. Washington Street stationery

April 17, 1979

Dear Arthur:

I'm sorry I had to miss the performance of your CHAMBER CON-CERTO in New York. The fact is that I was away on concert tour during that period. More conducting!

I hope the performance went off well (even though I know you're a difficult customer to please!)

Someday, somehow, I should be back in Boston. Look forward to seeing you and Esther[1] then.

All the best
[signed] Aaron

1. Copland's slip of memory for "Ellen." Copland repeats this slip in his letter of May 1, 1980.

———

Copland to Berger
Typed letter on 1538 L. Washington Street stationery

May 1, 1980

Dear Arthur:

I was astonished to get the invitation to the concert in honor of your retirement from Brandeis. Good Lord!—it was a shock for me to think of you as having arrived at such an end-of-the-road position. But knowing you as I do, I'm sure you will have plenty of projects to occupy yourself with.

Anyhow—all best to you, and love to Esther.

[in ink] As ever
Aaron

[in ink]: P.S. Sorry not to be able to be present at the concert.

———

Copland to Berger
Typed letter on 1538 L. Washington Street stationery

September 24, 1980

Dear Arthur,

I'm sure you know of (and probably personally know) my good friend, Vivian Perlis, of the Music Faculty at Yale. She is collaborating with me on the preparation of a book of memoires which we hope to publish within a reasonable time.

I trust you have no objection to seeing her in connection with our book. You will find her very knowledgeable and <u>sympathique</u>.

All best

[signed] Aaron

[typed] P.S. I understand that Vivian will be getting in touch with you in the very near future.

[ink] P.S. Hope all goes well with you.

———

Copland to Berger
Telegram dated April 25, 1982

CONGRATS ON YOUR ARRIVING AT AN IMPRESSIVE MILESTONE DATE.[1] HERE'S WISHING YOU MANY MORE YEARS OF ACCOM-PLISHMENT

AFFECTIONATELY

AARON

1. May 15, 1982 was Berger's seventieth birthday.

Berger to Copland
Handwritten card postmarked September 28, 1982, Boston, Mass.

You should be receiving any day now the announcement of a retrospective concert of my music at the Guild of Composers, <u>October 14</u>. I hope you can join us after the concert at a party given by Joseph Machlis,[1] at 303 East 57th St., Apt. 4F. Regards.

Arthur
RSVP—Berger, 9 Sparks St.
Cambridge, Ma. 02138

1. Musicologist; author of *Introduction to Contemporary Music* (New York: Norton, 1961), *American Composers of Our Time* (New York, Crowell, 1963), and *The Enjoyment of Music* (first ed. New York: Norton, 1963; many editions since).

PART IV

ANALYTIC PERSPECTIVES

War Drums, Tolling Bells, and
Copland's Piano Sonata

LARRY STARR

Aaron Copland's Piano Sonata (1939–1941) is unique in the composer's output in terms of genre, form, and expressive content. It is also fully representative of his compositional maturity. The Sonata is paradoxically that much more representative because of being unique, insofar as Copland made a specialty of producing remarkable, sui generis compositions. He inaugurated his career as a published composer with one such work, the character piece *The Cat and the Mouse* (1920). A list of analogously "exceptional" Copland works could continue with his major works of the 1920s: the Symphony for Organ and Orchestra composed specifically for Boulanger, the self-consciously "American" *Music for the Theatre*, the lone Piano Concerto, and the original version of *Symphonic Ode*. Compositions from the 1930s could follow: the Piano Variations, the orchestral *Statements*, *El Salón México*, and the "play opera" *The Second Hurricane*, among others. Each of these works is distinctive in terms of its genre, function, form, or instrumentation. (The Symphony for Organ and Orchestra, for example, is distinctive in all of these respects.) Many celebrated later works could readily be added to this list.

In the five years preceding the completion of his Piano Sonata, Copland was actively exploring a fresh "populist" style and approach, writing on commission for specific groups and occasions music that was designed to be accessible, and producing a significant body of work employing texts or programs. Conspicuously absent from his output during this period were new examples of "absolute music" and of works for solo instruments.[1] In the midst of all this "Americana," Copland turned abruptly to the European genre of the sonata, conceiving a work of absolute music with a considerably more complex and dissonant character than was typical of his output at the time.[2] The Piano Sonata stands out all the more because nothing remotely similar followed it; Copland's principal works of 1942 were *Lincoln Portrait*, *Fanfare for the Common Man*, and *Rodeo*, all of which fit readily into the Americana (or populist) category. Interestingly enough, when Copland in 1943 tackled the sonata genre for the second—and last—time with his Sonata for Violin and Piano, he produced a work whose style was much more obviously aligned with the diatonic, relatively consonant tendencies of his contemporaneous program pieces. Obviously the Piano Sonata represents a very special case.

While some commentators have viewed the Piano Sonata in terms of a rapprochement between the intensely severe style of Copland's earlier Piano Variations and the style of his populist music, I concur with Howard Pollack's estimation that the Sonata is an uncompromising and demanding work.[3] After all, it is not simply some measure of dissonance level that determines the character and "difficulty" of a composition. The Sonata may be less aggressively dissonant overall than the Variations, yet it shares with the earlier work a quality of unabated seriousness; both demand substantial attention and commitment from performers and listeners. Copland himself stressed, during a public discussion of his piano music, that the Sonata is "very serious" and he underlined this characterization of it in his autobiography: "It is a serious piece that requires careful and repeated study."[4] Copland's statement that the Sonata's second movement is "rhythmically American," the result of his familiarity with jazz, could suggest a point of contact between the Sonata and the composer's Americana works; however, the real musical distance between this movement and jazz may be gauged by the composer's description of how "the rhythmic units shift through 5/8, 6/8, 3/4, and 7/8."[5] It is difficult to imagine a metrical framework less characteristic of jazz, particularly the jazz commonly played and heard when the Piano Sonata was composed— at the height of the "swing era"! Any connection between the Sonata and Copland's more vernacular-based compositions seems tenuous at best.

A comparison between the Piano Variations and the Piano Sonata would seem more apposite, yet such a comparison ultimately reinforces an appreciation of the Sonata's distinctive character. Copland's typical economy in selection and development of musical materials is outstandingly exemplified by both works. However, the defining material of the Variations is its theme, a linear idea spun out from the four single notes proclaimed at the outset. The Sonata, by contrast, begins with three chords, as if the composer were determined to establish immediately that this ambitious new piano work will be constructed from a different basis entirely. (See Example 1.) In effect, the Sonata reverses the compositional strategy of the Variations; whereas the latter introduces a monophonic theme interrupted sporadically by chords, the former employs a chordal texture from which soloistic lines of melody occasionally emerge. The Variations retains its resolutely linear character, while the substantial opening movement of the Sonata is chordally conceived to a striking extent.

A common feature of the two works is a large-scale tempo progression in which the fastest music is positioned in the central part of the work, surrounded by slower-moving material. (This organizational procedure is another Copland trademark, characterizing many other works as well.) The tempo progression is employed in a highly individual way, however, in each of the two piano compositions. Although the theme, twenty variations, and coda that constitute the Piano Variations are to be performed as a continuous unit, there are a greater number of significant tempo changes within this work than in the three-movement Piano Sonata, which takes approximately twice as long to play. In the Variations, of course, tempo is a primary means of differentiating one variation from another, so the large number of individual variations helps account for the relatively frequent tempo changes. The overall range of tempo is also considerably wider in the Variations than in the Sonata. Both works employ the fastest metronome marking available, 208 beats per minute, with the quarter note as the unit of measurement. But the Variations commence at the other end of the dial, so to speak, grave, with the quarter note at 48, while the slowest metronome indication in the Sonata—the defining tempo for the finale's Andante sostenuto—situates the quarter note at 76. Although Copland himself described the tempo arrangement of the Sonata movements as "slow-fast-slow," the "slow" outer movements of the Sonata are slow only in comparison to the restless middle movement, a Vivace whose defining quarter-note tempo is the top-of-the-dial 208.[6] (The Variations reach this breakneck speed only briefly, just before the coda.) The sole movement of the Sonata to have major internal changes of tempo is the first; strikingly, its essential tempo progression is molto moderato—allegro—tempo I, anticipating the basic relationships among the three movements themselves and reinforcing Copland's characteristic strategy.

The Variations and the Sonata do share a distinctive approach to piano sonority. Complex, often clangorous and percussive, chordal sonorities occurring over the full range of the keyboard are juxtaposed with spare textures consisting of single melodic lines or, less frequently, widely spaced lines in counterpoint. This general description applies equally well to Copland's later Piano Fantasy (1955–57), the last of his three major keyboard works. Still, it must be stressed that these ambitious compositions employ similar textures to achieve markedly different expressive ends.

The Sonata plumbs remarkable emotional depths by exploring what, for this composer, seem to be the musical equivalents of "extreme conditions." The opening movement's fixation on chordal textures and the extreme tempo of the second movement have been mentioned. The Vivace is also metrically irregular to a degree that is striking for Copland, a composer who never shied away from rhythmic complexities; even the outer movements of *Short Symphony*, a work notorious for its rhythmic difficulty, are not as consistently inconsistent in meter as the Sonata's middle movement. (When the Vivace very occasionally settles into a steady meter for a few bars at a time, it is usually a meter of 5/8 or 7/8.) The finale of the Piano Sonata has its own exceptional qualities, beginning with its form—described by Copland himself as "free."[7] The free form is particularly striking insofar as the preceding two movements, extraordinary as they are, do correspond in some respects to traditional formal models: a substantial opening movement in sonata-allegro form is followed by a shorter, tripartite scherzo-like movement. In the finale, unusual form is in the service of unusual expression. Unlike the Piano Variations—or *Short Symphony*, or *Symphonic Ode*—all of which honor the long-standing tradition of ending ambitious instrumental pieces with loud, emphatic, climactic gestures, the Piano Sonata concludes by gradually yielding to stillness. In effect, the work closes inward, toward a cessation of melodic, rhythmic, and dynamic activity—another extreme condition. (See Example 18, page 252.)

What called forth such an intense work from Copland? The impulse might have originated simply with the desire to compose something deeply personal, original, and different from the other kinds of music that were occupying him at the time. However, it seems equally plausible that the Piano Sonata had its origins in the same kind of impulse to speak directly to, and of, his time that motivated Copland's Americana compositions. *The Second Hurricane*, *Quiet City*, the early film scores, and other works of this period are reflective of the Great Depression and the New Deal in America, and of Copland's desire as an artist to depict, and to respond to the needs of, his own country and people. But Copland was also very much a man of the world, who traveled frequently outside the United States and who could not have helped being aware of the global situation and of the war clouds enveloping Europe as the 1930s came to an end. As a Jewish American, he must have felt particular concern about the spread of European Fascism. The Piano Sonata was written during the three years that brought the outbreak of World War II in Europe and the subsequent triumphs of the German army, dark days indeed. Perhaps Copland turned to a great traditional European genre to express his personal feelings regarding events across the Atlantic and the threat that these events posed to all aspects of great European civilization—and to American civilization as well.[8]

Copland never claimed explicitly that the Piano Sonata was a response to the world events of 1939–41, but considering this possibility obviously helps illuminate the work's serious tone and its distinctive and extreme qualities. Howard Pollack asserts unequivocally that "the work certainly is a wartime work: grim, nervous, elegiac, with pervasive bell-like tollings of alarm and mourning."[9] The opening of the first movement seems to evoke pealing bells, culminating in the twelfth bar with a low, syncopated B-flat that resounds like a huge gong, or perhaps like the pounding of an enormous war drum. (Example 1.)

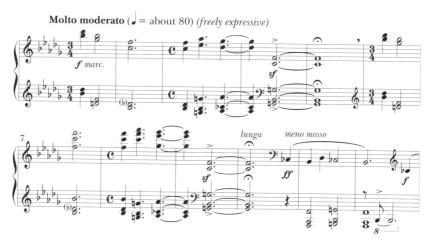

Example 1. Copland, Piano Sonata, first movement, mm. 1–12.

Listeners who, like myself, hear the sounds of bells and the echoes of war drums in Copland's Piano Sonata may gain indirect corroboration from what would seem an unlikely source—namely, the composer's own later setting of "I felt a funeral in my brain," the ninth of his *Twelve Poems of Emily Dickinson* (1949–50). In her wrenching poem, Dickinson employs a "drum" and a "bell" as similes to portray the feelings in her tortured mind. Examples 2 and 3 illustrate Copland's musical responses to these images.

Dickinson's "service like a drum" calls forth from Copland chord structures that are strikingly similar to those in the opening bars of the Piano Sonata, not only in terms of interval structure but even of specific pitch choices. (Compare Example 2 with Example 1.) Copland prominently employs the same low B♭, and creates an analogous sense of mixing B-flat

Example 2. Copland, "I felt a funeral in my brain," mm. 19–24.

major and B-flat minor coloring through the use of both D♮ and D♭. (G♭ and G♮, as well as C♭, are also important in both passages.) The analogy between the "bell" music (shown in Example 3) and the opening of the Sonata cannot be drawn with the same degree of exactitude. Nevertheless, significant similarities in sonority result from Copland's choices of intervals, chord spacing, and register.[10] An objection might be lodged that this all amounts to reasoning after the fact, since *Twelve Poems of Emily Dickinson* appeared nearly a decade after the Piano Sonata. Yet it could be claimed that this chronological relationship actually makes the argument all the more compelling. Long after composing the Sonata, when Copland was seeking in his compositional lexicon material suitable for "I felt a funeral in my brain," he was drawn naturally to the musical elements he had used previously in the Sonata—precisely because of their inherent emotional, psychological, and sonorous import.

The very particular sound world of Copland's Piano Sonata accounts for a good deal of its power. As a work of "absolute music," however, it ultimately communicates through the form by which Copland shapes his materials, and consequently it is the work's formal trajectory that now demands our attention.

Example 3. Copland, "I felt a funeral in my brain," mm. 39–46.

From the beginning, Copland's Sonata presents highly concentrated musical gestures that are immediately memorable and pregnant with possibilities.
Everything in the first twelve measures emerges directly from the three-
chord progression with which the work begins. (See Example 1.) In fact,
to an extent that can only be suggested here, the basic material of the entire
first movement proceeds with ineluctable logic from the first two bars, and
the echoes of these three chords continue to resound in various ways—
sometimes quite literally—throughout the remaining two movements of
the work. These chords expose three essential intervals in turn: the minor
third, the major third, and the perfect fourth. These are the intervals with
which the opening movement proves to be obsessed, and they are extremely
prominent in the other movements as well. An intense focus on particular intervals was consistently characteristic of Copland's economical
approach to composition. However, the first two measures of the Sonata
do not merely spell out the work's defining intervals. They also suggest a
harmonic frame of reference, one that establishes a rich and complex field
of play, both for the first movement and for the Sonata as a whole.

A general, if ambiguous, feeling of B-flat minor hovers over the opening chord progression. This is due to the doubled minor third on B♭ and

D♭ that initiates the progression, to the arpeggiation of a B-flat minor triad in the top voice of the progression, and to the third sonority—in effect, a B-flat minor triad in root position with the additional note C. The third chord also helps account for the sense of ambiguity, principally because the dissonant ninth seems to portend harmonic restlessness, but also because the F in the top voice (the fifth of the chord) seems to demand continuation. The greatest source of ambiguity, however, is the D♮ in the second chord, as the left hand's insistence on minor thirds creates a conflict with the five-flat "key signature" and engenders modal mixture in the progression; the second chord consists of the pitches of a B-flat *major* triad, in first inversion, with the additional note G♭. Thus the progression moves from a relatively "pure" consonance through a sonority that is intensely dissonant (both because of the minor ninth and because of the modal "cross-relation") to a relatively more stable, but still dissonant, sonority. Copland exposes, in this embryonic progression, significant musical issues with which the entire Sonata will grapple: triads and triad-like sonorities, modal mixture and ambiguity, relative consonance and dissonance, and the question of tonal center—all illuminated by the employment of specific intervals both to suggest and undermine conventional harmonic usage. The composer's impressive, modern, and distinctive engagement with the tonal traditions that played such a major role in the evolution of the sonata genre is evident in this work from the outset.[11]

The implication of a B-flat pitch center receives reinforcement with the strong low B♭ in m. 12. (See Example 1.) The melodic line in mm. 10–12, which emerges at last from the chordal texture, also emphasizes B-flat. (This little melodic motive comes directly from the top voice of the chords in mm. 3–4 and 8–9, here emphasizing F, and the motive assumes considerable importance as the movement develops.) But m. 12 provides no sense of real closure; Copland uses the new texture as a starting point for further elaboration, and the chord on the downbeat of the measure does not suggest finality on any level—the added, syncopated B♭ notwithstanding. In fact, this particular chord in this particular register recurs prominently, and arguably is resolved only in the final bars of the movement when it is allowed to progress directly to B♭ (as shown in Example 9). Yet not even at movement's end do we hear a pure B-flat minor triad. It is indicative of the complexity and subtlety of Copland's language that, although pure triads do occur in all three movements of the Sonata (only momentarily in the second), none of the movements concludes on a triad.

The smooth emergence of the solo line in mm. 10–12 of the first movement is in keeping with the unhurried, direct character of the opening music, a music of Coplandesque plain speaking that suggests careful declamation—or perhaps, considering the dynamics, proclamation. Occasionally, the chordal surface of this movement breaks apart abruptly, as if exposing a kind of emotional fissure through which material of a radically different character may pass. The first instance of this is brief but violent: the wildly cascading scale figure that erupts in mm. 48–49. This helps mark the climax of the first section of the movement and initiate the dissipation of tension that prepares the arrival of the second theme area. It may also help prepare the extended non-chordal passages in the central part of the movement, passages that break out suddenly with the octaves in m. 123 (più largamente) and cease even more abruptly with a bar of silence (m. 188, just before meno mosso). The textural character of the first movement is thus defined by chords, among which solo lines are interspersed and whose progressions these lines occasionally interrupt. This strategy is essentially inverted in the second movement and employed again at the beginning of the final movement, albeit to quite different effect.

The opening movement of Copland's Sonata, considered as a whole, may be seen as a rapprochement between the composer's characteristic techniques of thematic economy and harmonic complexity, on the one hand, and the traditional requirements of "a regular sonata allegro form with two themes," which is how Copland himself described the movement, on the other.[12] The second theme is derived directly from the first. (See Example 4.) In a manner reminiscent of Haydn, that first great master of traditional sonata allegro form, Copland differentiates his two thematic areas principally by means of harmony rather than melodic content. As Copland's change of key signature implies, the harmonic focus

Example 4. Copland, Piano Sonata, first movement, mm. 58–66.

of the second theme is an ambiguous G minor, with the recurring B♮s creating a modal ambiguity directly analogous to that characterizing the first theme. A comparison of mm. 58–59 with mm. 1–2 reveals additional kinships in register, chordal texture, choice of intervals, and the descending contour that initiates both themes. So close are they that mm. 58–59 may be heard as a varied transposition of mm. 1–2, incorporating but one additional pitch in the interest of providing material for four chords rather than three. (The F♮ in the second theme has no equivalent in the opening two bars, but its analogous A♭ is heard soon enough, in m. 3.) The interval of transposition—a minor third down—is surely no coincidence, and links the second theme area to that of the first theme in a harmonically structural manner insofar as the minor third is a crucial interval, arguably the defining interval, of the first theme. Here Copland brilliantly adapts the "classical" principle of tonal contrast in a sonata allegro exposition to the requirements of his own harmonic language and his preference for thematic economy. The sonata allegro form consequently emerges as a logical outgrowth of Copland's chosen material, not as a foreign element arbitrarily imposed on that material. And sonata allegro form itself is correspondingly enriched by Copland's consistent, convincing, and refreshingly personal approach. (It should come as no surprise that the recapitulation of the second theme is harmonically positioned a minor third *higher* than the B-flat minor of the first theme; see Example 8.)

Copland's second theme is further differentiated from the opening material by means of dynamic level and phrasing, and by the conspicuous absence of fourths. So economical is Copland's means of expression that only a few changes produce a complete alteration of mood; note his indication "with sentiment." The second theme area proceeds as a series of variations of a nine-measure unit (shown in Example 4). The variations all maintain the basic physiognomy and ambiguous modal coloring of the theme but alter its length and textural characteristics, and the implied harmonic center shifts from one variation to the next. (A kind of family resemblance to the Piano Variations may be felt here, a resemblance naturally accentuated by the close relationship this thematic material bears to the material that opens the Sonata.) Eventually, the music abandons its soft dynamic level and gentle quality, and a strong descending chord progression merges beautifully into a forceful, varied restatement of the opening theme in a new harmonic area, heralding clearly the start of a "development section." (See Example 5.) Developmental techniques are, of course, employed throughout the first movement and the Sonata as a whole, from the very opening measures; it is the direct and emphatic reminiscence of mm. 1–4 that operates to proclaim the development section in mm. 96–99.

Example 5. Copland, Piano Sonata, first movement, mm. 96–99.

At the beginning of this development, the first theme is transformed to incorporate an element from the second theme and a feeling of greater harmonic instability is introduced; these characteristics reflect traditional developmental techniques. The two chords in m. 96 suggest a C minor orientation, but in m. 97 the top voice ascends a whole step instead of descending the expected fourth (thus mimicking the motion in the second bar of the second theme—see Example 4, m. 59) and the chord in m. 97 suggests a G minor orientation. The motion of the top voice in mm. 96–97 prefigures the motive that will appear in the central section of this development, consisting of a descending fourth followed by an ascending major second. (See Example 6, m. 133.) This is preceded by the passage in octaves beginning at m. 123 (più largamente), which isolates as a four-note melodic motive the intervals articulated by the top voice in the chords that open the second theme (Example 4, mm. 58–59) and consequently encourages the listener to recognize that the motive in m. 133 is derived from that theme (by omitting the second of the four notes).

Sensing a connection on some level between the striking allegro passage in the development and the second theme material is important because the character of the Allegro seems initially so unanticipated. But

Example 6. Copland, Piano Sonata, first movement, mm. 133–36.

this Allegro, dominated by single-line passages (with octave doublings, as in Example 6), is part of a larger strategy on Copland's part for shaping the Sonata as a whole. In terms of both tempo and texture, it strongly anticipates the character of the second movement.[13] Interrelationships among the movements become more pronounced and direct as the work proceeds.

The Allegro stops abruptly, in effect hitting a chordal wall of bells (meno mosso) that heralds the overwhelming, climactic return of the first theme at tempo I (shown in Example 7). This recapitulation appropriately brings back the opening harmonic area. Copland, however, almost immediately resumes the ongoing developmental strategy of the movement, spreading the opening material over the entire range of the keyboard in an extraordinary passage requiring four staves for its notation. There could not be a greater contrast between this music and the

Example 7. Copland, Piano Sonata, first movement, mm. 196–203.

Example 8. Copland, Piano Sonata, first movement, mm. 223–26.

preceding light-textured, fleet-footed Allegro, and an implication of catastrophe—actual or impending—is virtually inescapable.

The fury subsides, and the brief, varied restatement of the second theme achieves an exquisite tenderness as Copland adds an obligato melody line above it. (See Example 8.) Then the range expands and the dynamics swell until a final pealing of bells brings the movement to the concluding cadence (shown in Example 9). Although the bass arrival on B♭ sounds definitive, Copland's concluding reiteration of the original three-chord progression is ambiguous in its implications. It is not so much the dissonance in the third chord that disturbs the sense of finality; the listener is by this time well accustomed to such chords, to the extent of accepting them as harmonic norms in this work. It is rather the sense that, for all the musical intensity and variety in this movement, the ending may only have brought us back to the point of departure; perhaps the major "action" in the Sonata has yet to come. The extent to which this interpretation

Example 9. Copland, Piano Sonata, first movement, mm. 237–42.

seems plausible is the extent to which Copland may have deviated, deliberately, from a basic animating principle of traditional sonata allegro forms: the principle of resolving established tensions. This line of reasoning may be pursued further, to help explain why Copland deviates progressively further from traditional architecture in each of the two succeeding movements (since he has to find his own way to resolve the tensions in the work) and why the finale must recall the first movement (in order to put that movement's enduring tensions to rest at last).

The second movement of Copland's Sonata evinces a compositional strategy very typical of the composer and already familiar from the first movement. A concentrated idea, composed of restricted pitch material and characteristic intervals, is gradually developed through repetition, variation, and expansion (as shown in Example 10). What accounts for the remarkable difference in effect between this music and that which opens the first movement is the sheer quantity of obsessive repetition (already evident in the fifteen measures of Example 10), coupled with the manic tempo; the metrical irregularity only enhances the impact.[14] In contrast to the "plain-spoken" declamation that begins the Sonata, this Vivace gives the impression of something like stuttering—having so much to

Example 10. Copland, Piano Sonata, second movement, mm. 1–15.

say, accompanied by so much anxiety, that it can scarcely articulate anything intelligible.[15]

The pitch material employed in the opening passages of the second movement shares certain characteristics with the material heard at the beginning
of the first, a fact that contributes to the overall coherence of the Sonata.
A similar sense of harmonic ambiguity obtains, due to the presence in the
Vivace of both D♮ and D♯; considering Copland's five-sharp key signature,
the suggestion here is of B major with an intruding minor-third scale
degree (which, in effect, reverses the modal implications of the first movement). The pitch collection that appears in the opening passages of the
Vivace approximates that employed in mm. 1–2 of the first movement,
transposed up a half step—with one exception and two additions. The exception results from Copland's choice of G♯ instead of G♮, a choice that seems
to reinforce the B major ambience somewhat, insofar as it accords with the
five-sharp signature. The additions are the E first heard in m. 1, and
the E♯ first heard in m. 6; together they add another cross-relation to the
already slippery harmonic surface, with the E♯ suggesting perhaps a Lydian
scale influence (although Copland seems most interested in the effect
created by parallel major sixths in the left hand of the piano). The sparse
texture, the continuous fixation of the basic motive on the pitch G♯, and
the absence of anything resembling a root position triad are additional factors contributing to the tonal insecurity here. Like its rhythm and tempo,
the harmony of the Vivace seems to have lost its moorings. The first
movement sounds remarkably stable by comparison.

In the music that follows after Example 10, the opening motive is subjected to further repetitions and expansions, and octave displacements are
introduced along with textural changes and one additional pitch (A♮). Still,
for all its restless racing, the music never seems able to get anywhere.
Following an abrupt bar of silence, bell sounds ring out once again. (See
Example 11.) A transposed version of the original idea attempts to extricate

Example 11. Copland, Piano Sonata, second movement, mm. 54–58.

itself from this dissonant clamor, and eventually does so, only to set off a bizarre machine-line passage in 7/8 (*A tempo*) together with additional variants of itself. The constant shifting of texture, register, and implied harmonic focus suggests a kind of development section; however, the absence of clear points of arrival or thematic differentiation renders this movement formally elusive—certainly much more so than the preceding one.

When at last the eighth-note rhythms temporarily relax, a wide-ranging melody employing much longer note values emerges briefly (as shown in Example 12). This expansive melody, so different from anything previously heard in the Sonata, reappears early in the third movement, where it receives sustained attention and introduces a radically new emotional tone. Here, however, it remains just the hint of an alternative to virtually all the music we have been hearing: leisurely, lyrical, and expressive, neither clangorous nor restless. The striking contrast is suggestive of a "trio" section for the "scherzo."[16] But the form remains skewed, just like everything else in this strange and disquieting movement: the trio is far too short to serve as a proper counterweight to the music that surrounds it on either side.

Example 12. Copland, Piano Sonata, second movement, mm. 201–09.

The movement soon resumes its familiar character, and earlier portions are restated, although not in their original order. The rearrangement allows Copland to end with the same material heard at the opening. Like the first movement, the second returns to its point of departure—which in this case seems particularly appropriate, given the tendency of this music to chase its own tail. In lieu of a real cadence, Copland collapses his original motive into a series of three dyads, paired with their transposition in the left hand at the lower fourth. (This transposition returns the left hand to the sixth on F♯ and D♯ so prominent in the movement's opening passages—see Example 13.) The chordal texture successfully prepares the strong chords which open the succeeding movement, and Copland indicates "attacca."

Example 13. Copland, Piano Sonata, second movement, mm. 306–10.

The finale begins with a three-chord progression, out of which emerges a "solo" line of melody—at first tentatively and then more extensively. The compositional process is by now typical of the work as a whole, while the specific textures, gestures, and tempo are clearly reminiscent of the music that begins the first movement. (See Example 14.) However, this is in no sense a return to the first movement. The chord progression has an emphatic "major" quality, as it ends on an inverted G-major triad. The characteristic cross-relation in this progression is between the F♯s in the first chord and the F♮ in the second, but this obviously doesn't affect the basic "major" ambience. The melody that emerges is the one previously heard in the trio of the second movement. (Compare Example 12 with Example 14.) Soon it is this melody, and its evolution into a two-part contrapuntal texture, that dominates the musical discourse as the chords cease to be heard.

Obviously, the work has taken a fresh turn. After linking the finale broadly to the first movement and directly to the second, Copland steers the Sonata into a new expressive landscape. "One thinks of the sonata as dramatic—a kind of play being acted out with plenty of time for self-expression," Copland wrote.[17] While there is much musical activity in both the first and second movements, neither one seems ultimately to move forward, to advance the action, so to speak. In creating an unprecedented kind of denouement for his "play," Copland permits his music at last to progress in unforeseen directions: new melodic ideas, new textures, and new harmonic realms ultimately generate a new "free" form. This all suggests intense "self-expression" on the part of a very careful composer. Many commentators have remarked on the singular nature of the Sonata's finale.[18] It is worth pondering why the Sonata seems to demand such an unusual conclusion.

Example 14. Copland, Piano Sonata, third movement, mm. 1–14.

The Sonata proclaims and declaims with tolling bells in the first movement and gives free rein to the expression of nervous restlessness in the
second. To be sure, there are respites of sentiment and gentle expressivity
in the former, and even the hint of a songlike passage in the trio section
of the latter. But it is only in the finale that Copland truly allows his music
to *mourn*, and in so doing to silence—if only temporarily—the harsh
sound-world of war. Copland marks the concluding passages of the
sonata "elegiac," a unique descriptive term, one that captures the essence
of the composer's intent.

Example 15. Copland, Piano Sonata, third movement, mm. 45–50.

The elegiac mood first appears in mm. 45–50, a passage representing the arrival point of the contrapuntal textures which flow out of the work's initial melodic statements. (See Example 15.) Two high voices in different registers call softly to each other, supported by a pedal point. Copland then develops this idea in a characteristic manner, gradually thickening the texture, expanding the range, and increasing the level of rhythmic activity. Eventually, in an astounding culmination, the music of mourning yields an emphatic reminder of its reason for being: bells peal once again, and the "first theme" music of the opening movement returns. (See Example 16. Interestingly, this return is modeled more closely on the "development" version of the theme—shown in Example 5—than on its initial presentation.) This climactic section gradually subsides, giving way to the sustained treatment of the elegiac material that brings the Sonata to a close.[19]

The presence of a five-flat key signature from m. 119 until the end of the finale betokens a general reminiscence of the pitch-world that characterized the first movement. At the same time, the pedal point on E♭ and suggestions of a new pitch center on A♭ illuminate the musical distance traveled from the opening of the Sonata. In the midst of the concluding elegy, the music from the first movement recurs. (See Example 17.) Here, however, it seems no longer an intrusion; now soft and expressive, it has itself become resigned and mournful in character, an integrated part of the elegy. Its C-flat/C-natural cross-relation persists into the movement's final bars (as shown in Example 18).

Example 16. Copland, Piano Sonata, third movement, mm. 79–92.

Example 17. Copland, Piano Sonata, third movement, mm. 144–52.

Example 18. Copland, Piano Sonata, third movement, mm. 165–71.

The Sonata's ending on an open fifth may be interpreted in different ways. In effect, it turns away from the issue of resolving the cross-relation by presenting a final chord with no third at all. Does this represent a kind of transcendence at the last, rising above and beyond all conflict? Or is it simply a kind of collapse from exhaustion, an admission that unambiguous resolution of conflict is impossible? That Copland avoids an unequivocal ending and presents instead a conclusion encouraging diverse readings and reactions is a strength of the work. Perhaps he is saying that this is the best, the most honest, thing an artist can do in music written in and for troubled times. Copland's unique Piano Sonata, his poignant gift to his own troubled times, retains its great power and eloquence in these troubled times of our own.

NOTES

1. The *Sextet* of 1937 does not constitute a real exception to this trend, since it is simply an arrangement of the earlier *Short Symphony* (no. 2, 1931–33), and the minor *Episode* for solo organ that Copland wrote in 1940 was apparently based on music from his score to *Our Town*. On the *Episode*, see Howard Pollack, *Aaron Copland: The Life and Work of an Uncommon Man* (New York: Henry Holt, 1999), p. 351.

2. Copland wrote an early piano sonata while studying composition with Rubin Goldmark; completed in 1921, the work was never included in the composer's own catalog of acknowledged works and was clearly a student effort. See ibid., p. 351.

3. Ibid., pp. 354–55.

4. See the transcription of a discussion between Copland and Leo Smit at Harvard University, November 1, 1977, on the jacket of the LP *Aaron Copland: The Complete Music for Solo Piano*, Columbia M2 35901, 1979; Aaron Copland and Vivian Perlis, *Copland: 1900 Through 1942* (New York: St. Martin's/Marek, 1984), p. 330.

5. Ibid., p. 332.

6. Ibid.

7. Ibid.

8. The Sonata's dedication to American playwright Clifford Odets, like Copland a very "engaged citizen" to borrow Howard Pollack's phrase (see Pollack, *Aaron Copland*, Chapter 16 title), is possibly relevant here. Although Odets commissioned the Sonata, it remains unclear whether the initial impetus for the work came from him or from Copland; see ibid., p. 330, and Pollack, *Aaron Copland*, p. 351.

9. Pollack, *Aaron Copland*, p. 351.

10. In the second song of Copland's Dickinson cycle, "There came a wind like a bugle," the passage in the piano that describes "the bell within the steeple wild" employs some related materials.

11. Readers interested in a thorough harmonic analysis of the Sonata may consult Charles Shadle's unpublished dissertation *Aaron Copland's* Piano Sonata: *An Analytical Analysis* (Waltham, Mass.: Brandeis University Press, 1997). Although I am in accord with Shadle's views concerning the large-scale tonal organization of the work, I find him too concerned with assigning temporary "keys" to virtually every passage—an approach that often seems antithetical to Copland's deliberately ambiguous ways of working with intervals and their complex implications.

12. Copland and Perlis, *Copland: 1900–1942*, p. 332.

13. Among commentators on the Sonata with whose work I am familiar, only David Schiff seems to think this worthy of comment; see his "Copland and the 'Jazz Boys'" in *Copland Connotations: Studies and Interviews*, ed. Peter Dickinson (Woodbridge, Suffolk, U.K.: The Boydell Press, 2002), p. 21.

14. If aspects of the first movement recall the Piano Variations, the rhythmic and textural character of the second movement may be said both to recall and to forecast: it is particularly reminiscent of variations 14, 15, and 16, and it anticipates many of the faster passages in the Piano Fantasy. (How appropriate, then, that the finale of the Sonata looks forward, in its wide-ranging expressivity and freedom of form, to the Fantasy. The Piano Sonata is in many respects Copland's central keyboard work.)

15. Wilfrid Mellers, whose writing Copland much admired, went so far as to describe the music of the Vivace as "hysterical" and "sickening"—in the context, it must be added, of praising it. See Mellers's *Music in a New Found Land* (1964; repr., New York: Hillstone, 1975), p. 92, and Copland and Perlis, *Copland: 1900–1942*, p. 332, where Copland cites with particular approval Mellers's interpretation of the Sonata's finale and his allusion to the sense of "immobility" at the work's conclusion.

16. Copland himself referred to the Sonata's Vivace as a "scherzo"; see Copland and Perlis, *Copland: 1900–1942*, p. 332.

17. Ibid., p. 330.

18. Pollack offers a good summary of these critical reactions; see Pollack, *Aaron Copland*, pp. 353–54. It is curious that, in seeking precedents for a sonata that concludes with unhurried, soft rumination, and an impression of great stillness, nobody has cited Ives's Piano Sonata no. 2 ("Concord"); the "Thoreau" finale of this work ends with some of the most quietly extraordinary, ethereal music in the sonata literature. The "Concord" Sonata received its first complete public performance in 1939, the same year in which Copland began work on his own Sonata, and it was in fact Copland's friend John Kirkpatrick who introduced Ives's work. Kirkpatrick went on to champion Copland's Sonata, both by performing it in public and by writing an appreciative article, "Aaron Copland's Piano Sonata," *Modern Music* 19 (1942): 246–50. For more on the relationship between Copland and Kirkpatrick, see Vivian Perlis, "Aaron Copland and John Kirkpatrick: 'Dear John, can you help me out?'" in Dickinson, *Copland Connotations*, ed. pp. 57–65.

19. David Schiff refers to this music as a *"berceuse"* (see his article "Copland and the 'Jazz Boys'" p. 21), a provocative and effective conceit so long as we grant that this is no ordinary lullaby and that it is not intended principally for children—although children are surely included among those who mourn, and who are mourned, in war.

Copland's Gift to Be Simple
Within the Cumulative Mosaic
Complexities of His Ballets

ELLIOTT ANTOKOLETZ

The intention in this study is to show how the American composer Aaron Copland created a new means of musical expression by the absorption and development of various American folk tunes into a contemporary musical language and style. His goal was to enhance the essence of these tunes and, by using contemporary rhythmic, textural, and structural techniques, to generate a new American compositional idiom that would satisfy the cultural and artistic demands for greater simplicity, accessibility, and familiarity that were part of the prevailing neoclassical musical tastes of the 1930s and 1940s. In order to bring out the essential simplicity of the tunes, he often needed, paradoxically, to employ complex harmonic and rhythmic procedures.

In the early twentieth century, many composers of varied national backgrounds absorbed authentic folk tunes into their compositional structures on a broadly tonal basis. Their inclinations toward scientific investigation of these tunes appear to be based on differing as well as similar reasons for employing authentic folk tunes in their own original compositions. As early as 1906, Béla Bartók began to collect his native Hungarian folk tunes with two aims in mind. One was to preserve a dying oral tradition, and the other was to find a musical mother tongue for his own original compositions. Bartók's need to look for his own national identity in music stems from the late-nineteenth-century reaction against the ultrachromaticism of the Wagner-Strauss period. Copland's motivations came later and were somewhat different from Bartók's. Copland turned to the use of American folk tunes during the more conservative period of the 1930s, when public reaction against avant-garde music led to the demand for more familiar, simpler styles of contemporary music. Nor did Copland appear to be concerned with the preservation of the folk sources as was

Bartók, but he did show an interest in developing an "Americana," originally instigated by his teacher Nadia Boulanger in the 1920s.

Bartók divided the transcription of folk music into three categories, in which (1) "the used folk melody is the more important part of the work" and "the added accompaniment and eventual preludes and postludes may only be considered as the mounting of a jewel"; (2) "the importance of the used melodies and the added parts is almost equal"; and (3) "the added compositional-treatment attains the importance of an original work, and the used folk melody is only to be regarded as a kind of motto."[1] Copland's approach seems most closely related to Bartók's first category, as seen in Copland's use of cowboy tunes in his ballet *Billy the Kid*, in which he often derives the sparsest harmonies (open fifths and octaves) from the simple harmonic constructions implied in the more important linearly stated tunes themselves. According to Bartók, "Many critics, especially West Europeans, objected to our transcriptions on the assumption that they are too complicated or too artificial and are not suited to the inherent simplicity of folk music."[2] This criticism might have applied to some extent to Copland's transcriptions, though the transcriptions of the tunes remained relatively simple. However, except for the Shaker tune in *Appalachian Spring*, his tunes are often somewhat modified by syncopation, metric changes, and altered durations. In the third category, Bartók uses the most daring chromatic harmonies against the subordinate thematic motto, in which the tune may undergo some kind of transformation. This may occur by means of bimodal extension, as in the fourth strain of the last of the *Eight Improvisations on Hungarian Peasant Tunes*, op. 20, for piano (1920), or, in the case of nonauthentic (that is, composed) folk-like tunes, by means of abstract chromatic compression of the tune's linear intervallic structure, as occurs with the "barrel organ" theme in the last movement of the *Fifth String Quartet* or the Romanian-like second theme of the second movement of the *Third String Quartet*, in which the quasi-diatonic mode of the theme is systematically compressed into chromatic intervals.

Although Copland does not, as a rule, employ Bartók's more radical procedures of folk-tune transformation, we may, nevertheless, observe a combination of the principles from Bartók's first and third categories in Copland's music. While the tunes themselves remain simple and clearly recognizable, they are sometimes set within complex textures. In both *Billy the Kid* and *Appalachian Spring*, the complex rhythmic and textural procedures surrounding the simple, unchanged tunes are based on convoluted, cyclical (fugal, etc.) interactions of several thematic statements that produce a static, ambiguous, and circuitous context rather than one of complex modifications of the tune itself. One example of this simpler thematic approach in Bartók's music, in which the unaltered tune is presented in a series of stretto entries, is the third strain of the last of the *Eight Improvisations*, op. 20. More often, however, Bartók will present extremely complex harmonies as accompaniment to variants of the folk tune.

Like Bartók, Copland's works show a capacity for creating a sense of coherence and integration within the mosaic compositional edifice. However, it was primarily Stravinsky's mechanistic, planed and layered neotonal textures that were to become the hallmark of Copland's American style, which had already begun to manifest itself in the early 1920s. Copland himself stated that he "was affected by the whole rhythmic side of [Stravinsky's] music, also by its dryness, its neo-Romanticism. He dominated the world of music at that time."[3] The principle of melodic repetition in the Russian folk sources, and its exploitation in art music by Stravinsky, was observed by Bartók: "From *Le Sacre du Printemps* onward, he . . . uses . . . short motives of two or three measures, and repeats them 'à la *ostinato*'. These short recurring primitive motives are very characteristic of Russian folk music of a certain category."[4] Such repetitions in the authentic Russian folk tunes are often based on structural reinterpretations within the pairings of phrases (Example 1), a phenomenon which served as a source for Stravinsky's own variational procedures in his Russian ballets.[5] These reinterpretations, based on a continual turning of the motivic figures around a few diatonic notes in cyclic repetition, produce a sense of variety within unity. According to the Russian folklorist, Evgeniia Linyova:

> The accent in folk song moves from one syllable to another within a word and from one word to another within a verse or of the melody. . . . In this mobility of accent one feels the urge to destroy monotony . . . it is very difficult to reconcile it [that is, the logical accent] with the metrical accent of contemporary art music (as marked by the bar lines), *which strives for mechanical regularity in the counting of the time units.*[6]

An exemplar of varied cyclic repetition is the opening rhapsodic folk tune of *Le Sacre* (Example 2), which Stravinsky had taken from an anthology of Lithuanian folk songs.[7] The quaternary folk-tune structure is determined by four different rhythmic segments, which encircle the tonic of the A-Aeolian mode mechanically.[8] While segments 1, 2, and 4 are identical in pitch construction (segment 3 altered at the caesura only slightly), their rhythms are varied in such a way as to create a sense of ambiguity within the characteristically-balanced, rounded-off quaternary outline. Segment 1, based on a held note and several short ones, is retrograded

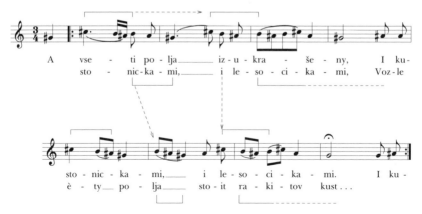

Example 1. Russian folk song. Structural reinterpretation within pairing of phrases.

Example 2. Stravinsky, *Le Sacre du Printemps,* opening bassoon theme, Lithuanian folk song. Rhythmic variation of cyclically repeated motif in quaternary structure.

by segment 4, while segment 3, based on 3 pairs of eighth notes, forms a converse relationship to segment 2, based on 2 sets of 3 triplets, to produce an internal balance. This balance is supported by the departure from, and return to, the strong placement of the initial pitch, C, in the successive segments, the first and fourth being the only ones to place the C at the bar line. While the rhapsodic parlando rubato quality of the tune would tend to obscure the proportions suggested by the explicit rhythmic notation, these rhythmic cells are defined by the strong contrapuntal entry of C♯ on the downbeat of the third rhythmic segment (3 x 2 eighths), thereby producing a conflict and ambiguity between the natural local cadences of the four thematic segments and the mechanical mathematical design of the four rhythmic cells.

Copland's American folk-tune (cowboy and Shaker) settings in his neo-classical ballets, while not in the same rhapsodic style as the Lithuanian tune in *Le Sacre*, similarly reveal cyclically repeated, metrically shifted rhythmic segments as the basis for the quaternary thematic structure. Copland's first work to reveal the anti-Romantic influence of Stravinsky as well as American jazz after his return to the United States was the short five-movement orchestral suite, *Music for the Theatre* (1925). The work combines blues thirds and bitonal progressions, the two tonal levels of which are defined by contrasting timbral layers, with complex syncopated, irregular multimetric schemes. The larger two-movement Concerto for Piano and Orchestra (1926–27) employs jazz elements in a more aggressively dissonant setting (the second movement especially), thereby drawing the work into a more modernistic milieu.[9] As Copland moved, temporarily, toward a more abstract (serial) approach to composition in the late 1920s, he became involved more directly in the institutional promotion of modern music. He and Roger Sessions inaugurated the Copland-Sessions Concerts in New York (1928–31) for the performance of new American music. It was during this time that he composed his Piano Variations (1930), which infused serial elements into his Stravinskian neoclassicism.[10] Although he was not to use the serial principle again until the 1950s, this piece heralded Copland's move toward a somewhat more abstract, though representative American style in the 1930s:

> The Piano Variations of 1930 mark a new direction towards absolute music. . . . The spare texture and fragmentary melodic features were at first so disconcerting that the significance of the work was not apparent. It introduced a radically new ascetic style that eliminated the earlier influence of jazz; gone too is diatonic melody and harmony.[11]

Regardless of Copland's use of programmatic elements in certain works since the 1930s, a more abstract musical plane is evident in his clearly defined, tightly constructed musical forms, as in the orchestral *Statements:* "Militant," "Cryptic," "Dogmatic," "Subjective," "Jingo," "Prophetic" (1932–35).[12] More abstract, however, are the *Short Symphony* (1932–33), later arranged as a Sextet for Piano, Clarinet, and Strings (1937), the Piano Sonata (1941), Sonata for Violin and Piano (1943), and the serial works since 1950.

With the onset of the economic depression, Copland and others had to modify their compositional approaches because of the loss of support from the small, yet special, musical public of the previous decade. In his efforts to reach the more conservative public at large, Copland moved toward a simplified contemporary idiom in works composed either for school performance, analogous to Hindemith's *Sing und Spiel* or *Gebrauchmusik* concepts, or for the more popular media of film, radio, and phonograph, a trend that had also been developing in other countries.

Among the most significant products of Copland's simpler style were the three ballets—*Billy the Kid* (1938), *Rodeo* (1942), and *Appalachian Spring* (1943–44)—which are imbued with Anglo-American folk music sources. His previous experience with the more complex structural conceptions of serialism was not to be lost in the folk-like idiom of the ballets. While their melodic and harmonic surface character contrasts with that of the Piano Variations of 1930, the larger relations of phrases and periods in the ballets were to maintain some of the complexity of structure and sophistication of serial conception, which reemerged in Copland's works after 1950.

Despite Copland's lack of sympathy with the "German music" of Schoenberg, Berg, and Webern during the interwar period, the concentrated use of the four-note motif that generates the chromatic context of the Piano Variations is reminiscent of Webern's pointillistic, angular approach to the row, although Copland himself suggested the influence of Schoenberg.[13] Copland lectured on serialism at the New School as early as 1928. As he pointed out subsequently, serial technique had provided him with a fresh view of his music, "somewhat like looking at a picture from a different angle so that you see things you might not have noticed otherwise."[14] Thus, in Copland's more accessible American style promoted during the 1930s and early 1940s, his clear tonalities were enriched both by his increased use of dissonance stemming from his previous serial concerns and by the complex structural interactions of the planed and layered phrases found in his neoclassical works of the era. This reveals that Copland was to maintain a certain continuity not only with the structures and textures of Stravinsky's neoclassical works, but also his own serial conception of the Piano Variations of 1930 and its twelve-tone serial development of the 1950s.

Appalachian Spring consists of nine continuous but contrasting sections, with suggestions as well as quotations from American folk sources. The seventh section employs a quoted Shaker dance tune (rehearsal number 55, with upbeat, to rehearsal number 56, clarinet I), entitled *The Gift to Be Simple,* as the basis for a set of dance variations.[15] The aesthetic significance of Copland's use of this authentic folk tune lies partly in its simple, clearly defined rhythmic construction within the larger, balanced thematic contour. Analysis of the double-period tune itself (i.e., two successive pairings of antecedent-consequent phrases, as shown in the complete presentation of the tune in Example 3) reveals two perfectly balanced, symmetrical quaternary patterns (i.e., four rhythmic figures that constitute each pair of phrases in a given period). In other words, each quaternary pattern occurs within a larger binary (antecedent-consequent) phrase construction. The clarity and simplicity of the A-flat major tonality is established both by the transparent accompaniment, based on open octaves, fifths (and fourths) that outline the tonic chord (A♭–E♭) exclusively, and the linear thematic outline based on tonic and dominant triads.

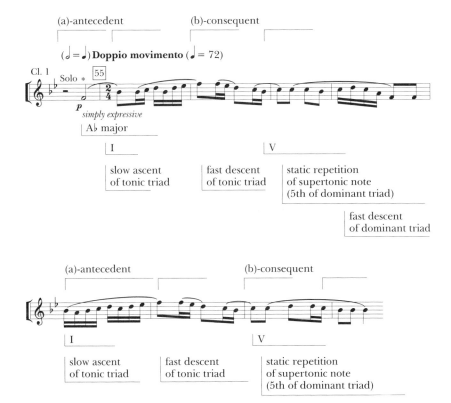

Example 3. Copland, *Appalachian Spring*, Shaker folk tune, "The Gift to Be Simple," rehearsal no. 55, with upbeat, to rehearsal no. 56, clarinet I, based on a balanced quaternary pattern within the larger binary (antecedent-consequent) phrase construction. The exclusive tonic-dominant harmonies in A-flat major as well as the distinctive melodic rhythm and balanced ascending-descending contour are essential in producing the simple, unambiguous melodic outline.

While the antecedent and consequent functions remain unambiguous in the initial thematic appearance, the highly modified repeat of this double period (rehearsal numbers 56–57, doubled clarinets) produces some sense of structural ambiguity. The immediate repeat of the first consequent (rehearsal number 56, mm. 3–4, clarinet II) by clarinet I (rehearsal number 56, mm. 5–7, first note) transforms the first consequent phrase into the antecedent phrase of the second period. This structural reinterpretation thus introduces some sense of circuity into the succession of symmetrical, quaternary thematic constructions.

After the first variation (rehearsal numbers 57–59), in which the tune is transposed down a whole step to G-flat major, the essentially clear, simple mood of the Shaker tune is drawn into a more complex unfolding of ambiguous mosaic constructions. In this second, extended variation (rehearsal numbers 59–61), the tune is employed in a more complex canonic sequence (Example 4), which further transforms the straightforward structure of the tune into a seemingly endless round of structural reversals and reinterpretations of antecedent and consequent phrases. Doubled between the trombone and viola (still in G-flat major) and now unfolding primarily in eighths rather than sixteenths, the first period (rehearsal number 59, m. 2, to rehearsal number 59, m. 9) is followed by a canonic compounding of the second period. The violas/trombones are answered two beats later by the horns/violins. While the staggered horns/violins form a single, balanced pair of antecedent and consequent phrases in stretto with the violas/trombones, the latter pair of instru-

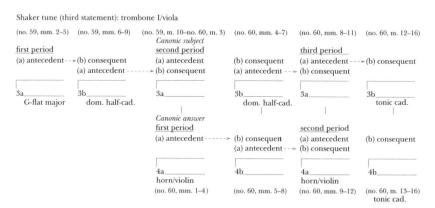

Example 4. Copland, *Appalachian Spring*, Shaker folk tune, as basis of second extended variation, rehearsal nos. 59–61, tune in more complex canonic sequence, further transforms tune (doubled in trombone and viola) into seemingly endless round of structural reversals and reinterpretations of antecedent and consequent phrases.

ments forms a complex structural relation with the preceding period. The very first period in trombones/violas (rehearsal number 59, m. 2) ends with a proper half-cadence that outlines the descending dominant triad (rehearsal number 59, mm. 8–9). The next period in the same instruments plays, therefore, a consequent role in relation to its antecedent. However, this consequent, which in turn initiates the stretto, also arrives at a half-cadence on the dominant harmony (rehearsal number 60, m. 7), reinforced by the arpeggiated dominant cadence of the horns/violins stretto answer. Thus, the antecedent phrase of the violas/trombones that initiates the stretto (rehearsal number 59, m. 9) has a dual, ambiguous function in that it is also the consequent of the second (consequent) phrase of the first period. The latter consequent itself also has the quality of an antecedent because of its half-cadence. Undoubtedly, the dual function of the violas/trombones cadences, which begin the second period and initiate the stretto, on the dominant harmony, is to accommodate the antecedent-consequent structure of the second period and the stretto.

The aura of "Americanness" that suffuses Copland's style in *Appalachian Spring* results not only from the pervasive allusions to American folk styles and the actual quotation of one tune but from the conservative handling of open diatonic sonorities, which are largely absent in his more dissonant and abstract musical scores. This permits a pastoral quality. The opening harmonizations are transparent and basic, suggested by the melodic disposition of the Shaker tune. Furthermore, the symmetrical quaternary structure of the Shaker tune lends itself ideally to Copland's concise structure. The use of contrasting variations, based on clearly articulated changes of texture, key, dynamics, and tempo, is perfectly suited to Copland's general inclination toward juxtaposition of structural blocks. At the same time, the internal construction of each variation is based on contrasting timbres and figures in distinct layers. The overall cumulative shape of the variations is produced, typically, by increased doublings that build to the full orchestra by the last variation.

With *Billy the Kid,* a western mood is established by the use of several cowboy tunes, each of which contains the same quaternary construction as the Shaker tune (See Example 3, earlier).[16] They are also parallel in exhibiting a larger binary (antecedent-consequent) form. Since Copland expressed disinterest toward cowboy tunes themselves, it is a tribute to his ingenuity that he was able to develop the structural and textural dimensions of these otherwise simple, "poverty-stricken" melodies:

I have never been particularly impressed with the musical beauties of the cowboy song as such. The words are usually delightful and the manner of singing needs no praise from me. But neither the words nor the delivery are of much use in a purely orchestral ballet score, so I was left with the tunes themselves, which I repeat, are often less than exciting.[17]

He confesses, however, that on a visit to France in 1938, he found that

perhaps there is something different about a cowboy song in Paris. But whatever the reason may have been, it wasn't very long before I found myself hopelessly involved in expanding, contracting, re-arranging and superimposing cowboy tunes on the rue de Rennes in Paris.[18]

For Copland, the key to the fascination of these tunes seems to lie in the challenge of "expanding, contracting, rearranging and superimposing" their simple structures onto larger mosaic patterns of a highly original, somewhat austere harmonic character. The opening scene of *Billy the Kid* is divided into two distinct sectional planes, with the lento maestoso establishing the lonely mood of the prairie and the more lively moderato the ambience of the frontier town. The first cowboy tune (rehearsal number 6, mm. 1–10), which initiates the latter section, "Street in a Frontier Town," in the piccolo and tin whistle, is derived from the song "Great Granddad." As part of Copland's vivid mood painting, this tune (marked "nonchalantly") appears against a transparent harmonic background of nothing but a sustained two-octave E♭ in the upper strings (Example 5). As the fifth degree of the key, this pitch-class contributes to the open quality of Copland's harmony and forms a contrasting layer against the lively tune. The symmetrical quaternary structure of the tune, which combines with a balanced overarching binary structure of (a)-antecedent (b)-consequent phrase pairings similar to the Shaker tune in *Appalachian Spring,* also lends itself to Copland's characteristic way of constructing a phrase through clear linearity. Together with its incessant encirclement of a few principal pitches (in this case the fifth degree, E♭, which begins and ends the tune), it produces a sense of being static tonally, which contributes further to the uniformity of the melody. All these characteristics are Stravinskian, establishing the basic framework for generating the distinct textural planes and layers of the larger form.

The initial cowboy tune is reiterated throughout the first half of the moderato (rehearsal number 6, mm. 1–10 and rehearsal number 7, mm. 1–16) as a kind of ostinato. Its cadential tone (E♭) is held at the end of each thematic occurrence, eventually providing a transparent but dissonant

Example 5. Copland, *Billy the Kid*, first cowboy tune (from "Great Granddad"), rehearsal no. 6, mm. 1–10, with transparent harmonic background of sustained two-octave E♭ in the upper strings.

harmonic accompaniment for the entry of the second cowboy tune (rehearsal number 7, upbeat to m. 5). The latter (Example 6) is derived from "The Streets of Laredo," and appears in alternation with the first tune, at the same time as its cadential tone (F) is held as a dissonance against it. The successive occurrences of these alternating tunes produce a series of contrasting thematic planes, but their close rhythmic and intervallic relations simultaneously contribute to the unity of the larger structure. The sequential rhythmic pattern of the second cowboy tune (Example 6, rehearsal number 7, mm. 4–8), based on a metrically articulated half note and two weak quarter notes, seems to be derived from the metric displacement of the three-note stretto figure that punctuates the first thematic cadence (rehearsal number 6, mm. 9ff.). This episodic figure, in turn, comes from the triadic segment, C-E♭-A♭, embedded near the opening of the first tune (rehearsal number 6, m. 2; see Example 5). Both tunes are prominently constructed of rising minor thirds, with the first tune outlined by C-E♭, B♭-D♭, and cadential C-E♭, and the second (see Example 6) by half notes, A to C (rehearsal number 7, mm. 5–7) and cadential grace note figure, E-G (rehearsal number 7, m. 15). By means of Copland's characteristic metric manipulations, these two contrasting but related themes become the basis of the more complex mosaic formal construction throughout.

Example 6. Copland, *Billy the Kid,* entry of the second cowboy tune (from "The Streets of Laredo"), at rehearsal no. 7, mm. 4–16, in alternation with first cowboy tune by overlapping its held cadential E♭.

The complexity of the combined blocks and planes, which are built from the simple, local symmetrical (quaternary or larger binary) constructions of the cowboy tunes, is made more ambiguous by the proportions of the phrases and periods (Example 5). The distance between the adjacent phrases (i.e., (a)-antecedent and (b)-consequent) of the initial appearance of the first cowboy tune (see Ia at rehearsal number 6, mm. 1–4) and Ib (rehearsal number 6, mm. 5–10), is expanded by the interpolated E-flat cadential extension between the antecedent and consequent phrases of the tune's second statement (see Ia at rehearsal number 7, mm.1–4 + 4 [E♭] and Ib at mm. 9–12 + 3 [E♭]). This interpolated extension suggests an interpretation of the second antecedent-consequent pairing as two separate tunes (Ia and Ib), thereby multiplying our perception of the number of actual thematic entities in this section to more than two.

Furthermore, the E-flat cadential extension of each phrase of the first tune serves as background against which the antecedent phrase (IIa) of cowboy tune II enters. This new antecedent is extended by the interpolated cadential F (rehearsal number 7, mm. 4–8 + 4) to delay and separate it from its consequent phrase (rehearsal number 7, mm. 12–16). Yet the mosaic structural ambiguity of the section does not end there but rather contributes to an overall effect of interactions that produce ambiguous circuity. The second statement of cowboy tune II (at rehearsal number 8) follows the consequent phrase (IIb) of the first statement directly, so the order of antecedent and consequent phrases gives the impression of being reversed (IIb seems like an antecedent to IIa). The real consequent (IIb) of the second statement then follows IIa directly, that is, without interpolation of the cadential F (rehearsal 8, mm. 1–5, rehearsal number 8, mm. 6–9). This relationship between the phrases of the second statement of cowboy tune II thereby represents a return to the relationship of phrases and cadential note in the first statement of cowboy tune I. Furthermore, while the two complete statements of cowboy tune I are separated from each other by the intervening held cadential E♭, the two complete statements of cowboy tune II are closer because there is no separation by any held cadential note. Thus the two thematic statements become adjacent now. This converse proportional relationship between the paired statements of the two tunes is essential for articulating the overall quasi-symmetrical construction. Also, the progressively decreasing distances between phrases as well as larger thematic statements contribute to closing off the section. The overall effect of these structural thematic interactions is one of ambiguous circuity. The first tune then initiates the next large sectional block (Example 7), where further thematic interactions and expansions occur through other reinterpretations of the proportions between phrases and periods.

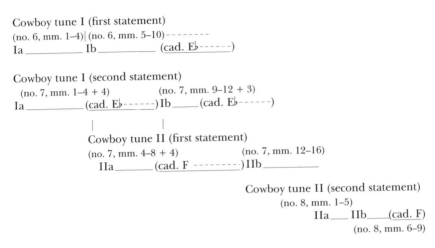

Example 7. Copland, *Billy the Kid*, expanding and contracting section (between nos. 6–9), based on converse proportional relation of (a)-antecedent/ (b)-consequent phrases (with cadential extensions) of the cowboy tunes I and II: "Street in a Frontier Town" and "Streets of Laredo." That is, overall symmetrical mosaic/periodic construction of two alternating and overlapping binary cowboy tunes.

While the first part of the moderato is almost exclusively based on open unisons and octave sonorities, Copland also achieves a sense of development and contrast by building timbral and harmonic materials, at the same time as he increases rhythmic complexity, further contributing to a sense of structural ambiguity and circuity. At the second occurrence of the first cowboy tune (rehearsal number 7), the piccolo line is doubled by the clarinet and unison fragments are added in the violins (Example 8). All these lines are doubled at the same two-octave range that was originally defined by the held E♭ octaves. By also doubling the violin fragments (E♭-C-F, C-E♭-A♭ and B♭-C-D♭), Copland articulates these figures as prominently outlined by the basic structural minor thirds (C-E♭ and B♭-D♭). A similar doubling procedure occurs in the ensuing thematic alternations until a larger instrumental combination is reached (rehearsal number 8, upbeat to m. 6). At this point (Example 9), the second tune progresses by half notes in parallel ninths rather than octaves. The cadential figure of this tune is then extended episodically for several measures and broken up into syncopated figures between upper and lower strings. The short, arch-shaped fragments that outline the minor thirds in the two cowboy tunes (in both Example 8 and Example 9) are articulated in metric positions that contradict one another.

Example 8. Copland, *Billy the Kid*, timbral and harmonic building of the first cowboy tune, rehearsal no. 7, mm. 1–3.

These syncopations continue against the next entry of the first cowboy tune (at rehearsal number 9) to produce the first heterophonic—that is, simultaneous—juxtaposition between contrasting planes of winds and strings (Example 10). The texture is made fuller by the striking addition of full triads. At the cadence of this thematic statement (rehearsal number 9, m. 8ff.), the original stretto figure (rehearsal number 6, m. 9ff.) from the end of the first occurrence of the tune is extended in the woodwinds in increased metric displacements and set against two other instrumental planes—one based on the syncopated grace note figure in the strings,

Example 9. Copland, *Billy the Kid,* timbral and harmonic building of the second cowboy tune, rehearsal no. 8, mm. 5–9.

the other on a replacement of the original E♭ pedal by fuller chords in the brass that are presented in a reiterated syncopated rhythm.

The next appearance of the first cowboy tune (rehearsal number 10, strings) is the fullest, accompanied by a more active waltz rhythm in the winds and piano (rehearsal number 10, m. 5ff.), which is harmonized in triads. The distinction between these simultaneously juxtaposed timbral planes (second cowboy tune in trombone and waltz in piano) is enhanced by polymetric conflict (the first of this section, in which the 4/4 meter of the tune is contradicted by the irregular 3+3+2 meter of the waltz (Example 11), the latter perhaps suggesting intoxicated cowboys. Based on cumulative juxtapositions of new blocks, planes, and layers, this increased textural and rhythmic complexity grows out of an additive process of proportional patterns that builds on the symmetrical pairings of conversely related periods (Example 7). The cyclical return of the first cowboy tune (at rehearsal number 9) begins a proportional pattern in a larger, seemingly endless succession of phrases and periods that alternate again with the second cowboy tune (rehearsal number 10, mm. 4–11). These structural complexities are increasingly compounded by the added juxtapositions of particular thematic (cadential, etc.) fragments from the two original cowboy tunes.

complete tertian harmonies

Example 10. Copland, *Billy the Kid*, from figural succession to heterophonic simultaneity, rehearsal no. 9, mm. 1–2.

This trend toward rhythmic complexity and increased use of textural planes continues in the remainder of the scene, resulting in a succession of thematic layers and timbral areas that interact to produce a cumulative mosaic form. Other folk or popular tunes—including allusions to "The Old Chisholm Trail," "Git Along Little Dogies," "Come Wrangle Yer

Example 11. Copland, *Billy the Kid*, polymetric distinction between simultaneously juxtaposed timbral planes (cowboy tunes I and II and waltz), rehearsal no. 10, mm. 2–6 in which the 4/4 meter of cowboy tunes is contradicted by the irregular 3+3+2 meter of the waltz.

Bronco," "Goodbye Old Paint," and "Oh Bury Me Not on the Lone Prairie"—are adapted in various passages and enhance the accessible American sound of the ballet. At the same time, they contribute to the larger structural mosaic.

In the early 1950s, Copland began to infuse the planed and layered textures of his earlier neoclassical style of *Billy the Kid* with twelve-tone serial principles, thereby allowing his typically angular rhythms, layered textures, and period constructions a stricter framework of pitch relations. Copland's adoption of the twelve-tone method in his Piano Quartet (1950) represents an abrupt change from the technical resources utilized in his popular film scores of the 1930s and 1940s, as well as in his orchestral suites, *Billy the Kid, Rodeo,* and *Appalachian Spring.* The fusion of features from both tendencies (serial and neoclassical) was to reach full fruition in his postwar compositions.

During this period, Copland continued to develop along the same stylistic lines as in his prewar compositions, not only in the sporadically occurring non-twelve-tone works of this period (including the diatonic *Old American Songs,* which appeared shortly after the Piano Quartet, and the Nonet of 1960), but also in the serial contexts of his orchestral *Connotations* (1962) and *Inscape* (1967). The bright sound of triads, open fifths, sixths, and especially tenths, which had been so characteristic of *Appalachian Spring* and *Billy the Kid,* are still evident in these more abstract serial contexts. But the most striking aspect of Copland's stylistic continuity is a gift for combining the clear and simple melodic surfaces of American folk idioms with complex phrase and period interactions, a synthesis of stylistic features that first became entirely evident in his neoclassical ballets.

NOTES

1. See Béla Bartók, "The Relation Between Contemporary Hungarian Art Music and Folk Music," in *Essays,* ed. Benjamin Suchoff (New York: St. Martin's Press, 1976), pp. 350–52. Lecture given at Columbia University in 1941.

2. Ibid., p. 353.

3. Aaron Copland, *Times* (London), November 14, 1970.

4. Elliott Antokoletz, "Modal and Structural Variation in Piano Works of Georg von Albrecht," *International Journal of Musicology* 1 (1992): 304–7. Also see Bartók, "The Influence of Peasant Music on Modern Music," in *Essays,* p. 343. For original publication, see "A parasztzene hatása az újabb mušzenére," *Új idošk* 37/23 (May 1931) (Budapest): 718–19.

5. This tune is from the Russian folk song collection by Fédor Istomin and Sergei Liapunov, eds., *Pesni russkogo naroda, sobrany v gubernijax: Vologodskoj Vjatskoj i Kostromskoj v 1893 godu* (St. Petersburg, 1899), p. 252. For a discussion of the authentic Russian folk sources in Stravinsky's Russian ballets, see Richard Taruskin, "Russian Folk Melodies in *The Rite of Spring." Journal of the American Musicological Society* 33, no. 3 (1980): 501–43.

6. Evgeniia Linyova, *Velikorusskie pesni v narodnoi garmonisatsii,* vol. I (Saint Petersburg, 1904), p. xvi; as cited in Richard Taruskin, "Stravinsky's 'Rejoicing Discovery' and What It Meant: In Defense of His Notorious Text Setting," *Stravinsky Retrospectives,* ed. Ethan Haimo and Paul Johnson (Lincoln/London: University of Nebraska Press, 1987), p. 179.

7. Anton Juszkiewicz, *Melodje ludowe Litewskie* (Lithuanian folk songs) (Cracow, 1900); in German, *Litauische Volks-Weisen* (Krakau: Verlag der Polnischen Akademie der Wissenschaften, 1900), no. 157.

8. Pierre Boulez outlines the cellular rhythmic properties of this tune, in *Notes of an Apprenticeship,* trans. Herbert Weinstock (New York: Alfred A. Knopf, 1968), pp. 80–81.

9. See Virgil Thomson, *American Music Since 1910* (New York: Holt, Rinehart and Winston, 1970, 1971), p. 52.

10. For further reference to this work, which foreshadowed Copland's turn to serialism after World War II, see Elliott Antokoletz, *Twentieth-Century Music* (Englewood Cliffs, N.J.: Prentice Hall, 1992), chap. 16.

11. Neil Butterworth, *The Music of Aaron Copland* (London: Toccata Press, 1985), p. 54.

12. See Thomson, *American Music Since 1910,* p. 52.

13. Aaron Copland and Vivian Perlis, *Copland: 1900 Through 1942* (New York: St. Martin's/ Marek, 1984), p. 182.

14. Ibid.

15. Originating in eighteenth-century England, Shakers were members of a religious society that believed in the dual nature of the Deity, practiced celibacy, community of possessions, pacifism, and equality of the sexes. Shaker worship included prayer dances and marches as well as songs. See this tune in Edward D. Andrews, *The Gift to Be Simple* (New York: Dover, 1940), p. 136.

16. These folk sources are identified in a concise descriptive survey of the work by Butterworth, *Music of Aaron Copland,* pp. 76–79.

17. See Aaron Copland, "Notes on a Cowboy Ballet," Aaron Copland Collection, Music Division, Library of Congress (1974), as cited in Howard Pollack, *Aaron Copland: The Life and Work of an Uncommon Man* (New York: Henry Holt, 1999), p. 320.

18. Ibid.

PART V

POLITICAL EDGES

Copland and the Politics of Americanism

ELIZABETH B. CRIST

In January 1953, Aaron Copland's *Lincoln Portrait* was pulled from President-elect Dwight D. Eisenhower's inaugural program because its composer was identified as a fellow traveler of the Communist Party. Representative Fred E. Busbey argued that Copland possessed a "known record" of "activities, affiliations, and sympathies with and for causes that seemed . . . more in the interest of an alien ideology than the things representative of Abraham Lincoln." Busbey offered no musical rationale but based his objections on political grounds: Copland's attachment to allegedly Communist causes was considered unpatriotic and, in the argot of postwar politics, un-American. "With all the music of fine, patriotic, and thoroughly American composers available to the concert committee of the Inauguration Committee," Busbey explained, "I not only questioned the advisability of using music by a composer with the long record of questionable affiliations of Mr. Copland . . . but protested the use of his music."[1]

Relying on the records of the House Committee on Un-American Activities, Busbey enumerated Copland's ties to Communist organizations. Among other things, Copland had "signed a statement to President Roosevelt defending the Communist Party"; belonged to the American Committee for Democracy and Intellectual Freedom, "a Communist front which defended Communist teachers"; judged a song contest sponsored by the American League Against War and Fascism; was linked to the Artists' Front to Win the War; belonged to the Committee of Professional Groups for Browder and Ford, the 1936 Communist presidential ticket; performed at benefits for *New Masses* and the American Music Alliance of the Friends of the Abraham Lincoln Brigade; reportedly spoke at a conference of the National Council of American-Soviet Friendship; and was a speaker at the Cultural and Scientific Conference for World Peace. The list goes on and on. Copland was also connected to the National Committee for People's Rights, the National Committee for the Defense of Political Prisoners, the Citizens Committee for Harry Bridges, the American Committee for the Protection of Foreign Born, the National Federation for Constitutional Liberties, and Frontier Films—all groups considered to be subversive communist fronts.[2]

Busbey cared only about the composer's affiliations, not his music, and by this measure, Copland's allegiance to the political Left is indisputable.[3] Copland himself characterized his beliefs as "democratic or liberal."[4] When asked by Vivian Perlis in 1979 about his political activities in the 1930s, he replied: "Well, I never joined anything. In that sense I wasn't aligned, but I was very sympathetic for the more radical side of things. It was a kind of feeling of the period, one was going to carry it along."[5] But Copland was not simply following a trend, and any equivocations about his political activities must be considered in the context of McCarthyism and the lasting influence of anticommunist ideology in American culture. In the years following World War II, many public figures faced enormous pressure to disavow their attachment to progressive causes in the 1930s. The vilification of the Left continued long after the 1950s, as contemporary political discourse still impugns leftist politics as un-American. Nevertheless, it is clear that Copland was for a time aligned with the Communist movement (if not the Party) and with left-wing politics more generally.

Furthermore, while it was of no matter to Busbey in particular or even the anticommunist movement more generally, Copland's music might also be heard to espouse a leftist political position. To interpret his works as invested with progressive or left-wing sympathies is to foreground a striking irony: at the same time the composer's politics were declared un-American, his music was widely perceived as quintessentially American. This apparent incongruity speaks both to music's ability to absorb as well as project a myriad of meanings and to the protean nature of Americanism. American and Americanism are political terms to be endlessly contested, whether used to describe political alignment or musical expression. They are empty symbols to be stolen back and forth and inscribed with various or possibly conflicting cultural values.[6] And while it may seem that Copland's music can be (or has been) attached to an unproblematic ideal of Americanness, his work actually provides an opportunity to interrogate the musical and political projects behind Americanism as but a single term for a variable set of ideals.

In what follows, representative pieces from the four decades up to and including the era of McCarthyism serve as illustrative points of intersection—moments when musical and cultural strands entangled to form a particular image of America. The jazzy style of *Music for the Theatre* captures the spirit of cosmopolitan modernism in the 1920s, while *Statements* resonates with the radical politics perceived as thoroughly American to leftists in the 1930s but categorically un-American to Busbey and his ilk. Composed in the midst of World War II, *Lincoln Portrait* implies support for the American war effort while advocating a progressive position on social justice. Finally, *The Tender Land* depicts a community fractured by the enmity characterizing the culture of McCarthyism. Separately, these pieces stand as specific examples of Copland's progressive politics as expressed in his music. Together, they advance a liberal, pluralistic notion of musical Americanism.

Returning to the United States in 1924 after three years abroad, Copland committed himself to writing music that was at once modern and American. The "desire to be 'American' was symptomatic of the period," he later recalled. Feeling "anxious to write a work that would immediately be recognized as American in character," Copland turned to jazz as "an easy way to be American in musical terms."[7] Aspects of the jazz idiom surface in his earliest significant compositions, including the Symphony for Organ and Orchestra (1924), *Music for the Theatre* (1925), and the Piano Concerto (1926), though the degree to which these works reflect an actual awareness of and engagement with jazz remains an issue much discussed in the literature on Copland.[8]

Like the idea of Americanism itself, the characteristics, qualities, and meanings of "jazz" are rather flexible. To white American and European modernists in the 1920s, it was a multifarious commercial music that captured the urban experience and epitomized the modern American city. "Manhattan is hot jazz in steel and stone," the French architect Le Corbusier wrote, while American critic Gilbert Seldes described jazz as "the symbol, or byword, for a great many elements in the spirit of the time—as far as America is concerned it is actually our characteristic expression."[9] The emphasis such critics, and Copland himself, placed on the inherent Americanness of jazz threatens to overwhelm the more cosmopolitan aspects of jazz as a dialect of international modernism. In addition to serving as a symbol of Americanism, jazz was a sonic marker of modernism and modernity, the former perhaps associated with the achievements of European artists, the latter with the dynamism of American society after the Great War. Copland described his use of jazz as a form of cultural nationalism and sign of musical Americanism, but his jazz idiom owes as much to the avant-garde in Paris as the music of New York, with Stravinsky and Milhaud alongside James Reese Europe and Paul Whiteman as certain influences.[10]

He extolled the rhythmic possibilities of jazz and popular music, but many jazzy passages in his works also draw on characteristic melodic and timbral effects.[11] In *Music for the Theatre,* the "Dance" movement features brassy timbres, muted trumpets, and solo breaks that exploit the pitch-shading of "blue" notes—especially the blue third. In the middle section of the movement, for instance, the E-flat clarinet emerges to take a solo turn that at once recalls the instrument's appearance in the first part of the suite, the grotesquerie of Berlioz's *Symphonie Fantastique* or Copland's own ballet *Grohg* (1924), and the exuberant clarinet lines of Sidney Bechet.[12] The persistent syncopation in the solo part contrasts with the steady staccato pulse of the piano vamp to suggest the rhythmic fabric of ragtime, and the adventurous performer might even be tempted to add a sense of swing by floating behind the beat or perhaps imbuing the dotted rhythms with a triplet feel (Example 1).[13]

Copland imitates the typical pitch inflections in jazz by juxtaposing the raised and lowered third scale degree and by indicating more ambiguous shadings. The clarinet is instructed to play its first F♮ "a little sharp," while four measures later the trumpet answers with the same pitch "a little flat." These are two perfectly prescribed and utterly characteristic bent thirds. The accompanying piano vamp features a semitone clash between the diatonic and blues third in vertical form, as F♮ and F♯ crunch together on the second beat of each measure. Another typical pitch inflection, the flatted fifth, makes a brief appearance in the solo part (six measures after rehearsal number 20), and Copland even tweaks the second scale degree, shaded a little sharp three measures before rehearsal number 21. Such melodic gestures, or metaphors, signaled jazz to listeners in the 1920s—as they do today.

"A squeaking clarinet and muted trumpet frankly carry a jazz tune," critic Henry Levine wrote of this passage in his review of the world premiere, concluding that "the effect is undoubtedly clever, and, though obvious, is never crude." Much of the audience was reportedly spurred to laughter, but "some staid listeners looked nonplussed."[14] Reviewer Philip Hale acknowledged that "someone may object to the entrance of 'jazz' in a symphonic concert room" but felt that it was typically American and thus appropriate material for an American composer. Apparently referring to the "Dance" in particular, Hale asserted: "American life with its restlessness, its haste, its snapping-of-fingers at ideals and spiritual things, its extravagance is 'jazz.' Why should not one movement in a suite be symbolic of American life as it now is?"[15]

The "Dance" movement not only captures the jazzy musical energy of the modern metropolis but also suggests, through its quotation of "The

Example 1. *Music for the Theatre*, second movement, "Dance," rehearsal numbers 20 to 21.

Example 1 continued

Example 1 continued

Sidewalks of New York," the richly textured social fabric of the American city. As Gayle Murchison has noted, the popular song from 1904 captures the diversity of New York City by describing a "merry group" of friends that includes Johnny Casey, Jimmy Crowe, Jakey Krause, and Nellie Shannon. All "tripped the light fantastic" to the music of the "Ginnie" organ grinder, an Italian-American musician.[16] This catalogue of ethnicities accurately reflects urban demographics and immigration patterns in the nineteenth and early twentieth centuries. The lyrics even mix representatives from two distinct waves of immigration. Between 1820 and 1880, immigrants to the United States were largely from Ireland and Germany. (African-Americans were, of course, already a presence on these shores.) Around the turn of the century, however, most new arrivals hailed from southern and eastern Europe; many were Italian or Jewish. The influx of people from these ethnic and religious groups prompted the rise of a politically conservative nativism, and laws were passed to restrict immigration based on nationality. In particular, the Emergency Quota Act of 1921 and the National Origins Act of 1924 set quotas that favored Anglo-Saxons and severely restricted the number of people allowed into the United States from southern and eastern Europe, particularly Italy, Bulgaria, and Russia. In addition, immigration from most Asian countries was prohibited entirely.[17] The reactionary sentiment behind such laws is countered by Copland's raucous setting of "The Sidewalks of New York" and its implied defense of cultural pluralism.[18]

The fourth movement of the suite, "Burlesque," also opposes conservative entrenchment and lends support to an attack on Victorian mores. The movement's title references the striptease, a dance incorporated into the burlesque show during the 1920s, and Copland's lascivious music suits its subject.[19] "It's whorehouse music," Roy Harris shouted upon hearing Copland's score, "it's whorehouse music!"[20] Both the burlesque and jazz, two genres associated with sexually expressive dance, were widely regarded by conservative forces as manifesting the immorality of modernity. At a time when conservative forces sought to challenge the move to modernity, *Music for the Theatre* seems an unqualified defense of the new, the modern, the progressive in musical and social terms.

"There is always a revolutionary period of the breaking down of old conventions and customs which follows after every great war," Anne Shaw Faulkner reasoned in an article for *The Ladies' Home Journal* in 1921. "So it is no wonder that young people should have become so imbued with this spirit that they should express it in every phase of their daily lives." And yet she wondered "whether this tendency should be demonstrated in jazz—that expression of protest against law and order, the bolshevik element of license striving for expression in music."[21] As Faulkner's language reveals, jazz threatened to do more than corrupt America's youth. Its exotic appeal and ethnic accent—so frequently associated with the African and the Jew—challenged the old order of white, Protestant, rural America.[22] If jazz were the characteristic music of America, it was a different kind of America than some were willing to accept. And as a jazz-inflected work by a gay, Russian-Jewish, leftist composer, *Music for the Theatre* declares its allegiance to this modern image of the nation.

In the late 1920s, Copland moved away from a frank engagement with the jazz idiom just as the economic prosperity and social energy of the Jazz Age began to wane. Change was in the air. Copland's friend Harold Clurman noticed that "between 1921 and 1927 society's headlong rush looked as if it would never end," but from 1927 to 1929, "a slowing down became perceptible" as "notes of doubt, fear, loneliness, stole into the picture."[23] By the time Copland was composing *Statements* for orchestra in the summer of 1932, the country was in the depths of the Great Depression. Amid the economic and social turmoil, many artists and intellectuals—Copland among them—were inspired to question the basic assumptions of American culture in the modern, industrial era, openly wondering whether the current crisis was but a symptom of a fundamental, systemic problem in American society.

The severity of the situation seems reflected in the musical language of *Statements*, which links a dissonant, fragmented musical idiom to radical political rhetoric. Eventually completed in 1935, the piece comprises six movements with descriptive titles, three of which—"Militant," "Dogmatic," and "Jingo"—are politically suggestive.[24] Copland had considered an even more explicit title for "Jingo": an autograph sketch identifies the movement under the title "Petty Bourgeois." These titles and the short movements they designate represent a conscious attempt on Copland's part to make his music more accessible. "The longer a piece was," he explained many years later, "the more difficulties it would present to the ordinary concert-goer. It occurred to me that if the movements of a work were pithy and compact, the music might seem more understandable. . . . I calculated that by giving each statement a suggestive sub-title, the listening public would have a better idea of what I had in mind when writing these pieces."[25]

One of the things that Copland seems to have had in mind was politics. During the summer of 1934 while composing *Statements* in Bemidji, Minnesota, Copland not only participated in a campaign meeting of the Communist Party but also ended up delivering his first political speech. He wrote about the experience to his friend Israel Citkowitz. "It began when Victor spied a little wizened woman selling a *Daily Worker* on the street corners of Bemidji," Copland recounted.

> From that, we learned to know the farmers who were Reds around these parts, attended an all-day election campaign meeting of the C.P. unit, partook of their picnic supper and made my first political speech! . . . When S. K. Davis, Communist candidate for Gov. in Minn. came to town and spoke in the public park, the farmers asked me to talk to the crowd. It's one thing to think revolution, or talk about it to one's friends, but to preach it from the streets—OUT LOUD— Well, I made my speech (Victor says it was a good one) and I'll probably never be the same!

"Now, when we go to town," Copland continued, "there are friendly nods from sympathizers" who "come up and talk as one red to another."[26]

At home in New York City during the early 1930s, Copland was also involved in the Communist-influenced Composers Collective, the Young Composers Group, and the Group Theater. He also appears to have been discussing politics in correspondence with friends. In May 1932, for instance, Harold Clurman wrote with news that he had been reading Marx and Lenin. This literature, along with his involvement in the John Reed clubs, had persuaded Clurman "that people like us are the real revolutionists in America to-day and that we are *revolutionists* in our function as artists and leaders." Arguing that the path had yet been paved for a proletarian revolution, he maintained that a change in institutional structure would first demand a change in cultural attitude. "Any revolution of social order that was not prepared for accompanied by and destined to a corresponding revolution *(conversion)* of men's hearts and mind[s] would be more monstrous than an earthquake and more meaningless," Clurman explained. And revolution was "doomed to death," he continued, "without the Aaron Coplands . . . and perhaps the Aaron Coplands—because they are as aware of the *World* as well as their art—are in the final analysis the greater *artists* as well as the greater revolutionaries." Clurman described revolutionary art as "an art which is personal and *objective,* individual and social, an art for All."[27]

This dialectical description offers a way to understand *Statements,* which unfolds as a series of paired movements.[28] The first two, "Militant" and "Cryptic," form a complementary pair that alternately evokes public pronouncement and private reflection. "Militant" is an oration that opens with a rhythmically square marcato theme in the winds and strings. This initial call is then answered by a sharp, one-measure retort in the trombones and tuba before the trumpets, horns, and strings offer their own response. The rhythmic profile of the movement is remarkably declamatory, the texture lean, and the dynamic nearly a constant forte or louder. By contrast, "Cryptic" withdraws into private thoughts. The movement begins with only a solo flute and horn, both marked dolce, misterioso. Any sure sense of meter or pulse is undermined by the slow-moving, unpredictable rhythms. The third and fourth movements follow a similar pattern. "Dogmatic" is loud and brash with a heavy, staccato opening. A rising eighth-note motto recurs almost obsessively throughout the movement; coupled with a stolid rhythmic profile, the limited melodic materials capture the inflexible stance implied by the title. But "Subjective" is an introspective essay drawn from music originally composed as a chamber piece titled *Elegies* and associated with the modernist poet Hart Crane.[29]

The fifth movement, "Jingo," pillories the same melody quoted in *Music for the Theatre,* though to a different end. Like the symbol of the flag or idea of Americanness, Copland's musical borrowings serve various functions depending on their musical and social contexts. In *Statements,* "The Sidewalks of New York" is not just a popular tune from the turn of the century or a familiar carousel melody but also evokes its role as the campaign song for Democrat Alfred E. Smith in the 1928 presidential election.[30] Smith was a product of New York's Tammany Hall, and the ironic setting of "Sidewalks" in *Statements* might be heard to reference the failed promise of Tammany itself as well as the cultural conflicts surrounding Smith's presidential bid. Founded in 1789 by middle-class New Yorkers to counter the political power of the social elite, by the late nineteenth century Tammany had evolved into a powerful political machine. Its potential as an instrument of social, economic, and political advancement to be achieved through collective organization was ultimately compromised by the individual will to power of its party bosses. While ensuring the immigrant poor and ethnic workingmen some measure of protection and advocacy at a time when the city government could not, Tammany's system of bossism also enabled fraud. In 1932, for example, just as Copland began work on *Statements,* scandals and investigations into the Tammany machine culminated in the resignation of New York City's mayor, James J. Walker, a Democrat elected with the help of then-governor Al Smith.[31] And by the time Copland had finished "Jingo" in 1934, Tammany's grip on democratic politics in New York City had finally been broken with the election of Fiorella LaGuardia, who ran for mayor on a Fusion ticket designed to defeat Tammany.

Having risen through the Tammany ranks, Al Smith served an unprecedented four terms as governor of New York. He was a progressive Democrat who fought to improve conditions for working men and women and secure the welfare of recent immigrants—especially Jewish émigrés.[32] Born in a tenement district on the Lower East Side of Manhattan, Smith was a second-generation Irish-Catholic. As such, he faced enormous religious bigotry during his unsuccessful presidential bid. Voters were warned that the pope would move from Rome to Washington, and the Ku Klux Klan burned crosses in the fields as he traveled across the country.[33] Smith and his opponent, Herbert Hoover, came to represent two conflicting visions of America during the presidential election of 1928: Hoover seemed a part of a traditional, Protestant, rural society, whereas Smith belonged to the modern, immigrant, urban world. The election thus became a contest, Smith's biographer Robert A. Slayton concludes, "over who had the right to be called 'American' and to choose its values."[34]

With this in mind, the appearance of Smith's campaign song in *Statements* might seem to express some compassion for the beleaguered Tammany politician. A snippet from the chorus ("East side, west side") is marked cantabile and given a long, lush phrasing. Though distorted, the melody remains a recognizable and perhaps even wistful fragment. Nearly all of the other musical material in "Jingo" is presented staccato or marcato, and such articulations lend a sharp, dry edge to the piece, alienating the brief, melodic quotation from its surrounding musical context. This discrepancy between the borrowed tune and original music might be heard to reflect the hostility Smith faced from jingoistic opponents and to capture his own sense of alienation from the American public.

But Smith proved a disappointment to progressive Democrats—his pro-business platform was nearly indistinguishable from the Republicans'—and the tone of "Jingo" is accordingly disillusioned. The modernist tendencies toward fragmentation, expressive objectivity, and ironic commentary strip "Sidewalks" of its power as either a sentimental popular song or political rallying cry. The satiric character of Copland's music undermines any potential nostalgia or sympathy that the quotation might hope to elicit, while the disjuncture between the borrowed melody and its musical context suggests at once a depiction of irrelevance and a frank portrayal of loss, whether of the simple bourgeois pleasure of the carousel ride or of faith in the established political system. "Jingo" offers a dim view of party politics, ultimately making a sardonic statement about belligerent patriotism and narrow-minded political sectarianism.

Statements was composed at a pivotal time for the country. In the summer of 1934 unemployment numbers were down and some economic indicators up, but severe storms ravaged the Midwestern Dust Bowl; a wave of strikes swept the country, including a general strike in San Francisco, an especially bloody conflict in Minneapolis, and a strike of some 350,000 textile workers in the South; the New Deal seemed incapable of solving the agricultural crisis in the Deep South; and Hitler was elected Führer. "Something is poisoned," Copland apparently wrote to Harold Clurman in July. Clurman responded, "When *I* speak of the unhappiness and maladjustment of a transition period I know I am talking about a reality,"

> but I always suspect that I am exaggerating a bit as far as the rest of the world goes which seems a little less sensitive to world currents, to moral atmosphere. But when you voice the same sense of difficulty I know that it is really universal, since you are not given to generalizations or to the expression of sentiments that you haven't

experienced directly. And tho it is a little sad for me to hear you say "something is poisoned" (because I would like for you never to live anywhere but in the most perfect atmosphere) it cheers me a little too—or rather it gives me some sense of exaltation—that what I hope to fight with is so tangible, and the objectives I propose to myself so clear.[35]

Copland's objectives may seem less clear, in part because his side of the correspondence no longer exists, but in the early 1930s what the composer had to fight with was tangible. Music was a weapon, an expression of a political alignment, and a way to prefigure a radically new form of American politics and culture.[36]

By 1938 the economic crisis of the Great Depression had begun to improve but the political situation in Europe had worsened. America was brought into the global conflict with the surprise bombing of Pearl Harbor on December 7, 1941. Some ten days after news of the attack had circulated throughout the country, conductor Andre Kostelanetz wrote to Jerome Kern, Virgil Thomson, and Aaron Copland with a commission. Kostelanetz hoped for three works that would have "a correlated idea in that they are to represent a musical portrait gallery of great Americans," suggesting George Washington, Paul Revere, Walt Whitman, Robert Fulton, Henry Ford, and Babe Ruth as suitable subjects to memorialize in music.[37] Copland first chose Walt Whitman, but Kern had already selected Mark Twain. Because Kostelanetz did not want two writers in the group of three portraits, Copland turned to Abraham Lincoln.

The sixteenth president was coupled in the public mind with Franklin Delano Roosevelt, who frequently invoked Lincoln to draw parallels between two wars and war leaders.[38] Roosevelt turned to Lincoln early and often in his presidency, first in reference to the Great Depression and later World War II. In a 1934 "fireside chat," for example, Roosevelt used Lincoln's words to defend the recovery programs of the New Deal. "I believe with Abraham Lincoln," Roosevelt declared, "that 'the legitimate object of government is to do for a community of people whatever they need to have done but cannot do at all or cannot do so well for themselves in their separate and individual capacities.'"[39] Roosevelt called on Americans to "renew our pledge of fidelity to the faith which Lincoln held in the common man" in a 1936 speech at Lincoln's birthplace, quoting Lincoln on the nature of democracy: "As I would not be a slave, so I would not be a master," Lincoln had written. "This expresses my idea of democracy. Whatever differs from this, to the extent of the difference, is no democracy."[40] (Copland later set this same passage in *Lincoln Portrait.*) In 1937 Roosevelt lauded Lincoln for having "fought for the morals of democracy" and opposed those "who thought first and last of their own selfish aims."[41] The president naturally referenced Lincoln when he dedicated the Gettysburg Memorial that summer.[42] After the United States entered the war, Lincoln became a potent symbol of authority for Roosevelt's administration as it worked to clarify the aims of the war effort, prepare the public for a protracted struggle, justify the military mobilization, and console the American people.[43] The Office of War Information produced a poster in the wake of Pearl Harbor with a quote from Lincoln's Gettysburg Address, obviously intended to motivate Americans to war as much as to commemorate the dead (Figure 1).

Lincoln was also an icon of the Left. His likeness hung behind the podium at the 1936 Communist national convention, and his legacy was invoked in the party platform of that same year. Asserting that Roosevelt was unwilling or unable to counter such conservative foes as the Republican Party, the Liberty League, and the Klan, the Communist platform called for a People's Front, an alliance of the workers, farmers, and middle class "to fight for and establish a People's government—a government of, for, and by the people."[44] The Party was eager to lay claim to an American revolutionary tradition that included Lincoln. "The Communist Party continues the traditions of 1776, of the birth of our country," the 1936 platform explains, "of the revolutionary Lincoln, who led the historic struggle that preserved our nation. In the greater crisis of today only the Communist Party shows a way to a better life now, and the future of peace, freedom, and security for all."[45]

By 1942, when Copland was writing *Lincoln Portrait,* the Communist Party had thrown its support behind Roosevelt and the war effort, but the left-wing social movement known as the Popular Front continued to be a significant presence in American political culture throughout the war years.[46] And if the rhetoric of reform had grown increasingly populist and patriotic as compared to the more radical pronouncements of the 1930s, this did not indicate a complete shift away from more progressive politics.[47] Likewise Copland's accessible, nationalist music from the war years can still be heard to resonate with his leftist sympathies. Lincoln, the people, and the common man were symbols to be filled with ideological content serving a range of political positions. In Copland's music, and especially in his choice of texts for *Lincoln Portrait,* these symbols of America remain attached to decidedly leftist ideas of social democracy.

The narration in *Lincoln Portrait* speaks eloquently to the wartime struggle against fascism and the potential for a better future after a bitter war.

Figure 1. Poster produced by the Office of War Information, 1942.

Although he remembered having consulted an immensely popular biography of Lincoln by Lord Charnwood, Copland actually appears to have relied on *The Life and Writings of Abraham Lincoln,* edited by Philip van Doren Stern.[48] Copland pulled quotes from a variety of Lincoln's writings and speeches, including the annual address to Congress on December 1, 1862, one month before the Emancipation Proclamation was to take effect. On that occasion Lincoln declared that "the dogmas of the quiet past are inadequate to the stormy present. The occasion is piled high with difficulty, and we must rise with the occasion. As our case is new, so we must think anew and act anew." Here is the ideal of the revolutionary Lincoln, as the quotation speaks to the concerns of those on the Left about the nature of the postwar world and seems to cast doubt on established cultural mores—the acceptance of economic injustice as part of the capitalist system, for example, or of a continuing racism in American society.

Copland set passages from Lincoln's writings that bring to mind not only the immediate context of World War II but also the Popular Front call for social justice and economic equity. In particular, the third of the five quotations in the narration emphasizes not a racial but a class-based conflict. Lincoln's reply to Stephen Douglas in one 1858 debate describes slavery as "the eternal struggle between two principles—right and wrong—throughout the world. . . . It is the same spirit that says, 'You toil and work and earn bread—and I'll eat it.'" Another quotation that Copland wrote out in his manuscript notes for the narration, but which he chose not to set, explicitly raises the issue of civil liberties. In the draft, Copland cobbled together the following from an 1860 letter from Lincoln to his friend Henry Asbury and an address delivered that same year at the Cooper Institute (Cooper Union) in New York City. "The fight must go on. The cause of civil liberty must not be surrendered at the end of one or even one hundred defeats. . . . Let us have faith that right makes might, and in that faith let us to the end dare to do our duty as we understand it."[49]

Music as well as text is quoted in *Lincoln Portrait*. Copland borrows two traditional American tunes: the eighteenth-century ballad "Springfield Mountain" and Stephen Foster's minstrel song "De Camptown Races."[50] In *Lincoln Portrait*, "Springfield Mountain" appears first, its arching melody arriving after an opening fanfare-like section. The simple tune is stated three times before snippets of the opening fanfare motif return as a brief transition to the next section. The key brightens, the tempo quickens, and jaunty rhythms enliven the music as fragments of "Camptown Races" emerge. The pitches and intervals of the song are altered, but its general rhythmic profile is clear enough.

In his choice and setting of these songs, Copland captures the two sides of Lincoln as portrayed by Sandburg's enormously popular biographies *Abraham Lincoln: The Prairie Years* (1926) and *Abraham Lincoln: The War Years* (1939). "Springfield Mountain" is a stately and plaintive lament that paints a picture of the solemn wartime president. Its title recalls Lincoln's hometown, and the tune's opening intervallic profile mimics "Taps," the bugle call used by the Union Army during the Civil War to signal lights out, which was adopted for military funerals.[51] "Camptown Races" is more exuberant and rough-hewn, like the young Lincoln himself. Moreover, as a blackface minstrel tune, "Camptown Races" recalls the subjects of race and slavery—key issues in Lincoln's presidency. The tune evokes the antebellum South and the history of racial repression, but its setting in *Lincoln Portrait* prevents the listener from easily identifying the melody. Such African-American musical traits in the song as syncopation and gapped melody have already passed through Stephen Foster's white filter, and Copland now runs these identifying characteristics through a process of modernist abstraction. His distorted borrowing keeps the song—and its associations—at a distance. While the unobjectionable "Springfield Mountain" is quoted almost exactly, Copland fragments Foster's minstrel song such that the melody calls up its cultural context but not its problematic lyrics. The song is so changed that it is difficult, if not impossible, to sing silently along and hear or silently voice the dialect-laden words. Thus Copland is able to borrow the song and exploit its connotations without becoming complicit in its offensive racial politics.

After each borrowed tune is presented separately, the two are brought together in counterpoint to offer a complete musical portrait of Lincoln as man and president (Example 2). "Springfield Mountain" resounds in the winds and brass, which feature the melody in a slow and stately three-part canon, while repeated snippets of "Camptown Races," with its characteristic dotted rhythm and ascending line, appear in the strings. Eventually the texture thins, so that only the triadic arch of "Springfield Mountain" remains. A *sforzando* downbeat in the bass and tuba along with a shimmering tam-tam crash precede the entrance of the speaker, intoning "Fellow citizens, we cannot escape history."

As Copland was composing the work during the spring of 1942, Andre Kostelanetz recalled that "our nation was in one of the darkest days in its history":

> Our Pacific Fleet had been all but destroyed. MacArthur, driven from Manila, was making a last-ditch stand on Corregidor. In Europe, our allies were beaten or facing defeat. France had fallen, Britain was reeling under a hail of firebombs, and Russia was fighting at the gates of Moscow. Copland finished the rough sketch around Lincoln's birthday, reworked and polished it that disastrous spring.[52]

Yet, Kostelanetz continued, "by the time he finished it in April the tide was starting to turn in the Pacific. Doolittle's daring men bombed Tokyo;

Example 2. "Springfield Mountain" and "Camptown Races" in *Lincoln Portrait*,
3 mm. before rehearsal number 150 to 3 mm. after.

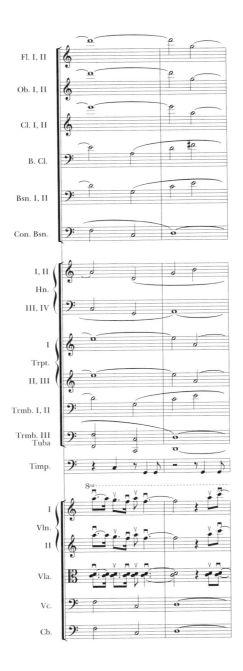

Example 2 continued

U.S. forces were grouping to push westward. Americans were breathing a bit easier." Just before the premiere in May, the United States triumphed in the Battle of the Coral Sea, and *Lincoln Portrait* was met with loud applause. "Lincoln's warning fell on victory-deadened ears," the conductor noted.[53]

But the fortunes of war were to turn again. When Kostelanetz led another performance in the summer of 1942 in Washington, D.C., with the First Lady and members of the Roosevelt administration in attendance, it was clear that the war would be long, hard, and costly. "Even as I raised my baton," Kostelanetz remembered, "President Roosevelt was in conference with Admiral King and General Marshall to chart our course." Copland's narration, Lincoln's words, "sounded with a terrible new clarity," and at the end of the performance there was silence.[54]

"Artists, by definition, hate all wars—hot or cold," Copland said in a speech delivered at the Conference for World Peace in 1949. The profound transformations in American society that accompanied the end of World War II affected Copland deeply, and he was clearly disturbed by the culture of the Cold War. "Lately I've been thinking that the cold war is almost worse for art than the real thing," he explained,

> for it permeates the atmosphere with fear and anxiety. An artist can function at his best only in a vital and healthy environment for the simple reason that the very act of creation is an affirmative gesture. An artist fighting in a war for a cause he holds just has something affirmative he can believe in. That artist if he can stay alive can create art. But throw him into a mood of suspicion, ill-will, and dread that typifies the cold war attitude and he'll create nothing.[55]

Soon enough Copland himself came under suspicion in the anticommunist fervor of the McCarthy era. Coverage of the Peace Conference in *Life* magazine ran Copland's picture under the heading "Dupes and fellow travelers dress up communist fronts."[56] His participation was included on the list of Communist activities compiled by HUAC and read into the *Congressional Record* by Representative Busbey.

Copland's opera *The Tender Land* (1952–54, rev. 1955) seems to capture the disappointment and hope that he articulated in his speech at the peace conference. Inspired by the landmark documentary book by James Agee and Walker Evans, *Let Us Now Praise Famous Men* (1941), the opera bids farewell to the world of the Popular Front and to the folkloric idiom that had brought Copland so much success during the 1930s and 1940s.[57]

But first *The Tender Land* envisions a transcendent community, as do so many of Copland's works from the era of depression and war. The libretto, by Copland's paramour Erik Johns (using the nom de plume Horace Everett), centers around Laurie Moss, a young girl who lives on a farm with her mother, grandfather, and younger sister. Laurie is about to graduate and is excited as well as anxious about her future. Just before her graduation party, two drifters arrive at the farm; Martin and Top are looking for work, and the pair are invited to stay. Act 1 culminates in "The Promise of Living," a quintet sung by the Moss family along with the new arrivals. To the soaring strains of the nineteenth-century hymn "Zion's Walls" and Copland's own memorable countermelody, mother, daughter, grandfather, and the two young men declare their solidarity. "The promise of growing / with faith and with knowing / is born of our sharing /our love with our neighbor," they sing. "The promise of ending/in right under-standing / is peace in our own hearts/a peace with our neighbor."

That peace is disrupted at Laurie's graduation party. Earlier in the day, a local girl had been assaulted, and Ma Moss harbors doubts about the two men who have suddenly appeared on her farm. She confesses her suspicions to a neighbor (Example 3). In the meantime, Laurie has quickly become smitten with Martin, but her mother and grandfather accuse him and Top of the attack. The allegations are proven false when a neighbor explains that the culprits are already in custody, but for Grandpa Moss, Martin and Top are "guilty all the same"—a clear reference to the politics of McCarthyism.

Martin quickly departs without saying good-bye to Laurie. When she then chooses to leave the farm and strike out on her own, she does so without romantic dreams of either her past or her future. The simple and secure world created in the first act and celebrated in "The Promise of Living" is shown to have been a naive ideal, as the fragile community of the farm is shattered by unnecessary worries and an oppressive insularity. Promises go unrealized. Laurie had hoped that her grandfather would stop meddling in her life and that she would find love; her mother seems to have wished Laurie would stay on the farm; Martin had dreamt of set-tling down. But in a climate of fear and suspicion, none of these things comes to pass.[58] As Laurie prepares to leave, she asks her distraught mother to "try to see / how changed this day must seem for me. / How changed I too have come to be" (Example 4).

Copland was in the midst of writing *The Tender Land* when *Lincoln Portrait* was pulled from Eisenhower's inaugural program. Five months after the controversy, the composer was called to appear before the Senate

Example 3. *The Tender Land,* Act 2, rehearsal number 39 to 2 mm. before number 40.

Example 3 continued

Permanent Subcommittee on Investigations. Copland testified before Senator Joseph McCarthy and the committee in a closed hearing on Tuesday, May 26, 1953.[59] The transcript reveals Copland to have been patient, polite, and shrewd. He avoided answering Senator McCarthy by puzzling over the questions and frequently responding "I don't know" or "I don't remember."

The various allegations made against Copland always concerned his political activities: Busbey and McCarthy focused on the organizations to which the composer belonged, not the music he wrote. But his music can nonetheless be heard to resonate with his politics and to express a rather liberal ideal of Americanism—liberal here indicating not a strictly partisan perspective but a magnanimous view of our national character. Even the stylistic pluralism that characterizes Copland's oeuvre as a whole and which has vexed many critics falls in line with this admittedly diffuse image of America. Copland's music projects an individual subjectivity and speaks with an identifiably American voice, but the accent is hard to place. As a result it seems especially easy to invest his works with a whole host of values and press compositions into the service of widely varying ideologies.

Recently, conservative writer and Cold War veteran William Safire has heard in Copland's music the reinscription of American exceptionalism. "Here is the sort of lesson I think needs teaching," Safire declares. "In the 20th century especially, American artists broke free from their formal European masters." Copland is mentioned, presumably because his music exemplifies those traits Safire ascribes to Americanism: "spare; daring; profoundly plain-spoken." One wonders, though, whether this list of qualities says more about a given political ideology than the general qualities of American expression. "We are getting far enough away from

Example 4. *The Tender Land*, Act 3, rehearsal numbers 71 to 73.

Example 4 continued

this," Safire concludes, obliquely referring back to his set of national characteristics, "to see how much it shapes our revolutionary character and affects our self-image today."[60] Yet in the midst of another war—one led by a plain-spoken president, marked by an atmosphere of fear, and justified as a magnanimous extension of our supposed national values to the world—it seems possible to accept these same adjectives of Americanness but hear in Copland's music a rather different idea of America from what the columnist might have in mind.

NOTES

1. Fred E. Busbey, "Aaron Copland and Inaugural Concert," January 16, 1953, 83rd Cong., 1st sess., *Congressional Record* 99, pt. 9, appendix, 169. Busbey's remarks in the *Congressional Record* followed a report by Paul Hume in the *Washington Post* (January 15, 1953) announcing the cancellation. On this incident, see Aaron Copland and Vivian Perlis, *Copland Since 1943* (New York: St. Martin's Press, 1989), pp. 184–89; Howard Pollack, *Aaron Copland: The Life and Work of an Uncommon Man* (New York: Henry Holt, 1999), pp. 452–54; and Jennifer L. DeLapp, "Copland in the Fifties: Music and Ideology in the McCarthy Era," Ph.D. diss., University of Michigan, 1997, pp. 123–29.

2. Busbey, "Aaron Copland and Inaugural Concert," appendix 169–171. On information compiled about Copland by the United States government and the cancellation of *Lincoln Portrait*, see DeLapp, "Copland in the Fifties," pp. 114–34. Many of these affiliations were also listed in *Red Channels: The Report on Communist Influence in Radio and Television* (New York: American Business Consultants, 1950), pp. 39–41.

3. See Aaron Copland and Vivian Perlis, *Copland: 1900 Through 1942* (New York: St. Martin's/Marek, 1984), pp. 217–30; Pollack discusses Copland's politics in *Aaron Copland*, pp. 270–87.

4. As quoted in Julia Smith, *Aaron Copland: His Work and Contribution to American Music* (New York: E. P. Dutton, 1955), p. 120.

5. Aaron Copland, interview by Vivian Perlis, September 16, 1979, Aaron Copland Collection, Music Division, Library of Congress, typescript, p. 324.

6. On "the stealing back and forth of symbols," see Kenneth Burke, *Attitudes Toward History*, vol. 2 (New York: The New Republic, 1937), p. 229. Burke was a prominent literary critic aligned with the left-wing politics of the Popular Front whose work in the 1930s reflects an engagement with Marxism. But like Copland, Burke was never a Communist with the capital *C* denoting a commitment to the Party. On Burke, see in particular Daniel Aaron, *Writers on the Left: Episodes in American Literary Communism* (New York: Harcourt, Brace & World, 1961), pp. 287–92; Armin Paul Frank, *Kenneth Burke* (New York: Twayne, 1969); Paul Jay, "Kenneth Burke," in *Dictionary of Literary Biography, Modern American Critics, 1920–55*, vol. 63, ed. Gregory S. Jay (Detroit: Gale Research, 1988), pp. 67–86; Jack Selzer, *Kenneth Burke in Greenwich Village: Conversing with the Moderns, 1915–1931* (Madison: University of Wisconsin Press, 1996). David Green discusses the changing nature of political rhetoric and the mutable definitions of political terms in *Shaping Political Consciousness: The Language of Politics in America from McKinley to Reagan* (Ithaca, N.Y.: Cornell University Press, 1987).

7. Aaron Copland, "Composer from Brooklyn," *Magazine of Art* (1939); repr. *Our New Music: Leading Composers in Europe and America* (New York: Whittlesey House/McGraw Hill, 1941); rev. and enl. as *The New Music: 1900–1960* (New York: W. W. Norton, 1968), pp. 158–59.

8. Copland's use of jazz is discussed in Arthur Berger, *Aaron Copland* (New York: Oxford University Press, 1953), pp. 48–51; Pollack, *Aaron Copland*, pp. 113–20; Gayle Minetta Murchison, "Nationalism in William Grant Still and Aaron Copland Between the Wars: Style and Ideology," Ph.D. diss., Yale University, 1998, pp. 219–92; David Schiff, "Copland and the 'Jazz Boys,'" in *Copland Connotations: Studies and Interviews*, ed. Peter Dickinson (Rochester, N.Y.: The Boydell Press, 2002), pp. 14–21; Gail Levin and Judith Tick, *Aaron Copland: A Cultural Perspective* (New York: Watson-Guptill, 2000), pp. 22–28, 134–35, 140–45; Judith Tick, "Origins and Style of Copland's *Mood for Piano* no. 3, 'Jazzy,'" *American Music* 20 (2002): 277–96; Stanley V. Kleppinger, "On the Influence of Jazz Rhythm in the Music of Aaron Copland," *American Music* 21 (2003): 74–111.

9. Le Corbusier as quoted in Peter Conrad, *The Art of the City: Views and Versions of New York* (New York: Oxford University Press, 1984); Gilbert Seldes, "Toujours Jazz," *Dial* 75 (August 1923): 151. See also Donna M. Cassidy, *Painting the Musical City: Jazz and Cultural Identity in American Art, 1910–1940* (Washington, D.C.: Smithsonian Institution Press, 1997), pp. 69–114.

10. On French modernism and American popular music, see in particular Murchison, "Nationalism in Still and Copland," pp. 194–97, 248–57; Nancy Perloff, *Art and the Everyday: Popular Entertainment and the Circle of Erik Satie* (Oxford, Eng.: Clarendon Press, 1991); also Carol J. Oja, *Making Music Modern: New York in the 1920s* (New York: Oxford University Press, 2000), pp. 313–60. Oja discusses Copland's internationalist perspective in *Making Music Modern*, pp. 237–51.

11. On the jazzy rhythms of *Music for the Theatre*, see Murchison, "Nationalism in Still and Copland," pp. 242–47. Kleppinger offers a detailed analysis of Copland's rhythmic practice in "On the Influence of Jazz Rhythm in the Music of Aaron Copland," pp. 74–111. Regardless of what Copland considered jazz and what we now do not, he was clearly most interested in the rhythmic and metric possibilities of current popular idioms. In his 1927 article "Jazz Structure and Rhythm," for example, he discusses the rhythms (and, tellingly, their notation) in George Gershwin's song "Clap Yo' Hands" and Zez Confrey's novelty piece "Kitten on the Keys." Aaron Copland, "Jazz Structure and Influence," *Modern Music* 4 (January–February 1927): 9–14; repr. in *Aaron Copland: A Reader, Selected Writings 1923–1972*, ed. Richard Kostelanetz (New York: Routledge, 2004), pp. 83–87.

12. The tripartite "Dance" can be considered an ABA form (Pollack, *Aaron Copland*, p. 129) or scherzo-trio-scherzo (Larry Starr, "The Voice of Solitary Contemplation: Copland's *Music for the Theatre* Viewed as a Journey of Self-Discovery," *American Music* 20 [2002]: 308). Murchison likewise hears an echo of Bechet in *Music for the Theatre* ("Nationalism in Still and Copland," p. 242). My discussion of *Music for the Theatre* is indebted to Howard Pollack's *Aaron Copland*, pp. 128–34.

13. Pollack notes that "how jazzily to play the work" is an open question and adds that Copland himself "thought that most musicians played his jazz works too squarely" (*Aaron Copland*, p. 133).

14. Henry Levine, "Copland Work in Boston Premiere Rouses Hearers," *Musical America*, November 28, 1925, p. 1.

15. Philip Hale, "Symphony Gives Copland Suite," *Boston Herald*, November 21, 1925. On the premiere of *Music for the Theatre*, see Copland and Perlis, *Copland: 1900–1942*, pp. 120–21.

16. Murchison, "Nationalism in Still and Copland," pp. 273–75.

17. The Emergency Quota Act decreed that the number of new immigrants from a given country could not exceed 3 percent of the total population of foreign-born nationals from that country residing in the United States in 1910. Under the provisions of the National Origins Act, operative until 1952, those limits were reduced to 2 percent of foreign-born residents from a particular country living in the United States as of 1890, with a total quota limit of 164,667. These percentages were legislated to change in 1927, but the new quotas went into effect only in 1929. At that point, quotas were based on the ethnic composition of the country in 1920. See the U.S. Citizenship and Immigration Services, http://uscis.gov/graphics/shared/aboutus/statistics/legishist/470.htm.

18. On immigration, assimilation, and cultural pluralism in the 1920s, see in particular Lawrence W. Levine, "Progress and Nostalgia: The Self-Image of the Nineteen Twenties," in *The Unpredictable Past: Explorations in American Cultural History* (New York: Oxford University Press, 1993), pp. 189–205; and Milton M. Gordon, *Assimilation in American Life: The Role of Race, Religion, and National Origins* (New York: Oxford University Press, 1964); Frederick M. Binder and David M. Reimers, *All the Nations Under Heaven: An Ethnic and Racial History of New York City* (New York: Columbia University Press, 1995); Leonard Dinnerstein and David M. Reimers, *Ethnic Americans: A History of Immigration*, 4th ed. (New York: Columbia University Press, 1999).

19. On the striptease in burlesque, see Robert Clyde Allen, *Horrible Prettiness: Burlesque and American Culture* (Chapel Hill: University of North Carolina Press, 1991), p. 243. Pollack notes that Copland's burlesque was also inspired by Fanny Brice, the Jewish singer and comedian known for her parodies of well-known theatrical figures. See Pollack, *Aaron Copland*, pp. 130–31.

20. As quoted in Pollack, *Aaron Copland*, p. 130; see also Levin and Tick, *Aaron Copland: A Cultural Perspective*, p. 144.

21. Anne Shaw Faulkner, "Does Jazz Put the Sin in Syncopation?" *The Ladies Home Journal*, August 1921; repr. in *Keeping Time: Readings in Jazz History*, ed. Robert Walser (New York: Oxford University Press, 1999), p. 35.

22. On the racialized response to jazz and to Copland, see Beth Ellen Levy, "Frontier Figures: American Music and the Mythology of the American West, 1895–1945," Ph.D. diss., University of California, Berkeley, 2002, pp. 237–51.

23. Harold Clurman, *The Fervent Years: The Story of the Group Theater and the Thirties* (New York: Alfred A. Knopf, 1945), p. 20.

24. Pollack, *Aaron Copland*, p. 296.

25. Aaron Copland, text for WNCN radio program "Aaron Copland Comments," December 9, 1968, typescript, Copland Collection.

26. Aaron Copland to Israel Citkowitz, [September] 1934, ibid.; also quoted in Copland and Perlis, *Copland: 1900–1942*, p. 229, and Pollack, *Aaron Copland*, p. 277.

27. Harold Clurman to Copland, May 24, 1932, Copland Collection.

28. Howard Pollack has likewise observed that the juxtaposition of movements "strikes one as dialectical" (*Aaron Copland*, p. 297), and my interpretation is greatly influenced by his analysis.

29. A sketch page among the manuscripts for *Elegies* is titled "Elegy for Hart Crane." Though the sketch is dated February 1932, the dedication could conceivably have been added after the poet committed suicide in April 1932. *Elegies* was later withdrawn from the composer's catalogue.

30. "Sidewalks of New York" is included on *Music of the Carousel*, Smithsonian Folkways Recordings, FW06128, 1961.

31. Robert A. Slayton, *Empire Statesman: The Rise and Redemption of Al Smith* (New York: The Free Press, 2001), pp. 222–24.

32. Ibid., pp. 170–88.

33. Ibid., pp. 311–13.

34. Ibid., pp. 315–16.

35. Harold Clurman to Copland, July 31, 1934, Copland Collection.

36. The notion of music as a weapon in the class struggle owes to the aesthetic policies of the Communist Party. Copland himself used the phrase in reviewing the first *Workers Song Book*, published by the Workers Music League, a Communist organization (Copland, "Workers Sing!" *New Masses*, June 5, 1934, 28; repr. *Aaron Copland: A Reader*, p. 88). On music in the American communist movement, see in particular Barbara A. Zuck, *A History of Musical Americanism* (Ann Arbor, Mich.: UMI Research Press, 1980), pp. 103–38; and Richard A. Reuss, *American Folk Music and Left-Wing Politics, 1927–1957* (Lanham, Md.: The Scarecrow Press, 2000), pp. 39–56.

37. Andre Kostelanetz to Copland, December 18, 1941, Copland Collection. The *Lincoln Portrait* commission is discussed in Copland and Perlis, *Copland: 1900–1942*, pp. 341–43, and Pollack, *Aaron Copland*, p. 357.

38. On the linkage of Roosevelt and Lincoln, see Alfred Hayworth Jones, *Roosevelt's Image Brokers: Poets, Playwrights, and the Use of the Lincoln Symbol* (Port Washington, N.Y.: Kennikat Press, 1974); also Charles Alexander, *Here the Country Lies: Nationalism and the Arts in Twentieth-Century America* (Bloomington: Indiana University Press, 1980), p. 195.

39. *The Public Papers and Addresses of Franklin D. Roosevelt*, vol. 3, *The Advance of Recovery and Reform, 1934* (New York: Random House, 1938), p. 422; also Jones, *Roosevelt's Image Brokers*, pp. 65–66.

40. As quoted by Roosevelt in *The Public Papers and Addresses of Franklin D. Roosevelt*, vol. 5, *The People Approve, 1936* (New York: Random House, 1938), p. 222.

41. *The Public Papers and Addresses of Franklin D. Roosevelt*, vol. 1938 (New York: Macmillan, 1941), p. 41; see also Jones, *Roosevelt's Image Brokers*, pp. 66–67.

42. Jones, *Roosevelt's Image Brokers*, pp. 71–72.

43. Barry Schwartz, "Memory as a Cultural System: Abraham Lincoln in World War II," *American Sociological Review* 61 (1996): 914–20.

44. "'Free, Prosperous, Happy . . .': The Text of the Communist Election Platform," *New Masses*, July 14, 1936, 17. See also Earl Browder, *The People's Front* (New York: International Publishers, 1938), p. 58. Copland supported the Communist ticket in 1936 (Pollack, *Aaron Copland*, p. 280).

45. "Text of the Communist Election Platform," 19.

46. On the Popular Front as an American left-wing social movement, see Michael Denning, *The Cultural Front: The Laboring of American Culture in the Twentieth Century* (London: Verso, 1997).

47. Ibid., p. 128.

48. Lord Charnwood, *Abraham Lincoln* (1916; 17th repr. New York: Henry Holt, 1928). *The Life and Writings of Abraham Lincoln*, ed. Philip van Doren Stern (New York: Random House, 1940). Passages in Copland's manuscript notes for the narration are keyed to particular page numbers in the Van Doren Stern collection.

49. Copland, autograph notes for the narration of *Lincoln Portrait*, Copland Collection; the first two sentences are found in *The Life and Writings of Abraham Lincoln*, p. 77; the concluding sentence appears on p. 85.

50. Copland found "Springfield Mountain" in S. Foster Damon's *Series of Old American Songs* (Providence, R.I.: Brown University Library, 1936) but also knew it from a recording of the Old Harp Singers of Nashville. See Pollack, *Aaron Copland*, pp. 358–59, and Copland, "Scores and Records," *Modern Music* 16 (1939): 186. "Camptown Races" is not in the Damon volume.

51. Lincoln was born in Kentucky but grew up in Springfield, Illinois. The events in the song "Springfield Mountain" take place in Massachusetts.

52. Andre Kostelanetz, "When I Heard Lincoln's Words," *Parade*, February 12, 1956, Copland Collection. This history, which Kostelanetz recalled from a distance of more than a decade, holds true in its broadest outlines. Copland's rough pencil sketches are dated February 24, 1942; the pencil sketch of the orchestration is dated April 13, a short score Feb.–Apr. 1942. The Battle of the Java Sea (February 27–March 1, 1942) was a crushing defeat for the Allies, and the Allied Forces in the Dutch East Indies soon surrendered to the Japanese. On March 11, General Douglas MacArthur was evacuated from Corregidor, famously announcing, "I shall return." The Germans began bombing British cathedral cities in April 1942, and Operation Barbarossa, the Nazi invasion of Russia launched in June 1941, continued to threaten Moscow.

53. Ibid.

54. Ibid.

55. Copland, "Effect of the Cold War on the Artist in the United States," speech delivered at the Fine Arts Panel of the Cultural and Scientific Conference for World Peace, March 27, 1949, Copland Collection. Copland and Perlis, *Copland Since 1943*, pp. 183–84; Pollack, *Aaron Copland*, pp. 283–84; DeLapp, "Copland in the Fifties," pp. 93–100. Of course, Copland created more than nothing during the Cold War, and, as DeLapp has argued, in works like the Piano Quartet he seemed even to defy the dichotomies of musical style and political ideology erected in the 1950s (DeLapp, "Copland in the Fifties").

56. "Red Visitors Cause Rumpus," *Life*, April 4, 1949, 39–43.

57. James Agee and Walker Evans, *Let Us Now Praise Famous Men* (Boston: Houghton Mifflin, 1941); see Pollack, *Aaron Copland*, pp. 471–72.

58. Pollack, *Aaron Copland*, p. 473. In a notable queer reading of *The Tender Land*, Daniel E. Mathers finds "challenges to social and political norms" of 1950s America in "the opera's insistence on issues of individual identity, expression and self-acceptance" ("Expanding Horizons: Sexuality and the Re-zoning of *The Tender Land*," in Schiff, *Copland Connotations*, p. 126).

59. Copland's experience with McCarthyism is described in Copland and Perlis, *Copland Since 1943*, pp. 181–203; Pollack, *Aaron Copland*, pp. 451–60; DeLapp, "Copland in the Fifties," pp. 134–51.

60. William Safire, "A Gioia to Behold," *New York Times*, op-ed, March 8, 2004.

From Orient to Occident: Aaron Copland and the Sagas of the Prairie

BETH E. LEVY

In 1932, Virgil Thomson began a remarkable assessment of his friend and colleague with this impressive overstatement: "Aaron Copland's music is American in rhythm, Jewish in melody, eclectic in all the rest." Later passages in this article expand on its pithy opening:

> Today we ape Stravinsky. Yesterday it was Debussy. Before it was Wagner. Copland's best recommendation is that he is less eclectic than his confrères. I reproach him with eclecticism all the same. . . . He has truth, force, and elegance. He has not quite style. There remain too many irrelevant memories of Nadia Boulanger's lessons, of the scores of Stravinsky and Mahler and perhaps Richard Strauss.[1]

Arguing that a cosmopolitan curriculum had left Copland with a multiplicity of European idioms that obscured his individual voice beyond recognition, Thomson concluded: "The music is all right but the man is not clearly enough visible through it. An American certainly, a Hebrew certainly. But his more precise and personal outline is still blurred by the shadows of those who formed his youth."[2] Whether he meant to or not, Thomson left some room for interpretation when he invoked the "shadows" of Copland's formative years, and in this essay I intend to make use of that interpretive space to explore what these shadows may have meant to critics in the 1930s–1940s and to suggest some of the larger forces that were operating as Copland's now-familiar silhouette emerged. Rather than undertaking a grand historiographical survey, I offer a detailed and sometimes speculative examination of what I believe to be one crucial turning point in the creation and reception of Copland's work.[3]

At first glance, the most prominent "shadow" in Thomson's text would seem to have been cast by Boulanger herself; however, his persistent emphasis on Copland as "a Hebrew" lends his closing critique a double meaning. While Copland's past may have been both Jewish and European, Thomson implied that Copland's future would involve moving in new directions. Copland's unfailing politeness and gift for understatement make it difficult to assess his response, but he appears to have been open to Thomson's suggestions. Although not exactly counting himself among the article's admirers, he replied in a letter: "Dear Virgil— Thanks for the article. All my friends thought it very swell. It made me understand your music much better. And it will help me make mine better I hope."[4] There may be a hint of protest in Copland's terse sentence structure or his observation that Thomson's essay revealed a great deal about its author, but (pending the discovery of more explicit correspondence) these few words leave many pressing questions unanswered. If Copland did take Thomson's words to heart, what avenues were open to him? If he objected to Thomson's portrayal, what might this objection have sounded like? And, more generally, which aspects of Copland's growing reputation were shaped by the composer himself and which were not?

Such questions lie at the heart of this study, and they are complicated not only by Copland's characteristic reserve but also by the fact that the relationships among Thomson's adjectives—the "American," the "Jewish," and the "eclectic"—have changed profoundly since 1932. Thanks to our overfamiliarity with the word *American,* it still seems relatively comfortable to consider Copland's music "American in rhythm" (or in melody, for that matter), but the terms *Jewish* and *eclectic* are more insistent in their demand for the historical contextualization that this essay provides. Copland lived through an unprecedented upheaval in the understanding of race in general and Jewishness in particular. By the middle of his career, the "Jewish" racial profile had been for the most part assimilated into "white" America through cultural and political processes outside Copland's immediate control.[5]

While he was virtually silent about critics' references to his Jewishness, Copland eventually played a much more active role in challenging those who viewed his stylistic eclecticism as evidence of immaturity or insincerity. Initially, he may have made little protest against Thomson and like-minded critics, but under the aegis of New Deal aesthetics he found both the occasion and the rhetoric to answer some of their lingering claims. Through such populist works as *El Salón México* and *The Second Hurricane* and the cowboy ballets *Billy the Kid* and *Rodeo,* Copland argued that his stylistic flexibility was a socially conscientious response to Depression-era circumstances, to the new media of radio and film, and to the diverse audiences that these new media could reach. In the process, he redeemed his supposed "eclecticism" by interpreting it as a symbol of civic responsibility rather than a sign of modernist rootlessness.

Remarkably, these changing relationships between and among nation, race, and style left their marks on a single piece that Copland completed on commission for CBS in 1937, *Music for Radio: Saga of the Prairie*.[6] Its compound title bears witness to its complicated genesis and the conflicting attractions of modern technology and agrarian nostalgia. Yet the title also leaves much unsaid, for the same forces that worked to reconfigure the "American," the "Jewish," and the "eclectic" were also at work behind its techno-pastoral surface. As one of several works signaling his turn toward a more accessible idiom, including *El Salón México* and *The Second Hurricane*, Copland's radio piece rekindled debates about his changeable style and his personal sincerity. As his first composition to bear a subtitle evoking the American West, it raised more specific questions about race and entitlement for some of its listeners, who wondered what claim the Russian-Jewish Copland could have on the stereotypically Anglo pioneer experience. In accepting the subtitle's suggestion of Anglo-Americana (despite its questionable relevance to his original intent), Copland allowed himself to be a man of many conversions—from modernism to populism, from urban to rural, from East to West. The fact that the imagery of the American West proved such a suitable backdrop for these cultural conversions is perhaps more surprising than it should be, for the West has always been a favorite site for experiences of self-discovery. Like the cowgirl heroine of *Rodeo* or the outlaw Billy the Kid, Copland found himself in the West. But unlike them, he had to travel to get there.

"Eclectic in All the Rest"

The ready availability today of music in many styles and the variety of phenomena associated with postmodernism may make it difficult for us to recapture the angst with which Copland and his contemporaries addressed the question of personal style. Though trends in composition had changed rapidly since the turn of the twentieth century, the rhetoric used to describe the creative process in the 1920s tended to rely on the Romantic tropes of originality, consistency, and an easily recognizable individual idiom. Copland's early oeuvre tested these tropes in several ways.

From the start, Copland may have been susceptible to charges of indiscriminate imitation because of the predilections of his primary teachers:

Rubin Goldmark, who encouraged Copland to "absorb," and "digest" before striking out on his own; and Nadia Boulanger, whose historical-analytical teaching style fostered an intimacy with past masterpieces in a variety of idioms.[7] Hard on the heels of the contrapuntal *Passacaglia* (1922) that Boulanger required of her students, came the asymmetrical meters and ostinato effects of the *Rondino* (1923) for string quartet, and the ballet *Grohg* (1924–25), which combines impressionist and expressionist elements, Stravinskian octatonicism and polytonality, microtones, and jazz polyrhythms—perhaps also courtesy of Stravinsky.[8] Arriving back in the United States in June 1924, Copland carried with him the first movement of the score that would fulfill his commission from Serge Koussevitzky for an organ work that Boulanger could play with the Boston Symphony Orchestra. The resulting Symphony for Organ and Orchestra, completed later that year in New York, celebrated Copland's musical and personal ties to France. Impressionist harmonies, references to the French organ tradition, and a parody of "Clair de la Lune" were reinforced by the work's dedication to Boulanger and by her physical presence as soloist. Copland himself called this work "too 'European' in derivation" early in his career, but he eventually discerned in its pages something akin to his "natural expressive idiom."[9] Indeed, the restless rhythmic energy of its middle movement calls to mind gestures that the composer would associate explicitly with jazz in his next work, *Music for the Theatre* (1925).

Although Copland made no secret of the fact that his European experiences had helped him discover the potential that jazz held for classical composers, he was also interested in jazz for its particularly American qualities.[10] His 1925 article, given the telling title "Jazz as Folk Music," suggests that he saw "jazz tunes and music of the 'Old Black Joe' variety" as his best hope for giving his own music an indigenous "folk-song foundation."[11] With this project in mind, Copland could hardly have ignored the lingering aftershocks of Paul Whiteman's notoriously successful "Experiment in Modern Music," staged a mere three months before he left Paris.[12] Although *Music for the Theatre* did not have the same kind of advance press promotion as George Gershwin's *Rhapsody in Blue*, it represented a related type of "experiment" in Copland's output and, together with the Piano Concerto (1926) it provided the musical counterpart to Copland's technical essays on jazz.[13] While the brash dissonances of the Piano Concerto and the racy "Burlesque" movement from *Music for the Theatre* predictably confounded certain segments of public taste,[14] Copland's syncopated revelry and allusions to Tin Pan Alley song linked his name with Gershwin's in many critics' minds, as MacDonald Smith Moore has shown in his book *Yankee Blues*.[15]

Today *Music for the Theatre* and the Piano Concerto are sometimes por-trayed rather simply as logical responses to the challenge of making a modern music that would be recognized as distinctively American. In their own time, however, they were more complicated and more contro-versial. Based on examination of little-known correspondence, it appears that Copland drew fire not just from conservative critics, but also from some of his supporters. In particular, two of his closest composer friends worried privately that he might be perceived as too "commercial" or too narrowly identified with New York. Roy Harris cautioned Copland against the dangers of adopting jazz elements in a letter written while the Piano Concerto was still in progress:

> A word of warning to you—dear brother Aaron—the Jazz idiom is too easily assumed and projected [—] as a serious expression it has nearly burned out already I believe. . . . Beware for that new piano concerto which so many Copeland [*sic*] enthusiasts are waiting for— Don't disappoint us with jazz— (Have I been harsh—if it might seem so—it is only because I have such belief in your integrity—<u>outside</u> the <u>jazz idiom</u>) [emphasis original].[16]

That same year, Roger Sessions expressed similar concerns, objecting vehemently to Copland's claim that *Music for the Theatre* was his most "characteristic" work. It was that assertion, Sessions wrote, "combined with what you said about being a New York composer etc. [that] led me to won-der whether you were not—temporarily, no doubt—going off on a vein which was smaller than your truest one." Presumably relieved by some conciliatory remark on Copland's part, Sessions continued, "But I am really happy that the 'New York composer' idea has been given up, perhaps partly for the purely personal reason that it identified you in my mind with cer-tain people whose work (in various fields of activity) is not for a moment to be compared with, or mentioned in the same breath with yours."[17]

Copland's answers to these letters have not to my knowledge been uncov-ered, but if we turn to his scores instead we can see that, even if he ignored his friends' advice, his subsequent works might have satisfied their concerns.[18] After finishing the Piano Concerto, his next large-scale com-position was the 1928 piano trio *Vitebsk (Study on a Jewish Theme)* and it was dedicated to Harris. While *Vitebsk* preserved and even intensified the dissonant language of his jazz-based works, Copland changed the frame of reference by aligning its quarter tones not with the jazzy realm of the "blue note," but with the vocal inflections of Hasidic song. The trio won approval from Harris, but its overt Jewishness remained rare in Copland's oeuvre.[19] Instead of pursuing this path, Copland's next compositions—including the *Symphonic Ode* (1929), Piano Variations (1930), and *Short Symphony* (1933)—sported a style that Sessions could have endorsed: dissonant, tightly constructed, and arguably free of explicit national or ethnic markers.

Variations on the same advice Copland had been receiving in private correspondence began to find their way into print before Thomson's 1932 essay. In 1930, for example, Theodore Chanler prepared to convey his thoughts on Copland to the readers of *The Hound and Horn*. After Copland sent Chanler scores of his most recent works, he received a letter of thanks and a glib warning from this fellow member of the "Boulangerie": "I finally started writing the article yesterday. Having no idea what I was going to say it came as something of a shock to me when I found myself positively <u>roasting</u> you. I hope you won't be annoyed. I've decided that your style is full of impurities. So there."[20] This accusation became the negative refrain in Chanler's otherwise complimentary text, which was later anthologized in Henry Cowell's influential collection, *American Composers on American Music* (1933). Stating from the outset that Copland's "architectural sense is in advance of his sense of style, which is still impure," Chanler deflated even his most enthusiastic praise with expressions of regret that Copland's own voice was insufficiently audible: "The zest which he manages to instill into certain rather jaded jazz *motifs*, the skilful disposition of the material, the humor and perfect timing of contrasts...save [the Piano Concerto] from being in any sense a *pastiche*, though one is aware of potentialities in Copland, not realized here, of achieving a more fruitfully personal style."[21] While Chanler does not say precisely what Copland needed to do to make his style more satisfying, he does suggest that the *Symphonic Ode,* while less "accomplished" than the Piano Concerto, nonetheless represented a positive step toward an "essential personality" that was "clearer and more decisively individual."[22]

We cannot know what "impurities" Chanler had in mind, but as the letters from Sessions and Harris suggest, Copland's reliance on urban and African-American elements sparked strong reactions. Henry Cowell shared this concern; in fact, when he reprinted Chanler's article in 1933, he felt compelled to add an editorial postscript that singled out the absence of jazz references in Copland's recent music as a sign of progress: "Since the foregoing article was written, Aaron Copland has produced a number of new works, and has materially broadened his tendencies in composition. For one thing, he no longer relies on jazz themes to animate his auditors."[23] Even Paul Rosenfeld, perhaps Copland's most vocal supporter during the first fifteen years of his career, made Copland's ties to jazz a prominent undercurrent in several of his multifaceted assessments of the composer. Unlike Harris or Sessions, Rosenfeld embraced the idea that Copland's music might reflect contemporary New York. He was also one of the first powerful advocates for the argument that Copland did have his own recognizable and independent idiom: "Mr. Copland's music has a thingness," he wrote in 1925.[24] But Rosenfeld quickly became convinced that many of Copland's limitations could be linked to his youthful preoccupation with "jazzing." As early as 1928, he greeted Copland as "a new colt in the American pasture" in an article titled "Aaron Copland Without the Jazz."[25] Here he described the two moods that had dominated Copland's expression: "a rather plaintive, wistful one" and "a wild, cackling state, full of machinery madness." Linking the first with the "nostalgic" blues and the second with "parodistic" jazz, he observed: "Both reflect more of a racial past than of a present."[26] What was the substance of this "racial past"? Rosenfeld gave an answer (of sorts) to this question in the 1929 collection, *An Hour with American Music*—a collection whose first words are "American music is not jazz. Jazz is not music."[27] In his essay, "Aaron Copland: George Gershwin," he emphasized the superiority of Copland's music over the merely "commercial" manifestations of jazz, but he also noted that Copland's "taste for hot colors and garish jazziness" was "perhaps a consequence of his oriental-American psyche."[28]

Rosenfeld was not alone in characterizing Copland's "racial" past as "Jewish." Although Copland himself usually chose to avoid calling attention to his ethnic background, many of his early critics did not share such inhibitions. Roger Sessions mentioned Copland's Jewishness rather casually, deeming it "interesting to note the occasional Jewish character of Copland's music."[29] Thomson made rather heavier weather of Copland's "penitential," Jewish *melos* ("When he sings it is as wailing before the wall"), his "ornamental" and "purely coloristic" chromaticism, and his stern Hebraic nature: "He is a prophet calling out her sins to Israel. His God is the god of battle, the Lord of Hosts, the jealous, the angry, the avenging god. . . . The gentler movements of his music are more like an oriental contemplation of infinity than like any tender depiction of the gentler aspects of Jehovah."[30] Although he never responded in detail to assertions about the Jewishness of his music, Copland himself seems on occasion to have accepted "Jewishness" as a meaningful musical category. At least he felt comfortable calling attention to Darius Milhaud's "profound nostalgia" and "deep sense of the tragedy of all life" as evidence of his "Jewish blood" and citing his "subjectivism," "violence," and "logic" as indications of his "Jewish spirit."[31] Given the rampant racial determinism of the age, Copland was particularly impressed by Milhaud's exceptional ability to display both "Jewish" and "French" traits—as he later put it, to "remain profoundly national and at the same time profoundly Jewish."[32]

In fact, both of the critical strains I have been describing—stylistic eclecticism in general and openness to jazz in particular—resonated strongly with contemporary perceptions of Jews and Jewish creativity, as Moore's *Yankee Blues* has persuasively argued. Some writers who focused on these controversial areas may have meant to imply a connection between Copland's music and his ethnicity; others probably had no such agenda. Regardless of authorial intent, I would suggest that critical emphasis on eclecticism and borrowing held a special danger for Jewish composers because these charges could so easily slip into related stereotypes about insincerity and commercialism that can be traced all the way back to the nineteenth century's most famous mouthpiece of anti-Semitism, Richard Wagner. According to Wagner's well-known tract "Das Judentum in der Musik" of 1850, Jews had become dangerously adept at assimilation because they had no true speech of their own. They were "parrots" condemned to babble "with quite distressing accuracy and deceptive likeness . . . but also with just as little real feeling and expression as these foolish birds." They rehashed the hard-won fruits of non-Jewish genius into a "mannered bricabrac" for sale at an oriental "art-bazaar" *(Kunstwarenwechsel):* "Just as words and constructions are hurled together in [poetic] jargon with wondrous inexpressiveness, so does the Jew musician hurl together the diverse forms and styles of every age and every master. Packed side by side, we find the formal idiosyncracies of all the schools, in motleyest chaos."[33] Such stereotypes proved quite durable among certain elements of the American press. In the 1920s, for example, at the height of American anti-Semitism, Henry Ford's *Dearborn Independent* voiced its view that "in this business of making the people's songs, the Jews have shown, as usual, no originality but very much adaptability . . . which is a charitable term used to cover plagiarism, which in its turn politely covers the crime of mental pocket-picking. The Jews do not create; they take what others have done, give it a clever twist, and exploit it."[34] Ford's extremism is relatively well known, but such Wagnerian sentiments were also expressed with shocking candor by Ernest Bloch, perhaps the century's best-known composer of "Jewish" music. In a 1917 interview, he told Sigmund Spaeth: "Some of the best writers of ragtime are Jews. But their creative work is a trick, or a spontaneous expression of self. Your Jew is a wonderful psychologist and a wonderful imitator. He can be more Parisian than a real Parisian and more German than a real German. And because he has always been willing to ape that which is popular, he has produced no characteristic secular music of his own."[35]

When it came to Copland, Thomson and Chanler were relatively charitable in their assertions about his stylistic hybridity. Lazare Saminsky, director of music at New York's Temple Emanu-El during the 1920s, was not. A practicing Jew and an authority on Jewish music, he divided Jewry into two camps: the pure, ancient "Hebraic" and the modern, degenerate "Judaic," which he lambasted with all manner of anti-Semitic critique. Defining the "Judaic" as an assimilationist idiom, "folksong born in the latest ghetto," "orientalized," and "showing an abundance of borrowed and neutralized traits," he observed: "It has emanated from an alien corner, acquired by the Jewish racial psyche; it flows from the mental agility, the calamitous gift of alert self-adaptation to a new cultural quarter."[36] Saminsky spared no pains when applying these complaints to Copland in passages that Howard Pollack has aptly described as "drenched in anti-Semitic and homophobic innuendos."[37] In Copland's case, "self-adaptation" had betrayed itself in the composer's chameleon style, and by 1934, Saminsky admitted that he had made up his mind—at least temporarily: "I am sorry to profess an eradicable conviction that Copland is of an observing, an absorbing nature, rather than a creative one."[38]

In the United States, there was no more intense locus for anxiety about stylistic eclecticism than the noisy collision of black and white represented by jazz. Perhaps it was this American anxiety that led Copland, in his treatment of Milhaud, to avoid making the connection between race and style that would probably have seemed most obvious to his contemporaries. While he praised Milhaud's jazz-inspired works, especially *La Création du Monde*, he did not describe Milhaud's jazziness as a corollary of Jewishness.[39]

MacDonald Smith Moore has identified a broad spectrum of writers who linked Jews with "the success of jazz" and "the fusion of jazz and classical music."[40] Henry Cowell, for one, admitted that Copland's Piano Concerto had the potential to improve jazz, but he remained convinced that such music should not and could not represent the "true America" because it lacked the Anglo-Saxon character represented by Ives or Ruggles. Complaining that "a pair of sophisticated Parisians" (Copland and Gershwin) had led young American composers astray by overemphasizing jazz, he concluded unequivocally: "The roots of jazz are the syncopation and rhythmic accents of the Negro; its modernization and present form is the work of Jews—mostly of New York 'Tin-Pan-Alley' Jews. Jazz is Negro music, seen through the eyes of these Jews."[41] Though far removed from Cowell politically, John Tasker Howard nonetheless agreed with this assessment, calling both Tin Pan Alley and jazz "Jewish interpretation[s] of the Negro."[42]

Contemporary racial reasoning affirmed and helped explain the link between Jews and jazz by positing a Jewish racial profile that fell between Negro and Anglo.[43] Along with Rosenfeld, Isaac Goldberg stated clearly that "the ready amalgamation of the American Negro and the American Jew goes back to something Oriental in the blood of both."[44] In other words, it was not merely their urban environment but their very blood that made Jews the ideal cultural middlemen, uniquely situated to perform the anarchic alchemy between "high" and "low" art represented by *Rhapsody in Blue* or *Music for the Theatre*. Thus when Daniel Gregory Mason labeled Copland "a cosmopolitan Jew," he positioned the composer on the dark side of a battle between "Oriental extravagance" and "the poignant beauty of Anglo-Saxon restraint." Still more vehement in his condemnations of jazz, Mason sounded an alarm against "the insidiousness of the Jewish menace to our artistic integrity" when he declared: "Our public taste is in danger of being permanently debauched . . . by the intoxication of what is, after all, an alien art."[45] For Mason, Copland's jazzy modernism and stylistic wandering represented a more serious sin than artistic immaturity: they were the musical embodiments of racial miscegenation.

As these opinions make clear, racially charged identities were not easy to cast off. Perhaps this is what Nadia Boulanger meant if in fact she remarked that Roy Harris would go further than Copland as a composer because he was not "handicapped" by being a Jew.[46] Her words might have reflected a sober awareness of prejudice in the world or a sobering reflection of the anti-Semitic attitudes prevalent in interwar Paris; either interpretation reveals the power of race and religious creed to predetermine attitudes, even among friends.[47] Copland was well aware that being recognized as a "Jewish composer" carried with it certain connotations. "People are certain to say—'Bloch,'" he warned the young Leonard Bernstein in 1939.[48] But while Jewishness remained a central feature of Bloch's reception, the same cannot be said of Copland. While never disavowing his heritage, by the late 1940s he had escaped these powerful stereotypes so completely that audiences today often remain unaware that Copland did not begin his career as a "common man."

How did this change take place? There is no simple answer to this question and no single moment at which the critical landscape surrounding Copland began to shift. By turning now to detailed examination of a specific work, *Music for Radio: Saga of the Prairie*, I do not mean to suggest that it holds the only key to understanding this multifaceted phase of his career or that it represents the "cause" or "effect" in a straightforward process. I do contend, however, that the forces at play in this piece are strikingly parallel to the forces that helped reconfigure Copland's reputation, making him appear less "Jewish" and more "American" and realigning his stylistic flexibility with responsible (American) populism rather than rootless (Jewish) eclecticism. In this way, *Music for Radio* can be considered one staging ground for a journey that transformed critical understanding of his life and work. The extent to which Copland forged his own paths during this journey and the degree to which his paths were dictated by others remain—and must remain—open to debate. In fact, the story of *Music for Radio* hinges on one of the clearest ironies of Copland's turn toward populism: while it may have helped his "precise and personal outline" to emerge from "the shadows of those who formed his youth," it also made it difficult to separate his own artistic preferences from the preoccupations of those around him.

The Sagas of the Prairie

Late in September of 1936, the Columbia Broadcasting System offered Copland his first radio commission, complete with a $500 honorarium and basic guidelines for length.[49] Curiously, Copland was not among the six composers originally chosen to participate in the network's commissioning project. As Susan Key has observed, Gershwin apparently turned down the job, leaving a slot open for his less predictable colleague.[50] Together with *El Salón México* (1932–36) and *The Second Hurricane* (1936), Copland's *Music for Radio* represents a turning point in his stylistic trajectory: the point at which he became interested in addressing the "new public . . . [that] had grown up around the radio and phonograph," and saying what he had to say "in the simplest possible terms."[51] Unlike his earlier shift from the international neoclassicism of the "Boulangerie" toward the urban landscape of *Music for the Theatre* or the dissonant abstraction of the Piano Variations, Copland's move toward accessibility quickly came to symbolize his progressive and socially responsible engagement with the mass audience and new technology.

Few advocates were more impassioned about the fruitful intersection of composition and radio than Davidson Taylor, the head of CBS's music division and the man responsible for the network's commissioning scheme. Writing in 1936, Taylor hailed the emerging role of radio companies as "the Brandenburgs, the Haffners, and the Esterhazys of today" and challenged composers to write music specifically "for the microphone."[52] Copland was right in line with such thinking. When he spoke on the air in 1940, for example, he welcomed a broadening of the "democratic bases of music," and proclaimed: "It is our job to give these new listeners a music that is fresh, direct, simple and profound. I can think of no better program for the composer of today."[53] Shortly after the first performance, a two-page advertisement in *Radio Daily* exaggerated the impact of the CBS project by claiming that the premiere of *Music for Radio* "wrote a new chapter in the history of serious music. For it belonged entirely to the radio audience; coming immediately to the whole of our people."[54]

It was thus no accident that the CBS commissions were slated for performance on a series called "Everybody's Music"—and no accident that this series was chosen for a unique experiment in audience participation.[55] Copland's initial title, *Radio Serenade,* was abruptly altered to the even more neutral *Music for Radio,* thanks to a clever public relations move by network officials: in order to increase audience interest, listeners would be asked to send in their suggestions for more descriptive titles after hearing the piece on the air. The response was staggering. CBS elicited more than a thousand suggested titles from every part of the United States— a scope that is all the more remarkable given that the sole prize offered was the composer's manuscript score.

Copland's piece had been framed as an homage to modern technology, and it exhibited twentieth-century timbres and special effects ranging from vibraphone, saxophones, and unusual brass mutes to solos at the microphone. As Pollack observes, the work also touched on many of "the kinds of music typically heard on the radio at that time: swing bands, folk song, and incidental music for serials, dramas, and news reports."[56] But apart from its association with the radio medium, Copland's piece was virtually a blank slate for its audience. At least two intrepid listeners seem to have grasped the peculiarity of this project. One apparently preferred to retain the title "Music for Radio." Another felt it necessary to explain his suggestion, "Notes in Search of a Program." According to a letter from Davidson Taylor to Copland, the listener's analysis went something like this:

A bunch of notes get together, deciding to be music. They go along enthusiastically for a while, then consternation overcomes them: my God, they have no program! What are they doing, being a piece of music without a program? They try several programs, none of which seems to fit. Then they strike out again without having found one, and at length they are satisfied just to be a piece of music.[57]

In addition to these self-conscious responses, more than 150 suggestions were sent to Copland in Mexico. A representative selection of these entries can be found in Table 1.[58]

Table 1. Selection from the more than 150 suggested titles sent to Copland in Mexico

Adventures in the Life of a Robot	A May of Victory
Agitation of the Masses	The Melting Pot
Airline Fantasy	Metropolis
An American Pippa Passes	Metropolitan Kaleidoscope
The Attack	Music for Radio
Autumn of the American Pioneer	New Mexican Village
Calling All Nations	Night in the City
Caprices of the Sea	1938
Cliff Dwellers	On Set in Hollywood
Commuters' Odyssey	Oriental Fantasy
Dance of the Mechanists	Peace Conference
Dawn in the Jungle	The Peasant's Fantasy
A Day's Work	A Psalm of Modern Life
Driving the Herd	Radionata
Early Morn in Bagdad	San Francisco
English Countryside	Sedative
Equinox	The Seraphic Triumph
Escape from the City	A Song of the Mechanical Age
Farewell Amelia	Spiritual Ecstasy
Futile Search for Order out of Chaos	Subway Traveler
Gypsy Caravan	Sunday Night in Manhattan
The Inca's Prayer to the Sun God	Sundayschool Carnival
Indecision	Sylvan Midsummernights Meditations
Journey of the British Patrol across Arabia	Thoughts while Strolling
The Jungle Storm	Tower and Turrets of the Mystic City of Sound
Lilacs in the Rain	Transatlantic Liner Ascending Ambrose Channel
Machine Modernistic	Trip through a National Park
The Majestic Mississippi	Urban Nocturne
Marconique Melody in the Air	Whims and Cries from the Great Tribulation
Marconi's World Message	World Variety

Ranging from total abstraction to remarkable specificity, encompassing both rural and urban imagery from around the globe, the titles are most striking for their diversity. One could hardly ask for a better illustration of instrumental music's polysemy. And Copland could hardly have wished for a greater variety of titles to choose from. Having looked over the entries, Copland telegraphed his response to CBS:

HAVE READ ALL TITLE SUGGESTIONS STOP ASTONISHED AND DELIGHTED BY NUMBER AND VARIETY STOP NO ONE TITLE COMPLETELY SATISFACTORY STOP ACCEPT GLADLY AS IMAGINATIVE SUBTITLE SAGA OF THE PRAIRIE STOP CLOSE RUNNERS UP PRAIRIE TRAVEL STOP JOURNEY OF THE EARLY PIONEERS STOP AMERICAN PIONEER[59]

Thus Copland christened his first work for national broadcast and one of his first with a descriptive title that invoked Americana. By keeping *Music for Radio* as the main title and making the colorful caption a "subtitle" instead, Copland and Taylor retained the reference to modern technology.[60] Notably, each of the titles Copland approved falls within the handful of suggestions related to westward expansion. After all, he remembered when compiling his memoirs in the 1980s, "I had used a cowboy tune in the second of the four sections, so the western titles seemed most appropriate."[61]

But there is more to this process than Copland's distant recollections suggest. One week before the premiere of *Music for Radio*, CBS issued a press release announcing that the piece "had a program, or scenario, that not even its composer . . . ventured to interpret," and that the composer was trusting the audience to name the composition. In fact, the network noted, the winning title would be the one that "is most successful in telling Mr. Copland what his music is."[62] This unusual view of artistic agency might be explained away as savvy advertising. But in the strange case of *Music for Radio*, the advertisement itself could be considered "amazing but true." Although it is unlikely that any listener could truly have told Copland "what his music is," the piece actually did have a scenario that Copland chose not to interpret—whether for personal, political, or artistic reasons, or some combination of the three.

Many of the melodies and textures that eventually found their way into *Music for Radio* appear in sketches preserved at the Library of Congress for a choral setting of Langston Hughes's poem "The Ballad of Ozie Powell." While this observation is not new, it has not sparked extensive interpretation in light of Copland's changing reception during the 1930s.[63]

Hughes's poem appeared in the left-wing journal *The American Spectator* in April 1936, and it pays tribute to one of the Scottsboro Boys, the nine black males falsely accused of raping two white prostitutes on an Alabama train in 1931.[64] The Scottsboro Boys barely escaped the lynch mob before encountering the judicial system: eight were sentenced to death, and the various legal battles that ensued left them in prison anywhere from six to nineteen years before they were all finally set free. During these extended trials, obtaining the release of the Scottsboro Boys became a rallying cry for Communists worldwide, but especially for the American Communist Party, which raised money and wrangled with the NAACP over control of the legal defense. Hughes visited Ozie Powell and the other men in prison and later wrote the "Ballad of Ozie Powell" when Powell's name resurfaced in the news after an altercation in which he slashed a sheriff's throat and was shot in the head.

Copland was not the only composer whose conscience was caught by the plight of the Scottsboro Boys. L. E. Swift (a.k.a. Elie Siegmeister) penned a mass song "The Scottsboro Boys Shall Not Die" for the first *Workers' Song Book,* which Copland reviewed for *New Masses* in 1934.[65] Like Siegmeister's "Scottsboro Boys" (and like Copland's own prize-winning mass song "Into the Streets, May First" of 1934), Copland's sketches for the "Ozie Powell" setting feature the carefully controlled dissonances, triadic harmonies, and forceful dotted rhythms that characterized the proletarian music making of the Composers' Collective. Unlike either mass song, the unfinished choral piece would have required coordinated ensemble work and vocal effects such as humming that seem more typical of a trained choir than a workers' chorus.

Copland began sketching his setting of Hughes's poem in mid-December 1936 (about eight months after the poem was published and almost three months after receiving the CBS commission). The most complete, and presumably latest, layer of sketches includes at least some vocal parts with scattered piano accompaniment for most of the couplets. As Table 2 shows, the most important modifications to the text involved omitting some of the refrain lines ("Ozie, Ozie Powell") in places where they were not required by the poem's syntax. Other alterations were minor, though not necessarily insignificant. In addition to misspelling "Ozie," Copland preferred the French *Ballade* to Hughes's *Ballad;* he also omitted, perhaps unintentionally, three of the poem's references to "black" and "white," retaining the adjective black only in the line "But nine black boys they know full well."[66]

The condensed refrain structure of the poem clearly dictated the form of Copland's piece: each instance of the text "Ozzie, Ozzie Powell" is

Table 2. Comparison of Langston Hughes's "Ballad of Ozie Powell" and the text for Copland's unfinished "Ballade of Ozzie Powell"

HUGHES: Ballad of Ozie Powell	COPLAND: Ballade of Ozzie Powell
Red is the Alabama road,	Red is the Alabama road
Ozie, Ozie Powell,	Ozzie, Ozzie Powell
Redder now where your blood has flowed,	[Redder now where your blood has flowed*]
Ozie, Ozie Powell.	Ozzie, Ozzie Powell
Strong are the bars and steel the gate,	Strong are the bars and steel the gates
Ozie, Ozie Powell.	Ozzie, Ozzie Powell
The High Sheriff's eyes are filled with hate,	The high sheriff's eyes are filled with hate
Ozie, Ozie Powell.	Ozzie, Ozzie Powell
The High Sheriff shoots and he shoots to kill	The high sheriff shoots And he shoots to kill
Black young Ozie Powell,	Ozzie, Ozzie Powell
The law's a Klansman with an evil will,	The laws a Klansman with an evil will,
Ozie, Ozie Powell.	
One of the nine in the law's clean claws,	
Penniless Ozie Powell,	
Not one of the nine who pass the laws,	
Ozie, Ozie Powell.	
Nine old men in Washington,	Nine old men in Washington
Ozie, Ozie Powell	
Never saw the High Sheriff's gun	never saw the Sheriff's gun
Aimed at Ozie Powell.	aimed at Ozzie Powell
Nine old men so rich and wise,	Nine old men so rich and wise
Ozie, Ozie Powell,	
They never saw the High Sheriff's eyes	Never saw the Sheriff's eyes
Stare at Ozie Powell.	stare at Ozzie Powell
But nine black boys know full well,	But nine black boys they know full well
Don't they, Ozie Powell?	
What it is to live in hell,	What it is to live in Hell
Ozie, Ozie Powell.	Don't they Ozzie Powell
The devil's a Kleagle with an evil will,	
Ozie, Ozie Powell,	
A white High Sheriff who shoots to kill	
Black young Ozie Powell.	
And red is that Alabama road,	
Ozie, Ozie Powell,	
But redder now where your life's blood's flowed,	
Ozie! Ozie Powell!	

* Although the text underlay is missing for this line in the most complete version of the sketches, these words are present in other sketches.

Example 1. Copland's sketches for "Ballade of Ozzie Powell."

declaimed using the melodic contour and echoing texture seen in Example 1, suggesting a religious litany or ritual incantation. The constricted, marchlike theme introduced in bar nine of the sketches likewise seems to take its inspiration from the tragic traveler on the "Alabama road" (see Example 2). His real imprisonment finds a haunting homology in the melody's inability to break free from the narrow confines of a minor third. Both these motives are strongly tied to the text and message of the poem, and both appear prominently in the sketches for *Music for Radio* and in its published score, which was eventually titled *Prairie Journal* (see Examples 3 and 4). Although the material associated with the repeated cry "Ozzie, Ozzie Powell" has lost its function as a literal refrain, it still punctuates *Music for Radio* periodically and audibly. Measures 84–85 even replicate the quasi-antiphonal texture of the "Ballade" sketches. While other instances may be more subtle—for example, when the "Ozzie" motif infiltrates the violin line at measures 264–70 (see Example 5)— Ozie Powell remains a palpable presence in Copland's *Music for Radio*.

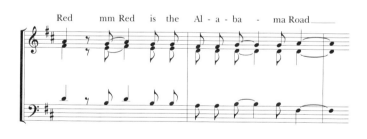

Example 2. Copland's sketches for "Ballade of Ozzie Powell."

Example 3. Copland's sketches for "Radio Serenade" (later *Music for Radio*).

As Pollack has noted in his biography of Copland, "It seems significant that *Prairie Journal,* widely considered the first of the composer's Western works, should have in its background, if not in its very genesis, a choral work about racial injustice in the rural South."[67] The significance of this transformation is worth exploring in greater detail. What did it mean when Copland shifted his attention away from Ozie Powell? Copland neither finished the choral setting nor made any allusion to Hughes or Scottsboro in the title or program note for the radio commission. Perhaps he became frustrated by the rigid refrain structure of Hughes's poem. Maybe the pressure of the radio commission did not allow him to complete this choral piece as

Example 4. *Music for Radio (Prairie Journal)*, mm. 75–86; condensed score with some instrumental parts deleted.

Example 4 continued

he would have liked; although he started the "Ozzie Powell" sketches after receiving the network's offer, it cannot be determined whether he began the "Ballade" with CBS in mind.[68] But one thing can be said for certain: as the network's deadline came and went, the "Ozzie Powell" sketches entered *Music for Radio* in such a way that a thousand listeners could devise a thousand wildly divergent interpretations, their imaginations unfettered by inconvenient texts or uncomfortable political references.[69]

Looking back on the rapidly changing politics of the 1930s, one might think that the Scottsboro affair would have proved too historically contingent or too ideologically charged to be an effective program for radio. Copland does not seem to have shared this view. In his essay "The Composer and Radio," published in *Our New Music* (1941), he devoted his most effusive language to the idea that radio was an ideal medium for exactly this kind of potent message. The impetus to communicate with "the widest possible audience," he noted,

is not without its political implications . . . for it takes its source partly from that same need to reaffirm the democratic ideal that already fills

Example 5. *Music for Radio (Prairie Journal)*, mm. 264–70, strings only.

our literature, our stage, and our screen. It is not a time for poignantly subjective lieder but a time for large mass singing. We are the men who must embody new communal ideals in a new communal music. And the radio is the natural outlet for that new music.[70]

Copland knew that even such lofty aims were not guaranteed to be above critical reproach, and he felt compelled to point out that his interest in connecting with audiences "should by no means be confused with mere opportunism. On the contrary, it stems from a healthy desire in every artist to find his deepest feelings reflected in his fellowman."[71]

Copland's continued commitment to progressive politics has been well documented by Elizabeth Bergman Crist, and his leftist ties easily spanned the years before and after *Music for Radio*.[72] His own mass song, and his review of the first *Workers' Songbook* were unabashed in their embrace of proletarian sentiments. And *The Second Hurricane*, which actually kept Copland from finishing his radio commission on time, carried a strong didactic message about cooperative brotherhood. But when Copland turned his attention to *Music for Radio*, he effectively erased a far more controversial program—one that had been openly co-opted by Communist agitators—in favor of imagery dictated neither by his own aesthetic intent nor by his political conscience. Literally (through the title contest) and figuratively (through the melting away of racial tension into a nostalgic national unity), *Music for Radio* gained a different kind of radical import through its deference to its listeners. In a way that Copland could never have imagined, it became a work that told the public precisely what it wanted to hear.

The fact that the erasure of Ozie Powell coincided with a westward reorientation and an embrace of rural Americana reveals several things about the cultural cachet of "westernness" during the Great Depression.[73] When Ruth Leonhardt of Grosse Pointe, Michigan, sent in the winning subtitle, she was responding to what she called the "typically American" sound of Copland's score, and as the symbol of that American sound she chose "the intense courage—the struggles and the final triumphs—of the early settlers, the real pioneers."[74] Leonhardt's reasoning would no doubt have struck a sympathetic chord with many of her contemporaries, raised on singing cowboys, Hollywood westerns, and Frederick Jackson Turner's frontier thesis, which posited the roots of the American character in westward expansion.

It was not the dreary Dust Bowl migrations, and certainly not the "Ballad of Ozie Powell," but rather the manifest destiny of the "early settlers, the real pioneers" that captured Leonhardt's imagination, and eventually Copland's, too. With his move from the explicit "Ballade" text to the implicit "Saga" narrative, came a transformation in storytelling mode—from lamenting an individual or regional plight to celebrating a triumph of nation building, from the actual Ozie to the legendary pioneers, from the urban to the rural, from a contemporary climate of racial and political conflict to an era of imaginary unity and resolve. This interpretation places *Music for Radio* in the midst of a long line of moments stretching through American history in which turning toward the West coincides with a turn away from black-white conflict. Just as westward expansion was driven in part by the antebellum desire to keep a balance of free and slave states, so western imagery and the myth of conquest could serve as positive replacements for unsettling depictions of civil strife and the messy realities of interracial coexistence. In this light, through a process neither Copland nor the listeners participating in the CBS contest could have anticipated, the metamorphosis of *Music for Radio* represents an uncanny recapitulation of America's desire to escape its racial dilemmas.

Given this history, it is not hard to hear "Ozie Powell" whispering from within the pages of *Music for Radio,* offering an eerie counterpoint to the "saga of the prairie." But of course no one was in a position to hear it this way in 1937—with the possible exception of Copland himself and any friends who might have had a peek at his sketchbook. Instead casual listeners and committed critics were faced with a piece that displayed two fairly distinct moods: the kinetic energy of its opening bars could easily be linked to Copland's existing, modernist works, but the pastoral strains of its mid-section seemed to suggest something new. When evaluating *Music for Radio,* professional critics tended to emphasize one or the other of these moods and, although the evidence is admittedly partial, one can see a shift in the work's reception during the 1930s.

In one of the earliest reviews of the piece, before the "Saga" subtitle was added, Bostonian critic Moses Smith greeted *Music for Radio* with assumptions that were clearly shaped by his understanding of Copland as the "Brooklyn Stravinsky."[75] The initial bars confirmed his expectations with their superimposition of irregular accent patterns over a steady pulse and occasionally layered textures as seen in Examples 6a and 6b. "For this listener," Smith wrote, "the more characteristically Coplandesque (or should it be 'Coplandish'?) portions are the fast parts, except for a few sequences that are a little too baldly Stravinskian and even Respighian. Particularly striking were the very opening measures. The nervous, fitful intensity of the rhythm (frequently heard later on) are quite worthy of the composer of 'Music for the Theatre' and the Piano Variations."[76] Some members of the general public also responded to these musical features with mechanistic or urban titles, but neither they nor Smith could have noticed that the melodic skeleton of the first two bars (D-C-D-A) is identical to the motivic contour originally associated with the utterance "Ozie Powell": down a whole step, up a whole step, down a perfect fourth.[77] Howard Pollack and Wayne Shirley have discussed the possibility that these opening bars actually depict the locomotive that had carried the Scottsboro Boys into trouble.[78] After all, Honegger's *Pacific 231* was a favorite score for Copland and he would later paint his own train picture in another radio piece, linked to another African-American character, the legendary railroader John Henry. Yet calling to mind these two scores underlines the openness of *Music for Radio* to alternate readings; had CBS

Example 6a. *Music for Radio (Prairie Journal)*, mm. 1–4; condensed score.

chosen *Pacific 231* or *John Henry* (1940) for its audience experiment, simulated whistles, hammers, engine noises, and the acceleration/deceleration of starting up and slowing down would probably have yielded a substantial number of railroading subtitles. For better or for worse, those listeners who associated the beginning of *Music for Radio* with transportation preferred the automobile, the subway, or even the airplane over the old-fashioned iron horse.

Though he had praised the motoric opening, Moses Smith expressed reservations about the quieter, more lyrical parts of the piece, calling

Example 6b. *Music for Radio (Prairie Journal)*, mm. 18–26; strings only.

them "sentimental" and questioning their "lasting qualities."[79] Ironically, it is exactly these "sentimental" parts that seem to have had the staying power Smith valued. In fact, for critics writing after the success of *Billy the Kid* in 1938, the challenge was to place the "Saga of the Prairie" in the context of Copland's popular western scores, not to link it with his modernist past. In 1939, for example, Marion Bauer could look back at the "amiable effects" and "straightforward melodies" of *Music for Radio* as signs that "Copland's new style may have been creeping up gradually on the public."[80] A closer examination reveals, however, that these ostensibly "straightforward" melodies in fact have a rather complicated tale to tell. For instance, the gentle tune that marks the work's central section (see Example 7) originally inspired such titles as "Lilacs in the Rain," "Thoughts While Strolling," or (one of Davidson Taylor's least favorite entries) "Sedative." But once the "Saga" subtitle was in place, the narrow

Example 7. *Music for Radio (Prairie Journal)*, mm. 95–106.

range and regular unfolding of the melody began to garner meanings more appropriate to the western backdrop that had suddenly appeared behind it. In retrospect, it became a cowboy song.

If its western origins were verifiable, this tune would be the first memento of Copland's cowboy career and powerful evidence that the composer's interest in the West arose independently of Lincoln Kirstein, John Steinbeck, or Agnes de Mille. But the cowboy pedigree is at best unlikely and Copland scholars have not discovered the tune in any of the usual sources.[81] Though perhaps not an entirely reliable witness, the eccentric Oscar Levant was probably on the mark in 1940 when he remembered Copland's surprise at the work's apparently western connotations.[82] The melody appears without text or comment in the sketches for the "Ballade of Ozzie Powell" and the first draft of *Music for Radio*. Table 3 outlines some of the stages in the gradual transformation of its meaning. In Copland's pencil and ink manuscripts, it gained only the designation "Cl[arinet] 1, subtone (at the mike)"—marking one of the moments where modern technology is supposed to come to the forefront of the soundscape.

Example 7 continued

continues on next page

After the title contest had reached its Americana conclusion, a program note (almost certainly by Copland) suggested that "the second theme . . . has an American folk-song quality" and that the work's subtitle "emphasized a certain frontier atmosphere derived from the nature of the themes themselves." The published score indicated that the melody should be played "simply, in the manner of a folk song." By the mid-1950s, when Copland's name could not be dissociated from his successful frontier ballets, Julia Smith remarked in her biography that the "folklike" theme of the central section was "presented in the manner of a cowboy song." Thus granted the authority of print, the cowboy connotation stuck and even though he protested against the "corny" subtitle in a letter to Eugene Ormandy in 1958, Copland dubbed the published score *Prairie Journal* ten years later.[83]

Is it merely the absence of onomatopoeia or a bona fide folk pedigree that enables the semantic openness of *Music for Radio*? Or is there a more pressing, more present explanation for its shape-shifting power? The enigma of "the Copland style" remains. But his "Saga of the Prairie" does

Example 7 continued

give us a few clues about its success. By avoiding a definitive depiction of the Alabama-bound train or the pioneers' covered wagon, *Music for Radio* actually became a vehicle for change, moving Copland metaphorically westward. And by eschewing straightforward identification with either Ozie Powell or the "early settlers" (not to mention the range-riding cowboy),

---

Table 3. A Timeline of Transformations in *Music for Radio*

1936	Sketches for "Ballade of Ozzie Powell"; theme appears with no marking.*
1937	Piano and open-score sketches for "Music for Radio"; theme appears with no marking.
1936–37	Pencil and ink scores for "Music for Radio"; theme is labeled "Cl[arinet] 1, subtone (at the mike)."
August 1937	"Saga of the Prairie" chosen as "imaginative subtitle."
After August 1937	Undated publicity most likely by Copland: "The second theme . . . has an American folk-song quality." "'Saga of the Prairee' *[sic]* . . . emphasized a certain frontier atmosphere derived from the nature of the themes themselves."
1937–38	The published score of *Music for Radio: Saga of the Prairie* (New York: Boosey & Hawkes) indicates that the theme should be played "simply, in the manner of a folk song."
1940	"To Copland's surprise, the piece had distinctly western overtones for a good many listeners, the winning title, eventually, being 'Saga of the Prairee' *[sic]*." Oscar Levant, *A Smattering of Ignorance* (New York: Doubleday, Doran), p. 241.
1955	"It was undoubtedly the . . . section, with its folklike theme presented in the manner of a cowboy song, and the general nostalgic character of the piece that suggested the winning subtitle." Julia Smith, *Aaron Copland* (New York: E. P. Dutton), p. 178.
1958	"I don't at all like the idea of being difficult about a mere title of a piece. After all, the music is the same whatever it is called. On the other hand, I must confess that I never liked the title 'Saga of the Prairie,' for the simple reason that it sounds too corny to me, and was not my idea in the first place." Copland to Eugene Ormandy, September 23.
1967	Published score retitled *Prairie Journal* (New York: Boosey & Hawkes).
1984	"I had used a cowboy tune in the second of the four sections, so the western titles seemed most appropriate." Copland with Vivian Perlis, *Copland 1900 Through 1942* (New York: St. Martin's/Marek 1984), p. 255.

* Unless attributed otherwise, timeline information is from the Aaron Copland Collection, Music Division, Library of Congress.

Copland's radio saga helped to change his own identity. Perhaps the magical melange of styles—the ones Pollack connected to radio broadcast—holds another key: "swing bands, folk song, and incidental music for serials, dramas, and news reports" conjure their own contexts while still requiring the listener's imagination to supply the details. Each sends a signal to audiences pointing to the world outside abstract symphonic writing, yet divorced from words or visual images, each remains allusive rather than prescriptive. But if this hybrid and inviting style is indeed part of what now sounds "Coplandish," then *Music for Radio: Saga of the Prairie* demonstrates that we are worlds away from the Wagnerian logic by which "imperfect" imitation and stylistic mixing seemed to cast the Jew as a perpetual outsider. In Copland's hands, these same features arguably enabled the assimilation of American identities that might otherwise have remained closed to him.

From Orient to Occident

Copland's prairie mood did not immediately become a safe haven against charges of stylistic vagary. On the contrary, its melodic warmth initially presented a challenge for many of his colleagues. "It doesn't sound as Aaron Copland use[d] to sound," composer (and former Goldmark pupil) Vittorio Giannini remarked to Davidson Taylor. "I am not sure, but perhaps he is more natural now and more himself than he has ever been before." Judging from his repeated protestations, Taylor himself seems to have been more than a little uneasy about Copland's newfound tunefulness: "Did you actually try to be popular?" he queried. "It's none of my affair, but I'm curious about it. Did you actually try to be popular in 'The Second Hurricane'? Anybody who can write as good tunes as you can ought to write good tunes. Your tunes sound sincere to me. 'Music for Radio' sounds sincere. I believe it is. I think you have imposed upon yourself some limitations of simplicity in both works, but I believe that you really care about simplicity. Am I near the facts?"[84] Questions remained after the first concert performance of *Music for Radio*, at least for A. J. Warner of the *Rochester Times Union*, who wondered publicly: "Perhaps this 'conspiracy' against the 'religion' of the modernists may have been an accident, and then again it may have been intentional. Who knows?"[85] The confusion had apparently not been laid to rest even in 1942, when Charles Mills hastened to reassure the readers of *Modern Music* that this "popular and amusing score, commonly supposed to be a concession to mass appeal" was really "a completely honest and natural expression of the composer."[86]

Of course, others could never be convinced by Copland's assimilation of the pastoral, and one would expect to find Lazare Saminsky among their number. Given his deep-seated distrust of Copland's "Judaic" tendencies, he remained predictably skeptical of the composer's sincerity and withering in his critique of what he considered blatant commercialism. Reviewing a concert performance of *Music for Radio* in the summer of 1941, Saminsky ridiculed the "prairie" subtitle and raised the "eclectic" banner once again: "He will not let us be. He everlastingly changes his style, his palette, his composer's technique and his advertising technique, too; and although he is always on the rostrum in one capacity or another, no one knows what it is he really stands for. His orchestral *Music for Radio*, sometimes given a patriotic name as Saga of the Prairies, which it is not, is painted in faint Slavonic colors. It is far below Copland's best." From Saminsky's perspective, the "pranks of polytonal jazz" and the "wistful, earnest and delicate slow melos of [*Music for the Theatre*] represented "the best and the Jewish Copland."[87]

Given Copland's success with such western scores as *Billy the Kid* and later *Rodeo*, Saminsky's assertion that the composer really ought to return to the jazz-influenced idiom of *Music for the Theatre* may seem surprising today. As this article shows, however, it directly reflects a prominent strand of racial reasoning inherited from the 1930s, which portrayed Copland as quintessentially urban, typically Jewish, and particularly open to African-American influences. Saminsky's voice was extreme, but that does not mean that his objections were ignored—or that his opinions found no echo in more moderate voices. Writing in 1941, John Tasker Howard was well within the mainstream, though still right of center, when he compared the musical proclivities of Roy Harris (who was born and bred in the West) with Copland (the "Composer from Brooklyn"): "While racially Harris seems to derive definitively from the Scotch-Irish element of his ancestry, Aaron Copland embodies the Russian-Jewish element transplanted to American soil. Thus we find that while Harris reflects the prairies and vastness of the West, Copland brings us the sophistication of the cosmopolitan cities on the seaboard."[88] For Howard, it was only natural that Harris's Anglo heritage allowed him to reflect the West while Copland's Russian-Jewish roots aligned him with the East.

Such entrenched racial and geographic determinism was, to its authors, axiomatic: it is hard to imagine that Howard (let alone Saminsky) would have changed his mind and celebrated Copland for his sincere engagement with Anglo-Americana. But just because they could not be convinced does not mean that these critics went answered. Their arguments were addressed in various ways by both Copland and his friends. Keeping these prominent preconceptions in mind sheds new light on many aspects of the composer's reputation, but I will mention only two: discussion of his more accessible works and his approach to folk materials.

As noted above, many writers grappled with a keen uneasiness about Copland's accessible works—beginning with *The Second Hurricane* and *Music for Radio* and continuing until the present. Even Rosenfeld, once Copland's champion, was taken aback in 1939 by such works as *Billy the Kid, An Outdoor Overture,* and the film score for *The City*. He heard in them "the carefree, exuberant, facile diffusion of energies so characteristic of the playboy spirit" and warned that Copland was "standing at the fork in the highroad, the two branches of which lead respectively to popular and to artistic success."[89] Arthur Berger, too, found it difficult to decide how to weigh in on his friend's so-called simple style. Most recently, he confessed his persistent belief in the distinction between Copland's "popular" and "tough" works (and his regret that Copland held him partly responsible for "his being cast forever in the role of Dr. Jekyll and Mr. Hyde").[90] Nevertheless, in the 1950s Berger made a point of discussing the common features in Copland's "stages of development," and he observed that his "striking transformations" had admirable causes: "a rare critical faculty" and "a sense of responsibility to musical audiences." "Copland," he wrote, "is not of the line of artists who, after following a dubious creative urge, justify their course by saying merely that they 'felt that way.'"[91]

Surrounded by the mixed feelings of his colleagues, Copland crafted his own solution to this critical conundrum—a solution that was both radical and, in a quiet way, courageous. Its roots stretch back at least as far as "The Composer and Radio" of 1941, in which Copland exclaimed: "The composer who is frightened of losing his artistic integrity through contact with a mass audience is no longer aware of the meaning of the word art."[92] In his Norton Lectures of 1951–52, he spoke of his disparate works as manifestations of his lifelong desire to make "a connection between music and the life about me." By 1967, in a new incarnation of his famous essay "A Composer from Brooklyn," his language was even more assured: "I prefer to think that I write my music from a single vision; when the results differ it is because I take into account with each new piece the purpose for which it is intended and the nature of the musical materials with which I begin to work."[93] Rather than framing his populist efforts as the products of isolated inspiration, Copland argued that sensitivity to external forces—such as radio commissions or audience input—could represent an equally powerful type of sincerity. He retained "consistency" as a cardinal value but changed the axis on which it should be measured: instead of a consistency of style, he claimed to have practiced a consistency of approach.

This credo, and the pressures that helped to shape it, are nowhere more apparent than in Copland's Americana works and the language he used to describe them. When it came to incorporating folk materials, he could hardly have ignored the fact that some of his harshest critics and dearest friends already thought he was overly inclined to absorb and assimilate. Furthermore, with both mainstream and leftist composers sharpening their focus on Anglo-American folklore, "Jazz as Folk Music" was a much less plausible article title in the mid-1930s than it had been in 1925.[94] In the process, Copland was allied with source material that many would have considered foreign to him. Consider Roy Harris's lament on the "mushroom exploitation" of folk song by those who failed to recognize that "it can't be reduced to a few formulas to stir and mix to taste": "America will have many folksong vendors in the next few years. Some city boys may take a short motor trip through our land and return to write the Song of the Prairies—others will be folksong authorities after reading in a public library for a few weeks."[95] Whether Harris intended to paraphrase Copland's "Saga of the Prairie" subtitle or not, he clearly felt that some composers were more entitled to dip into the folk music font than others. Copland, too, was well aware that the gaps separating a composer from his source material could be perilous. While writing *El Salón México,* he had wondered "what the Mexicans might think of a 'gringo' meddling with their native melodies."[96] As this essay has shown, things were no simpler when Copland cast his lot with Anglo folklore and crossed the Rio Grande. South of the border, his whiteness marked him as a foreigner; in his native land, his potential non-whiteness was the greater source of concern.

This may account in part for the occasional defensiveness that crept into Copland's descriptions of folk-based composition—descriptions that routinely emphasized the professional training of the composer and the intellectual effort required to integrate folk tunes into symphonic composition. For example, when describing his working method for *El Salón México,* he spoke of the "formal problem" that had to be overcome and the "modified potpourri" that resulted, "in which the Mexican themes or fragments and extensions thereof are sometimes inextricably mixed."[97] When dealing with cowboy song in *Billy the Kid,* Copland's initial reactions were famously lukewarm until he found himself in Paris, "hopelessly involved in expanding, contracting, rearranging and superimposing" the western tunes.[98] Had Copland chosen to portray himself as the natural conduit for some instinctive folk spirit, he could have been sure that his words would fall on more than a few disbelieving ears. Instead he invoked a more compatible story line: he was working to earn a legacy that he could not inherit.

Not every saga has a moral, but Copland's teaches us at least three lessons about the power of populism to transform both a piece and a career. First, the challenge of *Music for Radio* involved negotiating with conflicting notions of what it meant to be "modern" in Depression-era America. Did writing "modern music" mean using the most up-to-date media? Capturing the political consciousness of the time? Mirroring the aspirations of contemporary audiences? Struggling with these divergent demands helped Copland to put behind him an aesthetic whose problematic watchword was purity and to adopt a populist platform that embraced stylistic diversity. Second, the circumstances surrounding the creation and reception of *Music for Radio* show that incorporating folk or popular music makes a claim—whether active or passive, contested or accepted—to an identity that is usually more specific than can be accounted for by the general adjective "American." In Copland's case, association with western folklore—at first inadvertent, but later purposeful—seems to have overshadowed his engagement with African-American idioms and directed critical attention away from his Jewishness. Finally, examining the history and prehistory of Copland's populism reveals that inventing effective Americana requires group participation and symbolic fluidity, especially when racial and regional categories are at stake. The geographical and political reorientations of *Music for Radio* illustrate this with unusual clarity. As Ozie Powell receded into the unsung history of the piece, new but nameless pioneers appeared to take his place. As Copland relinquished the right to name his composition, hundreds of listeners volunteered to play their part. And as the work's most singable melody lost its status as an index of modern technology, it gained new significance as a souvenir of the Old West. The metamorphosis of *Music for Radio* into a "Saga of the Prairie" mirrors changes in Copland's career that make it more than a media experiment or a timely shift from black to white. It reminds us that America's national mask could show and shield many faces.

This essay is adapted from papers given at the meetings of the American Musicological Society in Atlanta (2001) and the Society for American Music in Lexington (2002). I am grateful to the many readers and audience members who contributed to my thinking on this topic, including Richard Taruskin, Katherine Bergeron, Danielle Fosler-Lussier, Nathaniel G. Lew, and Peter Schmelz. I would like to express my thanks for more recent input from Larry Starr and Klára Móricz and especially for the editorial advice of Judith Tick and Carol J. Oja.

1. Virgil Thomson, "Aaron Copland," *Modern Music* 9, no. 2 (1932): 71–72.

2. Ibid., 72.

3. Concerns about Copland's multifaceted style have persisted in Copland criticism, and numerous scholars have sought to identify the unifying features of his oeuvre or argued for stylistic heterogeneity as one of its defining traits. Among the many important considerations of these issues are: Arthur Berger's 1953 biography, *Aaron Copland* (New York: Oxford University Press, 1953), esp. p. 37ff.; two articles by Larry Starr: "Copland's Style," *Perspectives of New Music* 19 (Spring–Summer 1981): 68–89, and "Ives, Gershwin, and Copland: Reflections on the Strange History of American Art Music," *American Music* 12 (1994): 167–87; and, taken together, the explosion of Copland scholarship beginning in the late 1990s, including Howard Pollack's 1999 biography, *Aaron Copland: The Life and Work of an Uncommon Man* (New York: Henry Holt, 1999), esp. chaps. 5, 8, and 28; *Aaron Copland's America: A Cultural Perspective*, ed. Gail Levin and Judith Tick (New York: Watson-Guptill, 2002); and *Copland Connotations: Studies and Interviews*, ed. Peter Dickinson (Woodbridge, Suffolk, Eng.: The Boydell Press, 2002), pp. 3–13.

4. Aaron Copland to Virgil Thomson, January 27, 1932, Virgil Thomson Papers, Irving S. Gilmore Music Library, Yale University, MS 29, Box 33, Folder 1.

5. Matthew Frye Jacobson offers a historical perspective on changes in racial concepts in his *Whiteness of a Different Color: European Immigrants and the Alchemy of Race* (Cambridge, Mass.: Harvard University Press, 1998). On changing representations of whiteness in popular culture, see Richard Dyer's study, *White* (New York: Routledge, 1997).

6. *Music for Radio* has been recorded by Leonard Slatkin and the St. Louis Symphony Orchestra on their compact disc *Copland: Music for Films*, RCA Victor 9026-61699-2. To my knowledge, the most detailed analytical treatment of the piece can be found in Gayle Minetta Murchison, "Nationalism in William Grant Still and Aaron Copland Between the Wars: Style and Ideology," Ph.D. diss., Yale University, 1998, esp. 40ff.

7. Rubin Goldmark to Aaron Copland, April 26, 1921 and August 21, 1922, Aaron Copland Collection, Music Division, Library of Congress, Box 255, Folder 17. For Copland's impressions of his teachers, see esp. "Rubin Goldmark: A Tribute," *Juilliard Review* 3, no. 3 (Fall 1956): 15–16; and "The Teacher: Nadia Boulanger," in *Copland on Music* (Garden City, N.Y.: Doubleday, 1960), pp. 83–91. The substantial literature on Boulanger and her teaching methods includes Léonie Rosenstiel, *Nadia Boulanger: A Life in Music* (New York: W. W. Norton, 1982) and Mark DeVoto, "Copland and the 'Boulangerie,'" in Dickinson, *Copland Connotations*, pp. 3–13.

8. Pollack, *Aaron Copland*, p. 85. Perhaps the most significant bequest Copland received from the "Boulangerie" was his serious engagement with the music of Stravinsky. Critics of every era have commented on the Russian composer's possible influence on the young American in Paris. Thomson began the second half of his 1932 article with extended comments on Stravinsky's influence on Copland and others. Postwar assessments

include David Matthews, "Copland and Stravinsky," *Tempo* 95 (Winter 1950): 10–14; Arthur Berger, "Stravinsky and the Younger American Composers," *Score and I. M. A. Magazine* 12 (June 1955): 39–40; and many passages in Berger, *Aaron Copland*, esp. pp. 41–42, 70–71, 91, 94. Among more recent scholarship, see Carol J. Oja, "The Transatlantic Gaze of Aaron Copland," in *Making Music Modern: New York in the 1920s* (Oxford, Eng.: Oxford University Press, 2000), pp. 237–51; and Murchison, "Nationalism in William Grant Still and Aaron Copland," esp. p. 40ff.

9. Pollack, *Aaron Copland*, p. 125, citing Phillip Ramey's liner notes for Copland's *Symphony for Organ and Orchestra*, Columbia MS 7985.

10. Ibid., pp. 113–14.

11. Aaron Copland, "Jazz as Folk Music," *Musical America*, December 19, 1925, 18.

12. On the confluence of jazz and modernism, see esp. Oja, *Making Music Modern*, pp. 313–60.

13. These include "Jazz Structure and Influence," *Modern Music* 4 (January–February 1927): 9–14; and "The Jazz Interlude" in *Our New Music: Leading Composers in Europe and America* (New York: McGraw-Hill, 1941), pp. 86–100. For a thoughtful analysis of Copland's conflicted attitudes toward jazz, including consideration of his limited exposure to the improvisatory practices properly associated with the term "jazz" today, see David Schiff, "Copland and the 'Jazz Boys,'" in Dickinson, *Copland Connotations*, pp. 14–21.

14. For details, see Nicolas Slonimsky, *Lexicon of Musical Invective: Critical Assaults on Composers since Beethoven's Time* (New York: Colemann-Ross Company, 1953), pp. 86–87.

15. MacDonald Smith Moore, *Yankee Blues: Musical Culture and American Identity* (Bloomington: Indiana University Press, 1985); see esp."The Jewish Nexus," pp. 130–60. Among critics who chose to compare or contrast Copland and Gershwin were Henry Cowell and Paul Rosenfeld, as discussed below.

16. Roy Harris to Aaron Copland, July 26, 1926, Copland Collection, Box 256, Folder 8. Harris had apparently reacted strongly to the jazz idiom of *Music for the Theatre*, particularly to the "Burlesque" movement. According to Leo Smit ("A Conversation with Aaron Copland on His 80th Birthday," *Contemporary Keyboard* 6, no. 11 [1980]: 12), Harris made no secret of the associations such gestures evoked. Howard Pollack suggests that it was the "grotesco" music in the midsection of the aptly named "Burlesque" movement that inspired Harris's outburst at an early, informal hearing of the score: "It's whorehouse music! It's whorehouse music!" Pollack also points out possible resonances between the "Burlesque" movement and Copland's own biography. Copland himself cited the Jewish vaudeville and burlesque performer Fanny Brice as one of the influences on *Music for the Theatre;* more speculatively, Pollack has observed that Copland may have had in mind the burlesque houses that were part of homosexual social life in New York (*Aaron Copland*, p. 130).

17. Roger Sessions to Aaron Copland, (n.d., after August 26) 1926, Copland Collection, Box 262, Folder 5. Andrea Olmstead gives an overview and excerpts from the correspondence between these two men in "The Copland-Sessions Letters," *Tempo* 175 (1990): 2–5. Olmstead quotes from Sessions's letter of August 26, 1926, in which he objects to Copland's adoption of the term "New York composer." The undated letter cited above appears to be Sessions's response to Copland's response to the August 26 letter. In a later letter, dated February 25, 1927, Sessions hailed Copland's, "Jazz Structure and Influence," *Modern Music* 4 (January–February 1927) as "the final work [word?] in a tiresome and useless controversy."

18. From later letters, we can see that Copland took pains to reassure Sessions that his jazz days were over. On March 18, 1927, he wrote, "I'm glad you liked the Jazz article. It has helped considerably to get the whole business out of my system," and in a postscript to his letter of August 18, 1927, he exclaimed: "The Irony of Fate. Now that

I am done with jazz an article by I. Goldberg is to appear in the Sept. 'Mercury' on 'A. C. and his Jazz.'" Both letters are available online as part of the Library of Congress American Memory Project at http://memory.loc.gov/ammem/achtml/achome.html (digital ID numbers copland corr0088 and copland corr0092).

19. For further discussion of Jewishness in Copland's life and works, see Howard Pollack, "Copland and the Prophetic Voice," in this book; I am grateful to him for sharing his article with me prior to publication.

20. Theodore Chanler to Aaron Copland, August 16, 1930, Copland Collection, Box 249, Folder 21.

21. Theodore Chanler, "Aaron Copland Up to Now," *The Hound and Horn* 4, no. 1 (October–December 1930): 107; reprinted as "Aaron Copland," in *American Composers on American Music*, ed. Henry Cowell ([Stanford]: Stanford University Press, 1933), 51.

22. Chanler, "Aaron Copland Up to Now," p. 107.

23. Henry Cowell, postscript to Theodore Chandler [*sic*], "Aaron Copland," pp. 55–56.

24. Paul Rosenfeld, "Musical Chronicle," *Dial* 78 (1925): 258.

25. Paul Rosenfeld, "Aaron Copland Without the Jazz," in *By Way of Art: Criticisms of Music, Literature, Painting, Sculpture, and the Dance* (Freeport, N.Y.: Books for Libraries Press, 1967; first published 1928), pp. 266–72. Rosenfeld's description of this "new colt" is typically colorful: "You may call it Aaron Copland's musicianship, if you like, which however won't prevent it cantering past you on long uncertain stilts at your next encounter with it.... It's an amusing affair, in the incomplete assemblage of the organs, limbs and twinkling skin of the racer; charming with the awkwardness of the large young thing not long from the mother" (p. 266).

26. Rosenfeld, "Copland Without the Jazz," p. 270.

27. Paul Rosenfeld, "Jazz and Music: Music in America," in *An Hour with American Music* (Philadelphia: J. B. Lippincott Company, 1929), p. 11.

28. Paul Rosenfeld, "Aaron Copland: George Gershwin" in *An Hour with American Music*, pp. 130, 132. Many ideas in this essay are borrowed (sometimes verbatim) from "Aaron Copland Without the Jazz."

29. Roger Sessions, "An American Evening Abroad," *Modern Music* 4, no. 1 (1926): 34. Pollack discusses this and other excerpts under the heading "The Composer as Jew," in Pollack, *Aaron Copland*, pp. 518–531. See also MacDonald Smith Moore, *Yankee Blues*.

30. Thomson, "Aaron Copland," p. 67. In his biography, Pollack describes potentially anti-Jewish sentiments in Thomson's attitudes toward the League of Composers (Pollack, *Aaron Copland*, pp. 167, 173–74) and suggests that Thomson may have been the one to provide Chanler with one of his less flattering descriptions of Copland's economy of means: "Aaron Copland's ideas are like pennies shrewdly invested rather than pearls advantageously set." See also Oja, *Making Music Modern*, pp. 217–18.

31. Aaron Copland, "The Lyricism of Milhaud," *Modern Music* 6, no. 2 (January–February 1929): 14–19. Copland's sympathy with the racial determinism of the 1920s–1930s can be seen in his quasi-genealogical explanation of Milhaud's ability to sound French: "That he is not so racial a composer as Bloch or Mahler seems natural if we remember that his ancestors settled in Provence in the fifteenth century so that his Jewishness has been long tempered by the French point of view" (p. 16).

32. Aaron Copland, "What Is Jewish Music?" *New York Herald Tribune*, October 2, 1949. For more discussion of this article, see Murchison, "Nationalism in William Grant Still and Aaron Copland," pp. 281–83.

33. Richard Wagner, "Judaism in Music," in *Richard Wagner's Prose Work*, vol. 3, trans. William Ashton Ellis (New York: Broude Brothers, 1893), pp. 89, 82, 92. For the history and influence of this notorious document, see Jacob Katz, *The Darker Side of*

Genius: Richard Wagner's Anti-Semitism (Hanover, N.H./London: University Press of New England, 1986). Marc A. Weiner discusses the psychological and physiological manifestations of anti-Semitism in Wagner's works and writings in *Richard Wagner and the Anti-Semitic Imagination* (Lincoln/London: University of Nebraska Press, 1995). More generally, for provocative discussions of stereotyping about Jewish creativity, see the works of Sander L. Gilman, esp. *Smart Jews: The Construction of the Image of Jewish Superior Intelligence* (Lincoln/London: University of Nebraska Press, 1996).

34. *Jewish Influences in American Life: International Jew: The World's Foremost Problem,* vol. 3 (reprints from the *Dearborn Independent,* 1921), pp. 65, 70, 75–78; cited in Moore, *Yankee Blues,* p. 146.

35. Sigmund Spaeth, "Jews Interpreters More than Composers: Ernest Bloch Says It Is Because in Music, as in Everything, They Assimilate and Imitate—More Sincere Jewish Art to Come," *Evening Mail* (New York), April 26, 1917. I am grateful to Klára Móricz for bringing this quotation to my attention.

36. Lazare Saminsky, *Music of the Ghetto and the Bible* (New York: Bloch Publishing, 1934), pp. 67–69. As late as 1949, Saminsky described Copland as "a small, cool creative gift, but an ego of much frenetic drive, a devious personality with a feline *savoir faire,* with his fine commercial acumen and acute sense of the direction of today's wind"; "a shrewd manager of *musique à succès*"; "armed with a catalogue of swiftly garnered tricks of craft plucked from all successful stars of the day," in *Living Music of the Americas* (New York: Howell, Soskin, and Crown, 1949), p. 123.

37. Pollack, *Aaron Copland,* p. 520.

38. Saminsky, *Music of the Ghetto and the Bible,* p. 125.

39. Copland, "The Lyricism of Milhaud," 14, 17.

40. Moore, *Yankee Blues,* p. 131.

41. Henry Cowell, trans. Hanns Gutman, "Bericht aus Amerika: Amerikanische Musik?," *Melos* 9, nos. 8–9 (August–September 1930): 362–65; "Die beiden wirklichen Amerikaner: Ives und Ruggles," *Melos* 9, no. 10 (October 1930): 417–420; and "Die kleineren Komponisten," *Melos* 9, no. 12 (December 1930): 526–29. Cowell discusses Copland on p. 527 and makes the following remarks about jazz, pp. 363–64:

> Nun ist es zwar richtig, daß einige junge Amerikaner den Jazz mit Erfolg in ihren Werke benützt haben, aber es ist sehr lustig zu erfahren, daß die Führer diese Stiles den Anstoß hierzu in Paris gefunden haben. Ein paar sophistische Pariser haben diesen jungen Amerikanern eingeredet (Copland und Gershwin), der Jazz müsse die Grundlage der neuen amerikanischen Musik bilden; und sie nahmen sich das zu Herzen. Jazz ist eine der Entwicklungsstraßen der amerikanischen Musik, aber schwerlich von größerer Bedeutung als eine Reihe anderer Wege, die beschritten werden können. Die Vereinigten Staaten sind, trotz ihrer Zusammensetzung aus vielen Rassen, im Grunde angelsächsischer Herkunft. Keine Musik, die aller angelsächsischen Züge entbehrt, kann jemals das eigentliche Amerika ausdrücken, wenn sei auch natürlich einzelne Phasen des Lebens in Amerika darstellen kann. Die Grundlagen des Jazz sind die Synkopen und rhythmischen Akzente der Neger; ihre Modernisierung und gegenwärtige Form ist das Werk von Juden—zumeist von New Yorker "Tin-pan-alley"-Juden. Jazz ist Negermusik, gesehen durch die Augen dieser Juden.

42. John Tasker Howard, *Our Contemporary Composers: American Music in the Twentieth Century* (New York: Thomas Y. Crowell, 1941), p. 3. For some, the Jewish malady of cultural mixing actually corrupted jazz, rather than elevating it. See, for example, Paul Fritz Laubenstein's comment that if jazz had "not suffered the Jewish (Semitic!) direption [*sic*], it would probably have developed its own independent melody, rather than have become

a parasitic mannerism preying upon the classics." "Race Values in Aframerican Music," *Musical Quarterly* 16 (1930): 396, cited in Moore, *Yankee Blues,* 143.

43. The prevalence of the racial rhetoric associating Jews with blacks has been discussed in detail by Sander Gilman in *Jewish Self-Hatred: Anti-Semitism and the Hidden Language of the Jews* (Baltimore: Johns Hopkins University Press, 1986), see esp. pp. 5–12, 206–7, and 311.

44. Pollack, *Aaron Copland,* p. 518. Isaac Goldberg, "Aaron Copland and His Jazz," *American Mercury,* September 1927, 63–64. David Metzer discusses similar material in his provocative article "'Spurned Love': Eroticism and Abstraction in the Early Works of Aaron Copland," *Journal of Musicology* 15 (1997): 417–43, which tells a different story about the role of "the Orient" and stylistic change in Copland's early career.

45. Daniel Gregory Mason, ". . . And a Moral," *Tune in, America: A Study of Our Coming Musical Independence* (New York: Alfred A. Knopf, 1931), pp. 160–61. Parts of this essay are drawn from his earlier diatribe "Is American Music Growing Up? Our Emancipation from Alien Influences," in *Arts and Decoration,* November 1920. For more on Mason's racial rhetoric, see Moore, *Yankee Blues.*

46. Copland's longtime friend Harold Clurman recalls this episode in *All People Are Famous (Instead of an Autobiography)* (New York: Harcourt, Brace, Jovanovich, 1974), p. 33.

47. For more on prejudice against Jews in France, see Jane F. Fulcher, "The Preparation for Vichy: Anti-Semitism in French Musical Culture Between the Two World Wars," *Musical Quarterly* 79 (1995): 458–75. Like Léonie Rosenstiel, Fulcher points to Boulanger's association with the right-wing Action Française, which was both royalist and anti-Semitic. Fulcher endorses and provides a broader intellectual context for Rosenstiel's claims that Boulanger considered Jews a less creative race and "confide[d] her prejudices to Catholic friends," Rosenstiel, *Nadia Boulanger,* pp. 198–99. It is important to note that many Boulanger pupils, including Copland himself, vehemently disagreed with Rosenstiel's characterization. As Copland put it, " [Boulanger] and I became close friends, and there were other Jewish students who were Nadia's friends. It is impossible that one of us would not have noticed anti-Semitism in her behavior. Especially during the war years, we were very much aware of such things. I feel certain that anti-Semitism was not part of Nadia Boulanger's personality." (Aaron Copland and Vivian Perlis, *Copland: 1900 Through 1942* [New York: St. Martin's/Marek, 1984], p. 65.) According to Howard Pollack's interview with David Diamond, May 15, 1994, Copland also defended Boulanger after Diamond denounced her support for the reactionary leader Philippe Pétain. (Pollack, *Aaron Copland,* p. 574, n. 12.)

48. Pollack, *Aaron Copland,* p. 522. See also Klára Móricz, "The Confines of Judaism and the Illusiveness of Universality in Ernest Bloch's *Avodath Hakodesh* (Sacred Service)," *repercussions* 5, nos. 1–2 (1996): 184–241; and her book manuscript *Jewish Identities: Nationalism, Racism, and Utopianism in Twentieth-Century Music* (forthcoming). The critical fiasco of Bloch's orchestral *America* in 1928 could have impressed upon Copland the difficulty of writing music that would be embraced as a national rather than a racial expression. See Charles Brotman, "The Winner Loses: Ernest Bloch and His *America*," *American Music* 16, no. 4 (1998): 417–47.

49. Margaret Susan Key, "'Sweet Melody Over Silent Wave': Depression-Era Radio and the American Composer," Ph.D. diss., University of Maryland, 1995, pp. 129–30, 165–66.

50. Ibid., pp. 130–31. Copland's piece premiered in July. The other commissions were broadcast between May and October (Louis Gruenberg, *Green Mansions;* Howard Hanson, Symphony no. 3; Roy Harris, *Time Suite;* Walter Piston, *Concertino;* William Grant Still, *Lenox Avenue*).

51. Aaron Copland, "Composer from Brooklyn," in *Our New Music,* pp. 228–29.

52. Davidson Taylor, "Tomorrow's Broadcast," *North American Review* 241 (March 1936): 51.

53. Key, "Depression-Era Radio," pp. 136–37, citing "WABC: Howard Barlow Series," Copland Collection, Box 216, Folder 41. Similar themes—together with the notion that the radio audience would be freer from concert hall prejudices and more receptive to new music and the idealistic suggestion that radio networks should employ as many as ten "staff composers" each—are expressed at greater length in "The Composer and Radio," in *Our New Music,* pp. 233–42.

54. *Radio Daily,* September 27, 1937, n. p., as cited in Key, "Depression-Era Radio," p. 131. Even before Copland was asked to retitle his *Radio Serenade*, CBS was already contemplating how best to exploit the public relations potential of its commissioning project. "One caution," wrote Deems Taylor (then the network's "Consultant on Music") in the letter offering Copland the job, "please do not release any publicity on this thing that we are doing. We want to wait until we have all the acceptances in and then break a big story all over the country." Deems Taylor to Aaron Copland, September 28, 1936, Copland Collection, Box 335, Folder 9.

55. The program "Everybody's Music" was begun in 1936 to replace the New York Philharmonic–Symphony Society's broadcasts during the summer. Under the direction of Howard Barlow, it continued to offer opportunities for American composers until 1940. For details on the CBS commissions and more generally on new music written for radio, see Key, "Depression-Era Radio," esp. pp. 138–39.

56. Pollack, *Aaron Copland,* p. 311. Julia Smith, *Aaron Copland: His Work and Contribution to American Music* (New York: E. P. Dutton, 1955), pp. 177–78. See also Key, "Depression-Era Radio," pp. 182–83. For contemporary views on the unique musical possibilities of writing for radio, see R. Raven-Hart, "Composing for Radio," *Musical Quarterly* 16 (1930): 133–39 and two articles by Davidson Taylor: "Tomorrow's Broadcast," *North American Review* 241 (March 1936): 49–56; and "To Order, For Radio," *Modern Music* 14, no. 1 (November–December 1936): 12–17.

57. Davidson Taylor to Aaron Copland, July 30, 1937, Copland Collection, Box 335, Folder 9.

58. This typescript is preserved in the Copland Collection, Box 406, Folder 10. Jessica Burr has discussed this document and other important facets of Copland's association with the American West in "Copland, the West and American Identity," in Dickinson, *Copland Connotations,* pp. 22–28. In Table 1, I have attempted to roughly preserve the relative proportions of urban vs. rural and American vs. non-American titles while also conveying some of the more colorful entries.

59. Copland and Perlis, *Copland: 1900–1942,* p. 255.

60. This procedure is discussed in a letter from Taylor to Copland, July 30, 1937, Copland Collection, Box 335, Folder 9.

61. Copland and Perlis, *Copland: 1900–1942,* p. 255.

62. Smith, *Aaron Copland,* p. 178, paraphrasing and citing the *New York Times,* July 18, 1937.

63. In consultation with Wayne Shirley at the Library of Congress, scholars who have mentioned the connection between "Ozie Powell" and *Music for Radio* include Gayle Minetta Murchison, "Nationalism in William Grant Still and Aaron Copland," pp. 546–48; Jessica Burr, "Copland the West and American Identity," p. 25; Howard Pollack, *Aaron Copland,* pp. 312–13; and Elizabeth Bergman Crist, *Copland in Context: Aaron Copland's Music During the Depression and War* (Oxford: Oxford University Press, forthcoming).

64. Hughes's poem may be thought of as a pendant to his collection *Scottsboro Limited* (1932) which includes the poems "Scottsboro" and "Christ in Alabama" as well as a verse play about the Scottsboro Boys. "The Ballad of Ozie Powell" was later included in *A New*

Song (1938), the Hughes collection with the strongest communist ties. Many of the Scottsboro Boys wrote or co-wrote memoirs after their respective releases from prison. For more contextual information, see Dan T. Carter, *Scottsboro: A Tragedy of the American South* (Baton Rouge: Louisiana State University Press, 1969) and James Goodman, *Stories of Scottsboro* (New York: Pantheon Books, 1994).

65. Aaron Copland, "Workers Sing!" *New Masses* 11, no. 9 (1934): 28–29; reprinted in *Aaron Copland, A Reader: Selected Writings 1923–72*, ed. Richard Kostelanetz (New York: Routledge, 2004), pp. 88–90. Copland singled out Siegmeister's song in his review, attributing its popularity to the fact that "the issue of the Scottsboro Boys is close to the hearts of class-conscious workers." "To these workers," he continued, "the fact that the text of the song does not constitute great poetry, and that the music is effective only in a rather flat-footed and unimaginative fashion is of secondary significance." To Copland's ears, however, Siegmeister's contribution lacked the inspiring music that would make it "a more thrilling experience and thereby increase its political drive." Although it is possible that Copland intended his "Ballade" as a "correction" of Siegmeister's song, I find no compelling links in their musical materials. For more information about the mass song and its adoption by classically trained composers, see Carol J. Oja, "Marc Blitzstein's *The Cradle Will Rock* and Mass-Song Style in the 1930s," *Musical Quarterly* 73 (1989): 445–75, and Barbara Zuck, *A History of Musical Americanism* (Ann Arbor, Mich.: UMI Research Press, 1980).

66. Other alterations included the omission of a potentially tongue-twisting line ("One of the nine in the law's clean claws / Penniless Ozie Powell") and a possibly obscure reference to a ranking officer of the Ku Klux Klan ("The devil's a Kleagle with an evil will").

67. Pollack, *Aaron Copland*, p. 313.

68. According to a letter from Deems Taylor, September 28, 1936 (Copland Collection, Box 335, Folder 9), the work was to be "a major work for orchestra, with or without soloists" within which category Taylor included "a symphony, a suite, a cantata with solo or speaking voices, a concerto or a short serious opera or operetta." I infer that a work for chorus and orchestra would have been acceptable but not a work for chorus and piano. Because of Copland's habit of composing at the piano and the preliminary nature of the sketches, it is unclear whether the "Ballade" would have included orchestra or not.

69. A review by Moses Smith reveals that Copland offered a thumbnail sketch of the piece before it was aired: "In his thirteen-word description of his new work in advance Mr. Copland vouchsafed the information that the piece begins in fast time loudly and ends quietly. The performance further disclosed that there is considerable alternation between the loud and soft parts, between the fast and slow." "Music for the Radio," *Boston Evening Transcript*, July 26, 1937.

70. Copland, "The Composer and Radio," pp. 241–42. Interestingly, at least one listener suggested the overtly radical titles "Agitation of the Masses" or "The Agitator," and another proposed the implicitly revolutionary "A May of Victory."

71. Ibid. The artificiality of the populism generated by the CBS contest made it a less than ideal test case for pure altruism, however, and Oscar Levant could not help but quip that "this adaptation of a commercial device" almost suggested "that Copland was affiliating himself with 'Lucky Strike' or 'Old Gold,'" *A Smattering of Ignorance* (New York: Doubleday, Doran & Co., 1940), p. 241.

72. For a comprehensive study of Copland's political engagement and especially his lasting ties to the Popular Front, see Elizabeth Bergman Crist, "Aaron Copland and the Popular Front," *Journal of the American Musicological Society* 56 (2003): 409–65 and her forthcoming book, *Copland in Context*.

73. Burr discusses the appeal of the West in general and the Hollywood western in particular in "Copland, the West, and American Identity." See also Beth E. Levy, "Frontier

Figures: American Music and the Mythology of the American West, 1895–1945," Ph.D. diss., University of California, Berkeley, 2002.

74. "Copland Decides He Likes Own Name Best" (unsigned), *Boston Evening Transcript,* August 21, 1937. Copland Collection, Box 406, Folder 10. I am grateful to Elizabeth Bergman Crist for pointing out the likelihood that Leonhardt was inspired by the sub-title of O. E. Rölvaag's novel, *Giants in the Earth: A Saga of the Prairie* (New York: Harper & Row, 1927).

75. Looking back in 1953, Arthur Berger acknowledged the tendency in the 1920s to describe Copland as a "Brooklyn Stravinsky" but commented, "Today this seems curious, with both composers better known" (*Aaron Copland,* p. 42). Paul Rosenfeld also uses the phrase in "Aaron Copland's Growth," *The New Republic,* May 27, 1931, 46.

76. Moses Smith, "Music for the Radio."

77. This opening material appears on the penultimate page of the "Ballade of Ozzie Powell" sketches. Although there is neither text underlay nor any indication of where the passage might fit into the "Ballade," the motivic and physical connections (the page is attached to the rest of the sketch) strongly suggest that the material was conceived at the same time as or in relation to the choral setting.

78. Pollack, *Aaron Copland,* p. 313.

79. Moses Smith, "Music for the Radio."

80. Marion Bauer, "Aaron Copland: A Significant Personality in American Music," *American Music Lover* 4, no. 12 (April 1939): 429.

81. Pollack, *Aaron Copland,* p. 312.

82. Levant, *A Smattering of Ignorance,* p. 241. Both Howard Pollack and Jessica Burr have commented on the unlikelihood that *Music for Radio* contains any authentic cowboy material.

83. Copland Collection, Box 406, Folder 10; Smith, *Aaron Copland,* 178; Aaron Copland to Eugene Ormandy, September 23, 1958, Copland Collection, Box 260, Folder 10.

84. Davidson Taylor to Aaron Copland, July 30, 1937, New York, Copland Collection, Box 335, Folder 9.

85. A. J. Warner, "Philharmonic Program Pleases," April 29, 1938, *Rochester Times Union,* Copland Collection, Box 406, Folder 10. The concert premiere was given under Howard Hanson at the 1938 Eastman-Rochester American music festival.

86. Charles Mills, "Over the Air," *Modern Music* 20, no. 1 (November–December 1942): 63.

87. Lazare Saminsky, "'American' Phase of International Music Festival Revealed New Talent," *Musical Courier,* July 1941, 19; and, responding to *Vitebsk,* " [Copland] touches Jewish *melos* furtively. His is a back-door sort of communion; he does not wish, or is not able, to consecrate himself in earnest, deep submergence in the song of his race," *Music of the Ghetto and the Bible,* p. 124.

88. John Tasker Howard, *Our Contemporary Composers,* p. 145. For more on Harris and the West, see Beth E. Levy, "'The White Hope of American Music': Or, How Roy Harris Became Western," *American Music* 19, no. 2 (2001): 131–67.

89. Paul Rosenfeld, "Current Chronicle: Copland—Harris—Schuman," *Musical Quarterly* 25 (1939): 372, 374. According to Pollack, "By the 1940s [Rosenfeld] privately contended that the composer of *Rodeo* and *Appalachian Spring* had simply sold out" (*Aaron Copland,* p. 99).

90. Arthur Berger, "Composers and Their Audiences in the Thirties," in *Reflections of an American Composer* (Berkeley and Los Angeles: University of California Press, 2002), pp. 12–15.

91. Berger, *Aaron Copland,* p. 37.

92. Aaron Copland, "The Composer and Radio," p. 241.

93. Aaron Copland, "The Composer in Industrial America," in *Music and Imagination* (Cambridge, Mass.: Harvard University Press, 1952), pp. 99, 108–9; postscript to "Composer from Brooklyn," in *The New Music, 1900–1960* (New York: W. W. Norton, 1968), p. 168.

94. *The Second Hurricane* presents an interesting window on Copland's attitudes toward jazz and folk song at this juncture. His first experiment with Anglo folklore, a rather stilted rendering of the British ballad "The Capture of Burgoyne" sung by the operetta's stranded Caucasian teenagers, follows shortly after a catchy, syncopated tune initiated by its only African-American character, Jeff. For more on this moment, and the work as a whole, see Crist, *Copland in Context* (forthcoming).

95. Harris, "Folksong—American Big Business," *Modern Music* 18, no. 1 (November–December 1940): 11. As Harris's phrase "city boys" makes plain, race was not the only axis of difference that Copland had to contend with. His urban roots and European training continued to trouble Alan Lomax, who commissioned Copland's setting of *John Henry* for CBS's *School of the Air*. Lomax recalls, "I took all our best field recordings to one of our top-ranking composers, a very bright and busy man who generally thought he liked folk songs." Though this "busy man" remains nameless, there can be little doubt of his identity: "It took him about half an hour to learn all that 'John Henry,' our finest ballad, had to say to him, and I departed with my treasured records, not sure whether I was more impressed by his facility, or angry because he had never really listened to 'John Henry.' When his piece was played on the air, I was unsure no longer. My composer friend had written the tunes down accurately, but his composition spoke for the Paris of Nadia Boulanger, and not for the wild land and the heart-torn people who had made the song. The spirit and the emotion of 'John Henry' shone nowhere in this score because he had never heard, much less experienced them." "Saga of a Folksong Hunter," reprinted in *Alan Lomax: Selected Writings, 1934–1997*, ed. Ronald D. Cohen (New York: Routledge, 2003), p. 175. I am grateful to Judith Tick for bringing this citation to my attention.

96. Copland and Perlis, *Copland: 1900–1942*, p. 246.

97. Ibid.

98. Pollack, *Aaron Copland*, p. 320.

Aaron Copland, Norman Rockwell,

and the "Four Freedoms":

The Office of War Information's Vision and Sound

in *The Cummington Story* (1945)

NEIL LERNER

What is it for, now that dividing neither
Farm from farm nor field from field, it runs
Through deep impartial woods, and is transgressed
By boughs of pine or beech from either side?
　　　　　　　—"A Wall in the Woods: Cummington"
　　　　　　　　　　Richard Wilbur

Richard Wilbur's poem "A Wall in the Woods: Cummington" asks us to consider the old stone walls that divide farms and fields in rural New England, drawing attention to how those fixed markers of boundaries once held tangible meaning but have since been eclipsed as the terrain has developed and shifted around them. It invites reflection about not only literal walls but symbolic ones as well.[1] During World War II, the small town of Cummington, Massachusetts, provided a model of how to overcome stony social, political, and economic barriers by establishing a hostel for European war refugees, and the hostel, in turn, provided the impetus for a documentary film, *The Cummington Story*, produced by the Office of War Information (OWI) in 1942 with a score by Aaron Copland. The intertwining of immigration politics, local history, wartime propaganda, and musical style yield a fascinating story.[2]

The Cummington Refugee Hostel, initiated and run by Carl M. Sangree—a Congregational minister who had been a conscientious objector during World War I—saw over forty displaced Europeans pass through the doors of what was known as the "Little Red House" between 1940 and 1944.[3] Hailing mostly from Germany and Austria, the refugees included former lawyers (Paul L. Frank), former insurance managers (Werner Koenigsberger), former physicians (George E. Beer), former newspaper editors (Hans Kallman, who had been managing editor of the *Frankfurter Zeitung*), even former Olympic athletes (Julius Boehm, who in 1936 had carried the Olympic torch to Berlin for Austria).[4] That these individuals found a small community willing to take them in and offer a chance to succeed through hard work stands as a great testament to the United States' lofty ideals of limitless opportunity; that the actual circumstances involved xenophobia may balance out the reality of what happened.[5] Still, to provide a modern analogy, imagine a rural U.S. community in the early twenty-first century reacting to refugees from Afghanistan or Iraq. Would they be immediately greeted without suspicion or fear? Would they be offered sanctuary and relief from longtime residents who might know little about their country or religion? Cummington's hostel represented a remarkable transgressing of social boundaries and prejudices, a fact that made its story attractive to the federal government when its filmmaking branch wanted to explain American ideals to the rest of the world.

Just how the Cummington Refugee Hostel became the subject of a twenty-two minute OWI film rested in part on serendipity. Created in 1942, OWI had two chief aims: to attack enemy morale and to disseminate information about the United States within occupied and liberated countries. The film division screened thousands of commercial and documentary films outside of the United States, and early in 1944, the U.S. Army's Psychological Warfare Division requested the appointment of OWI film officers to their ranks.[6] Howard Smith Southgate, a screenwriter for the Overseas Motion Picture Bureau of OWI, had a home in nearby Goshen, Massachusetts, and knew Carl Sangree.[7] Southgate was in New England looking for ideas about a story that could be shown in a film series called *The American Scene*.[8] Sangree described the hostel, Southgate pitched the idea to his superiors at OWI, and on August 22, 1944, producers met with the townspeople and gave them a week to mull over the prospect of becoming movie stars.[9] The community agreed and from September to November of 1944, government crews shot footage; a seventeen and a half–ton truck, with two diesel motors to generate electrical power for the lighting, was brought to Cummington.[10] The community was unfazed by the bright lights and uncommon media attention; as one newspaper story reported, "in spite of suddenly finding itself in the nation's limelight via an OWI motion picture, Cummington is cool and blase about the filming, far more so than was Madison, Wis., where a similar movie was made."[11] Some of the refugees left Cummington before 1944, but the ones who were still around agreed to be filmed along with many longtime citizens.[12] After shooting and reshooting many scenes from across the region—one letter in the Cummington archives, from OWI official Ben Gradus to one of the refugee actors, Gustav Wolf, speaks of the need to reshoot scenes—the film entered into a lengthy period of processing and editing.[13] A series of polite but persistent communications between Sangree and OWI officials reveals the community's growing desire to see the finished product, which they finally did on January 28, 1946, nearly fourteen months after their role had ended.[14] A short blurb in *Time* described *The Cummington Story* as "OWI Overseas' proudest production."[15] During an international student exchange program with Columbia University during the 1950s, Cummington residents discovered that students from around the world had seen the film.[16] Even if the village had been aloof during production, an anonymous memoir about the film sums up the community's considerable pride regarding the film's reception:

> I think perhaps the most significant tribute that has come to our village through this film is the fact that at Columbia University Teachers College in New York this film is shown every year in the class on community. I do not know whether that is the exact title of the course. It may be a course in Community Relations, but in any event, our film figures in the education of young people still after these many years since it was made. I have friends who have told me that they have seen the film in Athens. Carl and Florence [Sangree] will testify to its being shown in France. And we do not know in how many other countries our little village has served to interpret America to other lands.[17]

Copland and Documentary Film Music

"Aaron Copland recently completed the score for a two-reel film, 'The Cummington Story,' produced by the Office of War Information," announced the *New York Times* on August 19, 1945. "Translated into twenty-four languages, the film, concerned with the experiences of a group of refugees settled in Cummington, Mass., is released exclusively for foreign distribution."[18] By the 1940s, the middle-period music of Aaron Copland had already been strongly attached to notions of U.S. patriotism for media consumers; this remains the case today. Indeed, it did not take long in those first shocked moments after the attacks of September 11, 2001, before Copland's music resounded through the media, and various tributes and memorials about the tragedy engaged familiar Copland works like *Appalachian Spring* and *Fanfare for the Common Man*, drawing on their established efficacy as signifiers for self-sacrifice, earnestness, and opportunity.[19] In particular, Copland's fondness in these middle-period works for disjunct melodies, brass and woodwind timbres, and diatonicism have long served Hollywood when it wants to evoke nostalgia for the pastoral space.[20] Beyond the commercial film industry, the U.S. government has also recognized the ideological potential of Copland's music, using it in a World War II film intended to sway international audiences. Copland's underscore for *The Cummington Story* strengthens the overall argument of the film, affirming the United States as a site of potential sanctuary, projecting a vision of New England related to the visual tableaux of Norman Rockwell, and offering the "Four Freedoms" as solace to displaced war refugees.

While some of the details behind Copland's involvement with *The Cummington Story* remain unknown, it is well known that in the 1930s Copland took advantage of the stylistic liberties available in noncommercial documentary film scoring to gain access into the world of Hollywood film.[21] After an unsuccessful trip to Southern California in June 1937 to secure a Hollywood contract, Copland landed his first cinematic assignment with *The City*, a short documentary film about suburban planning that was successfully screened at the 1939 New York World's Fair.[22] With the quickly ossified musical tastes of Hollywood in the 1930s—tastes dictated mostly by producers averse to the risk of including dissonant music in their product—many composers interested in writing for film turned to documentaries instead of fictional film, even though the latter were more lucrative. Film composer Irwin Bazelon bluntly described the situation in connection to concert-to-film-crossover composers like Copland: "Because the tensions and financial liabilities attending big-budget commercial ventures are absent, the documentary field offers an ideal atmosphere for the concert composer's participation."[23] In Copland's case, the story is often told: his score for *The City* convinced Hollywood producers that he could match images with compelling music, and he was quickly awarded a contract for *Of Mice and Men*, with several other Hollywood projects soon to follow.[24] During this same time Copland was transforming his style in other genres, and perhaps his delayed acceptance in Hollywood (1939 instead of 1937) played some role in that much discussed metamorphosis toward "imposed simplicity."[25] Only by publicly displaying a willingness to reduce the amount of dissonance and complexity in his work, as he did in his "trial" score for *The City*, was he able to gain access to Hollywood's gated community of stylistic conservatism. Forced to mute his modernist impulses toward abstraction, such as those that appear in works like the Piano Variations or the *Short Symphony*, Copland had to present himself as antimodern, but besides impressing Hollywood, his stylistic passing (if indeed that aptly characterizes his stylistic shift) had the further consequence of placing him in a position where the U.S. government also sought out his music as part of the war effort.[26] It was only through this calculated act of resisting abstraction that Copland's music became accessible enough for government use; it is laughable to imagine U.S. Navy recruiting commercials pairing the Piano Variations, instead of the *Fanfare for the Common Man*, with imposing shots of gleaming military ships.[27]

Copland worked for several government agencies during World War II, including service on the State Department's Music Advisory Committee, and he presented lectures on behalf of the War Department at army camps and colleges.[28] Officials with OWI were well acquainted with one of his Hollywood projects, *The North Star*, a film about Soviet peasants resisting German soldiers, and OWI published a short report by Copland in one of their regular publications.[29] OWI employed many of the most highly regarded documentary filmmakers of the 1940s, including Alexander Hammid, Irving Jacoby, Boris Kaufman, Irving Lerner, Lawrence Madison, Sidney Meyers, and Willard Van Dyke.[30] Given the need for effective films of persuasion during the war, and the recognized utility of music in such films, OWI producers also employed a number of well-recognized concert composers, including Copland, Virgil Thomson, Roy Harris, and Gail Kubik.[31] In his memoirs, Copland wrote that he had contacted OWI about two concerts of U.S. music in Paris in the spring of 1945, and when that plan collapsed, they put him in touch with their Overseas Motion Picture Bureau.[32]

No interviews or printed documents have surfaced to reveal what individuals were responsible for Copland's involvement with *The Cummington Story*, although two pieces of correspondence in the Copland Collection at the Library of Congress document aspects of his interactions with OWI. One is a letter dated May 14, 1945, from Copland to Irving Lerner, acting chief of production for the Overseas Motion Picture Bureau. The other is a letter from Lerner back to Copland, dated May 19, 1945, discussing specific suggestions Copland gave Lerner about editing the film:

One of the things which has been causing a slight delay on the final completion of The Cummington Story is the beginning. Following your suggestion for a method of introducing the town of Cummington I went ahead inserting such material. I soon discovered that it, strangely enough, destroyed the structure of the film.[33]

That Copland's editorial suggestions were even considered speaks to his reputation and the relatively uncommon freedoms of documentary film: in the assembly-line atmosphere of Hollywood at that time, composers did not give advice on editing. Lerner's letter ends by noting that he arranged to move a piano to their tenth floor projection room for Copland's use on an upcoming visit.

Copland composed music for The Cummington Story quickly, in seven days (June 21–28, 1945), orchestrating and recording it shortly thereafter.[34] (Table 1 lists the cues.) Copland expected to be paid $1,250 for the score, which he initially planned to deliver by June 18.[35] Although Copland never published any of this score as a concert suite, several sections of it resurfaced in his catalog under different titles (see Table 2). Cue I, "Title Music," found its way into a simple piano piece called Down a Country Lane in 1962 (orchestrated in 1964).[36] Cue II, "The Refugees Arrive," was

---

Table 1. Cues from The Cummington Story

I. Title Music
II. The Refugees Arrive
III. First Impressions
IV. Lullaby
V. Epilogue
VI. Going to Church
VII. Hymn Tune (incorporates "Wilmot" from The Southern Harmony)
VIII. The Visit
IX. Starting Work
X. Mozart Excerpt (arrangement of Mozart's Violin Concerto in A Major, third movement, K. 219)
XI. The Valley
XII. Interlude
XIII. The County Fair
XIV. The Solution

Table 2. Reappearances of Musical Material
from *The Cummington Story*

Original Cues	Reappearance
I. Title Music	*Down a Country Lane* (1962)
II. The Refugees Arrive	*An Evening Air* (1966)
II. The Refugees Arrive	*Mid-Day Thoughts* (1982)
XI. The Valley	Concerto for Clarinet (1947–48)
XIII. The County Fair	"Stomp Your Foot," *The Tender Land* (1952–54)

arranged as a piano solo called *An Evening Air* in 1966 when the Scribner Music Library commissioned a piece; the title came from a poem by Theodore Roethke, quoted in part in the score ("I see, in evening air, how slowly dark comes down on what we do"). The second half of the main phrase of cue II (the disjunct upper melody that is accompanied by a bass ascending twice by step) occurs throughout *Mid-Day Thoughts*, a piano piece that was assembled in 1982 after pianist Bennett Lerner found sketches from 1944 and asked Copland to complete them.[37] Elements of cue XI, "The Valley," reappear in the Concerto for Clarinet.[38] Howard Pollack has noted that some gestures from "The County Fair," cue XIII, are reused in "Stomp Your Foot" from *The Tender Land*.[39] Since the score for *The Cummington Story* was largely unknown to a U.S. audience, Copland may have felt freer to repackage this music; nevertheless, he had a long-standing habit of reworking musical material.[40]

Representing the Four Freedoms

The visual iconography in *The Cummington Story* also played a role in influencing Copland's overall approach to the scoring of this film. Some of the imagery in the film belongs to the political discourse of the time, and as we reflect upon it as well, we see Copland's responsiveness to the moment. In his January 6, 1941, State of the Union address, Franklin Roosevelt put forward "four essential human freedoms" (freedom of speech and worship, freedom from want and fear) as justification for greater U.S. engagement in World War II. OWI systematically advanced those "four freedoms" in defense of the war, and by 1943 they became a popular theme for U.S. artists, some of whom formed a consortium called

"Artists for Victory" that celebrated "Four Freedoms Days" on September 12–19, 1943.[41] Hugo Ballin created a Four Freedoms mural for the Burbank, California, City Hall, and Walter Russell sculpted the Four Freedoms as four angels.[42] The most familiar rendering of them, however, came from Norman Rockwell, who painted them in 1943.[43]

Figure 1. Norman Rockwell, *Freedom of Speech* (1943).

Questions of complexity, modernism, simplicity, and the ability to communicate engaged filmmakers, writers, and composers, as well as the government agencies charged with informing the U.S. public about the war. These issues reached a head in early 1943, when the Domestic Branch of OWI experienced internal divisions as power shifted from writers with academic and literary backgrounds to advertising executives. One such executive was Price Gilbert, a former vice president of Coca-Cola. Gilbert had argued against some of Ben Shahn's posters depicting German atrocities on the grounds that their gruesome iconography was too unappealing; he preferred the more reassuring images of Norman Rockwell, well-known by the 1940s as the creator of reassuring *Saturday Evening Post* covers and Boy Scout calendars. Convinced that Gilbert's approach was condescending and dangerous, the disgruntled graphics staff made a poster, for their eyes only, that showed the Statue of Liberty, with its arms holding four bottles of Coca-Cola instead of her traditional torch, and bearing the caption, "The War That Refreshes: The Four Delicious Freedoms!"[44] By invoking Coca-Cola's slogan of the day, "the

Figure 2. Joseph rises for the first time in a town meeting in *The Cummington Story* (1945). Note the prominence of the engaged listeners in both this shot and in Rockwell's *Freedom of Speech*.

pause that refreshes," the artists lampooned the encroachment of corporate interests in federal communications. Despite the considerable wit behind their satire, the in-house artists failed to persuade Gilbert, and OWI adopted Rockwell's simpler approach.

After their initial appearance in *The Saturday Evening Post*, Rockwell's four paintings representing the Four Freedoms were adopted by both the Treasury Department for war bond drives and the Office of War Information for massive distribution around the world as posters. They provided a crucial rallying call in 1943, prompting Four Freedoms war bond shows in sixteen cities where over a million people saw the images and bought over $133 million in bonds; the OWI distributed four million sets of the posters domestically and abroad.[45] The conceptual centrality of the Four Freedoms in the Office of War Information's campaign can be observed further from their appearance in print media such as the magazine *U.S.A.*, which was distributed by OWI around the globe. For example, a photo-essay entitled "Town Meeting in America" (1944) opens by listing the Four Freedoms and arguing that the first of the freedoms, that of speech and expression, is the most important for the acquisition of the other three.[46] The essay then cites the New England town meeting as a prime example of this element of U.S. culture.

In keeping with that model, *The Cummington Story* opens with a New England town meeting and continues with an unstated but unmistakable reference to each of the remaining Four Freedoms. Some of the shots from the film even parallel the composition of Rockwell's iconic paintings, as with those of the town meeting at the beginning of the film. Eventually the film brings to life all four of the freedoms: refugees representing various religions praying together, following Rockwell's Freedom of Worship;[47] a mother putting her infant to bed, mirroring Rockwell's Freedom from Fear; and tables full of produce at the town fair, suggesting the over-abundance of Rockwell's Thanksgiving meal in Freedom from Want. Copland's musical response to these images forms a musical analogue with the Four Freedoms, establishing musical moods that highlight heterophony, spirituality, reassurance, and abundance.

Figure 3. Freedom of Worship, *The Cummington Story.*

Figure 4. Freedom from Fear, *The Cummington Story.*

Figure 5. Freedom from Want, *The Cummington Story.*

Reading *The Cummington Story* Through Its Music

The Cummington Story's soundtrack allows only one human voice—the "voice-of-God" narration provided by Carl Sangree—and the drama of the Cummington refugees receives almost constant accompaniment by a mediating *melos*, Copland's largely pastoral score. The film opens in the middle of a town meeting, with the nervous rising of a European refugee named Joseph taking the floor for what will be his first and last time.[48] Sangree's narration explains that Joseph is a refugee and then launches into a flashback, beginning with the moment when a bus arrives with a small group of people headed to the hostel. Subsequent scenes detail the townspeople's initial coldness toward the refugees and their eventual acceptance into Cummington's religious, economic, and social spheres as they find work and produce goods worthy of display at the town fair. Early in the film, the citizens of Cummington appear to be unfriendly and petty. Sangree later explains that the harsh economic and environmental conditions of Cummington have made its residents suspicious of outsiders: "We're not the breadbasket of America, but if you work hard the earth will give you back enough for your family and a little left over to take to market. It's a hard life, and often a lonely life, and maybe that accounts for the way we act sometimes." Unaccustomed to newcomers, the Cummington townspeople lack skills for engaging the refugees, but the minister recognizes the breakdown in communication and begins connecting individuals with common needs and interests, determining each refugee's skills and taking the refugees to places where they can find work. A montage sequence shows them busy with several types of labor, culminating in a shared celebration, by longtime residents and refugees alike, at the Cummington Fair. The flashback ends, returning us to Joseph in the town meeting where he declares his plans to leave Cummington. The final shot shows a bus departing the town, as Sangree declares that "if the boys on the post office porch had been reluctant to welcome strangers . . . they were also reluctant to say good-bye to friends."

Copland's opening cue in *The Cummington Story* lacks the epic quality common to Hollywood features of the time but instead projects a pastoral introduction followed by Sangree's introductory words about the town meeting (Example 1). Rhythmically simple (all note values are either quarter note, half note, or whole note in common time) with no syncopation, the first eight measures demonstrate Copland's fondness for limiting his pitch choices to a discrete set, in this case, the diatonic collection on F major (not unlike the limitation to five pitches in the glimmering opening of *Appalachian Spring*). The regular rhythmic patterns and essentially major

Moderate tempo

Example 1. *The Cummington Story*, "Title Music," mm. 1–4.

character of most of the harmonies give this cue a tintinnabulary quality, although Copland's orchestration does not exploit bright, bell-like timbres (he uses no trumpets or percussion). This cue recurs subsequently with syncopation in cue VI, "Going to Church," where the bell-like quality of the music meshes with images of townspeople walking to church. It appears for yet a third time during the film's closing moments, as the refugees depart Cummington.

The bittersweet melody in the cue called "The Refugees Arrive" occurs nearly every time Joseph, the central refugee in the film, appears, and this motive functions as a marker for both Joseph and the entire group of refugees. When Sangree remarks that the town meeting at the start of the film is Joseph's first, this motive appears for the first time. The transition from the "Title Music" to "The Refugees Arrive" is remarkable in itself: while the first cue has a three-part texture (comprising lines of quarter, half, and whole notes), Joseph's motive begins with a single melody doubled at the interval of two octaves, moving from nonimitative polyphony to monophony as the town meeting goes from the organized din of several voices down to the one voice implied by Joseph's rising to address the town meeting. Thus the musical regulation of voices mirrors the speaking voices in the town meeting. The only human voice ever heard in the film belongs to Sangree. The first nine measures of this cue set up a call-and-response pattern, where the flute and clarinet, doubling the melody's "call," are then answered by chords in the strings, mm. 4–5, 8–9 (Example 2). Copland positions his voicings in ways that make sense in the context of the images, here suggesting a reaffirming response given in return for Joseph's participation in the community's conversation.

Sangree begins the flashback by recounting the first time he saw Joseph, and as the bus carrying the refugees pulls into the shot Copland breaks up the refugees' theme with octave B's that behave like "stingers" from

Example 2. *The Cummington Story,* "The Refugees Arrive," mm. 1–34, short score.

Example 2 continued

Hollywood practice, mm. 10–11 (Example 2). (Stingers are unexpectedly accented notes or chords that occur in direct association with an onscreen action, often a painful or shocking revelation.) Two more stinger octaves strike immediately in conjunction with a close-up of Joseph's face. By not explaining what specific circumstances forced Joseph's immigration to the United States, the film cleverly opens itself up to multiple refugee experiences, broadening its possible appeal to international audiences. Copland's music assists in the rhetorical maneuver here by encouraging audience sympathy for Joseph. The score manages to convey his emotional state, filling out the sketchy narrative details. The stinger chords accompanying Joseph's face bring out a stark, lonely quality, perhaps operating as a kind of musical Kuleshov effect.[49]

The refugees' theme returns four times, functioning like a leitmotif. During cue III, "First Impressions," the refugees, led by Sangree, walk to their new home, and Copland accompanies the melody of the refugee theme with eighth-note chords scored for bassoon, bass clarinet, and violas playing pizzicato, suggesting the convention of "mickey-mousing" footsteps with plucked strings.[50] In cue VI, "Going to Church," the refugee theme appears as the refugees enter church—it is similar to the first occurrence, without the stinger octaves. The refugee theme, which might also be called Joseph's theme since it is first heard when he is introduced, is withheld at a key moment, when Joseph enters the local general store and receives an icy silent treatment from the local loiterers. Sangree calls this group "the Old Stove League . . . [the]most exclusive club in America." The scene contains no music at all, providing an example of what Claudia Gorbman calls a "structural silence," meaning that a silence occurs at a point where, at previous corresponding structural moments, there had been sound.[51] The effect in *The Cummington Story* is powerful—it is the only time during the entire film where there is no music—and emphasizes with chilling precision the alienation between the town's longtime citizens and the refugees. In a corresponding scene later in the film, after the refugees have been accepted into the community, Joseph is invited to sit with the Old Stove League and his motive makes a triumphant return. The final statement of the refugees' theme occurs at the end of the film, when Sangree's flashback ends and Joseph explains he will be leaving soon to help rebuild his own country. For this final iteration of Joseph's theme (Example 3), Copland changes the melody, broadening the second half of its phrase by three beats, mm. 15–17 (as in Example 2). Both Joseph's character and the melody assigned to him are transformed into smoother, rounder, more relaxed entities by the end of the film.

The key moment in the integration of the refugees into the Cummington community comes during a visual montage of labor-intensive activities as they discover ways to work and make themselves economically productive. The film repeatedly comments on the refugees' surprise at finding various markers of European high culture—such as philosophy and chamber music—tucked away in rural New England. One refugee, Peter, wants to renew his vocation as a printer (the narration mentions book-burnings in his European hometown), and as he realizes that he could do similar work in Cummington—while visiting the homestead of New England poet William Cullen Bryant—a brief fugal passage occurs.[52] Copland's rough sketches for *The Cummington Story* suggest that he thought about including a fugue in the opening credits. Copland instead situated what he called the "Work Bench Fugue" at cue IX, "Starting Work"

(added notes)

Example 3. *The Cummington Story*, altered version of Joseph's/refugee's theme.

(Example 4). The subject of the "Work Bench Fugue" is melodically disjunct and centered around F. Its rhythmic simplicity suggests the purity of the values conveyed by the film. The fugue in *The Cummington Story* has an exposition where the subject, answer, and countersubject are initially stated, but then an episode occurs: in measures 16 to 34, Copland uses a series of repeated melodic phrases over a rhythmic ostinato derived from the opening of the subject (dotted quarter, eighth, quarter, quarter). Accompanying the divergent melodic lines are a series of crosscut scenes showing several of the refugees engaging in different labors. Copland's fugue conveys the synchronicity of narratives implied by the visual crosscutting. The fugue subject returns later in the film as we see the fruits of Peter's labor: an engraved title page for, appropriately enough, Ralph Waldo Emerson's essay *Self-Reliance*. Its message has political meaning, representing the multiple voices basic to democracy.

Copland makes inspired use of musical texture as a rhetorical device throughout the film. His skillful alternations—opening and closing with homophony, moments of nonimitative polyphony in the middle—offers a formal structure that reinforces the larger framing device incorporating

Example 4. *The Cummington Story*, "Starting Work," mm. 1–16.

a flashback during the town meeting. The presence of polyphony in the middle of the flashback provides an appropriate musical analogue for the democratic ideal. More complicated musical textures, after all, force a composer to consider the challenges of maintaining independence of voice and of being able to hear the individuals from within the din of the larger community. Copland's choice of a polyphonic texture, significant first because fugues rarely occur within Hollywood's conventional scoring practices, also complements the film's political message.

At three moments in the score, the music has the illusion of appearing from an on-screen source, creating what film scholars would call diegetic music. First, a mother puts her infant child to sleep and we hear a female voice singing a lullaby (cue IV); here, Copland used an unidentified Polish lullaby.[53] Then, during the refugees' first visit to a church service, the congregation joins the organist and choir in performing a hymn (cue VII), a rearrangement of the shape-note hymn "Wilmot" from *The Southern Harmony*.[54] Finally, Sangree joins Joseph and a person named as "the Hall girl" to play some chamber music (a reduction of the third movement of Mozart's Violin Concerto in A Major, K. 219, for flute, violin, and organ).[55] Each of these diegetic moments finds Copland borrowing from traditions that are thematically appropriate, mixing Polish, nineteenth-century Protestant, and Austrian musical signifiers to mirror the blending of these traditions at the Cummington hostel. Copland's familiar pastoral style— which dominates the majority of the score, representing a symbolic voice that the government found neutral enough to speak throughout the film— joins occasionally with these differently accented voices, representing American and European traditions. The music, in fact, offers a greater diversity of ethnic accents than does the speaking element of the soundtrack. In Sangree's voice-over narration, we never hear the multiple accents that must have been present in the speech of the various refugees.

Finally, Copland's documentary score runs against the grain of several Hollywood conventions, such as the tendency of fiction film to open with an epic-sounding, grandiose cue, usually employing a post-Romantic style in the tradition of Wagner or Strauss. It also countered Hollywood's tendency to force composers to follow the film's form, instead of structuring their musical ideas in more traditional, autonomous ways. Composers could not normally show up with a sonata or rondo and expect the editor to shape the images around the music. As a consequence of the priority of image over music, scores in narrative fiction films were usually expected to illustrate the image, instead of encouraging autonomous musical forms that might then inspire decisions of cinematography or editing. Some early commentators like Kurt Weill, Hanns Eisler, and Theodor Adorno lamented music's subordination to image and discussed how film scores contained few cues with familiar, recognizable musical forms.[56] *The Cummington Story* violates the convention of immediate postromantic grandiosity. Copland instead moves in the opposite direction, from the gentlest music of the score (for the main title) to the most energetic and dynamic near the end, running under the scenes of a county fair. For this cue Copland wrote a rondo in which no recurring section ever has an exact repetition. "The County Fair" (cue XIII) accompanies a rapid montage of various carnival scenes. The music is playful and optimistic, even though it contains sonorities that in other contexts might be perceived as dissonant, such as the opening measure's A♮ in the melody over the A♭ in the accompaniment (Example 5). Synchronous without being illustrative, it is the most technically complex cue in the score, featuring polymetric ostinati (Example 6) while maintaining a simplicity through triadic melodies.

Example 5. *The Cummington Story,* "The County Fair," mm. 65–81.

Example 6. *The Cummington Story,* "The County Fair," mm. 90–104.

Rockwell and Copland?

Rockwell and Copland both eschewed modernist disruptive strategies in the 1940s in favor of a more direct language. While Norman Rockwell does not appear to have had any direct personal involvement with the planning or production of *The Cummington Story,* his heavily distributed and popular vision of New England as a utopian space and his conception of the Four Freedoms find striking parallels in this obscure government film. Copland's middle-period sound, a style so attractive to Hollywood, to the federal government, and to audiences in search of nationalistic markers, taps into a larger tradition of narratives that mythologize the limitless opportunities available in the United States. *The Cummington Story*'s most remarkable feature may be the way that it reveals Rockwell's and Copland's 1940s work as falling within the same cultural-political orbit. Curiously, one almost never sees their names connected, even though their most famous works have significant affinities, from shared interests in narrative and storytelling to a genuinely optimistic outlook about the human condition.

In his 1966 survey of twentieth-century music, William W. Austin posited that Copland formed an important part of an "American school" of composers who formed "a worthy counterpart [to] the American poets and painters of the same generation," suggesting that "in the wider context of American poetry, fiction, and visual arts, and their world-wide importance, Copland more nearly than any other musician corresponds to an Ezra Pound, a Hemingway, or a Calder."[57] He did not link Rockwell with Copland but rather with the composer and arranger Robert Russell Bennett, citing Bennett's affinity not only for Rockwell but also for Stephen Foster as proof of his ostensibly unsophisticated tastes.[58] More recently, Gail Levin traced a series of connections between Copland and visual artists, including Thomas Hart Benton, Rufino Tamayo, Marc Chagall, Paul Strand, Ben Shahn, Grant Wood, and Alexander Calder, but she, too, did not mention Rockwell.[59] For many art historians, Rockwell falls into the category of "illustrator" rather than "artist," perhaps explaining why Copland's commentators have not pursued connections between the two: if Rockwell's artistic reputation stands on shaky ground, then linking him to Copland risks devaluing Copland's position within cultural hierarchies.[60] Rockwell, after all, was named by Clement Greenberg as an example of "kitsch" in his famous essay of 1939, "Avant-Garde and Kitsch," which was also the year of the founding of that other great monument to aesthetic modernism, the Guggenheim Museum in New York City.[61] That Rockwell might one day have an exhibition at the Guggenheim was probably unimaginable in 1939, yet in November 2001, such an event did occur, sparking critical outrage for those who believed modernism's boundaries had been transgressed.[62] At the same time, the still-smoldering memories of September 11 made Rockwell's unambiguous icons of heroism a source of comfort—the same impulse that also helps explain why Copland's works were so ubiquitous after the attacks.

Rockwell's optimistic and hopeful images obscured many urgent social problems in the United States during World War II, just as the Office of War Information's work with Hollywood film strove to promote a myth of racial, gender, and class unity—a myth that would be gradually dismantled after 1945.[63] *The Cummington Story* participates in that myth-making process while downplaying less flattering realities, such as the extent of the suspicion cast upon the refugees by townspeople and the FBI. While neither Copland nor Rockwell offered aggressive, explicit critiques of American life in their works, Copland may have employed more cynicism than Rockwell, who shied away from anything as extreme as

Copland's distortions of "The Star Spangled Banner" in *Hear Ye! Hear Ye!* (where Copland wanted "to convey the corruption of legal systems and courts of law").[64] But as World War II was winding down in 1945, Copland's accessible sounds matched Rockwell's visions, linking the two, albeit indirectly, in *The Cummington Story*. The works of Rockwell and Copland were well positioned to be highly effective tools in the government's campaign to persuade the citizens of the United States and the world at large about the reasons for, if not also the righteousness of, its participation in the war. Just as the Cummington wall in Richard Wilbur's poem no longer divides "farm from farm nor field from field," we can now start to look beyond the barrier separating Copland and Rockwell.

NOTES

I gratefully acknowledge the assistance and advice of Gasparo dell'Albera, Bryan Gilliam, Gloria Gowdy, Carol Oja, Howard Pollack, John Powell, and Judith Tick. Stephen Howes, chair of the Cummington Historical Commission, deserves special thanks for his assistance with the archives of the Cummington Refugee Hostel. Some of the research for this essay was supported by a grant from the Davidson College Faculty Study and Research Committee. At present, the film is not easily accessible. The National Archives will make copies of the film upon request; the community of Cummington has annual screenings. A concert suite of the film score, arranged by Jonathan Sheffer, appears on *Celluloid Copland: World Premiere Film Music*, Telarc CD-80583, 2001.

1. Richard Wilbur, *Mayflies: New Poems and Translations* (New York: Harcourt, 2000), p. 45.

2. The title credits, characteristically vague for this type of film, offer only one name behind its production: Aaron Copland. That only the composer and not even a director or screenwriter got a credit speaks to Copland's stature as a composer. New information from the Cummington Historical Commission archives clarifies the full credits, which have not before been fully outlined in any single scholarly source. The Commission materials include newspaper clippings, letters, and other papers in two folders and two scrapbooks. The story about the film that splashed across the front page of the Sunday *Springfield Union/Springfield Republican* (September 17, 1944) lists the following credits: director, Helen Grayson; producer, Frank Beckwith; production unit manager, Ben Gradus; director of photography, Lawrence Madison; cameraman, Benjamin Doniger; operating cameraman, Walter Harris; assistant cameraman, Walter Sachs; electrician, Anthony Gamiello; assistant electrician, Hugh Dinnen; generator operator, Louis Mucci; script girl [*sic*], Sylvia Dudowsky. Several sources in the archives, including an uncited clipping of an obituary for Howard Smith Southgate, name Southgate as the script writer.

3. Madeline Ball, "Movies Made in Cummington to Introduce New England to the World," *Spring Union/Springfield Republican*, September 17, 1944.

4. The Cummington Historical Archives in Cummington, Massachusetts, has detailed archives relating to the refugees and the hostel. Included among these papers are unpub-

lished histories by Carl Sangree and numerous newspaper clippings about the hostel and specific refugees. An overview of Sangree's work with the hostel may be found in Thelma P. Whiting, "Cummington Pastor Turns From War to God, Leaves Mark on World," *Daily Hampshire Gazette,* September 20, 1968. A brief accounting of the hostel and some of the individuals living there appears in Helen H. Foster and William W. Streeter, *Only One Cummington: A Book in Two Parts* (Cummington, Mass.: Cummington Historical Commission, 1974), pp. 113–16, and Olive Thayer, *A History of Cummington, Massachusetts, 1779–1979* (Pittsfield, Mass.: Cummington Souvenir Committee, 1979), pp. 48–49. After living in the Cummington hostel, former lawyer Paul Frank pursued musicology, studying at the University of Chicago and teaching at Otterbein College (uncredited clipping, "A Tribute to Paul L. Frank").

5. An uncredited clipping in the Cummington Historical Commission archives, "Cummington Refugee Haven Stirs Up Groundless Rumors," corroborates what Gloria Gowdy (August 13, 2004) and Stephen Howes (August 17, 2004) shared during personal interviews: some of the longtime residents in Cummington harbored suspicion that these European refugees might be spies. Several accounts refer to an FBI agent's visit to Cummington, following up reports that a Nazi had given a speech to a bund meeting of one hundred Germans; the investigation revealed that Hans Kallmann, a resident at the hostel, had addressed the local Parent Teacher Association about the democratic movement in Austria before the Anschluss (Whiting, "Cummington Pastor Turns from War to God," p. 15).

6. Philip C. Hamblet, *OWI in the ETO: A Report on the Activities of the Office of War Information in the European Theatre of Operations, January 1944–January 1945* (London: Reproduction Unit of OWI London, 1945), p. 12. Further information about the Office of War Information can be found in Clayton R. Koppes and Gregory D. Black, *Hollywood Goes to War: How Politics, Profits and Propaganda Shaped World War II Movies* (Berkeley: University of California Press, 1987); and Richard Dyer MacCann, *The People's Films: A Political History of U.S. Government Motion Pictures* (New York: Hastings House, 1973).

7. Whiting, "Cummington Pastor Turns from War to God."

8. A five-page typewritten document in the Cummington Historical Commission archives entitled "The Cummington Story" and attributed to Carl Sangree situates July 24, 1944, as the day Howard Southgate first appeared in Cummington, explaining that "he was looking for a story depicting life in a American village which could be used overseas" (p. 2). The title credits of *The Cummington Story* indicate that it is no. 14 in the series, *The American Scene.* Of the other parts of that series, we know that no. 13, *Tuesday in November*, is an explanation of voting procedures and has a score by Virgil Thomson. The manuscript for the full score, housed at the Yale Music Library, has the date June 6, 1945. The title page for the piano reduction of the *Tuesday in November* orchestral score states that the film was made by John Houseman and that the music was "recorded 1945 at the Paramount Studios, Los Angeles, for the United States Information Service." The film is available online as part of the Prelinger Archives, http://www.archive.org/movies/details-db.php?collection=prelinger&collectionid=01330.

9. Sangree, "The Cummington Story," p. 2.

10. Ball, "Movies Made in Cummington." Sangree reported that the same truck and generators had been used at the World's Fair to supply electricity for displays ("The Cummington Story," p. 4).

11. "Cummington Takes Movie Making in Stride," *Berkshire Evening Eagle,* September 22, 1944.

12. The Cummington Historical Commission archives contain a six-page handwritten document in which the people in each scene are identified. Locations are given as well; although the film presents itself as having been filmed entirely in Cummington, a few scenes were filmed in surrounding areas.

13. Cummington Historical Commission Archives; the letter is dated October 15, 1944.

14. Sangree, "The Cummington Story," p. 5. An uncredited newspaper clipping in the Cummington archives, with the title "Cummington Packs Town Hall to See Itself in the Films," explains that four shows, instead of the originally scheduled two, were necessary to accommodate the more than 700 persons who showed up to see the local premiere of the film. It has become an annual tradition in Cummington to screen the film.

15. "Cinema," *Time*, January 28, 1946, 102.

16. Foster and Streeter, *Only One Cummington*, p. 117.

17. The two-page, uncredited document appears in the Cummington Historical Commission's archives.

18. "Events in the World of Music," p. X4.

19. Williams Brooks describes a television show about September 11 that used *Appalachian Spring* in "Simple Gifts and Complex Accretions," *Copland Connotations*, ed. Peter Dickinson (Woodbridge, Suffolk, U.K.: The Boydell Press, 2002), p. 114. Elizabeth B. Crist notes the use of several Copland works in the HBO documentary *In Memoriam: New York City, 9/11/01*, in "Aaron Copland and the Popular Front," *Journal of the American Musicological Society* 56, no. 2 (Summer 2003): 412. For the 2002 Superbowl—the first Superbowl after September 11—the pre-game entertainment included a performance of *Lincoln Portrait* with all the then-living presidents reading the narration (Nancy Reagan read for Ronald), prompting a writer for the ESPN sports network to proclaim Copland one of the big winners of the day and declaring that the piece "deserved the nationwide props." See Dan Shanoff, "Superbowl's Real Winners and Losers," http://espn.go.com/page2/s/shanoff/020204.html (accessed June 7, 2004).

20. For a discussion of Copland's sound as one of Hollywood's chief musical codes for U.S. nationalism, see Neil Lerner, "Copland's Music of Wide Open Spaces: Surveying the Pastoral Trope in Hollywood," *Musical Quarterly* 85, no. 3 (Fall 2001): 477–515. Judith Tick traces several specific techniques used by Copland to "make the commonplace strange" in "The Music of Aaron Copland," in *Aaron Copland's America: A Cultural Perspective*, ed. Gail Levin and Judith Tick (New York: Watson-Guptill, 2000), p. 156.

21. Copland explains how his score for *The City* paved the way for future Hollywood assignments: "[It] seems that *The City* was playing in a movie theater out there and was seen by the producers, who earlier on had not been convinced by my symphonies, opera, and chamber music. Now I finally had a film credit, and I was in! (Aaron Copland and Vivian Perlis, *Copland: 1900 Through 1942* [New York: St. Martin's/Marek, 1984], p. 297. Howard Pollack observes that "*The City* opened up the doors to Hollywood." (*Aaron Copland: The Life and Work of an Uncommon Man* [New York: Henry Holt, 1999], p. 340).

22. Howard Pollack describes Copland's meetings with Hollywood music executives (*Aaron Copland*, p. 337), and Copland's version appears in his memoir (Copland and Perlis, *Copland: 1900–1942*, pp. 270–71). Two Ph.D. dissertations have chapters devoted to *The City*: Alfred Cochran, "Style, Structure, and Tonal Organization in the Early Film Scores of Aaron Copland," Catholic University, 1986; and Claudia Widgery, "The Kinetic and Temporal Interaction of Music and Film: Three Documentaries of 1930s America," University of Maryland, 1990.

23. Irwin Baselon, *Knowing the Score: Notes on Film Music* (New York: Van Nostrand Reinhold, 1975), p. 38. For further discussion of documentary film and music, see Neil Lerner, "The Classical Documentary Film in American Films of Persuasion: Contexts and Case Studies, 1936–1945," Ph.D. diss., Duke University, 1997; Neil Lerner, "Damming Virgil Thomson's Score for *The River*," in *Collecting Visible Evidence*, ed. Jane M. Gaines and Michael Renov (Minneapolis: University of Minnesota Press, 1999), pp. 103–15; and Julie Hubbert, "'Whatever Happened to Great Movie Music?': *Cinéma Vérité* and Hollywood Film Music of the Early 1970s," *American Music* 21, no. 2 (Summer 2003): 180–213.

24. His other film scores were *Our Town*; *The North Star*; *The Cummington Story*; *The Heiress*; *The Red Pony*; and *Something Wild*. Copland's pastoral idiom was quickly adopted by other Hollywood composers, such as Hugo Friedhofer and Jerome Moross, and finds its way into countless other film and television scores (see Lerner, "Copland's Music of Wide Open Spaces"). In addition to writing film music in Hollywood, Copland also wrote *about* film music in a series of articles aimed at both a mainstream (i.e., *New York Times*) and highly specialized audience (i.e., *Modern Music*). See Sally Bick, "Copland on Hollywood," in Dickinson, *Copland Connotations*, pp. 39–54.

25. Copland spoke of his change in style during the mid-to-late 1930s as a "tendency toward an imposed simplicity" in the frequently cited "Composer from Brooklyn" autobiography, reprinted in Copland, *Our New Music: 1900–1960*, rev. ed. (New York: W. W. Norton, 1968), p. 160. See Crist, "Aaron Copland and the Popular Front," p. 410.

26. Jennifer DeLapp addresses the reception of the *Short Symphony* against the rise of a middlebrow culture in "Speaking to Whom? Modernism, Middlebrow, and Copland's *Short Symphony*," in Dickinson, *Copland Connotations*, pp. 85–102.

27. During the 1990s the Navy ran televised recruiting commercials that juxtaposed images of naval vessels with Copland's *Fanfare for the Common Man*.

28. Aaron Copland and Vivian Perlis, *Copland Since 1943* (New York: St. Martin's Press, 1989), p. 8.

29. Koppes and Black, *Hollywood Goes to War*, pp. 209–15. Copland's essay was entitled "The American Composer Today," *U.S.A.* 2, no. 10 (1947): 23–27.

30. Richard Meran Barsam, *Nonfiction Film: A Critical History* (New York: E. P. Dutton, 1973), pp. 216–17. Erik Barnouw also observes that "unlike the army films [made during World War II], the OWI films were dominated by veteran documentarists, largely from the New York film world." In *Documentary: A History of the Non-Fiction Film*, 2nd ed. (New York: Oxford University Press, 1993), p. 164.

31. Kubik, who served as director of music for the domestic branch of the Office of War Information's Film Bureau from 1942 to 1943, also (like Bazelon) believed that Hollywood's obstinate reliance on a hegemonic musical vocabulary caused many concert composers to turn to documentaries. Further discussion of Kubik's work with OWI may be found in Alfred W. Cochran, "The Documentary Film Scores of Gail Kubik," in *Film Music: Critical Approaches*, ed. K. J. Donnelly (Edinburgh, U.K.: Edinburgh University Press, 2001), pp. 117–28.

32. Copland and Perlis, *Copland Since 1943*, p. 62.

33. Letter from Irving Lerner to Copland, May 19, 1945, Aaron Copland Collection, Music Division, Library of Congress.

34. On the front page of the short score, Copland wrote: "Begun June 21, 1945 / Composition finished June 28, 1945 Orchestration finished July 19, 1945 / Recorded July 24, 1945." Such speed was exceptional for Copland, who tended to write a work a year, although his accounting of the workdays overlooks the time beginning at least in May when he was in consultation with the producers over the film. The primary materials for the musical score, housed in the Copland Collection, include the 129-page full score, the cue sheets (6 pages) and narration (10 pages), a three-staff short score and thirteen pages of sketches. The score was conducted by Max Goberman, who also conducted Copland's score for *The City*.

35. Letter from Copland to acting chief of production, Irving Lerner, May 14, 1945, Copland Collection.

36. Copland and Perlis, *Copland Since 1943*, p. 259. The piano version was reprinted in *Life* (June 29, 1962).

37. In his preface to the 1984 edition, Copland wrote that "*Mid-Day Thoughts* is based on sketches for the slow movement of a projected *Ballade* for piano and orchestra dating

from early 1944 when I was finishing *Appalachian Spring*." Copland and Perlis credit Bennett Lerner with the editing of *Mid-Day Thoughts* from the 1944 sketch. Ibid., p. 263.

38. See Lerner, "Copland's Music of Wide Open Spaces," p. 500.

39. Pollack, *Aaron Copland*, p. 409.

40. Pollack discusses this practice (*Aaron Copland*, p. 11), summarizes many of Copland's borrowings (pp. 566–67), and cites Daniel Mathers's work on this topic.

41. Stuart Murray and James McCabe, *Norman Rockwell's "Four Freedoms"* (New York: Gramercy Books, 1993), pp. 40–43.

42. "Artists Interpret the Four Freedoms," *Art Digest* 17, no. 11 (March 1, 1943): 10.

43. For a history of Rockwell's engagement with the Four Freedoms, see Maureen Hart Hennessey's "The Four Freedoms," in *Norman Rockwell: Pictures for the American People*, ed. Maureen Hart Hennessey and Anne Knutson (New York: Harry N. Abrams, 1999), pp. 95–102.

44. Sydney Weinberg, "What to Tell America: The Writers' Quarrel in the Office of War Information," *Journal of American History* 55, no. 1 (June 1968): 85–86. Also, Koppes and Black, *Hollywood Goes to War*, pp. 134–35.

45. Rufus Jarman, "Profiles: U.S. Artist," *The New Yorker*, March 17, 1945, 41.

46. *U.S.A.* 1, no. 5 (1944): 44–51. A caption for one of the pictures in this essay reads, "When neighbors or friends get together, they can discuss subjects of their own choosing without fear that they are being secretly spied upon." Ironically, it would be only a few short years after working with OWI that Copland would find his private life scrutinized by Joseph McCarthy and the FBI. See Jennifer DeLapp, "Copland in the Fifties: Music and Ideology in the McCarthy Era," Ph.D. diss., University of Michigan, 1997. Also ironic is the film's later reception as Communist propaganda: what appears to be a sermon about *The Cummington Story* (it is a three-page typed document in the Cummington Historical Commission archives, signed by Carl Sangree) responds to an article by conservative journalist Fulton Lewis, Jr., in which Lewis attacked *The Cummington Story* as communist propaganda. Sangree's sermon states that Lewis's publication, "How Reds Get Messages Into Classrooms," appeared on July 9, 1953, and Sangree complains that Lewis singled out the film as "Red propaganda."

47. While it may appear that the refugees are all Jewish, as Jonathan Sheffer presumes in his liner notes for *Celluloid Copland: World Premiere Film Music* (Telarc CD-80583, 2001), Sangree states that the refugees "came from many different churches and denominations . . . Catholic, Jewish, Protestant" in his narration during the church scene. Some of the newspaper clippings in the Cummington Historical Commission archives refer to certain individuals as "racial refugees," referring to their Jewish heritage, and while a majority may have been Jewish, Sangree was not exaggerating when stressing the ecumenical mix represented within the hostel. In fact, Sangree took pains to welcome families with multiple religious backgrounds, finding that "religious agencies managed to provide help for their own people, so he decided that the Cummington hostel would cater to mixed marriages. A Jewish husband or wife with a Christian mate seemed to have nowhere to turn until the little red house offered them refuge." Whiting, "Cummington Pastor Turns from War to God."

48. The role of "Joseph" in the film was acted by Werner Koenigsberger, a refugee who, with his wife, had chosen to stay in Cummington after leaving the hostel (the couple set up a crafts business). Joseph's wife in the film, "Anna," was played by Leona Wolf, another former refugee and wife of Gustav Wolf, an artist of some reputation in Germany and the United States. A "Meet the Faculty" column from *The Northfield Star* (November 20, 1945) in the Cummington Historical Commission archives states that Wolf had been a professor at the State Academy for Fine and Applied Arts in Karlsruhe.

49. In Lev Kuleshov's famous editing experiment, audiences inferred meaning in originally unrelated images simply because of their juxtaposition: an old man's face next

to an image of a bowl of soup, although filmed separately, operated together to intensify a sense that the old man was hungry for the soup. One starting point for more detailed discussion of the Kuleshov effect is Norman N. Holland, "Film Response from Eye to I: The Kuleshov Experiment," in *Classical Hollywood Narrative: The Paradigm Wars*, ed. Jane Gaines (Durham, N.C.: Duke University Press, 1992), pp. 79–106.

50. "Mickey-Mousing" refers to compositional attempts to closely join musical gesture with image, as when an animated character's footsteps are each accompanied by a plucked string. The technique originated in animation but also found its way into early sound scores. Max Steiner's score for *King Kong*, 1933, contains many examples, including a scene where a nonanimated character's footsteps (those of the chief) are each accompanied by a short note in the orchestra.

51. Claudia Gorbman, *Unheard Melodies: Narrative Film Music* (Bloomington: Indiana University Press, 1987), p. 19.

52. Gustav Wolf played the role of Peter.

53. Copland and Perlis, *Copland Since 1943*, p. 63.

54. Copland's use of nineteenth-century Protestant hymn tunes as a means for making his score more authentic follows Virgil Thomson's similar technique in *The River* (1937). See Lerner, "Damming Virgil Thomson's Score for *The River*." Clifton Sears, whose blindness is mentioned by Sangree, was the organist at the Congregational Church in Cummington and also gave piano lessons ("Cummington Takes Movie Making in Stride").

55. The Cummington Historical Commission document identifying the people in the film names "the Hall girl" as Nancy Whitbread.

56. Weill detested "musical illustrating" and its abandonment of autonomous musical forms in "Musikalische Illustration oder Filmmusik?" originally in *Film-Kurier* 13, October 1927, reprinted in *Kurt Weill, Musik und Theater: Gesammelte Schriften*, ed. Stephen Hinton and Jürgen Schebera (Berlin: Henschelverlag Kunst und Gesellschaft, 1990), pp. 297–99. Eisler and Adorno established a dialectic between cinema music and "autonomous music," pointing out that in film, composers adopted compressed short forms (they cite Webern) but avoid the longer traditional forms. See Theodor Adorno and Hanns Eisler, *Composing for the Films* (London: Dennis Dobson Ltd., 1947), pp. 38–39.

57. William W. Austin, *Music in the Twentieth Century: From Debussy Through Stravinsky* (New York: W. W. Norton, 1966), p. 505.

58. Austin wrote that "Robert Russell Bennett (b. 1894) perfected with the help of Boulanger the skills that had already by 1926 brought him success as an arranger, but even in his six symphonies and other 'serious' works he stuck to the taste for Stephen Foster and Norman Rockwell that he shared with millions of his countrymen" (ibid., p. 506).

59. "Picturing Aaron Copland," in Levin and Tick, *Aaron Copland's America*.

60. Both art and film music criticism have used the concept of "illustration" as a pejorative label, although both do that without considering the reasons some creators may have employed more direct, illustrative methods over languages that rely on greater abstraction.

61. *Partisan Review* 6, no. 5 (Fall 1939): 43.

62. For more, see Alan Wallach, "*Norman Rockwell* at the Guggenheim," in *Art and Its Publics: Museum Studies at the Millennium* (Malden, Mass.: Blackwell Publishing, 2003), pp. 97–115.

63. Koppes and Black, *Hollywood Goes to War*, p. 325. Charles Rosen and Henri Zerner discuss Rockwell's blind spots and also give examples of what they regard to be his technical deficiencies in their review of the exhibition catalogue, "Scenes from the American Dream," *New York Review of Books*, August 10, 2000, 16–20.

64. Copland and Perlis, *Copland: 1900–1942*, p. 234.

Aaron Copland Meets the Soviet Composers

A Television Special

TRANSCRIBED AND INTRODUCED BY EMILY ABRAMS

In 1959, at the height of the Cold War, Copland took part in a television interview entitled *Aaron Copland Meets the Soviet Composers,* produced by WGBH in Boston. A transcript of the entire 30-minute show is included here. This intriguing program, brought about by an American-Soviet cultural exchange, was filmed during the visit of a group of Russian composers; the following year, Copland was selected to participate in a return visit to the USSR.

In many ways, Copland's participation in a Soviet-American project was entirely characteristic. He maintained an active interest in America's musical and political relations with Russia throughout his life. For a time during the 1930s he assumed a strong pro-Soviet position; during the 1940s he served on the music committee of the National Council of American-Soviet Friendship; and in 1949 he spoke at the Conference for World Peace in New York, where he criticized the United States for the detrimental effects of the Cold War on the arts.[1] Perhaps he felt some identification with the USSR because of his Russian-immigrant parents. Certainly he responded to the left-leaning tendencies of his generation of New York intellectuals.

Yet his connection to Russia—and to the communist ideology espoused there during his lifetime—was fraught and frequently in flux. Despite these previous connections with the Soviets, the timing of his involvement in the cultural exchange, and in *Aaron Copland Meets the Soviet Composers*, is rather puzzling. In 1953, six years prior to the filming of this program, Copland's previous political actions and affiliations had resulted in a summons to appear before Joseph McCarthy's Senate Permanent Subcommittee on Investigations to face charges of links with communism—an ordeal with many personal and professional consequences. Copland's case was dropped in 1955, yet just four years later he was chosen by WGBH to interview visiting Soviet composers and, a year after that, selected by the State Department to return to the USSR as a cultural ambassador. Considering where such activities had led him previously, it is somewhat surprising that he accepted both these offers. The State Department's actions are also intriguing in this context. A man so recently stigmatized in the "red scare" had suddenly become useful to the U.S. government.

American-Soviet cultural exchanges were initiated by the USSR following Premier Krushchev's call for more peaceful cooperation with the West at a 1956 Communist Party conference. Two years later, the countries signed an "Agreement . . . on Exchanges in the Cultural, Technical, and Educational Fields." Officially, the United States expressed the hope that the visits would improve cultural understanding between the two nations and decrease Soviet isolation and inwardness. But when one views the exchange program in tandem with the anti-Communist cultural propaganda campaign waged during the same period in Western Europe, it becomes clear that the Americans in all likelihood had far greater aspirations in Russia than official statements suggest.[2] In Europe, the CIA was secretly funding events that encouraged and promoted democratic values to help resist Communist infiltration. Meanwhile, in Russia, the U.S. State Department hoped that cultural exchanges would encourage change from within, by bringing capitalist thinking to Russian intellectuals via America's best and brightest.[3]

The first exchange of composers under the new agreement began with a thirty-day visit by Roy Harris, Ulysses Kay, Peter Mennin, and Roger Sessions to Russia, beginning on September 17, 1958. Before departing, the group was fully briefed by Americans who had previously visited the USSR and by a bevy of former officials from the American embassy in Moscow. The composers stayed together as a group, undertaking a tour that consisted primarily of concerts and receptions of a ceremonial nature. Visits to private homes were largely discouraged, although the composers did have some opportunities to interact with their Russian colleagues.[4] On his return, Roger Sessions called for further exchanges to help avert military conflict.[5]

On October 22, 1959, the corresponding Russian delegation arrived in New York. Five composers—Fikret Amirov, Kostyantyn Dankevych, Dmitry Kabalevsky, Tikhon Khrennikov, and Dmitry Shostakovich—were accompanied by the musicologist Boris Yarustovsky. This group was deliberately chosen to showcase the diversity of the Russian peoples, with representatives from a number of different republics. Touring New York, Washington, San Francisco, Los Angeles, Louisville, Philadelphia, Boston, and Chicago, they visited college campuses and attended concerts, movies, and receptions. As with the Americans in the USSR, the Soviet composers traveled as a group, a rule rigorously enforced. CBS's *Face the Nation* had planned an appearance by Shostakovich and Kabalevsky, which was canceled on very short notice by Khrennikov in his capacity as General Secretary of the Union of Soviet Composers. Khrennikov deemed that the network must interview the complete group or none at all, and the network opted for the latter.[6] Other signs of tension and controversy can be seen in *Aaron Copland Meets the Soviet Composers,* their only television interview during the visit, which was filmed on November 14 (Copland's birthday). Khrennikov voiced concerns about "the seductions of fashion trends" in composition that he believed were influencing American student composers, presumably referring to the predominance of serialism. On a separate occasion during the visit, Shostakovich was asked whether the Soviet Union had a hostile attitude toward American jazz. To this he replied, according to the *New York Times,* that he was not familiar with the "official position."[7] On his return to Russia, Khrennikov praised American composers and the exchange generally, but disparaged the prominence of the twin evils of jazz and serialism in America, thus clarifying the oblique criticisms he leveled in *Aaron Copland Meets the Soviet Composers.*[8]

Following the visit of the six Russians, two more Americans—Copland and Lukas Foss—were sent to the USSR, since the first American delegation had consisted of only four composers. They visited Moscow, Leningrad, and Riga in March and April of 1960. Copland recalled in his autobiography that before his departure for the USSR concerns remained about the validity of his passport: the McCarthy trauma was clearly still very present in his mind, even if apparently not overly troubling to government officials.[9] One can imagine that, by 1960, Copland's growing status as "Dean of American Music" was of greater importance to the State Department than the unproven claims of McCarthy. Furthermore, his involvement enabled them to demonstrate to the world America's growing tolerance of dissent, free speech, and "difference" (whether political or racial) following the discrediting of McCarthy and recent clashes over civil rights reform. By selecting as American cultural representatives figures such as the African-American Ulysses Kay and the left-leaning Copland, the State Department presented a clear message to the Russian people about the open-mindedness of a free society.[10]

Many questions remain, however, about Copland's motivations for involving himself in this exchange and about the exact nature of his interaction with the United States government on Soviet issues. *Aaron Copland Meets the Soviet Composers* points to some of these complexities, but nevertheless presents a fascinating snapshot of musical relations between the USSR and the West in 1959 and of cultural life under Soviet Socialist control. Despite outward courtesy among the participants, underlying tensions and differences of opinion are certainly apparent, although sometimes it is difficult to be sure whether the opinions of the Russians are their own or an official position. The program survives as a valuable illustration of the wide chasm of understanding that separated these two nations and their cultural representatives during this period.

Aaron Copland Meets the Soviet Composers

INTERVIEWERS: Aaron Copland (**AC**), Nicolas Slonimsky (**NS**).
GUESTS: Dmitry Shostakovich (**DS**), Tikhon Khrennikov (**TK**),[11] Dmitry Kabalevsky (**DK**),[12] Kostyantyn Dankevych (**KD**),[13] Fikret Amirov (**FA**),[14] Boris Yarustovsky (**BY**).[15]

The set is a mock concert hall stage, and the group sits in orchestra chairs. Placed in front of each is a music stand from which AC and NS read their questions. The extent to which the answers are scripted is unclear. The Russians appear to ad lib but do occasionally refer to their papers; on one occasion, for example, KD reads a list of names of young Russian composers. AC and NS ask their questions in English, and the Russians respond in Russian; all participants listen to a translator through an earpiece. The viewer hears a voice-over with a simultaneous English translation of the Russian statements—presumably the same translation heard by AC and NS. The Russian statements recorded below are therefore an exact transcription of the translator's speech and not my own translation of the Russian original. The translator's English is, owing to the "live" translation, not always entirely coherent or grammatically perfect. Finally, timings are inserted occasionally in brackets.

AC [standing away from the group and addressing the camera]: How do you do? I'm Aaron Copland. I'm very happy to have this opportunity to talk with six musician colleagues visiting from the Soviet Union. [Walks to seat next to **NS**] With me is my colleague the Russian-born American musicologist Nicolas Slonimsky. Nicolas, would you like to start the ball rolling by asking them the first question?

NS: Indeed. This question is addressed to Mr. Kabalevsky. What impression do you have about American music as you hear it in America and as you hear it in the Soviet Union? [On this occasion only, **NS** repeats his question in Russian.]

DK: To begin with, I should like to emphasize that we have been acquainted with American music well before we came here, of course, in various ways. Forty years ago, when I was studying music, we knew MacDowell from his piano works. Now the picture has changed. During the war there was a considerable change in that respect, and American music was performed in our country and Soviet musicians were better acquainted with American music. Especially in recent years our acquaintance with American music was developed, and this was promoted by the visits to the Soviet Union of the Boston, Philadelphia, and New York Philharmonic Orchestras. This was also promoted by the visit of the group of American composers. I could cite the names of numerous American composers who are well known in our country, not only by name but by their works. Gershwin, whose songs are very popular and whose magnificent opera *Porgy and Bess* was performed as early as the years of the war with success; I am thinking of Piston, I am thinking of Aaron Copland, I am thinking of Samuel Barber, [name unidentifiable],[16] Mennin,[17] Roy Harris, Sessions, Kay,[18] Leonard Bernstein and numerous other composers. We are very interested in a work, the opera [name unidentifiable].[19] A considerable group of composers in the United States may be regarded as very varied in their individualities. They all of course have a serious attitude to musical composition; they are remote from external fashion trends, and of course we are profoundly sympathetic to the creative endeavors of this group of composers and we would like to think that the same serious attitude to art will be developed among young composers in the United States. I venture to make that point because we have listened to the work of some younger composers here in universities and colleges, and it seemed to us occasionally that the very young composers have an insufficient care to avoid the seductions of fashion trends which are liable to divert the young from serious paths of art, the paths which their teachers and elder colleagues have been treading.[20] This is our impression: our general impression is a good one, and we are happy to have expanded our acquaintance with American music.

[4:48] **AC**: Thank you Mr. Kabalevsky. I'm very pleased to see that American music is not at all a new thing for you. Now I'd like to address a question to the musicologist and historian among the group of visitors, Mr. Yarustovsky. Tell us—we know, after all, that American novelists are much read and perhaps have some influence in the Soviet

Union. What about American music? Can you . . . do you think American music may have some influence on Soviet music?

BY: This is an interesting question. It seems to me that the mutual influence . . . the mutual fertilization of musical cultures is an important condition of the progress of universal musical culture. All the more intolerable would the isolation of national cultures be these days [*sic*]. The deeper the national roots of any musical culture, the clearer and the more fertile its influence on general musical progress. It is a happy coincidence that our coming to the United States coincided with a Jubilee: 100 years ago, the foot of the first Russian musician stepped on American soil—Yuri Golitzin.[21] Shortly after the arrival of this Russian Columbus to America, Anton Rubinstein—the first Russian composer—visited the United States.[22] Among the works he performed here were piano transformations of American melodies such as "Yankee Doodle." And when he came back to Russia he had great success in performing these American melodies in his own transcription before Russian audiences. I think this was the first time when American musical culture became known on Russian soil, and since that time no oceans have been able to sunder our cultures. All the time they continued to influence each other and to act upon each other. How about contemporary times? My colleague Dmitry Kabalevsky spoke good and truthful words about American composers and about how, especially recently, our influence from (and impressions from) American culture became deeper and better. The sensitive ear of the composer isn't just the membrane which hears the compositions. It harkens to them, it absorbs them, like a sponge for his own needs. And then this is recreated in his own compositions, willingly or otherwise. It is my impression . . . it is possible—perhaps controversial—that this influence was heard in the works of Aram Khachaturian, some of the works. I am not speaking of course of popular culture, I am thinking of my six-year-old son, who cannot be regarded as a representative of Soviet musical culture, but the American song "Mississippi" happens to be this six-year-old's favorite song. Soviet composers have been transcribing a good deal of American melodies, for example there is [name unidentifiable]'s great collection of American songs.[23] The same goes for light music: the rhythms of American light music have commanded great popularity in our country. The youth like that a lot—I am speaking of American good light music, which we have always listened to with great pleasure as performed by various ensembles.

[9:09] **AC**: Thank you Mr. Yarustovsky. Now, Mr. Khrennikov, we would like to know very much, what was the reaction toward the music and the personalities of the group of four American composers who visited the Soviet Union just about a year ago?

TK: We were very happy when our American colleagues visited our soil. I am thinking of composers Mennin, Sessions, Harris, Kay. These American composers visited a number of Soviet cities, they were given the opportunity of becoming acquainted with the work of Soviet musical institutions, they visited theaters and concert halls. In Moscow there was a large, great concert in which the works of American composers were performed.[24] Now, this concert of American music had tremendous success among Moscow listeners. The visit of American composers to the Soviet Union promoted the establishment of closer and friendlier contacts between American and Soviet composers, and I should like to express the hope that the visits of American composers to the Soviet Union, and of Soviet composers to America, will in the future proliferate.

AC: Thank you so much. Mr. Shostakovich—you know that we hear in our country a great deal of jazz. What about jazz in the Soviet Union, and how do you feel about its possible symphonic use?

[Pause—interjection in Russian on voice-over. Then, awkwardly, **NS** interjects before **DS** replies. **AC** seems nervous.]

NS: I should like to add that Aaron Copland himself produced quite a shock thirty-two years ago here when he played his celebrated so-called "Jazz Concerto" with the Boston Symphony Orchestra.

DS: I have a favorable attitude to good American jazz. Now, what is the meaning of "good American jazz?" Good jazz is the kind of jazz which executes well [*sic*] good music. As has been said, Aaron Copland, our prominent American colleague, has felt jazz influences, having written a jazz concerto. Also there is the prominent opera of Gershwin, a genius of an American composer, who wrote *Porgy and Bess*. This also shows jazz influence. It seems to me that good jazz music will continue to exert influence on the creativeness of American composers and Soviet composers and on the composers of other countries as well.

AC: Thank you Mr. Shostakovich. Mr. Dankevych: You know that I am very interested in the younger generation, both of my own country and in other countries. We would like to know who you think of as the most important members of the younger Soviet composers, and what they're writing, and why we don't hear their work in the United States more than we do.

KD: The great October Socialist Revolution gave freedom and self-determination to all the peoples of our great fatherland and created especially . . . exceptionally favorable conditions for the flowering of the culture and art of these peoples. The young, talented, gifted tribe in all fraternal republics of the Soviet Union, including the field of musical culture, is developing, is growing, and is gathering strength. The young, talented colleagues of ours are creating music in all genres of musical work: opera, ballet, symphonic creation, chamber music, choral music, songs, moving pictures, musical comedies. I must add that our talented composers, if they were to be listed, this would take a good deal of time. But since I was asked this courteous question by you, and since I am enjoying your hospitality, I should like to cite some names [reads from a paper on music stand]: Eshpay,[25] Shchedrin,[26] Andrei Volkonsky,[27] Andrei Petrov.[28] In the Ukraine: Kiraiko Shurovsky.[29] In Armenia: Jivan Ter-Tatevosian.[30] In Georgia: Taktakishvili,[31] Tsintsadze.[32] In Estonia: Tamberg.[33] In Lithuania: Balsys.[34] Burkhanov in Uzbekistan.[35] [Name unidentifiable],[36] [name unidentifiable] in Azerbaijan.[37] Now, this is a spring garden of young talent and you are quite right my dear colleague, Aaron Copland, that in America you have known the music of our younger talented composers much too little. We, the delegation of Soviet composers, are merely the first swallows from beyond the ocean. Of course I . . . it is difficult to call me personally a swallow, but I am confident that we will be followed by flights of younger Soviet composers from all the fraternal republics of our fatherland. They will follow us to this land and this will be the harbinger of the happy comradeship of the cultures of our two great countries in the musical realm.

[15:50] **AC**: I am very glad to hear you say that, Mr. Dankevych, because I too believe it is just as important to have the less well-known composers, both from the United States go to your country and to have return visits on that level of the younger people also. Nicolas, haven't you a question perhaps?

NS: Well, I should like to ask this question of Mr. Amirov. How can native materials be transposed into serious, symphonic and other music?

FA: As you are aware, utilization of popular folklore by professional composers has a worldwide history of its own. The Russian classics: Glinka; Rimsky-Korsakov; Tchaikovsky. Our Azerbaijanian classics: Hajibeyov[38]; Glière (the Russian composer) has lived and worked in Azerbaijan and has done a good deal for Azerbaijanian musical culture.[39] Their compositions have demonstrated not just the possibility but even the interesting potentialities of popular music when transformed into general European forms—I am thinking of operas, symphonies, quartets, etc. I am thinking of [the] year before last when I visited Egypt and Syria and I noted with what pleasure the Arabs named the name of Rimsky-Korsakov. And in Arab lands Rimsky-Korsakov is the most popular of all composers, of all Russian composers, especially because of his *Sheherazade*, of course. They spoke of him with great pleasure and admiration. He [they?] said that he did a great deal for Arab musical culture and he pointed the way to Arab composers. You may perhaps be interested in the fact that yesterday and today *mugam* was . . . will be performed . . . it has been performed.[40] Now, mugam is highly developed popular music as a genre and as a form. It is homophonic, essentially, but since a symphony orchestra was to perform it I sought to make it possible for a contemporary symphony orchestra to perform it in a manner which would be appropriate. I am thinking of Glinka's words, who said that music is composed by the people. We, the composers, merely arrange it. So perhaps it is proper to recall that I am utilizing Azerbaijan folklore. I play the *tar*, an Azerbaijani instrument, and I continue to do so. Love and admiration for popular music, which in my case means Azerbaijani music, of course, have made it possible for me to absorb and be filled with that music and, in turn, to yield it in my compositions. I think that we, the Soviet composers, are obliged not only to support but to develop this so generous form of musical creation.

[19:59] **AC**: Mr. Amirov: We are very glad that you came with the delegation because one thing is certain. In the United States, we simply do not know enough about the other parts of the Soviet Union where I am sure there are many very gifted, younger composers working in a folk idiom which itself is not sufficiently well-known here. Now, Nicolas, you are a musicologist—we have a musicologist here. Wouldn't you like to ask him some specific question on that subject?

NS: Yes. I should like to ask Mr. Yarustovsky this question. In the United States musicologists usually concentrate their labors on the music of the past. Now, is the same true in the Soviet Union, or is contemporary music given also consideration?

BY: Well, speaking of our sins, of course there is no shortage in the Soviet Union either of musicologists who are cabinet rats, but of course the time of the ivory tower science has passed. One cannot in fact understand the problems of the past without feeling the pulse of contemporary life. One cannot correctly understand numerous events of the contemporary scene without, for example, being acquainted with the whole history and background of musical culture. Now, in this connection I should like to add the following: It seems to me that the question asked can be solved by way of the correct education of young musicologists. In the Moscow Conservatory where I teach, in addition to an academic course where student musicologists are acquainted with contemporary musical culture in the Soviet Union in the past, in addition to that there are a number of, it seems to me, interesting factors which make it easier to bring musicologists closer to the contemporary scene. For example, there is the Student Scientific Society in our conservatory which periodically listens to contemporary music, both Soviet and Western, I repeat. At meetings of this student society, young musicologists present papers or written reports devoted to individual problems of contemporary musical creation. Moreover, our newspapers and periodicals act correctly when senior student musicologists are drawn into that work and asked to discuss contemporary music. This type of education, which makes it possible to interest musicologists in contemporary music and musical problems, this type of education I see as an important factor in resolving the sort of problem which you so interestingly and so aptly raised.

[23:19] **AC**: Thank you sir. We have only about four minutes left. Mr. Shostakovich, you know, I am sure, how very popular your music is in our country. Tell me—do you feel that your music is well understood here? Do you think there is any difference in the way it is understood here from the way it is understood in the Soviet Union?

DS: For me it is a great joy that my music is performed before audiences in the United States of America. It seems to me that if it is performed it stands to reason that it is understood by the audiences. I do not think that the question of the distinction between the understanding of my music in the Soviet Union and the United States is not apt. Quite the contrary, my music is of course heard and played a good deal in the Soviet Union and, please don't misunderstand me, but occasionally it does enjoy considerable success in the Soviet Union. Therefore that too can only occasion joy on my part.

[24:59] **AC**: Thank you. And as a final question in this too-brief séance we have together . . . Mr. Khrennikov, how do you feel that Soviet-American exchange in music can be encouraged still further?

TK: The present cultural agreement between the United States of America and the Soviet Union has made it possible to institute closer and more friendly relations between those active in culture and music in our countries. Over the past year and a half or two, this cultural exchange has been intensified. Musical ensembles and soloists have come to the Soviet Union: Soviet artistic groups—musicians, soloists—have come to the United States. I should like to express the hope on this occasion that the conclusion of subsequent cultural agreements will provide for an abiding expansion and intensification of our contacts and mutual visits. This is our common desire; surely, it is common ground between musical leaders and musicians in the United States and those of the Soviet Union.

AC: Thank you very much, Mr. Khrennikov. I wish there were more time so that we could continue with this discussion. There are obviously many questions we would like to ask you. We have many different kinds of curiosities concerning musical culture in your country, and we would also like to tell you about all the different phases of music in America, including some young composers who do not [laughing] write in the most advanced forms and whose music I feel sure you would find sympathetic. Thank you so much, Nicolas, for having helped us here with your Russian background and your good collegial feeling. [Stands up and walks to camera; speaks to camera] I hope that you've enjoyed as much as I have this brief yet unique meeting with these distinguished musicians from the Soviet Union. I want again to thank Mr. Slonimsky and I am glad that we have had this opportunity to share with you a portion of the experience of this important musical-cultural exchange.

NOTES

1. These are described in Howard Pollack, *Aaron Copland: The Life and Work of an Uncommon Man* (New York: Henry Holt, 1999), pp. 270–84.

2. The CIA's secret Cold War cultural propaganda program has been explored in Peter Coleman, *The Liberal Conspiracy: Cultural Freedom and the Struggle for the Mind of Postwar Europe* (New York: The Free Press; London: Collier Macmillan, 1989) and Frances Stonor Saunders, *Who Paid the Piper? The Cultural Cold War: The CIA and the World of Arts and Letters* (New York: The New Press, 1999).

3. For more information on American-Soviet cultural exchange see Yale Richmond, *Cultural Exchange and the Cold War: Raising the Iron Curtain* (University Park, Penn.: Pennsylvania State University Press, 2003). It is Richmond's thesis that Soviet-American cultural exchanges played a greater role in bringing down Communism in Russia and ending the Cold War than is generally recognized and that, in this way, they were far more successful than the State Department could ever have hoped.

4. Howard Taubman, "Exchange in Depth: Meetings with Russians on the Basic Issues," *New York Times,* November 22, 1959.

5. (Author unknown), "Music Exchanges with Reds Urged: Sessions, Back From Tour, Says Free Communication Could Avert Conflict," *New York Times*, November 2, 1958. Roger Sessions had also been outspoken on political issues and the ways in which music and musicians could positively impact on society. During World War II he frequently voiced his opinions on such issues in *Modern Music*. See, for example, "On the American Future," *Modern Music* 17, no. 2 (1940): 71–75; "American Music and the Crisis," *Modern Music* 18, no. 4 (1941): 211–17; and "Artists and This War," *Modern Music* 10, no. 1 (1942): 3–7.

6. According to one American report, Khrennikov "has been known to have prevented composers [in Russia] from talking freely with American music critics visiting the Soviet Union." Val Adams, "Soviet Composers Off Radio and TV: 'Face the Nation' Withdraws Its Invitation for Sunday to Shostakovich, Kabalevsky," *New York Times*, November 5, 1959.

7. (Author unknown), "Amity Is Voiced by Shostakovich: Soviet Composer, on Visit to U.S., Praises American People and Musicians," *New York Times*, October 25, 1959.

8. These criticisms were voiced in Khrennikov and Shostakovich's report on their trip published in *Pravda*, discussed in (author unknown), "Soviet Composers Describe U.S. Trip: Report in Pravda Praises Some Musicians but Scores [*sic*] Twelve-Tone Technique," *New York Times,* December 18, 1959.

9. See Aaron Copland and Vivian Perlis, *Copland Since 1943* (New York: St. Martin's Press, 1989), p. 283.

10. See Mary L. Dudziak, *Cold War Civil Rights: Race and the Image of American Democracy* (Princeton, N.J. / Oxford, Eng.: Princeton University Press, 2000). Many thanks to Jessica Gienow-Hecht for drawing my attention to this line of argument.

11. As Secretary of the Union of Composers from 1948, Tikhon Khrennikov (b. 1913) was responsible for enforcing Soviet policy on musical composition, a position which allowed him to criticize composers such as Prokofiev and Shostakovich. He wrote revolutionary operas as well as absolute music in a traditional, folk-inspired style and was also a successful virtuoso pianist. NOTE: This, and subsequent biographic information is based on articles from *Grove Music Online,* ed. L. Macy (accessed June 20, 2004), http://www.grovemusic.com, and *Baker's Biographical Dictionary of Musicians,* ed. Nicolas Slonimsky and Laura Kuhn (New York: Schirmer, 2001). Transliteration of names is also based on these sources.

12. Dmitry Kabalevsky (1904–1987) was employed by the Moscow Conservatory from 1932 and, although he composed operas, film music, and instrumental and vocal works, his principal successes were with music for children and musical education, through which he indulged his preference for a diatonic language.

13. Kostyantyn Dankevych (1905–1984), a Ukrainian composer, is chiefly known for his operas, which were composed in the Socialist Realist style on Ukrainian themes. His most famous opera, *Bohdan Khmelnytsky,* was criticized as overly nationalistic, but was universally acclaimed in its revised edition. His music shows the influence of Mussorgsky and Khachaturian.

14. Fikret Amirov (1922–1984) was an Azerbaijani composer, the son of a celebrated *tar* player and singer, and most famous for his works based on the folk *mugam* form, which combined Azerbaijani traditional music with Russian and European art music models.

15. Boris Yarustovsky (1911–1978) was a musicologist at the Moscow Conservatory from 1949 who focused largely on the music of Tchaikovsky. His writings attempted to appraise musical works within the context of socialist aesthetics and ideology. A member of the Union of Composers, Yarustovsky later became its secretary and also held important positions at UNESCO from the 1960s onward.

16. Name spoken by translator sounds like "Kirsten."

17. Peter Mennin.

18. Ulysses Kay.

19. Word spoken by translator sounds like "Robinson." The American composer Reginald De Koven's 1891 opera *Robin Hood* is the only possibility I could identify, although this seems unlikely, given its date.

20. It seems likely that Kabalevsky is here referring to the "fashion" of serialism.

21. Yuri Golitzin (1823–1872), Russian conductor and composer, organized tours of various countries with his choir and orchestra.

22. Anton Rubinstein (1829–1894), celebrated Russian pianist, conductor, and composer, made a tour of America in 1872–73, playing 215 concerts.

23. Name spoken by translator sounds like "Kavalya."

24. Concert on October 15, 1958: The Radio Symphony Orchestra played Kay's *Of New Horizons: Overture for Orchestra,* Sessions's *The Black Maskers,* Mennin's Sixth Symphony, and Roy Harris conducted his Fifth Symphony. See *New York Times,* October 16, 1958.

25. Andrey Eshpay (b. 1925). A student in composition at the Moscow Conservatory who later held many important administrative positions in composers' unions. His music includes a variety of genres, including many film scores.

26. Rodion Shchedrin (b. 1932). Important composer and academic in twentieth-century Russia. His music combines serial and avant-garde techniques with elements from Russian folk music. Especially important for his ballets and operas on Russian themes.

27. Volkonsky (b. 1933) was a harpsichordist, conductor, and composer. He trained in composition in Moscow, but was outspoken in his criticism of the direction Soviet music was taking and was expelled from the country in the 1970s.

28. Petrov (b. 1930) was a Communist Party member who wrote music in the Socialist Realist model, generally optimistic and energetic in style.

29. I was unable to obtain biographical information for Shurovsky.

30. Ter-Tatevosian (1926–1988) was an Armenian composer and violinist. His music combined national traditions with new techniques.

31. Otar Taktakishvili (1924–1989) was a composer and teacher who worked at the Tbilisi Conservatory in Georgia.

32. Sulkhan Tsintsadze (1925–1991) was a Georgian composer and teacher. In his string quartets he combined Georgian folk music with twentieth-century techniques.

33. Eino Tamberg (b. 1930): Estonian composer and pedagogue. His most important works are his symphonies, which utilize extended tonality and free atonality.

34. Eduardas Balsys (1919–1984) was a Lithuanian composer and teacher, and chairman of the composition department of the Lithuanian Conservatory. His music used classical forms while experimenting with some modern techniques.

35. Mutal Burkhanov (b. 1916) is an Uzbek composer who has written mainly choral works combining Uzbek monophony with Western polyphony, including the Uzbek Republic national anthem.

36. Name spoken by translator sounds like "Inmirnaseeva."

37. Name spoken by translator sounds like "Indra Nasayev."

38. Sultan Hajibeyov, or Gadzhibekov (1919–1974) was an Azerbaijani composer, conductor, and professor in composition at Azerbaijan State Conservatory. He wrote much music on Azerbaijani themes, but also utilized the folk material of other peoples.

39. Reinhold Glière (ca. 1875–1956) was a prolific Russian composer and pedagogue, principally employed at the Moscow Conservatory, who worked within the Russian national style.

40. See note 14.

PART VI

COPLAND AND HIS PUBLIC

Aaron Copland and the Composers'

Forum-Laboratory:

A Post-Concert Discussion, February 24, 1937

TRANSCRIBED AND INTRODUCED
BY MELISSA DE GRAAF

The New York City Composers' Forum, a series of weekly concerts of contemporary music, was established in 1935 under the auspices of the Federal Music Project (FMP) and Works Progress Administration (WPA). One of the New Deal's most successful endeavors, it showcased such diverse composers as Aaron Copland, Amy Beach, Henry Cowell, Ruth Crawford, Virgil Thomson, and Paul Hindemith.

Ashley Pettis, director of Social Music Education for the FMP, presented the idea of an American Composers' Forum to the FMP's director, Nicolai Sokoloff, in September of 1935. Inspired by a recent tour of the Soviet Union, Pettis visualized the Forum as a teaching tool for building a new educated audience. As music editor for the Communist weekly *New Masses,* as well as a pianist and composer, Pettis fervently believed in the use of music as a weapon in the class struggle, and sought a closer relationship between composer and audience.[1] Pettis and Copland had connected the previous year, when Copland won a competition sponsored by *New Masses* for a workers' song set to Alfred Hayes's poem, "Into the Streets May First," and Pettis wrote an article discussing Copland's setting.[2]

At the opening concert of the Forum, Pettis declared the goal of the entire endeavor:

> Not only are we interested in the composer and his work, per se, but in the development of a more definite understanding and relationship between the composer and the public. . . . We are hoping that through these evenings in intimate contact with composers, we may

do our part in removing the barrier which has always existed between the composer and the people who are or should be the consumers of his goods.[3]

The most immediate goal, however, from the composers' and musicians' points of view, was earning a living. Thousands of artists, painters, writers, and musicians subsisted on government handouts, alongside seamstresses, plumbers, and steelworkers. Rather than put them to work in fields outside their talents, Roosevelt in 1935 approved the creation of the Federal Arts Projects, including the Federal Theater Project, Federal Writers' Project, Federal Art Project, and Federal Music Project. These were intended not only to provide work for suffering artists but also to educate, at little or no cost, a new audience receptive to modern ideas.

Typically, composers interested in participating in the Forum submitted works to a selection committee, which included Pettis, Copland, and Edgard Varèse.[4] At first, the Forum presented one composer each week, but toward the end of the initial season, two composers shared each program. The concerts in following seasons continued to highlight two, sometimes three, composers. Concerts during the first season were held at the Federal Music Building at 110 West Forty-eighth Street, but growing audiences demanded that new quarters be found. On January 27, 1937, the new Theatre of Music opened at 254 West Fifty-fourth Street, which seated 1,200 people, 800 more than the Forty-eighth Street venue.[5] Nearly every session that season had a capacity audience.

At the beginning of each concert, Pettis introduced the composer or composers. Programs included slips of paper on which listeners could write questions and comments during the performance. Afterward, the audience passed forward their questions. Pettis, acting as intermediary, read the questions and comments to which the composers responded to the best of their ability.[6]

Although there were some concerts of orchestral music, the majority featured works for chamber groups or solo instruments.[7] In the first five seasons a total of 244 composers took part in 141 concerts. Performers were paid for their services, but composers were not. While the FMP acknowledged the difficulties that musicians faced and managed to provide jobs for thousands of performers, conductors, and teachers, they gave no direct financial assistance to composers. It was the one area in which the Composers' Forum and FMP truly fell short.

The New York Composers' Forum, more than other parallel local venues around the country, brought together the most disparate, conflicting set of people imaginable. The audience often included composers and performers, society types, music critics and journalists, artists and dancers, and even people off the streets.[8] Lehman Engel's concert attracted an impressive roster of luminaries, not only fellow composers and musicians, but also playwrights, poets, dancers, and patrons of music, including Martha Graham, e. e. cummings, the actress Mary Morris, and publisher W. W. Norton.[9]

The FMP administration's extremely generous attitude toward the audience was not always shared by composers. An official press release described the atmosphere of the forums as "delightfully friendly and informal" with a "large, intelligent, and appreciative" audience.[10] By contrast, Elliott Carter recalled the "pitiless questioning of the audience."[11] Olin Downes, of the *New York Times,* mentioned at various times the "frank and brutal treatment" composers were subjected to, and another *New York Times* writer described the "tussles between the prosecuting listener and the helpless defendant composer" in "Composers on the Grill."[12] No composers were exempt; audiences liberally attacked modernists and traditionalists, socialists and conservatives. Transcripts of these sessions survive nearly complete in the National Archives II, College Park, Maryland, representing an incredibly rich source of information about a time in American musical life that remains underexplored. Brief but valuable discussions of the Composers' Forum can be found in Barbara Zuck's *A History of Musical Americanism* and Cornelius Canon's *The Federal Music Project of the Works Progress Administration.*[13]

The success of the New York City Composers' Forum prompted cities across the country to institute similar programs. Boston and Philadelphia established highly flourishing forums that met weekly. Forums in Los Angeles and Chicago were only slightly less active, and Detroit, Cleveland, Milwaukee, Minneapolis, and San Francisco also held forums from time to time. Other activities by the New York branch included a collaboration with Lincoln Kirstein's Ballet Caravan to present an evening of "All-American" ballets, with music by Virgil Thomson, Robert McBride, and Paul Bowles. A special summer season of concerts, produced in conjunction with the 1939 World's Fair, was broadcast over WNYC, and a series of the regular concerts was broadcast over WQXR. Under the auspices of the Forum, Roy Harris presented a lecture series entitled "Let's Make Music" over WNYC, which attracted thousands of active listeners. After 1939, federal support for the forums ceased and various organizations assumed responsibility for maintaining the Forum, which exists to this day.[14]

On February 24, 1937, Aaron Copland appeared in the Composers' Forum in a rare evening of orchestral music, performed by the Municipal

Symphony Orchestra, with the composer conducting. On the program were his Two Pieces for String Orchestra, Lento Molto (1928) and Rondino (1923); the First Symphony (1924); and the Suite from his ballet *Hear Ye! Hear Ye!* (1934).[15] Also on the program, though not heard that evening, was the *Cortège Macabre*, from Copland's early ballet *Grohg* (1922–25, revised 1932). *Cortège* was not performed, for reasons unknown.

This performance of the Suite from *Hear Ye! Hear Ye!* marked the only time the ballet was heard in this form. Copland apparently created the Suite specifically for this occasion but decided to withdraw it, believing the music should not be performed independently from the choreography. The Suite score is presumed lost; scores of the original ballet exist, but have never been published.[16] Copland recycled one section for Blues No. 2 from *Four Piano Blues*. The Forum program included notes for the Suite, presumably written by Copland.

While not yet the American icon he would later become, by 1937 Copland was already well-known in New York City. In addition to teaching appointments at the New School for Social Research and the Henry Street Settlement, he was active in New York's League of Composers, often writing for its journal, *Modern Music*, as well as for *New Masses, Music Vanguard*, and other magazines and newspapers. His Copland-Sessions Concerts (1928–31) and Yaddo Festivals (1932–33) had been well received by critics and the public and, with his founding of the Young Composers' Group in 1932, won him recognition as a prominent spokesperson for American composers.

Copland received an enthusiastic welcome from the Composers' Forum audience and director, Ashley Pettis, and a lively question-and-answer session followed the concert. Such a warm reception was unusual for Forum composers, since the audience rarely hesitated to voice their dislikes. Although Copland expressed reluctance to discuss his music ("I'd much rather go home"), he nevertheless seems to have enjoyed engaging in a dialogue with the listeners and had much to say on the topics of modernism, jazz, the relationship between music and society, and the direction in which American music was heading.

Audiences routinely offered a critique of modernism at Forum concerts, with a split between those who criticized modernist composers for being too dissonant and those who attacked more traditional composers for writing music that failed to reflect the times. Though not criticized as harshly as Ruth Crawford or Johanna Beyer had been, Copland nevertheless found himself justifying his use of dissonance (see Questions 2 and 4 below) and failure to contribute to one listener's "evening relaxation" (Question 7).[17] Copland responded passionately that his music was not written to lull listeners into complacency, but rather was intended for those who desired to be "stirred and interested and awakened." Almost one-third of the total of thirty questions reflected the audience's resistance to the new modernist aesthetic. Copland himself remarked on the sense of "release" he felt to know that experimentation "did not seem any longer necessary" (see the second Question 20).[18]

Six questions about Copland's views on jazz prompted his most fasci-nating responses. Jazz was a frequent topic of discussion at Forum events, sparking debate over its use in concert hall music. Jazz's detractors saw signs of a degeneration of American culture, a disease affecting the ner-vous system. Many people considered "jazzing the classics"—as Forum composer Henry Brant had done—tantamount to sacrilege.[19] Composers such as Brant and Robert McBride fervently defended their continued use of jazz in Forum sessions.[20] Copland, on the other hand, expressed increasing ambivalence about jazz in his compositions, disavowing any use of jazz after 1928. He had considered it fruitful at one time, but as "a basis of serious composition" it would not "be so interesting anymore." The audience greeted his statement with a round of applause. Just a few years later, in *The New Music*, he expanded on this idea, recognizing the "severe limitations" of the two jazz "moods" (the "blues" mood and the "wild, aban-doned, almost hysterical and grotesque mood"). However, he also acknowledged the "wider implications" of the technical procedures of jazz.[21] By using the terms "hysterical and grotesque," Copland reflected the widely held view of jazz as "nerve music."[22]

At the center of the jazz controversy stood a figure with a strong pres-ence at Copland's Forum session—George Gershwin. Still alive at the time of the event, Gershwin died a few months later at thirty-nine from a brain tumor. Copland's comments on *Rhapsody in Blue* (Question 10) sug-gest Gershwin's influence on his own music, particularly the jazz-inspired *Music for the Theatre* (1925) and the Piano Concerto (1926). Yet, forced into making a direct comparison between himself and Gershwin, he betrayed dissatisfaction with Gershwin's music: "Gershwin is serious up to a point. My idea was to intensify it. Not what you get in the dance hall but to use it cubistically—to make it more exciting than ordinary jazz."[23]

Copland's use of the term "cubistic" deserves special comment. Borrowed from modernist revolutions in painting and associated with Picasso and Braque in the 1910s and twenties, the usage shows Copland's awareness of revolutionary painting techniques and his sense of affinity with them.[24] This may be the first time Copland used the cubistic metaphor; it would not be the last. From other comments Copland made about Cubism in following years, it becomes clear that this analogy applied to his and other composers' music in two distinct ways. The simultaneity of motifs in the juxtaposition of vaudeville melodies, Tin Pan Alley tunes, and stripper music in *Music for the Theatre* (1925) was one way Copland defined musical cubism.[25] His use of the term in the Forum, however, refers to polyrhythms, the element of jazz that had the most profound impact on Copland's aesthetic. In his well-known article on jazz for *Modern Music*, he declared, "The peculiar excitement they [polyrhythms] produce by clashing two definitely and regularly marked rhythms is unprecedented in occidental music. Its polyrhythm is the real contribution of jazz."[26] Copland undoubtedly referred to "the peculiar excitement" of polyrhythms when he made his cubistic comment in the Forum.[27]

Jazz was not the only controversial topic in the Forum. Audiences tended to be more left-wing than many of the composers, resulting in frequent and heated political discussions. Eight questions in Copland's Forum session reflect the tumultuous times of political ferment and Depression-era social consciousness. Copland's emphatic negative responses to questions such as, "Is it necessary for a composer to actively participate in political activity?" (Question 23) testify to his ambivalent relationship to politics.[28] A commitment to accessibility and relevance—elements inherent in Popular Front ideology—mark Copland's responses in the Forum. Stating that "all music that is any good has social significance" (Question 26), Copland nevertheless believed the most important direction in American music was "to get closer to the audience" (Question 20d). His new objective was "to write something that is simple, yet very good" (Question 20e).[29]

Questions about modernism and jazz were pervasive in the Forum, but Copland's status as an oracle of his time distinguished his experience from that of most other composers. Only composers perceived as leaders in the arts were expected to voice the character of American music on a grand scale.[30] Copland proclaimed, "The characteristics of American music are now in the making . . . one can already see a certain vigor and a certain rhythmic impulse which are recognizably American" (Question 28). Many of the remaining questions concerned general and detailed questions about Copland's music.

The following is a word-for-word transcript of Copland's discussion session at the Forum, as recorded by a stenographer.[31] Slight typographical errors are corrected silently.

Copland at the Composers' Forum:
Transcript of Post-Concert Discussion

On February 24th, 1937, at 8:35 P.M., Aaron Copland was the 21st composer to appear in the Second Series of the Composers' Forum-Laboratory, in the WPA Theatre of Music. A most distinguished audience numbering approximately 750 was present.[32]

ASHLEY PETTIS: It would be superfluous to speak at length concerning Mr. Aaron Copland. I wish merely to say that we are highly honored—that is, both the Federal Music Project and the Composers' Forum-Laboratory, to have Mr. Copland with us tonight. I shall permit Mr. Copland, both with his music and in the Forum to speak for himself.

To those unfamiliar with our procedure, I wish to say that the Forum follows immediately upon the conclusion of the program. Will you please keep your seats!

You will find slips in your programs, on which to write questions which will be answered by Mr. Copland immediately following the performance.

I have to announce that the "Cortege Macabre" is to be eliminated. There will be a short intermission after the third programmed number following the "Suite," which should read from "Hear ye! Hear ye!" Mr. Copland says his handwriting was responsible for the mistake.

[Concert Follows]

Prior to Forum Discussion:

ASHLEY PETTIS: The ushers will pass through the Auditorium for your questions. Will you please pass them forward at once?

The composer joins Ashley Pettis and says: "I'd much rather go home." To the audience he says: "This is not my idea. It is Mr. Pettis's." (laughter and amusement)

FORUM DISCUSSION

1. QUESTION: *Do you consider jazz a contribution to the development of modern music?*

ANSWER: The answer is "yes"!

2. QUESTION: *I like your kind of music. But how can the pedants in the audience tell when a player makes a mistake or plays badly? In old music, mistakes cause dissonance. In dissonant music, errors are indistinguishable. (laughter)*

ANSWER: Well! the answer is: "The melody is there for those who can hear it." (bravos from the audience) If you don't believe it, look at the score.

3. QUESTION: *How many symphonies did you write?*

ANSWER: Well, I have written only one that is called a "Symphony" but actually, I have written three. The other two besides the one you heard tonight are called "Dance Symphony" and "Symphonic Ode." They have symphonic proportions. (From the audience someone proffers: "A short symphony." Composer says: "Thank you.")

4. QUESTION: *Will you please explain what kind of chords you use in your compositions? Why do you use so many dissonances? Why did you write a jazz concerto? (Composer consults the question slip.)*

ANSWER: About the chords I use—too technical a question for a Forum. Dissonance? Well, I hear it that way. Why did I write a jazz concerto? Because I thought writing a piece based on jazz, at one time at any rate, was a very interesting thing to do. I am not sure that it would be so interesting anymore. (applause)

5. QUESTION: *In your estimation what are the outstanding contributions of American composers to serious music (excepting Africo-American [sic] and native Indian material); that is, in reference to new musical forms and distinctive rhythmic and harmonic conceptions?*

ANSWER: I'll write a book on that. (laughter and applause)[33]

6. QUESTION: *What do you think about Schoenberg?*

ANSWER: That has nothing to do with my compositions. (Turns to Ashley Pettis: "I don't have to answer that, do I?" Assured that he doesn't, Mr. Copland continues speaking to the audience.) I'm only being asked questions about my own music.[34]

7. **QUESTION:** *I have just had a hard working day. Your music does not contribute to my evening relaxation. Is that my fault? (uproarious laughter)*

   ANSWER: Well! It's your fault and it isn't your fault! It's your fault if you came here in order to be lured away into some far-off land, which my music isn't about, but if you came here in order to be stirred and interested and awakened, then I hope my music does that. (applause)

8. **QUESTION:** *Do you feel the chamber music compositions of yours which have been recorded adequately represent you as a creative artist?*

   ANSWER: Well, there has been only one thing recorded and only one chamber music work—and that represents 1929. Just one little thing.[35]

9. **QUESTION:** *I notice you have some short piano compositions. "A Cat and a Mouse" is one, I believe. About what grade is this and have you any third or fourth grade, so called? Do they lend themselves for teaching purposes?*

   ANSWER: Well, for the information of the person who asked that question: "The Cat and Mouse" is fairly well advanced pianistically but I have written two pieces especially designed for teaching purposes, and they are in a book of 30 compositions by various American composers. It's published by Carl Fischer, if you are interested.[36]

10. **QUESTION:** *What is the aesthetic value of jazz? Do you still find the Broadway product the legitimate basis for art forms—or the possible basis for an indigenous "American" culture?*

    ANSWER: That's an interesting question. Apparently that is troubling several people. My only relation to jazz finished in 1928. I feel I did all I could with it as a basis for serious composition when I had written my piano concerto. If anyone thinks he can use it interestingly, well and good! I used it when the "Rhapsody in Blue" was new. Since then it has become popular, and used by people here and abroad. However, it is not as fresh as when it was first played.

11. QUESTION: *Do you consider your later compositions a direct and rational evolution of your early work?*

ANSWER: I hope so!

12. QUESTION: *Why all the stormy music?*

ANSWER: Why not? (applause and laughter)

13. QUESTION: *I notice that occasionally the resolution of a note is given an octave above or below the normal position. What is the reason for the displacement and what effect is it intended to achieve?*

ANSWER: Too technical!

14. QUESTION: *Your music seems drenched in jazz. How do you compare it to Mr. Gershwin's jazz? And what do you think of his larger items? (Porgy and Bess, for instance)*

ANSWER: Well, the interesting part of your question is: "How do you compare to Gershwin?" I don't really know how it compares but I think I know how it compares with mine. Gershwin is serious up to a point. My idea was to intensify it. Not what you get in the dance hall but to use it cubistically—to make it more exciting than ordinary jazz. I have been interested in the new "swing" music where the musicians "let themselves go" a bit. The effects are what I was trying for in 1927.

15. QUESTION: *How many members are there in the orchestra?*

ANSWER: Eighty members in the orchestra. Eighty members in the last piece, that is. (Refers to Symphony.)

ASHLEY PETTIS: I have a question here which is illegible. Possibly Mr. Copland can decipher it. (Takes quite a few slips out of the collection of seeming question slips.) I seem to be discarding questions but they are addresses of people who have turned them in. I'll save some of the comments until the end.

16. QUESTION: *What do you think of Ferde Grofé's contribution, if any, to what is called "modern music"?*

ANSWER: I am not an expert on Mr. Grofé's music. I haven't heard enough of it.

17. QUESTION: *What do you think of the commercial possibilities for young composers in the field of incidental music for the theatre and the movies? (laughter)*

ANSWER: I think it has excellent possibilities, if you can get someone to hire you. (laughter)[37]

18. QUESTION: *Do you use such enormous tone color with that specific purpose or is it your superb structure created that makes your music so effective? [sic]*

ANSWER: I like the question, but I don't know the answer. (amusement)

19. QUESTION: *Do you admit to the similarities between a large part of your Symphony especially 1st and 2nd movements and the last portion of the finale, to the orchestral literature of the Debussy-Ravel school? (Emphatic "Nos" from the audience.)*

ANSWER: The audience seems to think not.

20. QUESTION: *Do you write at the piano? How do you plan your compositions? Do you wait for inspiration? (laughter)*

ANSWER: The first question—Yes! I do write at the piano. I might add to that that there is a part in Stravinsky's biography where he says that he writes at the piano and thinks that every composer should write at the piano. Because the composer should keep in contact with the sonorous. I might say it doesn't matter. So many people think you ought not write at the piano. My opinion is, it doesn't matter, just as long as you write! I plan them as every composer does. He gets an idea, then another one, another one, and another one, then he starts a movement,—another movement and then you have a symphony. You wait for inspiration every day. (applause)

ASHLEY PETTIS: This seems to be a series of 5 questions with an introduction of: "Let's hear more!" The questions seem to be interdependent, so I shall read them in sequence without interruption.

20. [sic] QUESTION: (a) *Is it true that the "ultra-modern" movement died in 1930?*[38]

ANSWER: In a sense, strangely enough it is true that "ultra-modern" music did die in 1930—in this sense only—that a certain period of development in sounds came to an end. I think Stravinsky brought that about. Everyone experimented and now it was time to dig in and do something with those experiments. It did not seem any longer necessary. One was released. It brought a reaction against ultra-modern music.

QUESTION: (b) *If so, how come the critics weren't informed?*

ANSWER: Well, I don't know. Ask the city editor. (laughter)

QUESTION: (c) *What has been done with the body?*

ANSWER: What's been done to the body? Well, that's all right! My answer to that is as good as anyone else's.

QUESTION: (d) *Is there any discernable and definite trend and aim in today's music?*

ANSWER: The trend is to get closer to the audience. To write things simpler so that the audience can build it without pulling it down.

QUESTION: (e) *What is your part in it?*

ANSWER: It is this: to write something that is simple, yet very good. It will take some time to do it. (as an afterthought) I have just written a high school operetta![39]

21. QUESTION: *Your music makes me feel nervous and restless. Is that how you felt when you wrote your compositions? (outbursts of laughter)*

ANSWER: Well! I imagine Beethoven must have written nervously when he wrote. You can't write restless music without feeling the sentiment yourself! (amusement)

22. QUESTION: *Did the orchestra do what you wanted it to do?*

ANSWER: Not always!

23. QUESTION: *Do you think it is necessary for a composer to actively participate in political activity?*

ANSWER: No! (emphatically)

24. QUESTION: *What, according to your own beliefs, are the salient characteristics of your own music?*

ANSWER: The salient characteristics, as I see them, are in the first place, a certain massive sense and a certain attempt at quite a large and grandiose effect. Not so much "effect" but a large and grandiose feeling in the music. The second, is an attempt to get an alive rhythmic vitality in the music. And the third characteristic, I should say, is an attempt to write music which is always logically constructed.

25. QUESTION: *Do you think that a composer has to be a political partisan in order to be able to compose?*

ANSWER: No!

26. QUESTION: *Does your music have any social significance?*

ANSWER: All music that is any good has social significance.

27. QUESTION: *Do you expect "modern music" to be fully appreciated in this generation?*

ANSWER: If you mean by "generation," the next 30 years—yes!

28. QUESTION: *In your opinion, by what characteristic do we recognize American music?*

ANSWER: The characteristics of American music are now in the making. Therefore, it is difficult to say with any certainty exactly what they are but one can already see a certain vigor and a certain rhythmic impulse which are recognizably American.

29. QUESTION: *Have the recent depression and economic upheaval and consequent changes in social thinking had any effect on your music in your opinion?*

ANSWER: Yes! It affected it very much.

30. QUESTION: *Do you think American music will develop out of and on the lines of the "jazz" part of your Suite from "Hear Ye! Hear Ye!"?*

ANSWER: Only one certain kind of American music. Not all kinds!

ASHLEY PETTIS: The balance is a series of comments:

"Your use of rhythms most striking and unusual and very effective."

"Your music is penetratingly beautiful and first-rate stuff. The best heard in a long time."

"I prefer very much Gershwin's Satire."[40]

"Couldn't the upstairs be open for those who wish to study the orchestra?"

I'll answer that one. It interferes with the Forum.

"Bravo! A splendid example for other American composers."

"Your music was lovely. We all enjoyed it so much. Come to us soon again. The orchestra played wonderfully well. Your last numbers reminded one of the old 'Town Criers of London.'"

[not read] *"Your Lento Molto sounds like a mono-maniac's nightmare. How about some tonal variety?"*[41]

ASHLEY PETTIS: Thank you so much. (to the composer and audience alike)

And so a memorable evening in the Composers' Forum-Laboratory came to a close.

Transcribed from stenographic notes by Gisella R. Silverman, 2/28/37

NOTES

1. Ashley Pettis (1892–n.d.) studied in San Francisco, New York, and Berlin, making his debut as pianist and composer in New York in 1922. From 1925 to 1931 he taught at the Eastman School of Music, and later at Sarah Lawrence College. In 1936 the Knickerbocker Little Symphony, under the auspices of the FMP, premiered his *March Hymn*. He coauthored *The Well-Tempered Accompanist* (Bryn Mawr, Penn.: T. Presser Co., 1949) with Coenraad Valentyn Bos, and wrote *Music: Now and Then* (New York: Coleman-Ross, 1955). In 1951 he entered the priesthood of the Catholic Church, residing in Rome for some years. Circa 1961 he became the chaplain at St. Mary Hospital in Nelsonville, Ohio.

2. Pettis, "Marching with a Song," *New Masses* (May 1, 1934): 15.

3. Composers' Forum Records, October 30, 1935. The Federal Music Project and Composers' Forum Records can be found at the National Archives II in Record Group (RG) 69.5.3. The Composers' Forum transcripts are a subsection within the records. Transcripts also exist for the Boston Composers' Forum at the Boston Public Library. Other cities did not maintain detailed records, although some descriptions are available for the Minneapolis-St. Paul Forum.

4. There are indications that some composers were able to bypass this supposedly blind selection process. Composer Paolo Gallico, commenting on the dates of his pieces, said he had "put them on a shelf and forgot all about them until my friend, Mr. Pettis, asked me to appear tonight." Composers' Forum Transcript, April 28, 1937.

5. The Forty-eighth Street venue was built by the Friars Club in 1916 to house their legendary "roasts." The world-famous Manny's Music Store opened there in 1935, sharing the block with the Fraternal Clubhouse, which hosted lectures, dances, and jazz concerts in the 1940s. The Fifty-fourth Street venue was built in 1927 as the San Carlo Opera House. It was also known briefly as the Gallo Theater, the Casino de Paree, and the Palladium, before its rebirth as the Federal Music Theater. After the demise of the FMP it became the CBS Radio Playhouse & Television Studio. In the seventies it was transformed into the infamous Studio 54, a star-studded nightclub rife with cocaine and corruption. Today the venue is once again a successful theater, where the smash-hit revival of *Cabaret* played for several years. (http://www.drakkar91.com/54).

6. Some transcripts indicate that composers knew whom the question had come from; composer Bernard Wagenaar addressed one questioner as "Madame." Composers' Forum Transcripts, December 2, 1936.

7. Musicians were drawn mainly from the Concert Division of the FMP. Frequent ensemble guests included the New String Quartet, the Gotham Symphony Orchestra, the Madrigal Singers under Lehman Engel, the Modern Art Quartet, and the Stringart Quartet. The pianist Richard Singer and soprano Louise Taylor were frequent soloists.

8. The free admission made the Composers' Forum a tempting venue for the poor and homeless. Ross Lee Finney recalled his first concert with the Forum: "Two-thirds of the people were there to get out of the cold. A lot of them were asleep!" Heidi Waleson, "Composers' Forum at 50," *High Fidelity* 36 (Musical America Edition) (April 1986): 14.

9. Composers' Forum Transcript, May 27, 1936.

10. "The American Composers' Forum—Have You Heard About It?" Press release, (ca. February 1936), Composers' Forum Records.

11. Carter quoted in Ashley Pettis, "The WPA and The American Composer," *Musical Quarterly* 36 (January 1940): 107.

12. Olin Downes, "Laboratory for Native Composers," *New York Times,* January 10, 1937: 159; n.a., "Composers on the Grill," *New York Times*, February 13, 1938.

13. Barbara Zuck, *A History of Musical Americanism* (Ann Arbor, Mich.: UMI Research Press, 1980); Cornelius B. Canon, *The Federal Music Project of the Works Progress Administration:*

Music in a Democracy (Minneapolis: University Microfilms International, University of Minnesota, 1963).

14. The New York Public Library and Juilliard School funded the 1939–40 season, after which Pettis moved the Forum to the West Coast for two years. Following a wartime hiatus, the Forum reestablished itself in New York, sponsored by the New York Public Library and Columbia University. Despite some financial ups and downs, the Forum has continued its tradition of introducing new, sometimes eclectic music to audiences. Composers with diverse backgrounds participate, and in recent years the Forum has included a tango marathon, video–live music, and computer music concerts, as well as retrospective concerts of music by composers who have long taken part in Forum events.

15. Lento molto and Rondino were originally written separately for string quartet but were grouped together and orchestrated in 1928. The First Symphony was a reorchestration of Copland's Symphony for Organ and Orchestra (1924). Scores and recordings are widely available for the Two Pieces for String Orchestra and Symphony no. 1.

16. The London Sinfonietta, with Oliver Knussen conducting, recorded the full ballet version of *Hear Ye! Hear Ye!* on a Decca/PolyGram Records compact disc in 1994, along with Copland's earlier ballet, *Grohg* (Argo 443 203-2). Manuscripts of the full ballet score exist for small and large orchestras and are located in the Library of Congress, as is a single printing by Boosey & Hawkes of Copland's two-piano arrangement. Neither a recording nor score seems to exist of the suite version of this ballet—Boosey & Hawkes has no record of it. The conductor Markand Thakar extracted numbers from the ballet to form a suite, which he conducted with the New York Philharmonic during the Completely Copland Festival in 1999. For Thakar's National Public Radio commentary on his suite, see http://www.markandthakar.com/Copland.htm (accessed July 23, 2004).

17. Ruth Crawford appeared in the Forum on April 6, 1938; Johanna Beyer's concerts took place on May 20, 1936, and May 19, 1937.

18. An error in the numbering of questions in the original transcript resulted in two questions numbered 20. The second one contains Copland's comments on ultra-modernism.

19. During Brant's Forum sessions audience members complimented his work on Benny Goodman's swing version of Bach. Composers' Forum Transcripts, February 15, 1939.

20. Brant first appeared in the Forum on March 4, 1936. McBride's concerts took place on April 21, 1937, and February 18, 1938. In *The New Music*, Copland listed McBride with some others as having "used jazz with greater or lesser degree of politeness." Copland, "Between the Wars," *Our New Music: Leading Composers in Europe and America* (New York/London: Whittlesey House, McGraw-Hill Book Company, 1941); republished as *The New Music: 1900–1960* (New York: W. W. Norton, 1968); as quoted in Copland, *Aaron Copland: A Reader: Selected Writings 1923–1972*, ed. Richard Kostelanetz (New York/London: Routledge, 2004), pp. 50–51.

21. Copland, "Between the Wars," as quoted in Kostelanetz, *Aaron Copland: A Reader,* p. 46.

22. See, for instance, Deems Taylor, *Of Men and Music* (New York: Simon and Schuster, 1938). Taylor maintained that jazz "stimulates the nervous system and the motor centres. . . . But jazz, as a class of music, is not moving. In the rare moments when it does attempt to stir the emotions it usually becomes merely sentimental and hollow" (p. 75).

23. In later comments Copland would temper this opinion of Gershwin, stating merely that Gershwin's works lacked "technical finish." See Copland, "Jazz Structure and Influence," *Modern Music* 4 (January–February 1927), as quoted in Kostelanetz, *Aaron Copland: A Reader,* 87. For the historiography of Copland and Gershwin, see Carol J. Oja,

"Gershwin and American Modernists of the 1920s," *Musical Quarterly* 78, no. 4 (Winter 1994): 646–68.

24. See Gail Levin and Judith Tick, *Aaron Copland's America: A Cultural Perspective* (New York: Watson-Guptill Publications, 2000). Levin recounts the numerous exchanges between Copland and painters, sculptors, photographers, and other artists in the twenties and thirties.

25. Tick, "The Music of Aaron Copland," *Aaron Copland's America*, p. 144. Copland applied the same analogy to Charles Ives's *Central Park in the Dark*, in which different musical strands sound simultaneously to create a realistic effect. Copland wrote, "The effect is almost that of musical cubism, since the music seems to exist independently on different planes. This so-called musical perspective makes use of musical realism in order to create an impressionistic effect." See Copland, "The Composer in Industrial America," *Music and Imagination: The Charles Eliot Norton Lectures* (Cambridge, Mass.: Harvard University Press, 1952), p. 106, as quoted in Levin, *Aaron Copland's America*, p. 10. Parallel to this description is Copland's discussion of Heitor Villa-Lobos, who, like Ives, "used impressionistic methods to suggest realistic scenes of homespun life"—in other words, musical cubism. See Aaron Copland, "Musical Imagination in the Americas," *Music and Imagination*, as quoted in Kostelanetz, *Aaron Copland: A Reader*, p. 81.

26. "Jazz Structure and Influence," *Modern Music*, as quoted in Kostelanetz, *Aaron Copland: A Reader*, p. 87.

27. Copland applied a rare negative inflection of the "cubistic" analogy to Stravinsky's ragtime-inspired music: *Piano-Rag Music*, *Ragtime* for eleven instruments, and the ragtime dance from *L'Histoire du soldat*. Referring to Stravinsky's juxtaposition of typical ragtime features and "other stock items," Copland saw in these works "a rather grotesque impression, as if Stravinsky were merely interested in making Cubistic caricatures out of the crudities of jazz." On a more positive note, Copland also observed the jazz-influenced polyrhythms in the first two sections of *L'Histoire*. Copland, "Music Between the Wars," *The New Music*, as quoted in Kostelanetz, *Aaron Copland: A Reader*, p. 81.

28. Although Copland participated in leftist enterprises such as the Pierre Degeyter Club, the Composers' Collective (infrequently), and the Workers' Music Olympiad, he avoided joining the American Communist Party.

29. A number of composers, including Ruth Crawford, expressed a desire to communicate more directly and simply with listeners. Crawford declared at her Forum (April 6, 1938) that her next music would be "simpler to play and to understand." See Melissa de Graaf, "The Reception of an Ultra-Modernist: Ruth Crawford in the Composers' Forum," *Ruth Crawford: A Reader* (Rochester University Press, forthcoming).

30. Roy Harris and Howard Hanson were two other composers who had achieved that level of status and respect, thereby inspiring similar questions. Harris's Composers' Forum Transcripts: 6 October 1937, 11 October 1938, 7 May 1939; Hanson's Composers' Forum Transcripts: 17 March 1937, 19 February 1939.

31. Composers' Forum Transcripts, February 24, 1937, National Archives II, Record Group (RG) 69.5.3.

32. He was actually the twenty-third composer that season. The twenty-two composers who preceded him were Lazare Saminsky, William Schuman, Werner Josten, Ross Lee Finney, Donald Tweedy, Rosalie Housman, Boris Levenson, Mabel Wood-Hill, Bernard Wagenaar, Robert W. Manton, Henry Hadley, Joseph Wagner, Marion Bauer, Daniel Gregory Mason, Alda Astori, A. W. Binder, Norman Cazden, Frederick Woltman, Nicolai Berezowsky, Seth Bingham, Paul Creston, and Quincy Porter.

33. Copland was only half joking. Not long after, Copland's lectures on "What to Listen for in Music" were published, and *Our New Music* came out in 1941.

34. By 1937 Schoenberg was already living in exile in the United States. He spent some months in New York and Boston in 1933 before moving to Los Angeles for health reasons in September of 1934.

35. Copland appears to have had a brief memory lapse in answering this question, since by 1937 there were several recordings of his music: *Nocturne,* Jacques Gordon violinist, Aaron Copland pianist, Columbia 68321-D, set X-48, 1935; *Ukelele Serenade,* Jacques Gordon violinist, Aaron Copland pianist, Columbia 68742-D, set X-68, 1935; *Vitebsk,* Ivor Karman violinist, David Freed cellist, Aaron Copland pianist, Columbia 68320/1-D, set X-48; *Vocalise,* Ethel Luening soprano, Aaron Copland pianist. *Recordings, New Music Quarterly,* number 1211 (1935).

36. With its modern harmonies and unconventional rhythms, *Humoristic Scherzo: The Cat and the Mouse* (1920) was the early piece that so puzzled Rubin Goldmark, Copland's teacher at the time, and caused the falling out between student and teacher. The children's pieces were "The Young Pioneers" and "Sunday Afternoon Music," both published in *Masters of Our Day: 18 Solos in the Contemporary Idiom for the Young Pianist,* ed. Lazare Saminsky and Isadore Freed (New York: Carl Fischer, 1936). The book also includes pieces by Cowell, Hanson, Milhaud, Sessions, and Thomson, among others.

37. Copland was to write his first film scores in 1939, for *The City* and *Of Mice and Men.* In 1937 he began composing for radio, with the CBS commission *Music for Radio.*

38. The term "ultra-modern" usually referred to experimental music represented in America by composers such as Ruth Crawford, Henry Cowell, and Johanna Beyer, who challenged the boundaries of musical aesthetics and techniques with serial-like elements, tone clusters, and the use of *Sprechstimme.*

39. In an important reference to his recent attempts at simplicity and accessibility, Copland alluded to *The Second Hurricane,* intended for students of the Henry Street Settlement and premiered in April of 1937 at the Grand Street Playhouse in New York— three months after his session in the Forum. The production was conducted by Lehman Engel and directed by Orson Welles.

40. This comment refers to Gershwin's politically inflected musicals of the early thirties, which include *Strike Up the Band* (1930), a caustic commentary on war; the Pulitzer Prize–winning *Of Thee I Sing* (1931), a satire that cast a harsh look at the Depression-era possibility of an American dictatorship; and the semi-operatic *Let 'Em Eat Cake* (1932). Such a comment from the audience indicates the radical political preferences of some listeners.

41. It was not uncommon for Pettis to omit comments or questions he felt were inappropriate or offensive.

Copland on Television: An Annotated List of Interviews and Documentaries

COMPILED BY EMILY ABRAMS

In October 1958, Aaron Copland made his television debut on the BBC program *Monitor*, marking the start of a successful new sideline for a composer whose career was already well established. Alongside ever more frequent conducting appointments, Copland's appearances in television documentaries and interviews provided a new outlet for his talents, particularly as his compositional inspiration began to wane.[1] With his distinctive facial profile, affable and straightforwardly articulate manner, and high standing in the music world, Copland must have seemed to television's early producers a guaranteed audience winner. His natural ability in front of the camera was evident from the outset, and he brought to the burgeoning medium decades of experience in lecturing, teaching, and speech making.

Copland's decision to get involved in television was surely influenced by the escalating success in the industry of his friend and disciple Leonard Bernstein. Copland must have realized, like Bernstein, the potential of television to promote American music and to increase public understanding of serious music in general. Bernstein made his first television appearance in 1954 on the CBS series *Omnibus* and rapidly rose to become a prominent television personality, making a large number of programs for which he is still much celebrated.[2] Copland, however, is less known in this capacity, despite taking part in over thirty interviews and documentaries during the second half of his life and conducting a large number of televised performances of music by himself and others. The annotated list of documentaries and television interviews of Copland published here amply demonstrates this important contribution and brings to Copland scholarship a wealth of previously unexplored primary source material.

An examination of the documentaries made about Copland, from the first in 1961 to the most recent posthumous production, reveals the almost immediate establishment, and subsequent reinforcement, of a stock narrative of Copland's life. Even when Copland was only in his sixties, a standard presentation of his biography had started to take shape. In this narrative, his life was divided into distinct periods separated by specific turning points, including, for example, his first composition lesson with Nadia Boulanger and his introduction to Koussevitsky. At the same time, viewers were encouraged to perceive certain dichotomies in Copland's music: city versus country, popular versus serious, and especially the national versus the personal. Copland's own description of his life obviously provided the basis for this biographical narrative, but it is clear that some elements were shaped by the writers, producers, and directors of the programs he took part in, who molded the narrative into an appealing form suitable for their audiences. The TV presentation of the Copland saga in the 1960s and 1970s differs little from its current manifestation (across all mediums), making the documentaries and interviews of these years of great importance in an analysis of the history of his reception.

One aspect deserving particular attention is the program makers' disproportionate concentration on Copland's early career. Most of the documentaries examine at some length Copland's childhood, presented as lacking in musical stimulus, his Paris education, and his early attempts to establish himself in America. An official announcement from Washington in celebration of Copland's eightieth birthday suggests a possible reason for this fascination with the early years:

> Aaron Copland, this country's greatest living composer, is the classic American success story: a man from modest beginnings who has reached the top of his profession solely by his own efforts.[3]

For television producers, as for the author of this statement, Copland's brand of "American success story" played into an appealing national myth of upward mobility. Additionally, Copland produced serious music in a language that a broad cut of Americans could understand. In a mass culture market that increasingly "homogenized" the highbrow and lowbrow (as the cultural critic Dwight Macdonald put it), producers saw in Copland the chance to bring a digestible form of high art to the masses, against the background of the heartwarming story of a very likable "common man."[4]

There is another important element of the Copland narrative for which he himself was largely responsible: his autobiography is primarily shaped not by facts and dates but by anecdotes of his connections with others. Vivian Perlis, coauthor of Copland's autobiography (in which most of these anecdotes can be found), coproduced one of the last documentaries in which Copland was actively involved. She alludes to his storytelling skills while praising his abilities in front of the camera: "Like a professional actor, he could repeat his favorite stories until the take was just right, yet each telling seemed fresh and spontaneous."[5] Copland allowed these stories to dominate his television interviews, quite probably to keep at bay more personal topics and excessive analytical discussion of his music, both of which he disliked. Another reason for their prevalence may well have been the gradual deterioration of his memory from the mid-seventies onward: he seems to have found anecdotes easier to recall than specific facts. Of course, for interviewers these stories also made Copland a fascinating and engaging subject, with an anecdote available for almost every major event of his life and every well-known figure with whom he came in contact. This may have been why these stories were so frequently requested.

Today we instinctively question a celebrity's reasons for making frequent media appearances. Was Copland seeking to create a particular public image of himself? This seems unlikely. He comes across on television, as in the literature, as a modest and straightforward man, and few signs indicate he was seeking to use the medium to promote himself or his music. Rather, he seemed to enjoy the work and his motivations appear to have been partly financial and partly altruistic—to further the cause of modern American music.

Reviewing all of Copland's television appearances, the earliest would seem to stand out as the most important for Copland scholarship, having been filmed at a time when he was fully immersed in the musical scene and was still able to engage intellectually and communicate with clarity and style. One of the first, *Aaron Copland Meets the Soviet Composers* (1959), is transcribed in this volume and provides an intriguing insight into American-Soviet musical relations. Both this program and *Music in the Twenties* (1965) highlight the remarkable intellectual depth of American educational television in the late 1950s and 1960s. In the twelve-part *Music in the Twenties* series, Copland presented the key musical, historical, and aesthetic issues of that decade while introducing his audience to both well-known and lesser-known music from the 1920s composed by a wide variety of composers. Another fascinating early program is the BBC's *Mr. Copland Comes to Town* (1964). Brilliantly made and highly entertaining, it also tells us much about Copland's reception in the United Kingdom. Although later programs continued to deliver interesting and important

Summary of Copland's Television Appearances

INTERVIEWS

1958 *Monitor*
1959 *Aaron Copland Meets the Soviet Composers*
1962 *Composers' Workshop*
1966 *Music in Close-up*
1966 *Salute to the League of Composers*
1966 *Sunday Showcase: Can Culture Explode?*
1966 *Wednesday Review*
1970 *Today Show*
1970 *Conversation: Aaron Copland, Composer*
1977 *Aaron Copland*
1978 *Dick Cavett Show*
1978 *Today Show*
1980 *Tomorrow*
1981 *Callaway Interviews: Aaron Copland*
1981 *Aaron Copland Interview*
1983 *The Levin Interviews: Aaron Copland*

DOCUMENTARIES

1961 *Contemporary American Composers: Aaron Copland*
1964 *Workshop: Mr. Copland Comes to Town*
1965 *Music in the Twenties*
1970 *60 Minutes: Aaron Copland at Seventy*
1974 *Copland in Cleveland*
1975 *A Copland Portrait*
1975 *Happy Birthday Aaron Copland*
1976 *Bill Moyer's Journal: Copland*
1976 *Marc Blitzstein: American Composer with a Message*
1979 *Are My Ears On Wrong? A Profile of Charles Ives*
1980 *Over Easy*
1980 *NBC Magazine*
1985 *Aaron Copland: A Self-Portrait*
1987 *Yehudi Menuhin—The Music of Man:*
      "The Known and the Unknown"
1987 *Vive La France!:*
      Mademoiselle—A Portrait of Nadia Boulanger
1996 *MacDowell: An American Artists' Colony*
2000 *Great Performances: Copland's America*
2001 *Fanfare for America: The Composer Aaron Copland*

new information—the two 1975 documentaries *A Copland Portrait* and *Happy Birthday Aaron Copland* are particularly noteworthy, as is the 1985 *Aaron Copland: A Self-Portrait* that he made with Perlis—it is Copland's contribution to television in the late 1950s and the 1960s that merits the closest scrutiny.

The list below is in chronological order and details all the television documentaries and interviews known to me in which Copland participated as well as posthumous productions that use historic footage of Copland. It does not include programs that are primarily concert performances, even if they contain some form of short speech by the composer. Each citation provides the following information: program title, program length, production team, first known broadcaster, first known transmission date, and location and call number of a known viewing copy (if available) or other relevant sources.[6] In cases where I have been able to view the film, or acquire a transcript of it, the first part of the annotation generally lists any other important people involved and describes the ordering of the program's material. The second part describes the most distinctive topics discussed by Copland (and others, where relevant), omitting the familiar anecdotes described above. When viewing the program has proved impossible, I have cited available descriptions of the program content.

Annotated List of Interviews and Documentaries

1. ***Monitor***. Length unknown. Producer and director unknown, BBC, London. Broadcast: BBC, UK, October 19, 1958. No known viewing copy.

   Interview with AC as part of a magazine-format show. Content unknown. According to correspondence with the BBC in the Copland Collection at the Library of Congress, this is AC's "first solo appearance" on television.[7]

2. ***Aaron Copland Meets the Soviet Composers***. 30 minutes. Produced by Jordan Whitelaw, directed by Paul Noble, WGBH-TV, Boston. Broadcast: NET,[8] November 15, 1959.[9] Viewing copy: Library of Congress, Washington, D.C., call number VAK 2092.

   AC and Nicolas Slonimsky interview Fikret Amirov, Kostyantyn Dankevych, Dmitry Kabalevsky, Tikhon Khrennikov, Dmitry

Shostakovich, and Boris Yarustovsky. See the background information and transcription included in this book.

3. ***Contemporary American Composers: Aaron Copland***. Two 30-minute programs. Produced and directed by John Ziegler, written by Colin Sterne, WQED, Pittsburgh. Broadcast: NET, August 20, 1961. Viewing copy: Library of Congress, Washington, D.C., call numbers VAK 3876 and VAK 3877.

> PROGRAM 1: Documentary-style introduction to AC's life with images of New York, Paris, and rural America: proposes a city-country dichotomy in AC's music. Copland in his Peekskill studio, addressing the camera. Topics discussed by AC: challenges presented by newly expanded audience, rise of functional music and its emotional and dramatic power (illustrated with reference to The Red Pony), personal motivations for composing.

> PROGRAM 2: Abbreviated version of introduction to Program 1. AC in his studio. AC at Tanglewood: rehearsal and performance of sections from Suite from *The Tender Land*. Topics discussed by AC: the experience of composing, personal compositional methods, justification for the use of folk material, evolution of original material in relation to folk material (with reference to finale of Suite from *The Tender Land*).

4. ***Composers' Workshop***. 60 minutes. Produced by David Epstein, director unknown, Educational Broadcasting Corporation, Washington, D.C. Broadcast: WNDT-TV, October 16, 1962. No known viewing copy.

> "Aaron Copland conducts a rehearsal and performance of his Nonet for Strings. Lester Trimble, composer and critic, interviews Mr. Copland."[10]

5. ***Workshop: Mr. Copland Comes to Town***. 60 minutes. Produced by Humphrey Burton, directed by Barrie Gavin, BBC, London. Broadcast: BBC, UK, June 20, 1964. Viewing copy: BBC, London; viewing is currently restricted.

> Documentary following AC on a visit to London in May 1964 to conduct the world premiere of *Music for a Great City* with the London Symphony Orchestra. Rehearsals with the LSO, including AC

making changes to the score, and private rehearsals of the Clarinet Concerto with a soloist and AC at the piano. Interview with AC while driving through London. In his dressing room and at social events. Filming a television interview during his visit (program unidentified), including a discussion of the content with the producer before filming. At the premiere of *Music for a Great City* and at the post-concert party. Members of the orchestra and audience and London newspaper critics give their opinions about AC and the piece. Topics discussed by AC: genesis of *Music for a Great City* and images suggested by each movement, new-music scene in American cities, thoughts on Benjamin Britten's *War Requiem*, intention to write a work about Walt Whitman.

6. ***Music in the Twenties***. Twelve 30-minute programs. Produced and directed by David M. Davis, WGBH-TV, Boston. Broadcast: NET, June 10, 1965. Viewing copies: Library of Congress, Washington, D.C., call numbers VBM 5704-8, 6409-10, 6869-73. Written transcripts of the preliminary tapes are at Houghton Library, Harvard University, call number *65M-94 (1-12). The preliminary tapes are lost.

   AC, alone and to camera, discusses developments in European and American music in the 1920s. Important composers and trends are described and personal anecdotes related. Each program includes a live performance of at least one musical work to illustrate the topic in question. The series is based on a course taught by AC at Harvard University during the spring term of 1952. The written transcripts of the preliminary tapes, which were donated by AC to Harvard University, include (for most programs) additional lengthy discussions on some topics between Copland, Curt Davis, and David Davis. These took place before and after the filming of each take and were not included in the broadcast programs.

   PROGRAM 1: **Background: 1910–19**
   Music performed:
   1. Arnold Schoenberg, *Pierrot lunaire,* sections 1, 4, 11, 12, 18, 21. Performed by: Bethany Beardslee, soprano; Robert Koff, violin; Peter Schenkman, cello; Martin Boykan, piano; Elinor Preble, flute; Felix Viscuglia, clarinet.
   Igor Stravinsky, *L'Histoire du Soldat.* Performed by: AC, conductor; Robert Koff, violin; Felix Viscuglia, clarinet; Donald Bravo,

bassoon; Ramon Parcells, cornet; Paul Gay, trombone; Everett Beale, percussion; William Curtis, contra-bass.

Topics discussed by AC in program: desire to be original as a key feature of the music of the 1920s, Schoenberg and Stravinsky as the most important rebels of the 1910s, the courage of their break with nineteenth-century Romanticism. Topics discussed only in extra material: originality now (in the 1960s) much more calculated than in the 1920s, whether the TV audience will appreciate *Pierrot lunaire*, comparison of Satie to Cage—both are "Much more amusing to talk about than to really listen to" (transcript of Program 1, p. 23).

PROGRAM 2: **Paris: Les Six**
Music performed:

1. Francis Poulenc, "Valse" from *Mouvements perpétuels* (from *The Album of the Six*) (excerpt). Performed by: AC, piano.

2. Arthur Honegger, Concertino for Piano and Orchestra. Performed by: Paul Jacobs, piano; AC, conductor; Cambridge Festival Orchestra.

Topics discussed by AC in program: The "Group of Six" and their new attitudes to composition and musical styles (Milhaud and Honegger most important, aesthetics of Satie). Topics discussed only in extra material: AC's love of Mahler (which came from Boulanger), Sibelius's lack of popularity with young American composers during 1920s, meeting Honegger at Tanglewood, contemporary composers swinging back from French to German music: "Boulez's generation thinks it was all nonsense" (transcript of Program 2, p. 20).

PROGRAM 3: **Jazz and Jazz Influences**
Music performed:

1. Darius Milhaud, *La Création du monde*. Performed by: AC, conductor; Cambridge Festival Orchestra.

Topics discussed by AC in program: impact of jazz on concert music, reasons why composers of serious music are interested in jazz, Milhaud as the European who best understood jazz. Topics discussed only in extra material: AC's interest in the rhythmic aspects of jazz ("the [harmonic] progressions are rather corny," transcript of Program 2, p. 20), American composers who used jazz in the 1920s, legitimacy of concert performances of AC's ballets.

PROGRAM 4: **Neoclassicism**

Music performed:

1. Igor Stravinsky, *Pulcinella Suite*, Vivo. Performed by: Igor Stravinsky, conductor; Boston Symphony Orchestra. Footage of concert at Boston Symphony Hall, December 1964.

2. Manuel de Falla, Concerto for Harpsichord. Performed by: AC, conductor; Sylvia Marlowe, harpsichord; Robert Brink, violin; Joan Brockway, cello; Elinor Preble, flute; Richard Summers, oboe; Felix Viscuglia, clarinet.

Topics discussed by AC in program: initial shock of Stravinsky's neoclassicism in Paris, reasons for growth of neoclassicism, parallels in Spain with Manuel de Falla. Topics discussed only in extra material: importance of de Falla.

PROGRAM 5: **Central Europe: Twelve-Tone Revolution**

Music performed:

1. Alban Berg, *Lyric Suite,* second and third movements. Performed by: Juilliard String Quartet (Robert Mann, violin; Isidore Cohen, violin; Raphael Hillyer, viola; Claus Adam, cello).

2. Anton Webern, Quartet, op. 22. Performed by: Luise Vosgerchian, piano; George Zazofsky, violin; Felix Viscuglia, clarinet; William Wrzesien, tenor saxophone.

Topics discussed by AC in program: fame of Paris blotted out successes in other European countries (especially Germany), radical nature of Schoenberg's *Pierrot lunaire*, Schoenberg's conception of twelve-tone composition, importance of judging Schoenberg's music through instinctive reaction while remaining open-minded, Webern as a composer who thought through the full implications of the system and was closer to today's musical aesthetic than Schoenberg. Topics discussed only in extra material: Webern's "cold-blooded" method of selecting notes (transcript of Program 4, p. 13), AC's and others' changing impressions of Schoenberg's methods, current serialist methods (of which the Second Viennese School would probably not have approved).

PROGRAM 6: **New Movements in Opera**

Music performed:

1. Kurt Weill, "Havanna Song" from *The Rise and Fall of the City of Mahagonny,* "Surabaya Johnny" from *Happy End*. Performed by: Lotte Lenya, vocalist; Milton Rosenstock, conductor; Cambridge Festival Orchestra.

2. Paul Hindemith, *Hin und zurück*. Performed by: Beverly Sills, soprano, "the wife"; Davis Cunningham, tenor, "the husband"; James Billings, tenor, "the sage"; Chester Ludgin, baritone, "the doctor"; Raymond Michalski, bass, "the orderly"; Bronia Stefan, "the aunt"; Patricia B. Hall, "the maid." Staged by Sarah Caldwell and David M. Davis; Sarah Caldwell, conductor; Cambridge Festival Orchestra.

Topics discussed by AC in program: generation following Schoenberg (especially Weill and Krenek) and their new attitudes toward opera in the 1920s, desire for new kind of opera, rise of the chamber opera (especially Hindemith). Topics discussed only in extra material: reasons for the bitterness in Weill's music, AC initially saw Weill's use of jazz in Mahagonny as old-fashioned and corny but ultimately realized it represented its time.

PROGRAM 7: **Nationalism: European Style**
Music performed:

1. Béla Bartók, Second Sonata for Violin and Piano, second movement. Performed by: Tossy Spivakovsky, violin; Arthur Balsam, piano.

Topics discussed by AC in program: two forms of nationalism (direct quotation of folk materials and "sense" of a place), Bartók's nationalism and influences, lack of popularity of nationalism among young contemporary composers. Topic discussed only in extra material: probability that nationalism in music will return.

PROGRAM 8: **Nationalism: New World Style**
Music performed:

1. Heitor Villa-Lobos, Suite for Voice and Violin, third movement. Performed by: Lauracy de Benevides, soprano; Robert Brink, violin.

2. Aaron Copland, *Music for the Theatre*, Prologue and Burlesque. Performed by: AC, conductor; Cambridge Festival Orchestra.

Topics discussed by AC in program: importance of Paris for American composers in the 1920s, reasons for American composers' move away from European styles, steps to building national musical styles in the New World, Villa-Lobos as a seminal figure, Americans inspired by European use of jazz, importance for AC of writing a music that was recognizably American, influence of North and South America on each other. Topic discussed only in extra material: serialism a big factor in the move away from nationalism in composition.

PROGRAM 9: **New Faces**

Music performed:

1. Paul Hindemith, Third String Quartet, op. 22, third and fifth movements. Performed by: Robert Brink, violin; Hanley Daws, violin; Eleftherios Eleftherakis, viola; Judith Davidoff, cello.

2. Sergey Prokofiev, Quintet op. 39, first movement. Performed by: Richard Summers, oboe; Felix Viscuglia, clarinet; Robert Brink, violin; Elftherios Eleftherakis, viola; William Curtis, contra-bass.

Topics discussed by AC in program: composers of the 1920s who were less innovative but quintessentially of their time have frequently turned out to be most popular in the long run (notably Hindemith and Prokofiev), Hindemith now seen as a rejuvenator of nineteenth-century Teutonic art but was shocking in the 1920s, Prokofiev a "naive creator" (transcript of Program 9, p. 9), hence his popularity. Topics discussed only in extra material: problems with Hindemith at Tanglewood, Hindemith "a true academician, deep-dyed" and "we didn't get on well" (transcript of Program 9, p. 13).

PROGRAM 10: **American Music in the 20s**

Music performed:

1. Roy Harris, Concerto for Piano, Clarinet, and String Quartet. Performed by: Luise Vosgerchian, piano; Felix Viscuglia, clarinet; Robert Brink, violin, Hanley Daws, violin; Eleftherios Eleftherakis, viola; Judith Davidoff, cello.

2. Virgil Thomson, "Pigeons on the Grass Alas" and "Procession of the Saints" from *Four Saints in Three Acts*. Performed by: Francis Hester, bass-baritone; Arimae Burrell, contralto; Alfred Nash Patterson, conductor; Cambridge Festival Orchestra.

Topics discussed by AC in program: Harris and Thomson as examples of two different types of American life in music (Harris from the Far West and a Whitmanesque idealist, Thomson from the Midwest and inclined to write plain, direct, sometimes nostalgic music). Topic discussed only in extra material: genesis of the Copland-Sessions Concerts.

PROGRAM 11: **Experimental Attitudes (I)**

Music performed:

1. Charles Ives, *The Unanswered Question*. Performed by: AC, principal conductor; Kalman Novak, associate conductor; Roger Voisin, trumpet; Cambridge Festival Orchestra.

2. Charles Ives, "Two Little Flowers," "Serenity," "Charlie Rutledge." Performed by: Donald Gramm, bass-baritone; Richard Cumming, piano.

3. Carl Ruggles, *Portals* for String Orchestra. Performed by: AC, conductor; Cambridge Festival Orchestra.

Topics discussed by AC in program: diversity of experimental directions in the 1920s, many of which didn't immediately lead anywhere (for example, innovations in microtonal music and use of mechanical instruments); music and personalities of Ives and Ruggles.

PROGRAM 12: **Experimental Attitudes (II)**
Music performed:

1. Leo Ornstein, "The Wild Men's Dance." Performed by: David Tudor, piano.

2. Henry Cowell, "Advertisement," "Banshee," "Aeolian Harp," "Tiger." Performed by: David Tudor, piano.

3. Edgard Varèse, *Ionisation*. Performed by: AC, conductor; Manhattan School of Music Percussion Ensemble.

Topics discussed by AC in program: Paul Rosenfeld's role in informing American composers about contemporary developments, Leo Ornstein primarily important as a virtuoso rather than as a composer, Cowell and his fresh approaches to the piano, Varèse and his interest in the science of acoustics, aspects of music of the 1960s that can be traced back to the 1920s. Topic discussed only in extra material: future of electronic music lies in its combination with live sound, e.g., Davidovsky and Babbitt.

7. *Music in Close-up*. 58 minutes. Produced by Allan Miller, directed by Roger Englander, WNDT, New York. Broadcast: WNDT-TV, March 11, 1966. Viewing copy: Library of Congress, Washington, D.C., call number VBR 4031.

Interview with AC (interviewer Hugo Weisgall) in a television studio about the *Twelve Poems of Emily Dickinson* interspersed with performances of the songs by Adele Addison, soprano, and AC, piano. Topics discussed by AC: factors influencing his choice of poetic material, structure of the cycle as a whole, balance of voice and accompaniment, setting the American language to music, effect of different musical interpretations.

8. **Salute to the League of Composers**. 60 minutes. Producer and director unknown, WNDT, New York. Broadcast: WNDT-TV, March 14, 1966. No known viewing copy.

   "Guests include Aaron Copland, composer; Paul Jacobs, pianist; William Schumann [*sic*], composer; others."[11]

9. **Sunday Showcase: Can Culture Explode?** 90 minutes. Produced by Edith Zornow and Lee Polk, directed by Lee Polk, WNDT, New York. Broadcast: WNDT-TV, May 8, 1966. No known viewing copy.

   "With the proliferation of cultural centers all over the country and the subsidizing of culture by state and government, Channel 13 takes a long, hard look at the results in *Can Culture Explode?* . . .
   "Featuring Stanley Kauffmann, Drama Critic of the *New York Times*, as host, the program will attempt to evaluate spoon-fed culture for the masses and whether there are any significant trends as a result of the efforts to 'popularize' culture.
   "Joining Mr. Kauffmann is a distinguished group of observers and participants in the cultural scene. They are: Buckminster Fuller, Designer and Architect and Professor of Design Science Exploration at Southern Illinois University; Aaron Copland, internationally famous composer; Hilton Kramer, Art News Editor of the *New York Times*; Robert Osborn, Artist and Author; and Theodore Solotaroff, Editor-in-Chief of *Book Week Magazine*."[12]

10. **Wednesday Review**. 60 minutes. Producer and director unknown, WNDT, New York. Broadcast: WNDT-TV, November 10, 1966. No known viewing copy.

   "Discussion of Leonard Bernstein's resignation as conductor of the NY Philharmonic. Aaron Copland, Winthrop Sargeant, Lukas Foss and others participate."[13]

11. **Today Show**. Length unknown. Producer and director unknown, NBC, New York. Broadcast: NBC, November 19, 1970. No known viewing copy.

   Interview with AC as part of a magazine-format news show. Content unknown.[14]

Sunday Showcase: Can Culture Explode?, WNDT, May 1966. From left to right: Stanley Kauffmann, drama critic, *N.Y. Times*; Hilton Kramer, Art News editor, *N.Y. Times*; Aaron Copland; Robert Osborn, artist and author; Theodore Solotaroff, editor *Book Week Magazine*; Buckminster Fuller, architect.

Sunday Showcase: Can Culture Explode?, WNDT, May 1966. Aaron Copland.

Sunday Showcase: Can Culture Explode?, WNDT, May 1966. Aaron Copland and Hilton Kramer.

12. ***60 Minutes: Aaron Copland at Seventy***. 5-minute segment of show. Produced by Don Hewitt, director unknown, CBS News, New York. Broadcast: CBS, November 24, 1970. Viewing copy: tape at Library of Congress, Washington, D.C.; no viewing copy available at time of publication.

> Birthday party speech for AC by Leonard Bernstein. AC and Bernstein play a two-piano duet. Mike Wallace interviews Copland. Topics discussed by AC: reasons for his longevity and good health, his motivations for becoming a composer.

13. ***Conversation: Aaron Copland, Composer***. 29 minutes. Produced by James Robert Davis, University of Wisconsin Milwaukee Instructional Media Laboratory, Milwaukee. Not broadcast (produced for Wisconsin classroom use), recorded January 30, 1970. Viewing copy: University of Wisconsin, Milwaukee, call number VHS-0307.

> "In an interview with Professor John Downey of the UWM Department of Music, Copland talks about the various people and musical trends which influenced him, divergent aspects of his own work, and future directions in American music."[15]

14. ***Copland in Cleveland***. 60 minutes. Producer and director unknown, WKYC-TV, Cleveland, Ohio. Broadcast: WKYC-TV, 1974 (exact date unknown). No known viewing copy.

> "Follows American composer Aaron Copland during his week's stay in Cleveland and shows the varied activities in which he participated."[16]

15. ***A Copland Portrait***. 30 minutes. Produced and written by Frieda Lee Mock and Terry Sanders, directed by Terry Sanders, United States Information Agency, Washington, D.C. Not for broadcast, produced in 1975. Viewing copy: Library of Congress, Washington, D.C., call number VAF 2047.

> AC tells life story against images of New York, Paris, and American countryside. At Tanglewood, in composition class and orchestral rehearsal. At Koussevitsky memorial service. At the piano, composing. At Kennedy Center in Washington, rehearsing and performing his First Symphony. Other participants: Harold Clurman and Michael Tilson-Thomas. Topics discussed by AC: reasons for becoming a composer, nationalism in music, method of composing.

16. ***Happy Birthday Aaron Copland***. 90 minutes. Produced by Rodney Greenberg, directed by Humphrey Burton, BBC, London. Broadcast: BBC, UK, November 16, 1975. Viewing copy: BBC, London; viewing is currently restricted.

> Hosted by Ludovic Kennedy (LK) and André Previn (AP). Other participants: Leonard Bernstein (LB), Nadia Boulanger (NB),

Benny Goodman (BG), and Lorin Maazel (LM) (all interviewed), with soloists Craig Sheppard (piano), Gervase de Peyer (clarinet), and Meriel Dickinson (mezzo soprano). Divided into titled sections: "Early Years," "The Jazz Influence," "Teacher," "Conductor," "Music for Movies," "Music for the Ballet," "Writer, Composer," "Pianist," "An American Voice," and "Copland at 75." Each section includes performances of works by AC, with AC either at the piano or conducting the London Symphony Orchestra; interviews with other participants; and interviews of AC by LK and AP. Some sections also include historic footage of AC, his films and ballets, as well as footage from a film by Terry Sanders, *A Copland Portrait* (1975), which shows AC at work in America (for example, at Tanglewood). Topics discussed by AC: Boulanger's teaching style, AC's combination of serious music with jazz in comparison with Gershwin's, opinions of his own conducting talents, intentions in writing popular scores, reasons for writing film music, frequently excessive complexity of contemporary music, ways in which music can be recognized as American, pros and cons of using serialist techniques. Topics discussed by other participants: AC's crusade for the cause of American music (LM), reasons why BG commissioned the clarinet concerto, Russian and Jewish aspects in AC's music (NB), hope that AC will start composing again (LB).

17. ***Bill Moyers' Journal: Copland***. 58 minutes. Produced by Charles Rose, written by Wayne Ewing, WNET, New York. Broadcast: PBS, March 14, 1976. Viewing copy: Library of Congress, Washington, D.C., call number VBP 1382.

> Bill Moyers interviews Copland in Aspen, Colorado. Richard Dufallo rehearses *Music for the Theatre* for a concert to celebrate AC's seventy-fifth birthday. AC discusses the piece with Dufallo. Question-and-answer session with students at Tanglewood. Copland rehearses orchestra at Tanglewood. Topics discussed by AC: reasons for composing, process of creating an American work of art, reasons for abandoning jazz, nature of musical inspiration, genesis of *Rodeo*, reasons for his variety of styles, importance of not trying too hard to define a work of art.

18. ***Marc Blitzstein: American Composer with a Message***. 27 minutes. Produced and directed by Muriel Balash, Camera Three/Creative Arts

Television, Kent, Conn. Broadcast: CBS, September 12, 1976. Viewing copy: Library of Congress, Washington, D.C., call number VAE 0414.

First of two programs examining the work of Marc Blitzstein (MB): AC features in the first only. Other participants: Arvin Brown, John Houseman, Brenda Lewis. Topics discussed by AC: importance of MB's innovations in the opera *No for an Answer*, MB's passion for writing music with a message that would last.

19. ***Aaron Copland***. 30 minutes. Producer and director unknown, Nebraska Educational Television Council for Higher Education, Lincoln, Neb. Broadcaster unknown, 1977 (exact date unknown). Viewing copy: Baptist College of Florida, Graceville, Fla., call number CVC ML 410 .C67 A37 1977 91352.

Interviewer Harold Shiffler. Content unknown (unable to obtain viewing copy).

20. ***Dick Cavett Show***. 29 minutes. Produced by Christopher Porterfield, directed by Richard Romagnola, Daphne Productions, New York. Broadcast: PBS, February 15, 1978. Viewing copy: Library of Congress, Washington, D.C., call number VBC 8810.

Studio interview with AC. AC shows signs of increasing memory loss, as in subsequent programs: his answers are shorter than previously, he mainly tells the familiar stories, and he is unable to recall the birthplace of his father. Topics discussed by AC: reasons for relative lack of women composers, growth in use of background music, tips to help listeners appreciate modern music, importance of Rosenfeld's reviews in his early career self-confidence, the meaning of music.

21. ***Today Show***. Length unknown. Producer and director unknown, NBC, New York. Broadcast: NBC, September 4, 1978. No known viewing copy.

Interview with AC as part of magazine-format news show. "Copland appears from Wolftrap, Virginia."[17]

22. ***The Rise of Modernism in Music 1890–1935: "Are My Ears On Wrong?" A Profile of Charles Ives.*** 24 minutes. Produced by David Thompson, directed by Robert Philip, The Open University, Milton

Keynes, UK. Broadcast: BBC, UK, April 3, 1979. Viewing copy: Learning Resource Center, Open University Library, Milton Keynes, UK, no call number, request at library reception desk.

Documentary about Charles Ives (CI) including historic interviews with him (audio only). Other participants: Elliot Carter, AC, and John Kirkpatrick. Topics discussed by AC: heroism of CI's ability to write in a vacuum, the effect of World War I on the American music scene, belief that CI, before his death, must have realized the mark he had made on American music.

23. ***Over Easy***. 30 minutes. Produced by Jules Power, directed by Vincent Casalaina, KQED, San Francisco. Broadcast: PBS, July 10, 1980. Viewing copy: Library of Congress, Washington, D.C., call number VBR 4032.

An interview of AC (interviewer Hugh Downes) in a New York studio interspersed with excerpts from Terry Sanders's film *A Copland Portrait* (1975). The program is aimed at senior citizens, so some of Downes's questions have to do with AC's achievements in old age. Topics discussed by AC (in the Downes interview): *Appalachian Spring* as a reflection of the personality of Martha Graham, reasons why he is no longer composing, opinions on contemporary composers, new passion for conducting.

24. ***Tomorrow***. Length unknown. Producer and director unknown, NBC, New York. Broadcast: NBC, November 6, 1980. No known viewing copy.

"Distinguished composer Aaron Copland explains how he has tried to write classical music with an American accent. He says he's always enjoyed popular music but preferred to pursue his natural talent for symphony and opera. He talks about conducting some of the world's finest orchestras and talks about his close friend Leonard Bernstein."[18]

25. ***NBC Magazine***. 30 minutes. Produced by Wallace Westfeldt, directed by George Paul, Copland segment produced by Robert Eaton, NBC, New York. Broadcast: NBC, November 11, 1980. Viewing copy: Library of Congress, Washington, D.C., call number VBB 5370.

Final segment in magazine-format news program. Interview with AC woven into a narrated documentary-style biography. At

Tanglewood: AC and Leonard Bernstein (LB) interviewed together and AC rehearses orchestra. Topics discussed by AC: musical nationalism, jazz in the concert hall, importance of fostering young talent (at Tanglewood). Topics discussed by AC and LB: importance of AC to LB's development, reasons why AC has stopped composing.

26. ***Callaway Interviews: Aaron Copland***. 60 minutes. Produced by Johanna Steinmetz, directed by Ken Voss, Chicago Educational Television Association, Chicago. Broadcast: WTTW Chicago, June 3, 1981. Viewing copy: Library of Congress, Washington, D.C., call number VBQ 8371.

John Callaway interviews AC in a television studio. Also see Callaway in locations pertinent to AC's life story. Topics discussed by AC: interest in writing film music, reasons for being active on the musical scene as well as composing, works of his he would like played more, personal compositional methods, opinions on the current scene in composition and music education, Jewish elements in his music, why he stopped composing.

27. ***Aaron Copland Interview***. 38 minutes. Production assistance WNET, New York. Produced to screen at a music festival at Umpqua Community College, Roseburg, Oregon, June 18–20, 1981, interview filmed April 3, 1981. Viewing copy: Library of Congress, Washington, D.C., call number VBQ 8370.

Interview filmed in AC's Peekskill studio. Interviewer Roberta Hall (from Umpqua Community College) asks AC some of her own questions as well as questions contributed by her faculty colleagues. On several occasions, AC replies that he cannot remember. Topics discussed by AC: Varèse and Stravinsky key influences on him, opinions of a variety of musical interpretations of his works, role of Koussevitsky in his rise to fame, collaborations with dancers, disinclination to predict musical developments of the future.

28. ***The Levin Interviews: Aaron Copland***. 30 minutes. Produced and directed by Chris Hunt, BBC, London. Broadcast: BBC, UK, July 2, 1983. Viewing copy: BBC, London, viewing is currently restricted.

Bernard Levin interviews AC in a television studio. Topics discussed by AC: reception of new American music in America in the 1920s, working with Martha Graham, respect that is due film music, what he is trying to express in his music.

29. ***Aaron Copland: A Self-Portrait***. 58 minutes. Produced by Ruth Leon, directed by Allan Miller, written by Vivian Perlis, Vintage Productions, Weston, Conn. Broadcast: PBS, October 16, 1985. Viewing copy: Library of Congress, Washington, D.C., call number VAC 6125. The complete, unedited interviews filmed for the program are in the Aaron Copland Collection, Music Division, Library of Congress.

Documentary about AC's life made by AC and Vivian Perlis. Other participants: Arthur Berger, Leonard Bernstein, Agnes de Mille, David Diamond, Jacob Druckman, Lukas Foss, Samuel Lipman, Ned Rorem, William Schuman, and Michael Tilson Thomas. Also includes material from *Music in the Twenties* (1965). Copland in Peekskill studio with a group of musicians rehearsing *Movement for String Quartet*. Copland and the narrator recount his life story against images of New York, Paris, etc. Performance of Piano Variations by Michael Tilson Thomas. Anecdotes and tributes from other participants. Features historic footage, including excerpts from the first production of Rodeo and from a performance of Lincoln Portrait with AC narrating and Bernstein conducting. AC also rehearses and performs various other works. Bernstein tribute at AC's seventieth birthday. Topics discussed by AC: reasons for writing Piano Variations, McCarthy allegations, new passion for conducting. Topics discussed by other participants: impact of AC's Piano Variations, AC's personality, AC's advocacy of young composers, AC at Tanglewood, AC's compositional advice.

30. ***Yehudi Menuhin—The Music of Man: "The Known and the Unknown."*** 60 minutes. Produced by Richard Bocking, Curtis W. Davis, and John Thomson, directed by Richard Bocking and John Thomson, written by Yehudi Menuhin and Curtis W. Davis with Charles Weir, Canadian Broadcasting Corporation, Toronto. Broadcast: CBC, Canada, 1987 (exact date unknown). Viewing copy: Wellesley Free Library, Wellesley, Mass., call number Video 780.9 Music.

Program seven of an eight-part series on the history of music in which Yehudi Menuhin (YM) examines music between the world wars. AC is briefly interviewed by YM in his Peekskill studio. Footage of AC conducting is also included. Topics discussed by AC: how it feels to be an American, diversity of influences, problems of the dominance of nineteenth-century European music in the repertoire.

31. *Vive La France! Mademoiselle—A Portrait of Nadia Boulanger*. 56 minutes. Produced by Dominique Parent-Altier, written by Shawn Altier, Crocus Films, Bloomington, Ind. Broadcast: PBS, April 5, 1987. Viewing copy: Library of Congress, Washington, D.C., call number VBG 3838.

Documentary about Nadia Boulanger (NB), with interviews of her and tributes from her pupils, including AC. Other participants: Philip Glass, David Diamond, Michel Legrand, Louise Talma, Virgil Thomson, Alice Hufstader, Emil Naoumoff (pianist). Topics discussed by NB that relate to AC: nature of her close relationship with him, his music "so original and so profoundly musical." Topics discussed by AC: NB should have been a composer, her influence on his music unidentifiable because her teaching approach was to seek to develop the individual personality of the composer.

32. *MacDowell: An American Artists' Colony*. 60 minutes. Produced by Fritz Wetherbee, directed and written by Marc Diessner, New Hampshire Public Television, Durham, NH. Broadcast: NHPTV, November 24, 1996. Viewing copy: Keene State College, Keene, N.H., call number N6535.N4 M3 1996.

Fritz Wetherbee narrates a history of the MacDowell Colony in Peterborough, N.H., and interviews many of its visitors, past and present. Wetherbee filmed the footage of AC at Peekskill in 1971: only a few minutes of this footage are used in the film. Topics discussed by AC: the benefits of the colony, his summer at the colony in 1938, Marion MacDowell's dedication to the Colony.

33. *Great Performances: Copland's America*. 56 minutes. Produced by John Walker, directed by David Horn, WNET/BBC, New York. Broadcast: CBS, January 21, 2000. Viewing copy: University of Denver, Denver, Colo., call number videocassette 2293.

"Biography of Aaron Copland and his music including historic film clips of performances and interviews with Copland. Copland is discussed by various composers, conductors, friends, etc. Excerpts from his various compositions are performed by Eos Orchestra and soloists, Jonathan Sheffer conducting."[19]

34. ***Fanfare for America: The Composer Aaron Copland***. 59 minutes. Produced by Swantje Ehrentreich, directed and written by Andreas Skipis, Hessischer Rundfunk, Frankfurt am Main, Germany. Broadcast: ITV2, UK, November 10, 2001. Viewing copy: Courtright Memorial Library, Westville, Ohio, call number ML410.C756 F36 2001.

Documentary about AC including interviews with Copland specialists, historic interviews of Copland (credited to Vivian Perlis Film Production and the Library of Congress), and performances of his works in various locations by the Frankfurt Radio Symphony Orchestra conducted by Hugo Wolff. Other participants: Howard Pollack, Hugo Wolff (both interviewed).

NOTES

I am greatly indebted to the staff of the Motion Picture and Television Reading Room at the Library of Congress, Washington, D.C., and in particular Rosemary Hanes, without whom this project would never have come about. My thanks also go to Bill Stea at the PBS archives and James McKelvey at the BBC for their help in locating programs, and to Anne C. Shreffler and especially Carol J. Oja for their invaluable advice and suggestions.

1. Many of the documentaries on this list examine Copland's conducting career, and a number include him conducting rehearsals or performances of his own music: *Composers' Workshop; Workshop: Mr. Copland Comes to Town; Music in the Twenties; A Copland Portrait; Bill Moyers' Journal: Copland; NBC Magazine;* and *Aaron Copland: A Self-Portrait*.

2. For a full list of original television scripts by Bernstein see Jack Gottlieb, ed., *Leonard Bernstein: August 25, 1918–October 14, 1990: A Complete Catalog of his Works: Celebrating his 80th Birthday Year 1998–99* (New York: Leonard Bernstein Music Publishing Company, Boosey & Hawkes Inc., 1998).

3. From the *Congressional Record*, quoted in Aaron Copland and Vivian Perlis, *Copland Since 1943* (New York: St. Martin's Press, 1989), p. 408.

4. Dwight Macdonald, "A Theory of Mass Culture," *Mass Culture: The Popular Arts in America*, ed. Bernard Rosenberg and David Manning White (Glencoe, Ill.: The Free Press, 1957), p. 62.

5. Copland and Perlis, *Copland Since 1943*, p. 404. Perlis wrote the 1985 documentary *Aaron Copland: A Self-Portrait*.

6. Where the first transmission date was not noted in library records or in Copland's correspondence, I have cited the program's first known transmission date in New York with the relevant channel, unless otherwise stated.

7. Letter from the BBC to Aaron Copland, October 28, 1958. Aaron Copland Collection, Music Division, Library of Congress, Folder 9 ("BBC"), Box 334.

8. National Educational Television (NET) was a non-commercial, educational station affiliated with Channel 13. WNET was sold to this new station in 1961. In 1969 NET was replaced by the Public Broadcasting Service.

9. This date is the first known transmission in Boston. I could not locate a New York transmission.

10. Television listing, *New York Times*, October 16, 1962.

11. "Television This Week," *New York Times*, March 13, 1966.

12. Sylvia Spence, press release, Public Information Department, Educational Broadcasting Corporation, April 27, 1966, National Public Broadcasting Archives, University of Maryland.

13. Television listing, *New York Times*, November 10, 1966.

14. Microfiche of NBC's Program Analysis File, Motion Picture and Television Reading Room, Library of Congress, Washington, D.C.

15. University of Wisconsin, UWM Libraries, Multimedia Library collection information.

16. "Copland in Cleveland," *Worldcat (FirstSearch)*, http://firstsearch.oclc.org (accessed May 18, 2004). The single known copy to which this entry refers is lost.

17. Microfiche of NBC's Program Analysis File, Library of Congress.

18. From NBC online news archives, http://www.footage.net/cgi-bin/FN/director. cgi?calling=docview&table=nbc_news&pkey=378866&query=$(aaron+and+copland).

19. "Copland's America," *Worldcat (FirstSearch)*, http://firstsearch.oclc.org (accessed May 20, 2004).

PART VII

RECONFIGURING COPLAND'S WORLD

Copland Reconfigured

LEON BOTSTEIN

I. Copland's Uniqueness

There is a remarkable symmetry between the way in which Aaron Copland was viewed at the height of his career and his posthumous reputation.[1] Virgil Thomson's understandable annoyance and thinly veiled envy notwithstanding, after World War II Copland emerged as the "dean" of American music and its composers.[2] He assumed a role in life he has not lost in history, as the undisputed central figure of American twentieth-century classical music. Charles Ives can be credited, as Copland himself did, for being the first major original American modernist. But Ives's output was comparatively restricted. His active career as a composer came to an end decades before his death, during the years Copland and his contemporaries were first making their mark in the 1920s. Like Gustav Mahler's, Ives's music is as closely linked with the nineteenth century as the twentieth. And Ives's music, despite its extensive use of American sources, in contrast to Copland's, never experienced either wide popularization or near-commercial imitation.[3]

Copland's centrality is due not only to the music and the place it maintains in the repertory but also to his public persona, which was exceptional for an individual with such success and fame. Particularly after 1945, Copland assumed a role as an avuncular and gentle senior figure, intent on assisting colleagues and students. He was a peacemaker in a highly contentious aesthetic environment in which avant-garde modernists, conservatives, and experimentalists all seemed inclined to controversy. Exponents of modernism were particularly explicit in their contempt both for traditionalists (who were no more tolerant) and the several worlds of commercial and popular music. Copland shunned these polemics and sought to bring together disparate factions.[4]

He defied the popular image of the self-consciously serious artist as eccentric, arcane, inaccessible, or rebellious. His self-presentation was one of middle-class modesty, frugality, absence of resentment, and generosity.[5] He taught and mentored a wide and diverse set of aspiring composers (primarily at Tanglewood). He was gracious in praise of younger colleagues and reticent in criticism. Except perhaps for an early sensitivity to the competitive prominence and popularity of George Gershwin, he displayed little envy of others.[6] Copland was eager to communicate with the broader public in a thoughtful manner, not only through his music but also as a writer on music. His restraint and studiously circumspect public self-image helped solidify his role as a benign and gentle leader among composers and musicians.

Copland, then, was the one figure in whom all in American musical life could find some grounds for admiration no matter the reservations some had about his music. For the crowd around *Perspectives of New Music* there was the Copland of the Piano Variations (1930), the *Short Symphony* (1933), the Piano Fantasy (1952–57), and the two final orchestral works, *Connotations* (1962) and *Inscape* (1967). For the public at large and enthusiasts of the musical theater and Hollywood there was the Copland of *Billy the Kid* (1938) and *Rodeo* (1942). Those with conservative tastes in serious music could be consoled that in the late works, particularly the Piano Fantasy and the two orchestral pieces, the use of modernist strategies associated with Arnold Schoenberg, Charles Ives, and Edgard Varèse still resulted in music that remained unmistakably Copland. For example, in the Piano Fantasy, as Arnold Whithall has observed, the familiar procedures of Copland are present beneath the work's modernism—the "declamatory and lyrical, forceful and tender, ceremonial chorale and intimate song."[7] They reside within an "association with consonance and dissonance" characteristic of tonality.[8] The allusions to chorale writing and the rhythmic dimensions of the Piano Fantasy evoke the Copland of *Appalachian Spring* (1944) and *The Red Pony* (1948). Likewise, the blocklike sonorities with which *Inscape* opens and the rhythmic elaboration in the central portion of the piece recall Copland's music of twenty years earlier.

Those who speculate that in his last years of productivity Copland felt marginalized and tried to emulate modernist fashions to show how up to date he was seem off the mark.[9] Copland retained a manner that mixed reserve and circumspection with self-confidence. His engagement with reigning fashions in the 1950s and 1960s was consistent with previous compositional habits. In the 1920s he borrowed from and adapted jazz. In the 1930s he largely gave up jazz (though it reappeared in the 1948 Clarinet Concerto) and followed others, primarily Thomson and Roy Harris, in using folk and popular song and dance materials. By the 1960s he turned to serialism as a method, much as he had used the genre of jazz forty years earlier. The end results, from the early works composed in Paris to the last pieces, betrayed audibly and unmistakably the consistent, distinctive hallmarks of Copland's musical rhetoric.

One reason Copland was a central figure in his lifetime and posthumously was that his craft as a composer has been universally admired. But far more significant is the widespread notion that he wrote music that has come to exemplify the modern American spirit and landscape. Copland helped define, if not create, the resounding clichés of America with which, in turn, he is credited. Copland's achievement is understood, therefore, not only in musical terms but as a prominent feature of American culture. On the musical side, particularly in the context of the disappearance, if not death, of radical musical modernism at the end of the twentieth century, Copland's aesthetic has come to represent a dominant rather than a peripheral American legacy from the twentieth century.[10]

American composers in the generations that followed Copland, beginning with David Del Tredici and John Adams, connect to him, rather than to John Cage, Roger Sessions, Milton Babbitt, or Elliott Carter. Links can be found between Copland's instinct for simplicity, formal clarity, and accessibility, and post-1970 minimalism. Qualities in the music of Steve Reich, Ellen Taaffe Zwilich, and Philip Glass suggest a common ground in the project of fashioning a distinctive American music between Copland and the legacy of Ives and Henry Cowell.[11] Postmodernism and neo-Romanticism echo the synthesis in Copland's music of accessible surface qualities, uncanny sensitive eclecticism, and openness to disparate styles and genres. Copland's appeal resides in his disciplined economy, refinement, and resistance to doctrines and catechisms. Arthur Berger's conviction that there might be two different personalities in the work can be countered by focusing more on the shared characteristics between his popular and more introverted and avant-garde music: the sonorities, use of characteristic rhythmic patterns, and the persistent suggestion of a narrative arc. Copland articulated early on (and adhered to) the necessity of a sustained musical line that justifies form and lends structure to musical logic: an allegiance to the "grand line" he developed in his studies with Nadia Boulanger.[12]

It can be argued further that the quality of Copland's output is admirably consistent when compared with that of his closest contemporary rivals, Thomson and Roy Harris.[13] However, Copland's catalog is not extensive. There are nominally three symphonies, but indeed only the third bears comparison with the grand symphonic achievement of, for example, Shostakovich, whose influence on Copland's Third is unmistakable. Copland's productivity cannot compare with Bohuslav Martinů's, not to speak of Nikolai Miaskovsky's. Set side by side even with Béla Bartók, Igor Stravinsky, and Arthur Honegger, let alone Copland's friend Darius Milhaud and sometime-colleague Paul Hindemith, the results are enviably elegant in their consistency, but restrained in range, genre, and number. Taking into account the amount of reutilization and cannibalizing in Copland's oeuvre, one is struck by the strategically economic compositional legacy. Copland seems to have had some difficulty composing. By his own admission, his muse shut down at midcareer, well before the onset of Alzheimer's. His turn to conducting was more of a symptom than a cause of the slowdown of his compositional output in the 1960s.[14]

Copland's music remains a defining part not only of history—twentieth-century American culture—but also of contemporary Americanism, and this ultimately sets it apart from that of all his contemporaries. The music that captured the imagination of listeners when first performed has been routinized so that for succeeding generations, Copland's musical rhetoric has become iconic. His music has helped generate a sense (perhaps the illusion) of historical and cultural unity and consistency. From the songs and piano works to the film scores, Copland's music has functioned as a mirror of America. It successfully bridges the widening audience gap between concert classical music and popular music.

But Copland did far more than reflect a pervasive sense of national identity in music. As the central figure of twentieth-century American music (only Gershwin and Duke Ellington are comparable), Copland helped shape the sense of the modern American spirit itself and helped define the modern consciousness of America's ideals, character, and sense of place. The notion that his music played not a subsidiary but a central role in the shaping of the national cultural consciousness makes Copland uniquely interesting, for the historian as well as for the musician.[15]

American nationalism as a construct did not emerge—in contrast to European counterparts—primarily from myths located in claims of linguistic, religious, demographic, ethnic, and geographical continuity, notions of blood and soil. This comparative historical vacuum generated an opportunity for a species of invention and dissemination in which the arts played a significant role. Music in the context of a diverse, dynamic, and pluralist American democracy became a primary historical force in the cultural politics of a national self-definition. Its role extended beyond a confirmation of a nativism rooted in claims of homogeneity characteristic of the European nineteenth century. Copland managed to exploit the inadequacy of the European nationalist model for the arts in modern America. He found a means to make serious concert music more than a supplemental or implicitly secondary phenomenon.

As scholars have noted, Copland's greatest success in fashioning a musical expression of national identity was inspired by the stylistic innovations of Thomson, particularly his *Symphony on a Hymn Tune* (1928).[16] But it was Copland's music from the late 1930s and 1940s (and not, as some might have predicted in the 1930s, that of Harris) that became widely celebrated as American in some exemplary and unifying fashion.[17] Copland's brand of Americanness has been understood as transcending class and region, the urban and the rural, and, above all, ethnicity and race. Spike Lee's elegant and powerful embrace of Copland's music in the 1998 film *He Got Game* only underscores the sustained role played by Copland's construct of America.

There are indeed very few comparable examples in history in which a composer of what Copland termed "serious" music is understood as having had a defining role in shaping national consciousness. More often than not, composers identified as articulating through music the sensibilities of a nation appropriated preexisting national elements into the high-art concert tradition. Copland engaged in such appropriations, but in his case the transformation and stylistic synthesis he fashioned became themselves the defining attributes. In contrast, composers deemed as expressing a national voice are most often not credited with inventing novel emblems of national consciousness. For example, in Russia beginning in the nineteenth century, premodern folk elements and materials were incorporated into musical works for the concert and operatic stage. Their function, however altered and camouflaged, was as authentic if not nostalgic signifiers of national groupings and distinct geographic regions.

These signifiers, even when radically transformed as in Stravinsky or Ives, helped define the composer's unique voice. But the results did not function as novel public redefinitions of the nation. In this sense, elements understood as "primitive" were adapted to an urban, avant-garde, and literate culture of music.[18]

More often than not, the recognition of nationalist elements was not disturbed by radical compositional transformation. The music of the "Mighty Five," Aleksandr Glazunov, and the early Stravinsky intentionally referenced musical elements understood in often quite controversial and polemical ways as nationalist. High-art transformations of fragments of a preliterate musical cultural heritage were cosmopolitan adaptations of reactionary and traditionalist symbolic indicators of nationhood, signifiers of a connection to a premodern rural community. The greater the modernist aesthetic originality, the more marginal the music became vis-à-vis its utility as a new vehicle of public national self-representation. It was this paradox that fueled, for example, the nasty and destructive shifts in official state aesthetics in the history of music during the Soviet era in Russia.[19]

A comparable argument can be made about the music of Bartók, who used his discovery, documentation, and construction of an authentic, preindustrial rural folk tradition (as opposed to the Gypsy tradition) to generate a vital and highly personal modernist musical vocabulary. His music was understood both as distinctly Hungarian and communicative to international audiences. It continues to be identified by audiences as recognizably Hungarian, but Bartók's music (as opposed to his status as a world-famous Hungarian personality) has assumed no role within Hungary in the definition of modern Hungarian national consciousness.[20] The same can be said of Leoš Janáček, despite his use of folk materials and Czech speech patterns in compositional practice. Even the synthetic allusion to and suggestion of authentic folk materials in the music of less radically nationalist figures—such as Pyotr Ilich Tchaikovsky, Karol Szymanowski, George Enescu, and Antonin Dvořák—confirmed rather than created emblems of national identity. These composers imitated recognizable sources with historical and geographical identities and legitimacy; they did not invent new markers of nationhood.

At first glance, the case of Copland seems to fit this pattern. During the 1930s Copland began to use American folk tunes, emblems of a rural frontier and a dynamic but yet not urbanized America. The role of "Simple Gifts" in *Appalachian Spring* and Stephen Foster songs in the *Lincoln Portrait* (1941) are later examples from the 1940s of the integration of authentic borrowed historical materials. This pattern is audible in the ballet scores *Billy the Kid* and *Rodeo* with their incorporation of cowboy and fiddle tunes.[21] In modern Western mass society, concert music has rarely been a powerful variable in the creation of a group consciousness. Yet it is Copland's musical style, not his use of folk materials, that sustains a defining role in the way Americans think of America, its history, and themselves as Americans. This manner transcends individual ethnic and regional personal identifications, as the use of Copland's music during the 1976 Bicentennial revealed. Folk fragments or their elaboration, despite their evident audibility, came to play a secondary role in lending Copland's music its apparent American character.[22]

It is striking how difficult it is to find comparable cases in which classical concert music played a leading and not secondary historical role in the formation of cultural and societal symbols. In this century, Shostakovich's original concert music may have briefly played such a role in the Soviet Union (notably during World War II). Richard Wagner's music had a comparable influence in shaping late-nineteenth-century and early-twentieth-century German nationalism, but much of its effectiveness derived not from the musical materials and practices per se but from the literary and mythic framework Wagner provided. Other parallels include Giuseppe Verdi's role in defining late-nineteenth-century Italian nationalism, Jean Sibelius's contribution to the construction of the modern self-image of the Finnish nation, and Edward Elgar's place in the shaping of the early-twentieth-century sense of England and its empire.[23]

The Sibelius and Elgar comparisons to Copland are particularly interesting because for Wagner and Verdi opera was the seminal medium, which inevitably cedes language and narrative a crucial role in defining the music's power. Copland's film and ballet scores and their unmistakably American scenarios (all of his film music except *North Star* is devoted to quintessentially American subjects) played a major role in establishing what we now hear as "the Copland sound." A story line is also suggested in the case of *Lincoln Portrait*, though the spoken text comes late in the work. Despite these ballet narratives and the movie plots, however, the "shaping force" in Copland's case (to borrow the potent phrase used by Ernst Toch) has been the character of the music, as his instrumental works without story lines and programmatic titles reveal. The analogy to Elgar and Sibelius may be therefore apt. The defining element of what we consider to be Finnish in the instrumental music of Sibelius's symphonies is the sound, not the narratives or programs of the tone poems, even though the narratives inspired the composer's sonic imagination.

Although Hungarians (and others) do not think of Bartók's music as defining the quintessentially Hungarian, domesticated, and commercialized premodern folk and Gypsy music, despite their use in classical composition, they retain their unchallenged centrality as expressive of Hungarianness. However, *Fanfare for the Common Man* (1942), the opening section of *Lincoln Portrait*, and fragments of *Appalachian Spring* (not just the use of "Simple Gifts") are heard as modern emblems of America, as expansive definitions of modern American consciousness. They have competed with and even supplanted and superseded folk music and popular music in their capacity to articulate America's uniqueness in the minds of a broad public in America and beyond. They do so in a manner that no fragment from Bartók or Janáček (and even Dvořák) does for the composer's nation.

The rarity of comparable examples extends beyond Europe. In the Western Hemisphere there is no comparable case even when one considers the legacy of Carlos Chávez in Mexico, Alberto Ginastera in Argentina, or Heitor Villa-Lobos in Brazil, all composers who were colleagues and in some cases close friends of Copland's. Their work, no matter what its debt to folk materials may be, has not been commercially exploited or utilized as part of state celebrations in a manner comparable to Copland's.

The special place that Copland's music holds in modern American cultural life has inspired the direction of contemporary Copland scholarship. The recent literature on Copland begins with the premise of his cultural significance. The task then becomes to illuminate the sources of the centrality and popularity of Copland's music. Four explanatory factors have come under scrutiny since the composer's death in 1990: Copland's homosexuality, his politics, his status as a Jew in America, and his links to the visual arts in America.[24]

II. Copland's Sexuality

The most novel and contested among the sources of explanation for his centrality concerns the interpretation of Copland's homosexuality. The argument has been made that for Copland and many of his prominent homosexual composer contemporaries—Virgil Thomson, Paul Bowles, Leonard Bernstein, David Diamond, Samuel Barber, Marc Blitzstein, Ned Rorem—music was a special and privileged medium. In this account, music was an expressive medium ideally suited for the composer in a society where being homosexual required camouflage, since music could be coded to conceal. Moreover, outsider status induced skepticism and freedom from majority norms and claims.[25] It gave the artist, and particularly the composer, an independence from a thoughtless allegiance to social and cultural conventions that may have been a necessary prerequisite for originality. This case has been made also for Charles Tomlinson Griffes, a key figure in the generation preceding Copland.[26]

Music, as Copland frequently argued, could be used to express private sentiments without revealing explicitly fixed intentional meanings of the sort communicated by images and words.[27] At the end of his autobiography written with Vivian Perlis, he wrote that he had the "privilege" of being a composer since that role gave him as an artist "the only place one can express in public the feelings ordinarily regarded as private."[28] The medium of serious music allowed Copland "to be completely honest."[29] Music allowed the homosexual composer, in Copland's words, not to "hide from ourselves or from others."[30]

The intriguing paradox was that while meaning in music could be precise from the vantage point of expressive intentions, it also allowed listeners to form quite different plausible interpretations. Music engendered both clarity and ambiguity. Its power was its unique capacity to say something with respect to "emotions, feelings, reactions" and at the same time to evade the limits of language.[31]

Copland never adhered to the nineteenth-century construct that contrasted absolute music with "program" music. He was at home writing music for films, ballets, and texts. He also wrote sonatas, concertos, and symphonies, often eagerly giving these instrumental compositions titles suggestive of images and places, without indicating any actual musical parallels or programmatic relationships. *Inscape*, a purely instrumental composition, is guided, albeit amorphously, in a manner reminiscent of Richard Strauss's use of texts, by the poetry of Gerard Manley Hopkins. (Strauss in *Don Juan* quotes Nikolaus Lenau in the front of the score; Copland prefaces *Inscape* with his explanation of the meaning of the word as it appears in Hopkins.)[32]

Although music generates a sense of meaning to its audience, for Copland the criteria for judging music were cast in purely musical terms, such as his beloved "grand line." Nevertheless, Copland wanted his well-crafted, serious music to communicate to as broad a public as possible. His judgment of the worth of a piece presumed the idea that good music communicates meaning and is cherished for that fact. He wanted the unique space of comprehension and communication that he believed music provided to be part of the experience of as many of his fellow human beings as possible. Music encouraged intimate feelings by rendering the private public, without threat of exposure; each individual took from the public hearing of music his or her own private meaning.

But music was not only a private transaction. It possessed a unique public function. It could be argued that for the homosexual music offered a particularly prized common public ground of social engagement. Music's meaning, in contrast to other art forms, appeared comparatively indirect and indeterminate, requiring a species of translation into language and images by listeners. If the homosexual understood himself to be marginalized or subject to prejudice, then music offered the possibility of candid public expression, a realm of participation in which equality as an artist was more readily achieved. Authentic expression could be achieved without disclosure and without the necessity to conceal or deny one's sense of self and one's identity. Music created the potential of a reconciliation between overt and covert communication. This potential was utilized by both homosexual and heterosexual composers, as suggested by the examples of Wagner in the *Siegfried Idyll* and Alban Berg in the *Lyric Suite,* where secret meanings are integrated with explicit ones.[33]

Performing and listening to music were therefore social acts with powers distinct from the act of reading. Reading was experienced as a solitary engagement, even when many people read the same, best-selling book. In the concert hall or on the ballet and opera stage, in a live radio broadcast, and most significantly through film, the writing of music aimed at a collective experience. It was realized in public spaces as a simultaneous and unique sound experience, often for sizable crowds. In concerts, each private individual had the dual benefit of a public event as well as an often inexpressible private experience. Music maintained an uncanny equilibrium between the intimate and the civic. Furthermore, for Copland, as for Ives before him, music's public role seemed uniquely suited to the advocacy of American democratic mores. The uniqueness of the individual, from the intentions of the composer to the meanings imputed by listeners, as well as a sense of community were underscored by music.

For the homosexual American composer in the mid-twentieth century living either in the closet or openly as an outsider or a pariah, the argument runs, the concealed aspect of music, vis-à-vis its precise meaning, was particularly appropriate. According to this line of reasoning, a radical opportunity for self-invention and innovation was specific to music, as opposed to literature and the visual arts. Furthermore, the social distance experienced by the homosexual offered, ironically, a privileged perspective. While the nature of music protected the privacy of the composer, it also created a detached perspective from which counterintuitive coherences and commonalities within the public realm could be invented or discovered. Music therefore became the medium in which a special kind of distance—created by sexual preference—was given a genuine voice.

This line of reasoning notwithstanding, scholars who focus on Copland as a homosexual are unclear about how that opportunity guided Copland from his work as a student of Rubin Goldmark to his studies in Paris with Nadia Boulanger, to his shift after composing *Statements* (1935) to writing his most successful populist works.[34] Likewise, they fail to explain why Copland's musical populism was far more successful than Thomson's or Blitzstein's, or why it led to an influential modernist construct symbolic of American identity.[35]

Nadine Hubbs has suggested that there might be some interplay between the homosexuality of Copland and his contemporaries and their preference for the French as opposed to the German traditions in music and letters.[36] But homosexuality may not be a dominant reason for the post–World War I affinity among young American artists for French culture. In Copland's case, Mahler figured as an important influence (in part inspired by Boulanger's advocacy). Furthermore, the importance of Copland's studies with Goldmark should not be overshadowed by the attention regularly paid to his years with Boulanger. The Great War had brought to an abrupt end the dominance and prestige of the German language and German culture in America; no deeper explanation may be required than the consequences of the war and the Treaty of Versailles. Add to that the Bolshevik Revolution of 1917, which made Paris a primary émigré locale for Russian exiles, and little mystery remains as to why Paris was alluring for young American musicians, artists, and writers, heterosexual and homosexual alike.[37]

Most significantly, Copland's life as a homosexual posed difficulties for him not particularly different from those heterosexuality would have posed. The wealth of biographical material confirms a consistent picture of Copland as discreetly but openly homosexual from the beginning of his career. Influenced by Havelock Ellis and André Gide, he came to understand himself, sympathetically, as a homosexual. He found a middle way, neither hiding it nor advertising it. Instead, he fashioned a pattern of self-presentation of refined discretion, in which his private life would not occupy center stage. He did not politicize his sexual preference, and did not closet it. He did not, like Bernstein, create a public image as a heterosexual. No pattern of allegiance based on sexual preference can be located in his social and political contacts as a teacher and colleague. And there is little evidence that he felt marginal (beyond the separateness and economic limitations that being a freelance composer brought him) as a result of the way he lived.

Copland was by nature an optimist. He came of age in a brief moment in the 1920s of openness and tolerance regarding sexuality. The popularization of modern psychology, including Freud, permitted him to internalize his choice without defensiveness. This stable sense of self served him in good stead when the vacuum created by the brief collapse of Victorian morality after 1918 was superseded by a growing intolerance that resurfaced in earnest during the 1940s and 1950s. By that time he was infamous only for his left-wing politics. And the historical connection between sexual preference and political ideology is tenuous, even for the 1950s, considering the homosexuality of Whittaker Chambers. Can it be said, then, that Copland's sexual life was so problematic, central, or specifically conceptualized that it becomes sufficient to define either the character of his music or his approach to composing? If the answer to this question is negative, then the claims made for his sexual preference as playing a significant role in his success in articulating a distinctive modern American voice through his status as a presumed outsider may be weak. His sexuality may not have been crucial to any particular distance essential to his capacity to generate, from the margins, an influential musical expression of American national identity.

III. Copland's Politics

Politics may hold more promise as a means to illuminate Copland's unique achievement. Elizabeth B. Crist has argued convincingly that Copland's populist if not radical progressive politics, which were first explicitly articulated in the 1930s, informed the most celebrated works of the 1940s, those for which he later became most renowned.[38] Despite the difficulties Copland encountered during the McCarthy era, his liberal sentiments seem to have remained with him to the end of his career. The consistency of his liberal populism stands somewhat in contrast to many left-wing contemporary intellectuals and artists who after 1939 drifted away from a 1930s radicalism and liberalism, often to become advocates of neoconservatism at the end of their careers.

Though Copland may have voted for the Communist candidate for president in the 1930s, his political allegiances were never doctrinaire or aligned with a party ideology.[39] He was, rather, a left-leaning liberal who, through the experience of World War II, came to embrace the ideals of Roosevelt and the New Deal. From the start, Copland's radicalism was rooted in an idealistic cultural rather than political conception of American democracy. He was, for example, not influenced intellectually by Marx or doctrinal versions of Marxism. Unlike some of his contemporaries, his habits of reading did not extend to tracts on economic theory and political thought. Democracy was understood consistently as a worthy alternative to fascism on the right and Stalinist totalitarianism on the left.[40]

By the same token, even if Copland's music has been recently appropriated as an emblem of a reflexive if not almost nativist patriotism, that was never the intent of the composer. The mix of grandeur and simplicity in Copland seems explicitly designed to reach the largest possible music-loving public, not merely, as some of his more strenuously communist colleagues might have wished, the historically "vanguard" working classes. Copland's genius was to create an "imposed simplicity" that retained the aspirations of both the classical tradition and musical modernism; Copland never abandoned the elite, privileged, and often conservative public for concert music, particularly Serge Koussevitzky's fans and devoted public.[41] Absent a disciplined radical political ideology, Copland embraced a generous liberal populism marked by a commitment to humanist ideals such as tolerance, freedom, and social justice, understood in common-sense terms consistent with the rhetoric of American history rather than a dialectical theory of history. The absence of any hint even early in his career of the enfant terrible or an aesthetic radical's conceit and pleasure at unmasking an older generation's presumed philistinism ran parallel with a commitment to the equality of citizenship in a free democracy, irrespective of race and class.[42]

Indeed, the nondoctrinaire but radically egalitarian political character of Copland's engagement with America holds promising clues to his enduring popularity. Unlike Hanns Eisler, Kurt Weill, or Marc Blitzstein, Copland's stylistic shift from the music of the 1920s to the music of the 1930s was less abrupt, less driven by partisan commitments to a particular movement and its claims. Copland's politics evolved and became more pointedly radical in the 1930s, but they, like his compositional development, reflected an evolution, not a series of conversions. No sharp deviation from prior ambitions was required. The early influence of French models such as Gabriel Fauré, or of Stravinsky, not to speak of his engagement with jazz, turned out to be natural, easy to absorb, and fortuitous. From the start, Copland had an instinct for form and clarity. The desire to succeed with the public was evident throughout.[43] The critical tradition of dividing Copland's music between serious modernist works and populist crowd pleasers overlooks a consistency throughout the music evident when one compares, for example, the early works for string quartet from the 1920s and his first success, "The Cat and the Mouse" (1920), with music written in the 1940s.

The affectation of simplicity and the embrace of a wholly new style characteristic of a politically inspired populism in the cases of Weill (who made a subsidiary and third stylistic shift upon his emigration to America), Eisler, and Blitzstein demanded more of a decisive stylistic change than Copland displayed. Copland consistently composed both accessible music and adventuresome music. Conversely, modernism was not wholly abandoned in the music directed at the wider public. Copland's musical style reflects a persistent gradualism. Even the works considered the most modernist never present a surface of obscurity, despite complex textures and compositional strategies. And the so-called popular works never strain artificially to achieve intelligibility. Consider the Piano Variations. Copland found nothing jarring or strange in refashioning them for orchestra in 1957, nearly thirty years after their composition for piano and long after he had written the ballet scores for which he was most famous.

Copland's engagement with politics has been justly compared to the political commitments of American modernist artists identified with Alfred Stieglitz and his circle. The relationship between photography and musical modernism in the early twentieth century deserves closer scrutiny.[44] Ernest Bloch was, for example, an accomplished photographer. Copland's aesthetic affinities in the visual arts led him less toward painting than to still photography and the moving picture, two media with strong modernist and political overtones in which Copland displayed a keen interest, particularly during his friendship with Rudy Burckhardt and Ralph Steiner. Copland's musical modernism can therefore be compared to the work of Paul Strand, Walker Evans, and Stieglitz, and the director William Wyler.

The conception of space and time in the seminal generation of American modernist photographers suggests an affinity between modern aesthetics and democratic politics. In their work, a realization of the American space and character comparable to Copland's, at once highly contoured, accessible, and direct, can be seen. The landscapes with which the photographers of the 1920s experimented were both urban and rural, just as Copland's musical evocations drew on both sources. The Walt Whitman–like assertion of the bold, open, and free democratic American spirit in Copland's music has its analogue in the pathbreaking use of the camera by photographers of his generation.[45]

If music could shape a sense of modern national consciousness, two novel media, both associated with industry, progress, and the machine—photography and the moving picture—were equally suited to a role in forging a unified sensibility out of a recent demographic amalgam. Both media possessed, like music, a private and public dimension. The camera was clearly a medium of seeing and art making with the capacity for wide public participation and reproduction. The movie was, like the concert, a public event (with music, even in the so-called silent movie era). Both encouraged the evolution of a distinctive modern American art form and voice that did not possess overwhelming residues of European models with their tradition of nondemocratic state patronage. Copland's music fit well into the film medium and, unlike that of most Hollywood composers (with a few exceptions, such as Bernard Hermann and Toch), remained original in its distance from late-Romantic gestures, patterns, and sonorities. Copland's film scores hint at a common ground of ambition between Copland and contemporary innovators in film.

The much-discussed presumed connection between politics and musical modernism argued by Adorno and heralded in the years immediately after 1945 has obscured the fact that the use of tonality between the 1930s and the mid-1960s cannot be reduced to a simple parallelism between musical style and political allegiances. The post–World War II radical generation of Pierre Boulez reacted to the musical aesthetics of fascism by adopting new techniques that rejected tonality and traditional practices. However, in Europe, an embrace of the avant-garde did not suggest progressive politics even before 1945, as the case of Anton Webern illustrates.[46] The experimentalists in America, from Ives and Cowell to Cage and Lou Harrison, similarly did not automatically share a common political point of view.

The modernist influence in Copland's music did not have political origins. Copland aimed to find a way to use modernism within the trajectory of compositional traditions, with tradition understood as necessarily progressive and innovative, not static. But the limitations and adaptations of modernism in his own music were influenced by strategic considerations regarding the public and in this sense were political, not aesthetic. Therefore Copland could speak of an "imposed simplicity." In the 1930s, he realized that to reach a wider audience in a democracy the composer had to become clearer, more disciplined, not less modern. Easy intelligibility was desirable in a democratic culture. Copland's redefinition of the public for whom he was writing took on a Whitman-like egalitarianism toward the broader public characteristic of the new art forms, film and photography.

Copland's lifelong interest in contemporary music, across a wide spectrum of styles, signaled a belief in the obligation of each composer to write music that was personally responsive to the historical moment. He opposed the notion of music written out of mere allegiance to tradition, or timeless aesthetic verities, or established schools of composition. Rather, Copland's willingness to experiment, incorporating contemporary elements within the idiosyncratic and personal voice he crafted as unmistakably his own, was consistent with the aim of maintaining a common ground with his listeners without sacrifice to individuality.

His uncanny capacity to reconcile the intimate with the monumental made Copland's voice distinct from the very beginning. In that sense Copland's affinity for Mahler becomes more understandable. The comparison rests not in the choice of compositional materials, strategies, or methods of orchestration. In Copland it lies, as in Shostakovich, in the powerful symbiosis in musical fabric between striking surface drama and intimate private sentiment—all flourishing in the framework of large-scale instrumental composition. In Copland, as in Mahler, the interplay of public gestures of grandiosity functions seamlessly with the restrained and disarmingly candid revelation of the personal.[47] What Copland, unlike Shostakovitch, rejected, however, is the dimension in Mahler of parody, irony, pessimism, and sarcasm. As Copland often reminded his listeners and readers, affirmation and optimism needed to be integral to music, particularly modern American music. An expansive cultural assertion of an open, socially fair, and egalitarian democracy helped define the character of new music in America and inspired the massive but translucent sonorities of Copland's use of the orchestra.

Considering Copland's political commitments does help illuminate the direction Copland took to fashion music that has come to reflect and even define the image of modern America. For Copland, the composer, like the photographer, was obligated to communicate both modernity and the promise of democracy.

IV. Copland's Jewish Identity

Unlike his homosexuality, Copland's status as a Jew was never an object of speculation. Nor did he make any effort to hide his Jewish identity. Even had he wanted to, it was at the front and center of his life and career, a public fact and an accepted, involuntary part of his identity in the world.[48]

Copland's Jewishness also informed the critical discourse about him from the start of his career. Homosexuality, historically, can remain hidden. The potential of secrecy or semipublic status was designed to mitigate the extent to which homosexuality marginalized the individual. The indelible and definitional, visible and public status of being Jewish within an overwhelmingly non-Jewish social and cultural structure presents a quite different factor in the development of one's self-image—particularly for someone of Copland's generation. Copland's sexual preferences remained quite private. His Jewishness was a basic public and social fact he could not avoid.

There is unfortunately a tendency to consider issues vis-à-vis Jewish identity in all too reductive a fashion. Being Jewish, "feeling Jewish," being seen as a Jew, and even anti-Semitism, particularly in America, were not social realities and historical experiences with stable meanings and fixed significance. Furthermore, it is crucial to consider the context in which Jewish identity is construed from the outside by non-Jews as well as internally by Jews. The overriding factor is that the American diaspora into which Copland was born was unique in modern Jewish history. Jewish immigrants from Europe to America after 1880, although poor, discovered that they were white and European in origin, creating decisive links to the majority. In America integration and equality appeared to be genuine possibilities since color and not religion defined the nation's primary objects of discrimination and racism. Jews were never the nation's politically decisive "other." Furthermore, they were not unique or dominant as immigrants.[49]

The contrast with the situation in Europe in the late nineteenth and early twentieth centuries was indeed startling. Despite key differences within Europe (generated by region and class structure, as well as by the role of religion among the majority populations and the variety of ways Jews chose to be Jewish), the Jew and anti-Semitism were at the very core of modern politics and nationalism.[50] Within European Jewry at one extreme were wealthy converts from Judaism in urban centers and their progeny. They had counterparts in America, the descendants of the mid–nineteenth-century German Jewish immigration. Yet the Viennese families Wittgenstein and Hofmannsthal retained their public status as Jews after 1900 despite wealth and religious conversion. This pattern was sustained by modern race-based political anti-Semitism. Even in the face of deep personal commitments by individual family members to the Christian faith, one's identity as a Jew persisted. In music history the most historic example of this paradox was Felix Mendelssohn, a believing Christian who in his lifetime and posthumously remained identified as a Jew. In America, by contrast, members of the Warburg family who converted all but vanished from public view as Jews.

At the other end of the European spectrum were Jews with active religious lives who were engaged members of the wider non-Jewish professional world. A Viennese example in music was the theorist, critic, and pianist Heinrich Schenker. An individual's relationship to his or her Jewish heritage in Europe was in political terms irrelevant; in all cases, from converts to adherents to Judaism, individuals of Jewish descent were considered apart and remained objects of public and official prejudice. They were blocked from gaining civic and social equality. Jews were Europe's defining minority.

The facts in Copland's case are relatively simple. He was born in the United States of parents who had come from eastern Europe relatively early in their lives. The parental language and the language of the home was English, not Yiddish or Russian, in stark contrast to that of Irving Berlin and, in a later generation, Morton Gould. Furthermore, Copland's parents were successful middle-class store owners in Brooklyn. Economic well-being distinguished Copland's home from those of Berlin and George Gershwin.[51] Copland's family circumstances growing up were perhaps most comparable in terms of social class and acculturation with those of Richard Rodgers.[52]

What was unusual and perhaps significant in Copland's case was that the elder Coplands were Brooklyn Jews with an experience of America that had brought them into contact with both Texas and Illinois. The vision of America in the Copland home was one that was less provincial vis-à-vis America than that of most New York Jews, for whom America meant only the city environment of New York. Yet they were eastern European Jews, not descendants of an older German Jewish community, as were Oscar Hammerstein and Jerome Kern. This social distinction remained strong for most of Copland's life, but it was relevant exclusively to internal dynamics within the Jewish community.[53]

The resolution of Jewish identity in the Copland house was entirely unexceptional. Holidays were kept, but there was no strict adherence to orthodoxy. Copland had a bar mitzvah and the family belonged to a synagogue. The home (in a not particularly Jewish neighborhood) offered a stable compromise between the Jewish and the American in a manner that fits well into categories of assimilation and acculturation.[54] The expectation was that Copland's generation would live in America as American citizens of Jewish descent and perhaps faith. Judaism as a religion became increasingly adhered to in an often nominal and merely symbolic manner.

America, as nearly every Jew in the generation of Copland's parents understood, was special. Jews knew they were not alone in coming to America with previous national and linguistic identities. In America the variety of religious practice and the extent of religious freedom were unparalleled, rendering the separation of church and state genuine and reducing religion to a private matter. Despite the persistence and even virulence of anti-Semitism in the United States, it never rivaled European prejudice or the discrimination directed at Americans of color. The tragic pride of place occupied by European anti-Semitism had been granted to the descendents of slavery, the African-American. Nonetheless the persistence of anti-Semitism created, particularly in Copland's New York, a significant bond between Jews and blacks that had its most memorable expression in musical culture.[55]

Integration into America for the Jew of Copland's generation was already uniquely possible even without a denial of one's status as a Jew. Disappearance and conversion did not seem inevitable if one sought to achieve stability in America. Even more crucial, the goal of social integration had been blurred by history. Despite the social conceits of so-called blue-blood descendants of the first English-speaking settlers (maintained by two prominent modernist composers, Carl Ruggles and Charles Ives), by 1920 America possessed no historically legitimate, uniform, politically dominant majority in terms of ethnicity, religion, or culture into which to disappear.

This reality made Thorstein Veblen's famous 1919 argument concerning the origins, persistence, and necessity of "intellectual preeminence" among Jews in modern Europe not applicable to modern America.[56] Although the decline in American anti-Semitism was gradual and accelerated significantly after 1945, integration and acceptance into American society and politics from the very start of the twentieth century, owing in part to the access to citizenship in a democracy, did not require exceptionalism on the part of the Jews. Jews could become normal, ordinary, and undistinguished Americans and, through becoming average, gain a secure place in society.

Apart from the involuntary recognition of one's status as a Jew emanating from the non-Jewish world, sustaining an active identity as a Jew in the era in which Copland lived did not depend entirely on the pursuit of religious practices, whether orthodox or reformed. Several forms of secular Jewish commitment flourished in America: from the socialist Jewish movement and the Bund, to a Yiddish language–based cultural nationalism, and to political Zionism in the post–Theodor Herzl sense. Early in Copland's career there were two Jewish composers who can be categorized as living quite public lives as Jews. The less well-known, one of Copland's severest critics, was the composer, physicist, and philosopher Lazare Saminsky, the longtime and prolific director of music at Temple Emanu-El in New York. And there was Copland's immediate predecessor, in terms of fame, as a Jewish composer in America, Ernest Bloch. Later in Copland's life Irving Fine, Arthur Berger, Harold Shapero, Lukas Foss, David Diamond, and Leonard Bernstein could be numbered among his Jewish colleagues. In this list were individuals with and without connections to religion, Zionism, anti-Zionist communal politics, and Yiddish culture.

Bernstein was perhaps the most famous and most overtly Jewish colleague in his conduct of life as a public Jew. Perhaps disappointing for those seeking clues in Copland's Jewishness, however, is the astonishing equanimity that Copland displayed vis-à-vis his being Jewish. He grew up in a professional context in which being Jewish was not exceptional. Many of his colleagues over a broad span of generations, from Koussevitzky to Mario Davidovsky, were also Jewish. He surrounded himself with contemporaries, many of Jewish origin, who mirrored versions of his smooth adaptation and integration into American life. Being Jewish was indelible but peripheral for him, as it was for others, and therefore he found it thoroughly unproblematic.

All indications are that to the end of his life Copland found no discomfort in the public acknowledgment of his being a Jew. Neither Copland nor his parents seemed to have been particular enthusiasts of Zionism, which was not uncommon among American Jews before 1933. But Copland was thrilled and proud during his first trip to Israel in 1951, and as a Jew he responded spontaneously as being somehow specially related to its inhabitants.[57] He had spent time before his bar mitzvah in a synagogue, but only periodically.[58] He emerged as an adult without an ongoing connection to religion. Despite the high level of acculturation in his immediate environment, growing up in New York left him with only a mild appreciation for Yiddish culture, and he had no active familiarity with the language. Copland did not push his status as a Jew onto center stage, as did Bernstein in both his music and through his enthusiastic embrace of Israel. Nor did Copland follow the path of Bloch, who sought to express his self-identification as a Jew explicitly through music.[59]

On the other hand, there is nothing in Copland's behavior or writings to hint at any internalization of anti-Semitism and its stereotypes. The literature on modern anti-Semitism is filled with explanatory categories such as self-hate. Scholars have developed a watchful eye and an acute ear for the way in which marginalization and prejudice are internalized, distorted, and appropriated by the victims of prejudice. In the hands of an ironist such as Karl Kraus, the great Jewish Viennese satirist who converted to Catholicism, the extensive language of anti-Semitic polemic was appropriated ironically in ways that have often been misread as literal examples of self-hate. It is all too easy to identify the victim of prejudice as unable to resist internalizing sentiments that mirror or reflect involuntarily the character of external prejudice.

Copland's self-awareness as an American came to the fore in Paris. Was this perhaps the result of the priority in France given to his status as a Jew? The Jew and the American were commonly linked in European anti-Semitic rhetoric, and a Jewish American from New York in the 1920s would inevitably be forced to grasp the contrast between the Old and the New World far more directly than would the non-Jewish American. It is hard to imagine that Copland and his friend (and cousin) Harold Clurman were not struck with the centrality of anti-Semitism in Europe and the contrast with their experience in New York. When Copland traveled to Germany it is likewise improbable that the realization that America was exceptional as a place for Jews, without a near rival on the European continent, did make itself apparent. The Jewish question, as articulated by European Jews and by anti-Semites, was central to the politics of the day in a manner that would have been strikingly unfamiliar to both men.

Nonetheless, within America, Copland's embrace of French culture and language helped attenuate his connection to most American Jews; it was a sign of the success of the comfortable acculturation and integration he experienced growing up. French language and culture were understood as divorced from anything characteristically Jewish, in contrast to German, Polish, and Russian culture. There were few French-speaking Jews in America. The Jewish community in France was legendary in its patriotism, despite the Dreyfus case and the visibility of French political anti-Semitism in the early twentieth century. Copland's Francophilism helped extend the process of his emancipation from common American markers of Jewish identity and allegiance.

Copland's apparent ease has to be understood in the context of both the praise and criticism he encountered early on as a Jewish voice in music. One of Copland's earliest advocates, the critic Paul Rosenfeld, himself a Jew, was a committed racialist who believed in categories such as Jewish traits. He believed that race, and in particular being Jewish, inevitably played a major role in the formation of a composer's character and the nature of his music. Rosenfeld's critical dismissal of Mahler is a case in point. For him Mahler fit Wagner's derisive description of the creative inadequacies of the Jew in the modern world. In the case of Leo Ornstein, Rosenfeld wrote, "The racial element is softened, become gentler and duskier and more romantic."[60] And not surprisingly, in discussing the work of Ernest Bloch, Rosenfeld argued that "as a Jew, Bloch carried within himself a fragment of the Orient; was in himself an outpost of the mother of continents. And he is one of the few Jewish composers really, fundamentally self-expressive. He is one of the few that have fully accepted themselves, fully accepted the fate that made them Jewish and stigmatized them."[61]

It is curious that Rosenfeld, who was revered by Copland and many of those in Copland's circle, had this to say about "the artist of Jewish extraction": "The whole world is open before him. He can express his day as he will. One thing, however, is necessary. He must not seek to inhibit any portion of his impulse. He must not attempt to deny his modes of apprehension and realization because they are racially colored. He must possess spiritual harmony. The whole man must go into his expression."[62] For Rosenfeld, Bloch was capable of providing "a poignant, an authentic expression of what is racial in the Jew."[63]

Rosenfeld followed the anti-Semitic Wagnerian lines of argument in considering Giacomo Meyerbeer and Mendelssohn to have been damaged. These Jews, he claimed, had failed to acquire and internalize the requisite "spiritual harmony" that was required to be a great artist. That acquisition was made more complicated in Rosenfeld's view by the barriers to social integration created by the continued presence of anti-Semitism and the stubborn adherence among Jews to their identity. One of the attractions of Marxism for Copland's Jewish contemporaries, in both Europe and America, was the promise it held to "solve" the Jewish question through socialism's historical transcendence of religious and national allegiances.

Rosenfeld's earliest writing on Copland properly located him as a distinctly American composer with an unerring capacity for control and a "leanness, slenderness of sound sharpened by the fact that it is found in connection with a strain of grandiosity."[64] Indeed, in 1929 Rosenfeld described the consistent quality of Copland's music (well before the onset of the explicitly populist phase). But Rosenfeld also found Copland's music also to be "finally Hebraic, harsh and solemn like the sentences of brooding rabbis."[65] To Rosenfeld, the rhetoric of the music, not its materials, seemed Jewish. Yet Copland, Rosenfeld believed, was destined to achieve the requisite spiritual harmony in his life.

Copland's place as a Jewish American was a significant factor in his reception among antimodernist anti-Semites like Daniel Gregory Mason, who from the beginning used Copland's Jewishness as a basis of criticism and derision. Other non-Jews, like Copland's friends Thomson and Leo Smit, believed they found Jewish or Hebraic traits in Copland's music. All agreed that there was nothing explicitly Jewish in the obvious sense, as was the case with Bloch or later with Bernstein. Yet there was something Jewish in the musical style nonetheless, as Howard Pollack has persuasively argued, in the almost didactic approach Copland took in seeking to express the modern and the American.[66] For Pollack (and many of his contemporaries, including Thomson), Copland's voice is evocative of the prophetic tone of the Old Testament.

Two interpretive traditions regarding the relationship between Jews (and their traditions) and the culture of host nations influenced the debate regarding Copland's Jewish identity. The first derives from Wagner's seminal essay, "Judaism in Music" (1850/1869). Its influence, as Rosenfeld's criticism indicates, extended well into the early twentieth century, in theories that suggested an interplay among Jewish identity, creativity, and gender. Jews, the argument went, were political pariahs with no organic connection to land and community and thus incapable of being creative or original, as true artists must be. Further, the absence of creativity among Jews could be ascribed to a racial propensity for the feminine. Contemporary pseudo-theories of race and psychology created a bizarre amalgam of notions that suggested an affinity between the Jewish character and the nonmasculine, and therefore the effeminate.[67]

In this manner masculinity and creativity, particularly aesthetic inspiration, became linked. This sort of logic makes its appearance in the writings of Charles Ives. The distinctions, curiously, did not necessarily overlap with national characteristics or compositional styles. Richard Strauss, for example, did not fare well in Ives's canon as masculine or muscular music. The French were not by definition feminine and the German, by contrast, masculine. Contrasts that appear in Nietzsche between the Apollonian and the Dionysian became bowdlerized, generating a dichotomy between the feminine-Apollonian-Jewish on the one hand and the Dionysian-ecstatic-inspired-Aryan on the other. Inverted, notably in the writings of Thomas Mann, these constructs suggested ways to link creativity with illness, genius with deviancy, and aesthetic refinement with homosexuality.

Copland resisted the allure of these categorical contrasts and ideas, although they captured the imagination of many of his contemporaries. He was not drawn to a celebration of decadence and degeneracy on the one hand or the critique of respectability and the bourgeois on the other. Instead he fashioned an assertive credo of the artist as participant citizen. From the 1920s on, his status as a Jew presented no barrier to his rapid assumption of leadership among a new generation of American composers—in organizing the Copland-Sessions concerts, for example, and pioneering the discovery of Ives. The assumption of leadership took place despite the fact that the anti-Semitism that appeared in reviews of his music in the eastern United States in the 1920s was reminiscent of late-nineteenth-century European anti-Semitic discourse. However, since the Ivesian notion that healthy American music needed to be manly and tied to native roots in New England, it is no coincidence that the American landscape and experience Copland turned to in fashioning his American style was largely urban or western. The cowboy was not only a pioneer but emblematically both masculine and marginal. Furthermore, the West was in the process of being defined culturally in Copland's youth. It, like the city, offered a fertile field for imaginative construction as new and distinctly open, subject to representation and evocation through modernism. The West and the city were an America for which no European settlers, not even the descendants of the *Mayflower,* could lay a claim of priority.

The second interpretive tradition regarding the interaction of Jewish identity and culture concerns the definition of the dynamics and significance of assimilation and acculturation among Jews.[68] These historical processes need to be differentiated, particularly in America, where Jewish identity came to be construed ironically in the public debate concerning modern American culture as an asset. In an essay entitled "Americans of Single and Dual Allegiance," for example, Saminsky sought to unravel the problems and paradoxes facing the composer in search of an American voice.[69] America, Saminsky argued, apart from the descendants of slaves and the Native American population, was essentially an immigrant nation made up of groups from varying European regions. The appeal to any native, premodern, musical traditions seemed limited. To Saminsky, in contrast to many proponents of the significance of jazz (including Louis Gruenberg), Dvořák's brief but influential intervention in the American scene in the 1890s was not convincing. Dvořák highlighted the challenge faced by Americans to achieve something beyond a pale imitation of European models. The most promising sources for Dvořák were the unique African-American and Native American roots of Americanism.[70]

Since eighteenth-century and nineteenth-century England could not boast a compositional tradition comparable to France and Germany, New Englanders, whom Saminsky termed "Anglo-Celtic," were viewed as the closest thing to Americans without a subsidiary loyalty to a non-American cultural past. For Saminsky the only traditional Americans in the Dvořák sense were these Anglo-Celtic individuals, particularly Harris, Ives, Sessions, and Ruggles. (He also included John Alden Carpenter and Griffes in this group.) These composers had a single allegiance but followed only one possible route to Americanism.

Saminsky rejected Deems Taylor's notion that America was more like a voluntary "club" than a nation demanding emotional loyalty. While the "civic" club model celebrated citizenship as an acquired status irrespective of race, religion, and birth, it was an inadequate metaphor for Saminsky, who felt that to be truly an American, one had to derive one's music from "an emotional and cultural allegiance."[71] In America that allegiance went beyond a "single racial fealty."[72] American composers needed to cultivate a "cultural loyalty" to "an empire . . . a commonwealth of races."[73] For Saminsky the true expression of such cultural loyalty would result in a "tonal culture grown from" an attachment to the landscape of America and its "native soil."[74]

Although Saminsky ceded some historical priority to the group of Christian Anglo-Celtics, he celebrated the America of Abraham Lincoln and Walt Whitman. So did the Stieglitz circle, Copland, and most Jewish Americans of his generation. Saminsky's formulation of an emotional commitment foresaw a special place for Americans of dual allegiances, particularly "Hebrew" Americans, since historically the driving forces of their emotions and creativity had been precisely cultural "allegiances," not race.[75] Unlike other immigrants, Jews could reconcile the Jewish with the American without sacrifice since they did not need to shed a competitive prior national loyalty. They were the ideal "test case" for Saminsky's model of a new American based on a deep loyalty to an emergent vision of America and an allegiance to a unique religious and historical experience.[76]

Saminsky believed that among the composers of his generation Copland possessed "the strongest Jewish traits, mental and creative. . . . His neurotic drive and stringent intellectualism are typically Jewish, but of the worst sort. . . . However, one senses in Copland's music a second, so to speak, Hebrew soul such as flows in the gentle, nobly warm and wistful melos of the slow movements in his *Music for the Theatre*."[77] Saminsky internalized the classic arsenal of anti-Semitic stereotypes in his view on Copland. He treated Bloch, Gruenberg, and Ornstein far more favorably. But even in Copland's case he considered Jewish attributes, when not distorted, as especially constructive to the creation of a musical Americanism. Saminsky conceded that Jews, a "race of extraordinary definiteness of *psyche*, race mentally polar to a nation aggressively Western, would preclude even a shade of sterling Americanism in a composer of recent adoption. In even a son or grandson of an outlander."[78] But he concluded, oddly enough, that ultimately "in spite of its definite and compelling Hebraism, the whole group of a double allegiance breathes all the moods and runs of creative Americanism. It turns on an American mental axis."[79]

The underlying point in Saminsky's hyperbolic rhetoric was that there was in modernity no native Americanism into which to assimilate. Rather, the immigrant Jew with at best weak ties to a nation of origin (as a result of European anti-Semitism) had special qualities that strengthened the embrace of America. Even for religious Jews, Americanism was a constructed cultural and civic ideal to which Jews had unique access. Best of all, the Jew, to be truly American, had to retain Jewish traits in some fashion; denial and assimilation were not required.

It would be all too convenient to dismiss Saminsky's words as the confused ranting of one of Copland's envious but ambitious contemporaries. But Saminsky's mode of thinking was not exceptional. How does a Jew function in America, particularly as an artist, yet remain visibly a Jew (without necessarily adhering to Jewish religion or nationalism)? This question was central to the debate among Jews eager to become part of America's culture when Copland came of age during the first two decades of the twentieth century.

Certainly a modernization of Jewish religious practices was required to enable full participation in American economic, social, and cultural life. This fact too often leads to a confusion between assimilation and acculturation.[80] There was more than one path from the ghetto of the mid-eighteenth century to integration in the larger American (or even European) society of the early twentieth.[81] The prevalence of normative usages of the terms *assimilation* and *acculturation* in Jewish historical scholarship compounds the confusion. Within the Jewish community, assimilation is usually viewed as a negative social process. Acculturation is somewhat less subject to criticism, because it implies the potential of reconciliation between Jewish law and customs and social and cultural integration. The modern orthodox can be said to seek acculturation but not assimilation. At the end of the process of assimilation many commentators assume conversion, intermarriage, and the disappearance of Jewish identity.

Since the definition of Jewish identity extended beyond religion and involved the notion of the Jewish people only as a distinct race, as Saminsky correctly surmised, a stable potential of dual allegiance existed among many Jews. Jewish identity not only did not compete with one's political and cultural sense of oneself as an American, it could deepen it. America was a diaspora in which one could as a Jew be an ideal citizen. The patriotism and loyalty of American Jews of Copland's parents' generation were extreme and widespread, and reflected this conceit.

This is the context in which Copland remarked that he discovered how American he was in Paris in the 1920s. Growing up in Brooklyn, it never occurred to him that he was anything less than thoroughly American, although he was also Jewish. The historical personage that defined America for Copland's parents' generation and Copland himself was Lincoln, whose vision of democracy and role in the emancipation of the slaves made him a unique hero and representative of America's potential for Jews. Copland's own pastiche of Lincoln's words and account of his life in *Lincoln Portrait* follows a time-honored tradition of a specific Jewish-American glorification of Lincoln that began with the central place given the Gettysburg Address in its Yiddish language translation for new immigrants.[82]

What, then, was the particular influence of Copland's stable but passive self-image as a Jew in America on his aesthetic construct of what America was or might be?[83] A possible clue can be located in the broadly disseminated ideas of the Anglo-Jewish writer Israel Zangwill.[84] On September 6, 1909, Zangwill's play *The Melting Pot* opened on Broadway. It ran for four months at the Comedy Theater and was regularly revived in New York through the 1930s. By any reasonable standard the play was a great success, although not with the critics. Before coming to Broadway, it had premiered in Washington in 1908, enjoyed a hugely successful run in Chicago, and become a particular favorite of Theodore Roosevelt, to whom Zangwill dedicated the published version. The play and its ideology became the subject of a wide and intense controversy, particularly within the American Jewish community, and helped to popularize the term "melting pot."[85]

It is not clear that anyone in Copland's family ever saw the play, but the issues it raised and the ideas behind the outlines of its plot were likely subjects of debate in the circles in which Copland grew up. The plot illuminates the special role a Jew who had suffered in Europe might assume as a modern composer in America. The play concerns a refugee from the Kishinev pogrom, the sole survivor in his family and a witness to the killings. That refugee is the central character David Quixano, an aspiring and visionary composer. His ambition is to write a grand symphonic musical tribute to America, a massive and musically novel work, an American Beethoven's Ninth celebrating a new modern utopia, the great melting pot. "Can't you hear the roaring and bubbling?" David asks his sweetheart Vera. He continues:

DAVID: There gapes her mouth [He points east.]—the harbour where a thousand mammoth feeders come from the ends of the world to pour in their human freight. Ah, what a stirring and a seething! Celt and Latin, Slav and Teuton, Greek and Syrian—black and yellow—

VERA: [Softly, nestling to him.] Jew and Gentile—

DAVID: Yes, East and West, and North and South, the palm and the pine, the pole and the equator, the crescent and the cross—how the great Alchemist melts and fuses them with his purging flame! Here shall they all unite to build the Republic of Man and the Kingdom of God. Ah, Vera, what is the glory of Rome and Jerusalem where all nations and races come to worship and look back, compared with the glory of America, where all races and nations come to labour and look forward!

[He raises his hands in benediction over the shining city.]
Peace, peace, to all ye unborn millions, fated to fill this giant continent—the God of our *children* give you Peace.[86]

David's ambition is to write serious orchestral music that expressed these sentiments. America required a new kind of instrumental and vocal music to match the noble vision of a new society and citizen, not evocations or imitations of light opera and commercial popular music. The music David seeks to create must emancipate itself therefore from its European models. It must be modern and adequate to the new utopian possibilities of America.

The play revolves around David's love for Vera, the idealistic daughter of the Russian nobleman responsible for the Kishinev pogroms. Vera has disavowed her aristocratic Russian past in disgust to become a political radical and a settlement house worker in America. She is entranced by David's talent. The play includes a character called Pappelmeister—a supportive, benign, and thinly veiled version of the great German conductor Anton Seidl, who played such an important role in New York's musical life. Pappelmeister, who has contempt for the superficial tastes of the New York elite, recognizes David's genius and becomes his champion.

Zangwill's amalgam of stock characters also includes David's Uncle Mendel, a musician and an apologetic, hardworking, grateful but anxious Jew; David's grandmother, a devout Jewess intent on maintaining her traditions; an Irish servant girl who learns to love strange Jewish rituals; and an aristocratic WASP, Quincy Davenport, a wealthy patron in love with Vera who ultimately overcomes his explicit social anti-Semitism. The play has a happy ending. David's paean to America, his grand symphony, is performed to acclaim, and David and the politically radical daughter of the aristocratic Russian bigot accept each other's love and vow to realize the unique promise of America as a melting pot.

The power of the plot of Zangwill's play was confirmed by history. The ambition to use large-scale symphonic music to express and communicate the political and social promise of America in the modern world, in an aesthetic form adequate to modernity, was harbored by more than one Jewish-American composer before the early 1930s. A massive work uncannily reminiscent of the one David Quixano dreams of was composed by Bloch, a symphonic extravaganza entitled *America: An Epic Rhapsody*. The work was completed in 1927 and enjoyed extraordinary but brief fame and popularity, catapulting Bloch to national prominence. Not surprisingly, Bloch's rhapsody offended many "Anglo-Celts," Daniel Gregory Mason among them. He dismissed it as a "long, brilliant, megalomaniac, and thoroughly Jewish symphony."[87] Yet the work won a competition sponsored by *Musical America* and earned Koussevitzky's praise. The composition is in three parts and uses quotes from American folk material. Its first two movements suggest the history of America. The third movement is a call to the future whose program is derived, predictably enough, from the words of Walt Whitman. The work ends with a simple anthem, intentionally accessible and "intelligible and singable."[88] Bloch's composition, like Quixano's imaginary equivalent, mirrored Zangwill's advocacy of the notion that the Jewish people had a special mission in history, one that could be accomplished only through acculturation with and integration into an America that Jews would help transform. And the arts, notably new modern music, had a central contributing role.

America, Zangwill wrote, was the "greatest idealistic experiment in government by the people that the world has ever tried. If it fails it will be the last great experiment of humanity. America is thus carrying mankind."[89] The Jews could contribute to this noble experiment their unique attachment to a universalizing, rational, and natural religion—one defined by Zangwill in large measure by the philosophy of Spinoza. Such a philosophy encouraged freedom, justice, and tolerance. Before it could bring its cultural influence to bear on the Christian world, however, the Jew would have to integrate into the surrounding American world and elevate the aspirations of the nation as a whole—by, as Zangwill himself put it, "melting up" into something superior.[90] America promised to become the ideal modern "mosaic" state, a representation of the vision of the prophets of the Old Testament. "The race that produced Moses, Isaiah, and Spinoza has still other messages to preach," Zangwill wrote.[91] By the "cross-fertilization" with Christianity, the Jews in America would bear "some new precious fruit for the human race, whose service is its highest ideal."[92]

Although taken to task by many Jews concerned about the pitfalls and illusions of assimilation, Zangwill's message in *The Melting Pot* did not suggest that acculturation meant a denial of a distinct Jewish heritage and legacy. Rather, the process of integration would create a new synthesis of cultures, fulfilling the task of Jewish history and redeeming Jewish suffering. Saminsky's ideas were reminiscent of Zangwill's. The Jewish contribution to modern society, politics, and culture rested for Zangwill in the creation of a new model citizen of the world. Although David and Vera marry at the end of the play, Zangwill was not arguing for conversion or intermarriage. Jews as a group would have to flourish, not atrophy, if their Hebraic influence was to be a vital constituent of a new society with a modern cultural center.

This Zangwill-like constructive conception of a "Hebraic" heritage (and the pride that went with it) was not uncommon among the class of Jews among whom Copland grew up. It provided a definition of Jewish exceptionalism different from Veblen's. It transcended religion and Jewish nationalism and was compatible with the embrace of democratic America. Religious faith, as Zangwill underscores in the play through the character of the old grandmother and the servant who gradually learns to love Jewish rituals emotionally and aesthetically as an outsider (without sharing the belief structure that sustains them), is no longer essential to a constructive Jewish identity in the American context. The distinct Jewish attributes that can help define democracy and modernity are, rather, the universal humanist political and social philosophy behind Judaic religious tradition, as well as the overriding rationalist epistemology of the Old Testament.

This universalized and secularized conception of Jewish tradition fit Copland's own political and aesthetic ambitions. What Copland had in common with Zangwill's vision was the conviction that a composer and therefore music and the arts could play a key role in shaping the new cultural synthesis. Many of Copland's populist and film scores can be considered variants of Quixano's dream. It is an open question whether Copland's particular credo regarding America and the role of the artist derived directly from Zangwill or indirectly from comparable sentiments within the Jewish milieu of his youth. Like Saminsky, Zangwill was not advocating the abandonment of Jewish identity and assimilation into a preexisting alternative. The Jewish experience and tradition through art would be in the vanguard, albeit transformed, of a new utopian world and culture.

Zangwill's vision suggests a context of origin for the synthesis between Americanism and the prophetic tone and character of Copland's music.

Copland's affinity for the ideals of Ralph Waldo Emerson, Henry Thoreau, and Whitman—figures cited also by Clurman, who came from a comparable Jewish milieu—may therefore have been strengthened by an implicit if not explicit acceptance of the notion of a compatible, contributory Jewish spirit. Indeed, Copland's champion as an American Jewish artist, Paul Rosenfeld, was himself closely allied to the traditions of American pragmatism through his association with John Dewey.[93]

The ideology and rhetoric of Zangwill's *The Melting Pot* also provide a framework for understanding how Copland's music came to be described as "Hebraic," reminiscent of the Old Testament and "brooding rabbis," or possessed of a "mosaic voice" and a "biblical air." The young Leonard Bernstein even expected Copland to look like Moses or a patriarch. Yet Bernstein, despite the persistent debt to Copland in his own music, chose a less secular and acculturated musical route to express his Jewishness. Bernstein, unlike Copland, returned to predictable ethnic musical and textual signifiers and symbols, rejecting Copland's secular and visionary modernist synthesis.

Copland became, more than Bloch or Bernstein, the Quixano of American history. His music eschewed explicit references to the Jews, but adopted a modernism and a communicative if not grandiloquent rhetoric inspired by social and political conceits commonplace within the New York community of acculturated Jews. The assimilation that Copland realized in his life—as an artist at once at ease with being Jewish and being understood in the public realm as a Jew, but with emotional allegiances not to religion but rather to a presumably Zangwill-like Hebraic conception of democracy—helped define his music and his idealized concept of America.

One notable exception concerning Copland's use of Jewish materials underscores the extent to which Copland echoed Zangwill's focus on the necessity for a modern, novel art for the citizen and society of the future. During the 1920s Copland became interested in the Yiddish theatre in New York. The 1920s was a period when Copland was most intrigued by jazz, a field in which Jews and blacks participated and that was perceived widely as influenced by both groups. There are references to Fanny Brice in *Music for the Theatre* (1925). They point to the Jewish aspect of Broadway and Jewish humor in popular entertainment. But the anti-Semitic dismissal of the piece by Edward Burlingame Hill did not pick up on that rare display of Jewish sources in Copland's music. Rather, Hill perceptively located what would become Copland's lifelong ambition, the pursuit of a secular modernist art as a vehicle by which to assert a particularly Jewish conception of America. Hill derided *Music for the Theatre* for its "usual clever Hebraic assimilation of the worst features of polytonalité." [94] Copland's Jewishness, for Hill, was not revealed by ethnic signifiers but tied to his appropriation of modernism in fashioning an American voice. The fact that Jewish materials and jazz played a role was secondary.

Much like Quixano, Copland, by combining modernism with a liberal patriotic allegiance to a vision of America, realized his own belief that music ought to be "a confirmation of life," even when the surface sounded tragic.[95] This is what separates the Jewish element in Mahler from that in Copland. The unifying core to his music was, in his words, "a sense of affirmation."[96] As Copland argued in his 1952 Norton Lectures at Harvard, "affirmative beliefs," not "fear or suspicion" and other "negative emotions," result in great music.[97] This was for him, as a Jew in twentieth-century America, a uniquely convincing claim contingent on the promise of American democracy.

Furthermore, like Quixano, Copland felt he needed to reach a wide audience if he wanted to engender a culture affirmative of America's potential. While Elliott Carter in 1955 mused about the challenges facing an American composer as a result of the "low grade of mass culture," Copland construed his civic task as elevating the standards of taste in a democracy.[98] Modern America demanded a counterweight to the downward pressure exerted by egalitarian democracy and mass communication. Copland chose to write serious music for the radio and for the movies because these media offered a novel chance to engage in a much-needed form of aesthetic mass education. He questioned the capacity of jazz to equal "serious music" in terms of "range of emotional expressivity" and "depth of feeling."[99] Despite its universal appeal, the "universality" of its language was limited.[100] Ever present in Copland's explanation of his own ambitions was the sort of unifying universalist optimism that sought to bring people of diverse classes, regions, and ethnicities together under the banner of America. At a Brooklyn College commencement in 1975, Copland asserted that his work as a composer was intended to generate a "positive" attitude toward life, to make one feel that life had meaning and that it was possible to help "one's fellow man" gain that same sense of meaning.[101]

Copland's belief that music could help others develop a positive sense of meaning for life defined serious music's public function. He was unsympathetic to the self-perception of the artist as neurotic, if not deviant, and therefore superior in the separateness of the artist's place in society. Music was not entirely justified by its evident interiority and subjectivity. Shostakovich and Bernstein embraced Mahler as the alienated and tortured artist par excellence. Copland did not. As H. Wiley Hitchcock noted,

Copland once "volunteered" that "agony, I don't connect with. Not even alienation."[102] Copland's discretion did not preclude him from using music to express the personal. Yet those feelings rarely were ones of suffering, sarcasm, pessimism, and anger. In Copland intimacy and sadness, memory and nostalgia occupy space alongside monumental optimism and energetic affirmation.

Copland's aversion to the categories of agony and alienation, and his ambition to use music and spread a sense of affirmation bear closer scrutiny. Copland showed little patience for the psychological crises and self-indulgent antics of even his closest friends and lovers. He urged several of his intimates to seek psychiatric help, even though there is no evidence that he himself ever felt the need to do so.[103] Copland's steadfast middle-class discipline and elegantly articulate and shrewd, if not efficient, character is reminiscent of Johannes Brahms on the one hand and Richard Strauss on the other. For all his associations with artists and writers considered outlandish or bohemian, notably Paul Bowles, Copland's self-image and manner remained tied to the hardworking, middle-class character of his immediate family. There was as little hostility for the bourgeois in Copland as in Brahms. In contrast to Strauss, Copland maintained modest tastes despite considerable business acumen and financial success.

Yet Copland's construct of himself and the task of the composer is revealingly therapeutic. It is reminiscent of a particular pattern in the early-twentieth-century American adaptation of the modern science of psychology. As Andrew R. Heinze has outlined in *Jews and the American Soul: Human Nature in the Twentieth Century* (2004), a series of seminal figures, all of Jewish origin, helped adapt modern psychology to influence the way twentieth-century Americans defined selfhood and mental health. The role of Jews in America in psychology runs strikingly parallel to the ideas of Zangwill and Saminsky and is remarkably similar to the impact and ambition of Copland.

Heinze argues that leading Jewish figures in the area of psychology, including Abraham Maslow, Erich Fromm, and Rabbi Joshua Liebman, succeeded in popularizing the notion that insights from modern psychology could be adapted in America to enable individuals to come to terms with themselves and their lives. Mental health—self-love and acceptance of self—became a key to realizing the promise of American life, the American dream. At the center was the notion of love as a central category of life. The key figure in Heinze's account is Rabbi Liebman, author of the best-selling 1946 book *Peace of Mind*. For Liebman Judaism was uniquely suited to enrich Christianity and America. Liebman echoed Zangwill; in Liebman's formulation it was Judaism that was the religion of love, not Christianity. Judaism was not legalistic but rather profoundly useful as a key to understanding human nature and the human condition in modernity.

Judaism offered a new route to finding the means by which to cope with the modern world.[104] Judaism as a religion of love was therefore ideally suited to encourage a universalist credo in America consistent with an embracing egalitarian democracy. Through psychological self-scrutiny and awareness, guilt and doubt could be supplanted by confidence, generosity, and healthy optimism. If one came to terms with oneself, one would then be able to accept the "other." Judaism encouraged an ideal of self-acceptance. This led not only to happiness, but also to a tolerant and open democracy.

Americans could pursue a program of mental hygiene that freed themselves of anxieties and disappointments. As Joseph Jastrow (one of the key figures in Heinze's analysis) argued, modern America represented the coming of age of psychology as a crucial component of public welfare. Ethical behavior and an enthusiasm for civic duty, a personal sense of well-being, and self-love could become widespread values without the necessity of the rarified opportunity of the psychoanalyst's couch. Through the dissemination of the writings of Fromm and Erik Erikson, a new democratic, American connection between psychology and politics and psychology and ethics was forged. A candid sense of self, defined in part by the capacity for adjustment to reality and self-improvement, became linked to the eighteenth-century civic virtues of happiness, justice, and tranquillity.

The interplay between psychology and politics ran parallel with Copland's career. It helps frame Copland's own search for a psychic equilibrium and his commitment to exploit the composer as civic force. Music became an instrument designed to encourage not political revolution but self-awareness and adjustment and a form of patriotic pride and love that in turn could form the basis of a progressive and inclusive democracy committed to social justice. The ideal American envisioned through the medium of Copland's music was a democratic citizen who was psychologically self-aware and idealistic, determined to shape a better world, and affirmative of modernity.

V. Architecture and the Civic Function of Art

Copland's eclectic construct of the American future as an expansive society marked by optimism, freedom, and justice seems bland. But it led him to be sympathetic with the more politically rigorous and philosophically grounded radicalism of many of his politically engaged contemporaries.

They, too, held the conviction that art possessed a visible civic role. His music therefore can be compared to the most public forms of art and architecture of the late 1920s and 1930s. The art includes the figurative public sculpture of the era and the art of the muralists, American and Mexican alike. Apart from Copland's personal attachment to Mexico, the narrative and modernist aspects of the work of José Clemente Orozco and Diego Rivera suggest the accessible narratives of Copland's scores from the late 1930s and early 1940s.[105] Likewise the murals of Thomas Hart Benton, despite the divergences in the politics of Copland and Benton, evoke the same sense of American monumentality without sacrifice to the cult of the individual.[106]

The connection between Copland and the visual arts extends beyond the link between Copland's modernism and the manipulation of realism in film and the photograph. Insofar as Copland construed the writing of music as a public act, an equally apt analogy is with architecture and the monument. The link between landscape, including the monument, and musical narrative connects Copland to the Ives of *Three Places in New England*. However, Copland did not emulate Ives in the use of music to evoke autobiographical memory. Place is invented by Copland in music without personal memory. In Ives, real events and symbolic moments, through recollection, are mediated through music. Consider, for example, the movements of *A Symphony: New England Holidays* or the *Second Orchestral Set*. They derive from the expression of the personal experience. Yet Ives's music assumes no shared, modern, therapeutic, political purpose.

A tradition with which Copland's music can then be properly compared is public sculpture and architecture. The work of Paul Manship, Daniel Chester French, and, to a lesser extent, William Zorach share with Copland elements of simplicity, a dominant formal line, and a visible debt to classicism. In both sculptors, quick readability and, particularly in the case of French, the attraction to the oversize gesture prevail. But it is the architecture of the era that can be most helpful as an analogy to Copland's music. In Rockefeller Center (1929–40), the height and the massive uniformity of material are broken up with hints of small-scale ornamentation. The entire complex reflects a modernist architectural interest in urban spaces in which multiple buildings are configured in a bold spatial gesture designed to be imposing and exhilarating. The scale implies mass democracy and shared usage, but in a manner that does not dwarf individuality. Instead it provides a common platform of experience, like the predictable white walls of the modern apartment that in their uniformity invite decorative individuation. The sculptures by Paul Manship chosen to adorn Rockefeller Center likewise echo an affirmative celebration of human effort and promise.

The American adaptation of an international modernist style in architecture—evident in the Chrysler Building (1930) and the Empire State Building (1930) as well—celebrated American modernity through its engineering, materials, and scale. As with Copland's music, the urban architecture in America stood apart from contemporary antimodernist European trends (as in Germany), folk-derived European modernism (as evident in Finland and Hungary), as well as from the far more stark and functionalist radical modernism characteristic of the Bauhaus and later Le Corbusier. Even the anonymous commercial and residential architecture of New York constructed in the 1940s and 1950s mirrors a clarity of line and modernist intelligibility, without a hint of either an extreme aesthetic radicalism or an aristocracy of wealth or station.

For Copland music was a form of aural architecture. Already in the 1924 *Symphony for Organ* (later in the 1929 *Symphonic Ode* and culminating in the 1946 Third Symphony), Copland's use of sonority is audibly architectural, in the spirit of the modern skyscraper or an urban complex such as Rockefeller Center. Although we are accustomed to marvel at how Copland invented a modernist language that evoked the open plains and the American West, the music's character, absent specific folk tune or cowboy references, is not inevitably rural. The wide registrations, the blocklike units of harmony, the alternation between static and active rhythmic components, and the interjections of small-scale intimate moments, are as much reflective of the contemporary urban landscape (for example, *Quiet City*, 1947, and *Music for a Great City*, 1964) as they are evocative of a construct of rural America. Commentators have noted how ironic the title *Appalachian Spring* is, since it bears so little relationship to the music or the scenario of the ballet. The ambivalences and contradictions surrounding the title for *Prairie Journal* (1937) suggest that the connection between Copland's music and its presumed programmatic aspect is located in the aesthetic invention of space and place, not, as in Ives, personal knowledge and experience.

Architecture, like the film medium, bridges the real and the imaginary. Buildings function to alter space and experience just as films, through the illusions of realism in a medium that uses sound and time, alter the public's sense of the real. Copland's aesthetic synthesis of modernism and populism ran on lines parallel to contemporary architects and filmmakers. This is why his film music illustrates best how Copland's adaptation of the French modernist preference for clarity in line, his allegiance to tonal functionality, and his distinctive use of complex rhythms became distinctly American. In *Our Town* (1940), *Of Mice and Men* (1939), *The Heiress* (1948), and *The Red Pony* (1948), music functioned to illuminate not only landscape but also the psychological within an experience of novelistic realism on film. The intelligibility of the story line, deepened by music in its film versions, assumed a didactic ethical dimension, even in the adaptation of Henry James's story. Copland's sense of music's power with the audience in modern America helped him refine techniques that he realized would resonate in the film medium with the psychology of his fellow citizens.

The film composer's role vis-à-vis the film is ironically much like the architect's role in relation to the client. The design (and by analogy, the music) responds to stated functions and purposes of a building, its so-called program of requirements. As with the film composer's relation to the director and the script, the architect adapts signature aesthetic techniques to realize and embody aspirations of a nascent reality. Architectural parallels to music extend to the way individual stylistic attributes (understood as strictly musical) are adjusted and reconfigured but repeated in contrasting contexts and with divergent overt meanings. The same gestures and rhetoric are employed over a vast array of real-life circumstances, aspirations, and functions. Architecture, film, and music—in Copland's formulation—all shared the ambition to influence the cultural construction of meaning of the nation in modernity.

VI. Copland's Triumph

Aaron Copland fashioned a popular modernism of subtlety, refinement, and intelligibility that did not sound reactionary, provincial, or old-fashioned. With and without narrative intent, the sounding result always bore his unique fingerprints: clarity, rhythmic vitality, a special sensibility for sonic clusters, a lean harmonic background that never obscured the overarching musical trajectory, a lyric intensity, and an immediacy of impact through economy of form. Copland possessed an unerring sense of drama vis-à-vis the listener, whether in the Emily Dickinson songs (1944–50), *Connotations*, or in the Piano Concerto (1926). All this was achieved with the unmistakable suggestion of a contemporary America marked by industry and urbanism as well as a sensibility for the nation's vast rural spaces and history.

It is not nostalgia or sentimentality that characterizes Copland's music. The America he inhabited possessed no genuine center. America was self-consciously still in the process of rapid national formation. The imputation of a vital and stable mainstream social and cultural tradition justified by a long sweep of history was far less plausible than in Europe. Modern nineteenth- and early-twentieth-century nationalism in Europe was relatively easy to cast within the reactionary framework of restoration and revival. By contrast, the modern American artist, even the immigrant, was in the unique position (as the character of David Quixano suggests) of fashioning and inventing a new progressive national cultural sensibility. Copland was the most influential and successful musical architect of that cultural center. He defined a mainstream that did not exist, a metaphorical, contemporary town square in musical terms that afforded him a place at its center and not the margin.

One can assume a critical stance to Copland's project and achievement. Copland's synthesis of Americanism sought to even out contradictions and diminish the darker underside of American life and politics. Copland's aversion to suffering and strife as sources of music is reminiscent of the popular psychology of adjustment and denial in which happiness becomes trivial and self-realization little more than a synthetic reconciliation of tensions and a superficial avoidance of any confrontation with evil. Suffering is buried under a quite American surface of cheerfulness and optimism. Copland's music can be found inadequate to the harsh realities of modernity of the years between the 1920s and the 1960s.

This suggestion cannot be easily dismissed. The charge can be made that Copland's music, particularly the most popular scores and the film music, contains vacuous grandiosity spelled by mere sentimentality, betrays craft but lacks emotional depth, and reeks of excess decorative beauty veiled under the artifice of simplicity. The absence of an audible engagement with the authentic character of tragedy and grief can make the affirmative cloying and the otherwise inspiring sonorities platitudinous.

The suggestion that the cultural center Copland sought to generate is at best a compromise and at worst a rationalized aesthetic accommodation to an unjust reality should be juxtaposed constructively with Copland's ambitions. He wished, through music, to encourage a sense of civic purpose and optimism—despite the brutal facts of modernity. This ambition was characteristic of the successful descendants of Jewish immigrants to America of Copland's generation. Their patriotism was an extension of an acute sense of gratitude for the extent to which America had, for its Jews, actually delivered on the social and economic promise of opportunity, justice, and equality. Above all, Copland's studied Americanism was a celebration of the radical contrast between Europe and America. The divergence in the fate of Jews on the two continents only underscored the validity of a call for the creation of a distinct new American voice.

Copland did not give expression to an existent America. Rather he shaped a normative sense of an Americanism we might all wish to share. Music's combination of meaning and indeterminacy allowed Copland to integrate an internationalist modernist style into an invented American sensibility. His sound synthesized the urban and the rural, the past and the present. Explanations for Copland's success that rely on the categories of outsider or social marginalization are too limited because in the America in which Copland lived he understood himself as neither marginal nor an outsider. Rather, he considered himself capable of fashioning a new vision of America based on its promise and history. That vision was democratic, but not politically, ethnically, or regionally sectarian. It was the sort of universalist America Zangwill dreamed of and the psychologist Rabbi Liebman urged modern Americans to embrace. Copland, by expressing a widely accessible sonic image of America that all varieties of American—emigrant and native, black and white, rich and poor—could identify with, filled a cultural vacuum for his generation.

Copland's synthetic, eclectic, creative accomplishment is comparable to the music of Johann Strauss Jr. in the power of its synthetic brilliance and symbolic resonance. Strauss's appropriation and extensions of Viennese local traditions resulted in a dramatic modernized dance form and an extension of the patterns of musical theatre. The "Blue Danube" and *Die Fledermaus* were innovations comparable to Copland's. Strauss created through music a common ground for the modern post-1848 Viennese that had not previously existed. A rapidly changing urban environment needed a quintessential, authentic voice of self-definition.[107] The achievement of Strauss and Copland was more than strictly musical. The wide popularity of their work vindicated the potential of complex musical systems, as forms of public art, to define an inclusive and affectionate civic sensibility.

1. I would like to thank Judith Tick, Carol J. Oja, Barbara Haskell, Cecile Kuznitz, Christopher Gibbs, Jane Smith, Richard Wilson, Joel Perlmann, and Paul De Angelis for their criticisms and assistance. This essay owes an enormous debt to Howard Pollack's *Aaron Copland: The Life and Work of an Uncommon Man* (New York: Henry Holt, 1999); Vivian Perlis's superb collaborations with the composer, *Copland: 1900 Through 1942* (New York: St. Martin's/Marek, 1984); and *Copland Since 1943* (New York: St. Martin's Press, 1989).

2. See Nadine Hubbs, *The Queer Composition of America's Sound: Gay Modernists, American Music, and National Identity* (Los Angeles: University of California Press, 2004), p. 86. On Virgil Thomson's complex attitude to Copland, see Anthony Tommasini, *Virgil Thomson: Composer on the Aisle* (New York: W. W. Norton, 1997), pp. 298–310; also Pollack, *Aaron Copland*, pp. 171–77. Thomson's angry 1947 reaction at Copland's being called the "dean" was one side of Thomson's mixture of admiration and criticism stemming not so much from rivalry but perhaps, as Hubbs has argued, from Thomson's belief that he had created aspects of the American style ultimately attributed to Copland. See Thomson's respectful review of the *Lincoln Portrait* in *The Musical Scene* (New York: Alfred A. Knopf, 1947), pp. 125–26, and his enthusiastic review of the music for *The Red Pony* in "Hollywood's Best" in *Music Right and Left* (New York: Henry Holt, 1951), pp. 120–23.

3. See J. Peter Burkholder's *All Made of Tunes: Charles Ives and the Uses of Musical Borrowing* (New Haven: Yale University Press, 1995), pp. 415–21; also his essay "Ives and the Nineteenth-Century European Tradition," in *Charles Ives and the Classical Tradition*, ed. Geoffrey Block and J. Peter Burkholder (New Haven: Yale University Press, 1996), pp. 11–33. See also Leon Botstein, "Innovation and Nostalgia: Ives, Mahler, and the Origins of Twentieth-Century Modernism," in *Charles Ives and His World*, ed. J. Peter Burkholder (Princeton, N.J.: Princeton University Press, 1996), pp. 35–74. For Copland on Ives, see "The Ives Case (1933, 1941, 1967)," in *Aaron Copland: A Reader—Selected Writings, 1923–1972*, ed. Richard Kostelanetz (New York: Routledge, 2003), pp. 151–57.

4. On Copland's generosity and diplomacy, see Copland and Perlis, *Copland Since 1943*, pp. 122–42.

5. Copland's behavior and self-image as a successful composer should be placed along-side Erich Wolfgang Korngold's ironic and cutting portrait of the twentieth-century composer in *Deception* (1946), starring Bette Davis. In this film, for which Korngold wrote his Cello Concerto, Claude Rains plays an egotistical composer who combines the per-sonalities of Richard Wagner, Arnold Schoenberg, and possibly Korngold himself. Bette Davis kills the composer at the end. In the postwar era, Copland was increasingly self-conscious about his influence and prominence and the ways they could be channeled constructively. If, after his death, he were to be inseparably tied to the identity of his nation, he wrote that "it would not make me happy to know that my own work engendered steril-ity in my progeny." Cited in Kostelanetz, *Aaron Copland: A Reader*, p. 294.

6. See Howard Pollack's comments on Copland's view of Gershwin in *Aaron Copland*, pp. 163–64, and in *Harvard Composers: Walter Piston and His Students, from Elliott Carter to Frederic Rzewski* (Metuchen, N.J.: The Scarecrow Press, 1992), p. 422.

7. Arnold Whithall, "Technique and Rhetoric in the *Piano Fantasy*," in *Copland Connotations: Studies and Interviews*, ed. Peter Dickinson (Woodbridge, Suffolk, U.K.: The Boydell Press, 2002), p. 147.

8. Ibid., p. 146. Varèse was one of the leading figures in the New York avant-garde between 1915 and 1928; his use of sonorities had a lasting influence even on Copland. See Carol J. Oja, *Making Music Modern: New York in the 1920s* (New York: Oxford University Press, 2000), pp. 25–43. Oja's book is the most comprehensive and outstanding account of the

musical culture of the 1920s into which Copland arrived and made his mark. It has been indispensable in the preparation of this essay. For a contemporary view of Varèse, see Paul Rosenfeld, *An Hour with American Music* (Philadelphia: J. P. Lippincott, 1929), pp. 160–79.

9. See Paul Henry Lang's remark about *Connotations* in Pollack, *Aaron Copland*, p. 501. The same has been suggested as an explanation for understanding *Inscape*. Leonard Bernstein's comments about Copland trying to "catch up" are cited in William W. Austin, "Aaron Copland," *The New Grove Dictionary of American Music*, vol. 1 (New York: Grove's Dictionaries of Music, 1986), p. 499.

10. See Elliott Carter's admiring analysis of Copland's use of rhythm and jazz influences (and the positive comparison vis-à-vis Roy Harris) in "The Rhythmic Basis of American Music" and also Carter's reflection on the American scene as he experienced it in "Life and Work." Both appear in *Elliott Carter: Collected Essays and Lectures, 1937–1995*, ed. Jonathan W. Bernard (Rochester, N.Y.: University of Rochester Press, 1997), pp. 57–62, 202–5.

11. See Kyle Gann, *American Music in the Twentieth Century* (New York: Schirmer Books, 1997), pp. 197–208; also David Nicholls, "Avant-Garde and Experimental Music," in *The Cambridge History of American Music,* ed. David Nicholls (Cambridge: Cambridge University Press, 1998), pp. 517–34.

12. For more on Copland's attachment to Boulanger's grand line, see Copland and Perlis, *Copland: 1900–1942*, p. 67; and Mark DeVoto, "Copland and the 'Boulangerie,'" in *Copland Connotations*, pp. 3–13. On Copland and Boulanger, see Léonie Rosenstiel, *Nadia Boulanger: A Life in Music* (New York: W. W. Norton, 1982), pp. 156–60, 183–84. It should be noted, however, that the argument of this essay is compatible with Arthur Berger's admiring and incisive analysis of Copland's compositions, the trajectory of his development, and his achievement. See Arthur Berger, *Aaron Copland* (New York: Oxford University Press, 1953), pp. 31–36, 95–96, as well as his *Reflections of an American Composer* (Berkeley: University of California Press, 2002), pp. 12–16, 25–28.

13. For example, though Harris's Third Symphony is powerful, there is a good deal of less convincing music in his catalogue. The same can be said for Thomson, where the disparity between very strong works, such as *The Plow That Broke the Plains* (1936), *Filling Station* (1937), *Four Saints in Three Acts* (1933), and *The Mother of Us All* (1947), and less memorable scores cannot be denied. In the 1920s, apart from Varèse, there were three figures who promised to play a significant role in shaping a decidedly American modern music: Leo Ornstein, George Antheil, and Dane Rudhyar. Their careers, however, did not result in a body of work that merits comparison with Harris, Thomson, Piston, and Copland. Of the composers in Copland's generation, Piston's music may in the long run experience a revival, giving him a more prominent presence in the heritage of American music. See Carter's excellent account of Piston's achievement, "Walter Piston," in *Elliott Carter*, pp. 158–75.

14. Pollack, *Aaron Copland*, pp. 532–49.

15. See Denise Von Glahn, *The Sounds of Place: Music and the American Cultural Landscape* (Boston: Northeastern University Press, 2003), pp. 110–27; and also the discussion of Copland in Beth Ellen Levy, "Frontier Figures: American Music and the Mythology of the American West, 1895–1945," Ph.D. diss., University of California, Berkeley, 2002, pp. 220–377.

16. For more about Thomson's influence on Copland, see Hubbs, *Queer Composition*, pp. 36–37, 40–43; and Tommasini, *Virgil Thomson*, pp. 156, 290–91.

17. Virgil Thomson was one of the few who did not participate in the enthusiasm for Harris; see *The Musical Scene*, pp. 14–15, 123–24. However, as Beth Levy argues in "Frontier Figures," because of his ethnicity Harris became the center of a charged controversy about whether he represented "the great white hope" of modern American music; see pp. 97–203.

18. On the discussion of Stravinsky's Russian roots, see Rosamund Bartlett, "Stravinsky's Russian Origins," in *The Cambridge Companion to Stravinsky,* ed. Jonathan Cross (Cambridge: Cambridge University Press, 2003), pp. 3–18; also Richard Taruskin's magisterial two-volume work, *Stravinsky and the Russian Traditions: A Biography of the Works Through Mavra* (Berkeley: University of California Press, 1996); and in his *Defining Russia Musically: Historical and Hermeneutical Essays* (Princeton, N.J.: Princeton University Press, 1997).

19. See Copland's comments on Shostakovich in Copland and Perlis, *Copland: 1900–1942,* p. 230. On the issues and import of Soviet policy, particularly with regard to Shostakovich, see Laurel E. Fay, *Shostakovich: A Life* (New York: Oxford University Press, 2000), esp. pp. 67–205.

20. On Bartók, see David S. Schneider, "Hungarian Nationalism and the Reception of Bartók's Music, 1904–1940," in *The Cambridge Companion to Bartók,* ed. Amanda Bayley (Cambridge: Cambridge University Press, 2001), pp. 177–89.

21. *Billy the Kid* incorporates six cowboy tunes: "Great Grandad," "Whoopee Ti Yi Yo, Git Along Little Dogies," "The Old Chisholm Trail," "Old Paint," "The Dying Cowboy," and "Trouble for the Range Cook." *Rodeo* draws from many more, among them "Sis Joe," "If He'd Be a Buckaroo," "I Ride an Old Paint," "Bonyparte," "McLeod's Reel," "Gilderoy," and "Tip Toe, Pretty Betty Martin." See Pollack, *Aaron Copland,* pp. 320, 367.

22. It is interesting to contrast Copland's influence on the shaping of a distinctive modern national sensibility with Debussy's. The difference lies in the absence of so-called traditional French musical materials in Debussy's music and the comparatively weak role his music plays as a symbol of modern French national consciousness outside of the world of serious music.

23. On Elgar, see Anna Nalini Gwynne, "Elephants and Moghuls, Contraltos and G-Strings: How Elgar Got His Englishness," in "India in the English Musical Imagination," Ph.D. diss., University of California, Berkeley, 2003, pp. 109–86; and Charles Edward McGuire, "Functional Music: Imperialism, the Great War, and Elgar as Popular Composer," in *The Cambridge Companion to Elgar,* ed. Daniel Grimley and Julian Rushton (Cambridge, Eng.: Cambridge University Press, 2004), pp. 214–24. On Sibelius, see Veijo Murtomäki, "'Symphonic Fantasy': A Synthesis of Symphonic Thinking in Sibelius's Seventh Symphony and *Tapiola,*" in *The Sibelius Companion,* ed. Glenda Dawn Goss (Westport, Conn.: The Greenwood Press, 1996), pp. 147–63. Copland recognized the similarities between his potential position in America and Sibelius's in Finland. He also pointed to the link between Grieg and Norway; see "From a Composer's Journal," in Kostelanetz, *Aaron Copland: A Reader,* p. 294. In the case of Grieg, however, the symbolic residue is probably limited to two tunes rather than a body of work and a particular sound and aesthetic.

24. The composer's homosexuality has been considered in scholarly work such as Hubbs, *Queer Composition.* On Copland's politics, see, for example, Elizabeth B. Crist, "Aaron Copland and the Popular Front," *Journal of the American Musicological Society* 56, no. 2 (Summer 2003): 409–65. Copland's Jewishness has been examined in Pollack's biography of the composer and in this volume. On the relationship between Copland's music and American visual arts, see, for example, Gail Levin, "Part I" in *Aaron Copland's America: A Cultural Perspective,* ed. Gail Levin and Judith Tick (New York: Watson-Guptill Publications, 2000), pp. 9–127.

25. See Hubbs, "Introduction: Composing Oneself," in *Queer Composition*, pp. 1–17.

26. See Edward Maisel, *Charles T. Griffes: The Life of an American Composer* (New York: Alfred A. Knopf, 1943; rev. 1984).

27. "I wouldn't want to translate [the language of music] into so many words," Copland wrote, "because that would be limiting it." See Copland and Perlis, *Copland Since 1943,* p. 426.

28. Ibid., p. 423.

29. Ibid.

30. Ibid.

31. Ibid., p. 426.

32. See Strauss, *Don Juan,* op. 20 (New York: E. F. Kalmus, 1980); and Copland, *Inscape* (New York: Boosey and Hawkes, 1968).

33. On the *Siegfried Idyll,* see Werner Breig, "The Musical Works," in *Wagner Handbook: The Full Story of the Man, His Music, and His Legacy,* ed. Ulrich Müller and Peter Wapnewski, trans. John Deathridge (Cambridge, Mass.: Harvard University Press, 1992), pp. 454–57. On Berg, see Douglas Jarman, *The Music of Alban Berg* (Berkeley: University of California Press, 1979), pp. 226–28.

34. Interestingly, *Statements* contains a movement entitled "Cryptic."

35. On Marc Blitzstein's career, see Eric A. Gordon, *Mark the Music: The Life and Work of Marc Blitzstein* (New York: St. Martin's Press, 1989).

36. Hubbs, *Queer Composition,* pp. 128–29, 132.

37. See Roger Nichols, *The Harlequin Years: Music in Paris, 1917–1929* (Berkeley: University of California Press, 2002); and Roger Shattuck, *The Banquet Years; The Arts in France, 1885–1918: Alfred Jarry, Henri Rousseau, Erik Satie, Guillaume Apollinaire* (New York: Doubleday, 1961).

38. Crist, "Aaron Copland and the Popular Front," pp. 409–65.

39. See "An Engaged Citizen," chap. 16 in Pollack, *Aaron Copland,* pp. 270–87.

40. See John Patrick Diggins, *The Rise and Fall of the American Left* (New York: W. W. Norton, 1992); Richard H. Pells, *Radical Visions and American Dreams: Culture and Social Thought in the Depression Years* (Urbana and Chicago: University of Illinois Press, 1998); and Waldo Frank, *The Re-Discovery of America: An Introduction to a Philosophy of American Life* (Westport, Conn.: Greenwood Press, 1929).

41. See Copland, "Composer from Brooklyn: An Autobiographical Sketch," in *The New Music: 1900–1960* (New York: W. W. Norton, 1968), p. 161.

42. Despite an awkward incident that triggered a correspondence between them, Copland had an admiring and perceptive understanding of Schoenberg. For Copland on Schoenberg's music and status as a revolutionary conservative, see "Schoenberg's Expressionism (1941, 1967)" in Kostelanetz, *Aaron Copland: A Reader,* pp. 158–61. The point here, however, is that Schoenberg and Ives shared an edge of anger and resentment against the musical establishment, which, for them, consisted of the conventional concert-going public, the critical press, and virtuoso performers. On Schoenberg, see two essays by Leon Botstein: "Arnold Schoenberg: Language, Modernism, and Jewish Identity," in *Austrians and Jews in the Twentieth Century: From Franz Joseph to Waldheim,* ed. Robert S. Wistrich (New York: St. Martin's Press, 1992), pp. 162–83; and "Music and the Critique of Culture: Arnold Schoenberg, Heinrich Schenker, and the Emergence of Modernism in Fin-de-Siècle Vienna," in *Constructive Dissonance: Arnold Schoenberg and Transformations of Twentieth-Century Culture,* ed. Juliane Brand and Christopher Hailey (Berkeley: University of California Press, 1997), pp. 3–22. For Copland on Ives, see "The Ives Case (1933, 1941, 1967)," in Kostelanetz, *Aaron Copland: A Reader,* pp. 151–57.

43. The most striking contrast to Copland's attitude can be found in Milton Babbitt's infamous 1953 essay, "Who Cares If You Listen?" reprinted in *Source Readings in Music History,* ed. Leo Treitler (New York: W. W. Norton, 1950; rev. 1998), pp. 1305–11.

44. See Katherine Hoffman, *Stieglitz: A Beginning Light* (New Haven: Yale University Press, 2004), esp. chap. 2, "The Twentieth Century," pp. 193–295.

45. See Barbara Haskell, *The American Century: Art & Culture, 1900–1950* (New York: Whitney Museum of American Art and W. W. Norton, 1999), pp. 172–77, 196–200.

46. See Mark Carroll's *Music and Ideology in Cold War Europe* (Cambridge: Cambridge University Press, 2003), esp. chap. 6, "Neither You Nor They: The Avant-Garde and Neutralité," pp. 87–102.

47. See Copland's assessment of Mahler in "From a Composer's Notebook (1929)," in Kostelanetz, *Aaron Copland: A Reader*, pp. 286–87.

48. Despite the striking social mobility America promised for Jews of Copland's generation—a claim that frames this section of the essay—the presence and power of American anti-Semitism, particularly before 1945, should not be underestimated. Jews were discriminated against in education and employment, notably college entrance at elite institutions and access to jobs in law and banking. In the hierarchy of the prejudices of the eastern Protestant elite against other white ethnicities, particularly Catholics, Jews held a disadvantaged place in the years in which Copland grew up. A pertinent instance is the contrast between the careers of Copland and Walter Piston, friends and colleagues and both students of Boulanger. Piston was six years older. Although he came from an Italian immigrant family on his father's side, he graduated from Harvard and came to be regarded (in large measure through his own self-representation) as the quintessential New England American in manner and reputation. Like Copland, his grandfather, not his parents, was an immigrant. Both families Americanized their names (*Copland* is a form of *Kaplan*, and *Pistone* became *Piston*). Piston was a professor at Harvard at a time when there were practically no Jews on the faculty. All traces of his status as an Italian-American essentially vanished. In Copland's generation, as his own career suggests and the contemporary reception of his music makes plain, being Jewish was not something Copland could have made disappear. The rapid and successful total assimilation exemplified by Piston's career would become possible over the span of the two generations of Jews after Copland. This comparison offers a helpful context for the broader argument in which the American and European diaspora experiences are compared. See Pollack, *Harvard Composers*, pp. 15–16, 420–21.

49. See Beth S. Wenger, *New York Jews and the Great Depression: Uncertain Promise* (Syracuse, N.Y.: Syracuse University Press, 1999); Hasia R. Diner, *The Jews of the United States: 1654 to 2000* (Berkeley: University of California Press, 2004).

50. See Hannah Arendt, *The Origins of Totalitarianism* (New York: Meridian Books, 1958), esp. "Part One: Antisemitism," pp. 3–120.

51. On the early life of Irving Berlin, see Charles Hamm, *Irving Berlin, Songs from the Melting Pot: The Formative Years, 1907–1914* (New York: Oxford University Press, 1997); and Laurence Bergreen, *As Thousands Cheer: The Life of Irving Berlin* (New York: Viking Press, 1990). On George Gershwin's beginnings, see William G. Hyland, *George Gershwin: A New Biography* (Westport, Conn.: Praeger Publishers, 2003).

52. On Richard Rodgers, see Andrea Most, *Making Americans: Jews and the Broadway Musical* (Cambridge, Mass.: Harvard University Press, 2004), pp. 12–31.

53. Interestingly, Copland's teacher in New York, Rubin Goldmark, a relative of Vienna's Karl Goldmark (who came originally from Hungary), represented a Jew in America with a higher social status within the Jewish community, one closer to the old German Jewish elite than to the milieu of Copland's parents.

54. On assimilation versus acculturation, see Jonathan Frankel's "Assimilation and the Jews in Nineteenth-Century Europe," in *Assimilation and Community: The Jews in Nineteenth-Century Europe*, ed. Jonathan Frankel and Steven J. Zipperstein (New York: Cambridge University Press, 1992), esp. pp. 21–23.

55. See Oja, *Making Music Modern*, pp. 318–60; Most, *Making Americans*, pp. 32–65; and Diner, *The Jews of the United States*, pp. 208–9.

56. Thorstein Veblen, "The Intellectual Preeminence of Jews in Modern Europe," *Political Science Quarterly* 32, no. 1 (March 1919): 33–42.

57. On Copland in Israel, see Pollack, *Aaron Copland*, p. 27; also Copland and Perlis, *Copland Since 1943*, pp. 171–73.

58. See Copland, "Conversation with Edward T. Cone (1967)," in Kostelanetz, *Aaron Copland: A Reader,* p. 346.

59. See "The Early Years" and "Return to Roots" in David Z. Kushner, *The Ernest Bloch Companion* (Westport, Conn.: Greenwood Press, 2002), pp. 13–42, 88–108.

60. Paul Rosenfeld, *Musical Portraits* (New York: Harcourt, Brace and Howe, 1920), p. 273. On Rosenfeld, see Oja, *Making Music Modern,* pp. 302–10.

61. Rosenfeld, *Musical Portraits,* p. 287.

62. Ibid., p. 288.

63. Ibid., p. 289.

64. Rosenfeld, *An Hour with American Music*, p. 128.

65. Rosenfeld, *Discoveries of a Music Critic* (New York: Harcourt Brace and Co., 1936), p. 334.

66. See Pollack, "Copland and the Prophetic Voice," in this volume; also Virgil Thomson, "Aaron Copland," *Modern Music* 9, no. 2 (1932): 67–72.

67. Consider, for example, the writings of Otto Weininger (1880–1903). On Weininger, see Chandak Sengoopta, *Otto Weininger: Sex, Science, and Self in Imperial Vienna* (Chicago: University of Chicago Press, 2000).

68. See Frankel, "Assimilation and the Jews in Nineteenth-Century Europe," pp. 1–37; Diner, *Jews of the United States,* esp. "A Century of Migration: 1820–1924," pp. 71–111.

69. Lazare Saminsky, *Music of Our Day: Essentials and Prophecies* (New York: Thomas Y. Crowell Company, 1939; repr. Freeport, N.Y.: Books for Libraries Press, 1970), pp. 147–63.

70. See Michael B. Beckerman, *New Worlds of Dvořák* (New York: W. W. Norton, 2003), esp. pp. 23–76, 123–73. On Louis Gruenberg, see Oja, *Making Music Modern,* pp. 71–176. In addition to his *Daniel Jazz,* Gruenberg wrote a work called *A Harlem Rhapsody,* op. 62, in 1953. It was later orchestrated by Jonathan Tunick and given its premiere in the 1990s by the American Symphony Orchestra. A considerable body of music in Gruenberg's catalog was inspired by jazz.

71. Saminsky, *Music of Our Day,* p. 162.

72. Ibid., p. 163.

73. Ibid.

74. Indeed this is, much to Saminsky's ire, what Copland achieved. Ibid.

75. Ibid., p. 152.

76. Ibid.

77. Ibid., pp. 152, 154.

78. Ibid., p. 161.

79. Ibid.

80. See Frankel, "Assimilation and the Jews in Nineteenth-Century Europe," pp. 15–27.

81. See, for example, Isaac Deutcher's legendary essays collected in *The Non-Jewish Jew and Other Essays,* ed. Tamara Deutscher (New York: Oxford University Press, 1968); and Yuri Slezkine's *The Jewish Century* (Princeton, N.J.: Princeton University Press, 2004).

82. Many examples can be found in the archives of YIVO Institute for Jewish Research in the Center for Jewish History. See Yudel Mark, "An Analysis of 21 Yiddish Translations of the Gettysburg Speech," *Yidishe Shprakh* (Yiddish Language) 3, nos. 1–2 (January–April 1943): 1–32.

83. This argument is designed to supplement Howard Pollack's fine essay in this volume.

84. For more about Zangwill, see Joseph H. Udelson's *Dreamer of the Ghetto: The Life and Works of Israel Zangwill* (Tuscaloosa, Ala.: University of Alabama Press, 1990); and Joseph Leftwich, *Israel Zangwill* (New York: Thomas Yoseloff, 1957).

85. On the play's reception and popularity, see Joe Kraus, "How the Melting Pot Stirred America: The Reception of Zangwill's Play and Theater's Role in the American

Assimilation Experience," *MELUS* 24, no. 3 (Autumn 1999): 3–19; see also Guy Szuberla, "Zangwill's 'The Melting Pot' Plays Chicago," *History and Memory* 20, no. 3 (Autumn 1995): 3–20.

86. Israel Zangwill, *The Melting Pot: A Drama in Four Acts* (New York: 1909), pp. 198–99.

87. Daniel Gregory Mason, *Tune In, America* (New York: Alfred A. Knopf, 1931; repr., Freeport, N.Y.: Books for Libraries Press, 1969), pp. 161–62.

88. Kushner, *Ernest Bloch Companion*, p. 76.

89. Quoted in Udelson, *Dreamer of the Ghetto*, p. 196.

90. See Leftwich, *Israel Zangwill*, p. 253.

91. Quoted in Udelson, *Dreamer of the Ghetto*, p. 193.

92. Quoted in ibid., pp. 193–94.

93. See Herbert A. Liebowitz, "Introduction," in *Musical Impressions: Selections from Paul Rosenfeld's Criticism*, ed. Herbert A. Leibowitz (London: George Allen & Unwin, 1969), pp. xvi–xix.

94. Letter from Edward Burlingame Hill to Virgil Thomson (then in Paris), December 5, 1925. Cited in Carol J. Oja, "Virgil Thomson's Harvard Years," in *A Celebration of American Music: Words and Music in Honor of H. Wiley Hitchcock*, ed. Richard Crawford, R. Allen Lott, and Carol J. Oja (Ann Arbor: University of Michigan Press, 1990), pp. 323–45.

95. Copland and Perlis, *Copland Since 1943*, p. 426.

96. Ibid.

97. Copland, *Music and Imagination: The Charles Eliot Norton Lectures, 1951–1952* (Cambridge, Mass.: Harvard University Press, 1975), p. 111.

98. Elliott Carter, *Collected Essays and Lectures, 1937–1995*, ed. Jonathan W. Bernard (Rochester, N.Y.: University of Rochester Press, 1997), p. 71.

99. Quoted in David Schiff's "Copland and the 'Jazz Boys'," *Copland Connotations*, p. 18. On Copland's reservations about the emotional expressiveness of jazz, see Dickinson, "Two Interviews with Aaron Copland (1976)," *Copland Connotations*, p. 192. Copland's attachment to jazz was connected with his attraction to polyrhythms. See his "Jazz Structure and Influence (1927)," in Kostelanetz, *Aaron Copland: A Reader*, pp. 83–87; and "Musical Imagination in the Americas," in *Music and Imagination*, esp. pp. 84, 86–88. See also *What to Listen for in Music* (New York: Signet, 2002), pp. 35–38.

100. Quoted in Schiff, "Copland and the 'Jazz Boys'," in *Copland Connotations*, p. 18.

101. See H. Wiley Hitchcock, "Forward," in *Copland Connotations*, p. xi.

102. Ibid.

103. See David Diamond's recollections in Copland and Perlis, *Copland: 1900–1942*, pp. 241–42. Also Copland and Perlis, *Copland Since 1943*, p. 65; here Copland deals with the problems of his longtime companion Victor Kraft.

104. Andrew R. Heinze, *Jews and the American Soul: Human Nature in the Twentieth Century* (Princeton, N.J.: Princeton University Press, 2004), p. 222.

105. See Levin, "Mexico," in Levin and Tick, *Aaron Copland's America*, pp. 61–64.

106. See Levin, "Explorations of Folk Idioms," in Levin and Tick, *Aaron Copland's America*, pp. 40–51; also Haskell, *The American Century*, pp. 220–24.

107. See Leon Botstein, "The Tragedy and Irony of Success: Locating Jews in the Musical Life of Vienna" and "Social History and the Politics of the Aesthetic: Jews and Music in Vienna, 1870–1938," in *Jews and the City of Music, 1870–1938*, ed. Leon Botstein and Werner Hanak (Frankfurt: Wolke Verlag, 2004), pp. 13–22, 43–63. Also Botstein, "Between Nostalgia and Modernity: Vienna 1848–1898," in *Pre-Modern Art of Vienna, 1848–1898*, ed. Leon Botstein and Linda Weintraub (Detroit, Mich.: Wayne State University Press, 1987), pp. 10–17.

INDEX AND CONTRIBUTORS

Index

Subject Index

For musical works, please refer to separate Musical Works Index.

Notes on the Contributors

Emily Abrams is currently studying for a Ph.D. in Historical Musicology at Harvard University and holds bachelor's and master's degrees from Durham and Oxford universities. Her interests include twentieth- and twenty-first-century American music, music and Cold War politics, and music and migration.

Paul Anderson recently completed his Ph.D. in Music Composition and Theory at Brandeis University. In his dissertation, he analyzed and contrasted the aesthetic views of Aaron Copland and Roger Sessions as revealed in their books, essays, and personal correspondence. His composition instructors include Salvatore Martirano, Yehudi Wyner, and Martin Boykan. His music has been performed by such groups as Speculum Musicae and the Lydian String Quartet, and his prose has been published in *Perspectives of New Music*. Paul currently works for Bank of America in Charlotte, North Carolina, where he lives with his wife, Kristen, and their five children.

Elliott Antokoletz is Professor of Musicology at the University of Texas at Austin, where he has held the Alice Mackie Scott Tacquard Endowed Centennial Chair (1983–84) and E. W. Doty Professorship in Fine Arts (1994–95). He is author of *The Music of Béla Bartók: A Study of Tonality and Progression in Twentieth-Century Music* (University of California Press, 1984); *Béla Bartók, A Guide to Research* (Garland, 1988, 1997); *Twentieth-Century Music* (Prentice Hall, 1992); and *Musical Symbolism in the Operas of Debussy and Bartók: Trauma, Gender, and the Unfolding of the Unconscious* (Oxford University Press, 2004). He received the Béla Bartók Memorial Plaque and Diploma from the Hungarian Government in 1981.

Leon Botstein is President and Leon Levy Professor in the Arts and Humanities at Bard College. He is the author of *Judentum und Modernität* (Vienna, 1991) and *Jefferson's Children: Education and the Promise of American Culture* (New York, 1997). He is the editor of *The Compleat Brahms* (New York, 1999) and *The Musical Quarterly*, as well as coeditor, with Werner Hanak, of *Vienna: Jews and the City of Music, 1870–1938* (Vienna and

New York, 2004). The music director of the American and the Jerusalem symphony orchestras, he has recorded works by, among others, Szymanowski, Hartmann, Bruch, Toch, Dohnányi, Bruckner, Popov, Shostakovich, Chausson, Richard Strauss, Mendelssohn, and Liszt for Telarc, CRI, Koch, Arabesque, and New World Records.

Martin Brody is Catherine Mills Davis Professor of Music at Wellesley College. He has written extensively about modern American music, focusing on composers such as Milton Babbitt, John Harbison, Roger Sessions, and Stefan Wolpe. As a composer, he has received awards from the Guggenheim and Fromm foundations, the National Endowment for the Arts, and the Aaron Copland Fund for Music. He has recently served as Paul Fromm Composer-in-Residence at the American Academy in Rome and Roger Sessions Memorial Fellow at the Ligurian Studies Center in Bogliasco, and he is President of the Stefan Wolpe Society.

Elizabeth B. Crist is Assistant Professor of Music at the University of Texas at Austin, where she teaches courses on twentieth-century music, especially of the United States. The author of *Music for the Common Man: Aaron Copland During the Depression and War* (Oxford, 2005) and coeditor (with Wayne Shirley) of *Selected Letters of Aaron Copland* (Yale, forthcoming), she is currently working on a collection of essays concerning music and cultural memory in postwar America, titled *Music in Memoriam.*

Melissa de Graaf is a doctoral candidate in the Department of Music at Brandeis University. Her dissertation, "Documenting Music in the New Deal: The New York Composers' Forum Concerts, 1935–40," explores issues of modernism, gender, race/ethnicity, and the intersection of vernacular and concert hall traditions. She has taught courses on twentieth-century music and gender and music at Brandeis and Northeastern universities. Her work has been published in *MLA Notes* and the *Institute for Studies in American Music Newsletter,* and she has essays forthcoming in *Musical Quarterly* and in *Ruth Crawford Seeger's Worlds: Innovation and Tradition in Twentieth-Century American Music* (University of Rochester Press).

Morris Dickstein is Distinguished Professor of English at the Graduate Center of the City University of New York, where he teaches courses in literature, film, and American cultural history. He is a senior fellow of the Center for the Humanities, which he founded in 1993. His books include a study of the 1960s, *Gates of Eden* (Basic Books, 1977), which was nominated for the National Book Critics Circle Award in criticism;

Double Agent: The Critic and Society (Oxford, 1992); and *Leopards in the Temple*, a widely reviewed social history of postwar American fiction, published in 2002 by Harvard University Press. His latest book is a collection of essays, *A Mirror in the Roadway: Literature and the Real World* (Princeton, 2005). He is completing a cultural history of the United States in the 1930s.

Lynn Garafola teaches dance history and criticism at Barnard College. She is the author of *Diaghilev's Ballets Russes* and, most recently, *Legacies of Twentieth-Century Dance*, a collection of articles, essays, and reviews. She has edited several books, including *José Limón: An Unfinished Memoir, Rethinking the Sylph: New Perspectives on the Romantic Ballet*, and *The Ballets Russes and Its World*. She has curated several exhibitions, including *Dance for a City: Fifty Years of the New York City Ballet*.

Neil Lerner is Associate Professor of Music at Davidson College, where he teaches courses on music history, film, and the humanities. A specialist in U.S. film music, he has recently published an analysis of Dimitri Tiomkin's score for *High Noon*, a study of John Williams's music in *Star Wars* and *Close Encounters of the Third Kind*, and an essay on barbarism in *The Birth of a Nation*, cowritten with Jane Gaines.

Gail Levin is Professor of Fine and Performing Arts, Art History, and American Studies at Baruch College and the Graduate Center of the City University of New York. Internationally known as a curator, in 2000 she organized the centennial exhibition *Aaron Copland's America* at the Heckscher Museum in Huntington, N.Y. She is coauthor with Judith Tick of *Aaron Copland's America: A Cultural Perspective* (Watson-Guptill, 2000; Toshindo, 2003). Her other books include *Edward Hopper: An Intimate Biography* and *Edward Hopper: A Catalogue Raisonné*. Levin is the author of recent articles in Jewish Studies, Asian Studies, and Women's Studies, and she is currently completing a biography of Judy Chicago.

Beth E. Levy is Assistant Professor of Music at the University of California, Davis. She is currently working on a book tentatively titled *Frontier Figures: American Music and the Mythology of the American West*.

Carol J. Oja is William Powell Mason Professor of Music at Harvard University. Her most recent book, *Making Music Modern: New York in the 1920s* (Oxford, 2000), won an ASCAP Deems Taylor Award and was named best book of the year by the Society for American Music. She first interviewed Aaron Copland in 1978, when doing research for an article on the Copland-Sessions Concerts. She is also author of *Colin McPhee: Composer in Two Worlds* (Smithsonian, 1990; University of Illinois, 2004), as well as articles on a variety of twentieth-century American composers, including George Antheil, Marc Blitzstein, Aaron Copland, Henry Cowell, Ruth Crawford, George Gershwin, Elie Siegmeister, William Grant Still, and Virgil Thomson. She is past-president of the Society for American Music and former director of the Institute for Studies in American Music at Brooklyn College. Currently, she is writing a book about Leonard Bernstein for the Yale Broadway Masters series.

Vivian Perlis is the founding director of Oral History, American Music at Yale University, a project devoted to collecting and preserving recorded interviews of major figures in American music. She is known for her writings and productions, among them articles, books, and documentary films on Aaron Copland, Eubie Blake, Leo Ornstein, and John Cage. Ms. Perlis is coauthor of the two-volume Copland autobiography and co-author of the forthcoming book and CD publication *Composers' Voices from Ives to Ellington*, to be published by Yale University Press.

Howard Pollack is Professor of Music and Director of Graduate Studies at the Moores School of Music at the University of Houston, where he has taught since 1987. His most recent book, *Aaron Copland: The Life and Work of an Uncommon Man* (1999), has been described as "a valuable model of what biography can and probably should be" (*Kirkus Reviews*) and "the definitive study of Aaron Copland's life and work, no doubt for a long time to come" (*New York Times*). He currently is completing a critical biography of George Gershwin.

Wayne D. Shirley was Music Specialist in the Library of Congress from 1965 to 2002. He has published articles on George Antheil, Henry Cowell, George Gershwin, Charles Ives, William Grant Still, and the spiritual "Deep River," and has edited Ives's "The Fourth of July" for publication by the Charles Ives Society. He is the editor, with Elizabeth Crist, of *Selected Letters of Aaron Copland* (Yale University Press, forthcoming). He served as a teaching assistant for Arthur Berger in the early 1960s, teaching sections in "Verdi and Wagner" and "Music of the Twentieth Century." His article in the present volume is an attempt at atonement for the grief he caused Berger during those classes!

Larry Starr is Professor of Music History at the University of Washington, Seattle. Specializing in twentieth-century and American music, he is the author of *A Union of Diversities: Style in the Music of Charles Ives* (Schirmer, 1992), and *The Dickinson Songs of Aaron Copland* (Pendragon, 2002), and coauthor (with Christopher Waterman) of *American Popular Music: From Minstrelsy to MTV* (Oxford, 2002). A contributor to *The Cambridge History of American Music* (1998), he has lectured widely on a broad range of musical topics, and is currently at work on the Gershwin volume for the new Yale Broadway Masters series.

Judith Tick, Matthews Distinguished University Professor of Music at Northeastern University, writes about American music, with a special focus on twentieth-century modernism and women's history. Her biography, *Ruth Crawford Seeger: A Composer's Search for American Music* (1997), won an ASCAP Deems Taylor Award and was named best book of the year by the Society for American Music. In collaboration with the art historian Gail Levin, she published *Aaron Copland's America: A Cultural Perspective* (2000). She has also contributed articles about Copland to the *Copland House Newsletter* and the journal *American Music*. Tick wrote the entries on "Women and Music" for *The New Grove Dictionary of American Music* (1986) and the 2001 revised edition of *The New Grove Dictionary of Music*. She is currently working on an anthology of primary sources for the study of American music and musical life, *America's Music: A Common Reader,* to be published by Oxford University Press. In 2000 she received a Distinguished Alumna Medal from Smith College, and in 2004 she was elected to the American Academy of Arts and Sciences.